THE COMPLETE RESULTS & LINE-UPS OF THE UEFA EUROPA LEAGUE 2015-2018

Marcel Haisma & Dirk Karsdorp

British Library Cataloguing in Publication Data
A catalogue record for this book is available from the British Library

ISBN: 978-1-86223-386-7

Copyright © 2018, SOCCER BOOKS LIMITED (01472 696226)
72 St. Peter's Avenue, Cleethorpes, N.E. Lincolnshire, DN35 8HU, England
Web site   www.soccer-books.co.uk
e-mail   info@soccer-books.co.uk

Printed in the UK by 4edge Ltd.

FOREWORD

Between the years of 1971 and 2009, the UEFA Cup was the second most important European Club competition, having itself superseded both the Fairs Cup and the European Cup-Winners' Cup competitions. From 1995 onwards, the Intertoto Cup also became an official UEFA competition and was, effectively, their third-ranked club competition until it ended in 2008.

From 2009, in an attempt to streamline their club tournaments, UEFA decided to end both the UEFA Cup and the Intertoto Cup competitions, replacing them with a single highly-ranked competition which was named the UEFA Europa League.

This publication provides a comprehensive statistical record of this competition from the first game in the qualifying stages of the 2015/16 competition through to the 2018 Final itself. Similar publications covering the Europa League from 2009-2012 and 2012-2015 are also available from Soccer Books Limited as are books covering the UEFA Cup and a selection of other European competitions including the Champions League and earlier European Cup. Please check the back page of this book for a listing of these and many other publications.

Although the contents of this book are, we believe, as accurate as possible, it is not always easy to obtain reliable statistics for such a pan-European competition. On occasions, different sources can provide different information for the same match, particularly in relation to attendances. In such cases as this the most trustworthy information which could be discovered was used in this book.

Michael Robinson
Editor

UEFA EUROPA LEAGUE 2015-2016

FIRST QUALIFYING ROUND

30.06.15   Hibernians Ground, Paola: Balzan Youths – Zeljeznicar Sarajevo 0-2 (0-2).
Balzan Youths: Christian Cassar, Justin Grioli, Steven Bezzina, Elkin Serrano, Edinson Bilbao, Dylan Grima (84' Ryan Darmanin), Clive Brincat, Terence Agius, Osa Guobadia, Lydon Micallef (90+1' Sean Cipriott), Luke Sciberras (78' Samir Arab). Coach: Oliver Spiteri.
Zeljeznicar Sarajevo: Marijan Antolovic, Josip Kvesic, Aleksandar Kosoric, Jasmin Bogdanovic, Rijad Bajic, Jovan Blagojevic, Ognjen Djelmic, Ivan Lavaja, Amir Hadziahmetovic (76' Enis Sadikovic), Dzenis Beganovic (56' Damir Sadikovic), Zoran Kokot (84' Secouba Diatta). Coach: Milomir Odovic.
Goals: 4',13' Rijad Bajic 0-1 (p), 0-2.
Referee: Dennis Antamo (FIN)   Attendance: 627.

30.06.15   Stade Municipal de Differdange, Differdange:
Progrès Niederkorn – Shamrock Rovers 0-0.
Progrès Niederkorn: Sebastian Flauss, Ismaël Bouzid, Jonathan Rigo (40' Adrien Ferino), David Soares, Samuel Dog, Valentin Poinsignon (80' Alessandro Fiorani), Olivier Cassan, Mickael Garos, Sébastien Thill, Hakim Menai (68' Lévy Rougeaux), Giuseppe Rossini. Coach: Oliver Ciancanelli.
Shamrock Rovers: Craig Hyland, Luke Byrne, David Webster, Simon Madden, Tim Clancy, Gary McCabe, Gavin Brennan, Patrick Cregg, Brandon Miele (81' Cian Kavanagh), Kieran Waters (75' Dylan Kavanagh), Michael Drennan. Coach: Pat Fenlon.
Referee: Zaven Hovhannisyan (ARM)   Attendance: 1,451.

30.06.15   Filip II. Makedonski, Skopje: FK Renova – Dacia Chisinau 0-1 (0-1).
FK Renova: Saljadin Mustafi, Agron Memedi, Visar Musliu, Nenad Miskovski, Jasmin Mecinovic (70' Lavdrim Skenderi), Izair Emini, Fisnik Nuhiu, Emran Ramadani (79' Remzi Selmani), Argjent Gafuri, Bashkim Velija (46' Medzit Neziri), Gjorgji Mojsov. Coach: Kjatip Osmani.
Dacia Chisinau: Artiom Gaiduchevici, Mihai Rosca, Sergiu Cojocari (46' Maksim Gavrilenko), Veaceslav Posmac, Volodymyr Zastavnyi, Abdoul Mamah, Evgeniy Lozoviy, Sapol Mani, Eugeniu Cociuc, Vyacheslav Pidnebennoy (46' Sergiy Zagynaylov), Vasili Pavlov (64' Maxim Mihailov). Coach: Igor Dobrovolskiy.
Goal: 12' Mihai Rosca 0-1.
Referee: Eiko Saar (EST)   Attendance: 1,500.

02.07.15   Kazhimukan Munaytpasov, Shymkent: Ordabasy Shymkent – Beitar Jerusalem 0-0.
Ordabasy Shymkent: Andrey Sidelnikov, Gafurzhan Suyombaev, Renat Abdulin, Sergiy Maliy, Talgat Adyrbekov, Aleksandaar Simcevic, Azat Nurgaliev, Kayrat Ashirbekov (75' Mardan Tolebek), Artem Kasyanov, Ivan Bozic, Aleksandr Geynrikh (90+3' Kyrylo Petrov). Coach: Viktor Kumykov.
Beitar Jerusalem: Boris Kleiman, Tal Kachila, Tomer Yeruham, Dusan Matovic, Daniel Askling, Omer Atzily (64' Omer Nachmani), Claudemir, Lidor Cohen (54' Ness Zamir), Liroy Zhairi, Ori Majabi (73' Itzhak Cohen), Dovev Gabay. Coach: Slobodan Drapic.
Referee: Dumitru Muntean (MOL)   Attendance: 11,600.

02.07.15   Gyumri City, Gyumri: Shirak FC – Zrinjski Mostar 2-0 (1-0).
Shirak FC: Vsevolod Ermakov, Arman Hovhannisyan, Milos Stamenkovic, Gevorg
Hovhannisyan, Tigran Davtyan, Gor Malakyan, Davit Hakobyan (59' Andranik Barikyan),
Edgar Malakyan, Aghvan Davoyan, Jean-Jacques Bougouhi (88' Aram Muradyan), Drissa
Diarrassouba (80' Viulen Ayvazyan). Coach: Vardan Bichakhchyan.
Zrinjski Mostar: Ratko Dujkovic, Zvonimir Blaic, Danijel Graovac, Pero Stojkic, Anto
Radeljic, Milan Muminovic, Milos Zeravica, Ognjen Todorovic, Milos Filipovic (71' Danijel
Stojanovic), Deni Simeunovic (46' Vucina Scepanovic), Stevo Nikolic (86' Milos Acimovic).
Coach: Vinko Marinovic.
Goals: 18',67' Jean-Jacques Bougouhi 1-0, 2-0.
Referee: Charalambos Kalogeropoulos (GRE)   Attendance: 2,774.

02.07.15   Hanrapetakan, Yerevan: Alashkert Martuni – St. Johnstone FC 1-0 (0-0).
Alashkert Martuni: Gevorg Kasparov, Sékou Fofana, Gevorg Poghosyan, Sergey Usenya (57'
Mihran Manasyan), Vahagn Minasyan, Karen Muradyan, Ararat Arakelyan, Khoren Veranyan,
Aram Bareghamyan, Artak Grigoryan (90+5' Aram Hovsepyan), Norayr Gyozalyan (80'
Héber). Coach: Abraham Khashmanyan.
St. Johnstone FC: Alan Mannus, David MacKay, Thomas Scobbie, Joe Shaughnessy, Brian
Easton, Simon Lappin, Murray Davidson (44' Scott Brown), David Wotherspoon, Steven
MacLean, John Sutton (60' Chris Kane), Michael O'Halloran. Coach: Tommy Wright.
Goal: 59' Mihran Manasyan 1-0.
Referee: Michael Johansen (DEN)   Attendance: 2,600.

02.07.15   Siauliu stadionas, Siauliai: FK Kruoja Pakruojis – Jagiellonia Bialystok 0-1 (0-0).
FK Kruoja Pakruojis: Martynas Matuzas, Horia Crisan, Valdas Pocevicius, Donatas Strockis,
Alfredas Skroblas, Tomas Salamanavicius (85' Boubakary Diarra), Tautvydas Eliosius,
Donatas Navikas, Darius Jankauskas, Ricardas Beniusis (80' Tomas Birskys), Aivaras
Bagocius (75' Tadas Eliosius). Coach: Divaldo.
Jagiellonia Bialystok: Bartlomiej Dragowski, Filip Modelski, Sebastian Madera, Konstantin
Vassiljev (64' Taras Romanchuk), Patryk Tuszynski (63' Lukasz Sekulski), Nika Dzalamidze
(80' Karol Swiderski), Igors Tarasovs, Rafal Grzyb, Piotr Tomasik, Karol Mackiewicz, Maciej
Gajos. Coach: Michal Probierz.
Goal: 90+3' Karol Swiderski 0-1.
Referee: Joao Capela (POR)   Attendance: 2,354.
Sent off: 82' Rafal Grzyb.

02.07.15   Stadium Laçi, Laçi: KF Laçi – Inter Baku 1-1 (1-0).
KF Laçi: Miroslav Vujadinovic, Emiliano Çela, Arjan Sheta, Elton Doku (56' Valdon Nimani),
Taulant Sefgjini, Agim Meto (78' Aldo Mitraj), Erjon Vucaj, Argjend Mustafa, Olsi Teqja,
Emiliano Veliaj, Segun Adeniyi. Coach: Armando Cungu.
Inter Baku: Sälahät Agayev, Juanfran, Lashar Kasradze, Zurab Khizanishvili, Abbas
Hüseynov, Nika Kvekveskiri, Mirsayib Abbasov (74' Ilkin Sadigov), Mirhuseyn Seyidov,
Fuad Bayramov, Rauf Aliyev (90+3' Mansur Nahavandi), Yuri Fomenko (43' Nizami
Hajiyev). Coach: Zaur Svanadze.
Goals: 20' Agim Meto 1-0, 47' Nika Kvekveskiri 1-1.
Referee: Carlos Del Cerro Grande (ESP)   Attendance: 850.

02.07.15 Klaipėdosmiesto Centrinis, Klaipeda: FK Atlantas – PFC Beroe 0-2 (0-0).

FK Atlantas: Mindaugas Malinauskas, Andrius Bartkus (46' Gerardas Zukauskas), Andrius Joksas, Rolandas Baravykas (69' Lukas Baranauskas), Aleksey Epifanov, Kazimieras Gnedojus, Dovydas Virksas, Dovydas Norvilas (65' Markas Beneta), Robertas Vezevicius, Maksim Maksimov, Andrey Panyukov. Coach: Konstantin Sarsaniya.

PFC Beroe: Blagoj Makendzhiev, Ivo Ivanov, Ventzislav Vasilev, Veselin Penev, Atanas Zehirov, Nemanja Milisavljevic, Elias (87' Tom), Igor Djoman, Junior M'Pia (81' Georgi Andonov), Georgi Bozhilov, Spas Delev (69' Ivan Kokonov). Coach: Petar Hubchev.

Goals: 60' Spas Delev 0-1, 84' Georgi Bozhilov 0-2.

Referee: Vilhjálmur Alvar Thorarinsson (ISL)   Attendance: 3,000.

02.07.15 Boris Pachaidze, Tbilisi: Dinamo Tbilisi – Gabala FK 2-1 (0-0).

Dinamo Tbilisi: Libor Hrdlicka, Lasha Totadze, Archil Tvildiani, Giorgi Gvelesiani, Mate Tsintsadze, Giorgi Papunashvili, Otari Kiteishvili (54' Rene), Jambul Jigauri, Zaza Chelidze, Vakhtang Chanturishvili (79' Lasha Parunashvili), Giorgi Kvilitaia (62' Aleksandr Iashvili). Coach: George Geguchadze.

Gabala FK: Dmitro Bezotosniy, Vitaliy Vernydub, Ricardinho, Urfan Abbasov, Rafael Santos, George Florescu (72' Räsad Sadiqov), Oleksiy Gay, Arif Dashdemirov (73' Dodô), Sergei Zenjov, Javid Hüseynov, Oleksiy Antonov. Coach: Roman Grygorchuk.

Goals: 65' Jambul Jigauri 1-0, 74' Javid Hüseynov 1-1, 84' Giorgi Papunashvili 2-1.

Referee: Roy Reinshreiber (ISR)   Attendance: 7,500.

Sent off: 51' Giorgi Gvelesiani.

02.07.15 Tsentralniy, Aktobe: FK Aktobe – JK Nõmme Kalju 0-1 (0-0).

FK Aktobe: Stas Pokatilov, Dele Adeleye, Dmitry Miroshnichenko, Viktor Dmitrenko, Yuriy Logvinenko, Arturas Zulpa, Marat Khayrullin, Ciprian Deac, Danilo Neco (87' Didar Zhalmukan), Marcos Pizelli (78' Almat Bekbaev), Danilo (81' Sergey Khiznichenko). Coach: Vladimir Gazzaev.

JK Nõmme Kalju: Vitali Teles, Alo Bärengrub, Jorge Rodrigues, Ken Kallaste, Borislav Topic (82' Tarmo Neemelo), Ats Purje, Allan Kimbaloula (90+2' Erik Listmann), Eino Puri, Karl Mööl, Hidetoshi Wakui (58' Joel Lindpere), Artjom Dmitrijev. Coach: Sergei Terehhov.

Goal: 72' Ats Purje 0-1.

Referee: Yuriy Mozharovsky (UKR)   Attendance: 10,870.

Sent off: 77' Stas Pokatilov.

02.07.15 Qemal Stafa, Tirana:FK Kukësi – Torpedo-BelAZ Zhodino 2-0 (1-0).

FK Kukësi: Dimitri Stajila, Gentian Muça, Rrahman Hallaçi, Renato Malota, Gledi Mici, Erick Flores, Edon Hasani (46' Besar Musolli), Birungueta (68' Jefferson), Felipe Moreira (60' Vilfor Hysa), Jean Carioca, Pero Pejic. Coach: Marcello Troisi.

Torpedo BelAZ Zhodino: Roman Stepanov, Vyacheslav Serdyuk (79' Aleksandr Selyava), Sergiy Melnik, Ihar Burko, Aleksey Pankovetds, Oleksandr Maksimov, Sergiy Datsenko, Artem Kontsevoy (67' Artiom Vaskov), Aleksandr Yatskevich, Dmitry Platonov (75' Anton Matveenko), Vyatcheslav Hleb. Coach: Igor Kriushenko.

Goals: 9' Jean Carioca 1-0, 54' Pero Pejić 2-0.

Referee: Sascha Amhof (SUI)   Attendance: 1,500.

7

02.07.15   A.Le Coq Arena, Tallinn: FC Flora – FK Rabotnicki 1-0 (0-0).
FC Flora: Mait Toom, Enar Jääger, Gert Kams, Nikita Baranov, Andre Frolov, Rauno
Sappinen (53' Zakaria Beglarishvili), Markus Jürgenson, German Slein (80' Karl-Eerik
Luigend), Irakliy Logue (72' Joonas Tamm), Rauno Alliku, Maksim Gussev.
Coach: Norbert Hurt.
FK Rabotnicki: Andreja Efremov, Goran Siljanovski, Milan Ilievski, Stephan Vujcic, Milovan
Petrovikj, Ivan Mitrov (46' Chuma Anene), Dusko Trajcevski (72' Miroslav Jovanovski), Mite
Cikarski, Suad Sahiti (62' Kire Markoski), Baze Ilijoski, Marijan Altiparmakovski.
Coach: Tomislav Franc.
Goal: 59' Maksim Gussev 1-0.
Referee: Mohammed Al Hakim (SWE)   Attendance: 1,236.

02.07.15   David Abashidze Stadium, Zestafoni: Dinamo Batumi – Omonia Nikosia 1-0 (1-0).
Dinamo Batumi: Mikheil Alavidze, Badri Tetunashvili, Anzor Sukhiashvili, Giorgi Kavtaradze
(83' Irakli Chirikashvili), Gela Gogitidze, Temur Shonia, Papuna Poniava, Boris Makharadze,
Georgi Beriashvili (87' Beka Varshanidze), Giorgi Gabedava, Dimitri Tatanashvili (75'
Valerian Tevdoradze). Coach: Shota Cheishvili.
Omonia Nikosia: Antonis Georgallides, Ucha Lobjanidze, Jackson Mendy (46' Margaca), Ivan
Runje, Nuno Assis, Giorgos Economides, Herold Goulon, Cristóvao, Gaoussou Fofana (58'
Andraz Kirm), André Schembri (70' Eze Okeuhie), Mickaël Poté. Coach: Costas Kaiafas.
Goal: 40' Giorgi Gabedava 1-0.
Referee: Mitja Zganec (SVN)   Attendance: 3,589.

02.07.15   Asim Ferhatović Hase, Sarajevo: Olimpik Sarajevo – Spartak Trnava 1-1 (1-0).
Olimpik Sarajevo: Dino Hamzic, Alem Merajic, Bojan Regoje, Jadranko Bogicevic, Filip
Gligorov, Veldin Muharemovic, Kenan Handzic, Ervin Jusufovic (80' Mahir Karic), Danijal
Brkovic, Dalibor Pandza (80' Stefan), Admir Rascic. Coach: Mirza Varesanovic.
Spartak Trnava: Bojan Knezevic, Milan Bortel, Milos Nikolic, Matús Conka, Boris Godál,
Lukas Gressák (46' José David Casado Garcia), Martin Mikovic (63' Cléber), Ján Vlasko, Erik
Sabo, Haris Harba, Ivan Schranz (70' Emir Halilovic). Coach: Juraj Jarábek.
Goals: 14' Dalibor Pandza 1-0, 70' Emir Halilovic 1-1.
Referee: Daniel Stefanski (POL)   Attendance: 2,622.

02.07.15   Skonto Stadion, Riga: Skonto FC – St. Patrick's Athetic 2-1 (1-1).
Skonto FC: Andrejs Pavlovs, Olegs Timofejevs, Renars Rode, Vitalijs Smirnovs, Iván Murillo
(90+1' Serge Tatiefang), Aleksejs Visnakovs (72' Vjaceslavs Isajevs), Igors Kozlovs, Edgars
Jermolaevs, Andrejs Kovalovs, Vladislavs Gutkovskis (83' Ivan Lukanyuk), Arturs
Karasausks. Coach: Tamaz Pertia.
St. Patrick's Athletic: Brendan Clarke, Ger O'Brien (46' Lee Desmond), Ian Bermingham,
Sean Hoare (67' Jason McGuinness), Kenny Browne, Greg Bolger, Killian Brennan, James
Chambers, Christopher Forrester, Aaron Greene, Chris Fagan (73' Jamie McGrath).
Coach: Liam Buckley.
Goals: 21' Aaron Greene 0-1, 38' Arturs Karasausks 1-1, 65' Vladislavs Gutkovskis 2-1.
Referee: Fran Jovic (CRO)   Attendance: 1,780.

8

02.07.15   Estadi Comunal, Andorra la Vella: UE Sant Julià – Randers FC 0-1 (0-1).

UE Sant Julia: Coca, Miguel Ruiz, Rafael Brito, Iván Vigo, Sebastian Varela, Francisco Rodriguez (67' Edu Peppe), Eric Rodriguez, Bruninho, Mario Spano (63' Alfonso Castellano), Fábio Serra, Ignacio Quirino (57' Arturo Madrazo). Coach: Raúl Canete.
Randers FC: Kalle Johnsson, Mads Fenger, Alexander Fischer. Christian Keller, Johnny Thomsen, Jeppe Tverskov, Mustafa Amini, Jonas Borring (82' Erik Marxen), Viktor Lundberg, Nikolaj Poulsen (62' Joel Allansson), Nicolai Brock-Madsen (85' Mikkel Thygesen). Coach: Colin Todd.
Goal: 22' Jonas Borring 0-1.
Referee: Tim Marshall (NIR)   Attendance: 350.
Sent off: 17' Viktor Lundberg, 81' Jeppe Tverskov.

02.07.15   Zemgalas Olimpiska Centra, Jelgava: FK Jelgava – PFC Litex Lovech 1-1 (0-0).
FK Jelgava: Kaspars Ikstens, Abdoulaye Diallo, Aleksandrs Gubins, Marcis Oss, Gints Freimanis, Rustam Sosranov, Dariusz Latka, Boriss Bogdaskins, Kennedy Eriba (69' Andrejs Kirilins), Glebs Kluskins (83' Artis Jaudzems), Vyachselav Sushkin (70' Olegs Malasenoks). Coach: Vitalijs Astafjevs.
PFC Litex Lovech: Vinicius, Rafael Pérez, Vasil Bozhikov, Ivan Goranov, Kristyan Malinov, Strahil Popov, Rumen Rumenov (57' Petrus Boumal), Arsénio (77' Milcho Angelov), Nikola Kolev, Björn Johnsen, Danilo Moreno (90' Alexandar Georgiev). Coach: Krassimir Balakov.
Goals: 50' Vasil Bozhikov 0-1, 83' Olegs Malasenoks 1-1.
Referee: Tiago Martins (POR)   Attendance: 1,560.

02.07.15   Sonera Stadium, Helsinki: SJK Seinäjoki – FH Hafnarfjördur 0-1 (0-0).
SJK Seinäjoki: Mihkel Aksalu, Richard Dorman, Pavle Milosavljevic, Zeljko Savic, Cèdric Gogoua, Johannes Laaksonen, Jussi Vasara (64' Bahrudin Atajic), Wayne Brown (81' Timo Tahvanainen), Mehmet Hetemaj, Toni Lehtinen (67' Ariel Ngueukam), Akseli Pelvas. Coach: Simo Valakari.
FK Hafnarfjördur: Róbert Oskarsson, Pétur Vidarsson, Tórarinn Valdimarsson, Kassim Doumbia, Bödvar Bödvarsson, Emil Pálsson, David Vidarsson, Gudmann Torisson, Brynjar Asgeir Gudmundsson, Steven Lennon (81' Kristján Finnbogason), Atli Gudnason (76' Bjarni Vidarsson). Coach: Heimir Gudjónsson.
Goal: 56' Steven Lennon 0-1.
Referee: Tihomir Pejin (CRO)   Attendance: 2,678.

02.07.15   Lahden, Lahti: FC Lahti – IF Elfsborg 2-2 (1-1).
FC Lahti: Henrik Moisander, Mikko Hauhia, Pyry Kärkkäinen, Maarkus Joenmäki, Petri Pasanen, Xhevdet Gela, Pekka Lagerblom (41' Hassan Sesay), Aleksi Paananen, Drilon Shala (78' Aleksi Ristola), Matheus (72' Rafael), Jussi Länsitalo. Coach: Toni Korkeakunnas.
IF Elfsborg: Kevin Stuhr-Ellegaard, Jon Jönsson, Adam Lundqvist, Marcus Rohdén, Anders Svensson, Simon Lundevall, Andreas Klarström (74' Jesper Manns), Victor Claesson, Henning Hauger, Simon Hedlund, Viktor Prodell (69' Per Frick). Coach: Magnus Haglund.
Goals: 15' Marcus Rohdén 0-1, 25' Pekka Lagerblom 1-1, 59' Viktor Prodell 1-2, 61' Matheus 2-2.
Referee: Nikola Dabanovic (MNE)   Attendance: 3,152.

9

02.07.15   Raatti, Oulo:Vaasan PS – AIK Solna 2-2 (1-0).
Vaasan PS: Henri Sillanpää, Timi Lahti, Ville Koskimaa, Jesper Engström, Denis Abdulahi, Tony Björk (84' Thomas Kula), Miika Niemi, Admir Catovic, Pyry Soiri, Jordan Seabrook (68' Eero Tamminen), Juho Mäkelä. Coach: Petri Vuorinen.
AIK Solna: Patrik Carlgren (28' Oscar Linnér), Per Karlsson, Nils-Eric Johansson, Haukur Hauksson, Noah Sonko Sundberg, Fredrik Brustad (64' Poborsky Bangura), Johan Blomberg, Ebenezer Ofori, Dickson Etuhu (78' Anton Jönsson Salétros), Henok Goitom, Nabil Bahoui. Coach: Andreas Alm.
Goals: 45' Admir Catovic 1-0, 65' Jordan Seabrook 2-0, 70',83' Nabil Bahoui 2-1, 2-2 (p).
Referee: Marius Avram (ROM)   Attendance: 2,180.

02.07.15   Bakcell Arena, Baku: Neftchi PFK – FK Mladost Podgorica 2-2 (1-1).
Neftchi PFK: Agil Mammadov, Melli, Ailton, Mahammad Kurbanov, Kamal Gurbanov, Elvin Badalov, Araz Abdullayev (73' Mirabdulla Abbasov), Rahman Hajiyev, Elshan Abdullayev (77' Kamran Najafzade), Ruslan Qurbanov, Samir Masimov (79' Nijat Gurbanov). Coach: Samir Aliyev.
FK Mladost Podgorica: Mileta Radulovic, Luka Pejovic, Milos S. Radulovic (90+1' Aldin Adzovic), Milos Lakic, Milos B. Radulovic, Dusan Lagator (63' Luka Mirkovic), Mirko Raicevic, Blazo Igumanovic, Milan Durisic (61' Marko Scepanovic), Ivan Novovic, Ivan Vukovic. Coach: Nikola Rakojevic.
Goals: 34' Dusan Lagator 0-1, 36' Kamal Gurbanov 1-1, 55' Araz Abdullayev 2-1, 87' Luka Mirkovic 2-2.
Referee: Ali Palabiyik (TUR)   Attendance: 9,866.

02.07.15   Nagyerdei, Debrecen: Debreceni VSC – FK Sutjeska 3-0 (1-0).
Debreceni VSC: István Verpecz, Norbert Mészáros, Dusan Brkovic, Mihály Korhut, Rene Mihelic, Adám Bódi (85' László Zsidai), József Varga, Péter Szakály, Tamás Kulcsár (66' Zsolt Horváth), Aleksandar Jovanovic, Norbert Balogh (46' Ibrahima Sidibe). Coach: Elemér Kondás.
FK Sutjeska: Marko Radovic, Dejan Ognjanovic, Aleksandar Sofranac, Slavko Lukic, Drasko Bozovic, Stevan Kovacevic, Jovan Nikolic, Nikola Stijepovic, Milos Vucic (59' Marko Vucic), Matija Vujovic, Masato Fukui. Coach: Aleksandar Nedovic.
Goals: 16' Rene Mihelic 1-0, 71' Dusan Brkovic 2-0, 74' Ibrahima Sidibe 3-0.
Referee: Raymond Crangle (NIR)   Attendance: 5,744.

02.07.15   Rakvere linnastaadion, Rakvere: JK Sillamäe Kalev – Hajduk Split 1-1 (1-1).
JK Sillamäe Kalev: Mikhail Starodubtsev, Marius Cinikas, Igor Cherminava, Igor Dudarev, Tihhon Sisov, Denis Vnukov (65' Daniil Ratnikov), Kyrylo Silich, Janar Toomet, Deniss Tjapkin, Giorgio Russo, Jaroslav Kvasov. Coach: Denis Ugarov.
Hajduk Split: Lovre Kalinic, Dino Mikanovic, Goran Milovic, Zoran Nizic, Fran Tudor, Nikola Vlasic, Mijo Caktas, Elvir Maloku (58' Artem Radchenko), Ante Roguljic (74' Maksim Beliy), Franck Ohandza, Andrija Balic. Coach: Damir Buric.
Goals: 6' Mijo Caktas 0-1 (p), 40' Kyrylo Silich 1-1.
Referee: Juan Martinez Munuera (ESP)   Attendance: 750.

02.07.15   Sheriff, Tiraspol: FC Sheriff – Odds BK 0-3 (0-3).

FC Sheriff: Bozhidar Mitrev, Marcel Metoua Kramin, Maxim Potimiche, Amer Dupovac (19'
Andrey Novicov), Ernandes, Mateo Susic, Igor Jugovic (63' Vyacheslav Sharpar), Cadu, Seidu
Yahaya, Juninho Potiguar (33' Ivan Crnov), Ricardinho. Coach: Lilian Popescu.

Odds BK: Sondre Rossbach, Espen Ruud, Emil Jonassen (52' Thomas Grøgaard), Steffen
Hagen, Lars-Kristian Eriksen, Ardian Gashi, Oliver Berg, Ole Halvorsen, Jone Samuelsen,
Frode Johnsen (18' Olivier Occean), Bentley (73' Havard Storbaek).
Coach: Dag-Eilev Fagermo.
Goals: 2' Bentley 0-1, 11' Frode Johnsen 0-2, 28' Steffen Hagen 0-3.
Referee: Tsvetan Krastev (BUL)   Attendance: 6,628.

02.07.15   Stade Municipal de Differdange, Differdange:
           FC Differdange 03 – Bala Town 3-1 (3-1).
FC Differdange 03: Julien Weber, André Rodrigues, Tom Siebenaler (78' Jean-Philippe
Caillet), Ante Bukvic, Pedro Ribeiro, Omar Er Rafik, Dejvid Sinani (69' Goncalo Almeida da
Silva), Phillipe Lebresne (46' Andy May), Gauthier Caron, Geoffrey Franzoni, Antonio Luisi.
Coach: Marc Thomé.
Bala Town: Ashley Morris, Ryan Valentine, Anthony Stephens, David Artell, Will Bell, Conall
Murtagh, Mark Connolly (82' Stephen Brown), Mark Jones, Rob Pearson (46' Mike Hayes),
Ian Sheridan, Kieran Smith. Coach: Stephen O'Shaughnessy.
Goals: 4' Omar Er Rafik 1-0, 7' Gauthier Caron 2-0, 26' Dejvid Sinani 3-0,
38' Ian Sheridan 3-1.
Referee: Milan Ilic (SER)   Attendance: 1,223.
Sent off: 83' Mike Hayes.

02.07.15   Brøndby Stadion, Brøndby: Brøndby IF – AC Juvenes/Dogana 9-0 (6-0).
Brøndby IF: Lukás Hrádecky, Frederik Holst, Johan Larsson, Dario Durmic, Patrick da Silva,
Martin Ornskov, Alexander Szymanowski, Lebogang Phiri (63' Rezan Corlu), Andrew
Hjulsager, Teemu Pukki (63' Daniel Stückler), Johan Elmander (46' Elbasan Rashani).
Coach: Thomas Frank.
AC Juvenes Dogana: Mattia Manzaroli, Daniele Villa, Mattia Merlini, Mirko Mantovani,
Giordo Bagli (76' Marco Ugolini), Riccardo Santini, Lorenzo Gasperoni, Manuel Battistini,
Thomas Cavalli (53' Nicola Canini), Cristian Maccagno, Giorgio Mariotti (59' Marco
Bernardi). Coach: Fabrizio Costantini.
Goals:6' Johan Elmander 1-0, 14' Patrick da Silva 2-0, 17' Johan Elmander 3-0,
22' Teemu Pukki 4-0, 23' Frederik Holst 5-0, 35' Johan Larsson 6-0, 56' Elbasan Rashani 7-0,
66' Rezan Corlu 8-0, 88' Elbasan Rashani 9-0.
Referee: Adrian Azzopardi (MLT)   Attendance: 8,408.

02.07.15   Dariaus ir Gireno, Kaunas: FK Trakai – HB Tórshavn 3-0 (1-0).
FK Trakai: Marius Rapalis, Linas Klimavicius, Justinas Janusevskis, Deividas Cesnauskis,
Ronalds Solomin, Vaidas Silenas, Eugen Zasavitchi, Aleksandr Bychenok, Yuriy Mamaev,
David Arshakyan, Lukas Kochanauskas (40' Donatas Segzda). Coach: Valdas Urbonas.
HB Tórshavn: Teitur Gestsson, Alex Dos Santos, Jóhan Davidsen (64' Gunnar Haraldsen),
Rógvi Holm, René Joensen, Heini Vatnsdal, Fródi Benjaminsen, Jógvan Davidsen, Arnbjørn
Hansen (79' Teit Jacobsen), Christian Mouritsen (74' Bartal Wardum), Levi Hanssen.
Coach: Hedin Askham.
Goals: 19' Aleksandr Bychenok 1-0, 61' David Arshakyan 2-0, 86' Ronalds Solomin 3-0.
Referee: Lasha Silagava (GEO)   Attendance: 1,070.
Sent off: 62' Alex Dos Santos.

11

02.07.15   Marienlyst, Drammen: Strømsgodset IF – FK Partizani 3-1 (1-0).
Strømsgodset IF: Espen Pettersen, Kim Madsen, Florent Hanin, Bismark Boateng, Marius
Hoibraten, Iver Fossum, Gustav Wikheim (79' Flamur Kastrati), Mohammed Abu, Lars-
Christopher Vilsvik, Oyvind Storflor, Marvin Ogunjimi (84' Péter Kovács).
Coach: Bjorn Petter Ingebretsen.
FK Partizani: Alban Hoxha (30' Dashamir Xhika), Arbnor Fejzullahu, Ditmar Bicaj, Labinot
Ibrahimi, Endrit Vrapi, Renaldo Kalari, Idriz Batha, Lorenc Trashi, Emiljano Vila, Sebino
Plaku (60' Astrit Fazliu), Stevan Racic (89' Alsid Tafili). Coach: Genc Tomorri.
Goals: 21' Lars-Christopher Vilsvik 1-0, 65' Marvin Ogunjimi 2-0, 68' Astrit Fazliu 2-1,
72' Lars-Christopher Vilsvik 3-1.
Referee: Paul McLaughlin (IRL)   Attendance: 3,273.

02.07.15   Stadionul Zimbru, Chisinau: FC Saxan – Apollon Limassol 0-2 (0-1).
FC Saxan: Anatolii Chririnciuc, Kouassi Kouadja, Dumitru Popovici, Ion Arabadji, Yacouba
Bamba, Mohamed Koné, Radu Catan, Victor Truhanov (79' Mamadou Fofana), Eric Né (89'
Sékou Doumbia), Artion Puntus (63' Andrey Bogdanov), Lassina Dao. Coach: Vlad Goian.
Apollon Limassol: Bruno Vale, Elizio, Nuno Lopes, Freire, Esteban Sacchetti, Marcos Gullón,
Joao Pedro, Luka Stojanovic (71' Alasdair Reynolds), Charis Kyriakou, Fotis Papoulis,
Giorgos Kolokoudias (90+1' Thodores Josephides). Coach: Pedro Emanuel.
Goals: 33' Joao Pedro 0-1, 88' Foris Pappoulis 0-2.
Referee: Denis Izmailov (KAZ)   Attendance: 2,535.

02.07.15   Municipal, Botosani: FC Botosani – Spartaki Tskhinvali 1-1 (1-0).
FC Botosani: Plamen Iliev, Andrei Cordos, Florin Plamada, Radoslav Dimitrov, Marius
Croitoru (74' Ciprian Brata), Petre Ivanovici (86' Paul Batin), Gabriel Vasvari, Raul Costin,
Quenten Martinus, Rashid Browne, Attila Hadnagy (46' Dan Roman). Coach: Leo Grozavu.
Spartaki Tskhinvali: Giorgi Nadiradze, Vasiko Bachiashvili, Giorgi Tsertsvadze, Levan
Kakubava, Varlam Kilasonia, Irakli Lekvtadze (63' Akaki Shulaia), Merab Gigauri (77' Ucha
Burdzenadze), George Ivanishvili (89' Giorgi Kachkachishvili), Rati Tsatskrialashvili, Bakar
Kardava, Nika Kacharava. Coach: Kakhaber Katcharava.
Goals: 21' Petre Ivanovici 1-0, 46' Nika Kacharava 1-1.
Referee: Lorenc Jemini (ALB)   Attendance: 6,031.

02.07.15   Victoria Stadium, Gibraltar: College Europe FC – Slovan Bratislava 0-6 (0-5).
College Europe FC: Mathew Caffer, Francisco Vargas, Boris Jukic (45' Aymen Mouelhi),
Pinero, Ante Sokol (72' Alejandro Orteg Flores), Alberto Merino, Javier Lopez, Hrvoje
Plazanic, Manuel Ledesma Carrill (51' Javi Fernández), Cristian Toncheff, Aaron Akrapovic.
Coach: Juan Gallardo Fernandez.
Slovan Bratislava: Martin Krnac, Boris Sekulic, Martin Dobrotka, Kornel Saláta, Adam Zrelak
(65' Lester Peltier), Marko Milinkovic, Samuel Stefánik (70' Filip Orsula), Slobodan Simovic,
Jakub Podany, Karol Meszáros (64' Frantisek Kubik), Tamás Priskin. Coach: Dusan Tittel.
Goals: 5',26',31' Karol Meszáros 0-1, 0-2, 0-3, 33' Slobodan Simovic 0-4,
41' Samuel Stefánik 0-5, 90+3' Tamás Priskin 0-6.
Referee: Ola Nilsen (NOR)   Attendance: 754.

12

02.07.15   Nantporth, Bangor: Airbus UK – Lokomotiva Zagreb 1-3 (1-0).
Airbus UK: James Coates, Michael Pearson, Andrew Jones, Lee Owens, Thomas Field, Wayne
Riley, Ryan Wignall (84' Ellis Healing), Jay Owen, Matty McGinn, Chris Budrys (83' Ricky
Evans), Tony Gray (74' Ryan Wade). Coach: Andrew Preece.
Lokomotiva Zagreb: Oliver Zelenika, Karlo Bartolec, Tomislav Mrcela, Karlo Brucic, Luka
Capan, Damir Sovsic (84' Josip Coric), Ivan Fiolic, Petar Misic (74' Sime Grzan), Franko
Andrijasevic, Jerko Leko, Mirko Maric (62' Marko Kolar). Coach: Ante Cacic.
Goals: 28' Wayne Riley 1-0, 48' Damir Sovsic 1-1, 61' Mirko Maric 1-2,
68' Marko Kolar 1-3.
Referee: Poroddur Hjaltalin (ISL)   Attendance: 543.

02.07.15   JENS Vesting, Emmen: Go Ahead Eagles – Ferencvárosi TC 1-1 (1-1).
Go Ahead Eagles: Erik Cummins, Bart Vriends, Xandro Schenk, Kenny Teijsse, Sven
Nieuwpoort, Sander Duits (74' Lars Lambooij), Deniz Türüc, Jerry van Ewijk (63' Jeffrey
Rijsdijk), Elvio van Overbeek, Randy Wolters, Teije ten Den (83' Alex Schalk).
Coach: Dennis Demmers.
Ferencvárosi TC: Dénes Dibusz, Michal Nalepa, Mateos, Cristian Ramirez, Leandro, Gábor
Gyömbér, Roland Lamah (80' Roland Ugrai), Dániel Böde, Zoltán Gera, Somália (86' Attila
Busai), Roland Varga (79' Dominik Nagy). Coach: Thomas Doll.
Goals: 3' Zoltán Gera 0-1, 45' Bart Vriends 1-1.
Referee: Craig Pawson (ENG)   Attendance: 6,248.

02.07.15   Sportni Park, Domzale: NK Domzale – FK Cukaricki-Stankom 0-1 (0-1).
NK Domzale: Nejc Vidmar, Darko Zec, Dejan Trajkovski, Gaber Dobrovoljc, Kenan Horic,
Rudi Vancas, Juninho (46' Lucas Horvat), Zan Majer (49' Ziga Kous), Uros Korun, Slobodan
Vuk (46' Matej Podlogar), Benjamin Morel. Coach: Luka Elsner.
FK Cukaricki-Stankom: Nemanja Stevanovic, Lucas, Filip Stojkovic, Bojan Ostojic, Dragojub
Srnic, Branislav Jankovic (89' Nenad Mirosavljevic), Igor Matic (82' Sasa Jovanovic),
Slavoljub Srnic, Rajko Brezancic, Andrija Pavlovic (90+4' Dorde Radovanovic), Petar Bojic.
Coach: Vladan Milojevic.
Goal: 43' Igor Matic 0-1.
Referee: Bart Vententen (BEL)   Attendance: 1,200.
Sent off: 47' Gaber Dobrovoljc.

02.07.15   Svangaskard, Toftir: Vikingur – Rosenborg BK 0-2 (0-0).
Vikingur: Tamas Túri Géza, Hanus Jacobsen, Atli Gregersen, Erling Jacobsen, Hans Djurhuus,
Solvi Vatnhamar, Bárdur Hansen, Andreas Olsen (87' Gert Aage Hansen), Hedin Hansen (80'
Gunnar Vatnhamar), Filip Dordevic (89' Dánjal Lervig), Finnur Justinussen.
Coach: Sigfridur Clementsen.
Rosenborg BK: André Hansen, Mikael Dorsin, Hólmar Eyjólfsson, Mike Jensen, Riku Riski
(80' Andreas Helmersen), Tobias Mikkelsen, Jørgen Skjelvik, Ole Selnæs, Fredrik Midtsjø,
Jonas Svensson, Tomás Malec (64' Alexander Søderlund). Coach: Kåre Ingebrigtsen.
Goals: 82',90+2' Alexander Søderlund 0-1, 0-2.
Referee: Bryn Markham-Jones (WAL)   Attendance: 1,057.

13

02.07.15   Petrol Arena, Celje: NK Celje – Slask Wroclaw 0-1 (0-1).

NK Celje: Matic Kotnik, Tilen Klemencic, Marko Jakolic, Soria, Mihovil Klapan, Tadej Vidmajer, Danijel Miskic, Matej Mrsic (70' Karlo Tezak), Ivan Firer, Gregor Bajde (63' Blaz Vrhovec), Valon Ahmedi (46' Sunny Omoregie). Coach: Simon Rozman.

Slask Wroclaw: Mariusz Pawelek, Piotr Celeban, Dudu Paraiba, Mariusz Pawelec, Pawel Zielinski, Tom Hateley, Tomasz Holota, Jacek Kielb, Flávio Paixao (78' Krzysztof Ostrowski), Peter Grajciar (69' Mateusz Machaj), Róbert Pich (90' Kamil Dankowski). Coach: Tadeusz Pawlowski.

Goal: 32' Róbert Pich 0-1.
Referee: Enea Jorgji (ALB)   Attendance: 4,900.

02.07.15   Latham Park, Newtown: Newtown AFC – Valletta FC 2-1 (1-0).

Newtown AFC: David Jones, Steffan Edwards, Kieran Mills-Evans, Shane Sutton (90+3' Gavin Cadwallader), Matty Owen (78' Sean Evans), Luke Boundford, Craig Williams, Tom Goodwin, Matthew Hearsey, Jason Oswell, Neil Mitchell (70' James Price). Coach: Chris Hughes.

Valletta FC: Nicholas Vella, Ian Azzopardi, Ryan Camilleri, Juan Gill, Dyson Falzon, Claudio Pani, Maxim Focsa, Abdelkarim Nafti (87' Daniel Camilleri), Uchenna Umeh (62' Jhonnattann), Luke Montebello (54' Jean-Pierre Triganza), Llywelyn Cremona. Coach: Paul Zammit.

Goals: 40' Luke Boundford 1-0, 73' Jhonnattann 1-1, 90+1' Jason Oswell 2-1.
Referee: Vladimir Vnuk (SVK)   Attendance: 1,420.
Sent off: 85' Ian Azzopardi.

02.07.15   Pod Goricom, Podgorica: FK Buducnost Podgorica – FK Spartaks 1-3 (1-2).

FK Buducnost Podgorica: Jasmin Agovic, Mihailo Tomkovic, Andija Vukcevic (71' Stefan Milosevic), Momcilo Raspopovic, Janko Simovic, Deni Hocko (77' Milos Raickovic), Flavio Junior, Marko Ilincic (60' Savo Gazivoda), Darko Nikac, Milos Pavicevic, Milivoje Raicevic. Coach: Miodrag Vukotic.

FK Spartaks: Aleksandrs Kolinko, Maksym Maksymenko, Dmitro Nazarenko, Toms Mezs, Nauris Bulvitis, Ingus Slampe (90+3' Elvis Stuglis), Daniil Ulimbasevs (90+1' Romans Bespalovs), Jevgenijs Kazacoks, Romans Mickevics, Francesco Vivacqua (81' Kevin Mena), Ferdinand Takyi. Coach: Roman Pylypchuk.

Goals: 6' Milivoje Raicevic 1-0, 22' Nauris Bulvitis 1-1, 42' Romans Mickevics 1-2, 74' Nauris Bulvitis 1-3 (p).
Referee: Oleksandr Derdo (UKR)   Attendance: 4,072.

02.07.15   Szusza Ferenc, Budapest: MTK Budapest – Vojvodina 0-0.

MTK Budapest: Lajos Hegedüs, Mato Grgic, Dragan Vukmir, Lyane Khaly, Marek Strestik (46' Myke), József Kanta, Dániel Vadnai, Adám Vass, Szabolcs Varga (59' Lorand Szatmári), Sandor Torghelle (90+3' Adám Schrammel), Barnabás Bese. Coach: Csaba László.

Vojvodina: Srdan Zakula, Jovica Vasilic, Darko Puskaric, Bojan Nastic, Igor Djuric, Dominik Dinga, Mirko Ivanic (90+3' Saleta Kordic), Aleksandar Palocevic (64' Uros Stamenic), Danilo Sekulic, Aleksandar Stanisavljevic, Milan Mrdakovic (89' Novica Maksimovic). Coach: Zlatomir Zagorcic.

Referee: Paolo Valeri (ITA)   Attendance: 902.

14

02.07.15   Olimpico di Serravalle, Serravalle: SP La Fiorita – FC Vaduz 0-5 (0-3).

SP La Fiorita: Gianmarco Pazzini, Andrea Martini, Davide Bugali, Sandro Macerata, Marco Gasperoni, Adrian Ricchiuti (69' Nicola Cavalli), Damiano Tommasi, Alessio Cangini (79' Andrea Righi), Danilo Rinaldi, Andy Selva, Tommaso Zafferani (89' Nicola Casadei).
Coach: Luigi Bizzotto.
FC Vaduz: Peter Jehle, Pavel Pergl, Nick von Niederhäusern (46' Nico Abegglen), Florian Stahel, Naser Aliji, Steven Lang, Diego Ciccone, Pascal Schürpf, Nicolas Hasler (65' Robin Kamber), Markus Neumayr, Manuel Sutter (72' Kristian Kuzmanovic).
Coach: Giorgio Contini.
Goals: 5' Pascal Schürpf 0-1, 26' Manuel Sutter 0-2, 41' Pavel Pergl 0-3, 79' Nico Abegglen 0-4, 90+2' Diego Ciccone 0-5.
Referee: Irfan Peljto (BIH)   Attendance: 649.

02.07.15   Mourneview Park, Lurgan: Glenavon FC – Shakhter Soligorsk 1-2 (0-2).
Glenavon FC: James McGrath, Simon Kelly, Rhys Marshall, Conor Dillon, David Elebert (64' Kris Lindsay), James Singleton, Andrew Kilmartin (67' Mark Patton), Andrew Hall (83' Gary Hamilton), Ciaran Martyn, Eoin Bradley, Kevin Braniff. CCoach: Gary Hamilton.
Shakhter Soligorsk: Vladimir Bushma, Aleksey Yanushkevich, Aleksandr Yurevich, Pavel Rybak, Ihar Kuzmianok, Siarhei Matveichyk, Mikhail Afanasiev (73' Nemanja Covic), Artem Stagorodskiy, Saulius Mikoliunas (52' Yuri Kovalev), Nikolai Yanush, Dmitriy Komarovskiy (84' Yaroslav Martinyuk). Coach: Sergey Nikiforenko.
Goals: 2' Mikhail Afanasiev 0-1, 30' Dmitriy Komarovskiy 0-2, 86' Mark Patton 1-2.
Referee: Dag Hafsas (NOR)   Attendance: 640.

02.07.15   Windsor Park, Belfast: Linfield FC – NSI Runavik 2-0 (0-0).
Linfield FC: Ross Glendinning, Chris Hegarty (65' Reece Glendinning), Mark Haughey, Aaron Burns, Sean Ward, Matthew Clarke, Stephen Lowry, David Kee, Ivan Sproule, Andrew Waterworth, Guy Bates (90' Kirk Millar). Coach: Warren Feeney.
NSI Runavik: András Gángó, Per Langgaard, Monrad Jacobsen, Jens Joensen (75' Hákun Edmundsson), Pól Justinussen, Arni Frederiksberg, Jóhan Jacobsen, Magnus Olsen, Haraldur Hojgaard (63' Jann Mortensen), Klaemint Olsen, Jónhard Frederiksberg (69' Jónleif Hojgaard). Coach: Trygvi Mortensen.
Goals: 57' Andrew Waterworth 1-0, 73' Guy Bates 2-0.
Referee: Petr Ardeleánu (CZE)   Attendance: 1,824.

02.07.15   Turners Cross, Cork: Cork City – KR Reykjavik 1-1 (1-1).
Cork City: Mark McNulty, Alan Bennett, Darren Dennehy, Colin Healy (66' Dan Murray), Kevin O'Connor, Billy Dennehy, Liam Miller, Gary Buckley, John O'Flynn (59' Mark O'Sullivan), Ross Gaynor (46' John Dunleavy), Karl Sheppard. Coach: John Caulfield.
KR Reykjavik: Stefán Magnússon, Rasmus Christiansen, Gonzalo Balbi (31' Aron Jósepsson), Skúli Jón Fridgeirsson, Gunnar Gunnarsson, Jónas Saevarsson, Pálmi Pálmason, Jacob Schoop, Oskar Hauksson (68' Gary Martin), Almarr Ormarsson (74' Þorsteinn Már Ragnarsson), Soren Frederiksen. Coach: Bjaarni Gudjónsson.
Goals: 19' Alan Bennett 1-0, 28' Oskar Hauksson 1-1.
Referee: Mads-Kristoffer Kristoffersen (DEN)   Attendance: 4,641.

15

02.07.15   Belfield Park, Dublin: UC Dublin – F91 Dudelange 1-0 (1-0).
UC Dublin: Niall Corbert, Mark Langtry, Michael Leahy, Ryan McLaughlin, Tomas Boyle,
Gary O'Neill, Chris Mulhall, Ryan Swan, Dylan Watts (90+2' Jack Watson), Robbie Benson,
Jamie Doyle. Coach: Collie O'Neill.
F91 Dudelange: Jonathan Joubert, Clayton De Sousa, Romain Ney, Tom Schnell, Jerry
Prempeh, Sofian Benzouien, Joël Pedro, Kevin Nakache, Grégory Adler (58' David Turpel),
Sanel Ibrahimovic (83' Patrik Teixeira Pinto), Daniël Da Mota (74' Alexandre Lauriente).
Coach: Michel Leflochmoan.
Goal: 45' Ryan Swan 1-0.
Referee: Petur Reinert (FRO)   Attendance: 1,075.

02.07.15   Stadion Rajko Mitić, Beograd: Crvena Zvezda – Kairat Almaty 0-2 (0-1).
Crvena Zvezda: Predrag Rajkovic, Savo Pavicevic, Milos Cvetkovic, Dusan Andelkovic, Zoran
Rendulic, Idan Vered, Vukan Savicevic, Aleksandar Kovacevic (5' Vukasin Jovanovic),
Aleksandar Katai (77' Mihailo Ristic), Josh Parker, Petar Orlandic (60' Luka Jovic).
Coach: Miodrag Bozovic.
Kairat Almaty: Vladimir Plotnikov, Bruno Soares, Mark Gorman, Zarko Markovic, Ermek
Kuantaev, Bauyrzhan Islamkhan (62' Serginho), Isael (81' Aslan Darabaev), Islambek Kuat
(85' Zhambyl Kukeev), Gerard Gohou, Sito Riera, Stanislav Lunin. Coach: Vladimir Weiss.
Goals: 45' Gerard Gohou 0-1, 64' Ermek Kuantaev 0-2.
Referee: Bartosz Frankowski (POL)   Attendance: 25,211.
Sent off: 3' Savo Pavicevic.

02.07.15   Upton Park, London: West Ham United – FC Lusitanos la Posa 3-0 (2-0).
West Ham United: Darren Randolph, James Tomkins, Reece Burke, Lewis Page, Matthew
Jarvis, Joey O'Brien (60' Josh Cullen), Morgan Amalfitano, Diego Poyet, Reece Oxford,
Mauro Zárate (74' Djair ParfittpWilliams), Diafra Sakho (62' Elliot Lee). Coach: Slaven Bilic.
FC Lusitanos la Posa: Gerardo Rubio, Carlos Acosta, Moises San Nicolas, Pedro Munoz,
Leonel Maciel, Alberto Molina, Franclim Soares (54' Oscar Sonejee), Jose Romero, Miguel,
José Aguilar (46' Edu Moya), Luigi San Nicolas (46' Alfi Conteh-Lacalle).
Coach: Xavier Roura.
Goals: 40',45' Diafra Sakho 1-0, 2-0, 58' James Tomkins 3-0.
Referee: Vadims Direktorenko (LAT)   Attendance: 34,966.

02.07.15   Hibernians Ground, Paola: Birkirkara FC – Ulisses FC 0-0.
Birkirkara FC: Justin Haber (37' Ini Akpan), Mauricio Mazzetti, Ryan Camenzuli, Nikola
Vukanac, Joseph Zerafa, Paul Fenech, Edmond Agius (72' Rafael Gaúcho), Zach Muscat,
Rowen Muscat, Vito Plut (65' Andrew Scicluna), Liliu. Coach: Giovanni Tedesco.
Ulisses FC: Arsen Beglaryan, Irakli Chezhiya, Ivan Mamakhanov, Rade Dugalic, Konstantin
Morozov, Levan Dzharkava, David Khurtsidze, Nika Piliev (62' Joël Tshibamba), Artak
Aleksanyan, Giorgi Khubua (79' Andrey Belomittsev), Irakli Geperidze (84' Rustem
Kalimullin). Coach: Suren Chakhalyan.
Referee: Erez Papir (ISR)   Attendance: 1,895.

02.07.15   The Oval, Belfast: Glentoran Belfast – MSK Zilina 1-4 (0-2).

Glentoran Belfast: Elliott Morris, Barry Holland, Calum Birney, Jay Magee, Steven McCullough, Marcus Kane, Francis McCaffrey (82' Stephen McAlorum), Jordan Stewart (63' Jonathan Addis), Kristian Gibson, Steven Gordon, Conor McMenamin.
Coach: Eddie Patterson.

MSK Zilina: Milos Volesak, Milan Skriniar, Denis Vavro, Ernest Mabouka, Miroslav Kácer, Jakub Paur (63' Jaroslav Mihalík), Viktor Pecovsky, Bojan Letic, László Bénes, Matej Jelic (89' William), Lukás Cmelik (78' Nikolas Spalek). Coach: Adrián Gula.
Goals: 13' Matej Jelic 0-1, 20' Jakub Paur 0-2, 59' Lukás Cmelik 0-3, 66' Conor McMenamin 1-3, 81' Marcus Kane 1-4 (og).
Referee: Jari Järvinen (FIN)   Attendance: 1,676.

02.07.15   Filip II. Makedonski, Skopje: KF Shkëndija 79 – Aberdeen FC 1-1 (0-0).

KF Shkëndija 79: Marko Jovanovski, Xhelil Abdulla (84' Hristijan Kirovski), Ardijan Cuculi, Armend Alimi, Artim Polozani, Besir Demiri, Blagoja Todorovski, Victor Juffo (80' Egzon Bejtulai), Ferhan Hasani, Bojan Vrucina (46' Besart Ibraimi), Stenio Júnior.
Coach: Shpëtim Duro.

Aberdeen FC: Danny Ward, Shaleum Logan, Graeme Shinnie, Andrew Considine, Mark Reynolds (69' Paul Quinn), Ash Taylor, Willo Flood (65' Peter Pawlett), Nial McGinn, Jonathan Hayes, Ryan Jack, Adam Rooney (65' David Goodwillie). Coach: Derek McInnes.
Goals: 79' Niall Mc Ginn 0-1, 84' Hristijan Kirovski 1-1.
Referee: Tolga Ozkalfa (TUR)   Attendance: 7,040.

02.07.15   Vikingsvöllur, Reykjavik: Vikingur Reykjavik – FC Koper 0-1 (0-0).

Vikingur Reykjavik: Thomas Nielsen, Dofri Snorrason (52' Hallgrimur Mar Steingrimsson), Milos Zivkovic, Alan Lowing, Igor Taskovic, Haukur Baldvinsson, Rolf Toft (64' Arnpór Ingi Kristinsson), Finnur Olafsson, Ivar Jónsson, Andri Rúnar Bjarnason (86' Viktor Arnarsson), David Atlason. Coach: Olafur Pordarson.

FC Koper: Vasja Simcic, Denis Srne, Denis Halilovic, Damir Hadzic, Ivica Guberac, Domen Crnigoj, Ante Tomic, Matej Palcic (67' Amar Rahmanovic), Josip Ivancic (82' Mitja Lotric), Goran Galesic (90+1' Miha Blazic), Matej Pucko. Coach: Rodolfo Vanoli.
Goal: 77' Matej Pucko 0-1.
Referee: Andrew Dallas (SCO)   Attendance: 1,010.

07.07.15   Tallaght Stadium, Dublin: Shamrock Rovers - Progrès Niederkorn 3-0 (2-0).

Shamrock Rovers: Craig Hyland, Luke Byrne, David Webster, Simon Madden, Tim Clancy, Gary McCabe, Gavin Brennan, Patrick Cregg, Brandon Miele, Kieran Waters (74' Ryan Brennan), Michael Drennan (87' Danny North). Coach: Pat Fenlon.

Progrès Niederkorn: Sebastian Flauss, Ismaël Bouzid, Adrien Ferino, Samuel Dog, Olivier Cassan, Alessandro Fiorani (75' Paul Bossi), Mickael Garos, Sébastien Thill (77' Oliver Thill), Hakim Menai, Giuseppe Rossini, Lévy Rougeaux (67' Valentin Poisignon).
Coach: Oliver Ciancanelli.
Goals: 21' David Webster 1-0, 41',57' Kieran Waters 2-0, 3-0.
Referee: Dominik Ouschan (AUT)   Attendance: 3,250.

17

09.07.15   SRC Bonifika, Koper: FC Koper – Vikingur Reykjavik 2-2 (1-0).

FC Koper: Vasja Simcic, Denis Srne, Miha Blazic, Damir Hadzic, Ivica Guberac, Domen Crnigoj, Ante Tomic, Matej Palcic, Josip Ivancic (58' Jaka Stromajer), Goran Galesic (90+2' Marko Krivicic), Matej Pucko. Coach: Rodolfo Vanoli.

Vikingur Reykjavik: Thomas Nielsen, Dofri Snorrason, Milos Zivkovic, Igor Taskovic, Tómas Gudmundsson, Haukur Baldvinsson, Arnpór Ingi Kristinsson, Finnur Olafsson (77' Halldór Sigurdsson), Ivar Jónsson, Andri Rúnar Bjarnason (73' Hallgrimur Mar Steingrimsson), David Atlason (57' Rolf Toft). Coach: Olafur Pordarson.

Goals: 18' Matej Pucko 1-0, 51' Arnpór Ingi Kristinsson 1-1, 61' Matej Palcic 2-1, 76' Arnpór Ingi Kristinsson 2-2.

Referee: István Kovács (ROM)   Attendance: 1,500.

09.07.15   Pittodrie Stadium, Aberdeen: Aberdeen FC - KF Shkëndija 79 0-0.

Aberdeen FC: Danny Ward, Shaleum Logan, Graeme Shinnie, Andrew Considine, Ash Taylor, Kenny McLean (67' Peter Pawlett), Willo Flood (79' David Goodwillie), Nial McGinn, Jonathan Hayes (80' Barry Robson), Ryan Jack, Adam Rooney. Coach: Derek McInnes

KF Shkëndija 79: Marko Jovanovski, Xhelil Abdulla (80' Hristijan Kirovski), Ardijan Cuculi, Armend Alimi, Artim Polozani, Besir Demiri, Blagoja Todorovski, Victor Juffo (71' Egzon Bejtulai), Ferhan Hasani, Stenio Júnior (85' Bojan Vrucina), Besart Ibraimi.
Coach: Shpëtim Duro.

Referee: Nikolaj Hänni (SUI)   Attendance: 14,112.

Aberdeen FC won on away goals.

09.07.15   Stadión pod Dubnom, Zilina: MSK Zilina – Glentoran Belfat 3-0 (1-0).

MSK Zilina: Milos Volesak, Milan Skriniar, Denis Vavro, Ernest Mabouka, Nikolas Spalek (59' Miroslav Kácer), Viktor Pecovsky (59' Lukás Cmelik), Michal Skvarka, Bojan Letic, László Bénes, Jaroslav Mihalík, Matej Jelic (79' Jakub Paur). Coach: Adrián Gula.

Glentoran Belfast: Elliott Morris, Barry Holland, Calum Birney, Jay Magee (79' William Garrett), Steven McCullough, Marcus Kane, Francis McCaffrey (76' Jonathan Addis), Stephen McAlorum (67' Kym Nelson), Kristian Gibson, Steven Gordon, Conor McMenamin.
Coach: Eddie Patterson.

Goals: 44',55',66' Matej Jelic 1-0, 2-0, 3-0.

Referee: Bardhyl Pashaj (ALB)   Attendance: 2,897.

09.07.15   Hanrapetakan, Yerevan: Ulisses FC – Birkirkara FC 1-3 (0-2).

Ulisses FC: Arsen Beglaryan, Ivan Mamakhanov, Rade Dugalic, Konstantin Morozov, Levan Dzharkava (70' Zamir Dzhanashiia), Igor Paderin, David Khurtsidze, Artak Aleksanyan, Giorgi Khubua, Joël Tshibamba (53' Nika Piliev), Irakli Geperidze. Coach: Suren Chakhalyan.

Birkirkara FC: Ini Akpan, Mauricio Mazzetti, Ryan Camenzuli, Nikola Vukanac, Joseph Zerafa, Paul Fenech, Zach Muscat, Rowen Muscat, Fabricio Miccoli (65' Edmond Agius), Liliu (68' Vito Plut), Edin Murga (71' Terence Vella). Coach: Giovanni Tedesco.

Goals: 21' Fabrizio Miccoli 0-1, 44' Mauricio Mazzetti 0-2, 71' Konstantin Morozov 1-2, 80' Paul Fenech 1-3 (p).

Referee: Nicolas Laforge (BEL)   Attendance: 3,500.

Sent off: 76' Terence Vella, 81' Artak Aleksanyan.

18

09.07.15 Estadi Comunal, Andorra la Vella:
FC Lusitanos la Posa – West Ham United 0-1 (0-1).

FC Lusitanos la Posa: Gerardo Rubio, Carlos Acosta (52' Edu Moya), Moises San Nicolas, Pedro Munoz, Leonel Maciel, Alberto Molina, Franclim Soares, Jose Romero (76' Alfi Cconteh-Lacalle), Miguel, José Aguilar, Luigi San Nicolas (74' Luis Pinto).
Coach: Xavier Roura.
West Ham United: Darren Randolph, James Tomkins, Lewis Page, Matthew Jarvis, Joey O'Brien (61' Reece Burke), Morgan Amalfitano (76' Djair Parfitt-Williams), Diego Poyet, Reece Oxford, Josh Cullen (86' Amos Nasha), Diafra Sakho, Elliot Lee. Coach: Slaven Bilic.
Goal: 21' Elliot Lee 0-1.
Referee: Anders Poulsen (DEN)   Attendance: 837.
Sent off: 14' Diafra Sakho.

09.07.15 Tsentralniy, Almaty: Kairat Almaty – Ccrvena Zvezda 2-1 (1-0).

Kairat Almaty: Vladimir Plotnikov, Bruno Soares, Mark Gorman, Zarko Markovic, Ermek Kuantaev, Bauyrzhan Islamkhan (66' Serginho), Isael, Islambek Kuat (84' Aslan Darabaev), Gerard Gohou (90+3' Zhambyl Kukeev), Sito Riera, Stanislav Lunin. Coach: Vladimir Weiss.
Crvena Zvezda: Predrag Rajkovic, Marko Petkovic (46' Milos Cvetkovic), Mamadou Mbodj, Dusan Andelkovic, Zoran Rendulic, Sasa Stojanovic, Idan Vered (70' Nenad Gavric), Vukan Savicevic, Luka Jovic, Aleksandar Katai, Josh Parker (60' Petar Orlandic).
Coach: Miodrag Bozovic.
Goals: 29' Bauyrzhan Islamkhan 1-0, 47' Islambek Kuat 2-0, 85' Vukan Savicevic 2-1 (p).
Referee: Baris Simsek (TUR)   Attendance: 21,550.

09.07.15 Stade Jos Nusbaum, Dudelange: F91 Dudelange – UC Dublin 2-1 (2-1).

F91 Dudelange: Jonathan Joubert, Clayton De Sousa (65' Sanel Ibrahimovic), Romain Ney, Tom Schnell, Jerry Prempeh, Sofian Benzouien (71' Grégory Adler), Joël Pedro, Stélvio, Kevin Nakache, Daniël Da Mota (76' Alexandre Lauriente), David Turpel.
Coach: Michel Leflochmoan.
UC Dublin: Niall Corbert, Sean Coyne, Mark Langtry, Michael Leahy (79' Adam Harney), Tomas Boyle, Gary O'Neill, Chris Mulhall, Ryan Swan (67' Samir Belhout), Dylan Watts (31' Maxim Kouogun), Robbie Benson, Jamie Doyle. Coach: Collie O'Neill.
Goals: 17' Ryan Swan 0-1, 43' Joël Pedro 1-1, 45' Kevin Nakache 2-1.
Referee: Rahim Hasanov (AZE)   Attendance: 1,245.
Sent off: 28' Sean Coyne.

UC Dublin won on away goals.

09.07.15 Alvogenvöllurinn, Reykjavik: KR Reykjavik – Cork City 2-1 (0-1, 1-1)
KR Reykjavik: Stefán Magnússon, Rasmus Christiansen, Skúli Jón Fridgeirsson, Gunnar Gunnarsson (71' Porsteinn Már Ragnarsson), Aron Jósepsson, Jónas Saevarsson (53' Almarr Ormarsson), Pálmi Pálmason, Jacob Schoop, Oskar Hauksson, Gary Martin (104' Grétar Sigurdsson), Soren Frederiksen. Coach: Bjaarni Gudjónsson.
Cork City: Mark McNulty, Alan Bennett, Darren Dennehy, Dan Murray, Colin Healy, Kevin O'Connor, Liam Miller (65' Liam Kearney), Mark O'Sullivan (107' Danny Morrissey), Gary Buckley, Ross Gaynor, Karl Sheppard (80' John O'Flynn). Coach: John Caulfield.
Goals: 13' Mark O'Sullivan 0-1, 75' Pálmi Pálmasonn 1-1, 99' Jacob Schoop 2-1.
Referee: Aleksandrs Anufrijevs (LAT)   Attendance: 1,145.
Sent off: 44' Skúli Jón Fridgeirsson.

KR Reykjavik won after extra time.

09.07.15   Svangaskard, Toftir: NSI Runavik – Linfield FC 4-3 (3-2).

NSI Runavik: András Gángó, Monrad Jacobsen, Jens Joensen, Einar Tróndargjogv, Pól Justinussen, Arni Frederiksberg, Jóhan Jacobsen, Magnus Olsen (81' Meinhard Olsen), Haraldur Hojgaard (55' Hakun Edmundsson), Klaemint Olsen, Jónhard Frederiksberg (68' Jann Mortensen). Coach: Trygvi Mortensen.

Linfield FC: Ross Glendinning, Chris Hegarty, Aaron Burns (83' Thomas Murray), Sean Ward, Matthew Clarke, Reece Glendinning, Stephen Lowry, David Kee, Ivan Sproule, Andrew Waterworth, Guy Bates (71' Ross Clarke). Coach: Warren Feeney.

Goals: 13' Reece Glendinning 0-1, 17' Klaemint Olsen 1-1, 19' Pól Justinussen 2-1, 33' Guy Bates 2-2, 45' Jens Joensen 3-2, 69' Andrew Waterworth 3-3, 85' Pól Justinussen 4-3.
Referee: Jovan Kaluderovic (MNE)   Attendance: 550.

09.07.15   Stroitel, Soligorsk: Shakhter Soligorsk – Glenavon FC 3-0 (1-0).

Shakhter Soligorsk: Vladimir Bushma, Aleksey Yanushkevich, Aleksandr Yurevich (75' Sergey Koseka), Pavel Rybak, Ihar Kuzmianok, Siarhei Matveichyk, Mikhail Afanasiev (59' Saulius Mikoliunas), Artem Stagorodskiy, Yuri Kovalev (82' Mikhail Sibun), Nikolai Yanush, Dmitriy Komarovskiy. Coach: Sergey Nikiforenko.

Glenavon FC: Jonny Tuffey, Simon Kelly, Kris Lindsay (69' Ciaran Caldwell), Rhys Marshall, Conor Dillon, James Singleton, Andrew Kilmartin (62' Gary Hamilton), Andrew Hall (35' Mark Patton), Ciaran Martyn, Eoin Bradley, Kevin Braniff. CCoach: Gary Hamilton.

Goals: 8' Aleksandr Yurevich 1-0, 66' Nikolai Yanush 2-0, 87' Dmitriy Komarovskiy 3-0.
Referee: Aleksander Gauzer (KAZ)   Attendance: 3,200.

09.07.15   Rheinpark, Vaduz: FC Vaduz – SP La Fiorita 5-1 (3-0).

FC Vaduz: Andreas Hirzel, Simone Grippo, Nick von Niederhäusern, Mario Bühler, Steven Lang, Diego Ciccone (57' Kristian Kuzmanovic), Ramon Cecchini, Pascal Schürpf (46' Manuel Sutter), Markus Neumayr, Philipp Muntwiler, Robin Kamber (58' Nicolas Hasler). Coach: Giorgio Contini.

SP La Fiorita: Gianmarco Pazzini, Andrea Martini, Sandro Macerata, Marco Gasperoni, Nicola Cavalli (70' Alessandro Guidi), Andrea Ricchiuti, Damiano Tommasi, Alessio Cangini, Andrea Righi (60' Nicola Casadei), Danilo Rinaldi (82' Thomas De Biagi), Tommaso Zafferani. Coach: Luigi Bizzotto.

Goals: 25',33' Robin Kamber 1-0, 2-0, 41' Pascal Schürpf 3-0, 71' Philipp Muntwiler 4-0, 74' Damiano Tommasi 4-1, 84' Steven Lang 5-1.
Referee: Suren Baliyan (ARM)   Attendance: 727.

09.07.15   Karadorde, Novi Sad: Vojvodina – MTK Budapest 3-1 (2-1).

Vojvodina: Srdan Zakula, Jovica Vasilic, Radovan Pankov, Bojan Nastic, Igor Djuric, Mirko Ivanic, Danilo Sekulic, Novica Maksimovic (55' Darko Puskaric), Aleksandar Stanisavljevic, Milan Mrdakovic (90' Aleksandar Palocevic), Uros Stamenic (77' Srdjan Babic). Coach: Zlatomir Zagorcic.

MTK Budapest: Lajos Hegedüs, Mato Grgic, Dragan Vukmir, Lyane Khaly, Marek Strestik (63' Lorand Szatmári), József Kanta, Dániel Vadnai, Adám Vass (90+3' Daniel Gera), Szabolcs Varga (53' Myke), Sandor Torghelle, Barnabás Bese. Coach: Csaba László.

Goals: 3' Marek Strestik 0-1, 14' Aleksandar Stanisavljević 1-1, 40' Milan Mrdakovic 2-1, 51' Mirko Ivanic 3-1.
Referee: Tore Hansen (NOR)   Attendance: 8,460.

20

09.07.15   Hibernians Ground, Paola: Valletta FC – Newtown AFC 1-2 (0-1).
Valletta FC: Nicholas Vella, Jonathan Caruana, Ryan Camilleri, Juan Gill, Dyson Falzon,
Roderick Briffa, Claudio Pani, Abdelkarim Nafti (87' Uchenna Umeh), Thierry Tazemeta (63'
Jean-Pierre Triganza), Jhonnattann, Llywelyn Cremona. Coach: Paul Zammit.
Newtown AFC: David Jones, Steffan Edwards, Kieran Mills-Evans, Shane Sutton, Matty
Owen (89' James Price), Luke Boundford, Craig Williams, Tom Goodwin, Matthew Hearsey
(68' Matthew Cook), Jason Oswell, Neil Mitchell (88' Gareth Partridge).
Coach: Chris Hughes.
Goals: 7' Jason Oswell 0-1, 46' Thierry Tazemeta 1-1, 85' Matty Owen 1-2.
Referee: Fabian Mihaly (HUN)   Attendance: 1,914.
Sent off: 74' Ryan Camilleri, 87' Matthew Cook.

09.07.15   Zemgalas Olimpiska Centra, Jelgava: FK Spartaks – FK Buducnost Podgorica 0-0.
FK Spartaks: Aleksandrs Kolinko, Maksym Maksymenko, Dmitro Nazarenko, Toms Mezs,
Nauris Bulvitis, Ingus Slampe, Daniil Ulimbasevs, Jevgenijs Kazacoks, Romans Mickevics,
Francesco Vivacqua (90+1' Ahmed Abdultaofik), Ferdinand Takyi (82' Elvis Stuglis).
Coach: Roman Pylypchuk.
FK Buducnost Podgorica: Jasmin Agovic, Mihailo Tomkovic, Andija Vukcevic (74' Stefan
Milosevic), Momcilo Raspopovic, Janko Simovic, Milos Raickovic (56' Marko Burzanovic),
Flavio Junior, Marko Ilincic, Darko Nikac, Milos Pavicevic (65' Savo Gazivoda), Milivoje
Raicevic. Coach: Miodrag Vukotic.
Referee: Peter Kralovic (SVK)   Attendance: 1,018.
Sent off: 82' Momcilo Raspopovic.

09.07.15   Meijski, Wroclaw: Slask Wroclaw – NK Celje 3-1 (0-0).
Slask Wroclaw: Mariusz Pawelek, Piotr Celeban, Dudu Paraiba, Mariusz Pawelec, Pawel
Zielinski, Tom Hateley, Tomasz Holota, Jacek Kielb (90+1' Kamil Dankowski), Flávio Paixao
(11' Krzysztof Ostrowski), Peter Grajciar (76' Michal Bartkowiak), Róbert Pich.
Coach: Tadeusz Pawlowski.
NK Celje: Matic Kotnik, Tilen Klemencic, Marko Jakolic, Soria, Mihovil Klapan, Tadej
Vidmajer, Blaz Vrhovec, Danijel Miskic (79' Valon Ahmedi), Matej Mrsic (70' Milan
Spremo), Ivan Firer, Sunny Omoregie (58' Gregor Bajde). Coach: Simon Rozman.
Goals: 46' Krzysztof Ostrowski 1-0, 56' Jacek Kielb 2-0, 80' Ivan Firer 2-1,
90' Jacek Kielb 3-1.
Referee: Anatoliy Zhabchenko (UKR)   Attendance: 12,364.

09.07.15   Lerkendal, Trondheim: Rosenborg BK – Vikingur 0-0.
Rosenborg BK: André Hansen, Mikael Dorsin, Hólmar Eyjólfsson, Riku Riski (74' Alexander
Søderlund), Jørgen Skjelvik, Ole Selnæs (66' Mike Jensen), Fredrik Midtsjø (84' Andreas
Helmersen), Jonas Svensson, John Hou Saeter, Tomás Malec, Emil Nielsen.
Coach: Kåre Ingebrigtsen.
Vikingur: Tamas Túri Géza, Hanus Jacobsen, Atli Gregersen, Erling Jacobsen, Hans Djurhuus,
Solvi Vatnhamar, Bárdur Hansen, Andreas Olsen (85' Sámal Jákup Joensen), Hedin Hansen
(75' Gert Aage Hansen), Filip Dordevic (64' Gunnar Vathamar), Finnur Justinussen.
Coach: Sigfridur Clementsen.
Referee: Sergejus Slyva (LTU)   Attendance: 4,572.

21

09.07.15   Cukaricki, Beograd: FK Cukaricki-Stankom – NK Domzale 0-0.
FK Cukaricki-Stankom: Nemanja Stevanovic, Lucas, Filip Stojkovic, Bojan Ostojic, Dragojub
Srnic, Branislav Jankovic, Igor Matic (69' Stanisa Mandic), Slavoljub Srnic, Rajko Brezancic,
Andrija Pavlovic (81' Nikola Stojiljkovic), Petar Bojic (90' Nenad Mirosavljevic).
Coach: Vladan Milojevic.
NK Domzale: Nejc Vidmar, Nejc Skubic, Dejan Trajkovski, Kenan Horic, Rudi Vancas (60'
Ernest Grvala), Lucas Horvat, Zan Majer (67' Slobodan Vuk), Uros Korun, Zeni Husmani (81'
Aladin Sisic), Matej Podlogar, Benjamin Morel. Coach: Luka Elsner.
Referee: Nikola Popov (BUL)   Attendance: 1,800.
Sent off: 90+5' Uros Korun.

09.07.15   Groupama Arena, Budapest: Ferencvárosi TC – Go Ahead Eagles 4-1 (3-0).
Ferencvárosi TC: Dénes Dibusz, Mateos, Emir Dilaver (28' Gábor Gyömbér), Cristian
Ramirez, Leandro, Attila Busai (72' Tamás Hajnal), Roland Lamah, Dániel Böde, Zoltán Gera,
Somália, Roland Varga (79' Zsolt Haraszti). Coach: Thomas Doll.
Go Ahead Eagles: Erik Cummins, Bart Vriends, Xandro Schenk, Kenny Teijsse, Sven
Nieuwpoort (76' Lars Lambooij), Sander Duits (73' Jerry van Ewijk), Deniz Türüc, Jeffrey
Rijsdijk, Elvio van Overbeek, Alex Schalk (59' Teije ten Den), Randy Wolters.
Coach: Dennis Demmers.
Goals: 4' Zoltán Gera 1-0, 20' Dániel Böde 2-0, 45' Attila Busai 3-0, 88' Zsolt Haraszti 4-0,
90+3' Deniz Türüc 4-1.
Referee: Bojan Pandzic (SWE).   *Match was played behind closed doors.*

Roland Lamah missed a penalty kick (64').

09.07.15   Maksimir, Zagreb: Lokomotiva Zagreb – Airbus UK 2-2 (0-0).
Lokomotiva Zagreb: Oliver Zelenika, Karlo Bartolec, Petar Mamic, Tomislav Mrcela, Luka
Capan, Damir Sovsic (90+2' Jakov Puljic), Luka Begonja, Ivan Fiolic (70' Sime Grzan), Petar
Misic (46' Marko Kolar), Franko Andrijasevic, Mirko Maric. Coach: Ante Cacic.
Airbus UK: James Coates, Michael Pearson, Andrew Jones, Lee Owens, Thomas Field (65'
Jordan Barrow), Wayne Riley (90+2' Jonathan Spittle), Ryan Wignall, Jay Owen, Matty
McGinn, Chris Budrys, Tony Gray (74' Ryan Wade). Coach: Andrew Preece.
Goals: 46' Chris Budrys 0-1, 65' Ivan Fiolic 1-1, 73' Damir Sovsic 2-1, 75' Andrew Jones 2-2.
Referee: Manuel Schüttengruber (AUT)   Attendance: 650.

09.07.15   Pasienky, Bratislava: Slovan Bratislava – College Europe FC 3-0 (2-0).
Slovan Bratislava: Martin Krnac, Boris Sekulic, Martin Dobrotka, Nicolas Gorosito (43'
Kornel Saláta), Frantisek Kubik, Adam Zrelak, Marko Milinkovic, Richard Lasik (46' Karol
Meszáros), Slobodan Simovic, Jakub Podany, Róbert Vittek (75' Tamás Priskin).
Coach: Dusan Tittel.
College Europe FC: Jose Camara Bellido, Diego Pacheco, Boris Jukic (64' Alejandro Ortega
Flores), Pinero, Alberto Merino, Javi Fernández, Javier Lopez, Javier Rodriguez Moreno (71'
Ante Sokol), Hrvoje Plazanic, Cristian Toncheff (86' Kelvin Morgan), Aaron Akrapovic.
Coach: Juan Gallardo Fernandez.
Goals: 20' Nicolas Gorosito 1-0, 35' Adam Zrelák 2-0, 68' Róbert Vittek 3-0 (p).
Referee: Alexandr Tean (MOL)   Attendance: 2,145.

09.07.15   Qemal Stafa, Tirana: FK Partizani – Strømsgodset IF 0-1 (0-0).

FK Partizani: Alban Hoxha, Arbnor Fejzullahu, Ditmar Bicaj, Endrit Vrapi, Renaldo Kalari (89' Dorian Bylykbashi), Idriz Batha, Mentor Mazrekaj (61' Nderim Nedzipi), Emiljano Vila, Astrit Fazliu, Sebino Plaku (77' Lorenc Trashi), Stevan Racic. Coach: Genc Tomorri.

Strømsgodset IF: Espen Pettersen, Kim Madsen, Gustav Valsvik, Mounir Hamoud, Martin Ovenstad, Iver Fossum, Gustav Wikheim, Mohammed Abu (84' Bassel Jradi), Lars-Christopher Vilsvik, Flamur Kastrati (58' Petter Moen), Marvin Ogunjimi (87' Thomas Sorum). Coach: Bjorn Petter Ingebretsen.

Goal: 90+5' Petter Moen 0-1.

Referee: Tobias Stieler (GER)   Attendance: 4,200.

09.07.15   Antonis Papadopoulos, Larnaca: Apollon Limassol – FC Saxan 2-0 (1-0).

Apollon Limassol: Bruno Vale, Elizio, Nuno Lopes, Freire, Esteban Sacchetti, Marcos Gullón, Joao Pedro (67' Christos Wheeler), Luka Stojanovic (57' Farley), Charis Kyriakou, Fotis Papoulis, Giorgos Kolokoudias (82' Thodores Josephides). Coach: Pedro Emanuel.

FC Saxan: Anatolii Chririnciuc, Kouassi Kouadja, Dumitru Popovici, Ion Arabadji, Yacouba Bamba (80' Mamadou Fofana), Mohamed Koné, Senin Sebai (62' Artion Puntus), Radu Catan (58' Andrey Bogdanov), Victor Truhanov, Eric Né, Lassina Dao. Coach: Vlad Goian.

Goals: 2' Luka Stojanovic 1-0, 61' Fotis Papoulis 2-0.

Referee: Srdan Jovanovic (SER)   Attendance: 3,800.

09.07.15   Mikheil Meshki, Tbilisi: Spartak Tskhinvali – FC Botosani 1-3 (0-1).

Spartaki Tskhinvali: Giorgi Nadiradze, Vasiko Bachiashvili, Giorgi Tsertsvadze, Levan Kakubava, Varlam Kilasonia, Merab Gigauri (63' Akaki Shulaia), Bidzina Makharoblidze, George Ivanishvili, Rati Tsatskrialashvili (78' Ucha Burdzenadze), Bakar Kardava (71' Zviad Lobzhanidze), Nika Kacharava. Coach: Kakhaber Katcharava.

FC Botosani: Plamen Iliev, Andrei Cordos, Florin Plamada, Stelian Cucu, Andrei Patache, Petre Ivanovici (46' Paul Batin), Gabriel Vasvari, Raul Costin, Quenten Martinus (53' Marius Croitoru), Dan Roman (74' Attila Hadnagy), Rashid Browne. Coach: Leo Grozavu.

Goals: 6',59' Dan Roman 0-1, 0-2, 65' Varlam Kilasonia 1-2 (p), 68' Paul Batin 1-3.

Referee: Nikolay Yordanov (BUL)   Attendance: 4,500.

Sent off: 38' Nika Kacharava, 50' Florin Plamada.

09.07.15   Tórsvollur, Tórshavn: HB Tórshavn – FK Trakai 1-4 (0-2).

HB Tórshavn: Teitur Gestsson, Rógvi Holm, Bartal Wardum, René Joensen, Heini Vatnsdal, Fródi Benjaminsen, Gunnar Haraldsen, Teit Jacobsen (67' Adrian Justinussen), Jógvan Davidsen, Arnbjorn Hansen (74' Poul Ingason), Levi Hanssen. Coach: Hedin Askham.

FK Trakai: Marius Rapalis, Linas Klimavicius (55' Nika Apakidze), Justinas Janusevskis, Deividas Cesnauskis, Ronalds Solomin, Vaidas Silenas, Eugen Zasavitchi (70' Rokas Stanuleviciux), Aleksandr Bychenok, Yuriy Mamaev (63' Rokas Masenzovas), Donatas Segzda, David Arshakyan. Coach: Valdas Urbonas.

Goals: 30' David Arshakyan 0-1, 38' Ronalds Solomin 0-2, 83' Aleksandr Bychenok 0-3 (p), 90' Levi Hanssen 1-3, 90+3' David Arshakyan 1-4 (p).

Referee: Sándor Andó-Szabó (HUN)   Attendance: 313.

Sent off: 22' Rógvi Holm.

09.07.15   Olimpico di Serravalle, Serravalle: AC Juvenes/Dogana – Brøndby IF 0-2 (0-0).
AC Juvenes Dogana: Mattia Manzaroli, Daniele Villa, Mattia Merlini, Mirko Mantovani, Riccardo Santini (65' Nicola Zafferani), Nicola Canini (85' Giordo Bagli), Lorenzo Gasperoni, Manuel Battistini, Marco Ugolini, Cristian Maccagno, Giorgio Mariotti (77' Alessandro Zonzini). Coach: Fabrizio Costantini.
Brøndby IF: Lukás Hrádecky, Martin Albrechtsen, Johan Larsson, Riza Durmisi, Dario Durmic, Alexander Szymanowski (46' Rezan Corlu), Lebogang Phiri (82' Svenn Crone), Andrew Hjulsager (71' Daniel Stückler), Teemu Pukki, Johan Elmander, Elbasan Rashani. Coach: Thomas Frank.
Goals: 49' Johan Elmander 0-1, 59' Elbasan Rashani 0-2.
Referee: Laurent Kopriwa (LUX)   Attendance: 814.

09.07.15   Belle Vue, Rhyl: Bala Town – FC Differdange 03 2-1 (0-0).
Bala Town: Ashley Morris, Ryan Valentine, Anthony Stephens, Tony Davies, David Thompson, Conall Murtagh, Mark Connolly, Mark Jones (90+2' Kennyi Lunt), Rob Pearson, Ian Sheridan, Kieran Smith. Coach: Stephen O'Shaughnessy.
FC Differdange 03: Julien Weber, André Rodrigues, Tom Siebenaler, Ante Bukvic, Mathias Jänisch, Pedro Ribeiro (72' Dejvid Sinani), Omar Er Rafik, Jordann Yéyé (63' Goncalo Almeida da Silva), Phillipe Lebresne (85' Antonio Luisi), Gauthier Caron, Geoffrey Franzoni. Coach: Marc Thomé.
Goals: 49' Conall Murtagh 1-0, 83' Ian Sheridan 2-0, 90+5' Omar Er Rafik 2-1.
Referee: Jens Maae (DEN)   Attendance: 1,049.

09.07.15   Skagerak Arena, Skien: Odds BK – FC Sheriff 0-0.
Odds BK: Sondre Rossbach, Espen Ruud, Thomas Grøgaard, Steffen Hagen, Lars-Kristian Eriksen, Ardian Gashi, Oliver Berg, Ole Halvorsen, Jone Samuelsen (82' Rafik Zekhnini), Olivier Occean (73' Vegard Bergan), Bentley (66' Havard Storbaek).
Coach: Dag-Eilev Fagermo.
FC Sheriff: Bozhidar Mitrev, Andrey Novicov, Maxim Potimiche, Ernandes, Valeriu Macritchii (67' Radu Ginsari), Mateo Susic (71' Andrei Macritchii), Mihajlo Cakic, Vyacheslav Sharpar, Seidu Yahaya, Juninho Potiguar (72' Wilfried Balima), Ricardinho. Coach: Lilian Popescu.
Referee: Dejan Jakimovski (MKD)   Attendance: 3,981.

09.07.15   Hrvatski vitezovi, Dugopolje: Hajduk Split - JK Sillamäe Kalev 6-2 (2-2).
Hajduk Split: Lovre Kalinic, Goran Milovic (81' Maksim Beliy), Zoran Nizic, Marko Pejic, Fran Tudor, Nikola Vlasic (87' Tomislav Kis), Mijo Caktas, Elvir Maloku, Ante Roguljic, Franck Ohandza (74' Anton Maglica), Andrija Balic. Coach: Damir Buric.
JK Sillamäe Kalev: Eduard Usikov, Marius Cinikas (78' Pavel Aleksejev), Igor Cherminava, Igor Dudarev, Tihhon Sisov (61' Aleksandr Ivanjusin), Denis Vnukov, Kyrylo Silich, Daniil Ratnikov, Janar Toomet (70' Jaroslav Kvasov), Deniss Tjapkin, Giorgio Russo.
Coach: Denis Ugarov.
Goals: 15' Andrija Balic 1-0, 36',41' Giorgio Russo 1-1, 1-2, 45' Mijo Caktas 2-2, 56',63' Franck Ohandza 3-2, 4-2, 72' Nikola Vlasic 5-2, 88' Anton Maglica 6-2.
Referee: Stavros Tritsonis (GRE)   Attendance: 4,500.

24

09.07.15   Gradski, Nikšić: FK Sutjeska – Debreceni VSC 2-0 (0-0).

FK Sutjeska: Marko Radovic, Dejan Ognjanovic, Aleksandar Sofranac, Slavko Lukic, Drasko Bozovic, Stevan Kovacevic, Jovan Nikolic, Nikola Stijepovic (84' Marko Vucic), Milos Vucic (71' Vladan Karadzic), Matija Vujovic (90+2' Filip Vorotovic), Masato Fukui.
Coach: Aleksandar Nedovic.
Debreceni VSC: István Verpecz, Norbert Mészáros, Dusan Brkovic, Mihály Korhut, Adám Bódi, József Varga, Péter Szakály (90+1' Igor Morozov), Tamás Kulcsár (73' Norbert Balogh), Aleksandar Jovanovic, Ibrahima Sidibe, Zsolt Horváth (46' Márk Szécsi).
Coach: Elemér Kondás.
Goals: 53' Masato Fukui 1-0, 81' Drasko Bozovic 2-0.
Referee: Erik Lambrechts (BEL)   Attendance: 1,214.

09.07.15   Pod Goricom, Podgorica: FK Mladost Podgorica – Neftchi PFK 1-1 (0-0).
FK Mladost Podgorica: Mileta Radulovic, Luka Pejovic, Milos S. Radulovic (80' Jasmin Muhovic), Milos Lakic, Milos B. Radulovic, Mirko Raicevic, Blazo Igumanovic, Milan Durisic, Luka Mirkovic (31' Ivan Novovic), Marko Scepanovic (89' Aldin Adzovic), Ivan Vukovic. Coach: Nikola Rakojevic.
Neftchi PFK: Agil Mammadov, Melli, Ailton, Mahammad Kurbanov (63' Elshan Abdullayev), Kamal Gurbanov, Elvin Badalov, Araz Abdullayev, Rahman Hajiyev, Caue, Ruslan Qurbanov, Samir Masimov (78' Nijat Gurbanov). Coach: Samir Aliyev.
Goals: 71' Araz Abdullayev 0-1, 90+1' Ivan Vukovic 1-1.
Referee: Kevin Clancy (SCO)   Attendance: 4,000.

FK Mladost Podgorica won on away goals.

09.07.15   Friends Arena, Solna: AIK Solna – Vaasan PS 4-0 (1-0).
AIK Solna: Oscar Linnér, Nils-Eric Johansson, Haukur Hauksson (70' Sam Lundholm), Alex (71' Anton Jönsson Salétros), Noah Sonko Sundberg, Johan Blomberg, Ebenezer Ofori, Dickson Etuhu, Niclas Eliasson, Henok Goitom (77' Marko Nikolic), Poborsky Bangura. Coach: Andreas Alm.
Vaasan PS: Henri Sillanpää, Timi Lahti, Ville Koskimaa, Mikko Viitikko, Jesper Engström, Denis Abdulahi (77' Samu Alanko), Tony Björk (63' Loorents Hertsi), Thomas Kula, Admir Catović, Pyry Soiri, Jordan Seabrook (46' Eero Tamminen). Coach: Petri Vuorinen.
Goals: 14' Henok Goitom 1-0, 55' Poborsky Bangura 2-0, 59' Henok Goitom 3-0, 85' Ebenezer Ofori 4-0.
Referee: Gunnar Jarl Jónsson (ISL)   Attendance: 8,430.

09.07.15   Boras Arena, Boras: IF Elfsborg – FC Lahti 5-0 (3-0).
IF Elfsborg: Kevin Stuhr-Ellegaard, Sebastian Holmén, Adam Lundqvist, Marcus Rohdén (59' Jon Jönsson), Anders Svensson, Arber Zeneli, Andreas Klarström, Victor Claesson, Per Frick (68' Simon Lundevall), Simon Hedlund (68' Lasse Nilsson), Viktor Prodell.
Coach: Magnus Haglund.
FC Lahti: Henrik Moisander, Mikko Hauhia, Pyry Kärkkäinen, Maarkus Joenmäki, Henri Toivomäki, Hassan Sesay (55' Rafael), Petri Pasanen, Xhevdet Gela, Aleksi Paananen, Drilon Shala (46' Aristote Mboma), Matheus (85' Aleksi Ristola). Coach: Toni Korkeakunnas.
Goals: 11 Anders Svensson 1-0, 21' Victor Claesson 2-0 (p), 33' Marcus Rohdén 3-0, 69' Viktor Prodell 4-0, 81' Lasse Nilsson 5-0.
Referee: Sandro Schärer (SUI)   Attendance: 3,304.

09.07.15   Kaplakrikavöllur, Hafnafjördur: FH Hafnafjördur – SJK Seinäjoki 1-0 (0-0).

FK Hafnarfjördur: Róbert Oskarsson, Pétur Vidarsson, Tórarinn Valdimarsson (81' Kristján Finnbogason), Kassim Doumbia, Bödvar Bödvarsson, Jonathan Hendrickx, Emil Pálsson, David Vidarsson, Gudmann Torisson, Steven Lennon (73' Bjarni Vidarsson), Atli Gudnason. Coach: Heimir Gudjónsson.

SJK Seinäjoki: Mihkel Aksalu, Pavle Milosavljevic, Henri Aalto, Cèdric Gogoua, Timo Tahvanainen, Johannes Laaksonen, Wayne Brown (65' Jussi Vasara), Mehmet Hetemaj, Ariel Ngueukam, Toni Lehtinen (45' Bahrudin Atajić), Akseli Pelvas (89' Emil Lidman). Coach: Simo Valakari.

Goal: 90+1' Kristján Finnbogason 1-0.

Referee: Mervyn Smith (NIR)   Attendance: 1,473.

09.07.15   Gradski, Lovech: PFC Litex Lovech – FK Jelgava 2-2 (1-1).

PFC Litex Lovech: Vinicius, Rafael Pérez, Vasil Bozhikov, Ivan Goranov, Kristyan Malinov (86' Milcho Angelov), Strahil Popov, Arsénio (61' Diogo Viana), Nikola Kolev (72' Alexandar Georgiev), Petrus Boumal, Björn Johnsen, Danilo Moreno. Coach: Krassimir Balakov.

FK Jelgava: Kaspars Ikstens, Valerijs Redjko (59' Vyacheslav Sushkin), Abdoulaye Diallo, Aleksandrs Gubins, Marcis Oss, Gints Freimanis, Rustam Sosranov, Dariusz Latka, Boriss Bogdaskins (90+1' Kennedy Eriba), Glebs Kluskins, Olegs Malasenoks (74' Andrejs Kirilins). Coach: Vitalijs Astafjevs.

Goals: 11' Marcis Oss 0-1, 25',56' Björn Johnsen 1-1, 2-1, 60' Abdoulaye Diallo 2-2.

Referee: Edin Jakupovic (BIH)   Attendance: 1,235.

FK Jelgava won on away goals.

09.07.15   Energi Viborg Arena, Viborg: Randers FC – UE Sant Julia 3-0 (1-0).

Randers FC: Kalle Johnsson, Erik Marxen, Mads Fenger, Alexander Fischer, Christian Keller, Johnny Thomsen (76' Jonas Bager), Mustafa Amini, Jonas Borring, Mikkel Thygesen (72' Mikkel Kallesoe), Joel Allansson (59' Edgar Babayan), Mikael Ishak. Coach: Colin Todd.

UE Sant Julia: Coca, Miguel Ruiz, Rafael Brito, Iván Vigo, Sebastian Varela, Francisco Rodriguez (61' Edu Peppe), Eric Rodriguez, Bruninho, Mario Spano (78' Fábio Serra), Arturo Madrazo, Ignacio Quirino (71' Alfonso Castellano). Coach: Raúl Canete.

Goals: 42' Mustafa Amini 1-0, 72' Edgar Babayan 2-0, 90+2' Mikael Ishak 3-0.

Referee: George Vadachkoria (GEO)   Attendance: 1,456.

09.07.15   Richmond Park, Dublin: St. Patrick's Athletic – Skonto FC 0-2 (0-1).

St. Patrick's Athletic: Brendan Clarke, Ger O'Brien, Ian Bermingham, Lee Desmond, Kenny Browne, Greg Bolger, Conan Byrne, Killian Brennan, Christopher Forrester, Aaron Greene (65' Morgan Langley), Chris Fagan (65' Jamie McGrath). Coach: Liam Buckley.

Skonto FC: Andrejs Pavlovs, Olegs Timofejevs, Renars Rode, Vitalijs Smirnovs, Vladislavs Sorokins, Iván Murillo (77' Vjaceslavs Isajevs), Igors Kozlovs, Edgars Jermolaevs, Andrejs Kovalovs, Vladislavs Gutkovskis (64' Aleksejs Visnakovs), Arturs Karasausks (83' Nikita Ivanovs). Coach: Tamaz Pertia.

Goals: 37' Vladislavs Sorokins 0-1, 59' Arturs Karasausks 0-2 (p).

Referee: Tomasz Musial (POL)   Attendance: 2,354.

26

09.07.15   Stadión FC ViOn Zlaté Moravce, Zlate Moravce:
Spartak Trnava – Olimpik Sarajevo 0-0.

Spartak Trnava: Adam Jakubech, Milos Nikolic, Martin Tóth, Matús Conka, Boris Godál, Martin Mikovic, Ján Vlasko (90' Lukas Gressák), Erik Sabo, Emir Halilovic (58' Ivan Schranz), Cléber (10' Haris Harba), José David Casado Garcia. Coach: Juraj Jarábek.
Olimpik Sarajevo: Dino Hamzic, Alem Merajic, Bojan Regoje, Jadranko Bogicevic, Filip Gligorov, Veldin Muharemovic, Sulejman Smajic (55' Mahir Karic), Kenan Handzic (80' Ervin Jusufovic), Danijal Brkovic (65' Stefan), Dalibor Pandza, Admir Rascic.
Coach: Mirza Varesanovic.
Referee: Robert Rogers (IRL)   Attendance: 3,011.

Spartak Trnava won on away goals.

09.07.15   Neo GSP, Nikosia: Omonia Nikosia – Dinamo Batumi 2-0 (0-0).
Omonia Nikosia: Kostas Panayi, Ucha Lobjanidze, Ivan Runje, Nuno Assis (88' Matias Pérez), Giorgos Economides, Margaca, Andraz Kirm (46' Gaoussou Fofana), Herold Goulon, Cillian Sheridan, Cristóvao, André Schembri (79' Eze Okeuhie). Coach: Costas Kaiafas.
Dinamo Batumi: Mikheil Alavidze, Badri Tetunashvili, Anzor Sukhiashvili, Giorgi Kavtaradze (80' Irakli Chirikashvili), Gela Gogitidze, Temur Shonia, Papuna Poniava (52' Beka Varshanidze), Boris Makharadze, Georgi Beriashvili, Giorgi Gabedava, Dimitri Tatanashvili (59' Vasha Koridze). Coach: Shota Cheishvili.
Goals: 57' Herold Goulon 1-0, 61' André Schembri 2-0.
Referee: Fábio Verissimo (POR)   Attendance: 13,532.
Sent off: 54' Badri Tetunashvili.

09.07.15   Filip II. Makedonski, Skopje: FK Rabotnicki – FC Flora 2-0 (0-0).
FK Rabotnicki: Daniel Bozinovski, Goran Siljanovski, Kire Ristevski, Milan Ilievski, Stephan Vujcic, Milovan Petrovikj, Mite Cikarski, Suad Shaiti (85' Miroslav Jovanovski), Chuma Anene, Baze Ilijoski (75' Ivan Mitrov), Marijan Altiparmakovski (80' Dusko Trajcevski).
Coach: Tomislav Franc.
FC Flora: Mait Toom, Enar Jääger, Gert Kams, Nikita Baranov (68' Kevin Aloe), Andre Frolov, Rauno Sappinen, Markus Jürgenson, German Slein, Irakliy Logue (55' Maksim Gussev), Rauno Alliku, Sakari Tukiainen (46' Joonas Tamm). Coach: Norbert Hurt.
Goals: 48' Chuma Anene 1-0, 54' Maarijan Altiparmakovski 2-0.
Referee: Markus Hameter (AUT)   Attendance: 1,690.

09.07.15   Torpedo, Zhodzina: Torpedo-BelAZ Zhodino - FK Kukësi 0-0.
Torpedo BelAZ Zhodino: Pavel Chesnovskiy, Vyacheslav Serdyuk, Sergiy Melnik, Ihar Burko, Aleksey Pankovetds, Aleksandr Selyava, Oleksandr Maksimov (61' Vitaliy Kibuk), Artiom Vaskov (67' Artem Kontsevoy), Sergiy Datsenko, Aleksandr Yatskevich (59' Dmitry Platonov), Vyatcheslav Hleb. Coach: Igor Kriushenko.
FK Kukësi: Dimitri Stajila, Ylli Shameti (56' Edon Hasani), Gentian Muça, Rrahman Hallaçi, Renato Malota, Gledi Mici, Erick Flores, Felipe Moreira (70' Birungueta), Jefferson (87' Besar Musolli), Jean Carioca, Pero Pejic. Coach: Marcello Troisi.
Referee: Serghei Derenov (MOL)   Attendance: 2,950.

09.07.15 A. Le Coq Arena, Tallinn: JK Nõmme Kalju – FZK Aktobe 0-0.
JK Nõmme Kalju: Vitali Teles, Alo Bärengrub, Jorge Rodrigues, Ken Kallaste, Borislav Topic (57' Réginald Mbu-Alidor), Ats Purje, Allan Kimbaloula, Eino Puri, Karl Mööl, Hidetoshi Wakui (61' Joel Lindpere), Artjom Dmitrijev (74' Tarmo Neemelo). Coach: Sergei Terehhov.
FK Aktobe: Almat Bekbaev, Dele Adeleye, Valeriy Korobkin, Dmitry Miroshnichenko, Yuriy Logvinenko, Arturas Zulpa, Ciprian Deac, Danilo Neco, Marcos Pizelli (78' Marat Khayrullin), Sergey Khiznichenko, Danilo. Coach: Vladimir Gazzaev.
Referee: Danilo Grujic (SER)   Attendance: 844.

09.07.15 Qäbälä Sähär Stadionu, Qäbälä: Gabala FK – Dinamo Tbilisi 2-0 (0-0).
Gabala FK: Dmitro Bezotosniy, Vitaliy Vernydub, Ricardinho, Urfan Abbasov (86' Arif Dashdemirov), Rafael Santos, George Florescu (77' Dodô), Räsad Sadiqov (81' Asif Mammadov), Oleksiy Gay, Sergei Zenjov, Javid Hüseynov, Oleksiy Antonov.
Coach: Roman Grygorchuk.
Dinamo Tbilisi: Libor Hrdlicka, Lasha Totadze, Archil Tvildiani (84' Giorgi Janelidze), Mate Tsintsadze, Giorgi Papunashvili, Rene, Jambul Jigauri, Zaza Chelidze, Vakhtang Chanturishvili, Aleksandr Iashvili (61' Otari Kiteishvili), Giorgi Kvilitaia (74' Giorgi Guruli).
Coach: George Geguchadze.
Goals: 88' Sergei Zenjov 1-0, 90+3' Oleksiy Antonov 2-0.
Referee: Amaury Delerue (FRA)   Attendance: 4,400.
Sent off: 71' Lasha Totadze.

09.07.15 Beroe, Stara Zagora: PFC Beroe – FK Atlantas 3-1 (2-0).
PFC Beroe: Blagoj Makendzhiev, Ivo Ivanov, Ventzislav Vasilev, Veselin Penev, Atanas Zehirov (54' Venelin Filipv), Nemanja Milisavljevic, Elias (63' Tom), Igor Djoman, Junior M'Pia (69' Stanislav Kostov), Georgi Bozhilov, Spas Delev. Coach: Petar Hubchev.
FK Atlantas: Mindaugas Malinauskas, Andrius Joksas, Rolandas Baravykas, Kazimieras Gnedojus, Edgaras Zarskis, Dovydas Virksas (57' Markas Beneta), Dovydas Norvilas (55' Ricardas Sveikauskas), Robertas Vezevicius, Ovidijus Verbickas, Maksim Maksimov, Andrey Panyukov (77' Lukas Baranauskas). Coach: Konstantin Sarsaniya.
Goals: 8',45' Spas Delev 1-0, 2-0, 65' Robertas Vezevicius 2-1, 67' Spas Delev 3-1.
Referee: Orkhan Mammadov (AZE)   Attendance: 7,432.

09.07.15 Shafa, Baku: Inter Baku – KF Laçi 0-0.
Inter Baku: Sälähät Agayev, Juanfran, Lashar Kasradze, Zurab Khizanishvili, Abbas Hüseynov, Nika Kvekveskiri, Nizami Hajiyev (80' Ilkin Sadigov), Mirsayib Abbasov (90+1' Denis), Mirhuseyn Seyidov, Fuad Bayramov, Rauf Aliyev (90+4' Mansur Nahavandi).
Coach: Zaur Svanadze
KF Laçi: Miroslav Vujadinovic, Emiliano Çela, Arjan Sheta, Elton Doku (76' Aldo Mitraj), Taulant Sefgjini, Agim Meto, Erjon Vucaj, Olsi Teqja, Emiliano Veliaj, Segun Adeniyi, Valdon Nimani (82' Mikelanxhelo Bardhi). Coach: Armando Cungu.
Referee: Aleksandr Aliyev (KAZ)   Attendance: 3,000.

Inter Baku won on away goals.

28

09.07.15   Bialystok City Stadium, Bialystok:
Jagiellonia Bialystok – FK Kruoja Pakruojis 8-0 (4-0).
Jagiellonia Bialystok: Bartlomiej Dragowski, Filip Modelski, Sebastian Madera, Taras
Romanchuk, Patryk Tuszynski (74' Lukasz Sekulski), Nika Dzalamidze, Igors Tarasovs, Piotr
Tomasik, Piotr Grzelczak (62' Przemyslaw Frankowski), Maciej Gajos, Karol Swiderski (55'
Konstantin Vassiljev). Coach: Michal Probierz.
FK Kruoja Pakruojis: Martynas Matuzas, Valdas Pocevicius, Oleksandr Tarasenko, Donatas
Strockis, Alfredas Skroblas, Tomas Salamanavicius (46' Tadas Eliosius), Tautvydas Eliosius,
Donatas Navikas, Darius Jankauskas, Ricardas Beniusis (59' Vadym Barba), Aivaras Bagocius
(57' Tomas Birskys). Coach: Divaldo.
Goals: 3' Maciej Gajos 1-0, 8' Karol Swiderski 2-0, 18',45',49' Patryk Tuszynski 3-0, 4-0,
5-0, 64',75',80' Przemyslaw Frankowski 6-0, 7-0, 8-0.
Referee: Domagoj Vuckov (CRO)   Attendance: 13,724.

09.07.15   McDiarmid Park, Perth: St. Johnstone FC – Alashkert Martuni 2-1 (1-0).
St. Johnstone FC: Alan Mannus, Thomas Scobbie, Frazer Wright (65' Brad McKay), Steven
Anderson (71' Liam Caddis), Joe Shaughnessy, Brian Easton, Scott Brown, Steven MacLean,
John Sutton (80' Graham Cummins), Chris Kane, Michael O'Halloran.
Coach: Tommy Wright.
Alashkert Martuni: Gevorg Kasparov, Sékou Fofana, Gevorg Poghosyan, Sergey Usenya,
Vahagn Minasyan, Karen Muradyan, Ararat Arakelyan, Khoren Veranyan (90+3' Andranik
Voskanyan), Aram Bareghamyan (90+5' Héber), Artak Grigoryan, Norayr Gyozalyan (75'
Mihran Manasyan). Coach: Abraham Khashmanyan.
Goals: 35' Michael O'Halloran 1-0, 74' Norayr Gyozalyan 1-1, 87' Brad McKay 2-1.
Referee: Fredy Fautrel (FRA)   Attendance: 5,764.
Sent off: 65' Karen Muradyan.

Alashkert Martuni won on away goals.

09.07.15   Bijeli Brijeg, Mostar: Zrinjski Mostar – Shirak FC 2-1 (0-0).
Zrinjski Mostar: Ratko Dujkovic, Zvonimir Blaic, Danijel Graovac, Danijel Stojanovic,
Aleksandar Radulovic (90+2' Milan Muminovic), Anto Radeljic, Milos Zeravica, Ognjen
Todorovic (69' Milos Filipovic), Goran Zakaric (76' Vucina Scepanovic), Jasmin Mesanovic,
Stevo Nikolic. Coach: Vinko Marinovic.
Shirak FC: Vsevolod Ermakov, Arman Hovhannisyan, Milos Stamenkovic, Gevorg
Hovhannisyan, Tigran Davtyan (83' Karen Aleksanyan), Gor Malakyan, Davit Hakobyan,
Edgar Malakyan, Aghvan Davoyan, Jean-Jacques Bougouhi, Drissa Diarrassouba (46'
Andranik Barikyan). Coach: Vardan Bichakhchyan.
Goals: 80' Jasmin Mesanovic 1-0 (p), 86' Milos Filipovic 2-0,
90+6' Jean-Jacques Bougouhi 2-1.
Referee: Zbynek Proske (CZE)   Attendance: 4,800.

09.07.15   Teddy Kollek Stadium, Jerusalem:
Beitar Jerusalem – Ordabasy Shymkent 2-1 (1-0).
Beitar Jerusalem: Boris Kleiman, Elazar Dasa (67' Tomer Yeruham), Tal Kachila, Dusan
Matovic, Daniel Askling, Omer Atzily, Claudemir, Dani Preda (53' Lidor Cohen), Liroy
Zhairi, Dovev Gabay, Omer Nachmani (74' Ori Majabi). Coach: Slobodan Drapic.
Ordabasy Shymkent: Andrey Sidelnikov, Gafurzhan Suyombaev, Renat Abdulin, Sergiy
Maliy, Talgat Adyrbekov (58' Kyrylo Petrov), Aleksandar Simcevic, Azat Nurgaliev, Kayrat
Ashirbekov (62' Yerkebulan Tunggyshbayev), Artem Kasyanov, Daurenbek Tazhimbetov,
Aleksandr Geynrikh. Coach: Viktor Kumykov.
Goals: 17' Omer Atzily 1-0, 60' Dovev Gabay 2-0, 66' Kyrylo Petrov 2-1.
Referee: Radek Prihoda (CZE)   Attendance: 14,000.
Sent off: 90+3' Artem Kasyanov.

09.07.15   Complexul Sportiv Raional, Orhei: Dacia Chisinau – FK Renova 4-1 (1-1).
Dacia Chisinau: Artiom Gaiduchevici, Mihai Rosca, Veaceslav Posmac, Volodymyr Zastavnyi,
Abdoul Mamah, Sapol Mani (52' Evgeniy Lozoviy), Eugeniu Cociuc, Maksim Gavrilenko,
Viorel Frunza (52' Vasile Jardan), Maxim Mihailov, Vasili Pavlov (75' Alexandru Bejan.
Coach: Igor Dobrovolskiy.
FK Renova: Saljadin Mustafi, Medzit Neziri, Agron Memedi, Visar Musliu, Nenad Miskovski,
Jasmin Mecinovic (71' Lavdrim Skenderi), Burim Sadiku, Izair Emini, Emran Ramadani (80'
Elmedin Redzepi), Argjent Gafuri, Gjorgi Mojsov (71' Fatjon Jusufi). Coach: Kjatip Osmani.
Goals: 8' Eugeniu Cociu 1-0, 32' Izair Emini 1-1, 55' Vasile Jardan 2-1, 60' Vasili Pavlov 3-1,
89' Evgeniy Lozoviy 4-1.
Referee: Denis Scherbakov (BLR)   Attendance: 800.

09.07.15   Asim Ferhatović Hase, Sarajevo: Zeljeznicar Sarajevo – Balzan Youths 1-0 (0-0).
Zeljeznicar Sarajevo: Marijan Antolovic, Josip Kvesic, Aleksandar Kosoric, Kerim Meija,
Jasmin Bogdanovic, Rijad Bajic, Jovan Blagojevic (70' Enis Sadikovic), Ognjen Djelmic,
Amir Hadziahmetovic, Dzenis Beganovic (64' Damir Sadikovic), Zoran Kokot (84' Amer
Hiros). Coach: Milomir Odovic.
Balzan Youths: Valerio Senatore, Justin Grioli, Samir Arab, Steven Bezzina, Elkin Serrano,
Ryan Fenech, Edinson Bilbao, Dylan Grima (79' Ryan Darmanin), Clive Brincat, Terence
Agius (73' Lydon Micallef), Osa Guobadia (90' Michael Borg). Coach: Oliver Spiteri.
Goal: 68' Damir Sadikovic 1-0.
Referee: Vasilis Dimitriou (CYP)   Attendance: 5,500.

SECOND QUALIFYING ROUND

16.07.15   Tsentralniy, Almaty: Kairat Almaty – Alashkert Martuni 3-0 (1-0).
Kairat Almaty: Vladimir Plotnikov, Bruno Soares, Zarko Markovic, Ermek Kuantaev,
Bauyrzhan Islamkhan (90' Zhambyl Kukeev), Isael, Islambek Kuat (64' Djordje Despotovic),
Anatoliy Tymoschchuk, Gerard Gohou (87' Mark Gorman), Sito Riera, Stanislav Lunin.
Coach: Vladimir Weiss.
Alashkert Martuni: Gevorg Kasparov, Sékou Fofana, Gevorg Poghosyan, Sergey Usenya,
Vahagn Minasyan, Ararat Arakelyan, Khoren Veranyan, Aram Bareghamyan (77' Gevorg
Karapetyan), Mihran Manasyan (57' Rafael Ghazaryan), Artak Grigoryan, Norayr Gyozalyan
(73' Héber). Coach: Abraham Khashmanyan.
Goals: 14' Bauyrzhan Islamkhan 1-0 (p), 55' Gerard Gohou 2-0, 69' Djordje Despotovic 3-0.
Referee: Sergey Ivanov (RUS)   Attendance: 22,100.

16.07.15   Zemgalas Olimpiska Centra, Jelgava: FK Jelgava – FK Rabotnicki 1-0 (0-0).
FK Jelgava: Kaspars Ikstens, Abdoulaye Diallo, Aleksandrs Gubins, Marcis Oss, Gints
Freimanis (86' Valerijs Redjko), Rustam Sosranov, Dariusz Latka, Boriss Bogdaskins,
Kennedy Eriba (56' Andrejs Kirilins), Glebs Kluskins, Vyacheslav Sushkin (63' Olegs
Malasenoks). Coach: Vitalijs Astafjevs.
FK Rabotnicki: Daniel Bozinovski, Goran Siljanovski, Kire Ristevski, Milan Ilievski, Stephan
Vujcic, Milovan Petrovikj, Dusko Trajcevski, Mite Cikarski (88' Ivan Mitrov), Chuma Anene,
Baze Ilijoski (65' Suad Sahiti), Marijan Altiparmakovski (79' Miroslav Jovanovski).
Coach: Tomislav Franc.
Goal: 87' Glebs Kluskins 1-0.
Referee: Tore Hansen (NOR)   Attendance: 1,510.

16.07.15   Stadionul Zimbru, Chisinau: Dacia Chisinau – MSK Zilina 1-2 (0-0).
Dacia Chisinau: Artion Gaiduchevici, Mihai Rosca, Vasile Jardan (68' Viorel Frunza),
Veaceslav Posmac, Volodymyr Zastavnyi, Abdoul Mamah, Evgeniy Lozoviy, Sapol Mani (46'
Maxim Mihaliov), Eugeniu Cociuc, Maksim Gavrilenko, Vasili Pavlov (57' Slaven
Stjepanovic). Coach: Igor Dobrovolskiy.
MSK Zilina: Milos Volesák, Milan Skriniar, Denis Vavro, Ernest Mabouka, Miroslav Kácer,
Jakub Paur (66' Jaroslav Mihalík), Viktor Pecovsky, Bojan Letic, László Bénes (89' Michal
Skvarka), Matej Jelic, Lukás Cmelik (85' Nikolas Spalek). Coach: Adrián Gula.
Goals: 53',59' Matej Jelic 0-1, 0-2, 80' Maxim Ihaliov 1-2.
Referee: Baris Simsek (TUR)   Attendance: 3,800.

16.07.15   AutoC Park Randers, Randers: Randers FC – IF Elfsborg 0-0.
Randers FC: Kalle Johnsson, Mads Fenger, Alexander Fischer, Christian Keller, Johnny
Thomsen, Jeppe Tverskov, Mustafa Amini, Jonas Bjorring (78' Erik Marxen), Nikolaj Poulsen,
Nicolai Brock-Madsen, Mikael Ishak (75' Edgar Babayan). Coach: Colin Todd.
IF Elfsborg: Kevin Stuhr-Ellegaard, Jesper Manns (19' Andreas Klarström), Sebastian
Holmén, Adam Lundqvist, Marcus Rohdén, Anders Svensson, Arber Zeneli (61' Simon
Lundevall), Victor Claesson, Henning Hauger, Per Frick, Simon Hedlund (75' Lasse Nilsson).
Coach: Magnus Haglund.
Referee: Ali Palabiyik (TUR)   Attendance: 3,151.

16.07.15   Skonto Stadion, Riga: Skonto FC – Debreceni VSC 2-2 (1-1).
Skonto FC: Andrejs Pavlovs, Olegs Timofejevs, Renars Rode, Vladislavs Sorokins, Iván
Murillo, Aleksejs Visnakovs (71' Ivan Lukanyuk), Igors Kozlovs, Edgars Jermolaevs, Andrejs
Kovalovs, Vladislavs Gutkovskis (57' Vjaceslavs Isajevs), Arturs Karasausks.
Coach: Tamaz Pertia.
Debreceni VSC: István Verpecz, Norbert Mészáros, Dusan Brkovic, Mihály Korhut, Ádám
Bódi, József Varga, Péter Szakály, Aleksandar Jovanovic, Norbert Balogh (90+3' Zsolt
Horváth), Ibrahima Sidibe (71' Geoffrey Castillion), Tibor Tisza (80' Márk Szécsi).
Coach: Elemér Kondás.
Goals: 9' Tibor Tisza 0-1, 27',47' Arturs Karasausks 1-1, 2-1, 72' Geoffrey Castillion 2-2.
Referee: Mads-Kristoffer Kristoffersen (DEN)   Attendance: 2,200.

31

16.07.15   Stroitel, Soligorsk: Shakhter Soligrosk – Wolfsberger AC 0-1 (0-0).
Shakhter Soligorsk: Vladimir Bushma, Aleksey Yanushkevich, Aleksandr Yurevich, Pavel
Rybak, Ihar Kuzmianok, Siarhei Matveichyk, Mikhail Afanasiev (63' Vitaliy Trubila), Artem
Stargorodskiy, Yuri Kovalev (72' Saulius Mikoliunas), Nikolai Yanush, Dmitriy Komarovskiy
(80' Sergey Koseka). Coach: Sergey Nikiforenko.
Wolfsberger AC: Alexander Kofler, Stephan Palla, Michael Berger, Michael Sollbauer, Daniel
Drescher, Manuel Weber (90+3' Boris Hüttenbrenner), Jacobo, Roland Putsche, Thomas
Zündel (82' Christopher Wernitznig), Silvio (71' Tadej Trdina), Philip Hellquist.
Coach: Dietmar Kühbauer.
Goal: 62' Jacobo 0-1.
Referee: Ilias Spathas (GRE)   Attendance: 3,200.

16.07.15   Beroe, Stara Zagora: PFC Beroe – Brøndby IF 0-1 (0-0).
PFC Beroe: Blagoj Makendzhiev, Ivo Ivanov, Ventzislav Vasilev, Veselin Penev, Atanas
Zehirov, Nemanja Milisavljevic (86' Ivan Kokonov), Elias, Igor Djoman (89' Tom), Junior
M'Pia (71' Georgi Andonov), Georgi Bozhilov, Spas Delev. Coach: Petar Hubchev.
Brøndby IF: Lukás Hrádecky, Martin Albrechtsen, Johan Larsson, Riza Durmisi, Dario
Durmic, Martin Ornskov, Lebogang Phiri, Christian Norgaard (84' Frederik Holst), Teemu
Pukki, Johan Elmander (73' Magnus Eriksson), Elbasan Rashami (60' Andrew Hjulsager).
Coach: Thomas Frank.
Goal: 85' Martin Albrechtsen 0-1.
Referee: Antonio Damato (ITA)   Attendance: 8,256.

16.07.15   Friends Arena, Solna: AIK Solna – Shirak FC 2-0 (1-0).
AIK Solna: Kenny Stamatopoulos, Per Karlsson (89' Sam Lundholm), Nils-Eric Johansson,
Noah Sonko Sundberg, Kenny Pavey, Ebenezer Ofori, Dickson Etuhu, Stefan Ishizaki, Niclas
Eliasson (67' Fredrik Brustad), Henok Goitom, Poborsky Bangura (67' Johan Blomberg).
Coach: Andreas Alm.
Shirak FC: Vsevolod Ermakov, Arman Hovhannisyan, Milos Stamenkovic, Gevorg
Hovhannisyan, Gor Malakyan, Davit Hakobyan (78' Andranik Barikyan), Karen Aleksanyan,
Edgar Malakyan, Aghvan Davoyan, Jean-Jacques Bougouhi (90+3' Viulen Ayvazyan), Drissa
Diarrassouba (90' Tigran Davtyan). Coach: Vardan Bichakhchyan.
Goals: 29', 83' Henok Goitom 1-0, 2-0 (p).
Referee: Vladimir Vnuk (SVK)   Attendance: 7,315.
Sent off: 69' Arman Hovhannisyan, 80' Gor Malakyan, 85' Andranik Barikyan.

16.07.15   Teddy Kollek Stadium, Jerusalem: Hapoel Be'er Sheva – FC Thun 1-1 (1-0).
Hapoel Be'er Sheva: David Goresh, Ben Biton, Shir Tzedek, Ofir Davidadze, Maharan Radi
(88' Roei Gordana), Maor Buzaglo, Ovidiu Hoban, Maor Melikson (77' Anthony Nuatuzor),
William Soares, John Ogu, Elyaniv Barda (61' Ben Sahar). Coach: Barak Bakhar.
FC Thun: Guillaume Faivre, Marco Bürki, Fulvio Sulmoni, Stefan Glarner, Gianluca Frontino,
Michael Siegfried (18' Nicola Sutter / 67' Enrico Schirinzi), Marco Rojas, Dennis Hediger,
Nelson Ferreira, Andreas Wittwer, Roman Buess (62' Simone Rapp). Coach: Ciriaco Sforza.
Goals: 26' Ovidiu Hoban 1-0, 87' Gianluca Frontini 1-1 (p).
Referee: Bart Vententen (BEL)   Attendance: 14,265.

16.07.15   Ludogorets Arena, Razgrad: Cherno More Varna – Dinamo Minsk 1-1 (1-0).
Cherno More Varna: Aleksandar Canovic, Mihail Venkov, Stefan Stanchev, Mamoutou
Coulibaly, Marc Klok, Marcin Burkhardt (67' Sténio), Mathias Coureur (72' Andreas Vasev),
Mehdi Bourabia, Todor Palankov, Simeon Raykov, Villyan Bizhev (58' Juan Varela).
Coach: Nikola Spasov.
Dinamo Minsk: Aleksandr Gutor, Maksim Vitus, Sergey Politevich, Roman Begunov, Artur
Yedigaryan (60' Shaloze Chigozie), Artem Bykov, Umaru Bangura, Nikita Korzun, Nenad
Adamovic (77' Vladimir Korytko), Gleb Rassadkin (87' Igor Voronkov), Fatos Beciraj.
Coach: Vuk Rasovic.
Goals: 11' Mathias Coureur 1-0, 71' Sergey Politevich 1-1.
Referee: Tobias Stieler (GER)   Attendance: 3,650.

16.07.15   Mestsky stadion, Mladá Boleslav: FK Mladá Boleslav – Strømsgodset IF 1-2 (1-1).
FK Mladá Boleslav: Robert Veselovsky, Antonin Krapka, Ondrej Kúdela, Jasmin Scuk, Jan
Kysela, Ondrej Zahustel, Jakub Rada, Gaston Mendu, Daniel Bartl (64' Ales Cermák), Jan
Chramosta (64' Lukás Magera), Stanislav Klobása (77' Jan Stohanzl). Coach: Karel Jarolim.
Strømsgodset IF: Espen Pettersen, Marius Hoibraten, Gustav Valsvik, Mounir Hamoud, Petter
Moen (61' Bassel Jradi), Iver Fossum, Gustav Wikheim, Mohammed Abu, Lars-Christopher
Vilsvik, Oyvind Storflor (85' Flamur Kastrati), Thomas Sorum (53' Thomas Olsen).
Coach: Bjorn Petter Ingebretsen.
Goals: 39' Daniel Bartl 1-0, 44' Thomas Sorum 1-1, 85' Bassel Jradi 1-2.
Referee: John Beaton (SCO)   Attendance: 4,756.

16.07.15   Antonis Papadopoulos, Larnaca: Apollon Limassol – FK Trakai 4-0 (1-0).
Apollon Limassol: Bruno Vale, Elizio, Nuno Lopes (80' Marios Stylianou), Freire, Esteban
Sacchetti, Marcos Gullón, Jaime, Joao Pedro, Luka Stojanovic (72' Alexandre), Fotis Papoulis
(68' Farley), Giorgos Kolokoudias. Coach: Pedro Emanuel.
FK Trakai: Marius Rapalis, Linas Klimavicius, Justinas Janusevskis, Deividas Cesnauskis,
Ronalds Solomin, Rokas Stanulevicius (68' Donatas Segzda), Vaidas Silenas, Eugen
Zasavitchi (88' Nika Apakidze), Aleksandr Bychenok, Yuriy Mamaev, David Arshakyan.
Coach: Valdas Urbonas.
Goals: 20' Giorgos Kolokoudias 1-0, 52' Luka Stojanovic 2-0, 64' G. Kolokoudias 3-0 (p),
86' Farley 4-0.
Referee: Nikola Dabanovic (MNE)   Attendance: 3,720.

16.07.15   SRC Bonifika, Koper: FC Koper – Hajduk Split 3-2 (3-1).
FC Koper: Vasja Simcic, Denis Srne, Denis Halilovic, Damir Hadzic, Ivica Guberac, Amar
Rahmanovic (60' Matej Pucko), Domen Crnigoj, Marko Krivicic, Matej Palcic, Josip Ivancic
(71' Jaka Stromajer), Goran Galesic. Coach: Rodolfo Vanoli.
Hajduk Split: Lovre Kalinic, Goran Milovic, Jefferson, Zoran Nizic, Marko Pejic, Fran Tudor,
Nikola Vlasic, Mijo Caktas, Ante Roguljic (70' Elvir Maloku), Anton Maglica (74' Artem
Radchenko), Andrija Balic (46' Tomislav Kis). Coach: Damir Buric.
Goals: 7' Denis Halilovic 1-0, 17' Amar Rahmanovic 2-0, 29' Goran Milovic 2-1,
40' Amar Rahmanovic 3-1, 90' Zoran Nizic 3-2.
Referee: Bartosz Frankowski (POL)   Attendance: 2,590.

33

16.07.15   Qemal Stafa, Tirana: FK Kukësi – FK Mladost Podgorica 0-1 (0-0).
FK Kukësi: Dimitri Stajila, Gentian Muça, Rrahman Hallaçi, Renato Malota, Gledi Mici, Erick Flores, Birungueta (36' Edon Hasani), Felipe Moreira (61' Semiao Granado), Jefferson, Jean Carioca (89' Ndriqim Halili), Pero Pejic. Coach: Marcello Troisi.
FK Mladost Podgorica: Mileta Radulovic, Luka Pejovic, Milos Lakic, Milos B. Radulovic, Mirko Raicevic, Blazo Igumanovic (77' Jasmin Muhovic), Milan Durisic, Ivan Novovic, Milos Radulovic, Marko Scepanovic (74' Luka Mirkovic), Ivan Vukovic. Coach: Nikola Rakojevic.
Goal: 52' Milos Lakic 0-1.
Referee: Kristo Tohver (EST)   Attendance: 2,500.

16.07.15   Stade du Pays, Charleroi: Sporting Charleroi – Beitar Jerusalem 5-1 (1-1).
Sporting Charleroi: Nicolas Penneteau, Sebastien Dewaest, Stergos Marinos, Francis N'Ganga, Martos, Damien Marcq, Enes Saglik (89' Roman Ferber), Clément Tainmont, David Pollet (80' Florent Stevance), Dieumerci Ndongala (90+1' Guillaume Francois), Neeskens Kebano. Coach: Felice Mazzu.
Beitar Jerusalem: Boris Kleiman, Elazar Dasa, Tal Kachila, Dusan Matovic, Daniel Askling, Omer Atzily (75' Lidor Cohen), Claudemir, Dani Preda (55' De Lucas), Liroy Zhairi, Dovev Gabay, Omer Nachmani (30' Ness Zamir). Coach: Slobodan Drapic.
Goals: 10' David Pollet 1-0, 35' Dovev Gabay 1-1, 47' Neeskens Kebano 2-1, 68' David Pollet 3-1, 88' Florent Stevance 4-1, 90+3' Neeskens Kebano 5-1.
Referee: Lee Probert (ENG)   Attendance: 10,175.
Sent off: 45' Elazar Dasa, 76' De Lucas.

16.07.15   Rheinpark, Vaduz: FC Vaduz – JK Nömme Kalju 3-1 (1-0).
FC Vaduz: Peter Jehle, Simone Grippo, Pavel Pergl, Florian Stahel, Naser Aliji, Steven Lang (84' Pascal Schürpf), Diego Ciccone, Ali Messaoud (66' Mauro Caballero Jr), Markus Neumayr, Stjepan Kukuruzovic (75' Robin Kamber), Philipp Muntwiler.
Coach: Giorgio Contini.
JK Nömme Kalju: Vitali Teles, Alo Bärengrub, Jorge Rodrigues, Ken Kallaste, Borislav Topic (46' Eino Puri), Réginald Mbu-Alidor, Ats Purje (70' Tarmo Neemelo), Allan Kimbaloula, Karl Mööl, Hidetoshi Wakui, Artjom Dmitrijev (63' Joel Lindpere). Coach: Sergei Terehhov.
Goals: 20' Diego Ciccone 1-0, 53' Markus Neumayr 2-0, 86' Hidetoshi Wakui 2-1, 90+2' Markus Neumayr 3-1.
Referee: Petur Reinert (FRO)   Attendance: 912.

16.07.15   Telia Parken, Kobenhavn: FC København – Newtown AFC 2-0 (1-0).
FC København: Stephan Andersen, Ludwig Augustinsson, Per Nilsson, Daniel Amartey, Peter Ankersen, Thomas Delaney, Kasper Kusk, Benjamin Verbic (90+3' Brandur Hendriksson), Nicolai Jorgensen, Marvin Pourie (82' Tom Hogli), Youssef Toutouh.
Coach: Ståle Solbakken.
Newtown AFC: David Jones, Steffan Edwards, Kieran Mills-Evans (78' Gavin Cadwallader), Shane Sutton, Matty Owen (80' James Price), Luke Boundford, Craig Williams, Tom Goodwin, Matthew Hearsey (69' Sean Evans), Jason Oswell, Neil Mitchell.
Coach: Chris Hughes.
Goals: 3' Benjamin Verbic 1-0, 74' Kasper Kusk 2-0.
Referee: Mete Kalkavan (TUR)   Attendance: 8,104.

34

16.07.15   Maksimir, Zagreb: Lokomotiva Zagreb – PAOK Saloniki 2-1 (2-0).

Lokomotiva Zagreb: Oliver Zelenika, Karlo Bartolec, Tomislav Mrčela, Karlo Brucic, Herdi Prenga, Damir Sovsic (90+3' Luka Capan), Luka Begonja, Franko Andrijasevic, Jerko Leko, Mirko Maric (73' Petar Misic), Marko Kolar (65' Jan Dolezal). Coach: Ante Cacic.

PAOK Saloniki: Robin Olsen, Giannis Skondras (79' Razvan Rat), Miguel Vitor, Ricardo Costa, Giorgos Tzavellas, Alexandros Tziolis (61' Hedwiges Maduro), Ergis Kaçe, Stelios Kitsiou, Dimitrios Pelkas, Róbert Mak, Dimitrios Salpingidis (68' Ioannis Mystakidis). Coach: Igor Tudor.

Goals: 30' Marko Kolar 1-0, 45' Franko Andrijasevic 2-0, 90+2' Róbert Mak 2-1.

Referee: Yuriy Mozharovsky (UKR)   Attendance: 1,000.

16.07.15   Hüseyin Avni Aker, Trabzon: Trabzonspor – FC Differdange 03 1-0 (1-0).

Trabzonspor: Onur Kivrak, Carl Medjani, Ugur Demirok, Mustafa Yumlu, Salih Dursun, Mehmet Ekici (84' Fatih Atik), Sefa Yilmaz, Soner Aydogdu, Musa Nizam, Erkan Zengin (64' Yusuf Erdogan), Waris Majeed (81' Zeki Yavru). Coach: Shota Arveladze.

FC Differdange 03: Julien Weber, André Rodrigues, Tom Siebenaler, Ante Bukvic, Mathias Jänisch, Pedro Ribeiro (90+3' Andy May), Omar Er Rafik, Dejvid Sinani (64' Phillipe Lebresne), Jordann Yéyé, Gauthier Caron (76' Jérémie Méligner), Geoffrey Franzoni. Coach: Marc Thomé.

Goal: 44' Mehmet Ekici 1-0.

Referee: Ivaylo Stoyanov (BUL)   Attendance: 9,254.

16.07.15   Stadión FC ViOn Zlaté Moravce: Zlaté Moravce:
Spartak Trnava – Linfield FC 2-1 (2-1).

Spartak Trnava: Adam Jakubech, Milos Nikolic, Martin Tóth (70' Lukás Gressák), Matús Conka, Boris Godál, Aldo Baéz, Martin Mikovic, Erik Sabo, Emir Halilovic, Haris Harba (46' Milan Bortel), José Casado (64' Tomás Mikinic). Coach: Juraj Jarábek.

Linfield FC: Ross Glendinning, Chris Hegarty, Mark Haughey, Aaron Burns (57' Ross Clarke), Matthew Clarke, Reece Glendinning, Stephen Lowry, David Kee, Ivan Sproule, Andrew Waterworth, Guy Bates. Coach: Warren Feeney.

Goals: 16' Erik Sabo 1-0 (p), 21' David Kee 1-1, 35' Martin Mikovic 2-1.

Referee: Mikhail Vilkov (RUS)   Attendance: 3,220.

Sent off: 45' Milos Nikolic.

16.07.15   Pasienky, Bratislava: Slovan Bratislava – UC Dublin 1-0 (0-0).

Slovan Bratislava: Ján Mucha, Boris Sekulic, Nicolas Gorosito, Kornel Saláta, Marko Milinkovic, Samuel Stefánik, Slobodan Simovic (44' Dávid Hudák), Jakub Podany, Adam Zrelak, Tamás Priskin (90+3' Timotej Zhaumensky), Róbert Vittek (46' Frantisek Kubik). Coach: Dusan Tittel.

UC Dublin: Niall Corbert, Mark Langtry, Michael Leahy, Tomas Boyle, Maxim Kouogun, Gary O'Neill, Chris Mulhall, Ryan Swan, Dylan Watts (85' Conor Cannon), Robbie Benson, Jamie Doyle. Coach: Collie O'Neill.

Goal: 84' Adam Zrelak 1-0.

Referee: Lasha Silagava (GEO)   Attendance: 3,050.

Sent off: 28' Nicolas Gorosito.

35

16.07.15   Groupama Arena, Budapest: Ferencvárosi TC – Zeljeznicar Sarajevo 0-1 (0-0).
Ferencvárosi TC: Dénes Dibusz, Michal Naelpa, Emir Dilaver, Cristian Ramirez (46' Tamás
Hajnal), Leandro, Zoltán Gera, Attila Busai (46' Stanislav Sesták), Roland Lamah (68' Gábor
Gyömbér), Dániel Böde, Somália, Roland Varga. Coach: Thomas Doll.
Zeljeznicar Sarajevo: Marijan Antolovic, Josip Kvesic, Aleksandar Kosoric, Kerim Memija,
Jasmin Bogdanovic, Rijad Bajic, Jovan Blagojevic, Ognjen Djelmic (71' Enis Sadikovic),
Amir Hadziahmetovic (53' Dzenis Beganovic), Damir Sadikovic, Zoran Kokot (87' Secouba
Diatta). Coach: Milomir Odovic.
Goal: 90' Dzenis Beganovic 0-1.
Referee: Gunnar Jarl Jónsson (ISL)   Attendance: 8,853.

16.07.15   Karadorde, Novi Sad: Vojvodina – FK Spartaks 3-0 (2-0).
Vojvodina: Srdan Zakula, Jovica Vasilic, Radovan Pankov, Bojan Nastic, Igor Djuric, Mirko
Ivanic, Danilo Sekulic, Novica Maksimovic (79' Darko Puskaric), Aleksandar Stanisavljevic,
Milan Mrdakovic (74' Ognjen Ozegovic), Uros Stamenic (72' Aleksandar Palocevic).
Coach: Zlatomir Zagorcic.
FK Spartaks: Aleksandrs Kolinko, Maksym Maksymenko, Dmitro Nazarenko, Nauris Bulvitis,
Ingus Slampe, Daniil Ulimbasevs, Romans Mickevics, Jevgenijs Kazacoks (46' Toms Mezs),
Elvis Stuglis (21' Ferdinand Takyi), Francesco Vivacqua, Ahmed Abdultaofik (75' Eriks
Punculs). Coach: Roman Pylypchuk.
Goals: 6' Aleksandar Stanisavljevic 1-0, 16' Milan Mrdakovic 2-0,
88' Romans Mickevics 3-0 (og).
Referee: Benoit Millot (FRA)   Attendance: 9,000.

16.07.15   Stadion Miejski, Bialystok: Jagiellonia Bialystok – Omonia Nikosia 0-0.
Jagiellonia Bialystok: Bartlomiej Dragowski, Filip Modelski, Sebastian Madera, Taras
Romanchuk (23' Konstantin Vassiljev / 85' Lukasz Sekulski), Patryk Tuszynski, Nika
Dzalamidze, Igors Tarasovs, Przemyslaw Frankowski (78' Karol Swiderski), Rafal Grzyb,
Piotr Tomasik, Maciej Gajos. Coach: Michal Probierz.
Omonia Nikosia: Kostas Panayi, Ucha Lobjanidze, Ivan Runje, Nuno Assis (89' Luciano
Bebe), Giorgos Economides, Margaca, Hérold Goulon, Cillian Sheridan, Cristóvao, Gaoussou
Fofana (81' Marios Demetriou), André Schembri (65' Andraz Kirm). Coach: Costas Kaiafas.
Referee: Bojan Pandzic (SWE)   Attendance: 16,067.

16.07.15   Cukaricki, Beograd: FK Cukaricki-Stankom – Gabala FK 1-0 (0-0).
FK Cukaricki-Stankom: Nemanja Stevanovic, Lucas, Filip Stojkovic, Bojan Ostojic, Dragoljub
Srnic, Branislav Jankovic, Slavoljub Srnic, Rajko Brezancic, Nikola Stojiljkovic (85' Nenad
Mirosavljevic), Andrija Pavlovic (67' Stanisa Mandic), Petar Bojic (90+1' Sasa Jovanovic).
Coach: Vladan Milojevic.
Gabala FK: Dmitro Bezotosniy, Vitaliy Vernydub, Ricardinho, Urfan Abbasov, Rafael Santos,
George Florescu (36' Dodô), Räsad Sadiqov, Oleksiy Gay, Sergei Zenjov (88' Asif
Mammadov), Javid Hüseynov, Oleksiy Antonov (46' Arif Dashdemirov).
Coach: Roman Grygorchuk.
Goal: 53' Nikola Stojiljkovic 1-0 (p).
Referee: Radu Petrescu (ROM)   Attendance: 3,550.

16.07.15   Miejski, Wroclaw: Slask Wroclaw – IFK Göteborg 0-0.

Slask Wroclaw: Mariusz Pawelek, Piotr Celeban, Mariusz Pawelec, Adam Kokoszka (59'
Marcel Gecov), Pawel Zielinski, Tom Hateley (67' Kamil Bilinski), Tomasz Holota, Jacek
Kielb (77' Flávio Paixao), Peter Grajciar, Róbert Pich. Coach: Tadeusz Pawlowski.
IFK Göteborg: John Alvbage, Emil Salomonsson, Haitam Aleesami, Sebastian Eriksson,
Thomas Rogne (86' Hjálmar Jónsson), Mattias Bjärsmyr, Jakob Ankersen, Martin Smedberg
(78' Soren Rieks), Gustav Svensson, Mikael Boman (78' Gustav Engvall), Lasse Vibe.
Coach: Jörgen Lennartsson.
Referee: Jesús Gil Manzano (ESP)   Attendance: 16,978.

16.07.15   Caledonian Stadium, Inverness: Inverness CT – Astra Giurgiu 0-1 (0-1).

Inverness CT: Owain Williams, Gary Warren, Josh Meekings (80' Dave Raven), Daniel
Devine, Nathaniel Wedderburn, Ross Draper (81' Jordan Roberts), Aaron Doran, Greg Tansey,
Danny Williams, Ryan Christie, Dani López (84' Richie Foran). Coach: John Hughes.
Astra Giurgiu: Silviu Lung jr., Geraldo Alves, Junior Maranhao, Valerica Gaman (47' Cristian
Oros), Pedro Queirós, Takayuki Seto, Gabriel Enache (71' Alexandru Stan), Rick, Filipe
Teixeira, Constantin Budescu (82' Daniel Florea), William Amorim. Coach: Marius Sumudica.
Goal: 24' Constantin Budescu 0-1.
Referee: Ken Johnsen (NOR)   Attendance: 5,534.

16.07.15   Upton Park, London: West Ham United – Birkirkara FC 1-0 (0-0).

West Ham United: Adrián, Winston Reid, Aaron Cresswell, James Tomkins, Kevin Nolan (79'
Diego Poyet), Matthew Jarvis, Mark Noble, Joey O'Brien, Morgan Amalfitano (59' Martin
Samuelsen), Mauro Zárate, Modibo Maiga (70' Elliot Lee). Coach: Slaven Bilic.
Birkirkara FC: Justin Haber, Mauricio Mazzetti, Ryan Camenzuli, Nikola Vukanac, Joseph
Zerafa, Paul Fenech (49' Kurt Zammit), Zach Muscat, Rowen Muscat, Fabrizio Miccoli, Liliu
(66' Vito Plut), Edin Murga (46' Edmond Agius). Coach: Giovanni Tedesco.
Goal: 90' James Tomkins 1-0.
Referee: Markus Hameter (AUT)   Attendance: 33,048.

16.07.15   Tallaght Stadium, Dublin: Shamrock Rovers – Odds BK 0-2 (0-0).

Shamrock Rovers: Craig Hyland, Luke Byrne, Conor Kenna, David Webster, Simon Madden,
Gary McCabe, Ryan Brennan (86' Cian Kavanagh), Gavin Brennan (80' Danny North), Patrick
Cregg, Kieran Waters (67' Brandon Miele), Michael Drennan. Coach: Pat Fenton.
Odds BK: Sondre Rossbach, Espen Ruud, Emil Jonassen, Steffen Hagen, Lars-Kristian
Eriksen, Ardian Gashi (46' Fredrik Jensen), Ole Halvorsen, Jone Samuelsen, Fredrik
Nordkvelle, Olivier Occéan (85' Vegard Bergan), Bentley (82' Havard Storbaek).
Coach: Dag-Eilev Fagermo.
Goals: 53', 67' Olivier Occéan 0-1 (p), 0-2.
Referee: Alain Bieri (SUI)   Attendance: 2,900.

16.07.15   Wojska Polskiego, Warszawa: Legia Warszawa – FC Botosani 1-0 (0-0).

Legia Warszawa: Dusan Kuciak, Michal Pazdan, Tomasz Jodlowiec, Tomasz Brzyski, Jakub
Rzezniczak, Lukasz Broz, Guilherme (67' Michal Zyro), Ondrej Duda (90+3' Michal
Maslowski), Dominik Furman, Nemanja Nikolic (68' Aleksandar Prijovic), Michal
Kucharczyk. Coach: Henning Berg.
FC Botosani: Plamen Iliev, Andrei Cordos, Andrei Miron, Stelian Cucu, Florin Acsinte,
Radoslav Dimitrov, Ciprian Brata (69' Petre Ivanovici), Gabriel Vasvari (64' Scott Robertson),
Raul Costin (84' Marius Croitoru), Dan Roman, Paul Batin. Coach: Leo Grozavu.
Goal: 77' Ondrej Duda 1-0.
Referee: Ante Vucemilovic-Simunovic (CRO)   Attendance: 10,446.

37

16.07.15   Kantrida, Rijeka: HNK Rijeka – Aberdeen FC 0-3 (0-1).

HNK Rijeka: Ivan Vargic, Marko Leskovic, Miral Samardzic, Marin Leovac, Marin Tomasov (46' Zoran Kvrzic), Anas Sharbini, Ivan Tomecak, Filip Bradaric (74' Ivan Mocinic), Josip Radosevic (55' Roman Bezjak), Moisés, Bekim Balaj. Coach: Matjaz Kek.

Aberdeen FC: Danny Ward, Shaleum Logan, Graeme Shinnie, Andrew Considine, Ash Taylor, Paul Quinn, Niall McGinn (69' Kenny McLean), Jonathan Hayes, Peter Pawlett (63' Willo Flood), Ryan Jack, David Goodwillie (83' Adam Rooney). Coach: Derek McInnes.

Goals: 38' Andrew Considine 0-1, 52' Peter Pawlett 0-2, 75' Kenny McLean 0-3.

Referee: Amaury Delerue (FRA)   Attendance: 9,000.

16.07.15   Alvogenvöllurinn, Reykjavik: KR Reykjavik – Rosenborg BK 0-1 (0-1).

KR Reykjavik: Stefán Magnússon, Grétar Sigurdsson, Rasmus Christiansen, Gunnar Gunnarsson, Aron Jósepsson, Jónas Saevarsson, Thorsteinn Már Ragnarsson (29' Gary Martin), Pálmi Pálmason, Jacob Schoop, Oskar Hauksson (80' Almarr Ormarsson), Soren Frederiksen (66' Hólmbert Fridjónsson). Coach: Bjarni Gudjónsson.

Rosenbog BK: André Hansen, Mikael Dorsin, Hólmar Eyjólfsson, Jørgen Skjelvik, Mike Jensen, Tobias Mikkelsen, Ole Selnæs, Fredrik Midtsjø, Jonas Svensson, Pål Helland (78' Riku Riski), Alexander Søderlund. Coach: Kåre Ingebrigtsen.

Goal: 56' Pål Helland 0-1 (p).

Referee: Adam Farkas (HUN)   Attendance: 1,550.

16.07.15   Kaplakrikavöllur, Hafnafjordur: FH Hafnafjördur – Inter Baku 1-2 (1-0).

FH Hafnarfjördur: Róbert Óskarsson, Pétur Vidarsson, Thórarinn Valdimarsson (83' Atli Björnsson), Kassim Doumbia, Bödvar Bödvarsson, Jonathan Hendrickx, Emil Pálsson (52' Kristján Finnbogason), David Vidarsson, Bjarni Vidarsson (70' Kristján Flóki Finnbogason), Gudmann Tórisson, Atli Gudnason. Coach: Heimir Gudjónsson.

Inter Baku: Sälahät Agayev, Juanfran, Lasha Kasradze, Zurab Khizanishvili, Abbas Hüseynov, Nika Kvekveskiri, Nizami Hajiyev (80' Stjepan Poljak, Mirsayib Abbasov (46' Dhiego), Mirhuseyn Seyidov, Fuad Bayramov (69' Denis), Rauf Aliyev. Coach: Zaur Svanadze.

Goals: 39' Atli Gudnason 1-0 (p), 54' Nika Kvekveskiri 1-1 (p), 61' Dhiego 1-2.

Referee: Michael Lerjéus (SWE)   Attendance: 1,020.

Sent off: 51' Róbert Óskarsson.

Note: There were 2 different players with the name Kristján Finnbogason, one a goalkeeper and the other, Kristján Flóki Finnbogason, a forward.

21.07.15   Boras Arena, Boras: IF Elfsborg – Randers FC 1-0 (0-0, 0-0).

IF Elfsborg: Kevin Stuhr-Ellegaard, Sebastian Holmén, Adam Lundqvist, Marcus Rohdén, Anders Svensson, Arber Zeneli (72' Viktor Prodell), Andreas Klarström (90' Simon Lundevall), Victor Claesson, Henning Hauger, Per Frick (106' Lasse Nilsson), Simon Hedlund. Coach: Magnus Haglund.

Randers FC: Kalle Johnsson, Erik Marxen (54' Edgar Babayan), Mads Fenger, Alexander Fischer, Christian Keller, Johnny Thomsen, Jeppe Tverskov, Mustafa Amini, Jonas Bjorring (80' Mikkel Thygesen), Nikolaj Poulsen, Nicolai Brock-Madsen. Coach: Colin Todd.

Goal: 94' Simon Lundevall 1-0.

Referee: Andreas Pappas (GRE)   Attendance: 5,197.

Sent off: 84' Nicolai Brock-Madsen.

IF Elfsborg won after extra time.

38

23.07.15   Shafa, Baku: Inter Baku – FH Hafnarfjördur 2-2 (1-0, 1-2).
Inter Baku: Sälahät Agayev, Juanfran, Lasha Kasradze, Zurab Khizanishvili, Abbas Hüseynov (87' Ilkin Qirtimov), Nika Kvekveskiri, Nizami Hajiyev, Mirhuseyn Seyidov (72' Stjepan Poljak), Fuad Bayramov, Rauf Aliyev, Dhiego (55' Mirsayib Abbasov). Coach: Zaur Svanadze.
FH Hafnarfjördur: Kristján Finnbogason, Sam Tillen (78' Bödvar Bödvarsson), Pétur Vidarsson, Thórarinn Valdimarsson, Kassim Doumbia, Jonathan Hendrickx, Emil Pálsson, David Vidarsson, Bjarni Vidarsson (37' Kristján Flóki Finnbogason), Jérémy Serwy, Atli Gudnason (97' Brynjar Asgeir Gudmundsson). Coach: Heimir Gudjónsson.
Goals: 45' Abbas Hüseynov 1-0, 47' Thórarinn Valdimarsson 1-1, 52' Kristján Flóki Finnbogason 1-2, 91' Rauf Aliyev 2-2.
Referee: Yaroslav Kozyk (UKR)   Attendance: 3,500.
Sent off: 56' Kristján Flóki Finnbogason.

Inter Baku won after extra time.

23.07.15   Lerkendal, Trondheim: Rosenborg BK – KR Reykjavik 3-0 (3-0).
Rosenbog BK: André Hansen, Mikael Dorsin, Hólmar Eyjólfsson, Jørgen Skjelvik, Mike Jensen, Tobias Mikkelsen, Ole Selnæs (37' Riku Riski), Fredrik Midtsjø, Jonas Svensson, Pål Helland (72' Emil Nielsen), Alexander Søderlund (79' Andreas Helmersen). Coach: Kåre Ingebrigtsen.
KR Reykjavik: Stefán Magnússon, Rasmus Christiansen, Skúli Jón Fridgeirsson, Gunnar Gunnarsson, Aron Jósepsson, Jónas Saevarsson (46' Grétar Sigurdsson), Pálmi Pálmason, Oskar Hauksson (61' Gonzalo Balbi), Gary Martin, Almarr Ormarsson, Hólmbert Fridjónsson (46' Kristinn Magnússon). Coach: Bjarni Gudjónsson.
Goals: 4' Fredrik Midtsjø 1-0, 7' Pål Helland 2-0, 17' Alexander Søderlund 3-0.
Referee: Athanasios Giachos (GRE)   Attendance: 6,371.

23.07.15   Pittodrie Stadium, Aberdeen: Aberdeen FC – HNK Rijeka 2-2 (0-0).
Aberdeen FC: Danny Ward, Shaleum Logan, Graeme Shinnie, Andrew Considine, Ash Taylor, Paul Quinn, Kenny McLean (73' Peter Pawlett), Niall McGinn (83' Willo Flood), Jonathan Hayes, Ryan Jack, David Goodwillie (75' Adam Rooney). Coach: Derek McInnes.
HNK Rijeka: Simon Sluga, Stefan Ristovski, Matej Mitrovic, Miral Samardzic, Marin Leovac, Marin Tomasov, Filip Bradaric (74' Bekim Balaj), Odise Roshi (52' Zoran Kvrzic), Josip Radosevic, Moisés, Roman Bezjak. Coach: Matjaz Kek.
Goals: 58' Marin Tomasov 0-1, 63' Zoran Kvrzic 0-2, 64' Niall McGinn 1-2, 72' Jonathan Hayes 2-2.
Referee: Marco Guida (ITA)   Attendance: 15,803.

23.07.15   Municipal, Botosani: FC Botosani – Legia Warszawa 0-3 (0-2).
FC Botosani: Plamen Iliev, Andrei Cordos (46' Gabriel Vasvari), Florin Plamada, Stelian Cucu, Andrei Patache (33' Quenten Martinus), Florin Acsinte, Radoslav Dimitrov, Ciprian Brata, Marius Croitoru, Raul Costin (73' Scott Robertson), Attila Hadnagy. Coach: Leo Grozavu.
Legia Warszawa: Dusan Kuciak, Michal Pazdan, Tomasz Jodlowiec (80' Michal Maslowski), Tomasz Brzyski (46' Michal Zyro), Jakub Rzezniczak, Lukasz Broz, Guilherme, Ondrej Duda, Dominik Furman, Nemanja Nikolic (70' Aleksandar Prijovic), Michal Kucharczyk. Coach: Henning Berg.
Goals: 7' Guilherme 0-1, 38' Nemanja Nikolic 0-2 (p), 84' Aleksandar Prijovic 0-3.
Referee: Alexandre Boucaut (BEL)   Attendance: 5,353.

23.07.15   Skagerak Arena, Skien: Odds BK – Shamrock Rovers 2-1 (0-0).

Odds BK: Sondre Rossbach, Espen Ruud, Emil Jonassen, Steffen Hagen, Lars-Kristian Eriksen (78' Vegard Bergan), Ardian Gashi, Oliver Berg, Ole Halvorsen, Fredrik Nordkvelle (62' Jone Samuelsen), Rafik Zekhnini, Bentley (46' Olivier Occéan). Coach: Dag-Eilev Fagermo.

Shamrock Rovers: Craig Hyland, Luke Byrne, Conor Kenna, David Webster, Simon Madden, Gary McCabe, Ryan Brennan, Gavin Brennan, Patrick Cregg (67' Cian Kavanagh), Brandon Miele (79' Danny North), Michael Drennan. Coach: Pat Fenton.

Goals: 72' Ole Halvorsen 1-0, 85' Steffen Hagen 2-0, 90+1' Gavin Brennan 2-1.

Referee: Marius Avram (ROM)   Attendance: 3,814.

23.07.15   National Stadium, Ta'Qali: Birkirkara FC – West Ham United 1-0 (1-0, 1-0).

Birkirkara FC: Justin Haber, Mauricio Mazzetti, Ryan Camenzuli, Nikola Vukanac, Joseph Zerafa, Paul Fenech, Zach Muscat, Rowen Muscat (70' Edmond Agius), Emerson (96' Kurt Zammit), Fabrizio Miccoli (77' Vito Plut), Liliu. Coach: Giovanni Tedesco.

West Ham United: Adrián, Aaron Cresswell, James Tomkins, James Collins, Kevin Nolan (59' Diego Poyet), Matthew Jarvis (120' Martin Samuelsen), Cheikhou Koyaté, Mark Noble, Joey O'Brien, Morgan Amalfitano (59' Modibo Maiga), Mauro Zárate. Coach: Slaven Bilic.

Goal: 15' Fabrizio Miccoli 1-0.

Referee: Enea Jorgji (ALB)   Attendance: 14,571.

Sent off: 45' James Tomkins, 108' Mauricio Mazzetti.

West Ham United won 5-3 on penalties following extra time.
Penalties: Noble 0-1, Fenech 1-1, Zárate 1-2, Plut 2-2, Cresswell 2-3, Vukanac missed,
*   O'Brien 2-4, Agius 3-4, Poyet 3-5.*

23.07.15   Stadionul Marin Anastasovici, Giurgiu: Astra Giurgiu – Inverness CT 0-0.

Astra Giurgiu: Silviu Lung Jr., Geraldo Alves, Junior Maranhao, Valerica Gaman, Pedro Queirós, Takayuki Seto, Gabriel Enache (80' Daniel Florea), Rick (84' Alexandru Dandea), Filipe Teixeira, Constantin Budescu (89' Florin Lovin), William Amorim. Coach: Marius Sumudica.

Inverness CT: Owain Williams, Dave Raven, Gary Warren, Josh Meekings, Daniel Devine, Nathaniel Wedderburn (79' Ross Draper), Aaron Doran, Greg Tansey, Danny Williams (78' Richie Foran), Ryan Christie, Dani López. Coach: John Hughes.

Referee: Artyom Kuchin (KAZ)   Attendance: 3,067.

23.07.15   Gamla Ullevi, Göteborg: IFK Göteborg – Slask Wroclaw 2-0 (0-0).

IFK Göteborg: John Alvbage, Emil Salomonsson, Haitam Aleesami, Sebastian Eriksson, Thomas Rogne, Mattias Bjärsmyr, Soren Rieks, Jakob Ankersen, Gustav Svensson, Mikael Boman (79' Martin Smedberg), Gustav Engvall (86' Tom Pettersson). Coach: Jörgen Lennartsson.

Slask Wroclaw: Mariusz Pawelek, Piotr Celeban, Dudu Paraiba, Adam Kokoszka, Pawel Zielinski (87' Mateusz Machaj), Tom Hateley, Tomasz Holota, Jacek Kielb, Flávio Paixao (76' Marcel Gecov), Peter Grajciar (68' Kamil Bilinski), Róbert Pich. Coach: Tadeusz Pawlowski.

Goals: 55' Gustav Engvall 1-0, 59' Mikael Borman 2-0.

Referee: Serdar Gözübüyük (HOL)   Attendance: 10,823.

40

23.07.15 Bakcell Arena, Baku: Gabala FK – FK Cukaricki-Stankom 2-0 (1-0).
Gabala FK: Dmitro Bezotosniy, Vojislav Stankovic, Ricardinho, Urfan Abbasov, Rafael
Santos, Räsad Sadiqov, Oleksiy Gay, Samir Zargarov (70' Arif Dashdemirov), Sergei Zenjov,
Javid Hüseynov, Oleksiy Antonov (89' Dodô)). Coach: Roman Grygorchuk.
FK Cukaricki-Stankom: Nemanja Stevanovic, Lucas, Filip Stojkovic, Bojan Ostojic, Dragoljub
Srnic (56' Obeng Regan), Branislav Jankovic (76' Igor Matic), Slavoljub Srnic (81' Stanisa
Mandic), Rajko Brezancic, Nikola Stojiljkovic, Andrija Pavlovic, Petar Bojic.
Coach: Vladan Milojevic.
Goals: 39', 53' Sergei Zenjov 1-0, 2-0.
Referee: Radek Prihoda (CZE)   Attendance: 8,500.

23.07.15 Neo GSP, Nikosia: Omonia Nikosia – Jagiellonia Bialystok 1-0 (1-0).
Omonia Nikosia: Kostas Panayi, Ucha Lobjanidze, Ivan Runje, Luciano Bebe, Nuno Assis,
Giorgos Economides, Margaca, Hérold Goulon (79' Gerasimos Fylaktou), Cillian Sheridan,
Cristóvao, André Schembri (84' Andraz Kirm). Coach: Costas Kaiafas.
Jagiellonia Bialystok: Bartlomiej Dragowski, Filip Modelski, Sebastian Madera, Taras
Romanchuk (75' Karol Swiderski), Patryk Tuszynski, Nika Dzalamidze (46' Piotr Grzelczak),
Igors Tarasovs, Przemyslaw Frankowski (62' Lukasz Sekulski), Rafal Grzyb, Piotr Tomasik,
Maciej Gajos. Coach: Michal Probierz.
Goal: 8' Cillian Sheridan 1-0.
Referee: Danilo Grujic (SER)   Attendance: 17,481.

23.07.15 Zemgalas Olimpiska Centra, Jelgava: FK Spartaks – Vojvodina 1-1 (0-0).
FK Spartaks: Pavels Davidovs, Maksym Maksymenko, Dmitro Nazarenko, Nauris Bulvitis,
Toms Mezs, Ingus Slampe, Daniil Ulimbasevs, Romans Bespalovs (54' Eriks Punculs),
Francesco Vivacqua, Ferdinand Takyi (71' Elvis Stuglis), Ahmed Abdultaofik (46' Romans
Mickevics). Coach: Roman Pylypchuk.
Vojvodina: Srdan Zakula, Radovan Pankov, Bojan Nastic, Igor Djuric, Mirko Ivanic (69'
Aleksandar Palocevic), Ivan Lakicevic, Sinisa Babic, Danilo Sekulic, Novica Maksimovic,
Aleksandar Stanisavljevic (73' Uros Stamenic), Ognjen Ozegovic (80' Saleta Kordic).
Coach: Zlatomir Zagorcic.
Goals: 86' Saleta Koric 0-1, 90+3' Francesco Vivacqua 1-1.
Referee: Richard Liesveld (HOL)   Attendance: 650.

23.07.15 Asim Ferhatović Hase, Sarajevo: Zeljeznicar Sarajevo - Ferencvárosi TC 2-0 (1-0).
Zeljeznicar Sarajevo: Marijan Antolovic, Josip Kvesic, Aleksandar Kosoric, Kerim Memija,
Jasmin Bògdanovic, Rijad Bajic, Jovan Blagojevic, Ognjen Djelmic, Amir Hadziahmetovic
(57' Enis Sadikovic), Damir Sadikovic (72' Dzenis Beganovic), Zoran Kokot (86' Joco
Stokic). Coach: Milomir Odovic.
Ferencvárosi TC: Dénes Dibusz, Michal Naelpa, Emir Dilaver, Tamás Hajnal (46' Stanislav
Sesták), Leandro, Gábor Gyömbér, Zoltán Gera, Roland Lamah, Dániel Böde (58' Attila
Busai), Somália, Roland Varga (41' András Radó). Coach: Thomas Doll.
Goals: 23' Zoran Kokot 1-0, 90+1' Ognjen Djelmic 2-0.
Referee: Orel Grinfield (ISR)   Attendance: 16,000.

23.07.15   Belfield Park, Dublin: UC Dublin – Slovan Bratislava 1-5 (0-1).

UC Dublin: Niall Corbert, Mark Langtry, Michael Leahy, Tomas Boyle, Maxim Kouogun, Gary O'Neill, Chris Mulhall (88' Samir Belhout), Ryan Swan, Dylan Watts (56' Conor Cannon), Robbie Benson, Jamie Doyle (76' Eoin Kirwan). Coach: Collie O'Neill.

Slovan Bratislava: Ján Mucha, Boris Sekulic, Martin Dobrotka (69' Dávid Hudák), Kornel Saláta, Frantisek Kubik (67' Filip Orsula), Marko Milinkovic (83' Lukás Gasparovic), Samuel Stefánik, Richard Lasik, Jakub Podany, Adam Zrelak, Róbert Vittek. Coach: Dusan Tittel.

Goals: 41' Róbert Vittek 0-1, 49' Marko Milinkovic 0-2, 57' Ryan Swan 1-2, 81' Kornel Saláta 1-3, 90+1', 90+3' Róbert Vittek 1-4, 1-5.

Referee: Ognjen Valjic (BIH)   Attendance: 1,361.

23.07.15   Windsor Park, Belfast: Linfield FC – Spartak Trnava 1-3 (1-0).

Linfield FC: Ross Glendinning, Chris Hegarty, Mark Haughey (76' Sean Ward), Aaron Burns, Matthew Clarke, Reece Glendinning, Stephen Lowry, David Kee, Ivan Sproule (63' Ross Clarke), Andrew Waterworth, Guy Bates. Coach: Warren Feeney.

Spartak Trnava: Adam Jakubech, Milan Bortel, Martin Tóth, Matús Conka, Lukás Gressák, Martin Mikovic, Erik Sabo, Emir Halilovic (76' Aldo Baéz), Haris Harba (70' Tomás Mikinic), Jakub Vojtus (88' Erik Jirka), José Casado. Coach: Juraj Jarábek.

Goals: 34' Stephen Lowry 1-0, 54' Erik Sabo 1-1, 60' Jakub Vojtus 1-2, 84' Erik Sabo 1-3.

Referee: Laurent Kopriwa (LUX)   Attendance: 3,001.

Sent off: 80' Milan Bortel.

23.07.15   Josy Barthel, Luxemburg: FC Differdange 03 – Trabzonspor 1-2 (0-1).

FC Differdange 03: Julien Weber, André Rodrigues (70' Phillipe Lebresne), Tom Siebenaler, Ante Bukvic, Mathias Jänisch, Pedro Ribeiro (79' Gilles Bettmer), Omar Er Rafik, Dejvid Sinani (57' Antonio Luisi), Jordann Yéyé, Gauthier Caron, Geoffrey Franzoni. Coach: Marc Thomé.

Trabzonspor: Onur Kivrak, Carl Medjani (90+4' Aytac Kara), Kevin Constant, Ugur Demirok, Mustafa Yumlu, Salih Dursun, Mehmet Ekici (58' Soner Aydogdu), Sefa Yilmaz, Yusuf Erdogan (72' Erkan Zengin), Musa Nizam, Waris Majeed. Coach: Shota Arveladze.

Goals: 19' Salih Dursun 0-1, 81' Omar Er Rafik 1-1, 90+3' Soner Aydogdu 1-2.

Referee: Marco Borg (MLT)   Attendance: 3,455.

23.07.15   Toumba, Saloniki: PAOK Saloniki – Lokomotiva Zagreb 6-0 (4-0).

PAOK Saloniki: Robin Olsen, Miguel Vitor, Ricardo Costa, Giorgos Tzavellas, Alexandros Tziolis (46' Hedwiges Maduro), Lucas Pérez (82' Ioannis Mystakidis), Ergis Kaçe, Stelios Kitsiou, Dimitrios Pelkas, Róbert Mak, Efthimos Koulouris (60' Razvan Rat). Coach: Igor Tudor.

Lokomotiva Zagreb: Oliver Zelenika, Karlo Bartolec, Tomislav Mrčela, Karlo Bručic, Herdi Prenga (25' Petar Misic), Damir Sovsic, Luka Begonja, Franko Andrijasevic, Jerko Leko (46' Jan Dolezal), Mirko Maric (57' Luka Capan), Marko Kolar. Coach: Ante Cacic.

Goals: 3' Lucas Pérez 1-0, 7' Róbert Mak 2-0, 14' Dimitrios Pelkas 3-0, 34' Stelios Kitsiou 4-0, 59' Franko Andrijasevic 5-0 (og), 84' Róbert Mak 6-0.

Referee: Carlos Xistra (POR)   Attendance: 11,923.

23.07.15   Latham Park, Newtown: Newtown AFC – FC København 1-3 (0-2).

Newtown AFC: David Jones, Steffan Edwards, Kieran Mills-Evans, Shane Sutton, Matty Owen (73' James Price), Luke Boundford, Craig Williams, Tom Goodwin (73' Matthew Cook), Matthew Hearsey (82' Craig Harris), Jason Oswell, Neil Mitchell.
Coach: Chris Hughes.
FC København: Stephan Andersen, Ludwig Augustinsson, Per Nilsson, Peter Ankersen, Mathias Jorgensen, Thomas Delaney, Kasper Kusk (65' Brandur Hendriksson), Benjamin Verbic, Nicolai Jorgensen (46' Tom Hogli), Marvin Pourie, Youssef Toutouh (46' Christoffer Remmer). Coach: Ståle Solbakken.
Goals: 28' Marvin Pourie 0-1, 40' Nicolai Jorgensen 0-2 (p), 51' Marvin Pourie 0-3, 70' Tom Goodwin 1-3.
Referee: Stanislav Todorov (BUL)   Attendance: 1,400.

23.07.15   A. Le Coq Arena, Tallinn: JK Nõmme Kalju – FC Vaduz 0-2 (0-0).
JK Nõmme Kalju: Vitali Teles, Alo Bärengrub, Jorge Rodrigues, Ken Kallaste, Ats Purje, Allan Kimbaloula, Eino Puri (63' Tarmo Neemelo), Karl Mööl, Hidetoshi Wakui, Artjom Dmitrijev (74' Vladimir Voskoboinikov), Joel Lindpere (72' Borislav Topic).
Coach: Sergei Terehhov
FC Vaduz: Oliver Klaus, Simone Grippo, Nick von Niederhäusern (62' Naser Aliji), Florian Stahel, Mario Bühler, Ramon Cecchini, Markus Neumayr (71' Stjepan Kukuruzovic), Philipp Muntwiler, Robin Kamber (62' Diego Ciccone), Manuel Sutter, Mauro Caballero Jr.
Coach: Giorgio Contini.
Goals: 59' Mauro Caballero Jr 0-1, 74' Naser Aliji 0-2.
Referee: Raymond Crangle (NIR)   Attendance: 1,030.

23.07.15   Teddy Kollek Stadium, Jerusalem: Beitar Jerusalem – Sporting Charleroi 1-4 (1-1).
Beitar Jerusalem: Boris Kleiman, Nisso Kapiloto, Tal Kachila, Dusan Matovic, Omer Atzily, Claudemir, Dani Preda (61' Ness Zamir), Liroy Zhairi (46' Itzhak Cohen), Ori Majabi, Avishay Cohen (61' Lidor Cohen), Dovev Gabay. Coach: Slobodan Drapic.
Sporting Charleroi: Nicolas Penneteau, Sebastien Dewaest, Stergos Marinos, Jessy Gálvez (57' Karel Geraerts), Francis N'Ganga, Martos, Damien Marcq, Enes Saglik (78' Florent Stevance), David Pollet, Dieumerci Ndongala, Neeskens Kebano (68' Benjamin Boulenger).
Coach: Felice Mazzu.
Goals: 16' Omer Atzily 1-0, 43' Neeskens Kebano 1-1, 53' Enes Saglik 1-2, 76' Dieumerci Ndongala 1-3, 90+2' Florent Stevance 1-4.
Referee: Stephan Klossner (SUI)   Attendance: 6,500.

23.07.15   Pod Goricom, Podgorica: FK Mladost Podgorica – FK Kukësi 2-4 (0-3).
FK Mladost Podgorica: Mileta Radulovic, Luka Pejovic, Milos Lakic, Milos B. Radulovic (80' Aldin Adzovic), Dusan Lagator (70' Luka Mirkovic), Mirko Raicevic, Milan Durisic, Ivan Novovic, Milos Radulovic (57' Jasmin Muhovic), Marko Scepanovic, Ivan Vukovic.
Coach: Nikola Rakojevic.
FK Kukësi: Dimitri Stajila, Gentian Muça, Rrahman Hallaçi, Renato Malota, Gledi Mici, Erick Flores, Edon Hasani (73' Besar Musolli), Felipe Moreira (60' Birungueta), Jefferson, Jean Carioca, Pero Pejic (79' Semiao Granado). Coach: Marcello Troisi.
Goals: 13' Pelipe Moreira 0-1, 19' Pero Pejic 0-2, 32' Erick Flores 0-3, 62' Marko Scepanovic 1-3, 72' Pero Pejic 1-4, 87' Aldin Adzovic 2-4.
Referee: Michael Tykgaard (DEN)   Attendance: 4,500.

43

23.07.15   Poljud, Split: Hajduk Split – FC Koper 4-1 (2-1).
Hajduk Split: Lovre Kalinic, Goran Milovic, Jefferson, Zoran Nizic, Marko Pejic, Fran Tudor, Nikola Vlasic, Mijo Caktas, Ante Roguljic (53' Elvir Maloku), Tomislav Kis (69' Anton Maglica), Andrija Balic (77' Tino-Sven Susic). Coach: Damir Buric.
FC Koper: Vasja Simcić, Denis Srne (71' Matej Pucko), Denis Halilovic, Damir Hadzic, Ivica Guberac, Amar Rahmanovic (77' Dalibor Radujko), Domen Crnigoj, Ante Tomic (81' Luka Vekic), Matej Palcic, Josip Ivancic, Goran Galesic. Coach: Rodolfo Vanoli.
Goals: 2' Tomislav Kis 1-0, 40' Jefferson 2-0, 45' Matej Palcic 2-1, 62' Mijo Caktas 3-1, 69' Anton Maglica 4-1.
Referee: Marco Fritz (GER)   Attendance: 22,800.

23.07.15   LFF Stadium, Vilnius: FK Trakai – Apollon Limassol 0-0.
FK Trakai: Marius Rapalis, Linas Klimavicius, Justinas Janusevskis, Deividas Cesnauskis, Ronalds Solomin (75' Edvardas Gaurilovas), Vaidas Silenas, Eugen Zasavitchi (78' Rokas Stanulevicius), Aleksandr Bychenok, Yuriy Mamaev, Donatas Segzda (59' Nika Apakidze), David Arshakyan. Coach: Valdas Urbonas.
Apollon Limassol: Bruno Vale, Elizio, Freire, Esteban Sacchetti, Marcos Gullón (63' Alexandre), Farley, Jaime, Joao Pedro, Luka Stojanović, Marios Stylianou, Giorgos Kolokoudias (87' Thodores Josephides). Coach: Pedro Emanuel.
Referee: Padraig Sutton (IRL)   Attendance: 930.

23.07.15   Marienlyst, Drammen: Strømsgodset IF – FK Mladá Boleslav 0-1 (0-1).
Strømsgodset IF: Espen Pettersen, Kim Madsen, Florent Hanin, Gustav Valsvik, Petter Moen (70' Martin Ovenstad), Iver Fossum, Gustav Wikheim, Mohammed Abu, Lars-Christopher Vilsvik, Oyvind Storflor (86' Flamur Kastrati), Thomas Sorum (69' Thomas Olsen). Coach: Bjorn Petter Ingebretsen.
FK Mladá Boleslav: Robert Veselovsky, Jan Boril, Antonin Krapka, Ales Cermák (79' Jasmin Scuk), Ondrej Kúdela, Jan Kysela, Ondrej Zahustel, Jakub Rada, Kevin Malpon (77' Jan Chramosta), Lukás Magera, Stanislav Klobása (67' Jiri Skalák). Coach: Karel Jarolim.
Goal: 31' Ales Cermák 0-1.
Referee: Aleksey Nikolaev (RUS)   Attendance: 4,371.

Strømsgotset IF won on away goals.

23.07.15   Traktor, Minsk: Dinamo Minsk – Cherno More Varna 4-0 (1-0).
Dinamo Minsk: Aleksandr Gutor, Maksim Vitus, Sergey Politevich, Roman Begunov, Mohamed El-Mounir (58' Sergiu Neacsa), Vladimir Korytko (88' Igor Voronkov), Umaru Bangura, Nikita Korzun, Nenad Adamovic (63' Artem Bykov), Gleb Rassadkin, Fatos Beciraj. Coach: Vuk Rasovic.
Cherno More Varna: Aleksandar Canovic, Mihail Venkov, Stefan Stanchev, Mamoutou Coulibaly, Marc Klok (46' Daniel Georgiev), Marcin Burkhardt (46' Sténio), Mathias Coureur, Mehdi Bourabia, Todor Palankov, Simeon Raykov, Villyan Bizhev (65' Andreas Vasev). Coach: Nikola Spasov.
Goals: 41' Vladimir Korytko 1-0, 58' Nenad Adamovic 2-0, 86', 90+2' Fatos Beciraj 3-0, 4-0.
Referee: Anatoliy Zhabchenko (UKR)   Attendance: 2,616.
Sent off: 45' Todor Palankov.

23.07.15 Stockhorn Arena, Thun: FC Thun – Hapoel Be'er Sheva 2-1 (1-1).

FC Thun: Guillaume Faivre, Fulvio Sulmoni, Thomas Reinmann, Stefan Glarner (60' Enrico Shirinzi), Gianluca Frontino (85' Ridge Munsy), Marco Rojas (90+4' Marco Bürki), Lotern Zino, Dennis Hediger, Nelson Ferreira, Andreas Wittwer, Simone Rapp. Coach: Ciriaco Sforza.

Hapoel Be'er Sheva: David Goresh, Ben Biton, Shir Tzedek, Ofir Davidadze, Maharan Radi, Maor Buzaglo, Ovidiu Hoban (75' Ben Sahar), Maor Melikson (83' Anthony Nuatuzor), William Soares, John Ogu, Elyaniv Barda (38' Loai Taha). Coach: Barak Bakhar.

Goals: 6' John Ogu 0-1, 40', 72' Nelson Ferreira 1-1, 2-1.
Referee: Craig Pawson (ENG)   Attendance: 4,017.
Sent off: 20' Shir Tzedek.

23.07.15 Gyumri City, Gyumri: Shirak FC – AIK Solna 0-2 (0-0).

Shirak FC: Vsevolod Ermakov, Artyom Mikaelyan, Milos Stamenkovic, Gevorg Hovhannisyan, Tigran Davtyan, Davit Hakobyan (58' Viulen Ayvazyan), Karen Aleksanyan (70' Mohamed Kaba), Edgar Malakyan, Aghvan Davoyan, Jean-Jacques Bougouhi (76' Aram Muradyan), Drissa Diarrassouba. Coach: Vardan Bichakhchyan.

AIK Solna: Kenny Stamatopoulos, Per Karlsson (13' Alex), Nils-Eric Johansson, Haukur Hauksson, Noah Sonko Sundberg, Fredrik Brustad (46' Niclas Eliasson), Johan Blomberg, Ebenezer Ofori, Dickson Etuhu (59' Anton Jönsson Salétros), Stefan Ishizaki, Henok Goitom. Coach: Andreas Alm.

Goals: 14' Henok Goitom 0-1, 25' Stefan Ishizaki 0-2.
Referee: Sándor Andó-Szabó (HUN)   Attendance: 2,820.

23.07.15 Brøndby Stadion, Brøndby: Brøndby IF – PFC Beroe 0-0.

Brøndby IF: Lukás Hrádecky, Martin Albrechtsen, Johan Larsson, Riza Durmisi, Dario Durmic, Martin Ornskov, Lebogang Phiri, Christian Norgaard, Andrew Hjulsager, Teemu Pukki (79' Frederik Holst), Johan Elmander, Elbasan Rashami (58' Magnus Eriksson). Coach: Thomas Frank.

PFC Beroe: Blagoj Makendzhiev, Ivo Ivanov, Ventzislav Vasilev, Veselin Penev, Atanas Zehirov, Nemanja Milisavljevic, Elias, Igor Djoman, Junior M'Pia, Georgi Bozhilov (79' Ivan Kokonov), Spas Delev. Coach: Petar Hubchev.

Referee: Nicolas Rainville (FRA)   Attendance: 9,550.

23.07.15 Wörthersee Stadion, Klagenfurt: Wolfsberger AC – Shakhter Soligorsk 2-0 (1-0).

Wolfsberger AC: Alexander Kofler, Stephan Palla, Michael Berger, Michael Sollbauer, Daniel Drescher (59' Boris Hüttenbrenner), Manuel Weber (45' Peter Tschernegg), Jacobo, Roland Putsche, Thomas Zündel (85' Christopher Wernitznig), Silvio, Philip Hellquist. Coach: Dietmar Kühbauer.

Shakhter Soligorsk: Vladimir Bushma, Aleksey Yanushkevich, Aleksandr Yurevich, Pavel Rybak, Ihar Kuzmianok, Siarhei Matveichyk (82' Nemanja Covic), Artem Stargorodskiy, Yuri Kovalev (65' Mikhail Afanasiev), Nikolai Yanush, Dmitriy Komarovskiy, Yaroslav Martinyuk (52' Kirill Vergeychik). Coach: Sergey Nikiforenko.

Goals: 19' Michael Sollbauer 1-0, 90' Philip Hellquist 2-0.
Referee: Dimitar Meckarovski (MKD)   Attendance: 6,400.

23.07.15   Nagyerdei, Debrecen: Debreceni VSC – Skonto FC 9-2 (5-0).

Debreceni VSC: István Verpecz, Norbert Mészáros, Dusan Brkovic, Mihály Korhut, Adám
Bódi (62' Zsolt Horváth), József Varga (46' László Zsidai), Péter Szakály, Aleksandar
Jovanovic, Norbert Balogh (56' Geoffrey Castillion), Ibrahima Sidibé, Tibor Tisza.
Coach: Elemér Kondás.

Skonto FC: Andrejs Pavlovs, Olegs Timofejevs, Iván Murillo (54' Dvis Indrans), Vladislavs
Sorokins, Reinars Rode, Aleksejs Visnakovs (46' Nikita Berenfelds), Igors Kozlovs, Edgars
Jermolaevs, Andrejs Kovalovs, Vladislavs Gutkovskis, Arturs Karasausks (61' Ivan
Lukanyuk). Coach: Tamaz Pertia.

Goals: 7' Tibor Tisza 1-0, 12' Norbert Balogh 2-0, 29', 31' Ibrahima Sidibe 3-0, 4-0,
45' Tibor Tisza 5-0, 51' Dusan Brkovic 6-0, 54' Péter Szakály 7-0 (p), 58' Adám Bódi 8-0,
59' Vladislavs Gutkovskis 8-1, 65' Renars Rode 8-2, 70' Geoffrey Castillion 9-2.
Referee: Vitaliy Meshkov (RUS)   Attendance: 8,532.
Sent off: 81' Andrejs Kovalovs.

23.07.15   Stadión pod Dubnom, Zilina: MSK Zilina – Dacia Chisinau 4-2 (1-0).

MSK Zilina: Milos Volesák, Milan Skriniar, Denis Vavro, Ernest Mabouka, Miroslav Kácer,
Viktor Pecovsky, Michal Skvarka (66' László Bénes), Bojan Letic, Jaroslav Mihalík (81'
Nikolas Spalek), Matej Jelic, Lukás Cmelik (73' Jakub Paur). Coach: Adrián Gula.

Dacia Chisinau: Artion Gaiduchevici, Mihai Rosca, Veaceslav Posmac, Volodymyr Zastavnyi,
Abdoul Mamah, Evgeniy Lozoviy, Sapol Mani (55' Maksim Gavrilenko), Eugeniu Cociuc,
Vyacheslav Pidnebennoy (55' Vasili Pavlov), Viorel Frunza (55' Petru Leuca), Maxim
Mihaliov. Coach: Igor Dobrovolskiy.

Goals: 15' Denis Vavro 1-0, 50' Miroslav Kácer 2-0, 62' Michal Skvarka 3-0,
64' Eugeniu Cociuc 3-1, 85' Jakub Paur 4-1, 98' Petru Leuca 4-2.
Referee: Sandro Schärer (SUI)   Attendance: 3,856.
Sent off: 31' Evgeniy Lozoviy.

23.07.15   Filip II. Makedonski, Skopje: FK Rabotnicki – FK Jelgava 2-0 (2-0).

FK Rabotnicki: Daniel Bozinovski, Goran Siljanovski, Kire Ristevski, Milan Ilievski, Stephan
Vujcic, Milovan Petrovikj, Mite Cikarski, Suad Sahiti, Chuma Anene (68' Dusko Trajcevski),
Baze Ilijoski (90+2' Kire Markoski), Marijan Altiparmakovski (86' Miroslav Jovanovski).
Coach: Tomislav Franc.

FK Jelgava: Kaspars Ikstens, Valerijs Redjko, Abdoulaye Diallo, Aleksandrs Gubins (60'
Andrejs Kirilins), Marcis Oss, Gints Freimanis, Rustam Sosranov, Dariusz Latka, Boriss
Bogdaskins, Glebs Kluskins (84' Artis Jaudzems), Vyacheslav Sushkin (79' Olegs
Malasenoks). Coach: Vitalijs Astafjevs.
Goals: 6' Baze Ilijoski 1-0, 17' Suad Sahiti 2-0.
Referee: István Kovács (ROM)   Attendance: 2,300.

23.07.15   Hanrapetakan, Yerevan: Alashkert Martuni – Kairat Almaty 2-1 (1-1).

Alashkert Martuni: Gevorg Kasparov, Sékou Fofana, Sergey Usenya, Vahagn Minasyan, Karen
Muradyan (78' Aram Hovsepyan), Ararat Arakelyan, Khoren Veranyan (58' Gevorg
Poghosyan), Aram Bareghamyan, Héber, Artak Grigoryan, Norayr Gyozalyan (58' Mihran
Manasyan). Coach: Abraham Khashmanyan.

Kairat Almaty: Vladimir Plotnikov, Bruno Soares, Zarko Markovic (85' Mark Gorman),
Ermek Kuantaev, Bauyrzhan Islamkhan, Isael, Islambek Kuat (67' Ulan Konysbaev), Anatoliy
Tymoschchuk, Gerard Gohou, Sito Riera (71' Djordje Despotovic), Stanislav Lunin.
Coach: Vladimir Weiss.
Goals: 28' Ararat Arakelyan 1-0, 45+3' Gerard Gohou 1-1, 90+4' Héber 2-1.
Referee: Joao Capela (POR)   Attendance: 2,500.

46

THIRD QUALIFYING ROUND

29.07.15   Chance Arena, Jablonec: FK Jablonec – FC Kobenhagen 0-1 (0-0).
FK Jablonec: Vlastimil Hruby, Tomás Hübschman, Ludek Perncia, Vyacheslav Karavaev, Vit
Benes, Filip Novák, Nermin Crnkic, Ján Gregus, Martin Pospisil (62' Michal Trávnik), Lukás
Masopust (62' Stanislav Tecl), Tomás Wágner (77' Martin Dolezal). Coach: Jaroslav Silhavy.
FC Kobenhagen: Stephan Andersen, Ludwig Augustinsson, Mikael Antonsson, Daniel
Amartey, Peter Ankersen, Mathias Jorgensen, Thomas Delaney, Benjamin Verbic (81' Kasper
Kusk), Nicolai Jorgensen, Federico Santander (88' Marvin Pourie), Youssef Toutouh (63'
William Kvist). Coach: Ståle Solbakken.
Goal: 51' Benjamin Verbic 0-1.
Referee: Mattias Gestranius (FIN)   Attendance: 4,830.
Sent off: 69' Stanislav Tecl.

30.07.15   Qemal Stafa, Tirana: FK Kukësi – Legia Warszawa 1-2 (0-1)
FK Kukësi: Dimitri Stajila, Rrahman Hallaçi, Gledi Mici, Renato Malota, Gentian Muça, Erick
Flores, Jean Carioca, Edon Hasani, Jefferson, Birungueta, Felipe Moreira.
Coach: Marcello Troisi.
Legia Warszawa: Dusan Kuciak, Tomasz Brzyski, Jakub Rzezniczak, Lukasz Broz, Michal
Pazdan, Tomasz Jodlowiec (42' Michal Maslowski), Guilherme, Michal Kucharczyk, Dominik
Furman, Ondrej Duda, Nemanja Nikolic. Coach: Henning Berg.
Goals: 29' Nemanja Nikolic 0-1, 49' Felipe Moreira 1-1, 51' Jakub Rzezniczak 1-2.
Referee: Stephan Klossner (SUI)   Attendance: 5,000

Match was abandoned in the 52nd minute after a Legia Warszawa player was hit on the head by
an object thrown from the crowd. Legia Warszawa were awarded a 3-0 victory by UEFA.

30.07.15   Tsentralniy, Almaty: Kairat Almaty – Aberdeen FC 2-1 (2-0).
Kairat Almaty: Vladimir Plotnikov, Bruno Soares, Mark Gorman (79' Serginho), Zarko
Markovic, Ermek Kuantaev, Mikhail Bakaev, Bauyrzhan Islamkhan, Isael, Anatoliy
Tymoshchuk, Stanislav Lunin, Djordje Despotovic (68' Ulan Konysbaev).
Coach: Vladimir Weiss.
Aberdeen FC: Danny Ward, Shaleum Logan, Graeme Shinnie, Andrew Considine, Ash Taylor,
Paul Quinn (85' Barry Robson), Niall McGinn, Jonathan Hayes, Peter Pawlett (46' Adam
Rooney), Ryan Jack, David Goodwillie (64' Kenny McLean). Coach: Derek McInnes.
Goals: 13' Mikhail Bakaev 1-0, 22' Bauyrzhan Islamkhan 2-0, 69' Kenny McLean 2-1.
Referee: Tamás Bognar (HUN)   Attendance: 23,500.

30.07.15   Boras Arena, Boras: IF Elfsborg – Odds BK 2-1 (1-1).
IF Elfsborg: Kevin Stuhr-Ellegaard, Sebastian Holmén, Adam Lundqvist, Marcus Rohdén,
Anders Svensson, Arber Zeneli, Andreas Klarström, Victor Claesson (87' Lase Nilsson),
Henning Hauger, Simon Hedlund (69' Simon Lundevall), Viktor Prodell (80' Per Frick).
Coach: Magnus Haglund.
Odds BK: Sondre Rossbach, Espen Ruud, Thomas Grøgaard, Steffen Hagen, Lars-Kristian
Eriksen, Ole Halvorsen, Jone Samuelsen, Fredrik Nordkvelle (43' Oliver Berg), Fredrik
Jensen, Pape Diouf (68' Bentley), Olivier Occéan. Coach: Dag-Eilev Fagermo.
Goals: 21' Olivier Occéan 0-1 (p), 43' Viktor Prodell 1-1, 76' Simon Lundevall 2-1.
Referee: Ognjen Valjić (BIH)   Attendance: 4,232.

30.07.15   Toumba, Saloniki: PAOK Saloniki – Spartak Trnava 1-0 (0-0).

PAOK Saloniki: Robin Olsen, Miguel Vitor, Ricardo Costa, Giorgos Tzavellas, Alexandros Tziolis (73' Kyriakos Savvidis), Lucas Pérez, Ergis Kaçe, Stelios Kitsiou, Dimitrios Pelkas, Róbert Mak (78' Ioannis Mystakidis), Efthimios Koulouris (5' Giannis Skondras). Coach: Igor Tudor.

Spartak Trnava: Lubos Kamenár, Marek Janecka, Milos Nikolic, Martin Tóth, Lukás Gressák, Martin Mikovic (20' Christián Steinhübel), Erik Sabo, Emir Halilovic (86' Aldo Baéz), Tomás Mikinic, Jakub Vojtus (74' Haris Harba), José Casado. Coach: Juraj Jarábek.

Goal: 82' Lucas Pérez 1-0.

Referee: Svein Edvartsen (NOR)   Attendance: 12,427.

Sent off: 3' Miguel Vitor.

30.07.15   U Nisy, Liberec: Slovan Liberec – Ironi Kiryat Shmona 2-1 (1-0).

Slovan Liberec: Tomás Koubek, Vladimír Coufal, Ondrej Svejdik, David Pavelka, David Hovorka, Isaac Sackey, Lukás Bartosák, Michael Rabusic (73' Marek Bakos), Milan Kerbr (53' Herolind Shala), Josef Sural, Dzon Delarge (86' Jiri Fleisman). Coach: Jindrich Trpisovsky.

Ironi Kiryat Shmona: Guy Haimov, Daniel Borchal, Cássio, Luis Gutiérrez, Oded Elkayam, Or Ostvind (75' Ofir Mizrachi), Roei Shukrani (51' Adrian Rochet), Ahmad Abed, Vladimir Broun, Bruno, Ido Exbard (46' Ugwu Chukwuma). Coach: Salah Hasarma.

Goals: 43' Dzon Delarge 1-0, 84' Herolind Shala 2-0, 89' Ahmad Abed 2-1.

Referee: Simon Evans (WAL)   Attendance: 5,400.

30.07.15   Antonis Papadopoulos, Larnaca: Apollon Limassol – Gabala FK 1-1 (1-0).

Apollon Limassol: Bruno Vale, Elizio, Nuno Lopes, Freire, Esteban Sacchetti, Marcos Gúllon, Alexandre (76' Thuram), Jaime, Joao Pedro (89' Marios Stylianou), Fotis Papoulis, Giorgos Kolokoudias (63' Abraham Guié-Guié). Coach: Pedro Emanuel.

Gabala FK: Dmitro Bezotosniy, Vojislav Stankovic, Ricardinho, Urfan Abbasov (85' Arif Dashdemirov), Rafael Santos, Räsad Sadiqov, Oleksiy Gay, Samir Zargarov (35' Dodô), Sergei Zenjov, Javid Hüseynov, Oleksiy Antonov (76' Ermin Zec). Coach: Roman Grygorchuk.

Goals: 14' Giorgos Kolokoudias 1-0, 90+5' Javid Hüseynov 1-1 (p).

Referee: Sergey Boyko (UKR)   Attendance: 4,540.

30.07.15   Friends Arena, Solna: AIK Solna – Atromitos 1-3 (0-2).

AIK Solna: Patrik Carlgren, Nisl-Eric Johansson, Alex, Noah Sonko Sundberg, Fredrik Brustad (57' Niclas Eliasson), Johan Blomberg (57' Henok Goitom), Kenny Pavey, Ebenezer Ofori, Dickson Etuhu, Stefan Ishizaki, Mohamed Bangura. Coach: Andreas Alm.

Atromitos: Andrey Gorbunov, Sokratis Fitanidis, Mariano Bíttolo, Nikolaos Lazaridis, Usero, Stefano Napoleoni (90+3' Panagiotis Ballas), Javier Umbides, Marcelinho (85' Eduardo Brito), Fernando Godoy, Kyriakos Kivrakidis, Sebastián García (75' Pape M'Bow). Coach: Michalis Grigoriou.

Goals: 3' Stefano Napoleoni 0-1, 15' Marcelinho 0-2, 70' Henok Goitom 1-2 (p), 80' Javier Umbides 1-3 (p).

Referee: Christian Dingert (GER)   Attendance: 9,771.

Sent off: 79' Noah Sonko Sundberg.

Kenny Pavey missed a penalty kick (49').

48

30.07.15 UPC-Arena, Graz: Sturm Graz – Rubin Kazan 2-3 (1-2).
Sturm Graz: Michael Esser, Michael Madl, Martin Ehrenreich, Christian Klem, Wilson Kamavuaka, Anel Hadzic (75' Sascha Horvath), Simon Piesinger, Kristijan Dobras, Thorsten Schick (68' Andreas Gruber), Josip Tadic (63' Romas Kienast), Donis Avdijaj.
Coach: Franco Foda.
Rubin Kazan: Sergey Ryzhikov, Oleg Kuzmin, Elmir Nabiullin, Solomon Kverkvelia, Guillermo Cotugno, Ruslan Kambolov (46' Blagoy Georgiev), Carlos Eduardo, Diniyar Bilyaletdinov (66' Sergey Kislyak), Magomed Ozdoev, Gökdeniz Karadeniz, Maksim Kanunnikov (46' Igor Portnyagin). Coach: Rinat Bilyaletdinov.
Goals: 14' Maksim Kanunnikov 0-1, 21' Donis Avdija 1-1, 25' Gökdeniz Karadeniz 1-2 (p), 56' Simon Piesinger 2-2, 61' Igor Portnyagin 2-3.
Referee: Daniel Stefanski (POL)   Attendance: 9,765.
Sent off: 69' Donis Avdija.

30.07.15 Tivoli Stadion Tirol, Innsbruck: SCR Altach – Vitória Guimaraes 2-1 (1-0).
SCR Altach: Andreas Lukse, Andreas Lienhart, Jan Zwischenbrugger, César Ortiz, Benedikt Zech, Philipp Netzer, Daniel Luxbacher, Boris Prokopic (90' Lukas Jäger), Hannes Aigner (78' Juan Barrera), Patrick Seeger (78' Martin Harrer), Louis N'Gwat-Mahop.
Coach: Damir Canadi.
Vitória Guimaraes: Douglas Jesus, Luis Rocha, Joao Afonso, Alvin Arrondel, Moreno, Montoya (52' Tózé), Bruno Alves, Ricardo Valente (70' Henrique), Tó Mané, Alex (90+3' Licá), Cafú. Coach: Armando Evangelista.
Goals: 24' Louis N'Gwat-Mahop 1-0, 50' Hannes Aigner 2-0 (p), 71' Tózé 2-1.
Referee: Aleksey Eskov (RUS)   Attendance: 3,267.

30.07.15 Kuba, Krasnodar: FK Krasnodar – Slovan Bratislava 2-0 (1-0).
FK Krasnodar: Andrey Dikan, Artur Jedrejczyk, Andreas Granqvist, Vitaliy Kaleshin, Ragnar Sigurdsson, Pavel Mamaev (68' Odil Akhmedov), Yuri Gazinskiy (81' Stefan Strandberg), Wanderson, Mauricio Pereyra, Ari, Fedor Smolov (62' Ricardo Laborde).
Coach: Oleg Kononov.
Slovan Bratislava: Ján Mucha, Boris Sekulic, Dávid Hudák, Kornel Saláta, Juraj Kotula, Mauro Ezequiel González (80' Samuel Stefanik), Marko Milinković, Jakub Podany, Adam Zrelak (73' Frantisek Kubik), Karol Mészáros (60' Filip Orsula), Róbert Vittek.
Coach: Dusan Tittel.
Goals: 45' Andreas Granqvist 1-0, 59' Pavel Mamaev 2-0 (p).
Referee: Halis Ozkahya (TUR)   Attendance: 10,420.

30.07.15 Letzigrund, Zürich: FC Zürich – Dinamo Minsk 0-1 (0-0).
FC Zürich: Yanick Brecher, Berat Djimsiti, Alain Nef, Philippe Koch, Cabral, Christian Schneuwly, Davide Chiumiento (46' Yacine Chikhaoui), Oliver Buff, Mike Kleiber (12' Cédric Brunner), Amine Chermiti (66' Mario Gavranovic), Armando Sadiku.
Coach: Urs Meier.
Dinamo Minsk: Aleksandr Gutor, Sergey Politevich, Oleg Veretilo, Roman Begunov, Mohamed El-Mounir (55' Jan Tigorev), Uladzimir Karytska (75' Sergiu Neacsa), Umaru Bangura, Nikita Korzun, Nenad Adamovic (90+1' Maksim Vitus), Gleb Rassadkin, Fatos Beciraj. Coach: Vuk Rasovic.
Goal: 63' Fatos Beciraj 0-1 (p).
Referee: Tom Hagern (NOR)   Attendance: 3,587.

49

30.07.15   Stadion pod Dupnom, Zilina: MSK Zilina – Vorskla Poltava 2-0 (1-0).

MSK Zilina: Milos Volesák, Milan Skriniar, Denis Vavro, Ernest Mabouka (20' Nikolas Spalek), Miroslav Kácer, Jakub Paur, Viktor Pecovsky, Bojan Letic, László Bénes (90+6' Michal Skvarka), Jaroslav Mihalík (83' William), Matej Jelic. Coach: Adrián Gula.

Vorkla Poltava: Stanislav Bogush, Sergiy Siminin, Armend Dallku, Volodimir Chesnakov, Evgen Tkachuk, Aleksandr Sklyar (85' Andriy Tkachuk), Artem Gromov (77' Mladen Bartulovic), Vadim Sapay, Sanzhar Tursunov, Anton Shynder, Oleksandr Kovpak (80' Oleg Barannik). Coach: Vasil Sachko.

Goals: 26' Matej Jelic 1-0, 73' Jakub Paur 2-0.

Referee: Marijo Strahonja (SVK)   Attendance: 4,757.

Sent off: 90' Stanislav Bogush.

Oleksandr Kovpak missed a penalty kick (63').

30.07.15   AFAS Stadion, Alkmaar: AZ Alkmaar – Medipol Basaksehir F.K 2-0 (1-0).

AZ Alkmaar: Sergio Rochet, Mattias Johansson, Jeffrey Gouweleeuw, Jop van der Linden, Ridgeciano Haps, Celso Ortiz, Joris van Overeem (46' Aron Jóhannsson), Markus Henriksen, Dabney dos Santos (86' Robert Mühren), Thom Haye, Vincent Janssen (74' Muamer Tankovic). Coach: John van den Brom.

Medipol Basakseehir F.K: Volkan Babacan, Yalcin Ayhan, Mahmut Tekdemir, Ugur Ucar, Gencer Cansev (65' Emre Belözoglu), Ferhat Oztorun, Edin Visca, Márcio Mossoró (15' Ufuk Ceylan), Doka Madureira (77' Cenk Alkilic), Stéphane Badji, Sokol Cikalleshi. Coach: Abdullah Avci.

Goals: 17' Jop van der Linden 1-0 (p), 63' Vincent Janssen 2-0.

Referee: Kevin Clancy (SCO)   Attendance: 11,723.

Sent off: 13' Volkan Babacan.

30.07.15   Stockhorn Arena, Thun: FC Thun – FC Vaduz 0-0.

FC Thun: Guillaume Faivre, Fulvio Sulmoni, Thomas Reinmann, Enrico Schirinzi, Sandro Wieser, Gianluca Frontino (56' Roman Buess), Marco Rojas (89' Ridge Munsy), Dennis Hediger, Nelson Ferreira, Andreas Wittwer, Simone Rapp. Coach: Ciriaco Sforza.

FC Vaduz: Oliver Klaus, Simone Grippo, Pavel Pergl, Nick von Niederhäuser, Naser Alji, Diego Ciccone, Ramon Cecchini (72' Ali Messaoud), Moreno Costanzo (78' Robin Kamber), Stjepan Kukuruzovic, Philipp Muntwiler, Mauro Caballero Jr (66' Markus Neumayr). Coach: Giorgio Contini.

Referee: Jakob Kehlet (DEN)   Attendance: 3,407.

30.07.15   Trans-Sil, Targu Mures: ASA Targu Mures – AS Saint-Etienne 0-3 (0-1).

ASA Targu Mures; Eduard Stancioiu, Sasa Balic, Iván González, Florin Bejan, Pawel Golanski, Gabriel Muresan (67' Ramiro Costa), Filip Jazvic, Pablo Brandán (61' Luis Pedro), Nicolás Gorobsov, Ousmane N'Doye, Mircea Axente (79' Miroslav Manolov). Coach: Vasile Miriuta.

AS Saint-Étienne: Stéphane Ruffier, Kévin Théophile-Catherine, Florentin Pogba, Moustapha Sall, Benoit Assou-Ekotto (61' Jonathan Brison), Jerémy Clément, Romain Hamouma (83' Kévin Monnet-Paquet), Loic Perrin, Ismaël Diomandé, Max Gradel, Nolan Roux (74' Yohan Mollo). Coach: Christophe Galtier.

Goals: 24' Ismaël Diomandé 0-1, 75', 83' Romain Hamouma 0-2, 0-3.

Referee: Pol van Boekel (HOL)   Attendance: 6,498.

30.07.15   Filip II. Makedonski, Skopje: FK Rabotnicki – Trabzonspor 1-0 (1-0).

FK Rabotnicki: Daniel Bozinovski, Goran Siljanovski, Kire Ristevski, Milan Ilievski, Stephan Vujcic, Milovan Petrovikj, Mite Cikarski, Suad Sahiti (85' Ivan Mitrov), Chuma Anene, Baze Ilijoski (63' Dusko Trajcevski), Marijan Altiparmakovski (82' Kire Markoski).
Coach: Igor Angelovski.
Trabzonspor: Ugurcan Cakir, Aykut Demir (75' Okay Yokuslu), Carl Medjani, Kévin Constant, Mustafa Yumlu, Salih Dursun, Sefa Yilmaz (62' Ozer Hurmaci), Yusuf Erdogan, Alper Uludag, Oscar Cardozo, Waris Majeed (80' Erkan Zengin). Coach: Shota Arveladze.
Goal: 23' Baze Ilijoski 1-0.
Referee: Pawel Gil (POL)   Attendance: 6,200.

30.07.15   Nagyerdei, Debrecen: Debreceni VSC – Rosenborg BK 2-3 (1-0).
Debreceni VSC: István Verpecz, Péter Máté, Dusan Brkovic, Mihály Korkut, Adám Bódi, József Varga, Péter Szakály (84' László Zsidai), Aleksandar Jovanovic, Norbert Balogh, Ibrahima Sidibe (64' Geoffrey Castillion), Tibor Tisza (84' Rene Mihelic).
Coach: Elemér Kondás.
Rosenborg BK: André Hansen, Mikael Dorsin, Hólmar Eyjólfsson, Jørgen Skjelvik, Mike Jensen, Tobias Mikkelsen (90+1' Riku Riski), Ole Selnæs, Fredrik Midtsjø, Jonas Svensson, Pål Helland (73' Yann-Erik De Lanlay), Alexander Søderlund (80' Matthias Vilhjálmsson).
Coach: Kåre Ingebrigtsen.
Goals: 33' Norbert Balogh 1-0, 52' Tobias Mikkelsen 1-1, 58' Pål Helland 1-2, 87' Tobias Mikkelsen 1-3, 90' Adám Bódi 2-3.
Referee: Neil Doyle (IRL)   Attendance: 10,532.

30.07.15   Brøndby Stadion, Brøndby: Brøndby IF – Omonia Nikosia 0-0.
Brøndby IF: Lukás Hrádecky, Martin Albrechtsen (43' Malthe Johansen), Frederik Holst, Johan Larsson, Riza Durmisi, Dcario Dumic, Lebogang Phiri, Teemu Pukki, Magnus Eriksson (81' Andrew Hjulsager), Johan Elmander (62' Ronnie Schwartz), Elbasan Rashani.
Coach: Thomas Frank.
Omonia Nikosia: Kostas Panayi, Ucha Lobjanidze, Ivan Runje, Luciano Bebe (89' Onisiforos Roushias), Nuno Assis, Giorgos Economides, Margaca, Cillian Sheridan, Cristovao, Gaoussou Fofana (75' Gerasimos Fylaktou), André Schembri (61' Andraz Kirm). Coach: Costas Kaiafas.
Referee: Libor Kovarik (CZE)   Attendance: 7,427.

30.07.15   Matmut Atlantique, Bordeaux: Girondins Bordeaux – AEK Larnaca 3-0 (0-0).
Girondins Bordeaux: Cédric Carrasco, Nicolas Pallois, Frédéric Guilbert, Maxime Poundje, Grégory Sertic, Henri Saivet, Clément Chantome, André Biyogo Poko, Wahbi Khazri (65' Nicolas Maurice-Belay), Thomas Touré (84' Robin Maulun), Cheick Diabaté (89' Isaac Thelin). Coach: Willy Sagnol.
AEK Larnaca: Tono, Adam Marciniak, Constantinos Mintikkis, Català, Emil Ninu, Jorge Larena (57' Juanma Ortiz), Joan Tomás, Tete (90' Kanté), Vladimir Boljevic, André Alves (69' Nestoras Mitidis), Monteiro. Coach: Thomas Christiansen.
Goals: 52' André Biyogo Poko 1-0, 74' Cheick Diabaté 2-0 (p), 80' Nic. Maurice-Belay 3-0.
Referee: Pavle Radovanovic (MNE)   Attendance: 30,174.

30.07.15   Stade du Pays, Charleroi: Sporting Charleroi – Zorya Lugansk 0-2 (0-0).
Sporting Charleroi: Nicolas Penneteau, Sebastien Dewaest, Stergos Marinos, Francis N'Ganga, Martos, Damien Marcq, Enes Saglik, Florent Stevance (74' Jessy Gálvez), David Pollet, Dieumerci Ndongala (79' Roman Ferber), Neeskens Kebano. Coach: Felice Mazzu.
Zorya Lugansk: Nikita Shevchenko, Nikita Kamenyuka, Evgeniy Opanasenko, Andriy Pilyavsky, Mikhail Sivakov, Igor Chaykovskiy (81' Dmytro Grechyshkin), Artem Gordienko (63' Zeljko Ljubenovic), Ruslan Malinovskiy, Oleksandr Karavayev (78' Ivan Petryak), Dmytro Khomchenovsky, Pylyp Budkovsky. Coach: Yuriy Vernydub.
Goals: 70', 89' Ruslan Malinovskiy 0-1, 0-2.
Referee: Radu Petrescu (ROM)   Attendance: 9,415.

30.07.15   Stade Sclessin, Liège: Standard Liège – Zeljeznicar Sarajevo 2-1 (2-0).
Standard Liège: Yohann Thuram-Ulien, Martin Milec, Alexander Scholz, Jelle Van Damme, Ricardo Faty, Beni Badibanga (67' Faysel Kasmi), Julien De Sart (54' Alexis De Sart), Eyong Enoh, Addrien Trebel, Anthony Knockaert (85' Mohamed Yattara), Ivan Santini. Coach: Slavoljub Muslin.
Zeljeznicar Sarajevo: Marijan Antolovic, Aleksandar Kosoric, Kerim Memija, Dusan Mladenovic, Jasmin Bogdanovic, Rijad Bajic, Jovan Blagojevic, Ognjen Djelmic, Amir Hadziahmetovic (90+3' Enis Sadikovic), Damir Sadikovic (90+1' Secouba Diatta), Zoran Kokot (78' Dzenis Beganovic). Coach: Milomir Odovic.
Goals: 16' Aleksandar Kosoric 1-0 (og), 28' Anthony Knockaert 2-0, 64' Ognjen Djelmic 2-1.
Referee: Arnold Hunter (NIR)   Attendance: 11,608.

30.07.15   San Mamés, Bilbao: Athletic Bilbao – Inter Baku 2-0 (1-0).
Athletic Bilbao: Iago Herrerín, Etxeita, Balenziaga, Eraso, Beñat, Iturraspe (46' Elustondo), Susaeta (81' Viguera), Gurpegi, De Marcos, Ibai (70' Aketxe), Aduriz. Coach: Valverde.
Inter Baku: Sälahät Agayev, Juanfran (46' Abbas Hüseynov), Lasha Kasradze, Denis, Zurab Khizanishvili, Ilkin Qirtimov (87' Elnur Abdullayev), Nika Kvekveskiri, Nizami Hajiyev, Stjepan Poljak (46' Yuri Fomenko), Fuad Bayramov, Rauf Aliyev. Coach: Zaur Svanadze.
Goals: 12', 48' Eraso 1-0, 2-0.
Referee: Stavros Tritsonis (GRE)   Attendance: 32,823.

30.07.15   Upton Park, London: West Ham United – Astra Giurgiu 2-2 (1-0).
West Ham United: Adrián, Aaron Cresswell, James Collins, Angelo Ogbonna, Cheikhou Kouyaté, Mark Noble, Joey O'Brien (35' Reece Burke), Reece Oxford, Mauro Zárate (76' Matthew Jarvis), Enner Valencia (37' Modibo Maiga), Dimitri Payet. Coach: Slaven Bilic.
Astra Giurgiu: Silviu Lung Jr., Geraldo Alves, Junior Maranhao, Valerica Gaman, Pedro Queirós, Takayuki Seto, Gabriel Enache, Rick (86' Alexandru Dandea), Filipe Teixeira, Constantin Budescu (90+1' Florin Lovin), William Amorim (76' Daniel Florea). Coach: Marius Sumudica.
Goals: 23' Enner Valencia 1-0, 51' Mauro Zárate 2-0, 71' Rick 2-1, 82' Angelo Ogbonna 2-2 (og).
Referee: Adrien Jaccottet (SUI)   Attendance: 33,858.
Sent off: 59' James Collins.

Coach Slaven Bilic sent to the stands (90').

52

30.07.15   Olimpico, Torino: Sampdoria – Vojvodina 0-4 (0-1).
Sampdoria: Emiliano Viviano, Mattia Cassani, Matias Silvestre, Ervin Zukanovic, Fernando, Edgar Barreto, Angelo Polombo (59' Vasco Regini), Nenad Krsticic (59' Pawel Wszolek), Roberto Soriano, Eder, Luis Muriel (73' Federico Bonazzoli). Coach: Walter Zenga.
Vojvodina: Srdan Zakula, Jovica Vasilic, Radovan Pankov, Bojan Nastic, Igor Djuric, Mirko Ivanic (87' Sinisa Babic), Darko Puskaric (71' Aleksandar Palocevic), Danilo Sekulic, Novica Maksimovic, Aleksandar Stanisavljevic (85' Uros Stamenic), Ognjen Ozegovic. Coach: Zlatomir Zagorcic.
Goals: 4' Mirko Ivanic 0-1, 49' Aleksandar Stanisavljevic 0-2, 58', 90+1' Ognjen Ozegovic 0-3, 0-4.
Referee: Andreas Ekberg (SWE)   Attendance: 4,200.

30.07.15   Poljud, Split: Hajduk Split – Strømsgodset IF 2-0 (0-0).
Hajduk Split: Lovren Kalinic, Goran Milovic, Jefferson, Zoran Nizic, Marko Pejic, Fran Tudor, Nikola Vlasic, Mijo Caktas, Ante Roguljic (61' Elvir Maloku), Franck Ohandza (78' Tomislav Kis), Andrija Balic (74' Tino-Sven Susic). Coach: Damir Buric.
Strømsgodset IF: Espen Pettersen, Kim Madsen, Gustav Valsvik, Mounir Hamoud, Martin Ovesntad, (82' Petter Moen), Iver Fossum, Gustav Wikheim, Mohammed Abu, Lars-Christopher Vilsvik, Flamur Kastrati (72' Bassel Jradi), Thomas Olsen (66' Thomas Sorum). Coach: Bjorn Petter Ingebretsen.
Goals: 67' Andrija Balić 1-0, 90+3' Tomislav Kis 2-0.
Referee: Kristo Tohver (EST)   Attendance: 28,000.

30.07.15   Estádio do Restelo, Lisboa: Os Belenenses – IFK Göteborg 2-1 (2-0).
Os Belenenses: Ventura, Amorim, Tonel, Geraldes, Brandão, Rúben Pinto, Miguel Rosa, André Sousa (67' Ricardo Dias), Fábio Sturgeon, Carlos Martins (86' Tiago Silva), Abel Camará (67' Fábio Nunes). Coach: Sá Pinto.
IFK Göteborg: John Alvbage, Emil Salomonsson, Haitam Aleesami, Sebastian Eriksson, Thomas Rogne, Mattias Bjärsmyr, Soren Rieks, Martin Smedberg (46' Jakob Ankersen), Gustav Svensson, Mikael Boman (71' Tom Pettersson), Gustav Engvall (81' Viktor Sköld). Coach: Jörgen Lennartsson.
Goals: 23', 41' Carlos Martins 1-0, 2-0, 58' Haitam Aleesami 2-1.
Referee: Vlado Glodovic (SER)   Attendance: 5,671.

30.07.15   Wörthersee Stadion, Klagenfurt: Wolfsberger AC – Borussia Dormund 0-1 (0-1).
Wolfsberger AC: Alexander Kofler, Stephan Palla, Michael Berger, Joachim Standfest (90' Peter Tschernegg), Michael Sollbauer, Boris Hüttenbrenner, Roland Putsche (70' Tadej Trdina), Manuel Seidl, Christopher Wernitzig (81' Jacobo), Thomas Zündel, Silvio. Coach: Dietmar Kühbauer.
Borussia Dortmund: Roman Bürki, Mats Hummels, Sokratis Papastathopoulos, Lukasz Piszczek, Marcel Schmelzer, Jonas Hofmann (66' Shinji Kagawa), Ilkay Gündogan, Henrikh Mkhitaryan, Marco Reus (79' Kevin Kampl), Julian Weigl (66' Gonzalo Castro), Pierre-Emerick Aubameyang. Coach: Thomas Tuchel.
Goal: 16' Jonas Hofmann 0-1.
Referee: Davide Massa (ITA)   Attendance: 30,250.

53

30.07.15   Saint Mary's, Southampton: Southampton FC – Vitesse 3-0 (2-0).
Southampton FC: Maarten Stekelenburg, Cédric Soares, Maya Yoshida, José Fonte, Matt
Targett, Jordy Clasie (62' Juanmi), Steven Davis, Victor Wanyama, Sadio Mané (85' Harrison
Reed), Dusan Tadic (62' Shane Long), Graziano Pellè. Coach: Ronald Koeman.
Vitesse: Eloy Room, Kelvin Leerdam, Kevin Diks (90+2' Julian Lelieveld), Rochdi Achenteh,
Guram Kashia, Valeri Qazaishvili (67' Danilo Pantic), Marvelous Nakamba, Lewis Baker,
Isaiah Brown, Uros Durdevic (61' Milot Rashica), Denys Oliynyk. Coach: Peter Bosz.
Goals: 36' Graziano Pellè 1-0, 45+1' Dusan Tadic 2-0, 84' Shane Long 3-0.
Referee: Jesús Gil Manzano (ESP)   Attendance: 30,850.

06.08.15   GelreDome, Arnhem: Vitesse – Southampton FC 0-2 (0-1).
Vitesse: Eloy Room, Maikel van der Werff (72' Rochdi Achenteh), Kelvin Leerdam, Kevin
Diks, Guram Kashia, Valeri Qazaishvili, Marvelous Nakamba, Lewis Baker (81' Danilo
Pantic), Isaiah Brown (69' Nathan), Denys Oliynyk, Milot Rashica. Coach: Peter Bosz.
Southampton FC: Maarten Stekelenburg, Maya Yoshida, José Fonte, Cuco Martina, Steven
Caulker, Steven Davis (78' Harrison Reed), Victor Wanyama, James Ward-Prowse, Sadio
Mané, Dusan Tadic (65' Juanmi), Graziano Pellè (72' Jay Rodriguez). Coach: Ronald Koeman.
Goals: 4' Graziano Pellè 0-1, 89' Sadio Mané 0-2.
Referee: Ilias Spathas (GRE)   Attendance: 20,550.

06.08.15   Signal Iduna Park, Dortmund: Borussia Dortmund – Wolfsberger AC 5-0 (0-0).
Borussia Dortmund: Roman Weidenfeller, Mats Hummels, Sokratis Papastathopoulos, Lukasz
Piszczek, Marcel Schmelzer, Ilkay Gündogan (77' Sven Bender), Henrikh Mkhitaryan, Marco
Reus (77' Jonas Hofmann), Shinji Kagawa (65' Gonzalo Castro), Julian Weigl, Pierre-Emerick
Aubameyang. Coach: Thomas Tuchel.
Wolfsberger AC: Alexander Kofler, Stephan Palla, Michael Berger, Joachim Standfest (86'
Peter Tschernegg), Michael Sollbauer, Manuel Weber, Jacobo, Boris Hüttenbrenner, Roland
Putsche (67' Tadej Trdina), Christopher Wernitzig (75' Peter Zulj), Silvio.
Coach: Dietmar Kühbauer.
Goals: 48' Marco Reus 1-0, 64' Pierre-Emerick Aubameyang 2-0,
73', 82', 86' Henrikh Mkhitaryan 3-0, 4-0, 5-0.
Referee: Marius Avram (ROM)   Attendance: 65,190.

06.08.15   Gamla Ullevi, Göteborg: IFK Göteborg – Os Belenenses 0-0.
IFK Göteborg: John Alvbage, Emil Salomonsson, Haitam Aleesami, Sebastian Eriksson (75'
Martin Smedberg), Thomas Rogne, Mattias Bjärsmyr, Soren Rieks, Jakob Ankersen, Gustav
Svensson, Mikael Boman (75' Tom Pettersson), Gustav Engvall. Coach: Jörgen Lennartsson.
Os Belenenses: Ventura, Amorim, Tonel, Geraldes, Brandão, Rúben Pinto, Miguel Rosa (68'
Dálcio), André Sousa, Fábio Sturgeon, Carlos Martins (78' Tiago Silva), Abel Camará (89'
João Afonso). Coach: Sá Pinto.
Referee: Jonathan Lardot (BEL)   Attendance: 12,976.

06.08.15   Marienlyst, Drammen: Strømsgodset IF – Hajduk Split 0-2 (0-0).
Strømsgodset IF: Espen Pettersen, Florent Hanin (30' Mounir Hamoud), Marius Hoibraten, Gustav Valsvik, Bassel Jradi (60' Oyvind Storflor), Iver Fossum, Gustav Wikheim, Mohammed Abu, Lars-Christopher Vilsvik, Flamur Kastrati (72' Thomas Sorum), Thomas Olsen. Coach: Bjorn Petter Ingebretsen.
Hajduk Split: Lovren Kalinic, Goran Milovic, Jefferson, Zoran Nizic, Marko Pejic, Fran Tudor, Nikola Vlasic, Mijo Caktas (83' Tino-Sven Susic), Elvir Maloku, Franck Ohandza (80' Anton Maglica), Andrija Balic (70' Josip Juranovic). Coach: Damir Buric.
Goals: 55' Mijo Caktas 0-1, 77' Franck Ohandza 0-2.
Referee: Oliver Drachta (AUT)   Attendance: 5,336.
Sent off: 53' Zoran Nizić.

06.08.15   Karadorde, Novi Sad: Vojvodina – Sampdoria 0-2 (0-1).
Vojvodina: Srdan Zakula, Jovica Vasilic, Radovan Pankov, Bojan Nastic, Igor Djuric, Mirko Ivanic (90+3' Sinisa Babic), Darko Puskaric (78' Aleksandar Palocevic), Danilo Sekulic, Novica Maksimovic, Aleksandar Stanisavljevic (87' Ivan Lakicevic), Ognjen Ozegovic. Coach: Zlatomir Zagorcic.
Sampdoria: Emiliano Viviano, Mattia Cassani, Andrea Coda, Matias Silvestre, Ervin Zukanovic, Fernando, Edgar Barreto, Nenad Krsticic (79' Dávid Ivan), Roberto Soriano (85' Pawel Wszolek), Eder, Luis Muriel (75' Federico Bonazzoli). Coach: Walter Zenga.
Goals: 15' Eder 0-1, 70' Luis Muriel 0-2.
Referee: Pawel Raczkowski (POL)   Attendance: 10,763.

06.08.15   Stadionul Marin Anastasovici, Giurgiu:
Astra Giurgiu – West Ham United 2-1 (2-1).
Astra Giurgiu: Silviu Lung Jr., Geraldo Alves (19' Cristian Oros), Junior Maranhao, Valerica Gaman, Pedro Queirós, Takayuki Seto, Gabriel Enache, Rick, Filipe Teixeira (67' Denis Alibec), Constantin Budescu (83' Florin Lovin), William Amorim. Coach: Marius Sumudica.
West Ham United: Darren Randolph, Carl Jenkinson, Doneil Henry, Lewis Page (90+2' Alex Pike), Kyle Knoyle, Kevin Nolan, Diego Poyet, Manuel Lanzini, Josh Cullen, Modibo Maiga, Elliot Lee (80' Jordan Brown). Coach: Slaven Bilic.
Goals: 4' Manuel Lanzini 0-1, 32', 36' Constantin Budescu 1-1, 2-1.
Referee: Paolo Valeri (ITA)   Attendance: 6,913.

06.08.15   Shafa, Baku: Inter Baku – Athletic Bilbao 0-0.
Inter Baku: Sälahät Agayev, Lasha Kasradze, Denis, Zurab Khizanishvili, Ilkin Qirtimov, Nika Kvekveskiri, Nizami Hajiyev (76' Elnur Abdullayev), Mirhuseyn Seyidov, Fuad Bayramov, Rauf Aliyev, Dhiego (78' Yuri Fomenko). Coach: Zaur Svanadze.
Athletic Bilbao: Iago Herrerín, Aymeric Laporte, San José, Etxeita, Balenziaga, Eraso (68' Sabin), Beñat (90' Elustondo), Susaeta (85' Ibai), Aketxe, De Marcos, Aduriz. Coach: Valverde.
Referee: Serdar Gözübüyük (HOL)   Attendance: 3,875.

06.08.15   Asim Ferhatović Hase, Sarajevo: Zeljeznicar Sarajevo – Standard Liège 0-1 (0-0).
Zeljeznicar Sarajevo: Marijan Antolovic, Aleksandar Kosoric, Kerim Memija, Dusan
Mladenovic, Jasmin Bogdanovic, Rijad Bajic, Jovan Blagojevic, Ognjen Djelmic, Amir
Hadziahmetovic (60' Enis Sadikovic), Damir Sadikovic (66' Dzenis Beganovic), Zoran Kokot
(76' Joco Stokic). Coach: Milomir Odovic.
Standard Liège: Yohann Thuram-Ulien, Ahmed El Messaoudi (59' Julien De Sart), Jorge
Teixeira, Martin Milec, Jelle Van Damme, Ricardo Faty, Beni Badibanga (79' Darwin
Andrade), Eyong Enoh, Adrien Trebel, Anthony Knockaert, Ivan Santini (70' Mohamed
Yattara). Coach: Slavoljub Muslin.
Goal: 68' Jelle Van Damme 0-1.
Referee: Georgi Kabakov (BUL)   Attendance: 19,721.

06.08.15   Valeriya Lobanovskovo, Kiev: Zorya Lugansk – Sporting Charleroi 3-0 (0-0).
Zorya Lugansk: Nikita Shevchenko, Nikita Kamenyuka, Evgeniy Opanasenko, Andriy
Pilyavsky, Mikhail Sivakov, Igor Chaykovskiy (46' Zeljko Ljubenovic), Artem Gordienko,
Ruslan Malinovskiy, Oleksandr Karavayev (59' Dmytro Grechushkin), Dmytro
Khomchenovsky, Pylyp Budkovsky (70' Ivan Petryak). Coach: Yuriy Vernydub.
Sporting Charleroi: Nicolas Penneteau, Steeven Willems, Benjamin Boulenger (57' Francis
N'Ganga), Sebastien Dewaest, Stergos Marinos, Karel Geraerts (63' Florent Stevance),
Damien Marcq, Enes Saglik, David Pollet, Roman Ferber (42' Dieumerci Ndongala), Neeskens
Kebano. Coach: Felice Mazzu.
Goals: 58', 68' Zeljko Ljubenovic 1-0, 2-0 (p), 90+3' Ruslan Malinovskiy 3-0.
Referee: Andris Treimanis (LAT)   Attendance: 3,966.

06.08.15   Antonis Papadopoulos, Larnaca: AEK Larnaca – Girondns Bordeaux 0-1 (0-1).
AEK Larnaca: Tono, Català, Emil Ninu (46' Jorge Larena), Elias Charalambous (74' André
Alves), Juanma Ortiz, Joan Tomás, Tete, Vladimir Boljević, Vincent Laban, Nestoras Mitidis,
Monteiro (64' Kanté). Coach: Thomas Christiansen.
Girondins Bordeaux: Cédric Carrasco, Milan Gajic, Diego Contento, Nicolas Pallois, Cédric
Yamberé, Abdou Traoré (79' André Biyogo Poko), Clément Chantome, Wahbi Khazri (54'
Thomas Touré), Robin Maulun (64' Grégory Sertic), Isaac Thelin, Nicolas Maurice-Belay.
Coach: Willy Sagnol.
Goal: 29' Isaac Thelin 0-1.
Referee: Tobias Stieler (GER)   Attendance: 2,517.
Sent off: 45' Clément Chantome, 82' Juanma Ortiz.

06.08.15   Neo GSP, Nikosia: Omonia Nikosia – Brøndby IF 2-2 (2-2).
Omonia Nikosia: Kostas Panayi, Ucha Lobjanidze, Ivan Runje, Luciano Bebe, Nuno Assis,
Giorgos Economides (86' Gerasimos Fylaktou), Margaca, Marios Demetriou (90+5' Jackson
Mendy), Cillian Sheridan, Gaoussou Fofana (69' Onisiforos Roushias), André Schembri.
Coach: Costas Kaiafas.
Brøndby IF: Lukás Hrádecky, Martin Albrechtsen, Frederik Holst, Johan Larsson, Riza
Durmisi, Dcario Dumic, Patrick da Silva (89' Malthe Johansen), Martin Ornskov, Teemu
Pukki (90+6' Elbasan Rashani), Magnus Eriksson, Johan Elmander (56' Lebogang Phiri).
Coach: Thomas Frank.
Goals: 2' Teemu Pukki 0-1, 16' Cillian Sheridan 1-1 (p), 39' Teemu Pukki 1-2,
45+3' Cillian Sheridan 2-2 (p).
Referee: Harald Lechner (AUT)   Attendance: 17,943.
Sent off: 90+8' Lukás Hrádecky, 90+13' Nuno Assis.

Brøndby IF won on away goals.

06.08.15 Lerkendal, Trondheim: Rosenborg BK – Debreceni VSC 3-1 (2-1).
Rosenborg BK: André Hansen, Hólmar Eyjólfsson, Johan Bjørdal, Jørgen Skjelvik, Mike
Jensen (90' Sivert Solli), Tobias Mikkelsen, Ole Selnæs, Fredrik Midtsjø (82' John Hou
Sæter), Jonas Svensson, Pål Helland, Alexander Søderlund (77' Matthias Vilhjálmsson).
Coach: Kåre Ingebrigtsen.
Debreceni VSC: István Verpecz, Norbert Méezáros, Péter Máté, Mihály Korkut, Adám Bódi,
József Varga, Aleksandar Jovanovic, Norbert Balogh (62' László Zsidai), Ibrahima Sidibe (77'
Rene Mihelic), Tibor Tisza (52' Igor Morozov), Geoffrey Castillion. Coach: Elemér Kondás.
Goals: 27' Alexander Søderlund 1-0, 40' Mike Jensen 2-0, 43' Geoffrey Castillion 2-1,
86' Matthias Vilhjálmsson 3-1.
Referee: Clayton Pisani (MLT)   Attendance: 12,919.
Sent off: 48' Péter Máté.

06.08.15 Hüseyin Avni Aker, Trabzon: Trabzonspor – FK Rabotnicki 1-1 (1-0, 1-1).
Trabzonspor: Onur Kivrak, Carl Medjani, Kévin Constant, Mustafa Yumlu, Luis Cavanda,
Okay Yokuslu (86' Aytac Kara), Ozer Hurmaci (76' Deniz Yilmaz), Stéphane Mbia, Yusuf
Erdogan (105' Sefa Yilmaz), Oscar Cardozo, Erkan Zengin. Coach: Shota Arveladze.
FK Rabotnicki: Daniel Bozinovski, Goran Siljanovski, Kire Ristevski, Milan Ilievski, Stephan
Vujcic, Milovan Petrovikj, Dusko Trajcevski, Mite Cikarski, Suad Sahiti (60' Marijan
Altiparmakovski), Chuma Anene (89' Kire Markoski), Baze Ilijoski (73' Ivan Mitrov).
Coach: Igor Angelovski.
Goals: 55' Okay Yokuslu 1-0, 112' Kire Markoski 1-1.
Referee: Steven McLean (SCO)   Attendance: 13,704.
Sent off: 65' Dusko Trajcevski.

FK Rabotnicki won after extra time.

06.08.15 Geoffroy Guichard, St. Étienne: AS Saint-Étienne – ASA Targu Mures 1-2 (0-1).
AS Saint-Étienne: Stéphane Ruffier, Florentin Pogba, Jonathan Brison, Moustapha Sall,
Francois Clerc (78' Kévin Théophile-Catherine), Jérémy Clément, Yohan Mollo, Loic Perrin,
Ismaël Diomandé (67' Fabien Lemoine), Nolan Roux, Kévin Monnet-Paquet (56' Romain
Hamouma). Coach: Christophe Galtier.
ASA Targu Mures: Eduard Stancioiu, Rubén Jurado (46' Pablo Brandán), Velayos, Sasa Balic,
Iván González, Pawel Golanski, Gabriel Muresan, Nicolás Gorobsov, Sergiu Hanca (60' Filip
Jazvic), Mircea Axente, Luis Pedro (71' Ramiro Costa). Coach: Vasile Miriuta.
Goals: 39' Luis Pedro 0-1, 62' Iván González 0-2, 72' Iván González 1-2 (og).
Referee: Craig Pawson (ENG)   Attendance: 27,284.

06.08.15 Rheinpark, Vaduz: FC Vaduz – FC Thun 2-2 (2-1).
FC Vaduz: Oliver Klaus, Simone Grippo, Pavel Pergl, Mario Bühler, Naser Alji, Diego
Ciccone, Ali Messaoud (77' Ramon Cecchini), Moreno Costanzo, Markus Neumayr, Stjepan
Kukuruzovic, Robin Kamber (69' Nicolas Hasler). Coach: Giorgio Contini.
FC Thun: Guillaume Faivre, Marco Bürki, Fulvio Sulmoni, Thomas Reinmann, Enrico
Schirinzi (58' Simone Rapp), Sandro Wieser, Gianluca Frontino (80' Nicola Sutter), Marco
Rojas (90+1' Nicolas Schindelholz), Dennis Hediger, Andreas Wittwer, Roman Buess.
Coach: Ciriaco Sforza.
Goals: 32' Moreno Costanzo 1-0, 38' Marcos Rojas 1-1, 45+1' Markus Neumayr 2-1,
65' Roman Buess 2-2.
Referee: István Kovács (ROM)   Attendance: 2,788.

FC Thun won on away goals.

06.08.15   Fatih Terim Stadium, Istanbul: Medipol Basaksehir F.K – AZ Alkmaar 1-2 (1-1).
Medipol Basakseehir F.K: Ufuk Ceylan, Yalcin Ayhan, Mahmut Tekdemir, Ugur Ucar (46'
Cenk Alkilic), Gencer Cansev, Ferhat Oztorun, Edin Visca, Márcio Mossoró (74' Mehmet
Batdal), Doka Madureira, Stéphane Badji, Emre Belözoglu (64' Mahmut Tekdemir), Sokol
Cikalleshi. Coach: Abdullah Avci.
AZ Alkmaar: Sergio Rochet, Mattias Johansson, Jeffrey Gouweleeuw, Jop van der Linden,
Ridgeciano Haps, Celso Ortiz, Joris van Overeem (86' Guus Hupperts), Markus Henriksen,
Dabney dos Santos (78' Achille Vaarnold), Thom Haye, Vincent Janssen (68' Robert Mühren).
Coach: John van den Brom.
Goals: 21' Markus Henriksen 0-1, 45' Doka Madureira 1-1, 75' Joris van Overeem 1-2.
Referee: Carlos Clos Gómez (ESP)   Attendance: 3,500.

06.08.15   Vorskla, Poltava: Vorskla Poltava – MSK Zilina 3-1 (0-0, 2-0).
Vorkla Poltava: Dmytro Nepogodov, Sergiy Siminin (46' Igor Perduta), Armend Dallku,
Evgen Tkachuk, Aleksandr Sklyar (87' Oleg Mishchenko), Vadim Sapay, Mladen Bartulovic
(60' Oleg Barannik), Sanzhar Tursunov, Anton Shynder, Oleksandr Kovpak.
Coach: Vasil Sachko.
MSK Zilina: Milos Volesák, Milan Skriniar, Denis Vavro, Miroslav Kácer, Jakub Paur,
Nikolas Spalek, Viktor Pecovsky, Bojan Letic (118' Tomás Hucko), László Bénes (73' Michal
Skvarka), Jaroslav Mihalík (78' William), Matej Jelic. Coach: Adrián Gula.
Goals: 67' Anton Shynder 1-0, 90+1' Evgen Tkachuk 2-0, 101' Sanzhar Tursunov 3-0 (p),
120+1' William 3-1.
Referee: Aliyar Agayev (AZE)   Attendance: 12,509.
Sent off: 99' Nikolas Spalek.

MSK Zilina won on away goals after extra time.

06.08.15   Dinamo, Brest: Dinamo Minsk – FC Zürich 1-1 (0-1, 1-1).
Dinamo Minsk: Aleksandr Gutor, Sergey Politevich, Oleg Veretilo, Roman Begunov,
Uladzimir Karytska (102' Igor Voronkov), Umaru Bangura, Nikita Korzun, Jan Tigorev (36'
Sergiu Neacsa), Nenad Adamovic (81' Mohamed El-Mounir), Gleb Rassadkin, Fatos Beciraj.
Coach: Vuk Rasovic.
FC Zürich: Yanick Brecher, Berat Djimsiti, Alain Nef, Philippe Koch, Cabral, Christian
Schneuwly (102' Artem Simonyan), Oliver Buff (73' Armando Sadiku), Burim Kukeli, Anto
Grgic, Mario Gavranovic (110' Sangoné Sarr), Amine Chermiti. Coach: Urs Meier.
Goals: 4' Amine Chermiti 0-1, 118' Fatos Beciraj 1-1.
Referee: Marcin Borski (POL)   Attendance: 9,437.

Dinamo Minsk won after extra time.

06.08.15   Pasienky, Bratislava: Slovan Bratislava – FK Krasnodar 3-3 (0-2).
Slovan Bratislava: Ján Mucha, Boris Sekulic, Dávid Hudák, Nicolas Gorosito, Kornel Saláta,
Frantisek Kubik (74' Filip Orsula), Mauro Ezequiel González (81' Samuel Stefanik), Marko
Milinkovic, Lester Peltier (46' Karol Mészáros), Jakub Podany, Róbert Vittek.
Coach: Dusan Tittel.
FK Krasnodar: Andrey Dikan, Artur Jedrejczyk, Andreas Granqvist, Ragnar Sigurdsson, Pavel
Mamaev (46' Dmitriy Torbinskiy), Yuri Gazinskiy (64' Stefan Strandberg), Odil Akhmedov,
Ricardo Laborde (78' Wanderson), Sergey Petrov, Ari, Fedor Smolov. Coach: Oleg Kononov.
Goals: 8', 11' Pavel Mamaev 0-1 (p), 0-2, 54', 59', 77' Róbert Vittek 1-2, 2-2, 3-2,
90+3' Fedor Smolov 3-3 (p).
Referee: Sebastien Delferiere (BEL)   Attendance: 2,852.

58

06.08.15   D.Afonso Henriques, Guimaraes: Vitória Guimaraes – SCR Altach 1-4 (0-1).
Vitória Guimaraes: Douglas Jesus, Luis Rocha (59' Tó Mané), Joao Afonso, Pedro Correia,
Moreno, Bruno Alves (46' Otávio), Tózé, Licá (69' Ricardo Valente), Alex, Cafú, Henrique.
Coach: Armando Evangelista.
SCR Altach: Andreas Lukse, Andreas Lienhart, Jan Zwischenbrugger, César Ortiz, Lukas
Jäger, Benedikt Zech, Philipp Netzer (62' Felix Roth), Daniel Luxbacher (86' Dominik
Hofbauer), Boris Prokopic, Patrick Seeger (67' Hannes Aigner), Louis N'Gwat-Mahop.
Coach: Damir Canadi.
Goals: 31' Philipp Netzer 0-1, 60' Pedro Correia 0-2 (og), 63' Boris Prokopic 0-3,
66' Tó Mané 1-3, 90+3' Andreas Lienhart 1-4.
Referee: Antony Gautier (FRA)   Attendance: 20,181.
Sent off: 73' Pedro Correia.

06.08.15   Tsentralniy, Kazan: Rubin Kazan – Sturm Graz 1-1 (0-0).
Rubin Kazan: Sergey Ryzhikov, Oleg Kuzmin, Elmir Nabiullin (79' Maksim Batov), Mauricio
Lemos, Solomon Kverkvelia, Ruslan Kambolov, Magomed Ozdoev, Gökdeniz Karadeniz (88'
Guillermo Cotugno), Blagoy Georgiev, Igor Portnyagin, Vladimir Dyadyun (60' Maksim
Kanunnikov). Coach: Rinat Bilyaletdinov.
Sturm Graz: Michael Esser, Charalampos Lykogiannis (45' Martin Ehrenreich), Michael Madl,
Marvin Potzmann, Lukas Spendlhofer, Wilson Kamavuaka, Daniel Offenbacher, Marc Andre
Schmerböck (46' Bright Edomwonyi), Kristijan Dobras (81' Roman Kienast), Thorsten
Schick, Josip Tadic. Coach: Franco Foda.
Goals: 68' Josip Tadic 0-1, 85' Oleg Kuzmin 1-1.
Referee: Liran Liany (ISR)   Attendance: 9,346.

06.08.15   Peristeri, Athen: Atromitos – AIK Solna 1-0 (0-0).
Atromitos: Andrey Gorbunov, Sokratis Fitanidis, Mariano Bíttolo, Nikolaos Lazaridis, Usero,
Stefano Napoleoni (85' Anthony Le Tallec), Javier Umbides (90' Dimitris Limnios),
Marcelinho, Fernando Godoy, Kyriakos Kivrakidis, Sebastián García (75' Eduardo Brito).
Coach: Michalis Grigoriou.
AIK Solna: Patrik Carlgren, Nisl-Eric Johansson, Haukur Hauksson, Alex (11' Johan
Blomberg), Fredrik Brustad (79' Marko Nikolic), Kenny Pavey, Dickson Etuhu, Stefan
Ishizaki, Niclas Eliasson (46' Mohamed Bangura), Anton Jönsson Salétros, Henok Goitom.
Coach: Andreas Alm.
Goal: 67' Marcelinho 1-0.
Referee: Artyom Kuchin (KAZ)   Attendance: 2,587.

06.08.15   Bakcell Arena, Baku: Gabala FK – Apollon Limassol 1-0 (0-0).
Gabala FK: Dmitro Bezotosniy, Vojislav Stankovic, Urfan Abbasov, Rafael Santos, Räsad
Sadiqov, Oleksiy Gay, Arif Dashdemirov, Sergei Zenjov, Dodô, Javid Hüseynov, Oleksiy
Antonov (71' Ermin Zec). Coach: Roman Grygorchuk.
Apollon Limassol: Bruno Vale, Elizio, Nuno Lopes (61' Thuram), Freire, Esteban Sacchetti,
Marcos Gúllon, Alexandre, Jaime (81' Farley), Joao Pedro, Fotis Papoulis, Giorgos
Kolokoudias (61' Abraham Guié-Guié). Coach: Pedro Emanuel.
Goal: 80' Javid Hüseynov 1-0 (p).
Referee: Duarte Gomes (POR)   Attendance: 9,537.
Sent off: 90+1' Urfan Abbasov.

06.08.15   Netanya Stadium, Netanya: Ironi Kiryat Shmona – Slovan Liberec 0-3 (0-2).
Ironi Kiryat Shmona: Guy Haimov, Daniel Borchal, Cássio, Luis Gutiérrez, Oded Elkayam, Or
Ostvind (54' Ofir Mizrachi), Adrian Rochet (78' Roei Shukrani), Ahmad Abed, Ugwu
Chukwuma, Vladimir Broun (61' Eden Shamir), Bruno. Coach: Salah Hasarma.
Slovan Liberec: Tomás Koubek, Vladimír Coufal, Lukás Pokorny, David Pavelka, Zdenek
Folprecht, David Hovorka, Lukás Bartosák, Herolind Shala (82' Milan Kerbr), Josef Sural,
Marek Bakos (80' Michael Rabusic), Dzon Delarge (76' Isaac Sackey).
Coach: Jindrich Trpisovsky.
Goals: 33' David Pavelka 0-1, 44' Josef Sural 0-2, 52' Marek Bakos 0-3.
Referee: Gediminas Mazeika (LTU)   Attendance: 1,218.

06.08.15   Stadión FC ViOn Zlaté Moravce, Zlate Moravce:
           Spartak Trnava – PAOK Saloniki 1-1 (1-0).
Spartak Trnava: Lubos Kamenár, Marek Janecka, Milan Bortel, Milos Nikolic, Martin Tóth,
Lukás Gressák, Martin Mikovic, Erik Sabo, Emir Halilovic (79' Aldo Baéz), Jakub Vojtus (62'
Haris Harba), José Casado (79' Tomás Mikinic). Coach: Juraj Jarábek.
PAOK Saloniki: Robin Olsen, Giannis Skondras, Ricardo Costa, Dimitrios Konstantinidis,
Giorgos Tzavellas, Nikos Korovesis, Alexandros Tziolis, Ergis Kaçe (81' Kyriakos Savvidis),
Dimitrios Pelkas, Róbert Mak, Ioannis Mystakidis (57' Efthimios Koulouris / 69' Achilleas
Poungouras). Coach: Igor Tudor.
Goals: 35' Erik Sabo 1-0 (p), 48' Dimitrios Konstantinidis 1-1.
Referee: Tobias Welz (GER)   Attendance: 3,555.
Sent off: 67' Giannis Skondras.

06.08.15   Skagerak Arena, Skien: Odds BK – IF Elfsborg 2-0 (1-0).
Odds BK: Sondre Rossbach, Espen Ruud, Thomas Grøgaard, Steffen Hagen, Lars-Kristian
Eriksen, Jone Samuelsen (82' Ardian Gashi), Fredrik Nordkvelle (84' Oliver Berg), Fredrik
Jensen, Pape Diouf (46' Ole Halvorsen), Olivier Océan, Bentley. Coach: Dag-Eilev Fagermo.
IF Elfsborg: Kevin Stuhr-Ellegaard, Sebastian Holmén, Adam Lundqvist, Marcus Rohdén,
Anders Svensson, Arber Zeneli, Andreas Klarström (46' Anton Lans), Victor Claesson,
Henning Hauger, Simon Hedlund (78' Lasse Nilsson), Viktor Prodell (78' Per Frick).
Coach: Magnus Haglund.
Goals: 27' Olivier Océan 1-0, 71' Bentley 2-0.
Referee: Sergey Ivanov (RUS)   Attendance: 6,106.

06.08.15   Pittodrie Stadium, Aberdeen: Aberdeen FC – Kairat Almaty 1-1 (0-0).
Aberdeen FC: Danny Ward, Shaleum Logan, Graeme Shinnie, Andrew Considine, Ash Taylor,
Kenny McLean, Niall McGinn, Jonathan Hayes (81' Paul Quinn), Peter Pawlett (68' Adam
Rooney), Ryan Jack, David Goodwillie (81' Willo Flood). Coach: Derek McInnes.
Kairat Almaty: Vladimir Plotnikov, Bruno Soares, Mark Gorman, Zarko Markovic, Ermek
Kuantaev, Mikhail Bakaev, Bauyrzhan Islamkhan, Isael (82' Serginho), Anatoliy Tymoshchuk,
Gerard Gohou (74' Djordje Despotovic), Stanislav Lunin (90+3' Islambek Kuat).
Coach: Vladimir Weiss.
Goals: 59' Gerard Gohou 0-1, 84' Kenny McLean 1-1.
Referee: Miroslav Zelinka (CZE)   Attendance: 20,317.

06.08.15   Wojska Polskiego, Warszawa: Legia Warszawa – FK Kukësi 1-0 (0-0).
Legia Warszawa: Dusan Kuciak, Michal Pazdan (61' Rafal Makowski), Igor Lewczuk, Tomasz
Brzyski, Bartosz Bereszynski, Jakub Rzezniczak, Ondrej Duda, Michal Zyro (45' Guilherme),
Dominik Furman, Michal Kucharczyk (68' Robert Bartczak), Aleksandar Prijovic.
Coach: Henning Berg.
FK Kukësi: Ervis Koci, Gentian Muça, Rrahman Hallaçi, Renato Maloca, Gledi Mici, Erick
Flores, Edon Hasani (50' Ndriqim Halili), Birungueta, Felipe Moreira (90+2' Edison Qafa),
Besar Musolli, Jean Carioca (83' Ylli Shameti). Coach: Marcello Troisi.
Goal: 47' Michal Kucharczyk 1-0.
Referee: Tony Chapron (FRA)   Attendance: 11,847.

06.08.15   Telia Parken, Kobenhavn: FC København – FK Jablonec 2-3 (0-1).
FC Kobenhagen: Stephan Andersen, Ludwig Augustinsson, Mikael Antonsson, Daniel
Amartey, Peter Ankersen (86' Per Nilsson), Mathias Jorgensen, William Kvist (61' Kasper
Kusk), Thomas Delaney, Benjamin Verbic, Nicolai Jorgensen, Federico Santander.
Coach: Ståle Solbakken.
FK Jablonec: Vlastimil Hruby, Tomás Hübschman, Ludek Perncia, Vyacheslav Karavaev, Vit
Benes, Filip Novák, Nermin Crnkic (88' Rossi), Ján Gregus, Martin Pospisil, Lukás Masopust
(72' Ruslan Mingazov), Tomás Wágner (82' Martin Dolezal). Coach: Jaroslav Silhavy.
Goals: 14' Tomás Wágner 0-1, 53' Ján Gregus 0-2, 72' Nicolai Jorgensen 1-2,
83' Martin Pospisil 1-3, 88' Federico Santander 2-3.
Referee: Leontios Trattou (CYP)   Attendance: 14,142.

FK Jablonec won on away goals.

PLAY-OFFS

20.08.15   Bakcell Arena, Baku: Gabala FK – Panathinaikos 0-0
Gabala FK: Dmitro Bezotosniy, Vojislav Stankovic, Ricardinho, Rafael Santos, Räsad
Sadiqov, Oleksiy Gay, Arif Dashdemirov, Ermin Zec (58' Samir Zargarov), Sergei Zenjov,
Dodô, Oleksiy Antonov (90' Asif Mammadov). Coach: Roman Grygorchuk.
Panathinaikos: Luke Steele, Georgios Koutroubis, Jens Wemmer, Efstathios Tavlaridis, Zeca,
Robin Lod (67' Abdul Ajagun), Nano, Danijel Pranjic, Nikolaos Karelis (58' Marcus Berg),
Nikolaos Kaltsas (76' Tasos Lagos), Mladen Petric. Coach: Yannis Anastasiou.
Referee: Andre Marriner (ENG)   Attendance: 10,950.

20.08.15   Stadionul Marin Anastasovici, Giurgiu: Astra Giurgiu – AZ Alkmaar 3-2 (3-2).
Astra Giurgiu: Silviu Lung Jr., Junior Maranhao, Cristian Oros, Valerica Gaman, Pedro
Queirós, Gabriel Enache, Florin Lovin, Rick (35' Alexandru Dandea), Denis Alibec (67'
Daniel Florea), Constantin Budescu, William Amorim (83' Alexandru Stan).
Coach: Marius Sumudica.
AZ Alkmaar: Sergio Rochet, Mattias Johansson, Jeffrey Gouweleeuw, Jop van der Linden,
Derrick Luckassen, Ridgeciano Haps, Celso Ortiz (65' Thom Haye), Joris van Overeem,
Markus Henriksen, Guus Hupperts (46' Fernando Lewis), Vincent Janssen (78' Robert
Mühren). Coach: John van den Brom.
Goals: 11' Markus Henriksen 0-1, 13' Vincent Janssen 1-1, 25' Rick 1-2,
40' Denis Alibec 2-2, 45' Alexandru Dandea 3-2.
Referee: Slavko Vincić (SVN)   Attendance: 3,712.

20.08.15   Dinamo, Brest: Dinamo Minsk – Red Bull Salzburg 2-0 (0-0).
Dinamo Minsk: Aleksandr Gutor, Maksim Vitus, Sergey Politevich, Umaru Bangura, Roman Begunov, Sergiu Neacsa (70' Mohamed El-Mounir), Uladzimir Karytska, Shaloze Chigozie (53' Nenad Adamovic), Nikita Korzun, Gleb Rassadkin (90+1' Igor Voronkov), Fatos Beciraj. Coach: Vuk Rasovic.
Red Bull Salzburg: Alexander Walke, Paulo Miranda, Duje Caleta-Car, Christian Schwegler, Andreas Ulmer, Naby Keita, Valon Berisha, Christoph Leitgeb, Yordy Reyna, Takumi Minamino (74' Valentino Lazaro), Dimitri Oberlin (59' David Atanga). Coach: Peter Zeidler.
Goals: 57' Gleb Rassadkin 1-0, 90+3' Nenad Adamovic 2-0.
Referee: Miroslav Zelinka (CZE)   Attendance: 9,952.

20.08.15   Amsterdam ArenA, Amsterdam: AFC Ajax – FK Jablonec 1-0 (0-0).
AFC Ajax: Jasper Cillessen, Joël Veltman, Jaïro Riedewald, Kenny Tete, Mitchell Dijks, Riechedly Bazoer, Daley Sinkgraven (72' Lasse Schöne), Davy Klaassen, Nemanja Gudelj, Arkadiusz Milik, Anwar El Ghazi (85' Vaclav Cerny). Coach: Frank de Boer.
FK Jablonec: Vlastimil Hruby, Tomás Hübschman, Ludek Perncia, Vyacheslav Karavaev, Vit Benes, Filip Novák, Nermin Crnkic, Ruslan Mingazov (67' Lukás Masopust), Ján Gregus, Martin Pospisil (72' Michal Trávnik), Tomás Wágner (84' Martin Dolezal).
Coach: Jaroslav Silhavy.
Goal: 53' Arkadiusz Milik 1-0 (p).
Referee: Tony Chapron (FRA)   Attendance: 30,898.

20.08.15   Molde idrettspark, Molde: Molde FK – Standard Liège 2-0 (2-0).
Molde FK: Ethan Horvath, Ruben Gabrielsen, Martin Linnes, Per-Egil Flo, Joona Toivio, Daniel Hestad, Harmeet Singh, Mattias Mostrøm, Erik Hestad (80' Sander Svendsen), Tommy Høiland (90' Magne Simonsen), Mohamed Elyounoussi. Coach: Erling Moe.
Standard Liège: Yohann Thuram-Ulien, Ahmed El Messaoudi (52' Julien De Sart), Jorge Teixeira, Martin Milec (46' Mohamed Yattara), Darwin, Andrade, Jelle Van Damme, Ricardo Faty, Eyong Enoh, Adrien Trebel, Anthony Knockaert, Ivan Santini (65' Beni Badibanga).
Coach: Slavoljub Muslin.
Goals: 23' Tommy Høiland 1-0, 28' Mohamed Elyounoussi 2-0.
Referee: Aleksey Kulbakov (BLR)   Attendance: 3,940.

20.08.15   Valeriya Lobanovskovo, Kiev: Zorya Lugansk – Legia Warszawa 0-1 (0-0)
Zorya Lugansk: Nikita Shevchenko, Nikita Kamenyuka, Ivan Petryak (46' Dmytro Khomchenovsky), Evgeniy Opanasenko, Vyacheslav Checher, Mikhail Sivakov, Igor Chaykovskiy (46' Zeljko Ljubenovic), Artem Gordienko, Ruslan Malinovskiy, Oleksandr Karavayev (70' Jaba Lipartia), Pylyp Budkovsky. Coach: Yuriy Vernydub.
Legia Warszawa: Dusan Kuciak, Michal Pazdan, Tomasz Brzyski, Bartosz Bereszynski, Jakub Rzezniczak, Tomasz Jodlowiec, Guilherme, Dominik Furman, Nemanja Nikolic (88' Marek Saganowski), Michal Kucharczyk, Aleksandar Prijovic (75' Ondrej Duda).
Coach: Henning Berg.
Goal: 48' Michal Kucharczyk 0-1.
Referee: Anasthasios Sidiropoulos (GRE)   Attendance: 16,000.

20.08.15　Toumba, Saloniki: PAOK Saloniki – Brøndby IF 5-0 (2-0)
PAOK Saloniki: Robin Olsen, Stelios Malezas, Miguel Vítor, Ricardo Costa, Dimitrios
Konstantinidis (83' Nikos Korovesis), Alexandros Tziolis, Garry Rodrigues (71' Ioannis
Mystakidis), Ergis Kaçe, Stelios Kitsiou, Dimitrios Pelkas (67' Kyriakos Savvidis), Róbert
Mak. Coach: Igor Tudor.
Brøndby IF: Frederik Rønnow, Martin Albrechtsen, Frederik Holst (42' Dario Dumic), Johan
Larsson, Riza Durmisi, Daniel Agger, Martin Ørnskov, Lebogang Phiri (75' Christian
Nørgaard), Teemu Pukki, Magnus Eriksson, Johan Elmander (58' Ronnie Schwartz).
Coach: Thomas Frank.
Goals: 17' Róbert Mak 1-0, 36' Dimitrios Pelkas 2-0, 51' Garry Rodrigues 3-0,
80' Róbert Mak 4-0, 82' Róbert Mak 5-0.
Referee: Alberto Undiano Mallenco (ESP)　　Attendance: 20,106.

20.08.15　U Nisy, Liberec: Slovan Liberec – Hajduk Split 1-0 (0-0)
Slovan Liberec: Tomás Koubek, Vladimír Coufal, David Hovorka, Lukás Bartosák, Lukás
Pokorny, David Pavelka, Zdenek Folprecht, Herolind Shala (79' Isaac Sackey), Josef Sural,
Marek Bakos (63' Michael Rabusic), Dzon Delarge (90+1' Milan Kerbr).
Coach: Jindrich Trpisovsky.
Hajduk Split: Lovren Kalinic, Maksim Beliy, Goran Milovic, Jefferson, Hrvoje Milic, Nikola
Vlasic, Josip Juranovic, Mijo Caktas, Tino-Sven Susic, Franck Ohandza, Andrija Balic (66'
Elvir Maloku). Coach: Damir Buric.
Goal: 79' Lukás Pokorny 1-0.
Referee: David Fernández Borbalán (ESP)　　Attendance: 8,530.

20.08.15　Kuban, Krasnodar: FK Krasnodar – HJK Helsinki 5-1 (2-1)
FK Krasnodar: Andrey Dikan, Stefan Strandberg, Andreas Granqvist, Vitaliy Kaleshin, Ragnar
Sigurdsson, Pavel Mamaev, Yuri Gazinskiy, Odil Akhmedov (58' Wanderson), Vladimir
Bystrov (58' Ari), Sergey Petrov, Fedor Smolov (74' Dmitriy Torbinskiy).
Coach: Oleg Kononov.
HJK Helsinki: Daniel Örlund, Gideon Baah (60' Tapio Heikkilä), Juhani Ojala, Roni Peiponen,
Formose Mendy (84' Obed Malolo), Markus Heikkinen, Atomu Tanaka (22' Toni
Kolehmainen), Rasmus Schüller, Erfan Zeneli, Guy Moussi, Ousman Jallow.
Coach: Mika Lehkosuo.
Goals: 8' Juhani Ojala 1-0 (og), 10' Pavel Mamaev 2-0 (p), 18' Ousman Jallow 2-1,
57' Fedor Smolov 3-1 (p), 62' Wanderson 4-1, 64' Yuri Gazinskiy 5-1.
Referee: Marijo Strahonja (CRO)　　Attendance: 15,425.

20.08.15　Generali Arena, Praha: Sparta Praha – FC Thun 3-1 (2-1)
Sparta Praha: David Bicík, Mario Holek, Costa Nhamoinesu, Matej Hybs, Lukás Vácha (29'
Martin Frydek), Borek Dockal, Lukás Marecek, Josef Husbauer (54' Tiémoko Konaté),
Ladislav Krejcí, Kehinde Fatai (71' Marco Paixão), David Lafata. Coach: Zdenek Scasny.
FC Thun: Guillaume Faivre, Fulvio Sulmoni, Kevin Bigler, Thomas Reinmann, Gianluca
Frontino, Dennis Hediger, Nelson Ferreira (72' Marco Rojas), Andreas Wittwer, Nicola Sutter,
Roman Buess (56' Gonzalo Zárate), Simone Rapp (83' Ridge Munsy). Coach: Ciriaco Sforza.
Goals: 5' Nicola Sutter 0-1, 43' Costa Nhamoinesu 1-1, 45+1', 90+4' Borek Dockal 2-1, 3-1.
Referee: Danny Makkelie (HOL)　　Attendance: 12,448.

20.08.15   Stadionul Zimbru, Chisinau: FC Milsami – AS Saint-Étienne 1-1 (0-1)
FC Milsami: Radu Mitu, Adil Rhaili, Iulian Erhan (64' Cornel Gheti), Petru Racu, Ovye
Monday, Artur Patras, Karlo Belak (69' Evgen Zarichnyuk), Denis Rassulov (73' Vadim
Bolohan), Andrei Cojocari, Igor Banovic, Cristian Bud. Coach: Iuri Osipenco.
AS Saint-Étienne: Stéphane Ruffier, Kévin Théophile-Catherine, Florentin Pogba, Moustapha
Sall, Benoît Assou-Ekotto, Benjamin Corgnet (80' Jonathan Bamba), Fabien Lemoine, Ismaël
Diomandé, Jean-Christophe Bahebeck (62' Kévin Monnet-Paquet), Nolan Roux (87' Jonathan
Brison), Romain Hamouma. Coach: Christophe Galtier.
Goals: 40' Romain Hamouma 0-1. 56' Cristian Bud 1-1.
Referee: Pawel Gil (POL)   Attendance: 6,072.
Sent off: 55' Romain Hamouma.

20.08.15   Arena Nationala, Bucuresti: Steaua Bucuresti – Rosenborg BK 0-3 (0-0)
Steaua Bucuresti: Valentin Cojocaru, Paul Papp, Lucian Filip, Alin Tosca, Guilherme, Jean
Alcénat (75' Gabriel Iancu), Jugurtha Hamroun (46' Nicolae Stanciu), Alexandru Chipciu,
Sulley Muniru (68' Aymen Tahar), Grégory Tadé, Adrian Popa. Coach: Mirel Radoi.
Rosenborg BK: André Hansen, Hólmar Eyjólfsson, Johan Bjørdal, Jørgen Skjelvik, Jonas
Svensson, Mike Jensen, Tobias Mikkelsen, Ole Selnæs, Fredrik Midtsjø (66' Anders
Konradsen), Pål Helland (76' Yann-Erik De Lanlay), Alexander Søderlund (89' Matthias
Vilhjálmsson). Coach: Kåre Ingebrigtsen.
Goals: 62' Tobias Mikkelsen 0-1, 67' Pål Helland 0-2, 90+3' Mike Jensen 0-3.
Referee: Luca Banti (ITA)   Attendance: 21,204.

20.08.15   Stade de Suisse, Bern: BSC Young Boys – Qarabag FK 0-1 (0-0)
BSC Young Boys: Yvon Mvogo, Milan Vilotic, Steve von Bergen, Jan Lecjaks, Scott Sutter,
Leonardo Bertone (80' Denis Zakaria), Milan Gajic, Raphaël Nuzzolo (69' Alexander
González), Miralem Sulejmani, Yūya Kubo (85' Haris Tabakovic), Guillaume Hoarau.
Coach: Harry Gämperle.
Qarabag FK: Ibrahim Sehic, Qara Qarayev, Rashad Sadygov, Ansi Agolli, Badavi Guseynov,
Reynaldo, Dani Quintana (75' Joshgun Diniyev), Alharbi El Jadeyaoui (87' Elvin Yunuszade),
Javid Tagiyev (80' Afran Ismayilov), Ilgar Gurbanov, Richard. Coach: Gurban Gurbanov.
Goal: 67' Richard 0-1.
Referee: Vladislav Bezborodov (RUS)   Attendance: 6,700.

20.08.15   Filip II. Makedonski, Skopje: FK Rabotnicki – Rubin Kazan 1-1 (0-0)
FK Rabotnicki: Daniel Bozinovski (90+6' Damjan Siskovski), Goran Siljanovski, Kire
Ristevski, Mite Cikarski, Milan Ilievski, Stephan Vujcic, Milovan Petrovikj, Miroslav
Jovanovski (70' Milan Ristovki), Chuma Anene (86' Leon Najdovski), Kire Markoski, Marijan
Altiparmakovski. Coach: Igor Angelovski.
Rubin Kazan: Sergey Ryzhikov, Oleg Kuzmin, Solomon Kverkvelia, Guillermo Cotugno,
Ruslan Kambolov, Carlos Eduardo (81' Sergey Kislyak), Diniyar Bilyaletdinov (58' Igor
Portnyagin), Magomed Ozdoev, Gökdeniz Karadeniz (71' Maksim Batov), Blagoy Georgiev,
Maksim Kanunnikov. Coach: Rinat Bilyaletdinov.
Goals: 68' Gökdeniz Karadeniz 0-1, 85' Kire Ristevski 1-1.
Referee: István Vad (HUN)   Attendance: 10,000.
Sent off: 55' Milovan Petrovikj.

20.08.15   Peristeri, Athen: Atromitos – Fenerbahçe 0-1 (0-0)
Atromitos: Andrey Gorbunov, Sokratis Fitanidis, Mariano Bíttolo, Nikolaos Lazaridis, Usero
(90+2' Pape M'Bow), Stefano Napoleoni, Javier Umbides, Marcelinho (76' Eduardo Brito),
Fernando Godoy, Kyriakos Kivrakidis, Sebastián García (85' Anthony Le Tallec).
Coach: Michalis Grigoriou.
Fenerbahçe: Volkan Demirel, Sener Özbayrakli, Bruno Alves, Abdoulaye Ba, Caner Erkin,
Souza, Diego, Raúl Meireles (71' Mehmet Topal), Moussa Sow (80' Robin van Persie),
Fernandão, Nani (87' Volkan Sen). Coach: Vítor Pereira.
Goal: 89' Robin van Persie 0-1.
Referee: Daniele Orsato (ITA)   Attendance: 3,328.

20.08.15   Stadion pod Dubnom, Zilina: MSK Zilina – Athletic Bilbao 3-2 (0-2)
MSK Zilina: Milos Volesák, Milan Skriniar, Denis Vavro, Ernest Mabouka (56' William),
Jakub Paur, Viktor Pecovsky, Bojan Letic, László Bénes (87' Michal Skvarka), Miroslav
Kácer, Matej Jelic, Lukás Cmelík (73' Jaroslav Mihalík). Coach: Adrián Gula.
Athletic Bilbao: Iago Herrerín, Eneko Bóveda, Elustondo, Aymeric Laporte, Mikel Rico (69'
Beñat), Gurpegi, Aketxe, Lekue, Kike Sola, Ibai, Sabin (74' Williams / 81' De Marcos).
Coach: Valverde.
Goals: 16' Sabin 0-1, 33' Kike Sola 0-2, 65' Jakub Paur 1-2, 77', 90+4' William 2-2, 3-2.
Referee: Ovidiu Hategan (ROM)   Attendance: 10,175.

20.08.15   Tivoli Stadion Tirol, Innsbruck: SCR Altach – Os Belenenses 0-1 (0-1)
SCR Altach: Andreas Lukse, Philipp Netzer, Andreas Lienhart, Jan Zwischenbrugger, César
Ortiz, Benedikt Zech, Patrick Salomon (65' Dominik Hofbauer), Boris Prokopic, Louis
N'Gwat-Mahop, Hannes Aigner (72' Martin Harrer), Patrick Seeger (80' Juan Barrera).
Coach: Damir Canadi.
Os Belenenses: Ventura, Amorim, Tonel, Geraldes, Brandão, Rúben Pinto, André Sousa (64'
Ricardo Dias), Tiago Silva (77' Fábio Nunes), Fábio Sturgeon, Miguel Rosa, Tiago Caeiro (66'
Abel Camará). Coach: Sá Pinto.
Goal: 13' Tiago Caeiro 0-1.
Referee: Matej Jug (SVN)   Attendance: 4,572.

20.08.15   Matmut Atlantique, Bordeaux: Girondins Bordeaux – Kairat Almaty 1-0 (1-0)
Girondins Bordeaux: Jérôme Prior, Diego Contento (14' Maxime Poundje), Nicolas Pallois,
Cédric Yamberé, Frédéric Guilbert, Abdou Traoré (71' Nicolas Maurice-Belay), Henri Saivet,
André Biyogo Poko, Wahbi Khazri, Diego Rolán (85' Enzo Crivelli), Isaac Thelin.
Coach: Willy Sagnol.
Kairat Almaty: Vladimir Plotnikov, Bruno Soares, Mark Gorman, Ermek Kuantaev, Mikhail
Bakaev, Bauyrzhan Islamkhan (68' Serginho), Isael, Islambek Kuat, Anatoliy Tymoshchuk
(90+3' Timur Rudosselskiy), Gerard Gohou, Sito Riera (83' Djordje Despotovic).
Coach: Vladimir Weiss.
Goal: 27' Wahbi Khazri 1-0.
Referee: Arnold Hunter (NIR)   Attendance: 24,795.

20.08.15   Skagerak Arena, Skien: Odds BK – Borussia Dortmund 3-4 (3-1)
Odds BK: Sondre Rossbach, Espen Ruud, Vegard Bergan, Thomas Grøgaard, Steffen Hagen, Jone Samuelsen (57' Oliver Berg), Fredrik Nordkvelle, Fredrik Jensen, Olivier Occéan (77' Ulrik Flo), Rafik Zekhnini, Bentley (65' Ole Halvorsen). Coach: Dag-Eilev Fagermo.
Borussia Dortmund: Roman Weidenfeller, Mats Hummels, Matthias Ginter, Marcel Schmelzer, Sven Bender (68' Julian Weigl), Ilkay Gündogan, Henrikh Mkhitaryan, Shinji Kagawa, Gonzalo Castro (46' Sokratis Papastathopoulos), Kevin Kampl (63' Adrián Ramos), Pierre-Emerick Aubameyang. Coach: Thomas Tuchel.
Goals: 1' Jone Samuelsen 1-0, 19' Fredrik Nordkvelle 2-0, 22' Espen Ruud 3-0, 34' Pierre-Emerick Aubameyang 3-1, 47' Shinji Kagawa 3-2, 76' Pierre-Emerick Aubameyang 3-3, 85' Henrikh Mkhitaryan 3-4.
Referee: Jorge Sousa (POR)   Attendance: 12,436.

20.08.15   Doosan Arena, Plzen: Viktoria Plzen – Vojvodina 3-0 (1-0)
Viktoria Plzen: Matús Kozácik, Roman Hubník, David Limbersky, Václav Procházka, Ondrej Vanek, Jan Kopic, Patrik Hrosovsky, Jan Kovarík (77' Milan Petrzela), Daniel Kolár (68' Tomás Horava), Frantisek Rajtoral, Michal Djuris (85' Jan Holenda). Coach: Karel Krejcí.
Vojvodina: Srdan Zakula, Jovica Vasilic, Radovan Pankov, Bojan Nastic, Igor Djuric, Mirko Ivanic, Darko Puskaric (68' Aleksandar Palocevic), Danilo Sekulic, Novica Maksimovic, Aleksandar Stanisavljevic (88' Sinisa Babic), Ognjen Ozegovic (88' Milan Pavkov).
Coach: Zlatomir Zagorcic.
Goals: 25' Jan Kopic 1-0, 51' Ondrej Vanek 2-0, 82' Jan Kopic 3-0.
Referee: Javier Estrada Fernández (ESP)   Attendance: 10,769.

20.08.15   INEA Stadion, Poznan: Lech Poznan – Videoton FC 3-0 (1-0)
Lech Poznan: Jasmin Buric, Barry Douglas, Tomasz Kedziora, Dariusz Dudka, Marcin Kaminksi, Lukasz Tralka, Karol Linetty, Szymon Pawlowski, Kasper Hämäläinen (83' Dariusz Formella), Gergö Lovrencsics (80' Marcin Robak / 89' Dávid Holman), Denis Thomalla.
Coach: Maciej Skorza.
Videoton FC: Branislav Danilovic, Paulo Vinicius, András Fejes, Ádám Lang, Filipe Oliveira, Máté Pátkai (71' Dinko Trebotic), Roland Szolnoki, Adám Gyurcsó (88' Viktor Sejben), Mirko Ivanovski, Alhassane Soumah (58' István Kovács), Ádám Simon. Coach: Tamás Petö.
Goals: 11' Karol Linetty 1-0, 57' Denis Thomalla 2-0, 68' Lukasz Tralka 3-0.
Referee: Oliver Drachta (AUT)   Attendance: 14,133.

20.08.15   Saint Mary's, Southampton: Southampton FC – FC Midtjylland 1-1 (0-1)
Southampton FC: Maarten Stekelenburg, Maya Yoshida, José Fonte, Steven Caulker, Matt Targett, Victor Wanyama, Oriol Romeu, James Ward-Prowse (83' Juanmi), Jay Rodriguez (76' Shane Long), Sadio Mané, Graziano Pellè. Coach: Ronald Koeman.
FC Midtjylland: Johan Dahlin, Kian Hansen, Erik Sviatchenko, Jesper Lauridsen, André Rømer, Tim Sparv, Jakob Poulsen, Petter Andersson (78' Kristoffer Olsson), Pione Sisto (71' Rilwan Hassan), Daniel Royer, Morten Rasmussen (89' Ebere Onuachu). Coach: Jess Thorup.
Goals: 45' Tim Sparv 0-1, 56' Jay Rodriguez 1-1 (p).
Referee: Clément Turpin (FRA)   Attendance: 28,890.

27.08.15   Stade Sclessin, Liège: Standard Liège – Molde FK 3-1 (1-1).

Standard Liège: Yohann Thuram-Ulien, Corentin Fiore, Ahmed, Darwin Andrade, Jelle Van Damme, Ricardo Faty, Christian Brüls (74' Jonathan Legear), Eyong Enoh, Adrien Trebel, Anthony Knockaert, Mohamed Yattara, Ivan Santini. Coach: Slavoljub Muslin.

Molde FK: Ethan Horvath, Ruben Gabrielsen, Martin Linnes, Per-Egil Flo, Vegard Forren, Daniel Hestad, Harmeet Singh, Mattias Mostrøm (70' Joona Toivio), Etzaz Hussain, Ola Kamara (77' Tommy Høiland), Mohamed Elyounoussi. Coach: Erling Moe.

Goals: 26' Anthony Knockaert 1-0, 42' Etzaz Hussain 1-1, 48' Ivan Santini 2-1, 90+5' Adrien Trebel 3-1.

Referee: Alexandru Tudor (ROM)   Attendance: 12,586.

Molde FK won on away goals.

27.08.15   Chance Arena, Jablonec: FK Jablonec – AFC Ajax 0-0.

FK Jablonec: Vlastimil Hruby, Tomás Hübschman, Ludek Perncia, Vyacheslav Karavaev, Vit Benes, Filip Novák, Nermin Crnkic (68' Martin Dolezal), Ruslan Mingazov, Ján Gregus (75' Michal Trávnik), Martin Pospisil, Tomás Wágner (46' Stanislav Tecl).
Coach: Jaroslav Silhavy.

AFC Ajax: Jasper Cillessen, Joël Veltman, Jaïro Riedewald, Kenny Tete, Mitchell Dijks, Riechedly Bazoer, Daley Sinkgraven (46' Viktor Fischer), Davy Klaassen, Nemanja Gudelj, Arkadiusz Milik (69' Ricardo van Rhijn), Anwar El Ghazi. Coach: Frank de Boer.

Referee: Kenn Hansen (DEN)   Attendance: 6,040.

Sent off: 59' Riechedly Bazoer.

Ján Gregus missed a penalty kick (58').

27.08.15   Red Bull Arena, Wals-Siezenheim:
         Red Bull Salzburg – Dinamo Minsk 2-0 (1-0, 2-0).

Red Bull Salzburg: Alexander Walke, Benno Schmitz, Duje Caleta-Car, Andreas Ulmer (106' Asger Sorensen), Stafan Lainer, Martin Hinteregger, Valon Berisha, Christoph Leitgeb (91' Christian Schwegler), Yordy Reyna (78' David Atanga), Takumi Minamino, Jonatan Soriano. Coach: Peter Zeidler.

Dinamo Minsk: Aleksandr Gutor, Maksim Vitus, Sergey Politevich, Umaru Bangura, Roman Begunov, Igor Voronkov (77' Oleg Veretilo), Sergiu Neacsa (84' Kirill Premudrov), Uladzimir Karytska, Nenad Adamovic, Gleb Rassadkin (62' Mohamed El-Mounir), Fatos Beciraj.
Coach: Vuk Rasovic.

Goals: 11' Takumi Minamino 1-0, 58' Jonatan Soriano 2-0.
Referee: Kevin Blom (HOL)   Attendance: 7,849.

Dinamo Minsk won 3-2 on penalties following extra time.

Penalties: Hinteregger 1-0, Beciraj 1-1, Soriano 2-1, Karytska missed, Minamoni missed, Begunov 2-2, Atanga missed, Politevich 2-3, Berisha missed.

27.08.15   AFAS Stadion, Alkmaar: AZ Alkmaar – Astra Giurgiu 2-0 (0-0).
AZ Alkmaar: Sergio Rochet, Mattias Johansson, Jeffrey Gouweleeuw, Jop van der Linden,
Derrick Luckassen (77' Muamer Tankovic), Ridgeciano Haps, Markus Henriksen, Dabney dos
Santos (89' Jan Wuytens), Thom Haye, Guus Hupperts, Vincent Janssen (78' Robert Mühren).
Coach: John van den Brom.
Astra Giurgiu: Silviu Lung Jr., Junior Maranhao, Cristian Oros, Valerica Gaman, Alexandru
Dandea, Pedro Queirós, Gabriel Enache (83' Alexandru Ionita), Florin Lovin (83' Daniel
Florea), Denis Alibec (62' Rick), Constantin Budescu, William Amorim.
Coach: Marius Sumudica.
Goals: 80' Jop van der Linden 1-0, 85' Robert Mühren 2-0.
Referee: Robert Schörgenhofer (AUT)   Attendance: 9,679.

27.08.15   Apostolos Nikolaidis, Athen: Panathinaikos – Gabala FK 2-2 (1-1).
Panathinaikos: Luke Steele, Georgios Koutroubis, Efstathios Tavlaridis, Sergio Sánchez, Zeca,
Nano, Christos Bourbos (77' Tasos Lagos), Sotiris Ninis, Danijel Pranjic (67' Viktor
Klonaridis), Marcus Berg, Nikolaos Karelis (67' Mladen Petric). Coach: Yannis Anastasiou.
Gabala FK: Dmitro Bezotosniy, Vojislav Stankovic, Vitaliy Vernydub, Ricardinho, Räsad
Sadiqov, Oleksiy Gay, Arif Dashdemirov, Ermin Zec (86' Elvin Jamalov), Sergei Zenjov,
Dodô, Oleksiy Antonov. Coach: Roman Grygorchuk.
Goals: 6' Dodô 0-1, 34' Marcus Berg 1-1, 60' Dodô 1-2, 78' Nano 2-2.
Referee: Ivan Kruzliak (SVK)   Attendance: 13,956.

Gabala FK won on away goals.

27.08.15   Wojska Polskiego, Warszawa: Legia Warszawa – Zorya Lugansk 3-2 (1-1)
Legia Warszawa: Dusan Kuciak, Michal Pazdan (7' Igor Lewczuk), Tomasz Brzyski, Bartosz
Bereszynski, Jakub Rzezniczak, Tomasz Jodlowiec, Guilherme, Dominik Furman, Nemanja
Nikolic (66' Ondrej Duda), Michal Kucharczyk, Aleksandar Prijovic (90+3' Marek
Saganowski). Coach: Henning Berg.
Zorya Lugansk: Nikita Shevchenko, Nikita Kamenyuka, Ivan Petryak, Evgeniy Opanasenko,
Andriy Pilyavsky (83' Vyacheslav Checher), Mikhail Sivakov, Artem Gordienko, Ruslan
Malinovskiy, Oleksandr Karavayev, Zeljko Ljubenovic (87' Jaba Lipartia), Dmytro
Khomchenovsky (58' Pylyp Budkovsky). Coach: Yuriy Vernydub.
Goals: 16' Tomasz Brzyski 1-0, 39' Dmytro Khomchenovsky 1-1, 62' Guilherme 2-1,
66' Ruslan Malinovsky 2-2, 90+5' Ondrej Duda 3-2 (p).
Referee: Tobias Welz (GER)   Attendance: 23,163.

27.08.15   Brøndby Stadion, Brøndby: Brøndby IF – PAOK Saloniki 1-1 (1-1)
Brøndby IF: Frederik Rønnow, Martin Albrechtsen, Johan Larsson, Riza Durmisi, Martin
Ørnskov, Lebogang Phiri (81' Frederik Holst), Christian Nørgaard, Andrew Hjulsager, Magnus
Eriksson (72' Teemu Pukki), Elbasan Rashani, Ronnie Schwartz (60' Johan Elmander).
Coach: Thomas Frank.
PAOK Saloniki: Panagiotis Glykos, Miguel Vítor, Ricardo Costa, Dimitrios Konstantinidis
(64' Kyriakos Savvidis), Giorgos Tzavellas, Alexandros Tziolis (64' Róbert Mak), Garry
Rodrigues, Ergis Kaçe, Stelios Kitsiou, Efthimios Koulouris (76' Panagiotis Deligiannidis),
Ioannis Mystakidis. Coach: Igor Tudor.
Goals: 21' Ricardo Costa 0-1, 27' Elbasan Rashani 1-1.
Referee: Paolo Tagliavento (ITA)   Attendance: 6,630.

27.08.15 Poljud, Split: Hajduk Split – Slovan Liberec 0-1 (0-1)
Hajduk Split: Lovren Kalinic, Goran Milovic, Jefferson, Zoran Nizic, Fran Tudor (73' Josip Juranovic), Hrvoje Milic, Nikola Vlasic, Mijo Caktas (49' Ante Roguljic), Tino-Sven Susic, Franck Ohandza, Andrija Balic (34' Elvir Maloku). Coach: Damir Buric.
Slovan Liberec: Tomás Koubek, Vladimír Coufal, David Hovorka, Lukás Bartosák, Lukás Pokorny, David Pavelka, Isaac Sackey (74' Jirí Fleisman), Herolind Shala (62' Daniel Soungole), Josef Sural, Marek Bakos, Dzon Delarge (49' Milan Kerbr).
Coach: Jindrich Trpisovsky.
Goal: 23' Josef Sural 0-1.
Referee: Artur Soares Dias (POR)   Attendance: 33,162.

27.08.15 Sonera Stadium, Helsinki: HJK Helsinki – FK Krasnodar 0-0
HJK Helsinki: Thomas Dähne, Alex Lehtinen, Juhani Ojala (64' Markus Heikkinen), Tapio Heikkilä, Roni Peiponen, Formose Mendy, Matti Klinga (77' Lucas Lingman), Rasmus Schüller, Erfan Zeneli, Guy Moussi, Ousman Jallow (68' Atomu Tanaka).
Coach: Mika Lehkosuo.
FK Krasnodar: Andrey Dikan, Stefan Strandberg, Andreas Granqvist, Nikolay Markov, Vitaliy Kaleshin (70' Artur Jedrzejczyk), Ragnar Sigurdsson, Dmitriy Torbinskiy, Odil Akhmedov, Wanderson (67' Ricardo Laborde), Sergey Petrov, Ari (75' Fedor Smolov). Coach: Oleg Kononov.
Referee: Felix Zwayer (GER)   Attendance: 2,952.

27.08.15 Stockhorn Arena, Thun: FC Thun – Sparta Praha 3-3 (1-2)
FC Thun: Guillaume Faivre, Fulvio Sulmoni, Nicolas Schindelholz, Kevin Bigler, Gianluca Frontino (46' Ridge Munsy), Marco Rojas (46' Enrico Schirinzi), Lotem Zino (55' Gonzalo Zárate), Dennis Hediger, Nelson Ferreira, Andreas Wittwer, Simone Rapp.
Coach: Ciriaco Sforza.
Sparta Praha: David Bicík, Markus Steinhöfer, Mario Holek, Costa Nhamoinesu, Matej Hybs (68' Michal Breznaník), Borek Dockal, Lukás Marecek, Martin Frydek, Josef Husbauer (27' Francis Litsingi), Ladislav Krejcí, David Lafata (82' Kehinde Fatai). Coach: Zdenek Scasny.
Goals: 10' Borek Dockal 0-1, 21' Josef Husbauer 0-2, 33' Nelson Ferreira 1-2, 50' Ridge Munsy 2-2, 71' Costa Nhamoinesu 2-3, 81' Nelson Ferreira 3-3.
Referee: Ruddy Buquet (FRA)   Attendance: 6,024.
Sent off: 85' Michal Breznaník.

27.08.15 Geoffroy Guichard, St.Étienne: AS Saint-Étienne – FC Milsami 1-0 (1-0)
AS Saint-Étienne: Stéphane Ruffier, Kévin Théophile-Catherine, Loïc Perrin, Moustapha Sall, Benoît Assou-Ekotto, Jérémy Clément, Benjamin Corgnet (63' Jonathan Bamba), Valentin Eysseric, Fabien Lemoine, Nolan Roux (75' Neal Maupay), Kévin Monnet-Paquet (89' Pierre-Yves Polomat). Coach: Christophe Galtier.
FC Milsami: Radu Mitu, Adil Rhaili, Iulian Erhan, Petru Racu, Cornel Gheti, Artur Patras, Karlo Belak (62' Evgen Zarichnyuk), Alexandru Antoniuc, Andrei Cojocari, Igor Banovic (78' Eugeniu Slivca), Cristian Bud (70' Vadim Bolohan). Coach: Iuri Osipenco.
Goal: 15' Benjamin Corgnet 1-0.
Referee: Aleksey Eskov (RUS)   Attendance: 22,456.

27.08.15   Sóstói, Székesfehérvár: Videoton FC – Lech Poznan 0-1 (0-0)
Videoton FC: Branislav Danilovic, Paulo Vinicius, Kees Luijckx (57' Ádám Simon), András
Fejes, Roland Juhász, István Kovács, Tamas Koltai (58' Adám Gyurcsó), Roland Szolnoki,
Dinko Trebotic, Róbert Feczesin (70' Gergely Rudolf), Mirko Ivanovski. Coach: Tamás Petö.
Lech Poznan: Jasmin Buric, Barry Douglas, Tomasz Kedziora, Tamás Kádár, Dariusz Dudka,
Marcin Kaminksi, Lukasz Tralka, Szymon Pawlowski (74' Gergö Lovrencsics), Kasper
Hämäläinen (72' Dávid Holman), Denis Thomalla (81' Piotr Kurbiel), Dariusz Formella.
Coach: Maciej Skorza.
Goal: 57' Tomasz Kedziora 0-1.
Referee: Stefan Johannesson (SWE)   Attendance: 2,815.

27.08.15   Lerkendal, Trondheim: Rosenborg BK – Steaua Bucuresti 0-1 (0-0)
Rosenborg BK: André Hansen, Hólmar Eyjólfsson, Johan Bjørdal, Jonas Svensson, Mike
Jensen, Tobias Mikkelsen, Ole Selnæs (29' Matthias Vilhjálmsson), Fredrik Midtsjø, Pål
Helland, Anders Konradsen, Alexander Søderlund. Coach: Kåre Ingebrigtsen.
Steaua Bucuresti: Florin Nita, Lucian Filip (75' Rares Enceanu), Alin Tosca, Guilherme, Jean
Alcénat (46' Paul Papp), Fernando Varela, Alexandru Chipciu, Nicolae Stanciu, Sulley
Muniru, Adrian Popa, Gabriel Iancu (46' Grégory Tadé). Coach: Mirel Radoi.
Goal: 54' Adrian Popa 0-1.
Referee: Bobby Madden (SCO)   Attendance: 14,645.

27.08.15   Tofig Bakhramov, Baku: Qarabag FK – BSC Young Boys 3-0 (2-0)
Qarabag FK: Ibrahim Sehic, Qara Qarayev (86' Vugar Mustafayev), Rashad Sadygov, Ansi
Agolli, Badavi Guseynov, Reynaldo, Dani Quintana, Afran Ismayilov (72' Rydell Poepon),
Javid Tagiyev (78' Joshgun Diniyev), Ilgar Gurbanov, Richard. Coach: Gurban Gurbanov.
BSC Young Boys: Yvon Mvogo, Florent Hadergjonaj, Milan Vilotic, Steve von Bergen, Scott
Sutter, Alexander González, Leonardo Bertone, Denis Zakaria, Miralem Sulejmani (65'
Raphaël Nuzzolo), Yüya Kubo (80' Milan Gajic), Guillaume Hoarau (54' Samuel Afum).
Coach: Harry Gämperle.
Goals: 4' Richard 1-0 (p), 43' Reynaldo 2-0, 61' Afran Ismayilov 2-0.
Referee: Gediminas Mazeika (LTU)   Attendance: 29,628.
Sent off: 4' Steve von Bergen.

27.08.15   Tsentralniy, Kazan: Rubin Kazan – FK Rabotnicki 1-0 (1-0)
Rubin Kazan: Sergey Ryzhikov, Oleg Kuzmin, Mauricio Lemos, Solomon Kverkvelia,
Guillermo Cotugno, Carlos Eduardo (79' Igor Portnyagin), Diniyar Bilyaletdinov, Magomed
Ozdoev, Blagoy Georgiev, Vladimir Dyadyun (90+3' Maksim Batov), Maksim Kanunnikov.
Coach: Rinat Bilyaletdinov.
FK Rabotnicki: Daniel Bozinovski, Goran Siljanovski, Kire Ristevski, Mite Cikarski, Milan
Ilievski, Suad Sahiti (46' Kire Markoski), Stephan Vujcic, Dusko Trajcevski (87' Miroslav
Jovanovski), Chuma Anene, Baze Ilijoski, Marijan Altiparmakovski. Coach: Igor Angelovski.
Goal: 35' Carlos Eduardo 1-0.
Referee: Hüseyin Göçek (TUR)   Attendance: 4,231.

27.08.15   Sükrü Saracoglu, Istanbul: Fenerbahçe – Atromitos 3-0 (1-0)
Fenerbahçe: Volkan Demirel, Simon Kjær, Sener Özbayrakli, Abdoulaye Ba, Caner Erkin, Mehmet Topal (77' Volkan Sen), Souza, Diego (67' Raúl Meireles), Fernandão, Robin van Persie (67' Alper Potuk), Nani. Coach: Vítor Pereira.
Atromitos: Andrey Gorbunov, Sokratis Fitanidis, Mariano Bíttolo (82' Alexandros Kouros), Nikolaos Lazaridis, Usero, Stefano Napoleoni, Javier Umbides, Marcelinho, Fernando Godoy (62' Panagiotis Ballas), Kyriakos Kivrakidis, Sebastián García (63' Anthony Le Tallec). Coach: Michalis Grigoriou.
Goals: 7' Fernandão 1-0, 59' Andrey Gorbunov 2-0 (og), 78' Fernandão 3-0.
Referee: Ivan Bebek (CRO)   Attendance: 33,121.

27.08.15   San Mamés, Bilbao: Athletic Bilbao – MSK Zilina 1-0 (1-0)
Athletic Bilbao: Iago Herrerín, Elustondo, Aymeric Laporte, De Marcos, Eraso (73' Aketxe), Beñat, Susaeta (85' Mikel Rico), Gurpegi, Lekue, Aduriz, Viguera (57' Sabin). Coach: Valverde.
MSK Zilina: Milos Volesák, Milan Skriniar, Róbert Mazán, Denis Vavro, Ernest Mabouka (80' Jaroslav Mihalík), Jakub Paur, Viktor Pecovsky, László Bénes, Miroslav Kácer (88' Nikolas Spalek), Matej Jelic (67' Lukás Cmelík), William. Coach: Adrián Gula.
Goal: 23' Elustondo 1-0.
Referee: Martin Strömbergsson (SWE)   Attendance: 38,688.

Athletic Bilbao won on away goals.

27.08.15   Estádio do Restelo, Lisboa: Os Belenenses – SCR Altach 0-0
Os Belenenses: Ventura, Amorim, Tonel, Geraldes, Brandão, Rúben Pinto (90+3' Ricardo Dias), André Sousa, Fábio Sturgeon, Miguel Rosa, Tiago Caeiro (87' João Afonso), Abel Camará (69' Tiago Silva). Coach: Sá Pinto.
SCR Altach: Andreas Lukse, Alexander Pöllhuber, Philipp Netzer (64' Felix Roth), Andreas Lienhart, Jan Zwischenbrugger, César Ortiz (83' Martin Harrer), Benedikt Zech, Patrick Salomon (57' Hannes Aigner), Boris Prokopic, Louis N'Gwat-Mahop, Patrick Seeger. Coach: Damir Canadi.
Referee: Anthony Taylor (ENG)   Attendance: 4,500.

27.08.15   Tsentralniy, Almaty: Kairat Almaty – Girondins Bordeaux 2-1 (1-0)
Kairat Almaty: Vladimir Plotnikov, Bruno Soares, Zarko Markovic, Ermek Kuantaev (87' Zhambyl Kukeev), Mikhail Bakaev, Bauyrzhan Islamkhan (82' Djordje Despotovic), Isael, Islambek Kuat, Anatoliy Tymoshchuk, Gerard Gohou, Sito Riera. Coach: Vladimir Weiss.
Girondins Bordeaux: Jérôme Prior, Nicolas Pallois, Cédric Yamberé, Frédéric Guilbert, Maxime Poundje, Abdou Traoré (69' Nicolas Maurice-Belay), Henri Saivet, André Biyogo Poko, Wahbi Khazri (86' Milan Gajic), Diego Rolán (69' Enzo Crivelli), Isaac Thelin. Coach: Willy Sagnol.
Goals: 1' Frédéric Guilbert 1-0 (og), 66' Islambek Kuat 2-0, 76' Enzo Crivelli 2-1.
Referee: Bas Nijhuis (HOL)   Attendance: 23,807.

Girondins Bordeaux won on away goals.

27.08.15   Signal Iduna Park, Dortmund: Borussia Dortmund – Odds BK 7-2 (4-1)
Borussia Dortmund: Roman Weidenfeller, Mats Hummels, Sokratis Papastathopoulos (64'
Lukasz Piszczek), Matthias Ginter, Marcel Schmelzer, Jonas Hofmann, Ilkay Gündogan (66'
Sven Bender), Henrikh Mkhitaryan (64' Pierre-Emerick Aubameyang), Shinji Kagawa, Julian
Weigl, Marco Reus. Coach: Thomas Tuchel.
Odds BK: Sondre Rossbach, Vegard Bergan, Thomas Grøgaard, Jarkko Hurme, Steffen Hagen,
Oliver Berg, Ole Halvorsen, Fredrik Nordkvelle (65' Ardian Gashi), Fredrik Jensen, Olivier
Occéan (46' Ulrik Flo), Rafik Zekhnini (77' Bentley). Coach: Dag-Eilev Fagermo.
Goals: 19' Ole Halvorsen 0-1, 25' Henrikh Mkhitaryan 1-1, 27', 32' Marco Reus 2-1, 3-1,
40' Shinji Kagawa 4-1, 51' Ilkay Gündogan 5-1, 57' Marco Reus 6-1, 64' Oliver Berg 6-2,
90' Shinji Kagawa 7-2.
Referee: Evgen Aranovskiy (UKR)   Attendance: 64,200.

27.08.15   Karadjordje, Novi Sad: Vojvodina – Viktoria Plzen 0-2 (0-1)
Vojvodina: Srdan Zakula, Jovica Vasilic, Nino Pekaric, Bojan Nastic (66' Slavisa Radovic),
Igor Djuric, Mirko Ivanic (80' Uros Stamenic), Aleksandar Palocevic, Sinisa Babic (64' Marko
Zocevic), Danilo Sekulic, Novica Maksimovic, Ognjen Ozegovic. Coach: Zlatomir Zagorcic.
Viktoria Plzen: Matús Kozácik, Roman Hubník (54' Jan Baránek), David Limbersky, Václav
Procházka, Ondrej Vanek, Jan Kopic, Milan Petrzela (72' Egon Vuch), Patrik Hrosovsky,
Daniel Kolár (81' Ajdin Mahmutovic), Frantisek Rajtoral, Michal Djuris. Coach: Karel Krejcí.
Goals: 19' Igor Djuric 0-1 (og), 60' Michal Djuris 0-2.
Referee: Michail Koukoulakis (GRE)   Attendance: 7,617.

27.08.15   MCH Arena, Herning: FC Midtjylland – Southampton FC 1-0 (1-0)
FC Midtjylland: Johan Dahlin, Kian Hansen, Erik Sviatchenko, Jesper Lauridsen, Kristian
Nielsen (83' André Rømer), Tim Sparv, Jakob Poulsen, Petter Andersson (80' Martin Pusic),
Pione Sisto (68' Rilwan Hassan), Daniel Royer, Morten Rasmussen. Coach: Jess Thorup.
Southampton FC: Maarten Stekelenburg, Maya Yoshida, José Fonte, Cuco Martina, Steven
Caulker (56' Dusan Tadic), Matt Targett, Steven Davis (82' Juanmi), Oriol Romeu, James
Ward-Prowse, Jay Rodriguez (75' Shane Long), Graziano Pellè. Coach: Ronald Koeman.
Goal: 28' Morten Rasmussen 1-0.
Referee: Liran Lany (ISR)   Attendance: 9,481.

GROUP STAGE

GROUP A

Molde FK	6	3	2	1	10 -	7	11
Fenerbahçe	6	2	3	1	7 -	6	9
AFC Ajax	6	1	4	1	6 -	6	7
Celtic FC	6	0	3	3	8 -	12	3

GROUP B

Liverpool FC	6	2	4	0	6 -	4	10
FC Sion	6	2	3	1	5 -	5	9
Rubin Kazan	6	1	3	2	6 -	6	6
Girondins Bordeaux	6	0	4	2	5 -	7	4

GROUP C

FK Krasnodar	6	4	1	1	9 -	4	13
Borussia Dortmund	6	3	1	2	10 -	5	10
PAOK Saloniki	6	1	4	1	3 -	3	7
Gabala FK	6	0	2	4	2 -	12	2

GROUP D

SSC Napoli	6	6	0	0	22 -	3	18
FC Midtjylland	6	2	1	3	6 -	12	7
Club Brugge KV	6	1	2	3	4 -	11	5
Legia Warszawa	6	1	1	4	4 -	10	4

GROUP E

Rapid Wien	6	5	0	1	10 -	6	15
Villarreal CF	6	4	1	1	12 -	6	13
Víktoria Plzen	6	1	1	4	8 -	10	4
Dinamo Minsk	6	1	0	5	3 -	11	3

GROUP F

Sporting Braga	6	4	1	1	7 -	4	13
Olympique Marseille	6	4	0	2	12 -	7	12
Slovan Liberec	6	2	1	3	6 -	8	7
FC Groningen	6	0	2	4	2 -	8	2

GROUP G

Lazio Roma	6	4	2	0	13 - 6	14
AS Saint-Étienne	6	2	3	1	10 - 7	9
Dnipro Dnipropetrovsk	6	2	1	3	6 - 8	7
Rosenborg BK	6	0	2	4	4 - 12	2

GROUP H

Lokomotiv Moskva	6	3	2	1	12 - 7	11
Sporting CP	6	3	1	2	14 - 11	10
Besiktas	6	2	3	1	7 - 6	9
KF Skënderbeu	6	1	0	5	4 - 13	3

GROUP I

FC Basel	6	4	1	1	10 - 5	13
ACF Fiorentina	6	3	1	2	11 - 6	10
Lech Poznan	6	1	2	3	2 - 6	5
Os Belenenses	6	1	2	3	2 - 8	5

GROUP J

Tottenham Hotspur	6	4	1	1	12 - 6	13
RSC Anderlecht	6	3	1	2	8 - 6	10
AS Monaco	6	1	3	2	5 - 9	6
Qarabag FK	6	1	1	4	4 - 8	4

GROUP K

FC Schalke 04	6	4	2	0	15 - 3	14
Sparta Praha	6	3	3	0	10 - 5	12
Asteras Tripolis	6	1	1	4	4 - 12	4
APOEL Nicosia	6	1	0	5	3 - 12	3

GROUP L

Athletic Bilbao	6	4	1	1	16 - 8	13
FC Augsburg	6	3	0	3	12 - 11	9
Partizan	6	3	0	3	10 - 14	9
AZ Alkmaar	6	1	1	4	8 - 13	4

The top 2 teams in each group advanced to the knockout phase of the competition.

GROUP STAGE – GROUP A

17.09.15   Amsterdam ArenA, Amsterdam: AFC Ajax – Celtic FC 2-2 (1-2)
AFC Ajax: Jasper Cillessen, Joël Veltman, Jaïro Riedewald, Kenny Tete, Mitchell Dijks, Daley
Sinkgraven (62' Thulani Serero), Davy Klaassen, Nemanja Gudelj, Viktor Fischer (75' Lasse
Schöne), Amin Younes (62' Arkadiusz Milik), Anwar El Ghazi. Coach: Frank de Boer.
Celtic FC: Craig Gordon, Emilio Izaguirre, Jozo Simunovic, Dedryck Boyata, Mikael Lustig
(69' Efe Ambrose), Nir Bitton, Scott Brown, Kris Commons (83' Saidy Janko), Stefan
Johansen, James Forrest (75' Tyler Blackett), Leigh Griffiths. Coach: Ronny Deila.
Goals: 8' Nir Bitton 0-1, 25' Viktor Fischer 1-1, 42' Mikael Lustig 1-2, 84' Lasse Schöne 2-2.
Referee: Luca Banti (ITA)   Attendance: 47,455.
Sent off: 74' Emilio Izaguirre.

17.09.15   Sükrü Saracoglu, Istanbul: Fenerbahçe – Molde FK 1-3 (1-1)
Fenerbahçe: Fabiano, Sener Özbayrakli, Bruno Alves, Michal Kadlec, Caner Erkin, Mehmet
Topal (58' Fernandão), Ozan Tufan, Raúl Meireles (69' Uygar Zeybek), Robin van Persie (69'
Alper Potuk), Nani, Volkan Sen. Coach: Vítor Pereira.
Molde FK: Ethan Horvath, Ruben Gabrielsen, Martin Linnes, Knut Rindarøy, Vegard Forren,
Daniel Hestad, Harmeet Singh, Mattias Mostrøm (87' Joona Toivio), Eirik Hestad (79' Etzaz
Hussain), Tommy Høiland (66' Ola Kamara), Mohamed Elyounoussi. Coach: Erling Moe.
Goals: 36' Tommy Høiland 0-1 (p), 42' Nani 1-1, 53' Mohamed Elyounoussi 1-2,
65' Martin Linnes 1-3.
Referee: Benoît Bastien (FRA)   Attendance: 35,500.
Sent off: 84' Mohamed Elyounoussi.

01.10.15   Celtic Park, Glasgow: Celtic FC – Fenerbahçe 2-2 (2-1)
Celtic FC: Craig Gordon, Efe Ambrose, Dedryck Boyata, Mikael Lustig, Kieran Tierney (82')
Tom Rogic, Nir Bitton, Scott Brown, Kris Commons, Stefan Johansen (82' Tyler Blackett),
James Forrest (90' Stuart Armstrong), Leigh Griffiths. Coach: Ronny Deila.
Fenerbahçe: Fabiano, Hasan-Ali Kaldirim, Simon Kjær, Sener Özbayrakli, Bruno Alves,
Mehmet Topal, Ozan Tufan (46' Diego), Raúl Meireles (78' Abdoulaye Ba), Robin van Persie,
Nani, Volkan Sen (40' Fernandão). Coach: Vítor Pereira.
Goals: 28' Leigh Griffiths 1-0, 32' Kris Commons 2-0, 43', 48' Fernandão 2-1, 2-2.
Referee: Kenn Hansen (DEN)   Attendance: 41,330.

01.10.15   Aker Stadion, Molde: Molde FK – AFC Ajax 1-1 (1-1)
Molde FK: Ethan Horvath, Ruben Gabrielsen, Martin Linnes (61' Joona Toivio), Knut
Rindarøy, Vegard Forren, Daniel Hestad, Harmeet Singh, Mattias Mostrøm, Etzaz Hussain,
Eirik Hestad (59' Sander Svendsen), Tommy Høiland (80' Ola Kamara). Coach: Erling Moe.
AFC Ajax: Jasper Cillessen, Joël Veltman, Jaïro Riedewald, Kenny Tete, Mitchell Dijks,
Riechedly Bazoer (88' Thulani Serero), Davy Klaassen, Nemanja Gudelj, Viktor Fischer,
Arkadiusz Milik (81' Amin Younes), Anwar El Ghazi. Coach: Frank de Boer.
Goals: 7' Eirik Hestad 1-0, 18' Viktor Fischer 1-1.
Referee: Pawel Raczkowski (POL)   Attendance: 7,890.

75

22.10.15   Sükrü Saracoglu, Istanbul: Fenerbahçe – AFC Ajax 1-0 (0-0)
Fenerbahçe: Fabiano, Simon Kjær, Abdoulaye Ba, Gökhan Gönül, Caner Erkin, Mehmet
Topal, Souza, Diego (73' Ozan Tufan), Lazar Markovic (84' Alper Potuk), Robin van Persie
(72' Fernandão), Nani. Coach: Vítor Pereira.
AFC Ajax: Jasper Cillessen, Ricardo van Rhijn (63' Kenny Tete), Joël Veltman, Jaïro
Riedewald, Mitchell Dijks, Riechedly Bazoer, Davy Klaassen, Nemanja Gudelj, Viktor Fischer
(63' Amin Younes), Lasse Schöne, Anwar El Ghazi (77' Daley Sinkgraven).
Coach: Frank de Boer.
Goal: 89' Fernandão 1-0.
Referee: David Fernández Borbalán (ESP)   Attendance: 35,292.

22.10.15   Aker Stadion, Molde: Molde FK – Celtic FC 3-1 (2-0)
Molde FK: Ethan Horvath, Martin Linnes, Knut Rindarøy (52' Per-Egil Flo), Vegard Forren,
Joona Toivio, Daniel Hestad, Harmeet Singh, Mattias Mostrøm, Etzaz Hussain, Ola Kamara
(74' Eirik Hestad), Mohamed Elyounoussi (84' Mushaga Bakenga).
Coach: Ole Gunnar Solskjær.
Celtic FC: Craig Gordon, Emilio Izaguirre, Efe Ambrose, Dedryck Boyata, Mikael Lustig, Nir
Bitton, Scott Brown, Stuart Armstrong (74' Gary Mackay-Steven), Kris Commons (76' Nadir
Çiftçi), Stefan Johansen, Leigh Griffiths. Coach: Ronny Deila.
Goals: 11' Ola Kamara 1-0, 18' Vegard Forren 2-0, 55' Kris Commons 2-1,
56' Mohamed Elyounoussi 3-1.
Referee: Vladislav Bezborodov (RUS)   Attendance: 9,166.

05.11.15   Amsterdam ArenA, Amsterdam: AFC Ajax – Fenerbahçe 0-0
AFC Ajax: Jasper Cillessen, Joël Veltman, Jaïro Riedewald, Kenny Tete, Nick Viergever,
Riechedly Bazoer, Davy Klaassen, Nemanja Gudelj (76' Thulani Serero), Viktor Fischer (52'
Amin Younes), Arkadiusz Milik, Anwar El Ghazi (33' Lasse Schöne). Coach: Frank de Boer.
Fenerbahçe: Volkan Demirel, Hasan-Ali Kaldirim, Simon Kjær, Bruno Alves, Gökhan Gönül,
Mehmet Topal, Souza, Diego (74' Ozan Tufan), Alper Potuk, Robin van Persie (80' Volkan
Sen), Nani (63' Fernandão). Coach: Vítor Pereira.
Referee: Liran Liany (ISR)   Attendance: 48,990.

05.11.15   Celtic Park, Glasgow: Celtic FC – Molde FK 1-2 (1-2)
Celtic FC: Craig Gordon, Jozo Simunovic (9' Tyler Blackett / 69' Nadir Çiftçi), Dedryck
Boyata, Mikael Lustig, Kieran Tierney, Nir Bitton, Stuart Armstrong, Kris Commons (46'
James Forrest), Tom Rogic, Stefan Johansen, Leigh Griffiths. Coach: Ronny Deila.
Molde FK: Ethan Horvath, Martin Linnes, Knut Rindarøy, Vegard Forren, Joona Toivio,
Daniel Hestad, Harmeet Singh, Mattias Mostrøm (62' Eirik Hestad), Etzaz Hussain (90' Ruben
Gabrielsen), Tommy Høiland (46' Ola Kamara), Mohamed Elyounoussi.
Coach: Ole Gunnar Solskjær.
Goals: 21' Mohamed Elyounoussi 0-1, 26' Kris Commons 1-1, 37' Daniel Hestad 1-2.
Referee: Slavko Vincic (SVN)   Attendance: 37,071.
Sent off: 77' Nir Bitton.

26.11.15   Celtic Park, Glasgow: Celtic FC – AFC Ajax 1-2 (1-1)
Celtic FC: Craig Gordon, Jozo Simunovic, Dedryck Boyata, Mikael Lustig, Kieran Tierney
(78' Emilio Izaguirre), Stuart Armstrong, Gary Mackay-Steven (72' Scott Allan), Tom Rogic
(66' Charlie Mulgrew), Callum McGregor, James Forrest, Leigh Griffiths.
Coach: Ronny Deila.
AFC Ajax: Jasper Cillessen, Mike van der Hoorn (80' Yaya Sanogo), Jaïro Riedewald, Kenny
Tete, Mitchell Dijks, Davy Klaassen, Nemanja Gudelj, Viktor Fischer (69' Vaclav Cerny),
Arkadiusz Milik, Amin Younes, Lasse Schöne (72' Donny van de Beek).
Coach: Frank de Boer.
Goals: 4' Callum McGregor 1-0, 22' Arkadiusz Milik 1-1, 88' Vaclav Cerny 1-2.
Referee: Felix Zwayer (GER)   Attendance: 44,118.

26.11.15   Aker Stadion, Molde: Molde FK – Fenerbahçe 0-2 (0-0)
Molde FK: Ethan Horvath, Martin Linnes, Knut Rindarøy, Vegard Forren, Joona Toivio,
Daniel Hestad (76' Eirik Hestad), Harmeet Singh, Etzaz Hussain, Fredrik Gulbrandsen (46'
Ola Kamara), Mohamed Elyounoussi, Sander Svendsen (86' Ruben Gabrielsen).
Coach: Ole Gunnar Solskjær.
Fenerbahçe: Fabiano, Hasan-Ali Kaldirim (74' Michal Kadlec), Simon Kjær, Bruno Alves,
Gökhan Gönül, Souza, Ozan Tufan, Diego, Alper Potuk, Fernandão (86' Robin van Persie),
Nani (82' Volkan Sen). Coach: Vítor Pereira.
Goals: 68' Fernandão 0-1, 84' Ozan Tufan 0-2.
Referee: Miroslav Zelinka (CZE)   Attendance: 8,235.
Sent off: 90' Knut Rindarøy.

10.12.15   Sükrü Saracoglu, Istanbul: Fenerbahçe – Celtic FC 1-1 (1-0)
Fenerbahçe: Fabiano, Hasan-Ali Kaldirim, Bruno Alves, Abdoulaye Ba, Gökhan Gönül,
Mehmet Topal, Souza, Diego, Alper Potuk, Lazar Markovic (83' Ozan Tufan), Fernandão (86'
Caner Erkin). Coach: Vítor Pereira.
Celtic FC: Craig Gordon, Jozo Simunovic, Dedryck Boyata, Mikael Lustig, Kieran Tierney,
Nir Bitton, Stuart Armstrong (63' James Forrest), Stefan Johansen (74' Tom Rogic), Callum
McGregor, Nadir Çiftçi, Scott Allan (74' Kris Commons). Coach: Ronny Deila.
Goals: 39' Lazar Markovic 1-0, 75' Kris Commons 1-1.
Referee: Serge Gumienny (BEL)   Attendance: 35,372.
Sent off: 67' Diego.

10.12.15   Amsterdam ArenA, Amsterdam: AFC Ajax – Molde FK 1-1 (1-1)
AFC Ajax: Jasper Cillessen, Ricardo van Rhijn, Joël Veltman, Jaïro Riedewald, Mitchell Dijks,
Davy Klaassen, Nemanja Gudelj, Donny van de Beek (64' Riechedly Bazoer), Viktor Fischer
(78' Lasse Schöne), Arkadiusz Milik, Amin Younes (62' Anwar El Ghazi).
Coach: Frank de Boer.
Molde FK: Ethan Horvath, Ruben Gabrielsen, Martin Linnes, Per-Egil Flo, Vegard Forren,
Joona Toivio (19' Daniel Hestad), Harmeet Singh, Mattias Mostrøm (76' Eirik Hestad), Etzaz
Hussain, Ola Kamara (52' Fredrik Gulbrandsen), Mohamed Elyounoussi.
Coach: Ole Gunnar Solskjær.
Goals: 14' Donny van de Beek 1-0, 29' Harmeet Singh 1-1.
Referee: Evgen Aranovskiy (UKR)   Attendance: 48,401.
Sent off: 90' Nemanja Gudelj.

77

GROUP B

17.09.15   Matmut Atlantique, Bordeaux: Girondins Bordeaux – Liverpool FC 1-1 (0-0)
Girondins Bordeaux: Cédric Carrasso, Milan Gajic (86' Frédéric Guilbert), Pablo, Nicolas
Pallois, Maxime Poundje, Henri Saivet (76' André Biyogo Poko), Clément Chantôme, Nicolas
Maurice-Belay, Wahbi Khazri (69' Jussiê), Diego Rolán, Enzo Crivelli. Coach: Willy Sagnol.
Liverpool FC: Simon Mignolet, Kolo Touré (27' Pedro Chirivella), Joe Gomez, Mamadou
Sakho, Alberto Moreno, Coutinho, Adam Lallana, Emre Can, Jordan Rossiter (80' Cameron
Brannagan), Divock Origi (73' Danny Ings), Jordon Ibe. Coach: Brendan Rodgers.
Goals: 65' Adam Lallana 0-1, 81' Jussiê 1-1.
Referee: Alberto Undiano Mallenco (ESP)   Attendance: 35,328.

17.09.15   Tourbillon, Sion: FC Sion – Rubin Kazan 2-1 (1-0)
FC Sion: Andris Vanins, Reto Ziegler, Léo Lacroix, Pa Modou Jagne, Elsad Zverotic, Xavier
Kouassi, Edimilson Fernandes, Vero Salatic, Carlitos, Moussa Konaté (89' Birama N'Doye),
Ebenezer Assifuah (68' Geoffrey Mujangi Bia). Coach: Didier Tholot.
Rubin Kazan: Sergey Ryzhikov, Oleg Kuzmin, Elmir Nabiullin, Solomon Kverkvelia, Ruslan
Kambolov, Carlos Eduardo (90' Vladimir Dyadyun), Diniyar Bilyaletdinov (46' Magomed
Ozdoev), Gökdeniz Karadeniz (86' Marko Devic), Blagoy Georgiev, Igor Portnyagin, Maksim
Kanunnikov. Coach: Valeriy Chaly.
Goals: 11' Moussa Konaté 1-0, 65' Maksim Kanunnikov 1-1, 82' Moussa Konaté 2-1.
Referee: Andreas Ekberg (SWE)   Attendance: 7,000.

01.10.15   Tsentralniy, Kazan: Rubin Kazan – Girondins Bordeaux 0-0
Rubin Kazan: Sergey Ryzhikov, Oleg Kuzmin, Elmir Nabiullin, Solomon Kverkvelia, Ruslan
Kambolov, Carlos Eduardo, Sergey Kislyak, Magomed Ozdoev, Igor Portnyagin (74' Vladimir
Dyadyun), Marko Devic (46' Diniyar Bilyaletdinov), Maksim Kanunnikov.
Coach: Valeriy Chaly.
Girondins Bordeaux: Cédric Carrasso, Diego Contento, Nicolas Pallois, Cédric Yamberé (89'
Lamine Sané), Frédéric Guilbert, Henri Saivet, Clément Chantôme, André Biyogo Poko (58'
Wahbi Khazri), Nicolas Maurice-Belay, Jussiê (58' Jaroslav Plasil), Enzo Crivelli.
Coach: Willy Sagnol.
Referee: Gediminas Mazeika (LTU)   Attendance: 17,642.
Sent off: 80' Sergey Kislyak.

01.10.15   Anfield, Liverpool: Liverpool FC – FC Sion 1-1 (1-1)
Liverpool FC: Simon Mignolet, Nathaniel Clyne (46' Alberto Moreno), Kolo Touré (76'
Mamadou Sakho), Joe Gomez, Adam Lallana, Emre Can, Joe Allen, Jordan Rossiter, Divock
Origi, Danny Ings (61' Coutinho), Jordon Ibe. Coach: Brendan Rodgers.
FC Sion: Andris Vanins, Reto Ziegler, Léo Lacroix, Pa Modou Jagne, Elsad Zverotic, Xavier
Kouassi, Edimilson Fernandes, Vero Salatic, Carlitos, Moussa Konaté (89' Geoffrey Mujangi
Bia), Ebenezer Assifuah (86' Birama N'Doye). Coach: Didier Tholot.
Goals: 4' Adam Lallana 1-0, 18' Ebenezer Assifuah 1-1.
Referee: Slavko Vincic (SVN)   Attendance: 37,252.

01.10.15   Anfield, Liverpool: Liverpool FC – Rubin Kazan 1-1 (1-1)
Liverpool FC: Simon Mignolet, Nathaniel Clyne, Mamadou Sakho, Alberto Moreno, Martin
Skrtel, James Milner, Coutinho (63' Christian Benteke), Adam Lallana, Emre Can, Joe Allen
(46' Lucas Leiva), Divock Origi (74' Roberto Firmino). Coach: Jürgen Klopp.
Rubin Kazan: Sergey Ryzhikov, Oleg Kuzmin, Elmir Nabiullin, Solomon Kverkvelia, Ruslan
Kambolov, Carlos Eduardo (64' Igor Portnyagin), Magomed Ozdoev, Gökdeniz Karadeniz
(81' Vladimir Dyadyun), Blagoy Georgiev, Marko Devic (46' Guillermo Cotugno), Maksim
Kanunnikov. Coach: Valeriy Chaly.
Goals: 15' Marko Devic 0-1, 37' Emre Can 1-1.
Referee: Robert Schörgenhofer (AUT)   Attendance: 42,951.
Sent off: 36' Oleg Kuzmin.

22.10.15   Matmut Atlantique, Bordeaux: Girondins Bordeaux – FC Sion 0-1 (0-1)
Girondins Bordeaux: Cédric Carrasso, Nicolas Pallois, Lamine Sané, Maxime Poundje, Henri
Saivet, Clément Chantôme, André Biyogo Poko, Jaroslav Plasil (64' Enzo Crivelli), Diego
Rolán, Thomas Touré (77' Adam Ounas), Cheick Diabaté (65' Wahbi Khazri).
Coach: Willy Sagnol.
FC Sion: Andris Vanins, Reto Ziegler, Léo Lacroix, Pa Modou Jagne, Elsad Zverotic,
Edimilson Fernandes, Vero Salatic, Carlitos, Birama N'Doye, Moussa Konaté, Ebenezer
Assifuah (77' Daniel Follonier). Coach: Didier Tholot.
Goal: 21' Léo Lacroix 0-1.
Referee: Aleksandar Stavrev (MKD)   Attendance: 18,318.
Sent off: 86' Wahbi Khazri.

05.11.15   Kazan Arena, Kazan: Rubin Kazan – Liverpool FC 0-1 (0-0)
Rubin Kazan: Sergey Ryzhikov, Elmir Nabiullin, Solomon Kverkvelia, Guillermo Cotugno
(81' Vitali Ustinov), Ruslan Kambolov, Carlos Eduardo (46' Magomed Ozdoev), Sergey
Kislyak (70' Ilzat Akhmetov), Gökdeniz Karadeniz, Blagoy Georgiev, Marko Devic, Maksim
Kanunnikov. Coach: Valeriy Chaly.
Liverpool FC: Simon Mignolet, Nathaniel Clyne, Dejan Lovren, Mamadou Sakho, Alberto
Moreno, James Milner (61' Adam Lallana), Roberto Firmino (81' Lucas Leiva), Emre Can
(90' Martin Skrtel), Joe Allen, Christian Benteke, Jordon Ibe. Coach: Jürgen Klopp.
Goal: 52' Jordon Ibe 0-1.
Referee: Kevin Blom (HOL)   Attendance: 41,585.

05.11.15   Tourbillon, Sion: FC Sion – Girondins Bordeaux 1-1 (0-0)
FC Sion: Andris Vanins, Reto Ziegler, Léo Lacroix, Vincent Rüfli, Elsad Zverotic, Edimilson
Fernandes, Vero Salatic, Carlitos (73' Martin Zeman), Birama N'Doye (87' Daniel Follonier),
Moussa Konaté, Ebenezer Assifuah (87' Gregory Karlen). Coach: Didier Tholot.
Girondins Bordeaux: Cédric Carrasso, Diego Contento, Nicolas Pallois, Lamine Sané, Cédric
Yamberé, Clément Chantôme, André Biyogo Poko, Jaroslav Plasil, Thomas Touré (90+1'
Henri Saivet), Cheick Diabaté (80' Enzo Crivelli), Jussiê (65' Nicolas Maurice-Belay).
Coach: Willy Sagnol.
Goals: 67' Thomas Touré 0-1, 90+4' Clément Chantôme 1-1 (og).
Referee: Ivan Kruzliak (SVK)   Attendance: 9,000.

26.11.15   Tsentralniy, Kazan: Rubin Kazan – FC Sion 2-0 (0-0)
Rubin Kazan: Sergey Ryzhikov, Elmir Nabiullin, Solomon Kverkvelia, Vitali Ustinov, Ruslan
Kambolov, Carlos Eduardo (70' Diniyar Bilyaletdinov), Sergey Kislyak (46' Vladimir
Dyadyun), Magomed Ozdoev, Blagoy Georgiev, Marko Devic (90+2' Ilzat Akhmetov),
Maksim Kanunnikov. Coach: Valeriy Chaly.
FC Sion: Andris Vanins, Reto Ziegler, Léo Lacroix, Vincent Rüfli, Elsad Zverotic, Edimilson
Fernandes, Vero Salatic (88' Geoffrey Mujangi Bia), Carlitos, Birama N'Doye, Moussa
Konaté (81' Gregory Karlen), Ebenezer Assifuah (80' Daniel Follonier). Coach: Didier Tholot.
Goals: 72' Blagoy Georgiev 1-0, 90' Marko Devic 2-0.
Referee: Halis Özkahya (TUR)   Attendance: 15,116.
Sent off: 34' Birama N'Doye.

26.11.15   Anfield, Liverpool: Liverpool FC – Girondins Bordeaux 2-1 (2-1)
Liverpool FC: Simon Mignolet, Nathaniel Clyne, Kolo Touré, Dejan Lovren, Alberto Moreno,
James Milner, Roberto Firmino (74' Adam Lallana), Lucas Leiva, Joe Allen (67' Emre Can),
Christian Benteke, Jordon Ibe (90+2' Divock Origi). Coach: Jürgen Klopp.
Girondins Bordeaux: Cédric Carrasso, Diego Contento, Lamine Sané, Cédric Yamberé, Henri
Saivet, Clément Chantôme, André Biyogo Poko, Jaroslav Plasil (84' Adam Ounas), Diego
Rolán, Jussiê (76' Nicolas Maurice-Belay), Enzo Crivelli (67' Cheick Diabaté).
Coach: Willy Sagnol.
Goals: 33' Henri Saivet 0-1, 38' James Milner 1-1 (p), 45+1' Christian Benteke 2-1.
Referee: Alon Yefet (ISR)   Attendance: 42,525.

10.12.15   Matmut Atlantique, Bordeaux: Girondins Bordeaux – Rubin Kazan 2-2 (0-1)
Girondins Bordeaux: Jérôme Prior, Cédric Yamberé, Frédéric Guilbert, Maxime Poundje,
Abdou Traoré (64' Kévin Soni), André Biyogo Poko, Valentin Vada, Robin Maulun, Diego
Rolán (83' Enzo Crivelli), Isaac Thelin, Gaëtan Laborde (72' Wahbi Khazri).
Coach: Willy Sagnol.
Rubin Kazan: Sergey Ryzhikov, Oleg Kuzmin (75' Vitali Ustinov), Elmir Nabiullin, Solomon
Kverkvelia, Ruslan Kambolov, Carlos Eduardo, Sergey Kislyak (46' Diniyar Bilyaletdinov /
77' Vladimir Dyadyun), Magomed Ozdoev, Blagoy Georgiev, Marko Devic, Maksim
Kanunnikov. Coach: Valeriy Chaly.
Goals: 31' Maksim Kanunnikov 0-1, 58' Gaëtan Laborde 1-1, 63' Diego Rolán 2-1,
76' Vitali Ustinov 2-2.
Referee: John Beaton (SCO)   Attendance: 13,640.
Sent off: 86' Frédéric Guilbert.

10.12.15   Tourbillon, Sion: FC Sion – Liverpool FC 0-0
FC Sion: Andris Vanins, Reto Ziegler, Léo Lacroix, Pa Modou Jagne, Vincent Rüfli (90+4'
Adão), Elsad Zverotic, Xavier Kouassi, Edimilson Fernandes, Vero Salatic, Carlitos, Ebenezer
Assifuah (73' Geoffrey Mujangi Bia). Coach: Didier Tholot.
Liverpool FC: Simon Mignolet, Nathaniel Clyne, Kolo Touré, Dejan Lovren, Brad Smith,
James Milner (61' Coutinho), Roberto Firmino (89' Cameron Brannagan), Jordan Henderson
(77' Jordan Rossiter), Adam Lallana, Emre Can, Divock Origi. Coach: Jürgen Klopp.
Referee: Michail Koukoulakis (GRE)   Attendance: 10,000.

GROUP C

17.09.15 Signal Iduna Park, Dortmund: Borussia Dortmund – FK Krasnodar 2-1 (1-1).
Borussia Dortmund: Roman Weidenfeller, Joo-ho Park, Mats Hummels, Sokratis
Papastathopoulos, Matthias Ginter, Marcel Schmelzer (46' Shinji Kagawa), Ilkay Gündogan,
Adnan Januzaj, Henrikh Mkhitaryan, Gonzalo Castro (61' Julian Weigl), Pierre-Emerick
Aubameyang (72' Adrián Ramos). Coach: Thomas Tuchel.
FK Krasnodar: Andrey Dikan, Stefan Strandberg, Artur Jedrzejczyk, Andreas Granqvist,
Ragnar Sigurdsson, Pavel Mamaev (81' Ari), Odil Akhmedov, Mauricio Pereyra (60' Ricardo
Laborde), Charles Kaboré (70' Yuri Gazinskiy), Sergey Petrov, Fedor Smolov.
Coach: Oleg Kononov.
Goals: 12' Pavel Mamaev 0-1, 45+1' Matthias Ginter 1-1, 90+2' Joo-ho Park 2-1.
Referee: Liran Liany (ISR)   Attendance: 55,200.

17.09.15 Bakcell Arena, Baku: Gabala FK – PAOK Saloniki 0-0
Gabala FK: Dmitro Bezotosniy, Vojislav Stankovic, Vitaliy Vernydub, Ricardinho, Oleksiy
Gay, Arif Dashdemirov, Derlis Meza Colli, Ermin Zec (46' Facundo Pereyra), Sergei Zenjov,
Dodô (83' Samir Zargarov), Oleksiy Antonov. Coach: Roman Grygorchuk.
PAOK Saloniki: Robin Olsen, Miguel Vítor, Ricardo Costa, Giorgos Tzavellas, Alexandros
Tziolis, Garry Rodrigues, Erik Sabo (84' Jairo), Stelios Kitsiou (76' Eyal Golasa), Dimitrios
Pelkas (76'), Róbert Mak, Stefanos Athanasiadis (59' Dimitar Berbatov). Coach: Igor Tudor.
Referee: Javier Estrada Fernández (ESP)   Attendance: 4,800.

01.10.15 Toumba, Saloniki: PAOK Saloniki – Borussia Dortmund 1-1 (1-0)
PAOK Saloniki: Robin Olsen, Miguel Vítor, Ricardo Costa, Dimitrios Konstantinidis, Giorgos
Tzavellas, Alexandros Tziolis, Garry Rodrigues, Ergis Kaçe (85' Charilaos Charisis), Erik
Sabo, Dimitar Berbatov (89' Dimitrios Pelkas), Róbert Mak (73' Jairo). Coach: Igor Tudor.
Borussia Dortmund: Roman Weidenfeller, Joo-ho Park, Neven Subotic, Lukasz Piszczek, Sven
Bender, Jonas Hofmann, Adnan Januzaj (84' Moritz Leitner), Henrikh Mkhitaryan (65' Adrián
Ramos), Gonzalo Castro, Julian Weigl (65' Marcel Schmelzer), Marco Reus.
Coach: Thomas Tuchel.
Goals: 34' Róbert Mak 1-0, 72' Gonzalo Castro 1-1.
Referee: Anthony Taylor (ENG)   Attendance: 25,663.

01.10.15 Kuban, Krasnodar: FK Krasnodar – Gabala FK 2-1 (1-0)
FK Krasnodar: Andrey Sinitsyn, Stefan Strandberg, Artur Jedrzejczyk, Andreas Granqvist,
Vitaliy Kaleshin, Pavel Mamaev (66' Ricardo Laborde), Yuri Gazinskiy (76' Joãozinho), Odil
Akhmedov, Wanderson, Charles Kaboré, Ari (60' Fedor Smolov). Coach: Oleg Kononov.
Gabala FK: Dmitro Bezotosniy, Vojislav Stankovic, Vitaliy Vernydub, Ricardinho, Oleksiy
Gay, Arif Dashdemirov, Derlis Meza Colli (46' Räsad Sadiqov / 90+1' Samir Zargarov),
Sergei Zenjov, Dodô, Facundo Pereyra, Oleksiy Antonov (74' Ermin Zec).
Coach: Roman Grygorchuk.
Goals: 8' Wanderson 1-0, 51' Dodô 1-1, 84' Fedor Smolov 2-1.
Referee: Marcin Borski (POL)   Attendance: 8,901.

22.10.15   Bakcell Arena, Baku: Gabala FK – Borussia Dortmund 1-3 (0-2)
Gabala FK: Dmitro Bezotosniy, Vojislav Stankovic, Vitaliy Vernydub, Ricardinho, Oleksiy Gay, Arif Dashdemirov, Derlis Meza Colli (83' Räsad Sadiqov), Sergei Zenjov (79' Ermin Zec), Dodô, Facundo Pereyra (60' Samir Zargarov), Oleksiy Antonov.
Coach: Roman Grygorchuk.
Borussia Dortmund: Roman Weidenfeller, Joo-ho Park (69' Marcel Schmelzer), Mats Hummels (63' Lukasz Piszczek), Sokratis Papastathopoulos, Matthias Ginter, Jonas Hofmann, Ilkay Gündogan (63' Sven Bender), Shinji Kagawa, Julian Weigl, Marco Reus, Pierre-Emerick Aubameyang. Coach: Thomas Tuchel.
Goals: 31', 38', 72' Pierre-Emerick Aubameyang 0-1, 0-2, 0-3, 90+3' Dodô 1-3.
Referee: Ivan Bebek (CRO)   Attendance: 10,500.

22.10.15   Toumba, Saloniki: PAOK Saloniki – FK Krasnodar 0-0
PAOK Saloniki: Panagiotis Glykos, Giannis Skondras, Stelios Malezas, Miguel Vítor (46' Marin Leovac), Ricardo Costa, Garry Rodrigues, Ergis Kaçe, Erik Sabo, Dimitrios Pelkas (72' Róbert Mak), Jairo, Stefanos Athanasiadis (57' Dimitar Berbatov). Coach: Igor Tudor.
FK Krasnodar: Andrey Dikan, Stefan Strandberg, Artur Jedrzejczyk, Andreas Granqvist, Vitaliy Kaleshin, Dmitriy Torbinskiy (82' Yuri Gazinskiy), Odil Akhmedov (65' Pavel Mamaev), Ricardo Laborde, Joãozinho, Charles Kaboré, Fedor Smolov (63' Ari).
Coach: Oleg Kononov.
Referee: Andreas Ekberg (SWE)   Attendance: 9,325.
Sent off: 88' Artur Jedrzejczyk, 89' Jairo.

05.11.15   Kuban, Krasnodar: FK Krasnodar – PAOK Saloniki 2-1 (1-0)
FK Krasnodar: Andrey Dikan, Andreas Granqvist, Vitaliy Kaleshin (69' Pavel Mamaev), Ragnar Sigurdsson, Dmitriy Torbinskiy, Odil Akhmedov (77' Yuri Gazinskiy), Ricardo Laborde (62' Fedor Smolov), Joãozinho, Charles Kaboré, Sergey Petrov, Ari.
Coach: Oleg Kononov.
PAOK Saloniki: Panagiotis Glykos, Giannis Skondras, Stelios Malezas, Ricardo Costa, Giorgos Tzavellas (81' Stelios Kitsiou), Alexandros Tziolis, Eyal Golasa (68' Stefanos Athanasiadis), Charilaos Charisis, Garry Rodrigues, Erik Sabo (58' Dimitrios Pelkas), Róbert Mak. Coach: Igor Tudor.
Goals: 33' Ari 1-0, 67' Joãozinho 2-0 (p), 90+1' Róbert Mak 2-1.
Referee: Arnold Hunter (NIR)   Attendance: 15,550.

05.11.15   Signal Iduna Park, Dortmund: Borussia Dortmund – Gabala FK 4-0 (2-0)
Borussia Dortmund: Roman Weidenfeller, Mats Hummels, Lukasz Piszczek, Matthias Ginter (62' Ilkay Gündogan), Marcel Schmelzer, Sven Bender, Henrikh Mkhitaryan, Gonzalo Castro, Julian Weigl, Marco Reus (46' Adnan Januzaj), Pierre-Emerick Aubameyang (68' Adrián Ramos). Coach: Thomas Tuchel.
Gabala FK: Dawid Pietrzkiewicz, Vojislav Stankovic, Vitaliy Vernydub, Ricardinho, Rafael Santos, Oleksiy Gay, Arif Dashdemirov, Derlis Meza Colli (76' Elvin Jamalov), Sergei Zenjov (86' Samir Zargarov), Dodô, Oleksiy Antonov (68' Facundo Pereyra).
Coach: Roman Grygorchuk.
Goals: 28' Marco Reus 1-0, 45' Pierre-Emerick Aubameyang 2-0, 67' Sergei Zenjov 3-0 (og), 70' Henrikh Mkhitaryan 4-0.
Referee: Sebastien Delferière (BEL)   Attendance: 57,009.

26.11.15   Kuban, Krasnodar: FK Krasnodar – Borussia Dortmund 1-0 (1-0)
FK Krasnodar: Andrey Dikan, Artur Jedrzejczyk, Andreas Granqvist, Vitaliy Kaleshin, Ragnar Sigurdsson, Pavel Mamaev (84' Ricardo Laborde), Odil Akhmedov (85' Dmitriy Torbinskiy), Mauricio Pereyra (74' Yuri Gazinskiy), Charles Kaboré, Ari, Fedor Smolov.
Coach: Oleg Kononov.
Borussia Dortmund: Roman Weidenfeller, Mats Hummels, Lukasz Piszczek (80' Matthias Ginter), Marcel Schmelzer, Sven Bender, Jonas Hofmann (68' Adnan Januzaj), Ilkay Gündogan, Henrikh Mkhitaryan, Gonzalo Castro, Julian Weigl (86' Moritz Leitner), Adrián Ramos. Coach: Thomas Tuchel.
Goal: 2' Pavel Mamaev 1-0 (p).
Referee: Serdar Gözübüyük (HOL)   Attendance: 30,150.

26.11.15   Toumba, Saloniki: PAOK Saloniki – Gabala FK 0-0
PAOK Saloniki: Panagiotis Glykos, Giannis Skondras, Stelios Malezas, Giorgos Tzavellas, Alexandros Tziolis, Garry Rodrigues, Ergis Kaçe, Stelios Kitsiou (78' Stefanos Athanasiadis), Dimitrios Pelkas (46' Erik Sabo), Dimitar Berbatov (71' Ioannis Mystakidis), Róbert Mak.
Coach: Igor Tudor.
Gabala FK: Dmitro Bezotosniy, Vojislav Stankovic, Ricardinho, Rafael Santos, Räsad Sadiqov (87' Elvin Jamalov), Oleksiy Gay, Arif Dashdemirov, Samir Zargarov (83' Magomed Mirzabekov), Ermin Zec, Sergei Zenjov (77' Vagif Javadov), Oleksiy Antonov.
Coach: Roman Grygorchuk.
Referee: Jakob Kehlet (DEN)   Attendance: 6,131.

10.12.15   Signal Iduna Park, Dortmund: Borussia Dortmund – PAOK Saloniki 0-1 (0-1)
Borussia Dortmund: Roman Weidenfeller, Joo-ho Park, Neven Subotic, Mats Hummels, Matthias Ginter, Pascal Stenzel, Sven Bender (46' Julian Weigl), Adnan Januzaj, Shinji Kagawa (66' Pierre-Emerick Aubameyang), Marco Reus (46' Henrikh Mkhitaryan), Adrián Ramos. Coach: Thomas Tuchel.
PAOK Saloniki: Panagiotis Glykos, Giannis Skondras, Stelios Malezas, Dimitrios Konstantinidis, Giorgos Tzavellas, Alexandros Tziolis, Gojko Cimirot, Ergis Kaçe, Dimitar Berbatov (71' Erik Sabo), Róbert Mak (66' Marin Leovac), Ioannis Mystakidis (77' Garry Rodrigues). Coach: Igor Tudor.
Goal: 33' Róbert Mak 0-1.
Referee: Mattias Gestranius (FIN)   Attendance: 55,200.

10.12.15   Bakcell Arena, Baku: Gabala FK – FK Krasnodar 0-3 (0-2).
Gabala FK: Andriy Popovich, Vojislav Stankovic, Ricardinho, Rafael Santos, Oleksiy Gay (76' Räsad Sadiqov), Arif Dashdemirov, Derlis Meza Colli, Sergei Zenjov (57' Samir Zargarov), Dodô, Facundo Pereyra (61' Ermin Zec), Oleksiy Antonov.
Coach: Roman Grygorchuk.
FK Krasnodar: Andrey Dikan, Andreas Granqvist, Vitaliy Kaleshin (65' Ricardo Laborde), Ragnar Sigurdsson, Pavel Mamaev, Odil Akhmedov, Wanderson (76' Fedor Smolov), Joãozinho, Mauricio Pereyra (69' Yuri Gazinskiy), Charles Kaboré, Sergey Petrov.
Coach: Oleg Kononov.
Goals: 26' Ragnar Sigurdsson 0-1, 41' Mauricio Pereyra 0-2, 75' Wanderson 0-3.
Referee: István Nagy (HUN)   Attendance: 3,000.

GROUP D

17.09.15 San Paolo, Napoli: SSC Napoli – Club Brugge KV 5-0 (3-0)
SSC Napoli: Pepe Reina, Elseid Hysaj, Kalidou Koulibaly, Faouzi Ghoulam, Raúl Albiol,
Jorginho, Marek Hamsík (62' Allan), David López, José Callejón, Gonzalo Higuaín (71'
Manolo Gabbiadini), Dries Mertens (75' Lorenzo Insigne). Coach: Maurizio Sarri.
Club Brugge KV: Sinan Bolat, Óscar Duarte, Thomas Meunier, Laurens De Bock, Brandon
Mechele, Boli Bolingoli-Mbombo (46' José Izquierdo), Timmy Simons, Víctor Vázquez (69'
Davy De fauw), Ruud Vormer, Abdoulaye Diaby (60' Claudemir), Leandro.
Coach: Michel Preud'homme.
Goals: 5' José Callejón 1-0, 19', 25' Dries Mertens 2-0, 3-0, 53' Marek Hamsík 4-0,
77' José Callejón 5-0.
Referee: István Vad (HUN)   Attendance: 13,043.

17.09.15 MCH Arena, Herning: FC Midtjylland – Legia Warszawa 1-0 (0-0)
FC Midtjylland: Mikkel Andersen, Kian Hansen, Erik Sviatchenko, Kristian Nielsen, Tim
Sparv, Jakob Poulsen, Petter Andersson (46' Kristoffer Olsson), Pione Sisto (81' Ebere
Onuachu), Filip Novák, Daniel Royer, Morten Rasmussen (88' Martin Pusic).
Coach: Jess Thorup.
Legia Warszawa: Dusan Kuciak, Igor Lewczuk, Tomasz Brzyski, Bartosz Bereszynski, Jakub
Rzezniczak, Guilherme, Stojan Vranjes (82' Rafal Makowski), Dominik Furman, Nemanja
Nikolic, Michal Kucharczyk (75' Ivan Trickovski), Aleksandar Prijovic. Coach: Henning Berg.
Goal: 60' Morten Rasmussen 1-0.
Referee: Hüseyin Göçek (TUR)   Attendance: 6,798.
Sent off: 88' Dominik Furman.

01.10.15 Wojska Polskiego, Warszawa: Legia Warszawa – SSC Napoli 0-2 (0-0)
Legia Warszawa: Dusan Kuciak, Michal Pazdan (89' Rafal Makowski), Igor Lewczuk, Tomasz
Brzyski, Bartosz Bereszynski, Jakub Rzezniczak, Tomasz Jodlowiec, Guilherme, Michal
Kucharczyk (62' Nemanja Nikolic), Ivan Trickovski (62' Ondrej Duda), Aleksandar Prijovic.
Coach: Henning Berg.
SSC Napoli: Gabriel, Christian Maggio, Vlad Chiriches, Kalidou Koulibaly, Faouzi Ghoulam,
Allan (83' Nathaniel Chalobah), Mirko Valdifiori, David López, José Callejón (76' Gonzalo
Higuaín), Dries Mertens (72' Omar El Kaddouri), Manolo Gabbiadini. Coach: Maurizio Sarri.
Goals: 53' Dries Mertens 0-1, 84' Gonzalo Higuaín 0-2.
Referee: Michail Koukoulakis (GRE)   Attendance: 26,357.

01.10.15 Jan Breydel Stadion, Brugge: Club Brugge KV – FC Midtjylland 1-3 (0-0)
Club Brugge KV: Sébastien Bruzzese, Davy De fauw (70' Thomas Meunier), Óscar Duarte,
Laurens De Bock, Brandon Mechele, Claudemir, Hans Vanaken, Ruud Vormer, Abdoulaye
Diaby (63' Jelle Vossen), José Izquierdo (71' Tuur Dierckx), Leandro.
Coach: Michel Preud'homme.
FC Midtjylland: Mikkel Andersen, Kian Hansen, Erik Sviatchenko, Kristian Nielsen (31'
André Rømer), Tim Sparv, Jakob Poulsen, Kristoffer Olsson, Pione Sisto (78' Marco Ureña),
Filip Novák, Daniel Royer, Morten Rasmussen (54' Ebere Onuachu). Coach: Jess Thorup.
Goals: 51' Pionen Sisto 0-1, 67' Ebere Onuachu 0-2, 74' Filip Novák 0-3,
79' Thomas Meunier 1-3.
Referee: Steven McLean (SCO)   Attendance: 14,126.

22.10.15   Wojska Polskiego, Warszawa: Legia Warszawa – Club Brugge KV 1-1 (0-1)
Legia Warszawa: Dusan Kuciak, Michal Pazdan, Igor Lewczuk, Tomasz Brzyski, Jakub
Rzezniczak, Lukasz Broz, Tomasz Jodlowiec, Guilherme (46' Ondrej Duda), Dominick
Furman (46' Ivan Trickovski), Nemanja Nikolic (76' Aleksandar Prijovic), Michal
Kucharczyk. Coach: Stanislav Cherchesov.
Club Brugge KV: Sébastien Bruzzese, Davy De fauw, Thomas Meunier, Stefano Denswil,
Brandon Mechele, Boli Bolingoli-Mbombo (68' Laurens De Bock), Timmy Simons, Hans
Vanaken, Jelle Vossen (80' Leandro), Abdoulaye Diaby (71' Tuur Dierckx), José Izquierdo.
Coach: Michel Preud'homme.
Goals: 39' Davy De fauw 0-1, 51' Michal Kucharczyk 1-1.
Referee: Harald Lechner (AUT)   Attendance: 16,320.

22.10.15   MCH Arena, Herning: FC Midtjylland – SSC Napoli 1-4 (1-3)
FC Midtjylland: Mikkel Andersen, Kian Hansen, Erik Sviatchenko, André Rømer, Tim Sparv,
Jakob Poulsen, Filip Novák, Daniel Royer, Morten Rasmussen (73' Marco Larsen), Martin
Pusic (62' Ebere Onuachu), Mikkel Dueland (73' Awer Mabil). Coach: Jess Thorup.
SSC Napoli: Pepe Reina, Christian Maggio, Vlad Chiriches, Kalidou Koulibaly, Faouzi
Ghoulam (80' Ivan Strinic), Allan (59' Marek Hamsík), Mirko Valdifiori, David López, Omar
El Kaddouri, José Callejón (64' Gonzalo Higuaín), Manolo Gabbiadini. Coach: Maurizio Sarri.
Goals: 19' José Callejón 0-1, 31', 40' Manolo Gabbiadini 0-2, 0-3, 43' Martin Pusic 1-3,
90+4' Gonzalo Higuaín 1-4.
Referee: Serdar Gözübüyük (HOL)   Attendance: 9,210.

05.11.15   Jan Breydel Stadion, Brugge: Club Brugge KV – Legia Warszawa 1-0 (1-0)
Club Brugge KV: Sébastien Bruzzese, Thomas Meunier, Stefano Denswil, Laurens De Bock,
Brandon Mechele, Timmy Simons, Claudemir, Víctor Vázquez (90+1' Hans Vanaken), Felipe
Conceição, Abdoulaye Diaby (82' Boli Bolingoli-Mbombo), Leandro (74' Jelle Vossen).
Coach: Michel Preud'homme.
Legia Warszawa: Dusan Kuciak, Michal Pazdan, Igor Lewczuk, Tomasz Brzyski, Bartosz
Bereszynski (67' Michal Kucharczyk), Jakub Rzezniczak, Tomasz Jodlowiec (62' Guilherme),
Ondrej Duda, Stojan Vranjes, Marek Saganowski (59' Aleksandar Prijovic), Ivan Trickovski.
Coach: Stanislav Cherchesov.
Goal: 38' Thomas Meunier 1-0.
Referee: Marijo Strahonja (CRO)   Attendance: 16,349.

05.11.15   San Paolo, Napoli: SSC Napoli – FC Midtjylland 5-0 (3-0)
SSC Napoli: Pepe Reina, Ivan Strinic (69' Elseid Hysaj), Christian Maggio, Vlad Chiriches,
Kalidou Koulibaly, Mirko Valdifiori, Marek Hamsík (53' Allan), David López, Omar El
Kaddouri, Manolo Gabbiadini, Lorenzo Insigne (57' José Callejón). Coach: Maurizio Sarri.
FC Midtjylland: Mikkel Andersen, Kian Hansen (46' Marco Ureña), Erik Sviatchenko, Patrick
Banggaard, André Rømer, Tim Sparv, Jakob Poulsen, Kristoffer Olsson (69' Pione Sisto), Filip
Novák, Daniel Royer, Ebere Onuachu (62' Martin Pusic). Coach: Jess Thorup.
Goals: 13' Omar El Kaddouri 1-0, 23', 38' Manolo Gabbiadini 2-0, 3-0,
54' Christian Maggio 4-0, 77' José Callejón 5-0.
Referee: Benoît Bastien (FRA)   Attendance: 18,475.

85

26.11.15   Jan Breydel Stadion, Brugge: Club Brugge KV – SSC Napoli 0-1 (0-1)
Club Brugge KV: Sébastien Bruzzese, Davy De fauw, Thomas Meunier, Stefano Denswil,
Brandon Mechele, Timmy Simons (88' Leandro), Víctor Vázquez (81' Hans Vanaken), Felipe
Conceição (81' Abdoulaye Diaby), Ruud Volmer, Jelle Vossen, José Izquierdo.
Coach: Michel Preud'homme.
SSC Napoli: Gabriel, Ivan Strinic, Christian Maggio, Vlad Chiriches, Kalidou Koulibaly,
Mirko Valdifiori, Marek Hamsík (69' Elseid Hysaj), David López, Omar El Kaddouri,
Nathaniel Chalobah (81' Allan), José Callejón (77' Faouzi Ghoulam). Coach: Maurizio Sarri.
Goal: 41' Vlad Chiriches 0-1.
Referee: Marius Avram (ROM)

Match was played behind closed doors.

26.11.15   Wojska Polskiego, Warszawa: Legia Warszawa – FC Midtjylland 1-0 (1-0)
Legia Warszawa: Arkadiusz Malarz, Igor Lewczuk, Bartosz Bereszynski, Lukasz Broz,
Tomasz Jodlowiec, Ondrej Duda, Stojan Vranjes, Nemanja Nikolic (90+1' Marek
Saganowski), Michal Kucharczyk, Ivan Trickovski (82' Michal Zyro), Aleksandar Prijovic
(64' Guilherme). Coach: Stanislav Cherchesov.
FC Midtjylland: Mikkel Andersen, Kian Hansen, Erik Sviatchenko, André Rømer, Tim Sparv,
Jakob Poulsen, Kristoffer Olsson (69' Martin Pusic), Pione Sisto (46' Awer Mabil), Filip
Novák, Daniel Royer, Morten Rasmussen (36' Ebere Onuachu). Coach: Jess Thorup.
Goal: 35' Aleksandar Prijovic 1-0.
Referee: Andre Marriner (ENG)   Attendance: 9,468.

10.12.15   San Paolo, Napoli: SSC Napoli – Legia Warszawa 5-2 (2-0)
SSC Napoli: Gabriel, Ivan Strinic, Christian Maggio, Vlad Chiriches (79' Sebastiano Luperto),
Kalidou Koulibaly (68' Raúl Albiol), Mirko Valdifiori, David López, Omar El Kaddouri,
Nathaniel Chalobah, Dries Mertens, Lorenzo Insigne (55' José Callejón).
Coach: Maurizio Sarri.
Legia Warszawa: Dusan Kuciak, Michal Pazdan, Igor Lewczuk, Bartosz Bereszynski, Lukasz
Broz, Tomasz Jodlowiec, Guilherme, Ondrej Duda (71' Ivan Trickovski), Stojan Vranjes,
Nemanja Nikolic (60' Aleksandar Prijovic), Michal Kucharczyk (79' Pablo Dyego).
Coach: Stanislav Cherchesov.
Goals: 32' Nathaniel Chalobah 1-0, 39' Lorenzo Insigne 2-0, 57' José Callejón 3-0,
62' Stojan Vranjes 3-1, 65', 90+1' Dries Mertens 4-1, 5-1, 90+2' Aleksandar Prijovic 5-2.
Referee: Aleksandar Stavrev (MKD)   Attendance: 7,922.

10.12.15   MCH Arena, Herning: FC Midtjylland – Club Brugge KV 1-1 (1-0)
FC Midtjylland: Mikkel Andersen, Kian Hansen, Erik Sviatchenko, André Rømer, Tim Sparv,
Jakob Poulsen, Kristoffer Olsson (90+2' Jesper Lauridsen), Pione Sisto (74' Marco Ureña),
Filip Novák, Daniel Royer, Martin Pusic (83' Ebere Onuachu). Coach: Jess Thorup.
Club Brugge KV: Sébastien Bruzzese, Davy De fauw, Thomas Meunier, Stefano Denswil,
Brandon Mechele (81' Björn Engels), Timmy Simons, Víctor Vázquez, Felipe Conceição (46'
Lior Refaelov), Ruud Volmer, Jelle Vossen, José Izquierdo (62' Leandro).
Coach: Michel Preud'homme.
Goals: 27' Pione Sisto 1-0, 68' Jelle Vossen 1-1.
Referee: Javier Estrada Fernández (ESP)   Attendance: 8,624.

86

GROUP E

17.09.15 Ernst-Happel-Stadion, Wien: Rapid Wien – Villarreal CF 2-1 (0-1)
Rapid Wien: Ján Novota, Christopher Dibon, Maximilian Hofmann, Mario Pavelic, Stefan Stangl (90+2' Stephan Auer), Stefan Schwab, Louis Schaub (64' Philipp Schobesberger), Steffen Hofmann, Florian Kainz (72' Philipp Huspek), Srdan Grahovac, Philipp Prosenik. Coach: Zoran Barisic.
Villarreal CF: Mariano Barbosa, Bojan Jokic, Víctor Ruiz, Antonio Rukavina, Daniele Bonera, Jonathan Dos Santos, Denis Suárez (79' Matías Nahuel), Bruno Soriano, Samuel (46' Samu Castillejo), Leo Baptistão, Adrián (69' Cédric Bakambu). Coach: Marcelino.
Goals: 45' Leo Baptistão 0-1, 50' Stefan Schwab 1-1, 53' Steffen Hofmann 2-1 (p).
Referee: Stefan Johannesson (SWE)   Attendance: 36,200.

17.09.15 Doosan Aréna, Plzen: Viktoria Plzen – Dinamo Minsk 2-0 (1-0)
Viktoria Plzen: Matús Kozácik, David Limbersky, Václav Procházka, Jan Baránek, Tomás Horava (90+1' Tomás Kucera), Ondrej Vanek, Jan Kopic, Patrik Hrosovsky, Jan Kovarík (73' Milan Petrzela), Frantisek Rajtoral, Michal Djuris (83' Jan Holenda). Coach: Karel Krejcí.
Dinamo Minsk: Aleksandr Gutor, Maksim Vitus, Sergey Politevich, Umaru Bangura, Roman Begunov, Igor Voronkov (78' Jan Tigorev), Sergiu Neacsa (72' Gleb Rassadkin), Uladzimir Karytska (61' Yaroslav Yarotski), Nikita Korzun, Nenad Adamovic, Fatos Beciraj. Coach: Vuk Rasovic.
Goals: 36' Tomás Horava 1-0, 75' Milan Petrzela 2-0.
Referee: Marius Avram (ROM)   Attendance: 10,784.

01.10.15 El Madrigal, Villarreal: Villarreal CF – Viktoria Plzen 1-0 (0-0)
Villarreal CF: Mariano Barbosa, Víctor Ruiz, Jaume Costa, Antonio Rukavina, Eric Bailly, Jonathan Dos Santos (76' Trigueros), Samu Castillejo, Bruno Soriano, Soldado, Leo Baptistão, Matías Nahuel (83' Samuel). Coach: Marcelino.
Viktoria Plzen: Matús Kozácik, David Limbersky, Václav Procházka, Jan Baránek, Tomás Horava, Jan Kopic (81' Lukás Hejda), Milan Petrzela (75' Ajdin Mahmutovic), Patrik Hrosovsky, Jan Kovarík (88' Egon Vuch), Frantisek Rajtoral, Michal Djuris. Coach: Karel Krejcí.
Goal: 54' Leo Baptistão 1-0.
Referee: Serdar Gözübüyük (HOL)   Attendance: 18,634.
Sent off: 80' Václav Procházka.

01.10.15 Borisov Arena, Borisov: Dinamo Minsk – Rapid Wien 0-1 (0-0)
Dinamo Minsk: Aleksandr Gutor, Maksim Vitus, Sergey Politevich, Umaru Bangura, Roman Begunov (90+2' Oleg Veretilo), Igor Voronkov (66' Mohamed El-Mounir), Uladzimir Karytska, Shaloze Chigozie, Nikita Korzun, Nenad Adamovic (72' Gleb Rassadkin), Fatos Beciraj. Coach: Vuk Rasovic.
Rapid Wien: Ján Novota, Mario Sonnleitner, Christopher Dibon, Mario Pavelic, Stefan Stangl, Stefan Schwab, Louis Schaub (46' Philipp Schobesberger), Steffen Hofmann (76' Deni Alar), Florian Kainz, Srdan Grahovac, Matej Jelic (86' Philipp Prosenik). Coach: Zoran Barisic.
Goal: 54' Steffen Hofmann 0-1.
Referee: Jakob Kehlet (DEN)   Attendance: 4,553.

22.10.15 Ernst-Happel-Stadion, Wien: Rapid Wien – Viktoria Plzen 3-2 (1-1)
Rapid Wien: Ján Novota, Christopher Dibon, Maximilian Hofmann, Mario Pavelic, Stefan
Stangl, Thanos Petsos, Stefan Schwab, Louis Schaub (80' Philipp Huspek), Steffen Hofmann
(62' Srdan Grahovac), Florian Kainz, Philipp Prosenik (68' Matej Jelic). Coach: Zoran Barisic.
Viktoria Plzen: Matús Kozácik, Lukás Hejda, David Limbersky, Jan Baránek, Tomás Horava
(58' Daniel Kolár), Ondrej Vanek (80' Jan Holenda), Jan Kopic (58' Milan Petrzela), Patrik
Hrosovsky, Jan Kovarík, Frantisek Rajtoral, Michal Djuris. Coach: Karel Krejcí.
Goals: 12' Michal Djuris 0-1, 34' Steffen Hofmann 1-1, 52' Louis Schaub 2-1,
68' Thanos Petsos 3-1, 76' Patrik Hrosovsky 3-2.
Referee: Craig Pawson (ENG)   Attendance: 39,400.

22.10.15 El Madrigal, Villarreal: Villarreal CF – Dinamo Minsk 4-0 (2-0)
Villarreal CF: Mariano Barbosa, Bojan Jokic, Víctor Ruiz, Antonio Rukavina, Eric Bailly, Pina
(62' Trigueros), Jonathan Dos Santos, Denis Suárez (67' Samu Castillejo), Samuel, Soldado,
Cédric Bakambu (46' Matías Nahuel). Coach: Marcelino.
Dinamo Minsk: Aleksandr Gutor, Maksim Vitus, Sergey Politevich, Umaru Bangura, Roman
Begunov, Kirill Premudrov, Uladzimir Karytska (46' Nenad Adamovic), Shaloze Chigozie
(74' Igor Voronkov), Nikita Korzun, Gleb Rassadkin, Fatos Beciraj (66' Mohamed El-
Mounir). Coach: Vuk Rasovic.
Goals: 17', 32' Cédric Bakambu 1-0, 2-0, 61' Sodado 3-0, 70' Eric Bailly 4-0.
Referee: Sergey Boyko (UKR)   Attendance: 14,025.

05.11.15 Doosan Aréna, Plzen: Viktoria Plzen – Rapid Wien 1-2 (0-1)
Viktoria Plzen: Matús Kozácik, Lukás Hejda, David Limbersky, Václav Procházka, Tomás
Horava, Milan Petrzela (63' Jan Kopic), Patrik Hrosovsky, Jan Kovarík, Daniel Kolár (70' Jan
Holenda), Frantisek Rajtoral (81' Ajdin Mahmutovic), Michal Djuris. Coach: Karel Krejcí.
Rapid Wien: Ján Novota, Mario Sonnleitner, Christopher Dibon (67' Maximilian Hofmann),
Mario Pavelic, Stefan Stangl, Thanos Petsos, Philipp Schobesberger, Stefan Schwab, Steffen
Hofmann (51' Srdan Grahovac), Florian Kainz, Philipp Prosenik (79' Matej Jelic).
Coach: Zoran Barisic.
Goals: 13' Philipp Schobesberger 0-1, 71' Jan Holenda 1-1, 77' Philipp Schobesberger 1-2.
Referee: Luca Banti (ITA)   Attendance: 11,691.

05.11.15 Borisov Arena, Borisov: Dinamo Minsk – Villarreal CF 1-2 (0-0)
Dinamo Minsk: Sergey Ignatovich, Sergey Politevich, Umaru Bangura, Roman Begunov,
Mohamed El-Mounir, Igor Voronkov (73' Uladzimir Karytska), Kirill Premudrov, Shaloze
Chigozie (78' Artur Yedigaryan), Nenad Adamovic (67' Maksim Vitus), Gleb Rassadkin,
Fatos Beciraj. Coach: Vuk Rasovic.
Villarreal CF: Mariano Barbosa, Mario, Bojan Jokic, Víctor Ruiz, Antonio Rukavina, Pina (62'
Jonathan Dos Santos), Trigueros, Samu Castillejo (73' Denis Suárez), Samuel, Cédric
Bakambu, Matías Nahuel (46' Soldado). Coach: Marcelino.
Goals: 69' Maksim Vitus 1-0, 72' Soldado 1-1 (p), 86' Sergey Politevich 1-2 (og).
Referee: John Beaton (SCO)   Attendance: 4,959.

26.11.15   Borisov Arena, Borisov: Dinamo Minsk – Viktoria Plzen 1-0 (0-0)
Dinamo Minsk: Aleksandr Gutor, Sergey Politevich, Umaru Bangura, Oleg Veretilo, Roman Begunov, Kirill Premudrov, Uladzimir Karytska (66' Mohamed El-Mounir), Shaloze Chigozie, Nikita Korzun, Gleb Rassadkin (76' Nenad Adamovic), Fatos Beciraj. Coach: Vuk Rasovic.
Viktoria Plzen: Petr Bolek, Ales Mateju, David Limbersky, Václav Procházka, Jan Baránek, Jan Kopic (73' Frantisek Rajtoral), Patrik Hrosovsky, Jan Kovarík (83' Jan Holenda), Daniel Kolár, Tomás Kucera, Ajdin Mahmutovic (63' Michal Djuris). Coach: Karel Krejcí.
Goal: 90+2' Nenad Adamovic 1-0.
Referee: Ognjen Valjic (BIH)   Attendance: 4,250.
Sent off: 90' Oleg Veretilo.

Nenad Adamovic missed a penalty kick (90+2').

26.11.15   El Madrigal, Villarreal: Villarreal CF – Rapid Wien 1-0 (0-0)
Villarreal CF: Mariano Barbosa, Mario, Víctor Ruiz, Jaume Costa, Antonio Rukavina, Jonathan Dos Santos (73' Denis Suárez, Samu Castillejo (83' Matías Nahuel), Bruno Soriano, Soldado, Cédric Bakambu (52' Samuel). Coach: Marcelino.
Rapid Wien: Ján Novota (61' Richard Strebinger), Mario Sonnleitner, Christopher Dibon (6' Maximilian Hofmann), Mario Pavelic, Stefan Stangl, Thanos Petsos, Philipp Schobesberger, Stefan Schwab, Steffen Hofmann, Florian Kainz, Philipp Prosenik (86' Matej Jelic). Coach: Zoran Barisic.
Goal: 78' Bruno Soriano 1-0.
Referee: Pawel Raczkowski (POL)   Attendance: 14,760.

10.12.15   Doosan Aréna, Plzen: Viktoria Plzen – Villarreal CF 3-3 (1-1)
Viktoria Plzen: Petr Bolek, Lukás Hejda, Ales Mateju, David Limbersky, Jan Baránek, Tomás Horava, Jan Kopic (83' Milan Petrzela), Jan Kovarík, Daniel Kolár, Tomás Kucera (88' Václav Procházka), Jan Holenda (71' Ajdin Mahmutovic). Coach: Karel Krejcí.
Villarreal CF: Mariano Barbosa, Bojan Jokic (43' Adrián Marín), Mateo Musacchio, Víctor Ruiz, Antonio Rukavina, Trigueros, Samu Castillejo (72' Denis Suárez), Bruno Soriano, Samuel (56' Jonathan Dos Santos), Soldado, Cédric Bakambu. Coach: Marcelino.
Goals: 8' Daniel Kolár 1-0 (p), 40' Cédric Bakambu 1-1, 62' Jonathan Dos Santos 1-2, 65' Jan Kovarík 2-2, 90' Tomás Horava 3-2, 90+4' Bruno Soriano 3-3.
Referee: Tony Chapron (FRA)   Attendance: 10,071.

10.12.15   Ernst-Happel-Stadion, Wien: Rapid Wien – Dinamo Minsk 2-1 (1-0)
Rapid Wien: Richard Strebinger, Mario Sonnleitner, Maximilian Hofmann, Mario Pavelic, Stephan Auer, Thanos Petsos, Stefan Schwab, Steffen Hofmann (65' Srdan Grahovac), Florian Kainz, Matej Jelic (71' Philipp Prosenik), Deni Alar (80' Stefan Stangl). Coach: Zoran Barisic.
Dinamo Minsk: Aleksandr Gutor, Maksim Vitus, Sergey Politevich, Umaru Bangura, Roman Begunov, Kirill Premudrov (61' Igor Voronkov), Uladzimir Karytska (85' Vitaly Bulyha), Shaloze Chigozie, Nikita Korzun, Nenad Adamovic (64' Mohamed El-Mounir), Fatos Beciraj. Coach: Vuk Rasovic.
Goals: 29' Maximilian Hofmann 1-0, 59' Matej Jelic 2-0, 65' Mohamed El-Mounir 2-1.
Referee: Äliyar Agayev (AZE)   Attendance: 34,800.

Steffen Hofmann missed a penalty kick (21').

89

GROUP F

17.09.15 U Nisy, Liberec: Slovan Liberec – Sporting Braga 0-1 (0-0)
Slovan Liberec: Tomás Koubek, Vladimír Coufal, David Hovorka, Lukás Bartosák, Lukás
Pokorny, David Pavelka, Daniel Soungole (65' Jan Sykora), Daniel Bartl, Herolind Shala (65'
Michael Rabusic), Josef Sural, Marek Bakos (75' Milan Kerbr). Coach: Jindrich Trpisovsky.
Sporting Braga: Matheus Magalhães, Willy Boly, André Pinto, Baiano, Djavan, Nikola
Vukcevic, Mauro, Crislan (62' Wilson Eduardo), Rui Fonte (86' Ricardo Ferreira), Rafa Silva,
Alan (75' Filipe Augusto). Coach: Paulo Fonseca.
Goal: 60' Rafa Silva 0-1.
Referee: Craig Pawson (ENG)   Attendance: 8,132.

17.09.15 Euroborg, Groningen: FC Groningen – Olympique Marseille 0-3 (0-2)
FC Groningen: Sergio Padt, Johan Kappelhof, Rasmus Lindgren, Abel Tamata, Hans Hateboer,
Albert Rusnák (70' Jesper Drost), Simon Tibbling, Hedwiges Maduro, Michael de Leeuw,
Danny Hoesen (66' Mimoun Mahi), Bryan Linssen. Coach: Erwin van de Looi.
Olympique Marseille: Steve Mandanda, Karim Rekik, Stéphane Sparagna, Mauricio Isla,
Benjamin Mendy (66' Paolo De Ceglie), Lucas Ocampos, Lucas Silva (82' Rolando), Romain
Alessandrini (75' Bouna Sarr), Alaixys Romao, André Zambo, Georges-Kévin N'Koudou.
Coach: Míchel.
Goals: 25' Georges-Kévin N'Koudou 0-1, 39' Lucas Ocampos 0-2,
61' Romain Alessandrini 0-3.
Referee: Evgen Aranovskiy (UKR)   Attendance: 21,520.

01.10.15 Vélodrome, Marseille: Olympique Marseille – Slovan Liberec 0-1 (0-0)
Olympique Marseille: Steve Mandanda, Karim Rekik, Rolando, Mauricio Isla (67' Brice Dja
Djedjé), Benjamin Mendy, Lucas Ocampos, Lucas Silva, Romain Alessandrini (82' Bouna
Sarr), Rémy Cabella (71' Abdelaziz Barrada), Alaixys Romao, Michy Batshuayi.
Coach: Míchel.
Slovan Liberec: Tomás Koubek, Vladimír Coufal, David Hovorka, Lukás Bartosák, Lukás
Pokorny, Jan Sykora, David Pavelka, Dmitri Efremov, Michael Rabusic (46' Marek Bakos),
Herolind Shala (73' Daniel Bartl), Josef Sural (89' Milan Kerbr). Coach: Jindrich Trpisovsky.
Goal: 84' Vladimír Coufal 0-1.
Referee: Aleksey Eskov (RUS)   Attendance: 10,040.

01.10.15 Estádio Municipal de Braga, Braga: Sporting Braga – FC Groningen 1-0 (1-0)
Sporting Braga: Matheus Magalhães, Willy Boly, Djavan (83' Pedro Santos), Arghus (40'
Mauro), Marcelo Goiano, Luíz Carlos, Nikola Vukcevic, Rui Fonte (71' Wilson Eduardo),
Rafa Silva, Ahmed Hassan, Alan. Coach: Paulo Fonseca.
FC Groningen: Sergio Padt, Johan Kappelhof, Etiënne Reijnen, Abel Tamata, Hans Hateboer,
Albert Rusnák (32' Kasper Larsen), Simon Tibbling, Hedwiges Maduro, Michael de Leeuw
(82' Danny Hoesen), Bryan Linssen, Mimoun Mahi (82' Jarchinio Antonia).
Coach: Erwin van de Looi.
Goal: 5' Ahmed Hassan 1-0.
Referee: Bobby Madden (SCO)   Attendance: 9,150.

22.10.15   Estádio Municipal de Braga, Braga:
Sporting Braga – Olympique Marseille 3-2 (0-0)
Sporting Braga: Matheus Magalhães, Willy Boly, Djavan, Ricardo Ferreira, Marcelo Goiano,
Nikola Vukcevic, Mauro, Rui Fonte (65' Wilson Eduardo), Rafa Silva (85' Luíz Carlos),
Ahmed Hassan (75' Crislan), Alan. Coach: Paulo Fonseca.
Olympique Marseille: Steve Mandanda, Karim Rekik, Stéphane Sparagna, Mauricio Isla,
Benjamin Mendy, Brice Dja Djedjé (64' Rémy Cabella), Lucas Silva, Lassana Diarra (83'
Lucas Ocampos), Romain Alessandrini, Abdelaziz Barrada (75' Georges-Kévin N'Koudou),
Michy Batshuayi. Coach: Míchel.
Goals: 61' Ahmed Hassan 1-0, 77' Wilson Eduardo 2-0, 84' Romain Alessandrini 2-1,
87' Michy Batshuayi 2-2, 88' Alan 3-2.
Referee: Alexandru Tudor (ROM)   Attendance: 10,495.

22.10.15   U Nisy, Liberec: Slovan Liberec – FC Groningen 1-1 (0-0)
Slovan Liberec: Tomás Koubek, Vladimír Coufal, Ondrej Svejdík, Lukás Bartosák, Lukás
Pokorny, David Pavelka, Zdenek Folprecht, Dmitri Efremov, Herolind Shala (84' Daniel
Bartl), Josef Sural (89' Isaac Sackey), Marek Bakos (61' Kevin Luckassen).
Coach: Jindrich Trpisovsky.
FC Groningen: Sergio Padt, Johan Kappelhof, Kasper Larsen (88' Jarchinio Antonia), Etiënne
Reijnen, Abel Tamata, Hans Hateboer, Albert Rusnák, Simon Tibbling, Hedwiges Maduro (78'
Michael de Leeuw), Bryan Linssen (70' Danny Hoesen), Mimoun Mahi.
Coach: Erwin van de Looi.
Goals: 87' Kevin Luckassen 1-0, 90+6' Danny Hoesen 1-1.
Referee: Christian Dingert (GER)   Attendance: 8,793.
Sent off: 83' Michael de Leeuw.

Danny Hoesen missed a penalty kick (90+6').

05.11.15   Vélodrome, Marseille: Olympique Marseille – Sporting Braga 1-0 (1-0)
Olympique Marseille: Steve Mandanda, Nicolas N'Koulou, Karim Rekik, Mauricio Isla,
Benjamin Mendy, Lucas Ocampos, Lucas Silva (70' Stéphane Sparagna), Rémy Cabella,
Alaixys Romao, Georges-Kévin N'Koudou (83' Abdelaziz Barrada), Michy Batshuayi (90+1'
Manquillo). Coach: Míchel.
Sporting Braga: Matheus Magalhães, Willy Boly, Baiano, Ricardo Ferreira, Marcelo Goiano,
Nikola Vukcevic, Mauro (53' Luíz Carlos), Rui Fonte, Rafa Silva, Ahmed Hassan (67'
Crislan), Alan (78' Wilson Eduardo). Coach: Paulo Fonseca.
Goal: 39' Georges-Kévin N'Koudou 1-0.
Referee: Hüseyin Göçek (TUR)   Attendance: 12,973.

05.11.15   Euroborg, Groningen: FC Groningen – Slovan Liberec 0-1 (0-0)
FC Groningen: Sergio Padt, Johan Kappelhof, Kasper Larsen, Lorenzo Burnet, Etiënne
Reijnen, Albert Rusnák, Simon Tibbling (83' Hans Hateboer), Hedwiges Maduro (78' Jesper
Drost), Jarchinio Antonia, Danny Hoesen (67' Juninho Bacuna), Bryan Linssen.
Coach: Erwin van de Looi.
Slovan Liberec: Tomás Koubek, Vladimír Coufal, Ondrej Svejdík, Lukás Bartosák (60' Jan
Sykora), Lukás Pokorny, David Pavelka, Zdenek Folprecht, Dmitri Efremov (90+4' Milan
Kerbr), Herolind Shala, Josef Sural, Marek Bakos (73' Michael Rabusic).
Coach: Jindrich Trpisovsky.
Goal: 81' Sergio Padt 0-1 (og).
Referee: Marcin Borski (POL)   Attendance: 18,693.

91

26.11.15   Estádio Municipal de Braga, Braga: Sporting Braga – Slovan Liberec 2-1 (1-1)
Sporting Braga: Matheus Magalhães, Willy Boly, Djavan, Ricardo Ferreira, Marcelo Goiano, Luíz Carlos, Nikola Vukcevic, Rui Fonte (59' Crislan), Rafa Silva, Ahmed Hassan (90+4' Wilson Eduardo), Alan (86' Pedro Santos). Coach: Paulo Fonseca.
Slovan Liberec: Tomás Koubek, Vladimír Coufal (85' Jan Sykora), David Hovorka, Lukás Bartosák, Lukás Pokorny, David Pavelka, Zdenek Folprecht, Dmitri Efremov (62' Michael Rabusic), Herolind Shala, Milan Kerbr (76' Jan Mudra), Marek Bakos.
Coach: Jindrich Trpisovsky.
Goals: 35' Dmitri Efremov 0-1, 42' Ricardo Ferreira 1-1, 90+2' Crislan 2-1.
Referee: Aleksey Kulbakov (BLS)   Attendance: 8,144.

26.11.15   Vélodrome, Marseille: Olympique Marseille – FC Groningen 2-1 (1-0)
Olympique Marseille: Steve Mandanda, Nicolas N'Koulou, Rolando (87' Abdelaziz Barrada), Mauricio Isla (65' Lucas Silva), Benjamin Mendy, Brice Dja Djedjé, Lucas Ocampos (57' Romain Alessandrini), Lassana Diarra, Rémy Cabella, Georges-Kévin N'Koudou, Michy Batshuayi. Coach: Míchel.
FC Groningen: Sergio Padt, Johan Kappelhof, Kasper Larsen, Etiënne Reijnen, Abel Tamata, Hans Hateboer, Albert Rusnák, Hedwiges Maduro, Jarchinio Antonia (84' Jesper Drost), Danny Hoesen, Bryan Linssen (71' Simon Tibbling). Coach: Erwin van de Looi.
Goals: 28' Georges-Kévin N'Koudou 1-0, 50' Hedwiges Maduro 1-1,
88' Michy Batshuayi 2-1.
Referee: Andris Treimanis (LAT)   Attendance: 9,107.

10.12.15   U Nisy, Liberec: Slovan Liberec – Olympique Marseille 2-4 (0-2)
Slovan Liberec: Tomás Koubek, Vladimír Coufal, David Hovorka, Ondrej Svejdík, Lukás Bartosák, Jan Sykora (89' Milan Kerbr), David Pavelka, Zdenek Folprecht (60' Michael Rabusic), Dmitri Efremov, Herolind Shala (66' Josef Sural), Marek Bakos.
Coach: Jindrich Trpisovsky.
Olympique Marseille: Steve Mandanda, Manquillo, Nicolas N'Koulou, Rolando, Mauricio Isla, Benjamin Mendy, Rémy Cabella (54' Lucas Silva), Abdelaziz Barrada, Alaixys Romao, Georges-Kévin N'Koudou (66' Stéphane Sparagna), Michy Batshuayi (73' Lucas Ocampos). Coach: Míchel.
Goals: 14' M. Batshuayi 0-1, 43' Georges-Kévin N'Koudou 0-2, 48' Abdelaziz Barrada 0-3, 75' Marek Bakos 1-3 (p), 76' Josef Sural 2-3, 90+4' Lucas Ocampos 2-4.
Referee: Robert Schörgenhofer (AUT)   Attendance: 9,600.

10.12.15   Euroborg, Groningen: FC Groningen – Sporting Braga 0-0
FC Groningen: Sergio Padt, Johan Kappelhof, Kasper Larsen, Etiënne Reijnen, Abel Tamata, Hans Hateboer, Albert Rusnák, Simon Tibbling, Hedwiges Maduro, Danny Hoesen (74' Michael de Leeuw, Bryan Linssen (74' Jarchinio Antonia). Coach: Erwin van de Looi.
Sporting Braga: Matheus Magalhães, Willy Boly, André Pinto, Baiano, Marcelo Goiano, Luíz Carlos, Nikola Vukcevic, Wilson Eduardo (90+3' Rui Fonte), Rafa Silva, Ahmed Hassan (65' Crislan), Alan (80' Pedro Santos). Coach: Paulo Fonseca.
Referee: Simon Evans (WAL)   Attendance: 15,715.

GROUP G

17.09.15   Dnipro, Dnipropetrovsk: Dnipro Dnipropetrovsk – Lazio Roma 1-1 (0-1)
Dnipro Dnipropetrovsk: Denis Boyko, Léo Matos, Douglas, Papa Gueye, Anderson Pico,
Artem Fedetskiy (61' John Ruiz), Edmar (86' Bruno Gama), Valeriy Fedorchuk (46' Danilo),
Ruslan Rotan, Evgen Seleznyov, Matheus. Coach: Miron Markevich.
Lazio Roma: Federico Marchetti, Wesley Hoedt, Santiago Gentiletti, Stefan Radu, Abdoulay
Konko, Felipe Anderson, Marco Parolo, Sergej Milinkovic-Savic (89' Stefano Mauri), Ogenyi
Onazi, Alessandro Matri (76' Antonio Candreva), Ricardo Kishna (76' Baldé Diao Keita).
Coach: Stefano Pioli.
Goals: 34' Sergej Milinkovic-Savic 0-1, 90+4' Evgen Seleznyov 1-1.
Referee: Arnold Hunter (NIR).

Match was played behind closed doors.

17.09.15   Geoffroy Guichard, St.Étienne: AS Saint-Étienne – Rosenborg BK 2-2 (1-1)
AS Saint-Étienne: Stéphane Ruffier, Loïc Perrin, Moustapha Sall, François Clerc, Benoît
Assou-Ekotto, Jérémy Clément, Valentin Eysseric (64' Benjamin Corgnet), Fabien Lemoine
(76' Vincent Pajot), Nolan Roux, Kévin Monnet-Paquet (71' Jonathan Bamba), Robert Beric.
Coach: Christophe Galtier.
Rosenborg BK: André Hansen, Hólmar Eyjólfsson, Jørgen Skjelvik, Jonas Svensson, Mike
Jensen, Tobias Mikkelsen, Ole Selnæs, Fredrik Midtsjø, Pål Helland (76' Yann-Erik De
Lanlay), Anders Konradsen, Alexander Søderlund. Coach: Kåre Ingebrigtsen.
Goals: 4' Robert Beric 1-0, 16' Tobias Mikkelsen 1-1, 79' Jonas Svensson 1-2,
87' Nolan Roux 2-2 (p).
Referee: Christian Dingert (GER)   Attendance: 22,826.

01.10.15   Olimpico, Roma: Lazio Roma – AS Saint-Étienne 3-2 (1-1)
Lazio Roma: Etrit Berisha, Wesley Hoedt, Dusan Basta, Stefan Radu, Mauricio (46' Santiago
Gentiletti), Stefano Mauri (64' Alessandro Matri), Felipe Anderson, Lucas Biglia, Sergej
Milinkovic-Savic, Ogenyi Onazi (74' Danilo Cataldi), Baldé Diao Keita. Coach: Stefano Pioli.
AS Saint-Étienne: Stéphane Ruffier, Pierre-Yves Polomat, Loïc Perrin, Moustapha Sall,
François Clerc, Vincent Pajot, Benjamin Corgnet (63' Ismaël Diomandé), Fabien Lemoine,
Nolan Roux (74' Kévin Monnet-Paquet), Romain Hamouma (63' Jean-Christophe Bahebeck),
Robert Beric. Coach: Christophe Galtier.
Goals: 6' Moustapha Sall 0-1, 22' Ogenyi Onazi 1-1, 48' Wesley Hoedt 2-1,
80' Lucas Biglia 3-1, 84' Kévin Monnet-Paquet 3-2.
Referee: Halis Özkahya (TUR)   Attendance: 11,039.
Sent off: 33' Robert Beric, 76' Moustapha Sall.

01.10.15   Lerkendal, Trondheim: Rosenborg BK – Dnipro Dnipropetrovsk 0-1 (0-0)
Rosenborg BK: André Hansen, Hólmar Eyjólfsson, Johan Bjørdal, Jørgen Skjelvik, Jonas
Svensson, Tobias Mikkelsen, Ole Selnæs, Fredrik Midtsjø (71' Mike Jensen), Pål Helland (46'
Yann-Erik De Lanlay), Anders Konradsen, Alexander Søderlund. Coach: Kåre Ingebrigtsen.
Dnipro Dnipropetrovsk: Denis Boyko, Léo Matos, Douglas, Papa Gueye, Artem Fedetskiy,
Edmar, Ivan Tomecak (71' Valeri Luchkevych), Valeriy Fedorchuk, Ruslan Rotan, Evgen
Seleznyov (84' Bruno Gama), Matheus (90+1' Evgeniy Cheberyachko).
Coach: Miron Markevich.
Goal: 79' Evgen Seleznyov 0-1.
Referee: Sebastien Delferière (BEL)   Attendance: 13,939.

22.10.15   Dnipro, Dnipropetrovsk: Dnipro Dnipropetrovsk – AS Saint-Étienne 0-1 (0-1)
Dnipro Dnipropetrovsk: Denis Boyko, Léo Matos, Douglas, Papa Gueye, Artem Fedetskiy (46'
Bruno Gama), Edmar, Ivan Tomecak, Valeriy Fedorchuk (59' Roman Bezus), Ruslan Rotan,
Evgen Seleznyov, Matheus (78' Anderson Pico). Coach: Miron Markevich.
AS Saint-Étienne: Stéphane Ruffier, Florentin Pogba, Loïc Perrin, François Clerc, Benoît
Assou-Ekotto, Vincent Pajot, Valentin Eysseric (80' Ismaël Diomandé), Fabien Lemoine,
Nolan Roux, Romain Hamouma (81' Jean-Christophe Bahebeck), Kévin Monnet-Paquet (87'
Pierre-Yves Polomat). Coach: Christophe Galtier.
Goal: 44' Romain Hamouma 0-1.
Referee: Alon Yefet (ISR).

Match was played behind closed doors.

22.10.15   Olimpico, Roma: Lazio Roma – Rosenborg BK 3-1 (1-0)
Lazio Roma: Etrit Berisha, Wesley Hoedt, Stefan Radu, Abdoulay Konko, Mauricio, Stefano
Mauri (75' Sergej Milinkovic-Savic), Felipe Anderson (70' Senad Lulic), Ogenyi Onazi (10'
Santiago Gentiletti), Danilo Cataldi, Antonio Candreva, Alessandro Matri.
Coach: Stefano Pioli.
Rosenborg BK: André Hansen, Mikael Dorsin (62' Tobias Mikkelsen), Hólmar Eyjólfsson,
Johan Bjørdal, Jørgen Skjelvik, Jonas Svensson (75' Anders Konradsen), Mike Jensen, Ole
Selnæs (89' Matthías Vilhjálmsson), Fredrik Midtsjø, Alexander Søderlund, Yann-Erik De
Lanlay. Coach: Kåre Ingebrigtsen.
Goals: 28' Alessandro Matri 1-0, 54' Felipe Anderson 2-0, 69' Alexander Søderlund 2-1,
79' Antonio Candreva 3-1.
Referee: Pawel Gil (POL)   Attendance: 8,630.
Sent off: 6' Mauricio.

Antonio Candreva missed a penalty kick (79').
Alexander Søderlund missed a penalty kick (90+4').

05.11.15   Geoffroy Guichard, St.Étienne:
            AS Saint-Étienne – Dnipro Dnipropetrovsk 3-0 (1-0)
AS Saint-Étienne: Stéphane Ruffier, Florentin Pogba, Loïc Perrin, François Clerc, Benoît
Assou-Ekotto, Vincent Pajot (70' Jérémy Clément), Valentin Eysseric (80' Benjamin Corgnet),
Fabien Lemoine, Nolan Roux, Kévin Monnet-Paquet (61' Romain Hamouma), Robert Beric.
Coach: Christophe Galtier.
Dnipro Dnipropetrovsk: Denis Boyko, Léo Matos, Evgeniy Cheberyachko (46' Roman Bezus),
Douglas, Papa Gueye, Artem Fedetskiy, Edmar, Ivan Tomecak (63' Valeri Luchkevych),
Ruslan Rotan, Evgen Seleznyov (78' Bruno Gama), Matheus. Coach: Miron Markevich.
Goals: 38' Kévin Monnet-Paquet 1-0, 52' Robert Beric 2-0, 65' Romain Hamouma 3-0.
Referee: Mattias Gestranius (FIN)   Attendance: 24,582.

94

05.11.15 Lerkendal, Trondheim: Rosenborg BK – Lazio Roma 0-2 (0-2)
Rosenborg BK: André Hansen, Tore Reginiussen (33' Johan Bjørdal), Hólmar Eyjólfsson, Jørgen Skjelvik, Jonas Svensson, Mike Jensen, Tobias Mikkelsen, Ole Selnæs, Fredrik Midtsjø (61' Anders Konradsen), Pål Helland, Alexander Søderlund (65' Matthías Vilhjálmsson).
Coach: Kåre Ingebrigtsen.
Lazio Roma: Etrit Berisha, Wesley Hoedt, Santiago Gentiletti, Stefan Radu, Abdoulay Konko, Ravel Morrison (76' Stefano Mauri), Ogenyi Onazi, Danilo Cataldi, Antonio Candreva (46' Baldé Diao Keita), Filip Djordjevic (66' Alessandro Matri), Ricardo Kishna.
Coach: Stefano Pioli.
Goals: 9', 29' Filip Djordjevic 0-1, 0-2.
Referee: Andre Marriner (ENG)   Attendance: 16,038.
Sent off: 83' Baldé Diao Keita.

26.11.15 Olimpico, Roma: Lazio Roma – Dnipro Dnipropetrovsk 3-1 (1-0)
Lazio Roma: Etrit Berisha, Santiago Gentiletti, Stefan Radu, Abdoulay Konko, Mauricio, Marco Parolo, Danilo Cataldi, Antonio Candreva, Miroslav Klose (65' Sergej Milinkovic-Savic), Alessandro Matri (70' Filip Djordjevic), Ricardo Kishna (81' Senad Lulic). Coach: Stefano Pioli.
Dnipro Dnipropetrovsk: Denis Boyko, Léo Matos, Dmitro Chigrinskiy, Douglas, Papa Gueye, Artem Fedetskiy (74' Yevhen Shakhov), Danilo, Roman Bezus (57' Roman Zozulya), Evgen Seleznyov, Bruno Gama, Matheus (41' Anderson Pico). Coach: Miron Markevich.
Goals: 4' Antonio Candreva 1-0, 65' Bruno Gama 1-1, 68' Marco Parolo 2-1, 90+3' Filip Djordjevic 3-1.
Referee: Gediminas Mazeika (LTU)   Attendance: 3,058.

26.11.15 Lerkendal, Trondheim: Rosenborg BK – AS Saint-Étienne 1-1 (1-0)
Rosenborg BK: Alexander Hansen, Hólmar Eyjólfsson, Johan Bjørdal, Jørgen Skjelvik, Jonas Svensson, Mike Jensen, Tobias Mikkelsen, Ole Selnæs, Pål Helland (81' Yann-Erik De Lanlay), Anders Konradsen (82' Matthías Vilhjálmsson), Alexander Søderlund.
Coach: Kåre Ingebrigtsen.
AS Saint-Étienne: Stéphane Ruffier, Pierre-Yves Polomat, Loïc Perrin, François Clerc, Benoît Assou-Ekotto, Vincent Pajot, Jérémy Clément, Renaud Cohade (71' Neal Maupay), Nolan Roux (87' Ismaël Diomandé), Romain Hamouma, Kévin Monnet-Paquet.
Coach: Christophe Galtier.
Goals: 40' Alexander Søderlund 1-0, 80' Nolan Roux 1-1 (p).
Referee: Vitaliy Meshkov (RUS)   Attendance: 15,038.

10.12.15 Geoffroy Guichard, St.Étienne: AS Saint-Étienne – Lazio Roma 1-1 (0-0)
AS Saint-Étienne: Jessy Moulin, Pierre-Yves Polomat, Florentin Pogba, Jonathan Brison, Benjamin Kantie Karamoko (27' Moustapha Sall), Jérémy Clément, Benjamin Corgnet (64' Benjamin Bamba), Valentin Eysseric, Ismaël Diomandé (57' Erin Pinheiro), Jean-Christophe Bahebeck, Neal Maupay. Coach: Christophe Galtier.
Lazio Roma: Etrit Berisha, Wesley Hoedt, Dusan Basta, Abdoulay Konko, Mauricio, Felipe Anderson, Marco Parolo, Danilo Cataldi, Chris Ikonomidis (84' Antonio Candreva), Filip Djordjevic, Alessandro Matri (74' Ravel Morrison). Coach: Stefano Pioli.
Goals: 52' Alessandro Matri 0-1, 76' Valentin Eysseric 1-1.
Referee: Kevin Blom (HOL)   Attendance: 28,954.

10.12.15   Dnipro, Dnipropetrovsk: Dnipro Dnipropetrovsk – Rosenborg BK 3-0 (1-0)
Dnipro Dnipropetrovsk: Denis Boyko, Léo Matos, Evgeniy Cheberyachko, Dmitro
Chigrinskiy, Papa Gueye, Artem Fedetskiy, Edmar, Yevhen Shakhov (80' Roman Bezus), John
Ruiz (85' Ivan Tomecak), Bruno Gama (77' Valeri Luchkevych), Matheus.
Coach: Miron Markevich.
Rosenborg BK: André Hansen, Mikael Dorsin (84' John Hou Sæter), Jørgen Skjelvik, Jonas
Svensson, Mike Jensen, Ole Selnæs, Fredrik Midtsjø, Pål Helland (69' Tobias Mikkelsen),
Matthías Vilhjálmsson, Alexander Søderlund, Yann-Erik De Lanlay (68' Anders Konradsen).
Coach: Kåre Ingebrigtsen.
Goals: 35', 60' Matheus 1-0, 2-0, 79' Yevhen Shakhov 3-0.
Referee: Stephan Klossner (SUI)   Attendance: 4,541.

Pål Helland missed a penalty kick (12').

GROUP H

17.09.15   Estádio José Alvalade, Lisboa: Sporting CP – Lokomotiv Moskva 1-3 (0-1)
Sporting CP: Rui Patricio, Jefferson, Paulo Oliveira, João Pereira, Tobias Figueiredo, Alberto
Aquilani (71' André Martins), Adrien Silva, Carlos Mané (63' Bryan Ruiz), Gelson Martins,
Fredy Montero (63' Islam Slimani), Teófilo Gutiérrez. Coach: Jorge Jesus.
Lokomotiv Moskva: Guilherme, Nemanja Pejcinovic, Vedran Corluka, Vitaliy Denisov,
Roman Shishkin, Manuel Fernandes (81' Aleksandr Kolomeytsev), Aleksandr Samedov,
Dmitriy Tarasov (86' Taras Mikhalik), Delvin N'Dinga, Maicon (82' Maksim Grigoriev),
Oumar Niasse. Coach: Igor Cherevtchenko.
Goals: 12' Aleksandr Samedov 0-1, 50' Fredy Montero 1-1, 56' Aleksandr Samedov 1-2,
65' Oumar Niasse 1-3.
Referee: Robert Schörgenhofer (AUT)   Attendance: 25,400.

17.09.15   Elbasan Arena, Elbasan: KF Skënderbeu – Besiktas 0-1 (0-1)
KF Skënderbeu: Orges Shehi, Ademir (67' Kristi Vangjeli), Marko Radas, Renato Arapi,
Blendi Shkëmbi, Leonit Abazi, Bernard Berisha, Liridon Latifi (46' Bakary Nimaga),
Esquerdinha, Sabien Lilaj, Peter Olayinka (70' Hamdi Salihi). Coach: Mirel Josa.
Besiktas: Tolga Zengin, Ismail Köybasi, Ersan Gülüm, Andreas Beck, Rhodolfo, José Sosa,
Atiba Hutchinson, Necip Uysal, Kerim Frei (54' Gökhan Töre), Ricardo Quaresma (83'
Mustafa Pektemek), Cenk Tosun (60' Mario Gómez). Coach: Senol Günes.
Goal: 28' José Sosa 0-1.
Referee: Tamás Bognar (HUN)   Attendance: 5,482.

01.10.15   Atatürk Olimpiyat, Istanbul: Besiktas – Sporting CP 1-1 (0-1)
Besiktas: Tolga Zengin, Ismail Köybasi, Ersan Gülüm, Andreas Beck, Rhodolfo, José Sosa
(68' Cenk Tosun), Gökhan Töre, Atiba Hutchinson, Necip Uysal (46' Oguzhan Özyakup),
Ricardo Quaresma (90+1' Kerim Frei), Mario Gómez. Coach: Senol Günes.
Sporting CP: Rui Patricio, Jonathan Silva, João Pereira, Naldo, Tobias Figueiredo, Alberto
Aquilani (78' Gelson Martins), William Carvalho, Bryan Ruiz, Carlos Mané, Matheus Pereira
(55' Adrien Silva), Teófilo Gutiérrez (70' Islam Slimani). Coach: Jorge Jesus.
Goals: 16 Bryan Ruiz 0-1, 61' Gökhan Töre 1-1.
Referee: Paolo Tagliavento (ITA)   Attendance: 25,827.

01.10.15   Lokomotiv, Moskva: Lokomotiv Moskva – KF Skënderbeu 2-0 (1-0)
Lokomotiv Moskva: Guilherme, Nemanja Pejcinovic, Vedran Corluka, Arseniy Logashov,
Manuel Fernandes (46' Aleksey Miranchuk), Aleksandr Kolomeytsev (66' Delvin N'Dinga),
Aleksandr Samedov, Dmitriy Tarasov, Renat Yanbaev, Maicon, Oumar Niasse (81' Petar
Skuletic). Coach: Igor Cherevtchenko.
KF Skënderbeu: Orges Shehi, Bajram Jashanica, Kristi Vangjeli, Marko Radas, Bakary
Nimaga, Leonit Abazi (77' Renato Arapi), Bernard Berisha, Liridon Latifi (71' Blendi
Shkëmbi), Sabien Lilaj, Hamdi Salihi, Peter Olayinka (87' Gerhard Progni). Coach: Mirel Josa.
Goals: 35' Oumar Niasse 1-0, 73' Aleksandr Samedov 2-0.
Referee: Orel Grinfeld (ISR)   Attendance: 10,340.

22.10.15   Lokomotiv, Moskva: Lokomotiv Moskva – Besiktas 1-1 (0-0)
Lokomotiv Moskva: Guilherme, Vedran Corluka, Taras Mikhalik, Vitaliy Denisov, Roman
Shishkin, Manuel Fernandes (73' Ján Durica), Aleksandr Kolomeytsev, Aleksandr Samedov,
Delvin N'Dinga, Maicon (79' Alan Kasaev), Oumar Niasse (88' Maksim Grigoriev).
Coach: Igor Cherevtchenko.
Besiktas: Tolga Zengin, Ismail Köybasi, Ersan Gülüm, Andreas Beck, Rhodolfo, José Sosa
(57' Necip Uysal), Gökhan Töre (65' Cenk Tosun), Atiba Hutchinson, Oguzhan Özyakup,
Ricardo Quaresma (87' Kerim Frei), Mario Gómez. Coach: Senol Günes.
Goals: 54' Maicon 1-0, 64' Mario Gómez 1-1.
Referee: Serge Gumienny (BEL)   Attendance: 19,124.
Sent off: 69' Vedran Corluka.

22.10.15   Estádio José Alvalade, Lisboa: Sporting CP – KF Skënderbeu 5-1 (2-0)
Sporting CP: Rui Patricio, Jonathan Silva, Ewerton, Ricardo Esgaio, Tobias Figueiredo,
Alberto Aquilani (72' William Carvalho), André Martins (59' Islam Slimani), Bruno Paulista,
Carlos Mané (65' Gelson Martins), Matheus Pereira, Fredy Montero. Coach: Jorge Jesus.
KF Skënderbeu: Orges Shehi, Bajram Jashanica, Tefik Osmani, Kristi Vangjeli, Renato Arapi,
Bakary Nimaga (66' Blendi Shkëmbi), Bernard Berisha, Esquerdinha (76' Leonit Abazi),
Sabien Lilaj, Gerhard Progni (67' Liridon Latifi), Hamdi Salihi. Coach: Mirel Josa.
Goals: 38' Alberto Aquilani 1-0 (p), 41' Fredy Montero 2-0 (p), 64' Matheus Pereira 3-0,
69' Tobias Figueiredo 4-0, 77' Matheus Pereira 5-0, 89' Bajram Jashanica 5-1.
Referee: Clayron Pisani (MLT)   Attendance: 20,567.
Sent off: 24' Hamdi Salihi.

05.11.15   Atatürk Olimpiyat, Istanbul: Besiktas – Lokomotiv Moskva 1-1 (0-0)
Besiktas: Tolga Zengin, Ismail Köybasi, Ersan Gülüm, Andreas Beck, Rhodolfo, José Sosa
(72' Necip Uysal), Gökhan Töre, Olcay Sahan (46' Ricardo Quaresma), Atiba Hutchinson,
Oguzhan Özyakup (83' Cenk Tosun), Mario Gómez. Coach: Senol Günes.
Lokomotiv Moskva: Guilherme, Ján Durica, Vitaliy Denisov, Roman Shishkin, Manuel
Fernandes (74' Anton Miranchuk), Aleksandr Kolomeytsev, Aleksandr Samedov, Renat
Yanbaev, Delvin N'Dinga, Maicon (90+3' Maksim Grigoriev), Oumar Niasse (90' Petar
Skuletic). Coach: Igor Cherevtchenko.
Goals: 58' Ricardo Quaresma 1-0, 76' Oumar Niasse 1-1.
Referee: Felix Zwayer (GER)   Attendance: 24,690.

05.11.15   Elbasan Arena, Elbasan: KF Skënderbeu – Sporting CP 3-0 (2-0)
KF Skënderbeu: Orges Shehi, Bajram Jashanica, Kristi Vangjeli, Marko Radas, Bakary
Nimaga, Leonit Abazi, Bernard Berisha (90+2' Renato Arapi), Liridon Latifi (82' Gerhard
Progni), Esquerdinha (90' Blendi Shkëmbi), Sabien Lilaj, Peter Olayinka. Coach: Mirel Josa.
Sporting CP: Rui Patricio, Jonathan Silva, Ewerton (71' Paulo Oliveira), Ricardo Esgaio,
Tobias Figueiredo, Adrien Silva (59' João Mário), Bruno Paulista, Carlos Mané, Matheus
Pereira, Junya Tanaka (19' Marcelo *goalkeeper*), Fredy Montero. Coach: Jorge Jesus.
Goals: 15', 19' Sabien Lilaj 1-0, 2-0 (p), 55' Bakary Nimaga 3-0.
Referee: Kristo Tohver (EST)   Attendance: 1,783.
Sent off: 17' Rui Patricio.

26.11.15   Lokomotiv, Moskva: Lokomotiv Moskva – Sporting CP 2-4 (1-3)
Lokomotiv Moskva: Guilherme, Taras Mikhalik, Ján Durica, Vitaliy Denisov, Roman
Shishkin, Manuel Fernandes (78' Aleksey Miranchuk), Aleksandr Samedov, Dmitriy Tarasov
(65' Aleksandr Kolomeytsev), Delvin N'Dinga, Maicon (81' Alan Kasaev), Oumar Niasse.
Coach: Igor Cherevtchenko.
Sporting CP: Marcelo, Jonathan Silva, Ewerton, Naldo, Ricardo Esgaio, João Mário (79'
Alberto Aquilani), Bryan Ruiz, Adrien Silva, Gelson Martins, Matheus Pereira (67' André
Martins), Fredy Montero (71' Islam Slimani). Coach: Jorge Jesus.
Goals: 5' Maicon 1-0, 20' Fredy Montero 1-1, 38' Bryan Ruiz 1-2, 43' Gelson Martins 1-3,
60' Matheus Pereira 1-4, 86' Aleksey Miranchuk 2-4.
Referee: Antonio Mateu Lahoz (ESP)   Attendance: 11,043.

26.11.15   Atatürk Olimpiyat, Istanbul: Besiktas – KF Skënderbeu 2-0 (1-0)
Besiktas: Tolga Zengin, Ismail Köybasi, Ersan Gülüm (33' Dusko Tosic), Andreas Beck,
Rhodolfo, Gökhan Töre (84' Olcay Sahan), Atiba Hutchinson, Oguzhan Özyakup, Necip
Uysal, Kerim Frei (68' Ricardo Quaresma), Cenk Tosun. Coach: Senol Günes.
KF Skënderbeu: Orges Shehi, Bajram Jashanica, Kristi Vangjeli, Marko Radas, Leonit Abazi,
Bernard Berisha (46' Renato Arapi), Liridon Latifi (79' Gerhard Progni), Esquerdinha, Sabien
Lilaj, Hamdi Salihi (83' Djair), Peter Olayinka. Coach: Mirel Josa.
Goals: 35', 78' Cenk Tosun 1-0, 2-0.
Referee: Pawel Gil (POL)   Attendance: 11,155.

10.12.15   Estádio José Alvalade, Lisboa: Sporting CP – Besiktas 3-1 (0-0)
Sporting CP: Rui Patricio, Jefferson, Paulo Oliveira, João Pereira, Naldo, William Carvalho,
João Mário, Bryan Ruiz, Adrien Silva (64' Teófilo Gutiérrez), Islam Slimani (88' Matheus
Pereira), Fredy Montero (46' Gelson Martins). Coach: Jorge Jesus.
Besiktas: Tolga Zengin, Ismail Köybasi (85' Kerim Frei), Dusko Tosic, Andreas Beck,
Rhodolfo, José Sosa (79' Cenk Tosun), Olcay Sahan (71' Necip Uysal), Atiba Hutchinson,
Oguzhan Özyakup, Ricardo Quaresma, Mario Gómez. Coach: Senol Günes.
Goals: 58' Mario Gómez 0-1, 67' Islam Slimani 1-1, 72' Bryan Ruiz 2-1,
77' Teófilo Gutiérrez 3-1.
Referee: Manuel Gräfe (GER)   Attendance: 28,211.

10.12.15 Elbasan Arena, Elbasan: KF Skënderbeu – Lokomotiv Moskva 0-3 (0-1)
KF Skënderbeu: Orges Shehi, Bajram Jashanica, Ademir, Marko Radas, Leonit Abazi, Bernard
Berisha, Liridon Latifi (72' Gerhard Progni), Esquerdinha (82' Djair), Sabien Lilaj, Hamdi
Salihi, Peter Olayinka. Coach: Mirel Josa.
Lokomotiv Moskva: Guilherme, Nemanja Pejcinovic, Taras Mikhalik (82' Ján Durica), Vitaliy
Denisov, Roman Shishkin, Alan Kasaev (75' Maicon), Aleksandr Kolomeytsev, Aleksandr
Samedov, Dmitriy Tarasov, Delvin N'Dinga, Oumar Niasse (90+1' Anton Miranchuk).
Coach: Igor Cherevtchenko.
Goals: 18' Dmitry Tarasov 0-1, 89' Oumar Niasse 0-2, 90' Aleksandr Samedov 0-3.
Referee: Marijo Strahonja (CRO) Attendance: 1,152.

GROUP I

17.09.15 Artemio Franchi, Firenze: ACF Fiorentina – FC Basel 1-2 (1-0)
ACF Fiorentina: Luigi Sepe, Gonzalo Rodríguez, Davide Astori (65' Manuel Pasqual), Marcos
Alonso, Facundo Roncaglia, Milan Badelj, Mati Fernández (66' Nenad Tomovic), Jakub
Blaszczykowski, Borja Valero, Josip Ilicic (46' Khouma Babacar), Nikola Kalinic.
Coach: Paulo Sousa.
FC Basel: Tomás Vaclík, Michael Lang, Marek Suchy, Daniel Høegh, Luca Zuffi, Birkir
Bjarnason, Mohamed Elneny, Taulant Xhaka, Marc Janko (87' Davide Callà), Breel Embolo,
Jean-Paul Boëtius (72' Matías Delgado). Coach: Urs Fischer.
Goals: 4' Nikola Kalinic 1-0, 71' Birkir Bjarnason 1-1, 79' Mohamed Elneny 1-2.
Referee: Michael Oliver (ENG) Attendance: 15,269.
Sent off: 65' Gonzalo Rodríguez.

17.09.15 INEA Stadion, Poznan: Lech Poznan – Os Belenenses 0-0
Lech Poznan: Jasmin Buric, Tamás Kádár, Dariusz Dudka, Kebba Ceesay, Paulus Arajuuri,
Marcin Kaminksi, Lukasz Tralka (46' Karol Linetty), Gergö Lovrencsics (68' Szymon
Pawlowski), Denis Thomalla, David Kownacki (60' Kasper Hämäläinen), Dariusz Formella.
Coach: Maciej Skorza.
Os Belenenses: Ventura, Amorim, Tonel, Geraldes, Brandão, Rúben Pinto, André Sousa (80'
Ricardo Dias), Fábio Sturgeon (63' Kuca), Carlos Martins (89' Dálcio), Miguel Rosa, Luís
Leal. Coach: Sá Pinto.
Referee: Sergey Boyko (UKR) Attendance: 7,934.

01.10.15 St.Jakob-Park, Basel: FC Basel – Lech Poznan 2-0 (0-0)
FC Basel: Tomás Vaclík, Michael Lang, Walter Samuel, Marek Suchy, Luca Zuffi, Birkir
Bjarnason, Mohamed Elneny, Taulant Xhaka, Davide Callà (80' Shkëlzen Gashi), Marc Janko,
Breel Embolo. Coach: Urs Fischer.
Lech Poznan: Maciej Gostomski, Tamás Kádár, Kebba Ceesay, Paulus Arajuuri, Marcin
Kaminksi, Karol Linetty, Darko Jevtic (54' Lukasz Tralka), Abdul Tetteh, Maciej Gajos (69'
Gergö Lovrencsics), David Kownacki (46' Kasper Hämäläinen), Dariusz Formella.
Coach: Maciej Skorza.
Goals: 55' Birkir Bjarnason 1-0, 90' Breel Embolo 2-0.
Referee: Ognjen Valjic (BIH) Attendance: 17,567.
Sent off: 49' Karol Linetty.

01.10.15 Estádio do Restelo, Lisboa: Os Belenenses – ACF Fiorentina 0-4 (0-2)
Os Belenenses: Ventura, Tonel, Geraldes, Brandão, Rúben Pinto, André Sousa, Kuca (63'
Fábio Nunes), Fábio Sturgeon (40' Dálcio), Filipe Ferreira, Carlos Martins (78' Tiago Caeiro),
Luís Leal. Coach: Sá Pinto.
ACF Fiorentina: Luigi Sepe, Nenad Tomovic, Davide Astori, Marcos Alonso, Matías Vecino,
Mati Fernández, Mario Suárez, Federico Bernardeschi (60' Milan Badelj), Ante Rebic (81'
Jakub Blaszczykowski), Giuseppe Rossi, Khouma Babacar (78' Vendú). Coach: Paulo Sousa.
Goals: 18' Federico Bernardeschi 0-1, 45+1' Khouma Babacar 0-2, 83' Tonel 0-3 (og),
90' Giuseppe Rossi 0-4.
Referee: Aleksandar Stavrev (MKD)   Attendance: 6,886.

22.10.15 Artemio Franchi, Firenze: ACF Fiorentina – Lech Poznan 1-2 (0-0)
ACF Fiorentina: Luigi Sepe, Nenad Tomovic, Davide Astori, Manuel Pasqual (68' Federico
Bernardeschi), Facundo Roncaglia, Mati Fernández, Mario Suárez (73' Josip Ilicic), Vendú
(65' Matías Vecino), Ante Rebic, Giuseppe Rossi, Khouma Babacar. Coach: Paulo Sousa.
Lech Poznan: Jasmin Buric, Tomasz Kedziora, Tamás Kádár, Dariusz Dudka, Marcin
Kaminksi, Lukasz Tralka, Dávid Holman (67' Kasper Hämäläinen), Abdul Tetteh, Gergö
Lovrencsics, Denis Thomalla (62' David Kownacki / 77' Maciej Gajos), Dariusz Formella.
Coach: Jan Urban.
Goals: 65' David Kownacki 0-1, 82' Maciej Gajos 0-2, 90' Giuseppe Rossi 1-2.
Referee: Gediminas Mazeika (LTU)   Attendance: 13,792.
Sent off: 90+1' Ante Rebic.

22.10.15 St.Jakob-Park, Basel: FC Basel – Os Belenenses 1-2 (1-2)
FC Basel: Germano Vailati, Michael Lang, Walter Samuel, Marek Suchy, Behrang Safari,
Matías Delgado (67' Luca Zuffi), Zdravko Kuzmanovic (78' Albian Ajeti), Taulant Xhaka,
Shkëlzen Gashi, Marc Janko, Breel Embolo (59' Birkir Bjarnason). Coach: Urs Fischer.
Os Belenenses: Ventura, Amorim, João Afonso, Brandão, Rúben Pinto, André Sousa (84'
Ricardo Dias), Tiago Silva (90+3' Gonçalo Silva), Kuca, Fábio Sturgeon, Filipe Ferreira, Luís
Leal (88' Tiago Caeiro). Coach: Sá Pinto.
Goals: 15' Michael Lang 1-0, 27' Luís Leal 1-1, 45+1' Kuca 1-2.
Referee: Simon Evans (WAL)   Attendance: 17,275.

05.11.15 INEA Stadion, Poznan: Lech Poznan – ACF Fiorentina 0-2 (0-1)
Lech Poznan: Jasmin Buric, Tomasz Kedziora, Tamás Kádár, Dariusz Dudka, Marcin
Kaminksi, Lukasz Tralka, Karol Linetty, Szymon Pawlowski, Kasper Hämäläinen (77' Maciej
Gajos), Abdul Tetteh (72' Denis Thomalla), Dariusz Formella (60' Gergö Lovrencsics).
Coach: Jan Urban.
ACF Fiorentina: Luigi Sepe, Gonzalo Rodríguez, Nenad Tomovic, Davide Astori, Matías
Vecino, Mati Fernández, Jakub Blaszczykowski (72' Marcos Alonso), Mario Suárez (79'
Milan Badelj), Josip Ilicic, Federico Bernardeschi, Giuseppe Rossi (63' Nikola Kalinic).
Coach: Paulo Sousa.
Goals: 42', 83' Josip Ilicic 0-1, 0-2.
Referee: Halis Özkahya (TUR)   Attendance: 22,343.

05.11.15 Estádio do Restelo, Lisboa: Os Belenenses – FC Basel 0-2 (0-1)
Os Belenenses: Ventura, Amorim, Brandão (28' Tonel), Gonçalo Silva, Rúben Pinto, André Sousa (66' Tiago Caeiro), Tiago Silva, Kuca (83' Fábio Nunes), Fábio Sturgeon, Filipe Ferreira, Luís Leal. Coach: Sá Pinto.
FC Basel: Tomás Vaclík, Michael Lang, Manuel Akanji, Marek Suchy, Behrang Safari, Luca Zuffi, Birkir Bjarnason, Mohamed Elneny, Taulant Xhaka, Marc Janko, Breel Embolo. Coach: Urs Fischer.
Goals: 45' Marc Janko 0-1 (p), 64' Breel Embolo 0-2.
Referee: Tamás Bognar (HUN)   Attendance: 4,802.

26.11.15 St.Jakob-Park, Basel: FC Basel – ACF Fiorentina 2-2 (1-2)
FC Basel: Germano Vailati, Michael Lang, Marek Suchy, Behrang Safari, Luca Zuffi, Birkir Bjarnason (88' Zdravko Kuzmanovic), Mohamed Elneny, Taulant Xhaka, Marc Janko, Breel Embolo, Jean-Paul Boëtius (60' Davide Callà). Coach: Urs Fischer.
ACF Fiorentina: Luigi Sepe, Gonzalo Rodríguez, Davide Astori, Marcos Alonso, Facundo Roncaglia, Milan Badelj (85' Gilberto), Matías Vecino, Borja Valero, Josip Ilicic (33' Nenad Tomovic), Nikola Kalinic, Federico Bernardeschi (85' Khouma Babacar). Coach: Paulo Sousa.
Goals: 23', 36' Federico Bernardeschi 0-1, 0-2, 40' Marek Suchy 1-2,
74' Mohamed Elneny 2-2.
Referee: Ivan Kruzliak (SVK)   Attendance: 22,550.
Sent off: 26' Facundo Roncaglia.

26.11.15 Estádio do Restelo, Lisboa: Os Belenenses – Lech Poznan 0-0
Os Belenenses: Ventura, Tonel, Geraldes, Brandão, Rúben Pinto, Tiago Silva (67' Carlos Martins), Kuca, Fábio Sturgeon (79' Dálcio), Ricardo Dias, Filipe Ferreira, Tiago Caeiro (76' Luís Leal). Coach: Sá Pinto.
Lech Poznan: Jasmin Buric, Barry Douglas, Tomasz Kedziora, Tamás Kádár, Dariusz Dudka, Lukasz Tralka (46' Abdul Tetteh), Karol Linetty, Gergö Lovrencsics, Maciej Gajos, Denis Thomalla (74' Kasper Hämäläinen), Dariusz Formella (65' Szymon Pawlowski). Coach: Jan Urban.
Referee: Arnold Hunter (NIR)   Attendance: 1,987.

Tiago Silva missed a penalty kick (36').

10.12.15 INEA Stadion, Poznan: Lech Poznan – FC Basel 0-1 (0-0)
Lech Poznan: Jasmin Buric, Tomasz Kedziora, Tamás Kádár, Paulus Arajuuri, Marcin Kaminski, Lukasz Tralka (46' Abdul Tetteh), Karol Linetty (61' Dariusz Formella), Szymon Pawlowski, Darko Jevtic (73' Kasper Hämäläinen), Maciej Gajos, David Kownacki. Coach: Jan Urban.
FC Basel: Germano Vailati (45+1' Mirko Salvi), Adama Traoré, Michael Lang (46' Adonis Ajeti), Walter Samuel, Luca Zuffi, Birkir Bjarnason (79' Robin Huser), Mohamed Elneny, Taulant Xhaka, Davide Callà, Albian Ajeti, Jean-Paul Boëtius. Coach: Urs Fischer.
Goal: 50' Jean-Paul Boëtius 0-1.
Referee: Bobby Madden (SCO)   Attendance: 10,457.

10.12.15   Artemio Franchi, Firenze: ACF Fiorentina – Os Belenenses 1-0 (0-0)
ACF Fiorentina: Luigi Sepe, Gilberto (57' Federico Bernardeschi), Nenad Tomovic, Davide
Astori, Manuel Pasqual, Marcos Alonso, Milan Badelj (79' Mario Suárez), Borja Valero (62'
Matías Vecino), Verdú, Giuseppe Rossi, Khouma Babacar. Coach: Paulo Sousa.
Os Belenenses: Ventura, Amorim, João Afonso, Gonçalo Silva, Rúben Pinto (79' Fábio
Nunes), André Sousa (56' Kuca), Fábio Sturgeon (83' Tiago Caeiro), Ricardo Dias, Filipe
Ferreira, Carlos Martins, Luís Leal. Coach: Sá Pinto.
Goal: 67' Khouma Babacar 1-0.
Referee: Vladislav Bezborodov (RUS)   Attendance: 12,756.

GROUP J

17.09.15   Constant Vanden Stock, Brussels: RSC Anderlecht – AS Monaco 1-1 (1-0)
RSC Anderlecht: Silvio Proto, Olivier Deschacht, Ivan Obradovic, Andy Najar, Dennis Praet,
Steven Defour (84' Michaël Heylen), Guillaume Gillet, Youri Tielemans (88' Imoh Ezekiel),
Leander Dendoncker, Matias Suárez (74' Frank Acheampong), Stefano Okaka.
Coach: Besnik Hasi.
AS Monaco: Danijel Subasic, Fabinho, Fábio Coentrão, Wallace, Elderson Echiéjilé (61'
Stephan El Shaarawy), Andrea Raggi, Almamy Touré, João Moutinho, Bernardo Silva, Mario
Pasalic (46' Lacina Traoré), Ivan Cavaleiro (76' Thomas Lemar). Coach: Leonardo Jardim.
Goals: 11' Guillaume Gillet 1-0, 85' Lacina Traoré 1-1.
Referee: Miroslav Zelinka (CZE)   Attendance: 15,576.

17.09.15   White Hart Lane, London: Tottenham Hotspur – Qarabag FK 3-1 (2-1)
Tottenham Hotspur: Hugo Lloris, Danny Rose, Toby Alderweireld, Kieran Trippier, Kevin
Wimmer, Érik Lamela, Eric Dier (75' Harry Winks), Andros Townsend (68' Clinton N'Jie),
Dele Alli, Tom Carroll, Heung-min Son (68' Harry Kane). Coach: Mauricio Pochettino.
Qarabag FK: Ibrahim Sehic, Qara Qarayev, Maksim Medvedev, Rashad Sadygov, Ansi Agolli,
Badavi Guseynov, Reynaldo, Dani Quintana (79' Michel), Afran Ismayilov (79' Alharbi El
Jadeyaoui), Javid Tagiyev (67' Samuel Armenteros), Richard. Coach: Gurban Gurbanov.
Goals: 7' Richard 0-1 (p), 28', 30' Heung-min Son 1-1, 2-1, 86' Érik Lamela 3-1.
Referee: Adrien Jaccottet (SUI)   Attendance: 26,463.

01.10.15   Stade Louis II, Monaco: AS Monaco – Tottenham Hotspur 1-1 (0-1)
AS Monaco: Danijel Subasic, Fabinho, Fábio Coentrão, Ricardo Carvalho (76' Nabil Dirar),
Andrea Raggi, João Moutinho, Bernardo Silva, Adama Traoré, Thomas Lemar (60' Stephan El
Shaarawy), Jérémy Toulalan, Lacina Traoré (68' Guido Carrillo). Coach: Leonardo Jardim.
Tottenham Hotspur: Hugo Lloris, Danny Rose, Toby Alderweireld, Jan Vertonghen, Kieran
Trippier, Érik Lamela (65' Clinton N'Jie), Eric Dier, Dele Alli, Christian Eriksen (90+1' Tom
Carroll), Harry Kane, Nacer Chadli (70' Andros Townsend). Coach: Mauricio Pochettino.
Goals: 35' Érik Lamela 0-1, 81' Stephan El Shaarawy 1-1.
Referee: Artur Soares Dias (POR)   Attendance: 7,216.

01.10.15   Tofiq Bakhramov, Baku: Qarabag FK – RSC Anderlecht 1-0 (1-0)
Qarabag FK: Ibrahim Sehic, Qara Qarayev, Maksim Medvedev, Rashad Sadygov, Ansi Agolli, Badavi Guseynov, Reynaldo, Dani Quintana (67' Joshgun Diniyev), Alharbi El Jadeyaoui (77' Elvin Yunuszade), Richard, Samuel Armenteros (61' Afran Ismayilov).
Coach: Gurban Gurbanov.
RSC Anderlecht: Silvio Proto, Olivier Deschacht, Serigne Mbodj, Ivan Obradovic (64' Frank Acheampong), Andy Najar, Dennis Praet (72' Matias Suárez), Steven Defour, Guillaume Gillet (72' Youri Tielemans), Leander Dendoncker, Imoh Ezekiel, Stefano Okaka.
Coach: Besnik Hasi.
Goal: 36' Richard 1-0.
Referee: Oliver Drachta (AUT)   Attendance: 25,000.

22.10.15   Constant Vanden Stock, Brussels: RSC Anderlecht – Tottenham Hotspur 2-1 (1-1)
RSC Anderlecht: Silvio Proto, Olivier Deschacht, Serigne Mbodj, Ivan Obradovic, Dennis Praet (90+2' Ibrahima Conté), Steven Defour, Guillaume Gillet, Youri Tielemans, Leander Dendoncker, Imoh Ezekiel (66' Frank Acheampong), Stefano Okaka (88' Idrissa Sylla).
Coach: Besnik Hasi.
Tottenham Hotspur: Hugo Lloris, Toby Alderweireld, Jan Vertonghen, Kieran Trippier, Ben Davies, Érik Lamela, Eric Dier, Andros Townsend (80' Joshua Onomah), Mousa Dembélé (65' Dele Alli), Christian Eriksen, Clinton N'Jie (59' Harry Kane). Coach: Mauricio Pochettino.
Goals: 4' Christian Eriksen 0-1, 13' Guillaume Gillet 1-1, 75' Stefano Okaka 2-1.
Referee: Pol van Boekel (HOL)   Attendance: 18,504.

22.10.15   Stade Louis II, Monaco: AS Monaco – Qarabag FK 1-0 (0-0)
AS Monaco: Danijel Subasic, Fabinho, Ricardo Carvalho, Wallace, Andrea Raggi, João Moutinho, Bernardo Silva (56' Mario Pasalic), Thomas Lemar (79' Nabil Dirar), Jérémy Toulalan, Lacina Traoré (90+1' Guido Carrillo), Stephan El Shaarawy.
Coach: Leonardo Jardim.
Qarabag FK: Ibrahim Sehic, Qara Qarayev, Maksim Medvedev, Rashad Sadygov, Ansi Agolli, Badavi Guseynov, Dani Quintana (59' Chumbinho), Afran Ismayilov (71' Rydell Poepon), Alharbi El Jadeyaoui (77' Elvin Mammadov), Richard, Samuel Armenteros.
Coach: Gurban Gurbanov.
Goal: 70' Lacina Traoré 1-0.
Referee: Jakob Kehlet (DEN)   Attendance: 6,165.

05.11.59   Tofiq Bakhramov, Baku: Qarabag FK – AS Monaco 1-1 (1-0)
Qarabag FK: Ibrahim Sehic, Qara Qarayev, Maksim Medvedev, Rashad Sadygov, Ansi Agolli, Badavi Guseynov, Dani Quintana (68' Chumbinho), Afran Ismayilov (64' Rydell Poepon), Alharbi El Jadeyaoui, Richard, Samuel Armenteros. Coach: Gurban Gurbanov.
AS Monaco: Danijel Subasic, Fabinho, Ricardo Carvalho, Wallace, Andrea Raggi, João Moutinho, Bernardo Silva, Mario Pasalic (61' Ivan Cavaleiro), Jérémy Toulalan, Lacina Traoré (78' Elderson Echiéjilé), Stephan El Shaarawy (70' Guido Carrillo). Coach: Leonardo Jardim.
Goals: 39' Samuel Armenteros 1-0, 72' Ivan Cavaleiro 1-1.
Referee: Cristian Balaj (ROM)   Attendance: 30,200.

05.11.15   White Hart Lane, London: Tottenham Hotspur – RSC Anderlecht 2-1 (1-0)
Tottenham Hotspur: Hugo Lloris, Toby Alderweireld, Jan Vertonghen, Kieran Trippier, Ben Davies, Ryan Mason (73' Mousa Dembélé), Érik Lamela, Eric Dier, Dele Alli (77' Joshua Onomah), Christian Eriksen (59' Heung-min Son), Harry Kane. Coach: Mauricio Pochettino.
RSC Anderlecht: Silvio Proto, Olivier Deschacht, Serigne Mbodj, Andy Najar, Steven Defour, Frank Acheampong (89' Idrissa Sylla), Fabrice N'Sakala (83' Ibrahima Conté), Guillaume Gillet, Youri Tielemans (69' Imoh Ezekiel), Leander Dendoncker, Stefano Okaka.
Coach: Besnik Hasi.
Goals: 29' Harry Kane 1-0, 72' Imoh Ezekiel 1-1, 87' Mousa Dembélé 2-1.
Referee: Orel Grinfeld (ISR)   Attendance: 33,479.

26.11.15   Stade Louis II, Monaco: AS Monaco – RSC Anderlecht 0-2 (0-1)
AS Monaco: Danijel Subasic, Fabinho, Fábio Coentrão, Ricardo Carvalho, Andrea Raggi, João Moutinho, Bernardo Silva, Mario Pasalic (62' Guido Carrillo), Jérémy Toulalan (29' Almamy Touré), Lacina Traoré (84' Elderson Echiéjilé), Stephan El Shaarawy.
Coach: Leonardo Jardim.
RSC Anderlecht: Silvio Proto, Olivier Deschacht, Serigne Mbodj, Andy Najar (65' Imoh Ezekiel), Dennis Praet (76' Frank Acheampong), Steven Defour, Fabrice N'Sakala, Guillaume Gillet, Youri Tielemans, Leander Dendoncker, Stefano Okaka (84' Matías Suárez).
Coach: Besnik Hasi.
Goals: 45+1' Guillaume Gillet 0-1, 78' Frank Acheampong 0-2.
Referee: Manuel Gräfe (GER)   Attendance: 5,913.

26.11.15   Tofiq Bakhramov, Baku: Qarabag FK – Tottenham Hotspur 0-1 (0-0)
Qarabag FK: Ibrahim Sehic, Qara Qarayev, Maksim Medvedev, Rashad Sadygov, Ansi Agolli, Badavi Guseynov, Dani Quintana, Afran Ismayilov (80' Elvin Mammadov), Javid Tagiyev (65' Chumbinho), Richard, Rydell Poepon (54' Samuel Armenteros).
Coach: Gurban Gurbanov.
Tottenham Hotspur: Hugo Lloris, Toby Alderweireld, Jan Vertonghen, Kieran Trippier, Ben Davies, Ryan Mason (73' Tom Carroll), Eric Dier, Dele Alli, Christian Eriksen (90+1' Joshua Onomah), Heung-min Son (80' Clinton N'Jie), Harry Kane. Coach: Mauricio Pochettino.
Goal: 78' Harry Kane 0-1.
Referee: Anasthasios Sidiropoulos (GRE)   Attendance: 28,000.

10.12.15   White Hart Lane, London: Tottenham Hotspur – AS Monaco 4-1 (3-0)
Tottenham Hotspur: Hugo Lloris, Toby Alderweireld, Kieran Trippier, Kevin Wimmer, Ben Davies, Érik Lamela (62' Nacer Chadli), Eric Dier (42' Nabil Bentaleb), Tom Carroll, Heung-min Son, Clinton N'Jie (79' Dele Alli), Joshua Onomah. Coach: Mauricio Pochettino.
AS Monaco: Danijel Subasic, Wallace, Elderson Echiéjilé, Nabil Dirar, João Moutinho (46' Thomas Lemar), Bernardo Silva (65' Raphaël Diarra), Tiemoué Bakayoko, Mario Pasalic, Jérémy Toulalan, Lacina Traoré (56' Kylian Mbappé), Stephan El Shaarawy.
Coach: Leonardo Jardim.
Goals: 2', 15', 38' Érik Lamela 1-0, 2-0, 3-0, 61' Stephan El Shaarawy 3-1, 78' Tom Carroll 4-1.
Referee: Ivan Bebek (CRO)   Attendance: 34,122.

10.12.15 Constant Vanden Stock, Brussels: RSC Anderlecht – Qarabag FK 2-1 (2-1)
RSC Anderlecht: Silvio Proto, Olivier Deschacht, Serigne Mbodj, Andy Najar, Dennis Praet
(90+1' Andy Kawaya), Fabrice N'Sakala, Guillaume Gillet, Youri Tielemans, Matías Suárez,
Imoh Ezekiel (66' Dodi Lukebakio), Stefano Okaka (81' Idrissa Sylla). Coach: Besnik Hasi.
Qarabag FK: Ibrahim Sehic, Qara Qarayev (75' Rydell Poepon), Maksim Medvedev, Rashad
Sadygov, Badavi Guseynov, Dani Quintana, Afran Ismayilov (63' Javid Tagiyev), Chumbinho
(71' Michel), Ilgar Gurbanov, Richard, Samuel Armenteros. Coach: Gurban Gurbanov.
Goals: 26' Dani Quintana 0-1, 28' Andy Najar 1-1, 31' Stefano Okaka 2-1.
Referee: Slavko Vincic (SVN)   Attendance: 16,075.

GROUP K

17.09.15 Neo GSP, Nicosia: APOEL Nicosia – FC Schalke 04 0-3 (0-2)
APOEL Nicosia: Boy Waterman, Carlão, Marios Antoniades (23' Kostakis Artymatas), Astiz,
Nuno Morais, Mário Sérgio, Tomás De Vincenti, Konstantinos Makrides, Vinicius (61' Semir
Stilic), Vander, Pieros Sotiriou (56' Fernando Cavenaghi). Coach: Temur Ketsbaia.
FC Schalke 04: Ralf Fährmann, Junior Caiçara, Dennis Aogo, Joel Matip, Johannes Geis (62'
Marco Höger), Max Meyer, Leon Goretzka, Leroy Sané (80' Sidney Sam), Roman Neustädter,
Franco Di Santo, Klaas-Jan Huntelaar (75' Pierre-Emile Højbjerg). Coach: André Breitenreiter.
Goals: 28' Joel Matip 0-2, 35', 71' Klaas-Jan Huntelaar 0-3.
Referee: Tony Chapron (FRA)   Attendance: 13,512.
Sent off: 77' Tomás De Vincenti.

17.09.15 Theodoros Kolokotronis, Tripoli: Asteras Tripolis – Sparta Praha 1-1 (1-0)
Asteras Tripolis: Tomás Kosicky, Fernando Alloco, Konstantinos Giannoulis, Brian Lluy,
Dorin Goian, Taxiarchis Fountas (66' Elin Dimoutsos), Facundo Bertoglio (71' Nico
Fernández), Matías Iglesias, Ederson (77' Rachid Hamdani), Pablo Mazza, Apostolos Giannou.
Coach: Staikos Vergetis.
Sparta Praha: David Bicík, Mario Holek, Costa Nhamoinesu, Matej Hybs, Marek Matejovsky,
Borek Dockal, Martin Frydek, Josef Husbauer (66' Kehinde Fatai), Ladislav Krejcí, Petr
Jirácek (83' Lukás Marecek), David Lafata. Coach: Zdenek Scasny.
Goals: 2' Pablo Mazza 1-0, 56' David Lafata 1-1.
Referee: Marijo Strahonja (CRO)   Attendance: 2,984.

01.10.15 Generali Arena, Praha: Sparta Praha – APOEL Nicosia 2-0 (1-0)
Sparta Praha: David Bicík, Jakub Brabec, Costa Nhamoinesu, Marek Matejovsky, Borek
Dockal, Lukás Marecek, Martin Frydek, Ladislav Krejcí (90+1' Markus Steinhöfer), Petr
Jirácek, Kehinde Fatai (86' Tiémoko Konaté), David Lafata. Coach: Zdenek Scasny.
APOEL Nicosia: Boy Waterman, Carlão, Marios Antoniades, Rafael Anastasiou, Nuno
Morais, Mário Sérgio, Kostakis Artymatas, Giorgos Efrem, Konstantinos Makrides (80' Costas
Charalambides), Vander (53' Semir Stilic), Mateusz Piatkowski (67' Fernando Cavenaghi).
Coach: Temur Ketsbaia.
Goals: 24' Kehinde Fatai 1-0, 60' Jakub Brabec 2-0.
Referee: Pawel Gil (POL)   Attendance: 9,130.

01.10.15   VELTINS-Arena, Gelsenkirchen: FC Schalke 04 – Asteras Tripolis 4-0 (3-0)
FC Schalke 04: Ralf Fährmann, Benedikt Höwedes, Sead Kolasinac, Sascha Riether, Joel
Matip, Johannes Geis (46' Kaan Ayhan), Leon Goretzka (73' Max Meyer), Leroy Sané, Pierre-
Emile Højbjerg, Franco Di Santo (63' Eric Maxim Choupo-Moting), Klaas-Jan Huntelaar.
Coach: André Breitenreiter.
Asteras Tripolis: Konstantinos Theodoropoulos, Khalifa Sankaré, Konstantinos Giannoulis,
Brian Lluy, Dorin Goian (70' Taxiarchis Fountas), Georgios Zisopoulos, Rachid Hamdani,
Matías Iglesias, Ederson (79' Dimitrios Kourbelis), Pablo Mazza (59' Tasos Tsokanis),
Apostolos Giannou. Coach: Staikos Vergetis.
Goals: 28', 37', 44' Franco Di Santo 1-0, 2-0, 3-0 (p), 84' Klaas-Jan Huntelaar 4-0.
Referee: Pol van Boekel (HOL)   Attendance: 42,447.

22.10.15   VELTINS-Arena, Gelsenkirchen: FC Schalke 04 – Sparta Praha 2-2 (1-0)
FC Schalke 04: Ralf Fährmann, Junior Caiçara, Benedikt Höwedes, Sead Kolasinac (83'
Dennis Aogo), Kaan Ayhan (61' Johannes Geis), Max Meyer, Leon Goretzka, Pierre-Emile
Højbjerg (61' Leroy Sané), Roman Neustädter, Franco Di Santo, Eric Maxim Choupo-Moting.
Coach: André Breitenreiter.
Sparta Praha: David Bicík, Jakub Brabec, Costa Nhamoinesu, Matej Hybs, Marek Matejovsky
(90+2' Josef Husbauer), Borek Dockal, Lukás Marecek, Tiémoko Konaté (62' David Lafata),
Ladislav Krejcí, Petr Jirácek, Kehinde Fatai (88' Mario Holek). Coach: Zdenek Scasny.
Goals: 6' Franco Di Santo 1-0, 50' Kehinde Fatai 1-1, 63' David Lafata 1-2,
73' Leroy Sané 2-2.
Referee: Artur Soares Dias (POR)   Attendance: 51,244.

22.10.15   Neo GSP, Nicosia: APOEL Nicosia – Asteras Tripolis 2-1 (1-1)
APOEL Nicosia: Boy Waterman, João Guilherme, Carlão, Marios Antoniades, Nuno Morais,
Kostakis Artymatas, Giorgos Efrem, Vinicius, Semir Stilic (87' Astiz), Vander (79' Costas
Charalambides), Fernando Cavenaghi (63' Mateusz Piatkowski). Coach: Temur Ketsbaia.
Asteras Tripolis: Konstantinos Theodoropoulos, Fernando Alloco, Khalifa Sankaré,
Konstantinos Giannoulis, Dimitrios Kourbelis (74' Manu Lanzarote), Brian Lluy, Elin
Dimoutsos (62' Nico Fernández), Facundo Bertoglio, Matías Iglesias, Pablo Mazza (88' Vasil
Shkurti), Apostolos Giannou. Coach: Staikos Vergetis.
Goals: 8' Brian Lluy 0-1, 45+8' Fernando Cavenaghi 1-1 (p), 59' Carlão 2-1.
Referee: Aleksey Eskov (RUS)   Attendance: 12,783.

05.11.15   Generali Arena, Praha: Sparta Praha – FC Schalke 04 1-1 (1-1)
Sparta Praha: David Bicík, Jakub Brabec, Costa Nhamoinesu, Matej Hybs, Marek Matejovsky,
Borek Dockal, Lukás Marecek, Ladislav Krejcí, Petr Jirácek, Kehinde Fatai (88' Tiémoko
Konaté), David Lafata (90' Lukás Julis). Coach: Zdenek Scasny.
FC Schalke 04: Ralf Fährmann, Junior Caiçara, Dennis Aogo, Kaan Ayhan, Johannes Geis,
Leon Goretzka (87' Sead Kolasinac), Leroy Sané (82' Max Meyer), Pierre-Emile Højbjerg,
Roman Neustädter, Eric Maxim Choupo-Moting, Klaas-Jan Huntelaar (77' Franco Di Santo).
Coach: André Breitenreiter.
Goals: 6' David Lafata 1-0, 20' Johannes Geis 1-1 (p).
Referee: Carlos Clos Gómez (ESP)   Attendance: 17,352.

106

05.11.15   Theodoros Kolokotronis, Tripoli: Asteras Tripolis – APOEL Nicosia 2-0 (2-0)
Asteras Tripolis: Konstantinos Theodoropoulos, Thanasis Panteliadis, Khalifa Sankaré,
Dimitrios Kourbelis, Brian Lluy, Georgios Zisopoulos, Facundo Bertoglio (64' Rachid
Hamdani), Matías Iglesias, Pablo Mazza, Manu Lanzarote (63' Taxiarchis Fountas), Apostolos
Giannou (77' Fernando Alloco). Coach: Staikos Vergetis.
APOEL Nicosia: Boy Waterman, Carlão, Marios Antoniades (64' Nektarios Alexandrou),
Astiz, Nuno Morais, Mário Sérgio, Kostakis Artymatas (77' Costas Charalambides), Vinicius,
Semir Stilic, Vander, Mateusz Piatkowski (46' Fernando Cavenaghi). Coach: Temur Ketsbaia.
Goals: 2' Facundo Bertoglio 1-0, 45+1' Apostolos Giannou 2-0.
Referee: Oliver Drachta (AUT)   Attendance: 3,624.

26.11.15   VELTINS-Arena, Gelsenkirchen: FC Schalke 04 – APOEL Nicosia 1-0 (0-0)
FC Schalke 04: Ralf Fährmann, Junior Caiçara (83' Sascha Riether), Dennis Aogo, Joel Matip,
Johannes Geis (79' Pierre-Emile Højbjerg), Leon Goretzka, Leroy Sané, Roman Neustädter,
Franco Di Santo (62' Max Meyer), Eric Maxim Choupo-Moting, Klaas-Jan Huntelaar.
Coach: André Breitenreiter.
APOEL Nicosia: Boy Waterman, João Guilherme, Carlão, Marios Antoniades (31' Astiz),
Nuno Morais, Mário Sérgio, Kostakis Artymatas, Tomás De Vincenti, Costas Charalambides
(77' Vander), Vinicius, Pieros Sotiriou (54' Konstantinos Makrides). Coach: Temur Ketsbaia.
Goal: 86' Eric Maxim Choupo-Moting 1-0.
Referee: Andreas Ekberg (SWE)   Attendance: 43,117.

Dennis Aogo missed a penalty kick (89').

26.11.15   Generali Arena, Praha: Sparta Praha – Asteras Tripolis 1-0 (1-0)
Sparta Praha: David Bicík, Jakub Brabec, Costa Nhamoinesu, Matej Hybs, Lukás Vácha,
Borek Dockal (86' Mario Holek), Lukás Marecek, Martin Frydek (90+2' Lukás Julis), Ladislav
Krejcí, Kehinde Fatai (80' Tiémoko Konaté), David Lafata. Coach: Zdenek Scasny.
Asteras Tripolis: Konstantinos Theodoropoulos, Khalifa Sankaré, Konstantinos Giannoulis,
Dimitrios Kourbelis (66' Elin Dimoutsos), Brian Lluy, Nico Fernández, Georgios Zisopoulos,
Taxiarchis Fountas (78' Manu Lanzarote), Matías Iglesias (81' Thanasis Panteliadis), Pablo
Mazza, Apostolos Giannou. Coach: Staikos Vergetis.
Goal: 33' Jakub Brabec 1-0.
Referee: Michael Oliver (ENG)   Attendance: 10,140.
Sent off: 82' Ladislav Krejcí.

10.12.15   Neo GSP, Nicosia: APOEL Nicosia – Sparta Praha 1-3 (1-0)
APOEL Nicosia: Boy Waterman, João Guilherme, Carlão (35' Vinicius), Nuno Morais, Mário
Sérgio, Kostakis Artymatas, Tomás De Vincenti, Semir Stilic, Vander (60' Giorgos Efrem),
Nektarios Alexandrou, Fernando Cavenaghi (80' Mateusz Piatkowski).
Coach: Temur Ketsbaia.
Sparta Praha: Marek Stech, Jakub Brabec, Mario Holek, Costa Nhamoinesu, Lukás Vácha (74'
David Lafata), Borek Dockal, Lukás Marecek, Martin Frydek, Tiémoko Konaté, Kehinde Fatai
(46' Marek Matejovsky), Lukás Julis (85' Francis Litsingi). Coach: Zdenek Scasny.
Goals: 6' Fernando Cavenaghi 1-0, 63' Lukás Julis 1-1, 77', 87' David Lafata 1-2, 1-3.
Referee: István Vad (HUN)   Attendance: 5,940.

10.12.15   Theodoros Kolokotronis, Tripoli: Asteras Tripolis – FC Schalke 04 0-4 (0-2)
Asteras Tripolis: Konstantinos Theodoropoulos, Thanasis Panteliadis, Khalifa Sankaré, Brian
Lluy, Dorin Goian (63' Georgios Zisopoulos), Nico Fernández, Tasos Tsokanis, Rachid
Hamdani, Matías Iglesias (69' Elin Dimoutsos), Manu Lanzarote (65' Facundo Bertoglio),
Apostolos Giannou. Coach: Staikos Vergetis.
FC Schalke 04: Ralf Fährmann, Junior Caiçara, Benedikt Höwedes (79' Marvin Friedrich),
Sead Kolasinac, Johannes Geis (65' Kaan Ayhan), Sidney Sam, Pierre-Emile Højbjerg, Roman
Neustädter, Franco Di Santo, Eric Maxim Choupo-Moting, Klaas-Jan Huntelaar (79' Max
Meyer). Coach: André Breitenreiter.
Goals: 29' Franco Di Santo 0-1, 37', 78' Eric Maxim Choupo-Moting 0-2, 0-3,
86' Max Meyer 0-4.
Referee: Liran Liany (ISR)   Attendance: 2,501.

GROUP L

17.09.15   San Mamés Barria, Bilbao: Athletic Bilbao – FC Augsburg 3-1 (0-1)
Athletic Bilbao: Iago Herrerín, Elustondo (46' Mikel Rico), Aymeric Laporte, De Marcos,
Etxeita, Beñat, Susaeta, Raúl García (80' Gurpegi), Lekue, Ibai (64' Sabin), Aduriz.
Coach: Valverde.
FC Augsburg: Marwin Hitz, Paul Verhaegh, Ragnar Klavan, Jan-Ingwar Callsen-Bracker,
Markus Feulner, Daniel Baier, Dominik Kohr (72' Piotr Trochowski), Halil Altintop (59' Ja-
cheol Koo), Alexander Esswein, Dong-won Ji, Tim Matavz (66' Tobias Werner).
Coach: Markus Weinzierl.
Goals: 15' Halil Antintop 0-1, 55', 66' Aduriz 1-1, 2-1, 90' Susaeta 3-1.
Referee: Vladislav Bezborodov (RUS)   Attendance: 37,838.

17.09.15   Partizan Stadion, Beograd: Partizan – AZ Alkmaar 3-2 (2-1)
Partizan: Zivko Zivkovic, Nikola Lekovic, Miroslav Vulicevic, Gregor Balazic, Fabrício,
Darko Brasanac, Stefan Babovic, Andrija Zivkovic (90+1' Nikola Ninkovic), Marko Jevtovic,
Aboubakar Oumarou (84' Sasa Ilic), Ivan Saponjic (66' Valeri Bozhinov).
Coach: Zoran Milinkovic.
AZ Alkmaar: Sergio Rochet, Mattias Johansson, Jeffrey Gouweleeuw, Rajko Brezancic, Jop
van der Linden, Joris van Overeem (64' Dabney dos Santos), Markus Henriksen, Ben Rienstra,
Thom Haye (73' Muamer Tankovic), Guus Hupperts, Vincent Janssen (73' Robert Mühren).
Coach: John van den Brom.
Goals: 11' Aboubakar Oumarou 1-0, 34' Jop van der Linden 1-1, 39' Aboubakar Oumarou 2-1,
89' Andrija Zivkovic 3-1, 90+3' Markus Henriksen 3-2.
Referee: Daniele Orsato (ITA)   Attendance: 7,949.
Sent off: 77' Guus Hupperts.

01.10.15   AFAS Stadion, Alkmaar: AZ Alkmaar – Athletic Bilbao 2-1 (0-0)
AZ Alkmaar: Gino Coutinho, Mattias Johansson, Jeffrey Gouweleeuw, Jop van der Linden,
Ridgeciano Haps, Joris van Overeem, Markus Henriksen, Ben Rienstra, Dabney dos Santos
(87' Thom Haye), Muamer Tankovic (76' Derrick Luckassen), Vincent Janssen (78' Alireza
Jahanbakhsh). Coach: John van den Brom.
Athletic Bilbao: Iago Herrerín, Eneko Bóveda, Aymeric Laporte, Eraso, Iturraspe (63' Raúl
García), Mikel Rico, Gurpegi, Aketxe (57' Williams), Lekue, Kike Sola (63' Aduriz), Viguera.
Coach: Valverde.
Goals: 55' Markus Henriksen 1-0, 65' Eneko Bóveda 2-0 (og), 75' Aduriz 2-1.
Referee: Ivan Kruzliak (SVK)   Attendance: 11,434.

01.10.15   WWK Arena, Augsburg: FC Augsburg – Partizan 1-3 (0-1)
FC Augsburg: Marwin Hitz, Paul Verhaegh, Jan-Ingwar Callsen-Bracker (75' Piotr
Trochowski), Jeong-ho Hong, Markus Feulner (46' Philipp Max), Daniel Baier, Ja-cheol Koo,
Halil Altintop, Dong-won Ji, Tim Matavz (46' Alexander Esswein), Raúl Bobadilla.
Coach: Markus Weinzierl.
Partizan: Zivko Zivkovic, Miroslav Vulicevic, Gregor Balazic (46' Milos Ostojic), Aleksandar
Subic, Fabrício, Darko Brasanac, Stefan Babovic, Andrija Zivkovic, Marko Jevtovic, Alen
Stevanovic, Aboubakar Oumarou (21' Valeri Bozhinov, 66' Nemanja Petrovic).
Coach: Zoran Milinkovic.
Goals: 31' Andrija Zivkovic 0-1, 54' Dong-won Ji 0-2 (og), 57' Raúl Bobadilla 1-2,
62' Andrija Zivkovic 1-3.
Referee: Alexandru Tudor (ROM)   Attendance: 22,948.
Sent off: 64' Aleksandar Subic.

22.10.15   AFAS Stadion, Alkmaar: AZ Alkmaar – FC Augsburg 0-1 (0-1)
AZ Alkmaar: Gino Coutinho, Mattias Johansson (77' Guus Hupperts), Jeffrey Gouweleeuw,
Jop van der Linden, Derrick Luckassen, Ridgeciano Haps, Joris van Overeem, Markus
Henriksen, Ben Rienstra (61' Thom Haye), Dabney dos Santos (70' Muamer Tankovic),
Vincent Janssen. Coach: John van den Brom.
FC Augsburg: Marwin Hitz, Paul Verhaegh, Ragnar Klavan, Jan-Ingwar Callsen-Bracker,
Philipp Max, Daniel Baier (58' Dominik Kohr), Tobias Werner, Piotr Trochowski (70' Markus
Feulner), Ja-cheol Koo, Caiuby, Raúl Bobadilla (80' Alexander Esswein).
Coach: Markus Weinzierl.
Goal: 43' Piotr Trochowski 0-1.
Referee: Miroslav Zelinka (CZE)   Attendance: 16,511.

22.10.15   Partizan Stadion, Beograd: Partizan – Athletic Bilbao 0-2 (0-1)
Partizan: Zivko Zivkovic, Nikola Lekovic, Miroslav Vulicevic, Nemanja Petrovic, Milos
Ostojic, Fabrício, Nikola Ninkovic (83' Nikola Trujic), Andrija Zivkovic, Sasa Lukic, Alen
Stevanovic (79' Ivan Saponjic), Valeri Bozhinov (65' Petar Grbic). Coach: Ljubinko Drulovic.
Athletic Bilbao: Iago Herrerín, Aymeric Laporte, San José, De Marcos, Etxeita, Balenziaga,
Beñat (90+1' Elustondo), Susaeta (55' Sabin), Raúl García, Williams (86' Eneko Bóveda),
Aduriz. Coach: Valverde.
Goals: 32' Raúl García 0-1, 85' Beñat 0-2.
Referee: Pawel Raczkowski (POL)   Attendance: 11,128.

05.11.15   WWK Arena, Augsburg: FC Augsburg – AZ Alkmaar 4-1 (2-1)
FC Augsburg: Marwin Hitz, Paul Verhaegh, Ragnar Klavan, Christoph Janker, Philipp Max,
Daniel Baier (65' Markus Feulner), Dominik Kohr, Caiuby, Dong-won Ji, Tim Matavz (55' Ja-
cheol Koo), Raúl Bobadilla (78' Tobias Werner). Coach: Markus Weinzierl.
AZ Alkmaar: Gino Coutinho, Mattias Johansson, Jeffrey Gouweleeuw, Jop van der Linden,
Derrick Luckassen, Ridgeciano Haps, Joris van Overeem, Markus Henriksen (37' Thom
Haye), Ben Rienstra (52' Celso Ortíz), Alireza Jahanbakhsh (76' Guus Hupperts), Vincent
Janssen. Coach: John van den Brom.
Goals: 24', 33' Raúl Bobadilla 1-0, 2-0, 45+1' Vincent Janssen 2-1, 66' Dong-won Ji 3-1,
74' Raúl Bobadilla 4-1.
Referee: Bobby Madden (SCO)   Attendance: 24,241.

05.11.15   San Mamés Barria, Bilbao: Athletic Bilbao – Partizan 5-1 (3-1)
Athletic Bilbao: Iago Herrerín, Eneko Bóveda, Aymeric Laporte, San José, Etxeita,
Balenziaga, Beñat (73' Elustondo), Susaeta, Raúl García (66' Eraso), Williams (63' De
Marcos), Aduriz. Coach: Valverde.
Partizan: Filip Kljajic, Miroslav Vulicevic, Gregor Balazic (26' Lazar Cirkovic), Aleksandar
Subic, Fabrício, Stefan Babovic, Petar Grbic, Sasa Lukic, Marko Jevtovic, Alen Stevanovic
(73' Nikola Ninkovic), Aboubakar Oumarou (46' Ivan Saponjic). Coach: Ljubinko Drulovic.
Goals: 15' Williams 1-0, 17' Aboubakar Oumarou 1-1, 19' Williams 2-1, 40 Beñat 3-1,
71' Aduriz 4-1, 81' Elustondo 5-1.
Referee: Michail Koukoulakis (GRE)   Attendance: 39,849.

26.11.15   WWK Arena, Augsburg: FC Augsburg – Athletic Bilbao 2-3 (1-1)
FC Augsburg: Marwin Hitz, Paul Verhaegh, Kostas Stafylidis, Ragnar Klavan, Christoph
Janker, Daniel Baier, Piotr Trochowski (55' Caiuby), Dominik Kohr, Halil Altintop (56' Raúl
Bobadilla), Alexander Esswein (76' Ja-cheol Koo), Dong-won Ji. Coach: Markus Weinzierl.
Athletic Bilbao: Iago Herrerín, Eneko Bóveda, Aymeric Laporte, San José (73' Iturraspe),
Balenziaga, Eraso (58' Raúl García), Susaeta, Mikel Rico, Gurpegi, Aduriz, Sabin (58'
Williams). Coach: Valverde.
Goals: 10' Susaeta 0-1, 41' Piotr Trochowski 1-1, 59' Raúl Bobadilla 2-1,
83, 86' Aduriz 2-2, 2-3.
Referee: Artur Soares Dias (POR)   Attendance: 23,741.

26.11.15   AFAS Stadion, Alkmaar: AZ Alkmaar – Partizan 1-2 (0-0)
AZ Alkmaar: Gino Coutinho, Mattias Johansson, Jeffrey Gouweleeuw, Rajko Brezancic,
Derrick Luckassen, Celso Ortíz (88' Guus Hupperts), Joris van Overeem (75' Muamer
Tankovic), Markus Henriksen, Dabney dos Santos, Alireza Jahanbakhsh (80' Robert Mühren),
Vincent Janssen. Coach: John van den Brom.
Partizan: Filip Kljajic, Ivan Bandalovski, Miroslav Vulicevic, Lazar Cirkovic, Aleksandar
Subic, Darko Brasanac, Stefan Babovic (75' Sasa Ilic), Nikola Ninkovic (84' Valeri
Bozhinov), Andrija Zivkovic (90+2' Petar Grbic), Marko Jevtovic, Aboubakar Oumarou.
Coach: Ljubinko Drulovic.
Goals: 48' Dabney dos Santos 1-0, 65' Aboubakar Oumarou 1-1, 89' Andrija Zivkovic 1-2.
Referee: Harald Lechner (AUT)   Attendance: 12,784.

10.12.15   San Mamés Barria, Bilbao: Athletic Bilbao – AZ Alkmaar 2-2 (1-1)
Athletic Bilbao: Iago Herrerín, Eneko Bóveda, Elustondo, San José (70' Iturraspe), Saborit,
Eraso (81' Aketxe), Susaeta, Mikel Rico, Gurpegi, Kike Sola (77' Viguera), Sabin.
Coach: Valverde.
AZ Alkmaar: Gino Coutinho, Mattias Johansson, Jeffrey Gouweleeuw, Derrick Luckassen,
Thomas Ouwejan (75' Pantelis Hatzidiakos), Celso Ortíz, Joris van Overeem (80' Robert
Mühren), Ben Rienstra, Thom Haye, Guus Hupperts (64' Muamer Tankovic), Vincent Janssen.
Coach: John van den Brom.
Goals: 26' Joris van Overeem 0-1, 43' Kike Sola 1-1, 47' San José 2-1 (p),
88' Vincent Janssen 2-2.
Referee: Benoît Bastien (FRA)   Attendance: 29,483.

10.12.15   Partizan Stadion, Beograd: Partizan – FC Augsburg 1-3 (1-1)
Partizan: Zivko Zivkovic, Ivan Bandalovski, Lazar Cirkovic, Aleksandar Subic (64' Nemanja Petrovic), Fabrício, Darko Brasanac, Stefan Babovic, Nikola Ninkovic (83' Petar Grbic), Andrija Zivkovic, Marko Jevtovic, Aboubakar Oumarou. Coach: Ljubinko Drulovic.
FC Augsburg: Marwin Hitz, Paul Verhaegh, Kostas Stafylidis (80' Philipp Max), Christoph Janker, Jan-Ingwar Callsen-Bracker (40' Jeong-ho Hong), Daniel Baier, Piotr Trochowski, Jacheol Koo (60' Caiuby), Dong-won Ji, Tim Matavz, Raúl Bobadilla. Coach: Markus Weinzierl.
Goals: 11' Aboubakar Oumarou 1-0, 45+2' Jeong-ho Hong 1-1, 51' Paul Verhaegh 1-2, 89' Raúl Bobadilla 1-3.
Referee: Paolo Tagliavento (ITA)   Attendance: 14,132.
Sent off: 81' Andrija Zivkovic.

ROUND OF 32

FC Porto, Olympiakos Piraeus, Manchester United, Bayer Leverkusen, Sevilla FC, Valencia CF, Galatasaray and Shakhtar Donetsk entered the UEFA Europa League after finishing in third-place in their respective UEFA Champions League groups.

16.02.16   Sükrü Saracoglu, Istanbul: Fenerbahçe – Lokomotiv Moskva 2-0 (1-0)
Fenerbahçe: Fabiano, Simon Kjær, Bruno Alves, Gökhan Gönül, Caner Erkin, Mehmet Topal, Souza (84' Michal Kadlec), Ozan Tufan, Robin van Persie (77' Fernandão), Nani, Volkan Sen (78' Alper Potuk). Coach: Vítor Pereira.
Lokomotiv Moskva: Guilherme, Nemanja Pejcinovic, Ján Durica, Vitaliy Denisov, Alan Kasaev (62' Maicon, 76' Taras Mikhalik), Manuel Fernandes, Aleksandr Samedov, Dmitriy Tarasov, Renat Yanbaev, Delvin N'Dinga, Petar Skuletic (79' Aleksey Miranchuk). Coach: Igor Cherevtchenko.
Goals: 18', 72' Souza 1-0, 2-0.
Referee: Martin Strömbergsson (SWE)   Attendance: 36,195.

18.02.16   Artemio Franchi, Firenze: ACF Fiorentina – Tottenham Hotspur 1-1 (0-1)
ACF Fiorentina: Ciprian Tatarusanu, Gonzalo Rodríguez, Nenad Tomovic, Davide Astori, Marcos Alonso, Tino Costa (68' Matías Vecino), Jakub Blaszczykowski (62' Nikola Kalinic), Borja Valero, Josip Ilicic (61' Milan Badelj), Mauro Zárate, Federico Bernardeschi. Coach: Paulo Sousa.
Tottenham Hotspur: Michel Vorm, Toby Alderweireld, Kieran Trippier, Kevin Wimmer, Ben Davies, Ryan Mason, Dele Alli, Christian Eriksen, Tom Carroll (46' Mousa Dembélé), Heung-min Son (69' Harry Kane), Nacer Chadli (79' Eric Dier). Coach: Mauricio Pochettino.
Goals: 38' Nacer Chadli 0-1 (p), 59' Federico Bernardeschi 1-1.
Referee: Felix Zwayer (GER)   Attendance: 15,200.

18.02.16   Signal Iduna Park, Dortmund: Borussia Dortmund – FC Porto 2-0 (1-0)
Borussia Dortmund: Roman Bürki, Mats Hummels, Sokratis Papastathopoulos, Lukasz Piszczek, Marcel Schmelzer, Henrikh Mkhitaryan, Nuri Sahin (57' Moritz Leitner), Shinji Kagawa (87' Matthias Ginter), Julian Weigl, Marco Reus (87' Christian Pulisic), Pierre-Emerick Aubameyang. Coach: Thomas Tuchel.
FC Porto: Iker Casillas, Bruno Martins Indi, José Ángel, Rúben Neves, Sérgio Oliveira (76' Evandro), Héctor Herrera, Miguel Layún, Varela, Yacine Brahimi (59' André André), Vincent Aboubakar (87' Hyun-jun Suk), Moussa Marega. Coach: José Peseiro.
Goals: 6' Lukasz Piszczek 1-0, 71' Marco Reus 2-0.
Referee: Luca Banti (ITA)   Attendance: 65,851.

18.02.16   Constant Vanden Stock, Brussels: RSC Anderlecht – Olympiakos Piraeus 1-0 (0-0)
RSC Anderlecht: Silvio Proto, Olivier Deschacht, Serigne Mbodj, Alexander Büttner (89'
Bram Nuytinck), Andy Najar, Stéphane Badji, Dennis Praet, Filip Djuricic (74' Youri
Tielemans), Steven Defour (89' Matías Suárez), Frank Acheampong, Stefano Okaka.
Coach: Besnik Hasi.
Olympiakos Piraeus: Roberto, Alberto Botía, Manuel Da Costa, Arthur Masuaku, Sasa Zdjelar
(69' Pajtim Kasami), Luka Milivojevic, Kostas Fortounis, Leandro Salino, Jimmy Durmaz (84'
Alejandro Domínguez), Sebá (81' Alan Pulido), Brown Odeye. Coach: Marco Silva.
Goal: 67' Serigne Mbodj 1-0.
Referee: Ivan Bebek (CRO)   Attendance: 15,397.

18.02.16   MCH Arena, Herning: FC Midtjylland – Manchester United 2-1 (1-1)
FC Midtjylland: Mikkel Andersen, Kian Hansen, Nikolaj Bodurov, André Rømer, Tim Sparv,
Kristoffer Olsson, Pione Sisto, Rilwan Hassan (67' Marco Ureña), Filip Novák, Martin Pusic
(60' Ebere Onuachu), Václav Kadlec (85' Daniel Royer). Coach: Jess Thorup.
Manchester United: Sergio Romero, Chris Smalling, Daley Blind, Paddy McNair, Donald
Love, Mata (78' Andreas Pereira), Michael Carrick, Ander Herrera (72' Morgan Schneiderlin),
Jesse Lingard, Memphis Depay, Anthony Martial. Coach: Louis van Gaal.
Goals: 38' Memphis Depay 0-1, 44' Pione Sisto 1-1, 77' Ebere Onuachu 2-1.
Referee: Artur Soares Dias (POR)   Attendance: 9,182.

18.02.16   Ramón Sánchez Pizjuán, Sevilla: Sevilla FC – Molde FK 3-0 (1-0)
Sevilla FC: David Soria, Timothée Kolodziejczak, Daniel Carriço, Escudero, Coke, Michael
Krohn-Dehli (73' Yevhen Konoplyanka), Sebastián Cristóforo (69' Iborra), Steven N'Zonzi,
Éver Banega, Vitolo, Llorente (57' Kevin Gameiro). Coach: Unai Emery.
Molde FK: Ethan Horvath, Ruben Gabrielsen, Per-Egil Flo, Vegard Forren, Joona Toivio,
Daniel Hestad, Mattias Mostrøm, Fredrik Aursnes (80' Sander Svendsen), Fredrik Gulbrandsen
(73' Agnaldo), Mohamed Elyounoussi (63' Eirik Hestad), Pape Diouf.
Coach: Ole Gunnar Solskjær.
Goals: 35, 49' Llorente 1-0, 2-0, 72' Kevin Gameiro 3-0.
Referee: Gediminas Mazeika (LTU)   Attendance: 28,920.

18.02.16   El Madrigal, Villarreal: Villarreal CF – SSC Napoli 1-0 (0-0)
Villarreal CF: Alphonse Aréola, Mario, Mateo Musacchio, Víctor Ruiz, Jaume Costa, Jonathan
Dos Santos (36' Samu Castillejo), Trigueros (74' Pina), Denis Suárez, Bruno Soriano, Soldado,
Leo Baptistão (61' Cédric Bakambu). Coach: Marcelino.
SSC Napoli: Pepe Reina, Elseid Hysaj, Ivan Strinic, Vlad Chiriches, Kalidou Koulibaly, Mirko
Valdifiori, Marek Hamsík, David López (83' Allan), José Callejón (73' Lorenzo Insigne),
Dries Mertens, Manolo Gabbiadini (67' Gonzalo Higuaín). Coach: Maurizio Sarri.
Goal: 82' Denis Suárez 1-0.
Referee: Bas Nijhuis (HOL)   Attendance: 17,686.

18.02.16   Geoffroy Guichard, St.Étienne: AS Saint-Étienne – FC Basel 3-2 (2-1)
AS Saint-Étienne: Stéphane Ruffier, Kévin Théophile-Catherine, Florentin Pogba, Moustapha
Sall, Jérémy Clément (67' Vincent Pajot), Renaud Cohade, Franck Tabanou, Fabien Lemoine,
Oussama Tannane, Nolan Roux (72' Jean-Christophe Bahebeck), Kévin Monnet-Paquet (75'
Romain Hamouma). Coach: Christophe Galtier.
FC Basel: Tomás Vaclík, Michael Lang, Walter Samuel, Marek Suchy, Behrang Safari, Luca
Zuffi, Birkir Bjarnason, Renato Steffen (64' Jean-Paul Boëtius), Taulant Xhaka, Marc Janko,
Breel Embolo (89' Davide Callà). Coach: Urs Fischer.
Goals: 9' Moustapha Sall 1-0, 39' Kévin Monnet-Paquet 2-0, 44' Walter Samuel 2-1,
56' Marc Janko 2-2 (p), 77' Jean-Christophe Bahebeck 3-2.
Referee: Anasthasios Sidiropoulos (GRE)   Attendance: 27,013.

18.02.16   Estadio de Mestalla, Valencia: Valencia CF – Rapid Wien 6-0 (5-0)
Valencia CF: Mathew Ryan, João Cancelo (76' Barragán), Rúben Vezo, Aderlan Santos, Gayà,
Parejo (59' Javi Fuego), Danilo, André Gomes (68' Rodrigo), Álvaro Negredo, Pablo Piatti,
Santi Mina. Coach: Gary Neville.
Rapid Wien: Richard Strebinger, Mario Sonnleitner, Maximilian Hofmann, Mario Pavelic,
Stefan Stangl, Thanos Petsos, Philipp Schobesberger (87' Deni Alar), Stefan Schwab, Steffen
Hofmann (45+1' Srdan Grahovac), Florian Kainz (46' Thomas Murg), Matej Jelic.
Coach: Zoran Barisic.
Goals: 4' Santi Mina 1-0, 10' Parejo 2-0, 25' Santi Mina 3-0, 29' Álvaro Negredo 4-0,
35' André Gomes 5-0, 89' Rodrigo 6-0.
Referee: Miroslav Zelinka (CZE)   Attendance: 28,831.

18.02.16   WWK Arena, Augsburg: FC Augsburg – Liverpool FC 0-0
FC Augsburg: Marwin Hitz, Paul Verhaegh, Kostas Stafylidis, Ragnar Klavan, Christoph
Janker, Markus Feulner, Tobias Werner (81' Dong-won Ji), Dominik Kohr, Halil Altintop (87'
Ja-cheol Koo), Alexander Esswein, Raúl Bobadilla (23' Caiuby). Coach: Markus Weinzierl.
Liverpool FC: Simon Mignolet, Nathaniel Clyne, Kolo Touré, Mamadou Sakho, Alberto
Moreno, James Milner (81' Jordon Ibe), Coutinho, Roberto Firmino, Jordan Henderson, Emre
Can, Daniel Sturridge (68' Divock Origi). Coach: Jürgen Klopp.
Referee: David Fernández Borbalán (ESP)   Attendance: 25,000.

18.02.16   Generali Arena, Praha: Sparta Praha – FK Krasnodar 1-0 (0-0)
Sparta Praha: David Bicík, Jakub Brabec, Mario Holek, Costa Nhamoinesu, Lukás Vácha,
Borek Dockal (80' Marek Matejovsky), Lukás Marecek, Ondrej Zahustel, Ladislav Krejci,
Kehinde Fatai (89' Petr Jirácek), Lukás Julis (78' Tiémoko Konaté). Coach: Zdenek Scasny.
FK Krasnodar: Andrey Dikan, Andreas Granqvist, Vitaliy Kaleshin, Ragnar Sigurdsson, Pavel
Mamaev, Odil Akhmedov, Joãozinho (82' Vladimir Bystrov), Mauricio Pereyra (66' Yuri
Gazinskiy), Sergey Petrov, Ari, Fedor Smolov (68' Wanderson). Coach: Oleg Kononov.
Goal: 64' Lukás Julis 1-0.
Referee: Slavko Vincic (SVN)   Attendance: 14,120.

18.02.16   Türk Telekom Arena, Istanbul: Galatasaray – Lazio Roma 1-1 (1-1)
Galatasaray: Fernando Muslera, Aurélien Chedjou, Hakan Balta, Lionel Carole (71' Olcan Adin), Koray Günter, Sabri Sarioglu (78' Umut Bulut), Jason Denayer, Selçuk Inan, Wesley Sneijder (89' Yasin Öztekin), Ryan Donk, Lukas Podolski. Coach: Mustafa Denizli.
Lazio Roma: Federico Marchetti, Wesley Hoedt, Stefan Radu, Abdoulay Konko, Mauricio, Felipe Anderson (58' Antonio Candreva), Marco Parolo, Senad Lulic (90' Stefano Mauri), Lucas Biglia, Sergej Milinkovic-Savic, Alessandro Matri (69' Miroslav Klose). Coach: Stefano Pioli.
Goals: 12' Sabri Sarioglu 1-0, 21' Sergej Milinkovic-Savic 1-1.
Referee: Michael Oliver (ENG)   Attendance: 33,353.

18.02.16   Tourbillon, Sion: FC Sion – Sporting Braga 1-2 (0-1)
FC Sion: Andris Vanins, Reto Ziegler, Léo Lacroix (24' Ebenezer Assifuah), Pa Modou Jagne, Vincent Rüfli, Edimilson Fernandes, Vero Salatic, Carlitos, Birama N'Doye, Geoffrey Mujangi Bia (70' Daniel Follonier), Moussa Konaté (77' Theofanis Gekas). Coach: Didier Tholot.
Sporting Braga: Matheus Magalhães, Willy Boly, André Pinto, Baiano, Luíz Carlos, Nikola Vukcevic, Wilson Eduardo, Rafa Silva, Nikola Stojiljkovic (90+2' Ricardo Ferreira), Ahmed Hassan (84' Josué), Alan (66' Pedro Santos). Coach: Paulo Fonseca.
Goals: 13' Nikola Stojiljkovic 0-1, 53' Moussa Konaté 1-1, 61' Rafa Silva 1-2.
Referee: Evgen Aranovskiy (UKR)   Attendance: 9,800.
Sent off: 89' Nikola Vukcevic.

18.02.16   Arena Lviv, Lviv: Shakhtar Donetsk – FC Schalke 04 0-0
Shakhtar Donetsk: Andriy Pyatov, Oleksandr Kucher, Maksym Malyshev (89' Sergiy Krivtsov), Ismaily, Darijo Srna, Yaroslav Rakitskiy, Taras Stepanenko, Marlos (74' Wellington Nem), Viktor Kovalenko, Oleksandr Gladkiy, Taison (79' Eduardo). Coach: Mircea Lucescu.
FC Schalke 04: Ralf Fährmann, Junior Caiçara, Sead Kolasinac, Joel Matip, Johannes Geis, Max Meyer (81' Alessandro Schöpf), Leon Goretzka, Younès Belhanda (88' Klaas-Jan Huntelaar), Leroy Sané (87' Sidney Sam), Roman Neustädter, Eric Maxim Choupo-Moting. Coach: André Breitenreiter.
Referee: Hüseyin Göçek (TUR)   Attendance: 23,615.
Sent off: 86' Oleksandr Kucher.

Shakhtar Donetsk played their home match at Arena Lviv, Lviv instead of their regular stadium, Donbass Arena, Donetsk, due to the ongoing conflict in Eastern Ukraine.

18.02.16   Vélodrome, Marseille: Olympique Marseille – Athletic Bilbao 0-1 (0-0)
Olympique Marseille: Steve Mandanda, Manquillo, Nicolas N'Koulou, Rolando, Mauricio Isla, Lassana Diarra, Romain Alessandrini (59' Michy Batshuayi), Abdelaziz Barrada (59' Florian Thauvin), Alaixys Romao, Steven Fletcher, Georges-Kévin N'Koudou (82' Bouna Sarr). Coach: Míchel.
Athletic Bilbao: Iago Herrerín, Aymeric Laporte, San José, De Marcos, Etxeita, Balenziaga, Eraso (58' Mikel Rico), Beñat (90+1' Elustondo), Williams, Aduriz, Sabin (75' Eneko Bóveda). Coach: Valverde.
Goal: 54' Aduriz 0-1.
Referee: Craig Thomson (SCO)   Attendance: 29,727.

18.02.16   Estádio José Alvalade, Lisboa: Sporting CP – Bayer Leverkusen 0-1 (0-1)
Sporting CP: Rui Patricio, Jefferson, Sebastián Coates (73' Ewerton), João Pereira, Rúben
Semedo, Alberto Aquilani (61' Adrien Silva), William Carvalho, João Mário, Bryan Ruiz,
Carlos Mané, Teófilo Gutiérrez (61' Islam Slimani). Coach: Jorge Jesus.
Bayer Leverkusen: Bernd Leno, Jonathan Tah, Tin Jedvaj (85' Roberto Hilbert), Wendell,
Ömer Toprak, Hakan Çalhanoglu, Julian Brandt (66' Kyriakos Papadopoulos), Christoph
Kramer, Karim Bellarabi, Stefan Kießling, Admir Mehmedi (79' Benjamin Henrichs).
Coach: Roger Schmidt.
Goal: 26' Karim Bellarabi 0-1.
Referee: Björn Kuipers (HOL)   Attendance: 26,201.
Sent off: 74' Rúben Semedo.

24.02.16   Estádio Municipal de Braga, Braga: Sporting Braga – FC Sion 2-2 (1-2)
Sporting Braga: Matheus Magalhães, Willy Boly, Baiano, Ricardo Ferreira, Marcelo Goiano,
Luíz Carlos, Josué (62' Pedro Santos), Mauro, Rafa Silva, Nikola Stojiljkovic (81' Rui Fonte),
Ahmed Hassan (90+2' André Pinto). Coach: Paulo Fonseca.
FC Sion: Andris Vanins, Pa Modou Jagne, Vilmos Vanczák, Vincent Rüfli, Edimilson
Fernandes, Vero Salatic, Carlitos, Birama N'Doye, Moussa Konaté, Ebenezer Assifuah (76'
Geoffrey Mujangi Bia), Theofanis Gekas (88' Martin Zeman). Coach: Didier Tholot.
Goals: 16' Theofanis Gekas 0-1, 27' Josué 1-1 (p), 29' Theofanis Gekas 1-2,
48' Nikola Stojiljkovic 2-2.
Referee: Liran Liany (ISR)   Attendance: 6,759.

25.02.16   Lokomotiv, Moskva: Lokomotiv Moskva – Fenerbahçe 1-1 (1-0)
Lokomotiv Moskva: Guilherme, Nemanja Pejcinovic, Vedran Corluka, Ján Durica, Vitaliy
Denisov, Alan Kasaev (81' Rifat Zhemaletdinov), Manuel Fernandes (73' Petar Skuletic),
Aleksandr Kolomeytsev, Aleksandr Samedov, Aleksey Miranchuk, Delvin N'Dinga (13' Taras
Mikhalik). Coach: Igor Cherevtchenko.
Fenerbahçe: Fabiano, Hasan-Ali Kaldirim, Simon Kjær, Bruno Alves, Gökhan Gönül (44'
Sener Özbayrakli), Mehmet Topal, Souza, Ozan Tufan (74' Michal Kadlec), Robin van Persie,
Nani (79' Alper Potuk), Volkan Sen. Coach: Vítor Pereira.
Goals: 45' Aleksandr Samedov 1-0, 83' Mehmet Topal 1-1.
Referee: Ivan Kruzliak (SVK)   Attendance: 15,695.

25.02.16   White Hart Lane, London: Tottenham Hotspur – ACF Fiorentina 3-0 (1-0)
Tottenham Hotspur: Hugo Lloris, Toby Alderweireld, Kieran Trippier, Kevin Wimmer, Ben
Davies, Ryan Mason (88' Harry Winks), Érik Lamela (76' Joshua Onomah), Eric Dier, Dele
Alli (85' Nabil Bentaleb), Christian Eriksen, Nacer Chadli. Coach: Mauricio Pochettino.
ACF Fiorentina: Ciprian Tatarusanu, Gonzalo Rodríguez, Nenad Tomovic, Davide Astori,
Marcos Alonso, Milan Badelj (82' Mati Fernández), Matías Vecino, Borja Valero (73' Jakub
Blaszczykowski), Josip Ilicic (62' Mauro Zárate), Nikola Kalinic, Federico Bernardeschi.
Coach: Paulo Sousa.
Goals: 26' Ryan Mason 1-0, 63' Érik Lamela 2-0, 81' Gonzalo Rodríguez 3-0 (og).
Referee: Ovidiu Hategan (ROM)   Attendance: 34,880.

25.02.16   Estádio Dragão, Porto: FC Porto – Borussia Dortmund 0-1 (0-1)
FC Porto: Iker Casillas, Maxi Pereira, Marcano, José Ángel, Rúben Neves, Evandro (71'
Héctor Herrera), Miguel Layún, Danilo, Varela (66' Yacine Brahimi), Vincent Aboubakar (56'
Hyun-jun Suk), Moussa Marega. Coach: José Peseiro.
Borussia Dortmund: Roman Bürki, Mats Hummels (46' Neven Subotic), Matthias Ginter,
Marcel Schmelzer, Sven Bender, Ilkay Gündogan (46' Nuri Sahin), Henrikh Mkhitaryan,
Shinji Kagawa, Julian Weigl, Marco Reus (70' Adrián Ramos), Pierre-Emerick Aubameyang.
Coach: Thomas Tuchel.
Goal: 23' Iker Casillas 0-1 (og).
Referee: Mark Clattenburg (ENG)   Attendance: 32,707.

25.02.16   Georgios Karaiskakis, Piraeus:
Olympiakos Piraeus – RSC Anderlecht 1-2 (1-0, 1-0)
Olympiakos Piraeus: Roberto, Alberto Botía, Manuel Da Costa, Omar Elabdellaoui, Arthur
Masuaku, Luka Milivojevic, Kostas Fortounis, Esteban Cambiasso (67' Sasa Zdjelar), Alan
Pulido (83' Sebá), Jimmy Durmaz (50' Alejandro Domínguez), Brown Odeye.
Coach: Marco Silva.
RSC Anderlecht: Silvio Proto, Olivier Deschacht, Serigne Mbodj, Alexander Büttner (90'
Bram Nuytinck), Andy Najar, Stéphane Badji, Dennis Praet, Filip Djuricic (82' Matías
Suárez), Frank Acheampong, Leander Dendoncker (97' Steven Defour), Stefano Okaka.
Coach: Besnik Hasi.
Goals: 29' Kostas Fortounis 1-0 (p), 103', 111' Frank Acheampong 1-1, 1-2.
Referee: Arnold Hunter (NIR)   Attendance: 31,005.

RSC Anderlecht won after extra time.

25.02.16   Old Trafford, Manchester: Manchester United – FC Midtjylland 5-1 (1-1)
Manchester United: Sergio Romero, Daley Blind, Guillermo Varela, Joe Riley (79' Marcos
Rojo), Mata, Michael Carrick, Ander Herrera (90+1' Regan Poole), Morgan Schneiderlin,
Jesse Lingard (86' Andreas Pereira), Memphis Depay, Marcus Rashford.
Coach: Louis van Gaal.
FC Midtjylland: Mikkel Andersen, Kian Hansen, Nikolaj Bodurov, André Rømer, Tim Sparv,
Jakob Poulsen, Kristoffer Olsson (79' Martin Pusic), Pione Sisto, Rilwan Hassan (67' Václav
Kadlec), Filip Novák, Marco Ureña (46' Ebere Onuachu). Coach: Jess Thorup.
Goals: 28' Pione Sisto 0-1, 32' Nokolaj Bodurov 1-1 (og), 64', 75' Marcus Rashford 2-1, 3-1,
88' Ander Herrera 4-1 (p), 90' Memphis Depay 5-1.
Referee: István Vad (HUN)   Attendance: 58,609.
Sent off: 89' André Rømer.

Mata missed a penalty kick (43').

25.02.16   Aker Stadion, Molde: Molde FK – Sevilla FC 1-0 (1-0)
Molde FK: Ethan Horvath, Ruben Gabrielsen, Per-Egil Flo, Vegard Forren, Joona Toivio,
Daniel Hestad (90+4' Kristian Strande), Mattias Mostrøm (80' Petter Strand), Fredrik Aursnes,
Sander Svendsen (68' Amidou Diop), Eirik Hestad, Mohamed Elyounoussi.
Coach: Ole Gunnar Solskjær.
Sevilla FC: David Soria, Timothée Kolodziejczak, Daniel Carriço, Federico Fazio, Escudero,
Mariano, Iborra, Reyes (54' Michael Krohn-Dehli), Éver Banega, Yevhen Konoplyanka (81'
Diogo), Llorente (62' Kevin Gameiro). Coach: Unai Emery.
Goal: 43' Eirik Hestad 1-0.
Referee: Bobby Madden (SCO)   Attendance: 7,284.

25.02.16   San Paolo, Napoli: SSC Napoli – Villarreal CF 1-1 (1-0)
SSC Napoli: Pepe Reina, Elseid Hysaj, Ivan Strinic (64' Christian Maggio), Vlad Chiriches,
Raúl Albiol, Mirko Valdifiori (75' Jorginho), Marek Hamsík, David López (78' Manolo
Gabbiadini), Gonzalo Higuaín, Dries Mertens, Lorenzo Insigne. Coach: Maurizio Sarri.
Villarreal CF: Alphonse Aréola, Mario, Mateo Musacchio, Víctor Ruiz, Jaume Costa, Antonio
Rukavina (77' Samu Castillejo), Pina (84' Trigueros), Denis Suárez, Bruno Soriano, Soldado
(70' Adrián), Cédric Bakambu. Coach: Marcelino.
Goals: 17' Marek Hamsík 1-0, 59' Pina 1-1.
Referee: Deniz Aytekin (GER)   Attendance: 23,928.

25.02.16   St.Jakob-Park, Basel: FC Basel – AS Saint-Étienne 2-1 (1-0)
FC Basel: Tomás Vaclík, Michael Lang, Walter Samuel (90+1' Alexander Fransson), Marek
Suchy, Behrang Safari (72' Adama Traoré), Luca Zuffi, Birkir Bjarnason, Matías Delgado (68'
Renato Steffen), Taulant Xhaka, Marc Janko, Breel Embolo. Coach: Urs Fischer.
AS Saint-Étienne: Stéphane Ruffier, Kévin Théophile-Catherine, Florentin Pogba, Moustapha
Sall, Jérémy Clément, Renaud Cohade, Franck Tabanou, Fabien Lemoine (75' Valentin
Eysseric), Oussama Tannane (60' Romain Hamouma), Jean-Christophe Bahebeck (55' Nolan
Roux), Kévin Monnet-Paquet. Coach: Christophe Galtier.
Goals: 15' Luca Zuffi 1-0, 89' Moustapha 1-1, 90+1' Luca Zuffi 2-1.
Referee: Danny Makkelie (HOL)   Attendance: 20,976.
Sent off: 83' Valentin Eysseric, 84' Breel Embolo.

FC Basel won on away goals.

25.02.16   Ernst-Happel-Stadion, Wien: Rapid Wien – Valencia CF 0-4 (0-0)
Rapid Wien: Richard Strebinger, Mario Sonnleitner, Maximilian Hofmann, Mario Pavelic,
Maximilian Wöber, Thanos Petsos, Stefan Schwab, Srdan Grahovac, Thomas Murg (82' Louis
Schaub), Deni Alar (70' Philipp Schobesberger), Philipp Prosenik (65' Matej Jelic).
Coach: Zoran Barisic.
Valencia CF: Mathew Ryan, Rúben Vezo, Shkodran Mustafi, Gayà (46' Lato), Barragán,
Sofiane Féghouli, Danilo, Javi Fuego (79' Tropi), Álvaro Negredo (65' Rafa Mir), Pablo Piatti,
Rodrigo. Coach: Gary Neville.
Goals: 59' Rodrigo 0-1, 64' Sofiane Féghouli 0-2, 72' Pablo Piatti 0-3, 88' Rúben Vezo 0-4.
Referee: Paolo Tagliavento (ITA)   Attendance: 39,800.

25.02.16   Anfield, Liverpool: Liverpool FC – FC Augsburg 1-0 (1-0)
Liverpool FC: Simon Mignolet, Nathaniel Clyne, Mamadou Sakho, Alberto Moreno, James
Milner, Coutinho (80' João Carlos), Roberto Firmino, Jordan Henderson, Lucas Leiva, Emre
Can, Daniel Sturridge (66' Divock Origi). Coach: Jürgen Klopp.
FC Augsburg: Marwin Hitz, Paul Verhaegh, Kostas Stafylidis, Ragnar Klavan, Christoph
Janker (90' Shawn Parker), Tobias Werner (72' Raúl Bobadilla), Ja-cheol Koo (80' Jan
Morávek), Dominik Kohr, Caiuby, Halil Altintop, Alexander Esswein.
Coach: Markus Weinzierl.
Goal: 5' James Milner 1-0 (p).
Referee: Clément Turpin (FRA)   Attendance: 43,081.

25.02.16   Kuban, Krasnodar: FK Krasnodar – Sparta Praha 0-3 (0-0)
FK Krasnodar: Andrey Dikan, Stefan Strandberg, Andreas Granqvist, Vitaliy Kaleshin, Pavel
Mamaev (62' Joãozinho), Odil Akhmedov, Mauricio Pereyra (62' Wanderson), Charles
Kaboré, Sergey Petrov, Ari, Fedor Smolov (75' Dmitriy Torbinskiy). Coach: Oleg Kononov.
Sparta Praha: David Bicík, Jakub Brabec, Mario Holek, Costa Nhamoinesu, Lukás Vácha,
Borek Dockal (83' Tiémoko Konaté), Lukás Marecek (79' Marek Matejovsky), Martin Frydek,
Ondrej Zahustel, Ladislav Krejci, Kehinde Fatai (76' Lukás Julis). Coach: Zdenek Scasny.
Goals: 51' Lukás Marecek 0-1, 57' Martin Frydek 0-2, 70' Kehinde Fatai 0-3.
Referee: Stefan Johannesson (SWE)   Attendance: 14,850.
Sent off: 68' Charles Kaboré.

25.02.16   Olimpico, Roma: Lazio Roma – Galatasaray 3-1 (0-0)
Lazio Roma: Federico Marchetti, Milan Bisevac, Stefan Radu, Abdoulay Konko, Mauricio,
Felipe Anderson, Marco Parolo, Senad Lulic (57' Antonio Candreva), Lucas Biglia, Sergej
Milinkovic-Savic, Alessandro Matri (70' Miroslav Klose). Coach: Stefano Pioli.
Galatasaray: Fernando Muslera, Aurélien Chedjou, Hakan Balta, Lionel Carole, Sabri Sarioglu
(66' Umut Bulut), Jason Denayer, Yasin Öztekin (76' Olcan Adin), Selçuk Inan, Wesley
Sneijder, Ryan Donk (85' Bilal Kisa), Lukas Podolski. Coach: Mustafa Denizli.
Goals: 59' Marco Parolo 1-0, 61' Felipe Anderson 2-0, 62' Yasin Öztekin 2-1,
72' Miroslav Klose 3-1.
Referee: Vladislav Bezborodov (RUS)   Attendance: 13,967.

25.02.16   VELTINS-Arena, Gelsenkirchen: FC Schalke 04 – Shakhtar Donetsk 0-3 (0-1)
FC Schalke 04: Ralf Fährmann, Junior Caiçara, Sead Kolasinac (46' Dennis Aogo), Joel Matip,
Johannes Geis, Leon Goretzka (45+2' Franco Di Santo), Younès Belhanda, Leroy Sané,
Alessandro Schöpf (58' Sidney Sam), Roman Neustädter, Klaas-Jan Huntelaar.
Coach: André Breitenreiter.
Shakhtar Donetsk: Andriy Pyatov, Maksym Malyshev, Ismaily, Darijo Srna, Sergiy Krivtsov,
Yaroslav Rakitskiy, Taras Stepanenko, Marlos (74' Wellington Nem), Viktor Kovalenko,
Facundo Ferreyra (89' Andriy Boryachuk), Taison (80' Eduardo). Coach: Mircea Lucescu.
Goals: 27' Marlos 0-1, 63' Facundo Ferreyra 0-2, 77' Viktor Kovalenko 0-3.
Referee: Matej Jug (SVN)   Attendance: 45,308.

25.02.16   San Mamés Barria, Bilbao: Athletic Bilbao – Olympique Marseille 1-1 (0-1)
Athletic Bilbao: Iago Herrerín, Aymeric Laporte, San José, De Marcos, Etxeita, Balenziaga,
Iturraspe, Susaeta (88' Mikel Rico), Raúl García (76' Sabin), Lekue (58' Muniain), Aduriz.
Coach: Valverde.
Olympique Marseille: Steve Mandanda, Manquillo (85' Florian Thauvin), Nicolas N'Koulou,
Karim Rekik (87' Romain Alessandrini), Mauricio Isla, Benjamin Mendy, Lassana Diarra,
Rémy Cabella, Steven Fletcher, Georges-Kévin N'Koudou, Michy Batshuayi. Coach: Míchel.
Goals: 40' Michy Batshuayi 0-1, 81' Sabin 1-1.
Referee: Aleksey Kulbakov (BLS)   Attendance: 38,259.

118

25.02.16   BayArena, Leverkusen: Bayer Leverkusen – Sporting CP 3-1 (1-1)
Bayer Leverkusen: Bernd Leno, Jonathan Tah, Kyriakos Papadopoulos (88' Robbie Kruse),
Tin Jedvaj, Wendell, Hakan Çalhanoglu, Julian Brandt (46' Admir Mehmedi), Christoph
Kramer, Karim Bellarabi, Javier Hernández, Stefan Kießling (63' André Ramalho).
Coach: Roger Schmidt.
Sporting CP: Rui Patricio, Jefferson, Ewerton, João Pereira, Naldo, Alberto Aquilani, Bruno
César (78' Gelson Martins), William Carvalho, João Mário, Carlos Mané (62' Bryan Ruiz),
Teófilo Gutiérrez (67' Islam Slimani). Coach: Jorge Jesus.
Goals: 30' Karim Bellarabi 1-0, 38' João Mário 1-1, 65' Karim Bellarabi 2-1,
87' Hakan Çalhanoglu 3-1.
Referee: Ruddy Buquet (FRA)   Attendance: 26,585.

ROUND OF 16

10.03.16   Arena Lviv, Lviv: Shakhtar Donetsk – RSC Anderlecht 3-1 (2-0)
Shakhtar Donetsk: Andriy Pyatov, Oleksandr Kucher, Maksym Malyshev, Ismaily, Darijo
Srna, Yaroslav Rakitskiy, Marlos (74' Wellington Nem), Viktor Kovalenko, Facundo Ferreyra,
Eduardo (88' Dentinho), Taison (46' Bernard). Coach: Mircea Lucescu.
RSC Anderlecht: Silvio Proto, Olivier Deschacht, Serigne Mbodj, Bram Nuytinck, Andy
Najar, Stéphane Badji (74' Youri Tielemans), Dennis Praet (67' Ibrahima Conté), Steven
Defour, Frank Acheampong, Matías Suárez (67' Filip Djuricic), Stefano Okaka.
Coach: Besnik Hasi.
Goals: 21' Taison 1-0, 24' Oleksandr Kucher 2-0, 69' Frank Acheampong 2-1,
79' Eduardo 3-1.
Referee: Artur Soares Dias (POR)   Attendance: 23,621.

*Shakhtar Donetsk played their home match at Arena Lviv, Lviv instead of their regular
stadium, Donbass Arena, Donetsk, due to the ongoing conflict in Eastern Ukraine.*

10.03.16   St.Jakob-Park, Basel: FC Basel – Sevilla FC 0-0
FC Basel: Tomás Vaclík, Michael Lang (46' Adama Traoré), Walter Samuel (90' Daniel
Høegh), Marek Suchy, Behrang Safari, Luca Zuffi, Birkir Bjarnason, Matías Delgado (83'
Alexander Fransson), Renato Steffen, Taulant Xhaka, Marc Janko. Coach: Urs Fischer.
Sevilla FC: David Soria, Benoît Trémoulinas, Adil Rami, Timothée Kolodziejczak, Coke,
Michael Krohn-Dehli, Sebastián Cristóforo, Steven N'Zonzi, Éver Banega (90+3' Daniel
Carriço), Kevin Gameiro (73' Llorente), Vitolo (64' Yevhen Konoplyanka).
Coach: Unai Emery.
Referee: Anthony Taylor (ENG)   Attendance: 22,403.
Sent off: 87' Steven N'Zonzi.

10.03.16   Signal Iduna Park, Dortmund: Borussia Dortmund – Tottenham Hotspur 3-0 (1-0)
Borussia Dortmund: Roman Weidenfeller, Mats Hummels, Lukasz Piszczek, Marcel
Schmelzer, Erik Durm, Sven Bender (58' Neven Subotic), Henrikh Mkhitaryan, Gonzalo
Castro, Julian Weigl, Marco Reus (82' Adrián Ramos), Pierre-Emerick Aubameyang (82'
Shinji Kagawa). Coach: Thomas Tuchel.
Tottenham Hotspur: Hugo Lloris, Toby Alderweireld, Kieran Trippier, Kevin Wimmer, Ben
Davies, Ryan Mason, Christian Eriksen (65' Érik Lamela), Tom Carroll, Heung-min Son (76'
Harry Kane), Nacer Chadli (58' Mousa Dembélé), Joshua Onomah.
Coach: Mauricio Pochettino.
Goals: 30' Pierre-Emerick Aubameyang 1-0, 61', 70' Marco Reus 2-0, 3-0.
Referee: Cüneyt Çakir (TUR)   Attendance: 65,848.

119

10.03.16 Sükrü Saracoglu, Istanbul: Fenerbahçe – Sporting Braga 1-0 (0-0)
Fenerbahçe: Volkan Demirel, Simon Kjær, Sener Özbayrakli, Bruno Alves, Caner Erkin,
Mehmet Topal, Souza, Ozan Tufan (72' Raúl Meireles), Alper Potuk (79' Fernandão), Robin
van Persie, Volkan Sen (65' Nani). Coach: Vítor Pereira.
Sporting Braga: Matheus Magalhães, André Pinto, Baiano, Ricardo Ferreira (15' Willy Boly),
Marcelo Goiano, Luíz Carlos, Josué, Nikola Vukcevic, Wilson Eduardo (72' Nikola
Stojiljkovic), Rafa Silva (85' Pedro Santos), Ahmed Hassan. Coach: Paulo Fonseca.
Goal: 82' Mehmet Topal 1-0.
Referee: Clément Turpin (FRA)   Attendance: 40,197.

10.03.16 El Madrigal, Villarreal: Villarreal CF – Bayer Leverkusen 2-0 (1-0)
Villarreal CF: Alphonse Aréola, Mario, Víctor Ruiz, Antonio Rukavina, Eric Bailly, Trigueros,
Denis Suárez, Samu Castillejo (80' Matías Nahuel), Bruno Soriano, Soldado (76' Léo
Baptistão), Cédric Bakambu (82' Adrián). Coach: Marcelino.
Bayer Leverkusen: Bernd Leno, Jonathan Tah, Kyriakos Papadopoulos, Tin Jedvaj, Wendell,
Hakan Çalhanoglu, Julian Brandt, Christoph Kramer (65' Marlon Frey), Karim Bellarabi (86'
Admir Mehmedi), Javier Hernández, Stefan Kießling (67' Robbie Kruse).
Coach: Roger Schmidt.
Goals: 4', 56' Cédric Bakambu 1-0, 2-0.
Referee: Gianluca Rocchi (ITA)   Attendance: 16,211.
Sent off: 90+4' Tin Jedvaj.

10.03.16 San Manés Barria, Bilbao: Athletic Bilbao – Valencia FC 1-0 (1-0)
Athletic Bilbao: Iago Herrerín, Aymeric Laporte, De Marcos, Etxeita, Balenziaga, Beñat,
Iturraspe (82' Mikel Rico), Susaeta (73' Elustondo), Raúl García, Muniain (53' Sabin), Aduriz.
Coach: Valverde.
Valencia CF: Mathew Ryan, Shkodran Mustafi, Gayà, Barragán, Aymen Abdennour, Parejo
(82' Paco Alcácer), Danilo, Javi Fuego, Álvaro Negredo, Pablo Piatti (70' André Gomes),
Rodrigo (86' Sofiane Féghouli). Coach: Gary Neville.
Goal: 20' Raúl García 1-0.
Referee: Björn Kuipers (HOL)   Attendance: 35,765.

10-03-16 Anfield, Liverpool: Liverpool FC – Manchester United 2-0 (1-0)
Liverpool FC: Simon Mignolet, Nathaniel Clyne, Dejan Lovren, Mamadou Sakho, Alberto
Moreno, Coutinho, Roberto Firmino (84' Divock Origi), Jordan Henderson, Adam Lallana,
Emre Can, Daniel Sturridge (64' Joe Allen). Coach: Jürgen Klopp.
Manchester United: De Gea, Marcos Rojo, Chris Smalling, Daley Blind, Guillermo Varela,
Mata (79' Ander Herrera), Marouane Fellaini, Morgan Schneiderlin (79' Bastian
Schweinsteiger), Memphis Depay, Anthony Martial, Marcus Rashford (46' Michael Carrick).
Coach: Louis van Gaal.
Goals: 20' Daniel Sturridge 1-0 (p), 73' Roberto Firmino 2-0.
Referee: Carlos Velasco Carballo (ESP)   Attendance: 43,228.

10.03.16   Generali Arena, Praha: Sparta Praha – Lazio Roma 1-1 (1-1)
Sparta Praha: David Bicík, Jakub Brabec, Mario Holek, Costa Nhamoinesu, Lukás Vácha,
Borek Dockal (59' Kehinde Fatai), Lukás Marecek, Martin Frydek, Ondrej Zahustel, Ladislav
Krejci, David Lafata (62' Lukás Julis). Coach: Zdenek Scasny.
Lazio Roma: Federico Marchetti, Wesley Hoedt, Milan Bisevac, Stefan Radu, Abdoulay
Konko (46' Dusan Basta, 66' Mauricio), Marco Parolo, Lucas Biglia, Sergej Milinkovic-Savic,
Antonio Candreva, Baldé Diao Keita, Alessandro Matri (55' Senad Lulic).
Coach: Stefano Pioli.
Goals: 13' Martin Frydek 1-0, 38' Marco Parolo 1-1.
Referee: Alberto Undiano Mallenco (ESP)   Attendance: 17,482.

17.03.16   Constant Vanden Stock, Brussels: RSC Anderlecht – Shakhtar Donetsk 0-1 (0-0)
RSC Anderlecht: Silvio Proto, Olivier Deschacht, Serigne Mbodj, Bram Nuytinck (78' Idrissa
Sylla), Andy Najar, Stéphane Badji (71' Youri Tielemans), Dennis Praet, Steven Defour, Frank
Acheampong, Imoh Ezekiel (71' Trézéguet), Stefano Okaka. Coach: Besnik Hasi.
Shakhtar Donetsk: Andriy Pyatov, Oleksandr Kucher, Maksym Malyshev, Ismaily, Darijo
Srna, Yaroslav Rakitskiy, Taras Stepanenko, Marlos (90+1' Eduardo), Viktor Kovalenko (88'
Ivan Ordets), Facundo Ferreyra, Taison (83' Dentinho). Coach: Mircea Lucescu.
Goal: 90+3' Eduardo 0-1.
Referee: Antonio Mateu Lahoz (ESP)   Attendance: 13,785.
Sent off: 84' Oleksandr Kucher, 86' Serigne Mbodj.

17.03.16   Ramón Sánchez Pizjuán, Sevilla: Sevilla FC – FC Basel 3-0 (3-0)
Sevilla FC: David Soria, Benoît Trémoulinas, Adil Rami, Timothée Kolodziejczak, Mariano,
Michael Krohn-Dehli (52' Escudero), Iborra (61' Grzegorz Krychowiak), Reyes, Sebastián
Cristóforo, Éver Banega, Kevin Gameiro (70' Llorente). Coach: Unai Emery.
FC Basel: Tomás Vaclík, Michael Lang, Marek Suchy, Behrang Safari, Daniel Høegh, Luca
Zuffi, Birkir Bjarnason (62' Alexander Fransson), Matías Delgado (60' Breel Embolo), Renato
Steffen, Taulant Xhaka, Marc Janko (71' Cedric Itten). Coach: Urs Fischer.
Goals: 35' Adil Rami 1-0, 44', 45' Kevin Gameiro 2-0, 3-0.
Referee: Deniz Aytekin (GER)   Attendance: 35,546.

17.03.16   White Hart Lane, London: Tottenham Hotspur – Borussia Dortmund 1-2 (0-1)
Tottenham Hotspur: Hugo Lloris, Toby Alderweireld, Kieran Trippier, Kevin Wimmer, Ben
Davies (13' Danny Rose), Ryan Mason, Érik Lamela (74' Joshua Onomah), Eric Dier, Dele
Alli (70' Tom Carroll), Heung-min Son, Nacer Chadli. Coach: Mauricio Pochettino.
Borussia Dortmund: Roman Weidenfeller, Neven Subotic, Sokratis Papastathopoulos (54' Erik
Durm), Lukasz Piszczek, Matthias Ginter, Marcel Schmelzer, Henrikh Mkhitaryan (72' Shinji
Kagawa), Gonzalo Castro, Julian Weigl, Marco Reus (60' Christian Pulisic), Pierre-Emerick
Aubameyang. Coach: Thomas Tuchel.
Goals: 24', 71' Pierre-Emerick Aubameyang 0-1, 0-2, 74' Heung-min Son 1-2.
Referee: Nicola Rizzoli (ITA)   Attendance: 34,943.

17.03.16   Estádio Municipal de Braga, Braga: Sporting Braga – Fenerbahçe 4-1 (1-1)
Sporting Braga: Matheus Magalhães, Willy Boly, André Pinto, Baiano, Marcelo Goiano,
Josué, Nikola Vukcevic (73' Pedro Santos), Mauro, Rafa Silva, Nikola Stojiljkovic (90' Filipe
Augusto), Ahmed Hassan. Coach: Paulo Fonseca.
Fenerbahçe: Volkan Demirel, Simon Kjær, Sener Özbayrakli, Bruno Alves, Caner Erkin,
Mehmet Topal, Souza, Diego (73' Michal Kadlec), Alper Potuk, Robin van Persie (78'
Fernandão), Nani (72' Volkan Sen). Coach: Vítor Pereira.
Goals: 11' Ahmed Hassan 1-0, 45+3' Alper Potuk 1-1, 69' Josué 2-1 (p),
74' Nikola Stojiljkovic 3-1, 83' Rafa Silva 4-1.
Referee: Ivan Bebek (CRO)   Attendance: 16,431.
Sent off: 67' Mehmet Topal, 87' Alper Potuk, 90+7' Volkan Sen.

Coach Vítor Pereira was sent to the stands (44').

17.03.16   BayArena, Leverkusen: Bayer Leverkusen – Villarreal CF 0-0
Bayer Leverkusen: Bernd Leno, Jonathan Tah, Kyriakos Papadopoulos (79' André Ramalho),
Wendell, Hakan Çalhanoglu, Julian Brandt, Christoph Kramer (68' Vladlen Yurchenko),
Marlon Frey, Karim Bellarabi, Javier Hernández, Admir Mehmedi (59' Robbie Kruse).
Coach: Roger Schmidt.
Villarreal CF: Asenjo, Mario, Víctor Ruiz, Antonio Rukavina, Eric Bailly, Pina, Denis Suárez
(89' Pedraza), Samu Castillejo (61' Trigueros), Bruno Soriano, Soldado (74' Adrián), Cédric
Bakambu. Coach: Marcelino.
Referee: William Collum (SCO)   Attendance: 23,409.

17.03.16   Estadio de Mestalla, Valencia: Valencia FC – Athletic Bilbao 2-1 (2-0)
Valencia CF: Mathew Ryan, Rúben Vezo, Aderlan Santos, Shkodran Mustafi, Gayà, Danilo,
Javi Fuego (68' Parejo), André Gomes (83' Paco Alcácer), Álvaro Negredo, Rodrigo (74'
Sofiane Féghouli), Santi Mina. Coach: Gary Neville.
Athletic Bilbao: Iago Herrerín, Aymeric Laporte, San José, De Marcos, Etxeita, Balenziaga
(75' Lekue), Beñat, Raúl García, Muniain (25' Susaeta), Aduriz, Sabin (75' Iturraspe).
Coach: Valverde.
Goals: 13' Santi Mina 1-0, 37' Aderlan Santos 2-0, 76' Aduriz 2-1.
Referee: Daniele Orsato (ITA)   Attendance: 31,681.

Coach Gary Neville was sent to the stands (78').

Athletic Bilbao won on away goals.

17.03.16   Old Trafford, Manchester: Manchester United – Liverpool FC 1-1 (1-1)
Manchester United: De Gea, Marcos Rojo (62' Matteo Darmian), Chris Smalling, Daley Blind,
Guillermo Varela (46' Antonio Valencia), Mata, Michael Carrick (70' Bastian
Schweinsteiger), Marouane Fellaini, Jesse Lingard, Anthony Martial, Marcus Rashford.
Coach: Louis van Gaal.
Liverpool FC: Simon Mignolet, Nathaniel Clyne, Dejan Lovren, Mamadou Sakho, James
Milner, Coutinho, Roberto Firmino (85' Christian Benteke), Jordan Henderson (71' Joe Allen),
Adam Lallana, Emre Can, Daniel Sturridge (68' Divock Origi). Coach: Jürgen Klopp.
Goals: 32' Anthony Martial 1-0 (p), 45' Coutinho 1-1.
Referee: Milorad Mazic (SER)   Attendance: 75,180.

17.03.16   Olimpico, Roma: Lazio Roma – Sparta Praha 0-3 (0-3)
Lazio Roma: Federico Marchetti, Wesley Hoedt, Milan Bisevac, Abdoulay Konko (67'
Mauricio), Stefano Mauri (58' Felipe Anderson), Marco Parolo, Senad Lulic, Lucas Biglia,
Antonio Candreva, Miroslav Klose (58' Alessandro Matri), Baldé Diao Keita.
Coach: Stefano Pioli.
Sparta Praha: David Bicík, Jakub Brabec, Mario Holek, Costa Nhamoinesu, Lukás Vácha (70'
Marek Matejovsky), Borek Dockal, Lukás Marecek, Martin Frydek, Ondrej Zahustel, Ladislav
Krejci (83' Kehinde Fatai), Lukás Julis (58' Tiémoko Konaté). Coach: Zdenek Scasny.
Goals: 10' Borek Dockal 0-1, 12' Ladislav Krejci 0-2, 44' Lukás Julis 0-3.
Referee: Ruddy Buquet (FRA)   Attendance: 18,827.

QUARTER-FINALS

07.04.16   Estádio Municipal de Braga, Braga: Sporting Braga – Shakhtar Donetsk 1-2 (0-1)
Sporting Braga: Matheus Magalhães, Willy Boly, Baiano, Ricardo Ferreira, Marcelo Goiano,
Luíz Carlos, Pedro Santos, Nikola Vukcevic (87' Filipe Augusto), Rafa Silva, Nikola
Stojiljkovic (75' Wilson Eduardo), Ahmed Hassan. Coach: Paulo Fonseca.
Shakhtar Donetsk: Andriy Pyatov, Maksym Malyshev, Ivan Ordets, Ismaily, Darijo Srna,
Yaroslav Rakitskiy, Taras Stepanenko, Marlos (82' Eduardo), Viktor Kovalenko (88' Bernard),
Facundo Ferreyra, Taison (79' Dentinho). Coach: Mircea Lucescu.
Goals: 44' Yaroslav Rakitskiy 0-1, 75' Facundo Ferreyra 0-2, 89' Wilson Eduardo 1-2.
Referee: Jonas Eriksson (SWE)   Attendance: 21,645.

07.04.16   El Madrigal, Villarreal: Villarreal CF – Sparta Praha 2-1 (1-1)
Villarreal CF: Asenjo, Mario, Víctor Ruiz, Jaume Costa (77' Adrián Marín), Eric Bailly,
Trigueros, Denis Suárez, Samu Castillejo (62' Léo Baptistão), Bruno Soriano, Soldado, Cédric
Bakambu (82' Adrián). Coach: Marcelino.
Sparta Praha: David Bicík, Jakub Brabec, Mario Holek (28' Radoslav Kovác), Costa
Nhamoinesu, Marek Matejovsky (88' David Lafata), Borek Dockal, Lukás Marecek, Martin
Frydek, Tiémoko Konaté, Ladislav Krejci, Lukás Julis (73' Kehinde Fatai).
Coach: Zdenek Scasny.
Goals: 3' Cédric Bakambu 1-0, 45+4' Jakub Brabec 1-1, 63' Cédric Bakambu 2-1.
Referee: Ovidiu Hategan (ROM)   Attendance: 15,803.

07.04.16   San Mamés Barria, Bilbao: Athletic Bilbao – Sevilla FC 1-2 (0-0)
Athletic Bilbao: Iago Herrerín, Eneko Bóveda, San José, De Marcos, Etxeita, Balenziaga,
Eraso (69' Viguera), Beñat, Williams (63' Susaeta), Muniain (63' Lekue), Aduriz.
Coach: Valverde.
Sevilla FC: David Soria, Benoît Trémoulinas (12' Federico Fazio), Adil Rami, Timothée
Kolodziejczak, Coke, Grzegorz Krychowiak, Michael Krohn-Dehli (68' Yevhen
Konoplyanka), Steven N'Zonzi, Éver Banega (74' Iborra), Kevin Gameiro, Vitolo.
Coach: Unai Emery.
Goals: 48' Aduriz 1-0, 56' Timothée Kolodziejczak 1-1, 83' Iborra 1-2.
Referee: Mark Clattenburg (ENG)   Attendance: 40,856.

07.04.16   Signal Iduna Park, Dortmund: Borussia Dortmund – Liverpool FC 1-1 (0-1)
Borussia Dortmund: Roman Weidenfeller, Mats Hummels, Lukasz Piszczek, Marcel
Schmelzer, Erik Durm (46' Nuri Sahin), Sven Bender (76' Sokratis Papastathopoulos),
Henrikh Mkhitaryan, Gonzalo Castro, Julian Weigl, Marco Reus, Pierre-Emerick Aubameyang
(76' Christian Pulisic). Coach: Thomas Tuchel.
Liverpool FC: Simon Mignolet, Nathaniel Clyne, Dejan Lovren, Mamadou Sakho, Alberto
Moreno, James Milner, Coutinho, Jordan Henderson (46' Joe Allen), Adam Lallana (77'
Roberto Firmino), Emre Can, Divock Origi (84' Daniel Sturridge). Coach: Jürgen Klopp.
Goals: 36' Divock Origi 0-1, 48' Mats Hummels 1-1.
Referee: Carlos Velasco Carballo (ESP)   Attendance: 65,848.

14.04.16   Arena Lviv, Lviv: Shakhtar Donetsk – Sporting Braga 4-0 (2-0)
Shakhtar Donetsk: Andriy Pyatov, Oleksandr Kucher, Maksym Malyshev, Ivan Ordets,
Ismaily, Darijo Srna, Taras Stepanenko, Marlos (77' Eduardo), Viktor Kovalenko (86'
Bernard), Facundo Ferreyra, Taison (78' Dentinho). Coach: Mircea Lucescu.
Sporting Braga: Matheus Magalhães, Willy Boly (77' André Pinto), Djavan, Ricardo Ferreira,
Marcelo Goiano, Luíz Carlos (77' Mauro), Josué, Nikola Vukcevic, Wilson Eduardo (56'
Nikola Stojiljkovic), Rafa Silva, Ahmed Hassan. Coach: Paulo Fonseca.
Goals: 25' Darijo Srna 1-0 (p), 42' Ricardo Ferreira 2-0 (og), 50' Viktor Kovalenko 3-0,
74' Ricardo Ferreira 4-0 (og).
Referee: Pavel Královec (CZE)   Attendance: 33,617.

*Shakhtar Donetsk played their home match at Arena Lviv, Lviv instead of their regular
stadium, Donbass Arena, Donetsk, due to the ongoing conflict in Eastern Ukraine.*

14.04.16   Generali Arena, Praha: Sparta Praha – Villarreal CF 2-4 (0-3)
Sparta Praha: David Bicík, Radoslav Kovác, Marek Matejovsky, Borek Dockal, Lukás
Marecek, Martin Frydek, Tiémoko Konaté, Ladislav Krejci, Kehinde Fatai, David Lafata,
Lukás Julis. Coach: Zdenek Scasny.
Villarreal CF: Alphonse Aréola, Mario (57' Jaume Costa), Víctor Ruiz, Antonio Rukavina,
Eric Bailly, Trigueros (61' Jonathan Dos Santos), Denis Suárez (66' Léo Baptistão), Samu
Castillejo, Bruno Soriano, Soldado, Cédric Bakambu. Coach: Marcelino.
Goals: 5' Cédric Bakambu 0-1, 43' Samu Castillejo 0-2, 45+1' David Lafata 0-3 (og),
49' Cédric Bakambu 0-4, 6' Borek Dockal 1-4, 71' Ladislav Krejci 2-4.
Referee: Martin Atkinson (ENG)   Attendance: 18,201.

14.04.16   Ramón Sánchez Pizjuán, Sevilla: Sevilla FC – Athletic Bilbao 1-2 (0-0, 1-2)
Sevilla FC: David Soria, Adil Rami, Timothée Kolodziejczak, Escudero, Mariano (100' Coke),
Grzegorz Krychowiak, Michael Krohn-Dehli (51' Yevhen Konoplyanka), Iborra (67' Sebastián
Cristóforo), Steven N'Zonzi, Kevin Gameiro, Vitolo. Coach: Unai Emery.
Athletic Bilbao: Iago Herrerín, Eneko Bóveda (60' Iturraspe), San José, De Marcos, Etxeita,
Balenziaga, Beñat, Susaeta, Raúl García, Lekue (54' Muniain), Aduriz (70' Viguera).
Coach: Valverde.
Goals: 57' Aduriz 0-1, 59' Kevin Gameiro 1-1, 80 Raúl García 1-2.
Referee: Damir Skomina (SVN)   Attendance: 38,567.

Sevilla FC won 5-4 on penalties following extra time.

*Penalties: Raúl García 0-1, Coke 1-1, Viguera 1-2, Krychowiak 2-2, San José 2-3,
    Konoplyanka 3-3, Beñat missed, N'Zonzi 4-3, Susaeta 4-4, Gameiro 5-4.*

14.04.16   Anfield, Liverpool: Liverpool FC – Borussia Dortmund 4-3 (0-2)
Liverpool FC: Simon Mignolet, Nathaniel Clyne, Dejan Lovren, Mamadou Sakho, Alberto Moreno, James Milner, Coutinho, Roberto Firmino (62' Daniel Sturridge), Adam Lallana (62' Joe Allen), Emre Can (80' Lucas Leiva), Divock Origi. Coach: Jürgen Klopp.
Borussia Dortmund: Roman Weidenfeller, Mats Hummels, Sokratis Papastathopoulos, Lukasz Piszczek, Marcel Schmelzer, Henrikh Mkhitaryan, Shinji Kagawa (77' Matthias Ginter), Gonzalo Castro (82' Ilkay Gündogan), Julian Weigl, Marco Reus (83' Adrián Ramos), Pierre-Emerick Aubameyang. Coach: Thomas Tuchel.
Goals: 5' Henrikh Mkhitaryan 0-1, 9' Pierre-Emerick Aubameyang 0-2, 48' Divock Origi 1-2, 57' Marco Reus 1-3, 66' Coutinho 2-3, 78' Mamadou Sakho 3-3, 90+1' Dejan Lovren 4-3.
Referee: Cüneyt Çakir (TUR)   Attendance: 42,984.

SEMI-FINALS

28.04.16   Arena Lviv, Lviv: Shakhtar Donetsk – Sevilla FC 2-2 (2-1)
Shakhtar Donetsk: Andriy Pyatov, Oleksandr Kucher, Maksym Malyshev, Ismaily, Darijo Srna, Yaroslav Rakitskiy, Taras Stepanenko, Marlos (90+2' Bernard), Viktor Kovalenko, Facundo Ferreyra (90+1' Eduardo), Taison (90+1' Wellington Nem). Coach: Mircea Lucescu.
Sevilla FC: David Soria, Adil Rami, Daniel Carriço, Escudero, Mariano, Grzegorz Krychowiak, Steven N'Zonzi, Éver Banega, Yevhen Konoplyanka (59' Michael Krohn-Dehli, 72' Coke), Kevin Gameiro, Vitolo. Coach: Unai Emery.
Goals: 6' Vitolo 0-1, 23' Marlos 1-1, 36' Taras Stepanenko 2-1, 82' Kevin Gameiro 2-2 (p).
Referee: Szymon Marciniak (POL)   Attendance: 34,267.

Shakhtar Donetsk played their home match at Arena Lviv, Lviv instead of their regular stadium, Donbass Arena, Donetsk, due to the ongoing conflict in Eastern Ukraine.

28.04.16   El Madrigal, Villarreal: Villarreal CF – Liverpool FC 1-0 (0-0)
Villarreal CF: Asenjo, Mario, Víctor Ruiz, Jaume Costa, Eric Bailly (76' Mateo Musacchio), Pina, Jonathan Dos Santos (72' Samu Castillejo), Denis Suárez, Bruno Soriano, Soldado (74' Adrián), Cédric Bakambu. Coach: Marcelino.
Liverpool FC: Simon Mignolet, Nathaniel Clyne, Kolo Touré, Dejan Lovren, Alberto Moreno, James Milner, Coutinho (46' Jordon Ibe), Roberto Firmino (90' Christian Benteke), Adam Lallana, Lucas Leiva, Joe Allen. Coach: Jürgen Klopp.
Goal: 90+2' Adrián 1-0.
Referee: Damir Skomina (SVN)   Attendance: 21,606.

05.05.16   Ramón Sánchez Pizjuán, Sevilla: Sevilla FC – Shakhtar Donetsk 3-1 (1-1)
Sevilla FC: David Soria, Benoît Trémoulinas (73' Escudero), Adil Rami, Daniel Carriço, Coke, Mariano, Grzegorz Krychowiak, Steven N'Zonzi, Éver Banega (89' Sebastián Cristóforo), Kevin Gameiro (82' Iborra), Vitolo. Coach: Unai Emery.
Shakhtar Donetsk: Andriy Pyatov, Oleksandr Kucher, Maksym Malyshev, Ismaily, Darijo Srna, Yaroslav Rakitskiy, Taras Stepanenko, Marlos (84' Wellington Nem), Viktor Kovalenko, Eduardo (84' Dentinho), Taison (76' Bernard). Coach: Mircea Lucescu.
Goals: 9' Kevin Gameiro 1-0, 44' Eduardo 1-1, 47' Kevin Gameiro 2-1, 59' Mariano 3-1.
Referee: Björn Kuipers (HOL)   Attendance: 41,286.

05.05.16   Anfield, Liverpool: Liverpool FC – Villarreal CF 3-0 (1-0)
Liverpool FC: Simon Mignolet, Nathaniel Clyne, Kolo Touré, Dejan Lovren, Alberto Moreno, James Milner, Coutinho (82' Joe Allen), Roberto Firmino (89' Christian Benteke), Adam Lallana, Emre Can, Daniel Sturridge (90+2' Lucas Leiva). Coach: Jürgen Klopp.
Villarreal CF: Alphonse Aréola, Mario, Mateo Musacchio, Víctor Ruiz, Jaume Costa, Pina (60' Trigueros), Jonathan Dos Santos (73' Daniele Bonera), Denis Suárez, Bruno Soriano, Soldado (68' Adrián), Cédric Bakambu. Coach: Marcelino.
Goals: 7' Bruno Soriano 1-0 (og), 63' Daniel Sturridge 2-0, 81' Adam Lallana 3-0.
Referee: Viktor Kassai (HUN)   Attendance: 43,074.
Sent off: 71' Víctor Ruiz.

FINAL

18.05.16   St.Jakob-Park, Basel: Liverpool FC – Sevilla FC 1-3 (1-0)
Liverpool FC: Simon Mignolet, Nathaniel Clyne, Kolo Touré (83' Christian Benteke), Dejan Lovren, Alberto Moreno, James Milner, Coutinho, Roberto Firmino (69' Divock Origi), Adam Lallana (73' Joe Allen), Emre Can, Daniel Sturridge. Coach: Jürgen Klopp.
Sevilla FC: David Soria, Adil Rami (78' Timothée Kolodziejczak), Daniel Carriço, Escudero, Coke, Mariano, Grzegorz Krychowiak, Steven N'Zonzi, Éver Banega (90+3' Sebastián Cristóforo), Kevin Gameiro (89' Iborra), Vitolo. Coach: Unai Emery.
Goals: 35' Daniel Sturridge 1-0, 46' Kevin Gameiro 1-1, 64', 70' Coke 1-2, 1-3.
Referee: Jonas Eriksson (SWE)   Attendance: 34,429.

TOP SCORERS 2015-2016

Aduriz	Athletic Bilbao	10
Cédric Bakambu	Villarreal CF	9
Kévin Gameiro	Sevilla FC	8
Pierre-Emerick Aubameyang	Borussia Dortmund	8
Raúl Bobadilla	FC Augsburg	6
Érik Lamela	Tottenham Hotspur	6
Aboubakar Oumarou	Partizan	5
Dries Mertens	SSC Napoli	5
José Callejón	SSC Napoli	5
Franco Di Santo	FC Schalke 04	5
David Lafata	Sparta Praha	5
Aleksandr Samedov	Lokomotiv Moskva	5
Marco Reus	Borussia Dortmund	5

Top scorer statistics exclude qualifying rounds and the play-off round.

UEFA EUROPA LEAGUE 2016-2017

FIRST QUALIFYING ROUND

28.06.16   Filip II Makedonski, Skopje: FK Rabotnicki – FK Buducnost Podgorica 1-1 (0-1).
FK Rabotnicki: Damjan Siskovski, Leon Najdovski, Dejan Mitrev, Goran Siljanovski, Mite
Cikarski, Suad Sahiti, Bojan Najdenov (63' Elif Elmas), Ivan Galić (55' Filip Duranski),
Dusko Trajcevski, Kire Markoski (78' Sebastián Herera), Marijan Altiparmakovski.
Coach: Tomislav Franc.
FK Buducnost Podgorica: Milos Dragojević, Nikola Vukcević, Filip Mitrović, Ermin Seratlić
(57' Marko Raicević), Milos Raicković (88' Danilo Marković), Ivan Pejaković, Deni Hocko,
Luka Mirković, Velizar Janketić (64' Driton Camaj), Milan Vusurović, Radomir Djalović.
Coach: Miodrag Vukotic.
Goals: 36' Velizar Janketić 0-1, 80' Elif Elmas 1-1.
Referee: Zbynek Proske (CZE)   Attendance: 1,500.

28.06.16   Elbasan Arena, Elbasan: FK Partizani – Slovan Bratislava 0-0.
FK Partizani: Alban Hoxha, Gëzim Krasniqi, Labinot Ibrahimi, Renaldo Kalari (87' Sodiq
Atanda), Realdo Fili (88' Ardit Jaupaj), Renato Arapi, Idriz Batha, Ylber Ramadani, Lorenc
Trashi, Emiljano Vila, Agustin Torassa (84' Jurgen Bardhi). Coach: Genc Tomori.
Slovan Bratislava: Jan Mucha, Boris Sekulic, Lorenzo Burnet, Ruben Ligeon, Kornel Salata,
Joeri de Kamps, Richard Lasik (62' Vukan Savicevic), Seydouba Soumah, Adam Zrelak, Lesly
de Sa (76' Frantisek Kubik), Mitchell Schet. Coach: Nicky Papavasiliou.
Referee: Erez Papir (ISR)   Attendance: 1,350.

The second leg was not played because FK Partizani entered the Champions League after
KF Skenderbeu were banned from European competition over match-fixing allegations.
Slovan Bratislava progressed to the second qualifying round.

28.06.16   Dalga Arena, Baku: FK Kapaz – Dacia Chisinau 0-0.
FK Kapaz: Tadas Simaitis, Karim Diniyev, Vugar Baybalayev (73' Jeyhun Javadov), Dário
Júnior, Nijat Gurbanov (70' Orkhan Aliyev), Tural Akhundov, Shahriyar Aliyev, Renan Alves,
Shahriyar Rahimov, Sérginho (79' Tural Qurbatov), Julien Ebah. Coach: Shakhin Diniyev.
Dacia Chisinau: Dumitru Celeadnic, Andrii Slinkin, Simeon Bulgaru, Veaceslav Posmac,
Abdoul Mamah, Rinar Valeev (40' Maksim Gavrilenko), Denis Kozhanov, Eugeniu Cociuc,
Igor Bugaev (61' Sapol Mani), Alexandru Bejan (83' Andrey Bugneac), Maksim Feshchuk.
Coach: Veaceslav Semionov.
Referee: Aleksander Gauzer (KAZ)   Attendance: 2,000.

28.06.16   Richmond Park, Dublin: St Patrick's Athletic – Jeunesse Esch 1-0 (1-0).
St Patrick's Athletic: Brendan Clarke, Ger O'Brien, Ian Bermingham, Darren Dennehy, Sean
Hoare, Keith Treacy, David Cawley, Conan Byrne (60' Mark Timlin), Graham Kelly, Billy
Dennehy, Chris Fagan. Coach: Liam Buckley.
Jeunesse Esch: Marc Oberweis, Milos Todorovic, Adrien Portier, Ricardo Delgado, Emmanuel
Lapierre, Martin Ontiveros (81' Andrea Deidda), Ken Corral (21' Ashot Sardaryan), René
Peters, Giancarlo Pinna, Robin Mertinitz, Patrick Stumpf. Coach: Carlo Weis.
Goal: 7' Chris Fagan 1-0.
Referee: Pavel Orel (CZE)   Attendance: 1,200.

30.06.16   Tengiz Burjanadze, Gori: Dila Gori – Shirak FC 1-0 (1-0).
Dila Gori: Mikheil Mujrishvili, Giga Samkharadze, Dato Kvirkvelia, Teimuraz Gongadze, Givi
Karkuzashvili, Luka Razmadze, Tengiz Tsikaridze (68' Tamaz Kikabidze), Levan
Nonikashvili (89' Irakli Katamadze), Giorgi Eristavi (79' Levan Sabadze), Grigol Dolidze,
Irakli Modebadze. Coach: Ucha Sosiashvili.
Shirak FC: Anatoly Ayvazov, Arman Hovhannisyan, Artyom Mikaelyan, Gevorg
Hovhannisyan, Robert Darbinyan, Rumyan Hovsepyan (58' Drissa Diarrassouba), Davit
Hakobyan (78' Kouadia Brou), Solomon Udo, Mohamed Kaba, Nemanja Stoskovic, Konan
Kouakou (87' Aram Muradyan). Coach: Vardan Bichakhchyan.
Goal: 36' Irakli Modebadze 1-0.
Referee: Anatoliy Zhabchenko (UKR)   Attendance: 2,512.

30.06.16   Tsentralniy, Aktobe: FK Aktobe – MTK Budapest 1-1 (1-1)
FK Aktobe: Samat Otarbaev, Marat Sitdikov, Kouassi Kouadja, Bagdat Kairov, Viktor
Kryukov, Sandro Tsveiba, Egor Sorokin, Didar Zhalmukan (83' Kirill Shestakov), Vuk
Mitosevic, Nikita Bocharov, Lassina Dao (62' Dmitriy Golubov). Coach: Yuri Utkulbaev.
MTK Budapest: Lajos Hegedüs, Akos Baki, Mato Grgic, Daniel Vadnai, Patrik Poor, Lorand
Szatmari (88' Balint Borbely), Jozsef Kanta, Adam Vass, Darko Nikac (90+1' Bence Deutsch),
Sandor Torghelle, Daniel Gera. Coach: Vaszilisz Teodoru.
Goals: 30' Sandor Torghelle 0-1, 43' Didar Zhalmukan 1-1 (p).
Referee: Sascha Amhof (SUI)   Attendance: 8,600.

30.06.16   Estadi Comunal, Andorra la Vella:
            UE Santa Coloma – Lokomotiva Zagreb 1-3 (0-1)
UE Sant Coloma: Ivan Perianez, Alexandre Martinez, Miguel Ruiz, Jesus Rubio, Josep Ayala,
Boris Anton (74' Walid Bousenine), Pedro Reis, Juan Salomo (62' Jordi Rubio), Victor Bernat,
Gerard Aloy (81' Cristian Orosa), Sergi Crespo. Coach: Emilio.
Lokomotiva Zagreb: Ivan Filipovic, Karlo Bartolec, Karlo Brucic, Dino Peric, Herdi Prenga,
Luka Capan, Ivan Fiolic, Luka Ivanusec (60' Josip Coric), Endri Cekici, Eros Grezda (76'
Lovro Majer), Mirko Maric (79' Jakov Puljic). Coach: Valentin Barisic.
Goals: 20' Mirko Maric 0-1, 65' Herdi Prenga 0-2, 73' Mirko Maric 0-3,
90+3' Pedro Reis 1-3.
Referee: Donatas Rumsas (LTU)   Attendance: 250.

30.06.16   Ventspils Stadions, Ventspils: FK Ventspils – Vikingur 2-0 (2-0)
FK Ventspils: Maksims Uvarenko, Alans Sinelnikovs, Nikita Kolesovs, Nikola Boranijasevic,
Antons Jemelins, Simonas Paulius, Eduards Tidenbergs, Vitalijs Recickis, Ritvars Rugins,
Aleksey Alekseev (46' Ndue Mujeci), Girst Karlsons (90+2' Kaspars Pavlovs).
Coach: Paul Ashworth.
Vikingur: Tamas Turi Geza, Atli Gregersen, Erling Jacobsen, Hans Djurhuus, Gert Aage
Hansen, Sølvi Vatnhamar, Bardur Hansen, Andreas Olsen (75' Jon Krossla Poulsen), Filip
Djordjevic (86' Jakup Olsen), Hans Pauli Samuelsen (62' Sorin Anghel), Finnur Justinussen.
Coach: Samal Hentze.
Goals: 5' Girts Karlsons 1-0, 37' Girts Karlsons 2-0.
Referee: Mikhail Vilkov (RUS)   Attendance: 1,982.

128

30.06.16   NV Arena, Sankt Pölten: FC Admira Wacker – Spartak Myjava 1-1 (1-0)
FC Admira Wacker: Jörg Siebenhandl, Stephan Zwierschitz, Thomas Ebner, Markus Wostry, Markus Lackner, Christoph Knasmüllner, Daniel Toth, Eldis Bajrami, Srdan Spiridonovic, Christoph Monschein (58' Toni Vastic), Dominik Starkl (74' Markus Pavic).
Coach: Ernst Baumeister.
Spartak Myjava: Matus Hruska, Ivan Ostojic, Jaroslav Machovec, Adi Mehremic, Lukas Beno, Tomas Kona, Lubos Kolar (65' Stefan Pekar), Denis Duga (65' Peter Sladek), Frederik Bilovsky (89' Tomas Marcek), Erik Daniel, Vladimir Kukol. Coach: Mikulas Radvanyi.
Goals: 34' Elsid Bajrami 1-0, 73' Tomas Kona 1-1.
Referee: Fran Jovic (CRO)   Attendance: 1,300.

30.06.16   Lugova, Budva: FK Bokelj – Vojvodina 1-1 (1-1)
FK Bokelj: Milan Mijatovic, Sinisa Mladenovic, Ilija Bogdanovic, Miroslav Zlaticanin, Dejan Ognjanovic, Mirko Todorovic, Danilo Tomic (64' Dejan Kotorac), Aleksandar Macanovic, Dejan Djenic, Jovan Vucinic (72' Luka Maras), Dejan Pepic (76' Lazar Pajovic).
Coach: Slobodan Draskovic.
Vojvodina: Marko Kordic, Vladimir Kovacevic, Nikola Antic, Darko Puskaric, Sinisa Babic (70' Nikola Asceric), Nikola Kovacevic (59' Dusan Micic), Filip Malbasic, Dusan Jovancic (59' Aleksandar Palocevic), Nemanja Miletic, Nikola Trujic, Dejan Meleg.
Coach: Nenad Lalatovic.
Goals: 5' Dejan Djenic 1-0, 6' Dejan Meleg 1-1.
Referee: Alejandro Hernandez Hernandez (ESP)   Attendance: 1,403.

30.06.16   Kadrioru Staadion, Tallinn: FC Levadia – HB Torshavn 1-1 (0-1)
FC Levadia: Sergei Lepmets, Luc Tabi, Maksim Podholjuzin, Igor Morozov, Ilja Antonov, Pavel Marin, Marcelin Gando, Anton Miranchuk (70' Alan Gatagov), Daniil Ratnikov, Evgeni Kobzar (46' Siim Luts), Rimo Hunt. Coach: Sergei Ratnikov.
HB Torshavn: Teitur Gestsson, Johan Davidsen, Ari Jonsson, Magnus Egilsson (66' Bartal Wardum), Frodi Benjaminsen, Trondur Jensen, Teit Jacobsen, Rokur Jespersen (90+3' Adrian Justinussen), Jogvan Davidsen, Christian Mouritsen, Ari Mohr Olsen (84' Pal Joensen).
Coach: Jan Christian Dam.
Goals: 21' Luc Tabi 0-1 (og), 65' Pavel Marin 1-1.
Referee: Filip Glova (SVK)   Attendance: 730.

30.06.16   Puskas Akademia Pancho Arena, Felcsut: Videoton FC – FC Zaria 3-0 (1-0)
Videoton FC: Adam Kovacsik, Paulo Vinicius, Andras Fejes, Loïc Nego, Mate Patkai, Adam Bodi, Roland Szolnoki, Krisztian Geresi (84' Istvan Kovacs), Asmir Suljic, David Barczi (72' Robert Feczesin), Adam Simon. Coach: Henning Berg.
FC Zaria: Serghei Pascenco, Victor Golovatenco, Andrey Novicov, Iulian Erhan, Alexandru Onica (81' Vadim Rata), Igor Tigirlas, Ruben Gomez, Alexandru Grosu (72' Alexandru Suvorov), Igor Picusceac, Georgi Ovsyannikov (69' Gheorghe Boghiu), Maxim Mihaliov.
Coach: Igor Rakhaev.
Goals: 18' Krisztian Geresi 1-0, 88', 90+4' Robert Feczesin 2-0, 3-0.
Referee: Enea Jorgji (ALB)   Attendance: 2,321.
Sent off: 53' Igor Picusceac, 90+3' Alexandru Suvorov.

30.06.16   Klaipedosmiesto Centrinis, Klaipeda: FK Atlantas – HJK Helsinki 0-2 (0-0)
FK Atlantas: Povilas Valincius, Rolandas Baravykas, Aleksey Epifanov, Kazimieras Gnedojus, Rokas Gedminas (67' Andrius Bartkus), Domantas Simkus (67' Donatas Kazlauskas), Markas Beneta, Ovidijus Verbickas, Oleg Dmitriev (77' Marius Papsys), Abdoul Karim Sylla, Maksim Maksimov. Coach: Konstantin Sarsaniya.
HJK Helsinki: Thomas Dähne, Taye Taiwo, Lum Rexhepi, Ivan Tatomirovic, Ville Jalasto, Medo, Obed Malolo, Atomu Tanaka, Nnamdi Oduamadi (88' Toni Kolehmainen), Nikolai Alho (24' Richard Gadze, 82' Sebastian Sorsa), Alfredo Morelos. Coach: Mika Lehkosuo.
Goals: 53', 85' Alfredo Morelos 0-1, 0-2.
Referee: Alexandros Aretopoulos (GRE)   Attendance: 2,500.

Abdoul Karim Sylla missed a penalty kick (18').

30.06.16   Bilino Polje, Zenica: Sloboda Tuzla – Beitar Jerusalem 0-0
Sloboda Tuzla: Kenan Piric, Ivan Kostic, Aldin Djidic, Samir Efendic, Zajko Zeba, Amer Ordagic, Nemanja Stjepanovic, Miljan Govedarica (80' Mladen Veselinovic), Damir Mehidic (85' Vladimir Grahovac), Samir Merzic, Mahir Karic. Coach: Husref Musemic.
Beitar Jerusalem: Boris Kleiman, Jesus Rueda, Dan Mori, Snir Mishan, Dan Einbinder, Omer Atzily, Claudemir, Kobi Moyal (66' Lidor Cohen), Ori Majabi, Itay Shechter (80' Ya'akov Berihon), Arsenio Valpoort (89' Omer Nachmani). Coach: Slobodan Drapic.
Referee: Glenn Nyberg (SWE)   Attendance: 2,762.

30.06.16   LFF Stadium, Vilnius: FK Trakai – JK Nõmme Kalju 2-1 (0-1)
FK Trakai: Marius Rapalis, Justinas Janusevskis, Modestas Vorobjovas, Deividas Cesnauskis, Vaidas Silenas, Eugen Zasavitchi, Artem Gurenko (79' Titas Vitukynas), Aleksandr Bychenok, Dmitriy Rekish (76' Lukas Kochanauskas), David Arshakyan, Nerijus Valskis (86' Rokas Masenzovas). Coach: Valdas Urbonas.
JK Nõmme Kalju: Vitali Teles, Maximiliano Ugge, Jorge Rodrigues, Andrei Sidorenkov, Reginald Mbu-Alidor, Janar Toomet (77' Andre Järva), Peeter Klein (80' Tarmo Neemelo), Karl Mööl, Hidetoshi Wakui, Damiano Quintieri (45' Vlasiy Sinyavskiy), Artjom Dmitrijev. Coach: Sergey Frantsev.
Goals: 6' Hidetoshi Wakui 0-1 (p), 69' Nerijus Valskis 1-1, 78' David Arshakyan 2-1.
Referee: Vladimir Vnuk (SVK)   Attendance: 500.

30.06.16   Hibernians Ground, Paola: Balzan Youths – Neftci PFK 0-2 (0-1)
Balzan Youths: Ivan Janjusevic, Steven Bezzina, Elkin Serrano, Oliveira, Paul Fenech, Dylan Grima (81' Samir Arab), Clive Brincat (74' Justin Grioli), Dê, Borce Manevski (65' Lydon Micallef), Alfred Effiong, Bojan Kaljevic. Coach: Oliver Spiteri.
Neftci PFK: Krsevan Santini, Jairo, Vance Sikov, Magsad Isayev, Dario Melnjak, Araz Abdullayev (81' Fahmin Muradbayli), Elshan Abdullayev, Murad Agaev, Rahman Hajiyev (75' Javid Imamverdiyev), Edson Castillo (90+4' Rahil Mammadov), Ruslan Qurbanov. Coach: Veli Kasumov.
Goals: 14' Rahman Hajiyev 0-1, 84' Ruslan Qurbanov 0-2 (p).
Referee: Jovan Kaluderovic (MNE)   Attendance: 357.

30.06.16   Traktor, Minsk: Dinamo Minsk – FK Spartaks 2-1 (1-0)
Dinamo Minsk: Sergey Ignatovich, Yuriy Ostroukh, Kirill Premudrov, Artem Bykov,
Uladzimir Karytska (66' Luka Rotkovic), Valeriy Zhukovskiy (86' Anton Shramchenko),
Oleksandr Noyok, Yuriy Gabovda, Nikita Kaplenko, Gleb Rassadkin, Vladimir
Khvashchinskiy. Coach: Vuk Rasovic.
FK Spartaks: Vladislavs Kurakins, Sergey Pushnyakov, Pavels Mihadjuks, Ingus Slampe,
Jevgenijs Kazacoks, Evgeny Kozlov, Sergey Koseka, Ridwaru Adeyemo, Moshtagh Yaghoubi,
Vladislavs Kozlovs, Dmitry Platonov (35' Daniil Ulimbasevs). Coach: Oleg Kubarev.
Goals: 18' Artem Bykov 1-0, 80' Daniil Ulimbasevs 1-1, 82' Artem Bykov 2-1.
Referee: Zaven Hovhannisyan (ARM)   Attendance: 1,700.

30.06.16   Hanrapetakan, Yerevan: FC Banants – Omonia Nikosia 0-1 (0-1)
FC Banants: Stepan Ghazaryan, Soslan Kachmazov, Aslan Kalmanov, Vlatko Drobarov,
Hakob Hakobyan, Layonel Adams, Valter Poghosyan (78' Oleksandr Ohanisian), Claudio
Torrejon, Zaven Badoyan (85' Edgar Movsesyan), Vahagn Ayvazyan (81' Petros Avetisyan),
Atsamaz Buraev. Coach: Tito Ramallo.
Omonia Nikosia: Kostas Panayi, Carlitos, Thanasis Panteliadis, Gerasimos Fylaktou, Margaça,
George Florescu, Dimitris Christofi (17' Amir Agajev), Marin Orsulic, Cillian Sheridan (70'
Cleyton), Matt Derbyshire, Ziguy Badibanga (90+1' Antreas Panayiotou). Coach: John Carver.
Goal: 26' Matt Derbyshire 0-1.
Referee: Mario Zebec (CRO)   Attendance: 1,520.

30.06.16   Gamla Ullevi, Göteborg: IFK Göteborg – Llandudno FC 5-0 (3-0)
IFK Göteborg: John Alvbåge, Emil Salomonsson, Haitam Aleesami, Sebastian Eriksson (76'
Tom Pettersson), Thomas Rogne, Mattias Bjärsmyr, Mads Albæk, Søren Rieks, Martin
Smedberg (53' Patrik Karlsson-Lagemyr), Mikael Boman (65' Tobias Hysén), Gustav Engvall.
Coach: Jörgen Lennartsson.
Llandudno FC: Dave Roberts, Danny Taylor, James Joyce (77' Connor Tierney), Danny
Hughes, Mike Williams, Danny Shaw, Tom Dix, Lee Thomas (57' Liam Dawson), Marc
Williams, Jamie Reed, Lewis Buckley (70' John Owen). Coach: Alan Morgan.
Goals: 11' Gustav Engvall 1-0, 12' Søren Rieks 2-0, 36' Emil Salomonsson 3-0,
79' Tobias Hysén 4-0, 81' Tobias Hysén 5-0.
Referee: Martin Lundby (NOR)   Attendance: 6,074.

30.06.16   Tele2 Arena, Stockholm: AIK Solna – Bala Town 2-0 (1-0)
AIK Solna: Patrik Carlgren, Per Karlsson, Nils-Eric Johansson, Patrick Kpozo, Ebenezer
Ofori, Daniel Sundgren, Stefan Ishizaki, Christos Gravius (74' Anton Saletros), Amin Affane
(68' Johan Blomberg), Carlos Strandberg, Alexander Isak (83' Denni Avdic).
Coach: Rikard Norling.
Bala Town: Ashley Morris, Ryan Valentine, Anthony Stephens, Stuart Jones, Stuart Jones,
Tony Davies, David Thompson (56' Mike Hayes), Nathan Burke (83' Jamie Crowther), Mark
Connolly (69' Mark Jones), Ian Sheridan, Kieran Smith. Coach: Stephen O'Shaughnessy.
Goals: 27' Amin Affane 1-0, 52' Nils-Eric Johansson 2-0.
Referee: Kirill Levnikov (RUS)   Attendance: 6,127.

131

30.06.16   Victoria Stadium, Gibraltar: Europa FC – Pyunik FC 2-0 (2-0)
Europa FC: Javi Muñoz, Toni (58' José Gonzalez), Toscano, Vazquez, Ivan Moya, Felix
Lopez, Guille Roldan, Alex Quillo (66' Eloy), Martin Belfortti, Alberto Merino, Pedro Carrion
(76' Copi). Coach: Juan Gallardo Fernandez.
Pyunik FC: Gor Manukyan, Serob Grigoryan, Artur Kartashyan, Armen Manucharyan, Kamo
Hovhannisyan, Davit Manoyan, Alik Arakelyan, Vardges Satumyan (46' Hovhannes
Harutyunyan), Taron Voskanyan, Ramzik Hakobyan (46' Erik Petrosyan), Artur Yuspashyan
(71' Robert Minasyan). Coach: Sargis Hovsepyan.
Goals: 32' Pedro Carrion 1-0, 39' Felix Lopez 2-0.
Referee: Markus Hameter (AUT)   Attendance: 850.
Sent off: 79' Serob Grigoryan.

30.06.16   Vasil Levski, Sofia: Slavia Sofia – Zaglebie Lubin 1-0 (0-0)
Slavia Sofia: Mario Kirev, Georgi Pashov, Stefan Velkov, Emil Martinov, Nikita Sergeev,
Omar Khamis, Borislav Baldzhiyski (55' Yanis Karabelyov), Bozhidar Vasev, Serder
Serderov, Kaloyan Krastev (56' Ivailo Dimitrov), Georgi Yomov (90' Petko Hristov).
Coach: Aleksandr Tarkhanov.
Zaglebie Lubin: Martin Polacek, Maciej Dabrowski, Djordje Cotra, Aleksandar Todorovski,
Lubomir Guldan, Jaroslaw Kubicki, Lukasz Piatek, Jan Vlasko (83' Adrian Rakowski),
Arkadiusz Wozniak, Lukasz Janoszka (74' Krzysztof Janus), Krzysztof Piatek (68' Michal
Papadopulos). Coach: Piotr Stokowiec.
Goal: 85' Serder Serderov 1-0.
Referee: Aliyar Agayev (AZE)   Attendance: 1,160.

30.06.16   MCH Arena, Herning: FC Midtjylland – FK Sūduva 1-0 (0-0)
FC Midtjylland: Johan Dahlin, Kian Hansen, Patrick Banggaard, Rasmus Nissen, Tim Sparv
(90+1' Markus Halsti), Jakob Poulsen, Kristoffer Olsson (55' Mikkel Duelund), Pione Sisto
(77' Vaclav Kadlec), Filip Novák, Martin Pusic, Ebere Onuachu. Coach: Jess Thorup.
FK Sūduva: Ivan Kardum, Algis Jankauskas, Miljan Jablan, Povilas Leimonas, Andro
Svrljuga, Eligijus Jankasukas (90+2' Domantas Antanavicius), Vaidas Slavickas, Nermin
Jamak, Predrag Pavlovic, Admir Kecap, Karolis Laukzemis (51' Paulius Janusauskas).
Coach: Aleksander Veselinovic.
Goal: 56' Ebere Onuachu 1-0.
Referee: Srdan Jovanovic (SRB)   Attendance: 4,347.

30.06.16   Stadionul Zimbru, Chisinau: FC Zimbru – Chikhura Sachkhere 0-1 (0-1)
FC Zimbru: Denis Rusu, Luan, Emerson, Ion Jardan, Izaldo, Diego Lima (46' Veaceslav
Zagaevschii), Gheorghe Anton, Alex Bruno, Amancio Fortes, Mohamed Coulibaly (81' Erick),
Dan Spataru (86' Daniel Jalo). Coach: Flavius Stoican.
Chikhura Sachkhere: Dino Hamzic, Tornike Grigalashvili, Levan Kakubava, Lasha
Chikvaidze, Shota Kashia, Giorgi Rekhviashvili, Giorgi Ganugrava, Saba Lobzhanidze (66'
Irakli Lekvtadze), George Ivanishvili (90+2' Besik Dekanoidze), Giorgi Gabedava (57' Denis
Dobrovolski), Dimitri Tatanashvili. Coach: Soso Pruidze.
Goal: 39' Dimitri Tatanashvili 0-1.
Referee: Jari Järvinen (FIN)   Attendance: 2,500.
Sent off: 36' Gheorghe Anton, 61' Giorgi Ganugrava.

30.06.16   Antonis Papadopoulos, Larnaca: AEK Larnaca – SS Folgore/Falciano 3-0 (3-0)
AEK Larnaca: Mateusz Taudul, Constantinos Mintikkis, Català, Elias Charalambous (84'
Nikos Englezou), Daniel Mojsov (74' Murillo), Jorge Larena, Joan Tomas, Tete (63' Costas
Charalambides), Vincent Laban, André Alves, Ivan Trickovski. Coach: Thomas Christiansen.
SS Folgore/Falciano: Simone Montanari, Luca Righi (69' Cristian Brolli), Andrea Nucci (59'
Michael Angelini), Christofer Genestreti, Matteo Camillini, Francesco Quintavalla, Manuel
Muccini, Luca Bezzi (86' Luca Rossi), Michael Traini, Francesco Perrotta, José Hirsch.
Coach: Luciano Mularoni.
Goals: 22' Ivan Trickovski 1-0, 31' André Alves 2-0, 34' Ivan Trickovski 3-0.
Referee: Aleksandrs Golubevs (LAT)   Attendance: 2,100.

30.06.16   Elbasan Arena, Elbasan: FK Kukësi – FK Rudar Pljevlja 1-1 (1-0)
FK Kukësi: Enea Kolici, Ylli Shameti, Gentian Muça (82' Bedri Greca), Rrahman Hallaçi,
Renato Malota, Gledi Mici, Izair Emini, Besar Musolli, Jean Carioca (75' Philippe Guimaraes),
Rangel, Matija Dvornekovic (65' Bekim Dema). Coach: Hasan Lika.
FK Rudar Pljevlja: Milos Radanovic, Ermin Alic, Dusan Nestorovic, Mirko Radisic, Radule
Zivkovic, Ryota Noma (90+4' Ivan Markovic), Alphonse Soppo, Ivan Ivanovic (90+1' Stevan
Reljic), Drasko Bozovic (78' Miroje Jovanovic), Predrag Brnovic, Nedeljko Vlahovic.
Coach: Srdan Bajic.
Goals: 32' Rangel 1-0, 71' Milos Radanovic 1-1 (p).
Referee: Roy Reinshreiber (ISR).

Match was played behind closed doors.

30.06.16   Rheinpark Stadion, Vaduz: FC Vaduz – Sileks Kratovo 3-1 (2-0)
FC Vaduz: Peter Jehle, Simone Grippo, Axel Borgmann, Mario Bühler, Diego Ciccone,
Moreno Costanzo, Maurice Brunner, Stjepan Kukuruzovic, Philipp Muntwiler (76' Nicolas
Hasler), Dejan Janjatovic (63' Albion Avdijaj), Gonzalo Zarate (70' Marco Mathys).
Coach: Giorgio Contini.
Sileks Kratovo: Nikola Vujanac, Nemanja Ivanov, Blagoj Gucev, Gligor Gligorov, Angel
Timovski (52' Kristijan Filipovski), Marjan Mickov, Gjorgje Dzhonov, Andrej Acevski (61'
Antonio Kalanoski), Gjorgji Tanusev (90+2' Stojan Stojcevski), Aleksandar Panovski, Igor
Nedeljkovic. Coach: Gordan Zdravkov.
Goals: 36' Moreno Costanzo 1-0, 45+2' Moreno Costanzo 2-0, 86' Marjan Mickov 2-1,
90+5' Simone Grippo 3-1.
Referee: Thoroddur Hjaltalin (ISL)   Attendance: 928.

30.06.16   Stade Municipal de Differdange, Differdange:
         FC Differdange 03 – Cliftonville FC 1-1 (1-0)
FC Differdange 03: Julien Weber, André Rodrigues, Tom Siebenaler (71' Ante Bukvic), David
Vandenbroeck, Mathias Jänisch, Geoffrey Franzoni, Andy May, Pedro Ribeiro (67' Dejvid
Sinani), Omar Er Rafik, Jordann Yéyé (81' Jeff Lascak), Antonio Luisi. Coach: Marc Thomé.
Cliftonville FC: Jason Mooney, Levi Ives, Caoimhin Bonner, Jason McGuinness, Christopher
Curran (85' Darren Murray), James Knowles, Martin Donnelly (67' Ross Lavery), Ryan
Catney, Jude Winchester, Daniel Hughes (56' David McDaid), Jay Donnelly.
Coach: Gerry Lyttle.
Goals: 38' Omar Er Rafik 1-0, 89' Ross Lavery 1-1.
Referee: Ignasi Villamayor (AND)   Attendance: 1,355.

133

30.06.16   Skagerak Arena, Skien: Odds BK – IFK Mariehamn 2-0 (0-0)
Odds BK: Sondre Rossbach, Espen Ruud, Thomas Grøgaard (75' Fredrik Jensen), Joakim
Nilsen, Steffen Hagen, Lars-Kristian Eriksen, Oliver Berg (55' Olivier Occean), Ole
Halvorsen, Fredrik Nordkvelle, Henrik Johansen (55' Rafik Zekhnini), Bentley.
Coach: Dag-Eilev Fagermo.
IFK Mariehamn: Walter Viitala, Albin Granlund, Kristian Kojola, Jani Lyyski, Bobbie Friberg
da Cruz, Gabriel Petrovic, Amos Ekhalie (90' Tommy Wirtanen), Anthony Clement Dafaa (59'
Philip Sparrdal Mantilla), Diego Assis (69' Aleksei Kangaskolkka), Dever Orgill, Brian Span.
Coaches: Kari Virtanen & Peter Lundberg.
Goals: 63' Thomas Grøgaard 1-0, 86' Olivier Occean 2-0.
Referee: Mohammed Al Hakim (SWE)   Attendance: 3,701.

30.06.16   Pecara, Siroki Brijeg: Siroki Brijeg – Birkirkara FC 1-1 (1-1)
Siroki Brijeg: Antonio Soldo, Boris Pandza, Dino Coric, Slavko Brekalo, Stipo Markovic, Jure
Ivankovic (70' Zoran Plazonic), Josip Corluka (46' Wagner Lago), Ivan Sesar, Ivan Crnov,
Ivan Krstanovic, Ivan Baraban (85' Luka Menalo). Coach: Slaven Musa.
Birkirkara FC: Miroslav Kopric, Christian Bubalovic, Joseph Zerafa (63' Matthew
Guillaumier), Predrag Jovic, Gareth Sciberras, Ryan Camenzuli (57' Shaun Bajada), Srdan
Dimitrov, Ryan Scicluna (76' Edinson Bilbao), Cain Attard, Emerson, Vito Plut.
Coach: Drazen Besek.
Goals: 15' Cain Attard 0-1, 45' Ivan Baraban 1-1.
Referee: Sandro Schärer (SUI)   Attendance: 3,000.

30.06.16   Bakcell Arena, Baku: Gabala FK – FC Samtredia 5-1 (3-0)
Gabala FK: Dmitro Bezotosniy, Vojislav Stankovic, Vitaliy Vernydub, Ricardinho, Urfan
Abbasov, Räsad Sadiqov, Nika Kvekveskiri, Filip Ozobic, Theo Weeks (86' Gismat Aliyev),
Sergei Zenjov (83' Tellur Mutallimov), Bagaliy Dabo (77' Rashad Eyyubov).
Coach: Roman Grygorchuk.
FC Samtredia: Omar Migineishvili, Jemal Gogiashvili, Nika Sandokhadze, Lasha
Shergelashvili, Giorgi Mtchedlishvili, Giuli Manjgaladze (71' Dachi Tsnobiladze), Davit
Razhamashvili, Georgi Datunaishvili, Bachana Arabuli, Budu Zivzivadze (59' Teimurazi
Markozashvili), Davit Jikia (46' Giorgi Gamkrelidze). Coach: Giorgi Tsetsadze.
Goals: 16' Vojislav Stankovic 1-0, 19' Sergei Zenjov 2-0, 30' Theo Weeks 3-0,
59' Lasha Shergelashvili 3-1, 69', 72' Theo Weeks 4-1, 5-1.
Referee: Denis Scherbakov (BLS)   Attendance: 5,850.

30.06.16   Netanya Stadium, Netanya: Maccabi Tel Aviv – ND Gorica 3-0 (2-0)
Maccabi Tel Aviv: Predrag Rajkovic, Eitan Tibi, Omri Ben Harush (82' Avi Rikan), Carlos
Garcia, Haris Medunjanin, Gal Alberman, Nosa Igiebor, Dor Peretz, Tal Ben Haim (II) (78'
Eden Ben Basat), Dor Mikha, Orlando Sá (70' Barak Itzhaki). Coach: Shota Arveladze.
ND Gorica: Grega Sorcan, Matija Skarabot, Miha Gregoric, Tine Kavcic, Alen Jogan, Andrej
Kotnik, Jaka Kolenc, Gianluca Franciosi (58' Sandi Arcon), Rifet Kapic, Miran Burgic (85'
Theodore Wilson), Bede Osuji (70' Tilen Nagode). Coach: Miran Srebrnic.
Goals: 13' Nosa Igiebor 1-0, 45' Orlando Sá 2-0, 69' Nosa Igiebor 3-0.
Referee: Jonathan Lardot (BEL)   Attendance: 7,982.

134

30.06.16   Beroe, Stara Zagora: PFC Beroe – Radnik Bijeljina 0-0
PFC Beroe: Blagoj Makendzhiev, Ventzislav Vasilev, Veselin Penev, Iliya Milanov, Vasil
Panayotov (54' Tom), Aleksandar Vasilev (83' Pedro Marques), Nemanja Milisavljevic (71'
Stanislav Dryanov), Hristofor Hubchev, Erik Pochanski, Alexander Kolev, Georgi Bozhilov.
Coach: Plamen Lipenski.
Radnik Bijeljina: Mladen Lucic, Nikola Celebic (59' Stanko Ostojic), Samir Memisevic,
Mladen Zeljkovic, Jovo Kojic, Dusan Martinovic, Aleksandar Vasic, Velibor Djuric (65' Dejan
Jankovic), Stefan Rakic, Joco Stokic (79' Demir Peco), Marko Obradovic.
Coach: Slavko Petrovic.
Referee: Giorgi Kruashvili (GEO)   Attendance: 2,918.

30.06.16   Sportni Park, Domzale: NK Domzale – FC Lusitanos la Posa 3-1 (3-1)
NK Domzale: Adnan Golubovic, Matija Sirok, Dejan Trajkovski, Gaber Dobrovoljc, Kenan
Horic, Matic Crnic, Lucas Horvat (57' Jan Repas), Zan Majer, Luka Zinko, Slobodan Vuk (75'
Juninho), Benjamin Morel (87' Luka Volaric). Coach: Luka Elsner.
FC Lusitanos la Posa: Coca, Carlos Acosta (66' Christopher Pousa), Moises San Nicolas,
Pedro Muñoz, Leonel Maciel, Luis Pinto, Alberto Molina, Bruninho, Luizão (84' Luigi San
Nicolas), Miguel (56' Lucas Sousa), José Aguilar. Coach: Raúl Cañete.
Goals: 5' Luizão 0-1, 11' Gaber Dobrovoljc 1-1, 26' Kenan Horic 2-1), 43' Matic Crnic 3-1.
Referee: Orkhan Mammadov (AZE)   Attendance: 1,000.

30.06.16   Svangaskard, Toftir: NSI Runavik – Shakhter Soligorsk 0-2 (0-1)
NSI Runavik: Simun Rogvi Hansen, Per Langgaard, Monrad Jacobsen, Jens Joensen, Pol
Justinussen, Jann Mortensen (71' Jannik Mathias Olsen), Nicolaj Køhlert, Johan Jacobsen,
Petur Knudsen (88' Jann Benjaminsen), Høgni Madsen, Klæmint Olsen (52' Magnus Olsen).
Coach: Anders Gerber.
Shakhter Soligorsk: Vladimir Bushma, Siarhei Matveichyk, Aleksandr Yurevich, Igor Burko
(65' Mikhail Shibun), Nikola Ignjatijevic, Pavel Rybak, Igor Kuzmenok, Sergiy Rudika (58'
Aleksandr Pavlov), Artem Stargorodskiy, Yuri Kovalev, Dmitriy Osipenko (79' Yevgeniy
Elezarenko). Coach: Sergey Nikiforenko.
Goals: 45', 84' Artem Stargorodskiy 0-1 (p), 0-2 (p).
Referee: Timothy Marshall (NIR)   Attendance: 350.
Sent off: 47' Jens Joensen.

30.06.16   Niko Dovana, Durrës: KF Teuta Durrës – Kairat Almaty 0-1 (0-0)
KF Teuta Durrës: Shpejtim Moçka, Silvester Shkalla, Rustem Hoxha, Blerim Kotobelli, Arber
Çyrbja, Nijaz Lena (65' Eri Lamçja), Erand Hoxha, Ardit Hila, Emiljano Musta, Bledar Hodo
(82' Nazmi Gripshi), Artur Magani (76' Jasmin Rraboshta).
Coaches: Hito Hitaj & Julian Ahmataj.
Kairat Almaty: Vladimir Plotnikov, Lukas Tesak, Zarko Markovic, Ermek Kuantaev, Mikhail
Bakaev, Bauyrzhan Islamkhan, Isael (80' Islambek Kuat), Anatoliy Tymoshchuk, Gerard
Gohou (90+2' Leandre Tawamba), Stanislav Lunin, Andrey Arshavin (78' Gerson Acevedo).
Coach: Kakhaber Tskhadadze.
Goal: 70' Andrey Arshavin 0-1.
Referee: Vasilis Dimitriou (CYP)   Attendance: 500.

135

30.06.16   Belle Vue, Rhyl: Gap Connah's Quay FC – Stabæk IF 0-0
Gap Connah's Quay FC: John Danby, John Disney, Ian Kearney, George Horan, Callum
Morris, Wes Baynes, Danny Harrison, Nathan Woolfe, Jay Owen, Lewis Short, Michael Wilde
(89' Les Davies). Coach: Andrew Morrison.
Stabæk IF: Gurpreet Singh Sandhu (30' Mandé Sayouba), Morten Skjønsberg, Nicolai Næss,
Jeppe Moe, Birger Meling, Cole Grossman, Giorgi Gorozia, Kamal Issah, Ohi Omolijuanfo,
Ernest Asante, Moussa Njie (65' Agon Mehmeti). Coach: Billy McKinlay.
Referee: Johnny Casanova (SMR)   Attendance: 573.

30.06.16   Anton Malatinsky, Trnava: Spartak Trnava – Hibernians FC 3-0 (2-0)
Spartak Trnava: Adam Jakubech, Filip Deket (46' Matus Paukner), Peter Cögley, Matus
Conka, Boris Godal, Lukas Gressak, Martin Mikovic, Emir Halilovic (71' Kouakou Privat
Yao), Bello Babatounde, Ivan Schranz (81' Erik Jirka), Robert Tambe.
Coach: Miroslav Karhan.
Hibernians FC: Justin Haber, Jonathan Pearson, Diosdado Mbele (62' Renan), Andrei Agius,
Jackson, Rodolfo Soares, Andrew Cohen, Johan Bezzina (88' Joseph Mbong), Marcelo Dias,
Clayton Failla, Juan Varea (76' Jean Farrugia). Coach: Mark Miller.
Goals: 7' Robert Tambe 1-0, 40' Martin Mikovic 2-0, 83' Robert Tambe 3-0.
Referee: Edin Jakupovic (BIH)

Match was played behind closed doors.

30.06.16   San Marino Stadium, Serravalle: SP La Fiorita – Debreceni VSC 0-5 (0-2)
SP La Fiorita: Gianluca Vivan, Andrea Martini, Davide Bugali, Gianluca Bollini (75' Alberto
Mazzola), Marco Gasperoni, Tommaso Zafferani (89' Alessandro Guidi), Nicola Cavalli (65'
Simon Parma), Damiano Tommasi, Alessio Cangini, Marco Martini, Danilo Rinaldi.
Coach: Luigi Bizzotto.
Debreceni VSC: Bozidar Radosevic, Norbert Meszaros, Dusan Brkovic, David Holman, Janos
Ferenczi, Jozsef Varga, Peter Szakaly, Aleksandar Jovanovic, Karol Meszaros (58' Ognjen
Djelmic), Tibor Tisza (68' Danilo Sekulic), Geoffrey Castillion (46' Tamas Kulcsar).
Coach: Elemer Kondas.
Goals: 5' Peter Szakaly 0-1, 34', 49' Tibor Tisza 0-2, 0-3, 83' Peter Szakaly 0-4,
89' Tamas Kulcsar 0-5.
Referee: Juri Frischer (EST)   Attendance: 402.

30.06.16   Cukaricki, Beograd: FK Cukaricki-Stankom – Ordabasy Shymkent 3-0 (0-0)
FK Cukaricki-Stankom: Nemanja Stevanovic, Lucas Piasentin, Filip Stojkovic, Djordje Djuric,
Stefan Zivkovic, Branislav Jankovic (60' Marko Docic), Asmir Kajevic, Dusan Lagator,
Stanisa Mandic (46' Igor Matic), Ismaël Fofana, Filip Knezevic (71' Alen Petric).
Coach: Milan Lesnjak.
Ordabasy Shymkent: Sergey Boychenko, Mukhtar Mukhtarov, Renat Abdulin, Talgat
Adyrbekov, Aleksandar Simcevic, Dominic Chatto (86' Bekzat Beysenov), Mardan Tolebek
(59' Aleksandr Geynrikh), Abdoulaye Diakhaté, Gogita Gogua, Filip Kasalica (84' Bakdaulet
Kozhabaev), Yerkebulan Tunggyshbayev. Coach: Bakhtiyar Baiseitov.
Goals: 49' Igor Matic 1-0 (p), 53' Asmir Kajevic 2-0, 68' Igor Matic 3-0.
Referee: Fabio Verissimo (POR)   Attendance: 2,214.
Sent off: 20' Mukhtar Mukhtarov.

Lucas Piasentin missed a penalty kick (9').

30.06.16   Pittodrie Stadium, Aberdeen: Aberdeen FC – CS FOLA Esch 3-1 (0-0)
Aberdeen FC: Joe Lewis, Shaleum Logan, Graeme Shinnie, Andrew Considine, Ash Taylor, Kenny McLean, Willo Flood (55' Adam Rooney), Jonathan Hayes, Ryan Jack, Niall McGinn, Jayden Stockley. Coach: Derek McInnes.
CS FOLA Esch: Thomas Hym, Massimo Martino, Billy Bernard (70' Cedric Sacras), Tom Laterza (67' Gerson Rodrigues), Mehdi Kirch (82' Ernes Mahmutovic), Julien Klein, Veldin Muharemovic, Jakob Dallevedove, Emmanuel Francoise, Samir Hadji, Stefano Bensi. Coach: Jeff Strasser.
Goals: 68' Shaleum Logan 1-0, 70' Julien Klein 1-1, 90+3' Niall McGinn 2-1, 90+7' Adam Rooney 3-1 (p).
Referee: Mads-Kristoffer Kristoffersen (DEN)   Attendance: 12,570.

30.06.16   Windsor Park, Belfast: Linfield FC – Cork City 0-1 (0-0)
Linfield FC: Roy Carroll, Mark Stafford, Mark Haughey, Reece Glendinning, Niall Quinn, Stephen Lowry, Jamie Mulgrew (56' David Kee), Andrew Waterworth, Kirk Millar (84' Ross Clarke), Ross Gaynor, Paul Smyth (72' Aaron Burns). Coach: David Healy.
Cork City: Mark McNulty, Alan Bennett, Kenny Browne, Greg Bolger, Stephen Dooley, Kevin O'Connor, Gearoid Morrissey, Garry Buckley (60' Mark O'Sullivan), Steven Beattie, Karl Sheppard (46' Danny Morrissey), Sean Maguire (90' Colin Healy). Coach: John Caulfield.
Goal: 63' Sean Maguire 0-1 (p).
Referee: Bart Vertenten (BEL)   Attendance: 2,093.

30.06.16   Tallaght Stadium, Dublin: Shamrock Rovers – Rovaniemi PS 0-2 (0-1)
Shamrock Rovers: Craig Hyland, Robert Cornwall, David O'Connor, Simon Madden, Sean Heaney, Brandon Miele, Killian Brennan (75' Gary McCabe), Gavin Brennan (56' Dean Clarke), Patrick Cregg, Stephen McPhail (86' Sean Boyd), Gary Shaw. Coach: Pat Fenlon.
Rovaniemi PS: Reguero, Jarkko Lahdenmäki, Abdou Jammeh, Janne Saksela, Juha Pirinen, Robert Taylor, Manut Saine (82' Mika Mäkitalo), Michal Mravec, Juuso Hämäläinen, Will John (68' Aleksandr Kokko), Jean Nganbe (70' Eetu Muinonen). Coach: Juha Malinen.
Goals: 26' Robert Taylor 0-1, 74' Janne Saksela 0-2.
Referee: Georgios Kominis (GRE)   Attendance: 1,908.

30.06.16   Tynecastle, Edinburgh: Heart of Midlothian – FC Infonet 2-1 (2-1)
Heart of Midlothian: Jack Hamilton, Callum Paterson, Alim Öztürk, John Souttar, Faycal Rherras, Prince Buaben (79' Perry Kitchen), Arnaud Sutchuin Djoum, Sam Nicholson, Jamie Walker, Conor Sammon, Juanma (65' Billy King). Coach: Robbie Neilson.
FC Infonet: Matvei Igonen, Andrei Kalimullin, Vladimir Avilov, Michael Ofosu-Appiah, Aleksandr Volodin, Dmitriy Kruglov, Jevgeni Harin (83' Aleksandr Kulinits), Sergei Mosnikov, Aleksandr Dmitrijev, Nikolai Masitsev (61' Draman Haminu), Vladimir Voskoboinikov. Coach: Aleksander Putsov.
Goals: 21' Jevgeni Harin 0-1, 28' Prince Buaben 1-1 (p), 36' Andrei Kalimullin 2-1 (og).
Referee: Vulhjalmur Alvar Thorarinsson (ISL)   Attendance: 14,417.

30.06.16   Nacionalna Arena Filip II Makedonski, Skopje:
KF Shkëndija 79 – Cracovia Krakow 2-0 (1-0)
KF Shkëndija 79: Kostadin Zahov, Egzon Bejtulai, Ardijan Cuculi, Armend Alimi (73' Artim Polozani), Ferhan Hasani (87' Victor Juffo), Besir Demiri, Blagoja Todorovski, Stephan Vujcic, Besart Ibraimi, Marjan Radeski, Stenio Junior (84' Sciprim Taipi).
Coach: Bruno Akrapovic.
Cracovia Krakow: Grzegorz Sandomierski, Robert Litauszki, Florin Bejan, Hubert Wolakiewicz (77' Anton Karachanakov), Deleu, Jakub Wojcicki, Mateusz Cetnarski (61' Miroslav Covilo), Damian Dabrowski, Marcin Budzinski, Tomas Vestenicky (61' Mateusz Wdowiak), Erik Jendrisek. Coach: Jacek Zielinski.
Goals: 41' Besart Ibraimi 1-0, 68' Stenio Junior 2-0.
Referee: Sandor Szabo (HUN)   Attendance: 4,539.

30.06.16   Alvogenvöllurinn, Reykjavik: Breidablik – FK Jelgava 2-3 (1-3)
Breidablik: Gunnleifur Gunnleifsson, Damir Muminovic, Elfar Helgason, Alfons Sampsted, Oliver Sigurjonsson, David Kristjan Olafsson, Daniel Bamberg, Arnthor Ari Atlason (62' Gisli Eyjolfsson), Jonathan Glenn (62' Solon Leifsson), Ellert Hreinsson, Andri Yeoman (78' Agust Edvald Hlynsson). Coach: Arnar Gretarsson.
FK Jelgava: Kaspars Ikstens, Vitalijs Smirnovs, Valerijs Redjko, Abdoulaye Diallo, Gints Freimanis, Ryotaro Nakano, Boriss Bogdaskins (90' Olegs Malasenoks), Mindaugas Grigaravicius (78' Vladislavs Sorokins), Glebs Kluskins, Artis Lazdins, Daniils Turkovs (70' Kyrylo Silich). Coach: Saulius Sirmelis.
Goals: 10' Glebs Kluskins 0-1, 13' Daniel Bamberg 1-1, 33' Valerijs Redjko 1-2, 44' Mindaugas Grigaravicius 1-3, 90+6' Oliver Sigurjonsson 2-3.
Referee: Anders Poulsen (DEN)   Attendance: 531.

30.06.16   Kopavogsvöllur, Kopavogur: KR Reykjavík – Glenavon FC 2-1 (1-1)
KR Reykjavík: Stefan Magnusson, Michael Præst Møller, Gunnar Gunnarsson, Skuli Jon Fridgeirsson (82' Aron Josepsson), Indridi Sigurdsson, Morten Beck, Finnur Margeirsson, Palmi Palmason, Oskar Hauksson (87' Denis Fazlagic), Morten Andersen (72' Holmbert Fridjonsson), Kennie Chopart. Coach: Willum Thorsson.
Glenavon FC: Jonny Tuffey, Simon Kelly, Kris Lindsay (56' Andrew Doyle), Rhys Marshall, Joel Cooper, Andrew Hall, Mark Patton, Mark Sykes, Ciaran Martyn (82' Andrew Kilmartin), Eoin Bradley, Gregory Moorhouse (71' Gary Hamilton). Coach: Gary Hamilton.
Goals: 14' Simon Kelly 0-1, 40' Palmi Palmason 1-1, 78' Holmbert Fridjonsson 2-1 (p).
Referee: Nicolas Laforge (BEL)   Attendance: 502.

30.06.16   Valsvöllur, Reykjavik: Valur Reykjavik – Brøndby IF 1-4 (0-0)
Valur Reykjavik: Anton Ari Einarsson, Sigurdur Larusson, Rasmus Christiansen, Bjarni Eiriksson, Gudjon Lydsson (66' Einar Karl Ingvarsson), Haukur Sigurdsson (77' Baldvin Sturluson), Kristinn Halldorsson (73' Rolf Toft), Kristinn Sigurdsson, Orri Omarsson, Andri Stefansson, Nikolaj Hansen. Coach: Olafur Johannesson.
Brøndby IF: Frederik Rønnow, Jesper Juelsgård, Benedikt Röcker, Johan Larsson, Svenn Crone, Christian Nørgaard, Kamil Wilczek, Andrew Hjulsager (83' Frederik Holst), Christian Jakobsen, Teemu Pukki (69' Jonas Borring), David Bousen (46' Lebogang Phiri).
Coach: Alexander Zorniger.
Goals: 47', 54' Kamil Wilczek 0-1, 0-2, 61' Teemu Pukki 0-3, 79' Christian Jakobsen 0-4, 90+3' Einar Karl Ingvarsson 1-4.
Referee: Ali Palabiyik (TUR)   Attendance: 728.

138

05.07.16   La Frontière, Esch: Jeunesse Esch – St Patrick's Athletic 2-1 (1-0).
Jeunesse Esch: Marc Oberweis, Milos Todorovic, Adrien Portier, Johannes Kühne, Ricardo Delgado, Emmanuel Lapierre (80' Ashot Sardaryan), Martin Ontiveros (88' Andrea Deidda), René Peters, Giancarlo Pinna, Robin Mertinitz, Patrick Stumpf. Coach: Carlo Weis.
St Patrick's Athletic: Brendan Clarke, Ger O'Brien, Ian Bermingham, Darren Dennehy, Sean Hoare, Keith Treacy (82' Sam Verdon), David Cawley, Conan Byrne, Billy Dennehy, Chris Fagan, Mark Timlin (79' Graham Kelly). Coach: Liam Buckley.
Goals: 22' Patrick Stumpf 1-0, 73' Darren Dennehy 1-1, 87' Patrick Stumpf 2-1.
Referee: Irfan Peljto (BIH)   Attendance: 1,378.
Sent off: 90+4' Adrien Portier.

05.07.16   David Abashidze Stadium, Zestafoni: Chikhura Sachkhere – FC Zimbru 2-3 (1-1)
Chikhura Sachkhere: Dino Hamzic, Tornike Grigalashvili, Levan Kakubava, Lasha Chikvaidze, Shota Kashia, Giorgi Rekhviashvili, Saba Lobzhanidze (78' Besik Dekanoidze), Giorgi Koripadze, George Ivanishvili (71' Irakli Lekvtadze), Denis Dobrovolski, Dimitri Tatanashvili (90+2' Tornike Mumladze). Coach: Soso Pruidze.
FC Zimbru: Denis Rusu, Luan, Emerson, Ion Jardan, Izaldo, Amancio Fortes (88' Stefan Burghiu), Erick (80' Veaceslav Zagaevschii), Alex Bruno, Mohamed Coulibaly (39' Diego Lima), Dan Spataru, Ilie Damascan. Coach: Flavius Stoican.
Goals: 13' George Ivanishvili 1-0, 45' Emerson 1-1, 55' Levan Kakubava 2-1, 61' Ion Jardan 2-2, 90+3' Emerson 2-3.
Referee: Suren Baliyan (ARM)   Attendance: 1,500.

05.07.16   Hibernians Ground, Paola: Birkirkara FC – Siroki Brijeg 2-0 (1-0)
Birkirkara FC: Miroslav Kopric, Christian Bubalovic, Joseph Zerafa, Predrag Jovic (78' Ryan Camenzuli), Gareth Sciberras, Srdan Dimitrov (75' Edinson Bilbao), Shaun Bajada, Ryan Scicluna (65' Matthew Guillaumier), Cain Attard, Emerson, Vito Plut. Coach: Drazen Besek.
Siroki Brijeg: Antonio Soldo, Boris Pandza (46' Josip Barisic), Dino Coric, Slavko Brekalo, Stipo Markovic, Zoran Plazonic (46' Jure Ivankovic), Wagner Lago, Ivan Sesar, Ivan Crnov, Ivan Krstanovic, Ivan Baraban (78' Luka Menalo). Coach: Slaven Musa.
Goals: 29' Srdan Dimitrov 1-0, 76' Stipe Markovic 2-0 (og).
Referee: Rahim Hasanov (AZE)   Attendance: 1,152.

06.07.16   A. Le Coq Arena, Tallinn: FC Infonet – Heart of Midlothian 2-4 (0-3)
FC Infonet: Matvei Igonen, Andrei Kalimullin, Vladimir Avilov (45' Draman Haminu), Michael Ofosu-Appiah, Aleksandr Volodin (75' Aleksandr Kulinits), Dmitriy Kruglov, Jevgeni Harin, Sergei Mosnikov (45' Pavel Dõmov), Aleksandr Dmitrijev, Nikolai Masitsev, Vladimir Voskoboinikov. Coach: Aleksander Putsov.
Heart of Midlothian: Jack Hamilton, Callum Paterson, Igor Rossi, Alim Öztürk, Liam Smith, Faycal Rherras, Perry Kitchen, Prince Buaben (74' John Souttar), Arnaud Sutchuin Djoum (89' Juanma), Jamie Walker (70' Sam Nicholson), Conor Sammon. Coach: Robbie Neilson.
Goals: 2' Callum Paterson 0-1, 9' Igor Rossi 0-2, 45' Alim Öztürk 0-3, 51' Jevgeni Harin 1-3, 52' Igor Rossi 1-4, 63' Vladimir Voskoboinikov 2-4.
Referee: Petr Ardeleanu (CZE)   Attendance: 1,354.

07.07.16   Stadionul Moldova, Speia: Dacia Chisinau – FK Kapaz 0-1 (0-0).
Dacia Chisinau: Dumitru Celeadnic, Andrii Slinkin, Simeon Bulgaru, Veaceslav Posmac,
Abdoul Mamah, Denis Kozhanov (77' Igor Bugaev), Sapol Mani (67' Rinar Valeev), Eugeniu
Cociuc, Makssim Gavrilenko, Alexandru Bejan (72' Andrey Bugneac), Maksim Feshchuk.
Coach: Oleg Bejenari.
FK Kapaz: Tadas Simaitis, Karim Diniyev, Vugar Baybalayev (67' Jeyhun Javadov), Dário
Júnior, Nijat Gurbanov (82' Azad Karimov), Tural Akhundov, Shahriyar Aliyev, Renan Alves,
Shahriyar Rahimov, Sérginho (73' Tural Qurbatov), Julien Ebah. Coach: Shakhin Diniyev.
Goal: 56' Dário Júnior 0-1.
Referee: Lasha Silagava (GEO)   Attendance: 620.

07.07.16   Pod Goricom, Podgorica: FK Buducnost Podgorica – FK Rabotnicki 1-0 (1-0).
FK Buducnost Podgorica: Milos Dragojević, Risto Radunović, Nikola Vukcević, Filip
Mitrović, Momcilo Raspopović, Milos Raicković (82' Danilo Marković), Ivan Pejaković (73'
Ermin Saratlić), Deni Hocko, Luka Mirković (77' Velizar Janketić), Milan Vusurović,
Radomir Djalović. Coach: Miodrag Vukotic.
FK Rabotnicki: Damjan Siskovski, Leon Najdovski, Dejan Mitrev, Sebastián Herera (55' Elif
Elmas), Goran Siljanovski (46' Luka Tomas), Mite Cikarski, Suad Sahiti, Filip Duranski (75'
Ivan Galić), Bojan Najdenov, Dusko Trajcevski, Marijan Altiparmakovski.
Coach: Tomislav Franc.
Goal: 18' Risto Radunović 1-0 (p).
Referee: Jørgen Burchardt (DEN)   Attendance: 2,000.
Sent off: 17' Leon Najdovski.

07.07.16   Gyumri City, Gyumri: Shirak FC – Dila Gori 1-0 (0-0, 1-0)
Shirak FC: Anatoly Ayvazov, Artyom Mikaelyan, Gevorg Hovhannisyan, Robert Darbinyan,
Rumyan Hovsepyan, Davit Hakobyan, Solomon Udo, Aghvan Davoyan (71' Arman
Hovhannisyan), Nemanja Stoskovic (65' Vahan Bichakhchyan), Konan Kouakou (69' Viulen
Ayvazyan), Drissa Diarrassouba. Coach: Vardan Bichakhchyan.
Dila Gori: Mikheil Mujrishvili, Giga Samkharadze, Lasha Japaridze (91' Tamaz Kikabidze),
Dato Kvirkvelia, Teimuraz Gongadze, Givi Karkuzashvili, Luka Razmadze, Tengiz Tsikaridze
(72' Levan Sharikadze), Giorgi Eristavi (68' Levan Nonikashvili), Grigol Dolidze, Irakli
Modebadze. Coach: Ucha Sosiashvili.
Goal: 83' Vahan Bichakhchyan 1-0.
Referee: Sergejus Slyva (LTU)   Attendance: 2,400.

Shirak FC won 4-1 on penalties following extra time.

*Penalties: Hovsepyan 1-0, Kvirkvelia missed, Darbinyan 2-0, Gongadze missed, Ayvazyan 3-0,
Razmadze 3-1, Hakobyan 4-1.*

07.07.16   Alcufer Stadion, Györ: MTK Budapest – FK Aktobe 2-0 (1-0)
MTK Budapest: Lajos Hegedüs, Akos Baki, Mato Grgic, Barnabas Bese, Patrik Poor, Lorand
Szatmari (62' Balint Borbely), Jozsef Kanta (90+1' David Jakab), Adam Vass, Darko Nikac
(83' Adam Hrepka), Daniel Gera, Sandor Torghelle. Coach: Vaszilisz Teodoru.
FK Aktobe: Samat Otarbaev, Marat Sitdikov, Kouassi Kouadja, Bagdat Kairov, Viktor
Kryukov, Sandro Tsveiba, Egor Sorokin, Didar Zhalmukan, Vuk Mitosevic, Nikita Bocharov,
Lassina Dao (57' Dmitriy Golubov, 81' Abilkhan Abdukarimov). Coach: Yuri Utkulbaev.
Goals: 8' Darko Nikac 1-0, 84' Barnabas Bese 2-0.
Referee: Nikolay Yordanov (BUL)   Attendance: 601.

07.07.16   Kranjcevicevoj, Zagreb: Lokomotiva Zagreb – UE Santa Coloma 4-1 (2-0)
Lokomotiva Zagreb: Ivan Filipovic, Karlo Bartolec, Fran Karacic, Dino Peric, Herdi Prenga
(81' Maksim Oluic), Luka Capan (60' Lovro Majer), Ivan Fiolic, Josip Coric, Endri Cekici
(72' Jan Dolezal), Eros Grezda, Mirko Maric. Coach: Valentin Barisic.
UE Sant Coloma: Ricardo Fernandez, David Maneiro (69' Juan Salomo), Alexandre Martinez,
Jordi Rubio, Miguel Ruiz, Walid Bousenine, Cristian Orosa, Jesus Rubio, Boris Anton, Victor
Bernat (59' Aitor Pereira), Sergi Crespo (62' Roger Nazzaro). Coach: Emilio.
Goals: 8' Josip Coric 1-0, 19' Herdi Prenga 2-0 (p), 48' Mirko Maric 3-0, 57' Dino Peric 4-0,
89' Juan Salomo 4-1.
Referee: Veaceslav Banari (MOL)   Attendance: 294.

07.07.16   Svangaskard, Toftir: Vikingur – FK Ventspils 0-2 (0-0)
Vikingur: Tamas Turi Geza, Atli Gregersen, Erling Jacobsen, Hans Djurhuus, Sorin Anghel
(71' Gunnar Vatnhamar), Gert Aage Hansen, Sølvi Vatnhamar, Bardur Hansen, Andreas
Olsen, Filip Djordjevic (68' Jakup Olsen), Finnur Justinussen. Coach: Samal Hentze.
FK Ventspils: Maksims Uvarenko, Alans Sinelnikovs (64' Jurijs Zigajevs), Nikita Kolesovs,
Nikola Boranijasevic, Antons Jemelins, Simonas Paulius, Eduards Tidenbergs, Vitalijs
Recickis (63' Abdullahi Alfa), Ritvars Rugins, Aleksey Alekseev (76' Rashid Abdul Obuobi),
Girst Karlsons. Coach: Paul Ashworth.
Goals: 57' Antons Jemelins 0-1 (p), 90+2' Girts Karlsons 0-2.
Referee: Nikolaj Hänni (SUI)   Attendance: 369.
Sent off: 52' Andreas Olsen, 58' Hans Djurhuus.

07.07.16   Stadion Myjava, Myjava: Spartak Myjava – FC Admira Wacker 2-3 (1-2)
Spartak Myjava: Matus Hruska, Ivan Ostojic, Jaroslav Machovec, Adi Mehremic, Tomas
Kona, Lubos Kolar, Denis Duga (46' Stefan Pekar), Frederik Bilovsky, Tomas Marcek (46'
Peter Sladek), Erik Daniel, Vladimir Kukol (84' Martin Cernacek). Coach: Mikulas Radvanyi.
FC Admira Wacker: Jörg Siebenhandl, Fabio Strauss, Stephan Zwierschitz, Thomas Ebner,
Markus Pavic, Markus Wostry, Markus Lackner, Christoph Knasmüllner (66' Daniel Toth),
Lukas Grozurek (46' Maximilian Sax), Eldis Bajrami, Dominik Starkl (80' Christoph
Monschein). Coach: Oliver Lederer.
Goals: 2' Markus Wostry 0-1, 27' Dominik Starkl 0-2, 30' Lubos Kolar 1-2,
57' Stephan Zwierschitz 1-3, 89' Stefan Pekar 2-3.
Referee: Alper Ulusoy (TUR)   Attendance: 2,057.

07.07.16   Karadjordje, Novi Sad: Vojvodina – FK Bokelj 5-0 (2-0)
Vojvodina: Marko Kordic, Nikola Antic, Darko Puskaric, Aleksandar Palocevic (69' Lazar
Zlicic), Ivan Lakicevic, Sinisa Babic (69' Uros Stamenic), Filip Malbasic (68' Marko Djurisic),
Novica Maksimovic, Nemanja Miletic, Nikola Trujic, Dejan Meleg. Coach: Nenad Lalatovic.
FK Bokelj: Milan Mijatovic, Sinisa Mladenovic, Ilija Bogdanovic, Miroslav Zlaticanin, Dejan
Ognjanovic, Mirko Todorovic, Danilo Tomic (64' Milos Nikezic), Aleksandar Macanovic (52'
Luka Maras), Dejan Djenic, Jovan Vucinic, Dejan Pepic (52' Dejan Kotorac).
Coach: Slobodan Draskovic.
Goals: 9', 42' Filip Malbasic 1-0, 2-0, 60' Dejan Meleg 3-0, 63', 87' Nikola Trujic 4-0, 5-0.
Referee: Andrew Dallas (SCO)   Attendance: 4,388.
Sent off: 90+2' Jovan Vucinic.

07.07.16   Gundadalur, Torshavn: HB Torshavn – FC Levadia 0-2 (0-0)
HB Torshavn: Teitur Gestsson, Johan Davidsen, Ari Jonsson, Magnus Egilsson, Frodi
Benjaminsen, Trondur Jensen, Teit Jacobsen, Jogvan Davidsen, Christian Mouritsen (37'
Bartal Wardum), Adrian Justinussen (79' Pal Joensen), Ari Mohr Olsen (79' Øssur Dalbud).
Coach: Jan Christian Dam.
FC Levadia: Sergei Lepmets, Luc Tabi, Maksim Podholjuzin, Igor Morozov, Ilja Antonov,
Marcelin Gando, Anton Miranchuk, Siim Luts, Marek Kaljumäe, Evgeni Kobzar (75' Andreas
Raudsepp), Rimo Hunt. Coach: Sergei Ratnikov.
Goals: 71' Evgeni Kobzar 0-1, 90+2' Anton Miranchuk 0-2.
Referee: Radek Molacek (CZE)   Attendance: 580.

07.07.16   Stadionul Zimbru, Chisinau: FC Zaria – Videoton FC 2-0 (2-0)
FC Zaria: Serghei Pascenco, Victor Golovatenco, Andrey Novicov, Iulian Erhan, Alexandru
Onica, Igor Tigirlas, Ruben Gomez, Georgi Ovsyannikov, Gheorghe Boghiu, Maxim Mihaliov,
Alexandru Grosu. Coach: Vlad Goian.
Videoton FC: Adam Kovacsik, Paulo Vinicius, Loïc Nego, Adam Lang, Stopira, Filip Oliveira
(87' Andras Fejes), Adam Bodi (67' Robert Feczesin), Roland Szolnoki, Krisztian Geresi,
Asmir Suljic, Adam Simon. Coach: Henning Berg.
Goals: 9' Maxim Mihaliov 1-0, 29' Georgi Ovsyannikov 2-0.
Referee: Fyodor Zammit (MLT)   Attendance: 2,097.

07.07.16   Sonera Stadium, Helsinki: HJK Helsinki – FK Atlantas 1-1 (1-0)
HJK Helsinki: Thomas Dähne, Taye Taiwo, Lum Rexhepi, Ivan Tatomirovic, Ville Jalasto,
Medo, Obed Malolo, Toni Kolehmainen, Nikolai Alho (82' Sebastian Sorsa), Alfredo Morelos
(67' Mikael Forssell), Richard Gadze (75' Nnamdi Oduamadi). Coach: Mika Lehkosuo.
FK Atlantas: Marius Adamonis, Vytas Gaspuitis, Andrius Bartkus (67' Donatas Kazlauskas),
Rolandas Baravykas, Aleksey Epifanov, Skirmantas Rakauskas (39' Marius Papsys), Markas
Beneta, Ovidijus Verbickas, Oleg Dmitriev (54' Domantas Simkus), Abdoul Karim Sylla,
Maksim Maksimov. Coach: Konstantin Sarsaniya.
Goals: 30' Taye Taiwo 1-0 (p), 76' Marius Papsys 1-1.
Referee: Bryn Markham-Jones (WAL)   Attendance: 3,501.

07.07.16   Teddy Kollek Stadium, Jerusalem: Beitar Jerusalem – Sloboda Tuzla 1-0 (0-0)
Beitar Jerusalem: Boris Kleiman, Jesus Rueda, Dan Mori, Snir Mishan, Omer Atzily, Dan
Einbinder, Claudemir, Kobi Moyal (85' Lidor Cohen), Ori Majabi, Itay Shechter (78' David
Keltjens), Arsenio Valpoort (72' Ya'akov Berihon). Coach: Ran Ben-Shimon.
Sloboda Tuzla: Kenan Piric, Ivan Kostic, Aldin Djidic, Samir Efendic, Zajko Zeba, Amer
Ordagic, Nemanja Stjepanovic (81' Sulejman Krpic), Damir Mehidic (73' Miljan Govedarica),
Mladen Veselinovic, Samir Merzic, Mahir Karic. Coach: Husref Musemic.
Goal: 67' Omer Atzily 1-0 (p).
Referee: Oleksandr Derdo (UKR)   Attendance: 9,010.
Sent off: 87' Aldin Djidic.

07.07.16 Kadrioru staadion, Tallinn: JK Nõmme Kalju – FK Trakai 4-1 (0-1)
JK Nõmme Kalju: Vitali Teles, Maximiliano Ugge, Jorge Rodrigues, Andrei Sidorenkov, Reginald Mbu-Alidor, Janar Toomet, Peeter Klein (46' Tarmo Neemelo), Karl Mööl, Hidetoshi Wakui (66' Eino Puri), Damiano Quintieri (59' Ats Purje), Artjom Dmitrijev.
Coach: Sergey Frantsev.
FK Trakai: Marius Rapalis, Justinas Janusevskis, Modestas Vorobjovas, Deividas Cesnauskis, Titas Vitukynas, Vaidas Silenas, Eugen Zasavitchi, Artem Gurenko (87' Lukas Kochanauskas), Aleksandr Bychenok, Dmitriy Rekish, David Arshakyan. Coach: Valdas Urbonas.
Goals: 14' David Arshakyan 0-1, 66' Jorge Rodrigues 1-1, 69' Andrei Sidorenkov 2-1, 87', 90+2' Tarmo Neemelo 3-1, 4-1.
Referee: Erik Lambrechts (BEL)   Attendance: 465

Andrei Sidorenkov missed a penalty kick (69').

07.07.16 Bakcell Arena, Baju: Neftci PFK – Balzan Youths 1-2 (1-0)
Neftci PFK: Krsevan Santini, Jairo, Vance Sikov, Magsad Isayev, Dario Melnjak, Araz Abdullayev (77' Fahmin Muradbayli), Elshan Abdullayev (90' Rahil Mammadov), Murad Agaev, Rahman Hajiyev, Edson Castillo, Ruslan Qurbanov (69' Javid Imamverdiyev).
Coach: Veli Kasumov.
Balzan Youths: Christian Cassar, Justin Grioli, Steven Bezzina, Elkin Serrano, Oliveira, Paul Fenech, Dylan Grima (82' Clive Brincat), Dê, Borce Manevski (46' Lydon Micallef), Alfred Effiong, Bojan Kaljevic. Coach: Oliver Spiteri.
Goals: 20' Jairo 1-0, 50', 67' Lydon Micallef 1-1, 1-2.
Referee: Yaroslav Kozyk (UKR)   Attendance: 7,650.

Paul Fenech missed a penalty kick (57').

07.07.16 Slokas, Jurmala: FK Spartaks – Dinamo Minsk 0-2 (0-1)
FK Spartaks: Vladislavs Kurakins, Sergey Pushnyakov, Pavels Mihadjuks, Ingus Slampe, Daniil Ulimbasevs (71' Elvis Stuglis), Jevgenijs Kazacoks, Evgeny Kozlov, Sergey Koseka, Ridwaru Adeyemo (81' Dmitry Platonov), Moshtagh Yaghoubi, Vladislavs Kozlovs (66' Ricards Korzans). Coach: Oleg Kubarev.
Dinamo Minsk: Sergey Ignatovich, Yuriy Ostroukh, Kirill Premudrov, Artem Bykov, Uladzimir Karytska, Valeriy Zhukovskiy (82' Mohamed El-Mounir), Oleksandr Noyok, Yuriy Gabovda, Nikita Kaplenko, Gleb Rassadkin (90+3' Luka Rotkovic), Vladimir Khvashchinskiy (68' Anton Shramchenko). Coach: Vuk Rasovic.
Goals: 11' Vladimir Khvashchinskiy 0-1, 90+1' Mohamed El-Mounir 0-2.
Referee: Alexandr Tean (MOL)   Attendance: 1,100.

07.07.16 Neo GSP, Nikosia: Omonia Nikosia – FC Banants 4-1 (0-0, 0-1)
Omonia Nikosia: Kostas Panayi, Carlitos, Thanasis Panteliadis, Amir Agajev (85' Onisiforos Roushias), Gerasimos Fylaktou, Margaça, George Florescu (73' Fanos Katelaris), Marin Orsulic, Cillian Sheridan, Matt Derbyshire, Ziguy Badibanga (73' Cleyton).
Coach: John Carver.
FC Banants: Stepan Ghazaryan, Aslan Kalmanov, Hakob Hakobyan, Soslan Kachmazov (100' Petros Avetisyan), Jasmin Mecinovic, Vlatko Drobarov, Layonel Adams, Valter Poghosyan (56' Vahagn Ayvazyan), Claudio Torrejon, Zaven Badoyan (89' Edgar Movsesyan), Atsamaz Buraev. Coach: Tito Ramallo.
Goals: 71' Atsamaz Buraev 0-1, 93', 108' Onisiforos Roushias 1-1, 2-1, 113' Matt Derbyshire 3-1, 120' Cleyton 4-1.
Referee: Aleksandrs Anufrijevs (LAT)   Attendance: 8,042.

07.07.16   Nantporth, Bangor: Llandudno FC – IFK Göteborg 1-2 (0-1)
Llandudno FC: Dave Roberts, Danny Taylor, James Joyce, Gareth Evans (70' Liam Dawson),
Danny Hughes, Mike Williams, Danny Shaw (58' Nathan Peate), Tom Dix, Marc Williams,
John Owen (65' Leo Riley), Lewis Buckley. Coach: Alan Morgan.
IFK Göteborg: Pontus Dahlberg, Hjalmar Jonsson, Billy Nordström, Mattias Bjärsmyr,
Alexander Leksell, Mads Albæk (63' Sebastian Eriksson), Tobias Hysén (80' Søren Rieks),
Martin Smedberg, Tom Pettersson, Viktor Sköld, Patrik Karlsson-Lagemyr (80' Mikael
Boman). Coach: Jörgen Lennartsson.
Goals: 36' Martin Smedberg 0-1, 53' Viktor Sköld 0-2, 72' Danny Hughes 1-2.
Referee: Tiago Martins (POR)   Attendance: 841.

07.07.16   Belle Vue, Rhyl: Bala Town – AIK Solna 0-2 (0-2)
Bala Town: Ashley Morris, Ryan Valentine, Anthony Stephens, Stuart Jones, Stuart Jones,
Tony Davies (65' David Thompson), Nathan Burke, Mark Connolly, Mark Jones (65' Jamie
Crowther), Ian Sheridan, Kieran Smith (74' Mike Hayes). Coach: Stephen O'Shaughnessy.
AIK Solna: Patrik Carlgren, Nils-Eric Johansson, Sauli Väisänen, Patrick Kpozo, Johan
Blomberg, Ebenezer Ofori (72' Amin Affane), Daniel Sundgren, Stefan Ishizaki (46' Ahmed
Yasin), Anton Saletros, Denni Avdic, Carlos Strandberg (63' Alexander Isak).
Coach: Rikard Norling.
Goals: 8' Denni Avdic 0-1, 24' Carlos Strandberg 0-2.
Referee: Fedayi San (SUI)   Attendance: 890.

07.07.16   Hanrapetakan, Yerevan: Pyunik FC – Europa FC 2-1 (1-1)
Pyunik FC: Gor Manukyan, Artur Kartashyan, Armen Manucharyan, Robert Hakobyan, Kamo
Hovhannisyan, Hovhannes Panosyan, Davit Manoyan, Alik Arakelyan, Hovhannes
Harutyunyan (90+3' Narek Aslanyan), Artur Yuspashyan (54' Ramzik Hakobyan), Robert
Minasyan (64' Vardges Satumyan). Coach: Sargis Hovsepyan.
Europa FC: Javi Muñoz, Toni, Toscano, Vazquez, Ivan Moya (4' José Gonzalez, 75' Copi),
Felix Lopez, Guille Roldan, Alex Quillo, Martin Belfortti, Alberto Merino, Pedro Carrion (61'
Eloy). Coach: Juan Gallardo Fernandez.
Goals: 10' José Gonzalez 0-1, 25' Alik Arakelyan 1-1, 56' Razmik Hakobyan 2-1.
Referee: Boris Marhefka (SVK)   Attendance: 2,000.

07.07.16   Stadion Zaglebie, Lubin: Zaglebie Lubin – Slavia Sofia 3-0 (1-0)
Zaglebie Lubin: Martin Polacek, Maciej Dabrowski, Djordje Cotra, Aleksandar Todorovski,
Lubomir Guldan, Jaroslaw Kubicki, Lukasz Piatek, Jan Vlasko (61' Adrian Rakowski),
Arkadiusz Wozniak, Lukasz Janoszka (85' Jakub Tosik), Krzysztof Piatek (77' Michal
Papadopulos). Coach: Piotr Stokowiec.
Slavia Sofia: Mario Kirev, Georgi Pashov, Stefan Velkov, Emil Martinov (82' Kaloyan
Krastev), Nikita Sergeev, Abdud Omar, Borislav Baldzhiyski, Bozhidar Vasev, Yanis
Karabelyov (46' Georgi Yomov), Serder Serderov, Ivailo Dimitrov (67' Martin Stankev).
Coach: Aleksandr Tarkhanov.
Goals: 20' Lubomir Guldan 1-0, 65' Lukasz Piatek 2-0, 81' Maciej Dabrowski 3-0.
Referee: Yuriy Mozharovsky (UKR)   Attendance: 5,817.

07.07.16   Marijampoles m.stadionas, Marijampole: FK Sūduva – FC Midtjylland 0-1 (0-1).
FK Sūduva: Ivan Kardum, Algis Jankauskas, Miljan Jablan, Povilas Leimonas, Andro
Svrljuga, Paulius Janusauskas, Vaidas Slavickas, Nermin Jamak (46' Eligijus Jankasukas),
Predrag Pavlovic (89' Karolis Laukzemis), Tomas Radzinevicius (62' Ernestas Veliulis),
Admir Kecap. Coach: Aleksander Veselinovic.
FC Midtjylland: Johan Dahlin, Kian Hansen (64' Kristian Riis), Markus Halsti (76' André
Rømer), Patrick Banggaard, Rasmus Nissen, Jakob Poulsen, Kristoffer Olsson, Pione Sisto,
Rilwan Hassan (55' Vaclav Kadlec), Filip Novák, Martin Pusic. Coach: Jess Thorup.
Goal: 16' Filip Novák 0-1.
Referee: Peter Kralovic (SVK)   Attendance: 1,738.

07.07.16   San Marino Stadium, Serravalle: SS Folgore/Falciano – AEK Larnaca 1-3 (1-0)
SS Folgore/Falciano: Simone Montanari, Luca Righi (72' Luca Rossi), Christofer Genestreti,
Marco Berardi (67' Cristian Brolli), Francesco Quintavalla, Matteo Camillini, Manuel
Muccini, Luca Bezzi, Michael Traini, Michael Angelini (87' Achille Della Valle), Francesco
Perrotta. Coach: Luciano Mularoni.
AEK Larnaca: Mateusz Taudul, Català, Murillo, Elias Charalambous, Constantinos Mintikkis,
Jorge Larena, Joan Tomas, Vincent Laban (73' Vladimir Boljevic), Costas Charalambides (67'
Tete), André Alves, Ivan Trickovski (86' Konstantinos Konstantinou). Coach: Imanol Idiakez.
Goals: 35' Michael Traini 1-0, 51', 55' Ivan Trickovski 1-1, 1-2, 65' André Alves 1-3 (p).
Referee: Jens Maae (DEN)   Attendance: 319.

07.07.16   Gradski, Niksic: FK Rudar Pljevlja – FK Kukësi 0-1 (0-0)
FK Rudar Pljevlja: Milos Radanovic, Ermin Alic, Dusan Nestorovic, Mirko Radisic (86'
Marko Vukovic), Radule Zivkovic, Ryota Noma (73' Miroje Jovanovic), Alphonse Soppo (81'
Ivan Markovic), Ivan Ivanovic, Drasko Bozovic, Predrag Brnovic, Nedeljko Vlahovic.
Coach: Dragan Radojicic.
FK Kukësi: Enea Kolici, Ylli Shameti, Rrahman Hallaçi, Renato Malota, Gledi Mici, Izair
Emini, Bekim Dema (54' Bedri Greca), Besar Musolli (77' Gentian Muça), Jean Carioca,
Rangel, Matija Dvornekovic (63' Sindri Guri). Coach: Hasan Lika.
Goal: 79' Sindri Guri 0-1.
Referee: João Capela (POR)   Attendance: 486
Sent off: 66' Bedri Greca.

07.07.16   Filip II. Makedonski, Skopje: Sileks Kratovo – FC Vaduz 1-2 (1-0)
Sileks Kratovo: Nikola Vujanac, Nemanja Ivanov, Blagoj Gucev, Gligor Gligorov, Gjorgje
Dzhonov, Marjan Mickov, Kristijan Filipovski (72' Lutfi Bilali), Gjorgji Tanusev, Aleksandar
Panovski (83' Nikola Georgiev), Antonio Kalanoski (56' Andrej Acevski), Igor Nedeljkovic.
Coach: Gordan Zdravkov.
FC Vaduz: Benjamin Siegrist, Simone Grippo, Axel Borgmann, Mario Bühler, Diego Ciccone,
Moreno Costanzo, Marco Mathys (72' Pascal Schürpf), Nicolas Hasler (62' Albion Avdijaj),
Maurice Brunner, Stjepan Kukuruzovic, Gonzalo Zarate (82' Ali Messaoud).
Coach: Giorgio Contini.
Goals: 31' Marjan Mickov 1-0, 89' Moreno Costanzo 1-1 (p), 90+4' Ali Messaoud 1-2.
Referee: Paul McLaughlin (IRL)   Attendance: 450.

145

07.07.16   Solitude, Belfast: Cliftonville FC – FC Differdange 03 2-0 (1-0)
Cliftonville FC: Jason Mooney, Levi Ives (66' Ross Lavery), Caoimhin Bonner, Jason
McGuinness, Christopher Curran, Martin Donnelly, Ryan Catney, Jude Winchester (72' James
Knowles), Tomas Cosgrove, David McDaid (84' Daniel Hughes), Jay Donnelly.
Coach: Gerry Lyttle.
FC Differdange 03: Julien Weber, André Rodrigues, Tom Siebenaler, David Vandenbroeck,
Geoffrey Franzoni, Andy May, Pedro Ribeiro (78' Antonio Luisi), Omar Er Rafik, Dejvid
Sinani (49' Jeff Lascak), Jordann Yéyé, Gauthier Caron. Coach: Pascal Carzaniga.
Goals: 2' David McDaid 1-0, 75' Jay Donnelly 2-0.
Referee: Ferenc Karako (HUN)   Attendance: 1,168.
Sent off: 57' Tom Siebenaler.

07.07.16   Wiklöf Holding Arena, Mariehamn: IFK Mariehamn – Odds BK 1-1 (1-0)
IFK Mariehamn: Walter Viitala, Albin Granlund, Kristian Kojola, Philip Sparrdal Mantilla
(88' Thomas Mäkinen), Jani Lyyski, Bobbie Friberg da Cruz, Gabriel Petrovic (80' Diego
Assis), Amos Ekhalie, Dever Orgill, Brian Span (70' Robin Sid), Aleksei Kangaskolkka.
Coach: Kari Virtanen.
Odds BK: Sondre Rossbach, Espen Ruud, Fredrik Semb Berge (86' Vegard Bergan), Joakim
Nilsen, Steffen Hagen, Lars-Kristian Eriksen, Oliver Berg, Ole Halvorsen, Fredrik Jensen (82'
Olivier Occean), Henrik Johansen, Rafik Zekhnini (72' Bentley). Coach: Dag-Eilev Fagermo.
Goals: 4' Philip Sparrdal Mantilla 1-0, 78' Bentley 1-1.
Referee: Peter Kjærsgaard-Andersen (DEN)   Attendance: 1,402.

07.07.16   David Abashidze Stadium, Zestafoni: FC Samtredia – Gabala FK 2-1 (1-1)
FC Samtredia: Omar Migineishvili, Jemal Gogiashvili, Nika Sandokhadze, Lasha
Shergelashvili, Giorgi Mtchedlishvili, Dachi Tsnobiladze (75' Davit Razhamashvili), Georgi
Datunaishvili, Tornike Gorgiashvili (46' Giuli Manjgaladze), Giorgi Gamkrelidze (63' Davit
Jikia), Bachana Arabuli, Budu Zivzivadze. Coach: Giorgi Tsetsadze.
Gabala FK: Dmitro Bezotosniy, Vojislav Stankovic, Vitaliy Vernydub (46' Rafael Santos),
Ricardinho, Urfan Abbasov, Räsad Sadiqov (69' Elvin Jamalov), Nika Kvekveskiri, Filip
Ozobic (52' Tellur Mutallimov), Theo Weeks, Sergei Zenjov, Bagaliy Dabo.
Coach: Roman Grygorchuk.
Goals: 14' Budu Zivzivadze 1-0 (p), 42' Theo Weeks 1-1, 90+2' Lasha Shergelashvili 2-1.
Referee: Georgios Kyzas (GRE)   Attendance: 847.

07.07.16   Sportni Park, Nova Gorica: ND Gorica – Maccabi Tel Aviv 0-1 (0-1)
ND Gorica: Grega Sorcan, Matija Skarabot, Miha Gregoric, Tine Kavcic, Matija Boben,
Andrej Kotnik (71' Rok Grudina), Jaka Kolenc, Leon Marinic (77' Sandi Arcon), Rifet Kapic,
Miran Burgic (66' Theodore Wilson), Tilen Nagode. Coach: Miran Srebrnic.
Maccabi Tel Aviv: Predrag Rajkovic, Eitan Tibi (64' Egor Filipenko), Omri Ben Harush, Tal
Ben Haim (I), Haris Medunjanin, Gal Alberman, Nosa Igiebor, Dor Peretz, Yossi Benayoun,
Dor Mikha (71' Tal Ben Haim (II)), Orlando Sá (46' Eden Ben Basat).
Coach: Shota Arveladze.
Goal: 10' Yossi Benayoun 0-1.
Referee: Manuel Schüttengruber (AUT)   Attendance: 700.

146

07.07.16 Gradski, Banja Luka: Radnik Bijeljina – PFC Beroe 0-2 (0-0)
Radnik Bijeljina: Mladen Lucic, Nikola Celebic, Samir Memisevic, Mladen Zeljkovic, Jovo Kojic, Dusan Martinovic, Dino Besirevic (76' Demir Peco), Aleksandar Vasic, Velibor Djuric, Joco Stokic (76' Dejan Jankovic), Marko Obradovic. Coach: Slavko Petrovic.
PFC Beroe: Blagoj Makendzhiev, Ivo Ivanov, Ventzislav Vasilev, Veselin Penev, Iliya Milanov, Vasil Panayotov, Nemanja Milisavljevic, Pedro Marques (89' Aleksandar Vasilev), Tom (85' Georgi Dinkov), Erik Pochanski (90+2' Alexander Kolev), Georgi Bozhilov. Coach: Aleksandar Dimitrov.
Goals: 79', 80' Erik Pochanski 0-1, 0-2.
Referee: Dimitrios Massias (CYP)   Attendance: 2,832.

07.07.16 Estadi Comunal, Andorra la Vella: FC Lusitanos la Posa – NK Domzale 1-2 (1-2)
FC Lusitanos la Posa: Coca, Moises San Nicolas, Lucas Sousa, Pedro Muñoz, Leonel Maciel, Luis Pinto, Alberto Molina, Bruninho (82' Luigi San Nicolas), Christopher Pousa (68' Carlos Acosta), Luizão (69' Miguel), José Aguilar. Coach: Raúl Cañete.
NK Domzale: Adnan Golubovic, Matija Sirok, Dejan Trajkovski, Gaber Dobrovoljc (48' Miha Blazic), Kenan Horic, Matic Crnic, Zan Majer, Luka Zinko (84' Juninho), Zeni Husmani (65' Lucas Horvat), Benjamin Morel, Antonio Mance. Coach: Luka Elsner.
Goals: 5' Zan Majer 0-1, 18' Luizão 1-1, 41' Benjamin Morel 1-2.
Referee: Stanislav Todorov (BUL)   Attendance: 500.

07.07.16 Stroitel, Soligorsk: Shakhter Soligorsk – NSI Runavik 5-0 (2-0)
Shakhter Soligorsk: Vladimir Bushma, Aleksey Yanushkevich, Aleksandr Yurevich (67' Yevgeniy Elezarenko), Igor Burko (69' Mikhail Shibun), Nikola Ignjatijevic, Pavel Rybak, Igor Kuzmenok, Sergiy Rudika, Artem Stargorodskiy, Yuri Kovalev, Dmitriy Osipenko (79' Aleksandr Pavlov). Coach: Sergey Nikiforenko.
NSI Runavik: Simun Rogvi Hansen, Per Langgaard, Monrad Jacobsen, Pol Justinussen, Jann Mortensen (75' Jann Benjaminsen), Nicolaj Køhlert, Johan Jacobsen, Petur Knudsen (87' Morits Heini Mortensen), Magnus Olsen, Høgni Madsen (84' Jakup Gaardbo), Klæmint Olsen. Coach: Anders Gerber.
Goals: 20' Igor Burko 1-0, 42' Sergiy Rudika 2-0, 81' Mkhail Shibun 3-0 (p), 86' Yevgeniy Elezarenko 4-0, 90+1' Aleksey Yanishkevich 5-0.
Referee: George Vadachkoria (GEO)   Attendance: 1,100.

07.07.16 Tsentralniy, Almaty: Kairat Almaty – KF Teuta Durrës 5-0 (2-0)
Kairat Almaty: Vladimir Plotnikov, Zarko Markovic, Yan Vorogovskiy, Islambek Kuat, Mikhail Bakaev, Bauyrzhan Islamkhan (66' Gerson Acevedo), Isael, Anatoliy Tymoshchuk, Gerard Gohou (69' Leandre Tawamba), Stanislav Lunin, Andrey Arshavin (76' Bauyrzhan Turysbek). Coach: Kakhaber Tskhadadze.
KF Teuta Durrës: Shpejtim Mocka, Silvester Shkalla (66' Nazmi Gripshi), Rustem Hoxha, Blerim Kotobelli, Arber Cyrbja (52' Jasmin Rraboshta), Nijaz Lena, Erand Hoxha (54' Dajan Shehi), Ardit Hila, Emiljano Musta, Bledar Hodo, Artur Magani. Coach: Hito Hitaj.
Goals: 27' Gerard Gohou 1-0, 45' Mikhail Bakaev 2-0, 61' Gerard Gohou 3-0, 72' Leandre Tawamba 4-0, 79' Bauyrzhan Turysbek 5-0.
Referee: Dag Hafsås (NOR)   Attendance: 20,700.

147

07.07.16 Fredrikstad Stadion, Fredrikstad: Stabæk IF – Gap Connah's Quay FC 0-1 (0-1)
Stabæk IF: Mandé Sayouba, Morten Skjønsberg (72' Eirik Haugstad), Nicolai Næss, Jeppe Moe (66' Shadrach Eghan), Birger Meling, Cole Grossman, Giorgi Gorozia (54' Agon Mehmeti), Kamal Issah, Ohi Omolijuanfo, Ernest Asante, Moussa Njie.
Coach: Billy McKinlay.
Gap Connah's Quay FC: John Danby, John Disney (68' Matty Owen), Ian Kearney, George Horan, Callum Morris, Wes Baynes, Danny Harrison, Nathan Woolfe (80' Sean Smith), Jay Owen, Lewis Short, Michael Wilde (84' Les Davies). Coach: Andrew Morrison.
Goal: 15' Callum Morris 0-1.
Referee: Laurent Kopriwa (LUX)   Attendance: 384.
Sent off: 51' Kamal Issah, 78' John Disney.

07.07.16 Hibernians Ground, Paola: Hibernians FC – Spartak Trnava 0-3 (0-1)
Hibernians FC: Justin Haber, Jonathan Pearson, Andrei Agius (30' Diosdado Mbele), Jackson, Rodolfo Soares, Bjorn Kristensen, Marcelo Dias, Clayton Failla (72' Joseph Mbong), Juan Varea (80' Jurgen Degabriele), Renan, Jorghino. Coach: Mark Miller.
Spartak Trnava: Adam Jakubech, Peter Cögley, Matus Conka (44' Andrej Kadlec), Boris Godal, Lukas Gressak, Martin Mikovic, Emir Halilovic, Eder (50' Matej Oravec), Bello Babatounde, Ivan Schranz (64' Erik Jirka), Robert Tambe. Coach: Miroslav Karhan.
Goals: 4' Martin Mikovic 0-1, 57' Matej Oravec 0-2, 90+2' Bello Babatounde 0-3.
Referee: Anastasios Papapetrou (GRE)   Attendance: 322.

07.07.16 Nagyerdei, Debrecen: Debreceni VSC – SP La Fiorita 2-0 (1-0)
Debreceni VSC: Bozidar Radosevic, Csaba Szatmari, Dusan Brkovic, Mihaly Korhut, David Holman (68' Danilo Sekulic), Ognjen Djelmic (46' Karol Meszaros), Jozsef Varga, Peter Szakaly (61' Janos Ferenczi), Aleksandar Jovanovic, Tibor Tisza, Geoffrey Castillion.
Coach: Elemer Kondas.
SP La Fiorita: Gianluca Vivan, Davide Bugali, Gianluca Bollini, Marco Gasperoni, Tommaso Zafferani, Damiano Tommasi, Alessio Cangini (89' Andrea Righi), Simon Parma (71' Nicola Cavalli), Andy Selva (83' Alessandro Guidi), Marco Martini, Danilo Rinaldi.
Coach: Luigi Bizzotto.
Goals: 41' Tibor Tisza 1-0, 51' David Holman 2-0.
Referee: Stavros Mantalos (GRE)   Attendance: 8,632.

07.07.16 Kazhimukan Munaytpasov, Shymkent:
Ordabasy Shymkent – FK Cukaricki-Stankom 3-3 (1-3)
Ordabasy Shymkent: Sergey Boychenko, Branislav Trajkovic, Temirlan Yerlanov, Talgat Adyrbekov, Aleksandar Simcevic, Dominic Chatto, Mardan Tolebek, Abdoulaye Diakhaté (46' Gogita Gogua), Dauren Kaykibasov (46' Filip Kasalica), Yerkebulan Tunggyshbayev (78' Bekzat Beysenov), Aleksandr Geynrikh. Coach: Bakhtiyar Baiseitov.
FK Cukaricki-Stankom: Nemanja Stevanovic, Lucas Piasentin, Nikola Jankovic, Djordje Djuric, Stefan Zivkovic, Dragoljub Srnic (75' Erhan Masovic), Asmir Kajevic, Dusan Lagator, Stanisa Mandic (59' Igor Matic), Ismaël Fofana (80' Sasa Jovanovic), Filip Knezevic.
Coach: Milan Lesnjak.
Goals: 10', 15' Stanisa Mandic 0-1, 0-2, 21' Asmir Kajevic 0-3, 45' Aleksandr Geynrikh 1-3, 67' Yerkebulan Tunggyshbayev 2-3, 90+3' Temirlan Yerlanov 3-3.
Referee: Denis Scherbakov (BLS)   Attendance: 5,100.

148

07.07.16   Josy Barthel, Luxembourg: CS FOLA Esch – Aberdeen FC 1-0 (1-0)
CS FOLA Esch: Thomas Hym, Billy Bernard, Tom Laterza, Mehdi Kirch, Ryan Klapp (71'
Gerson Rodrigues), Julien Klein, Veldin Muharemovic (87' Stefan Rocha), Jakob Dallevedove,
Emmanuel Francoise (78' Basile Camerling), Samir Hadji, Stefano Bensi. Coach: Jeff Strasser.
Aberdeen FC: Joe Lewis, Shaleum Logan, Graeme Shinnie, Andrew Considine, Ash Taylor,
Anthony O'Connor (46' Mark Reynolds), Kenny McLean, Jonathan Hayes, Peter Pawlett (46'
Willo Flood), Ryan Jack, Jayden Stockley (63' Adam Rooney). Coach: Derek McInnes.
Goal: 45' Samir Hadji 1-0.
Referee: Ola Nilsen (NOR   Attendance: 1,789.

07.07.16   Turners Cross, Cork: Cork City – Linfield FC 1-1 (0-0)
Cork City: Mark McNulty, Alan Bennett, Michael McSweeney (56' Mark O'Sullivan), Kenny
Browne, Gavan Holohan (56' Danny Morrissey), Stephen Dooley, Kevin O'Connor, Gearoid
Morrissey, Garry Buckley (65' Colin Healy), Steven Beattie, Sean Maguire.
Coach: John Caulfield.
Linfield FC: Roy Carroll, Mark Stafford, Mark Haughey, Matthew Clarke (88' Michael
McLellan), Niall Quinn, Stephen Lowry, Jamie Mulgrew, Andrew Waterworth, Kirk Millar
(78' Aaron Burns), Ross Gaynor, Paul Smyth. Coach: David Healy.
Goals: 49' Sean Maguire 1-0 (p), 52' Mark Stafford 1-1.
Referee: Bartosz Frankowski (POL)   Attendance: 3,521.

07.07.16   Keskuskenttä, Rovaniemi: Rovaniemi PS – Shamrock Rovers 1-1 (1-1)
Rovaniemi PS: Reguero, Jarkko Lahdenmäki, Abdou Jammeh, Janne Saksela, Juha Pirinen,
Robert Taylor, Eetu Muinonen, Manut Saine (46' Aleksandr Kokko), Michal Mravec, Juuso
Hämäläinen, Will John (46' Mika Mäkitalo, 53' Jean Nganbe). Coach: Juha Malinen.
Shamrock Rovers: Craig Hyland, Robert Cornwall, Simon Madden, Sean Heaney, Gary
McCabe, Brandon Miele (67' Trevor Clarke), Killian Brennan, Gavin Brennan, Patrick Cregg,
Gary Shaw (74' Sean Boyd), Dean Clarke (74' Aaron Dobbs). Coach: Stephen Bradley.
Goals: 22' Gary McCabe 0-1 (p), 26' Eetu Muinonen 1-1.
Referee: Dejan Jakimovski (MKD)   Attendance: 1,525.

07.07.16   Marszalek Pilsudski, Krakow: Cracovia Krakow – KF Shkëndija 79 1-2 (0-1)
Cracovia Krakow: Grzegorz Sandomierski, Hubert Wolakiewicz, Piotr Polczak, Deleu,
Miroslav Covilo, Jakub Wojcicki, Damian Dabrowski (46' Mateusz Cetnarski), Marcin
Budzinski, Anton Karachanakov (50' Sebastian Steblecki), Tomas Vestenicky (46' Mateusz
Wdowiak), Erik Jendrisek. Coach: Jacek Zielinski.
KF Shkëndija 79: Kostadin Zahov, Egzon Bejtulai, Ardijan Cuculi, Armend Alimi (71' Artim
Polozani), Ferhan Hasani, Besir Demiri, Blagoja Todorovski, Stephan Vujcic, Besart Ibraimi
(88' Victor Juffo), Marjan Radeski (83' Sciprim Taipi), Stenio Junior.
Coach: Bruno Akrapovic.
Goals: 12' Besart Ibraimi 0-1, 68' Mateusz Cetnarski 1-1, 90+3' Ferhan Hasani 1-2.
Referee: Gunnar Jarl Jonsson (ISL)   Attendance: 7,122.

07.07.16   Zemgalas Olimpiska Centra, Jelgava: FK Jelgava – Breidablik 2-2 (1-2)
FK Jelgava: Kaspars Ikstens, Vitalijs Smirnovs (46' Igors Savcenkovs), Valerijs Redjko,
Abdoulaye Diallo, Gints Freimanis, Ryotaro Nakano, Boriss Bogdaskins, Mindaugas
Grigaravicius, Glebs Kluskins, Artis Lazdins, Daniils Turkovs (84' Andrejs Kovalovs).
Coach: Saulius Sirmelis.
Breidablik: Gunnleifur Gunnleifsson, Damir Muminovic, Elfar Helgason, Arnor Adalsteinsson,
Oliver Sigurjonsson, Gisli Eyjolfsson (83' Jonathan Glenn), David Kristjan Olafsson, Daniel
Bamberg (77' Agust Edvald Hlynsson), Arnthor Ari Atlason, Ellert Hreinsson, Andri Yeoman
(77' Atli Sigurjonsson). Coach: Arnar Gretarsson.
Goals: 15' Daniils Turkovs 1-0, 31' Ellert Hreinsson 1-1, 33' Daniel Bamberg 1-2 (p),
70' Abdoulaye Diallo 2-2.
Referee: Petur Reinert (FAR)   Attendance: 1,560.

07.07.16   Mourneview Park, Lurgan: Glenavon FC – KR Reykjavík 0-6 (0-2)
Glenavon FC: Jonny Tuffey, Simon Kelly, Rhys Marshall, Andrew Doyle, Joel Cooper,
Andrew Hall (79' Jack O'Mahony), Mark Patton, Mark Sykes, Ciaran Martyn (71' Andrew
Kilmartin), Gary Hamilton (64' Gregory Moorhouse), Eoin Bradley. Coach: Gary Hamilton.
KR Reykjavík: Stefan Magnusson, Michael Præst Møller (80' Valtyr Mar Michaelsson),
Gunnar Gunnarsson, Indridi Sigurdsson, Aron Josepsson, Morten Beck, Finnur Margeirsson,
Palmi Palmason, Oskar Hauksson, Holmbert Fridjonsson (56' Morten Andersen), Kennie
Chopart (58' Denis Fazlagic). Coach: Willum Thorsson.
Goals: 6', 29' Kennie Chopart 0-1, 0-2, 53' Holmbert Fridjonsson 0-3 (p),
68' Morten Andersen 0-4, 78' Oskar Hauksson 0-5, 80' Denis Fazlagic 0-6.
Referee: Dennis Antamo (FIN)   Attendance: 1,250.

07.07.16   Brøndby Stadion, Brøndby: Brøndby IF – Valur Reykjavik 6-0 (3-0)
Brøndby IF: Frederik Rønnow, Jesper Juelsgård, Benedikt Röcker, Johan Larsson, Svenn
Crone, Lebogang Phiri (61' Frederik Holst), Christian Nørgaard, Kamil Wilczek (46' Daniel
Stückler), Andrew Hjulsager, Christian Jakobsen (73' Patrick da Silva), Teemu Pukki.
Coach: Alexander Zorniger.
Valur Reykjavik: Ingvar Thor Kale, Sigurdur Larusson (77' Dadi Bergsson), Rasmus
Christiansen, Bjarni Eiriksson, Gudjon Lydsson, Haukur Sigurdsson, Kristinn Halldorsson,
Kristinn Sigurdsson (76' Einar Karl Ingvarsson), Orri Omarsson, Andri Stefansson, Nikolaj
Hansen (60' Rolf Toft). Coach: Olafur Johannesson.
Goals: 5' Kamil Wilczek 1-0, 15' Andrew Hjulsager 2-0, 26', 57' Teemu Pukki 3-0, 4-0,
71', 90+3' Daniel Stückler 5-0, 6-0.
Referee: Tihomir Pejin (CRO)   Attendance: 6,227.

150

SECOND QUALIFYING ROUND

14.07.16 Gyumri City, Gyumri: Shirak FC – Spartak Trnava 1-1 (1-0)
Shirak FC: Anatoly Ayvazov, Artyom Mikaelyan, Gevorg Hovhannisyan, Robert Darbinyan, Davit Hakobyan, Solomon Udo, Aghvan Davoyan (83' Arman Hovhannisyan), Mohamed Kaba, Nemanja Stoskovic (63' Vahan Bichakhchyan), Konan Kouakou, Drissa Diarrassouba (75' Ghukas Poghosyan). Coach: Vardan Bichakhchyan.
Spartak Trnava: Adam Jakubech, Andrej Kadlec, Denis Hornik, Boris Godal, Lukas Gressak, Martin Mikovic, Anton Sloboda, Emir Halilovic (90+1' Matej Oravec), Eder, Kouakou Privat Yao (58' Erik Jirka), Ivan Schranz (76' Matus Paukner). Coach: Miroslav Karhan.
Goals: 16' Davit Hakobyan 1-0, 87' Erik Jirka 1-1.
Referee: Artyom Kuchin (KAZ)   Attendance: 2,747.

14.07.16 Tsentralniy, Almaty: Kairat Almaty – Maccabi Tel Aviv 1-1 (1-0)
Kairat Almaty: Vladimir Plotnikov, Zarko Markovic, Ermek Kuantaev, Gafurzhan Suyombaev, Mikhail Bakaev, Bauyrzhan Islamkhan, Isael, Anatoliy Tymoshchuk, Gerard Gohou (83' Leandre Tawamba), Stanislav Lunin, Andrey Arshavin (77' Islambek Kuat).
Coach: Kakhaber Tskhadadze.
Maccabi Tel Aviv: Predrag Rajkovic, Eitan Tibi, Tal Ben Haim (I), Haris Medunjanin (90+1' Eyal Golasa), Gal Alberman, Avi Rikan, Nosa Igiebor (86' Barak Itzhaki), Dor Peretz, Tal Ben Haim (II) (73' Yossi Benayoun), Dor Mikha, Orlando Sá. Coach: Shota Arveladze.
Goals: 29' Andrey Arshavin 1-0, 90+1' Yossi Benayoun 1-1.
Referee: Antti Munukka (FIN)   Attendance: 22,500.
Sent off: 90+4' Bauyrzhan Islamkhan.

14.07.16 Traktor, Minsk: Dinamo Minsk – St Patrick's Athletic 1-1 (1-0)
Dinamo Minsk: Sergey Ignatovich, Yuriy Ostroukh, Kirill Premudrov, Artem Bykov, Uladzimir Karytska (79' Anton Shramchenko), Valeriy Zhukovskiy (70' Luka Rotkovic), Oleksandr Noyok, Yuriy Gabovda, Nikita Kaplenko, Gleb Rassadkin, Vladimir Khvashchinskiy (57' Mohamed El-Mounir). Coach: Vuk Rasovic.
St Patrick's Athletic: Brendan Clarke, Ger O'Brien, Ian Bermingham, Darren Dennehy, Sean Hoare, Keith Treacy (72' David Cawley), Conan Byrne, Graham Kelly, Billy Dennehy, Chris Fagan (79' Sam Verdon), Mark Timlin (79' Dinny Corcoran). Coach: Liam Buckley.
Goals: 25' Uladzimir Karytska 1-0, 54' Chris Fagan 1-1.
Referee: Srdan Jovanovic (SER)   Attendance: 1,286.

14.07.16 Keskuskenttä, Rovaniemi: Rovaniemi PS – Lokomotiva Zagreb 1-1 (0-0)
Rovaniemi PS: Reguero, Abdou Jammeh, Janne Saksela, Juha Pirinen, Robert Taylor, Eetu Muinonen, Michal Mravec, Juuso Hämäläinen, Will John (81' Ransford Osei), Jean Nganbe (74' Antti Okkonen), Aleksandr Kokko (59' Aapo Heikkilä). Coach: Juha Malinen.
Lokomotiva Zagreb: Ivan Filipovic, Karlo Bartolec, Sinisa Rozman, Dino Peric, Herdi Prenga, Luka Capan, Ivan Fiolic (90+4' Jakov Puljic), Josip Coric (81' Ivan Sunjic), Endri Cekici, Eros Grezda (65' Petar Bockaj), Mirko Maric. Coach: Valentin Barisic.
Goals: 72', 86' Abdou Jammeh 0-1 (og), 1-1.
Referee: Thorvaldur Arnason (ISL)   Attendance: 1,812.

14.07.16   Traktor, Minsk: Neftci PFK – KF Shkëndija 79 0-0
Neftci PFK: Krsevan Santini, Jairo, Vance Sikov, Magsad Isayev, Dario Melnjak, Araz
Abdullayev, Murad Agaev (78' Javid Imamverdiyev), Rahman Hajiyev, Edson Castillo,
Ruslan Qurbanov (86' Elshan Abdullayev), Fahmin Muradbayli. Coach: Veli Kasumov.
KF Shkëndija 79: Kostadin Zahov, Egzon Bejtulai, Ardijan Cuculi, Armend Alimi, Ferhan
Hasani, Besir Demiri, Blagoja Todorovski, Stephan Vujcic, Besart Ibraimi (90+2' Artim
Polozani), Marjan Radeski, Stenio Junior. Coach: Bruno Akrapovic.
Referee: Sergey Tsinkevich (BLS)   Attendance: 6,891.

14.07.16   Kadrioru staadion, Tallinn: FC Levadia – Slavia Praha 3-1 (1-0)
FC Levadia: Sergei Lepmets, Luc Tabi, Maksim Podholjuzin, Igor Morozov, Ilja Antonov,
Marcelin Gando, Anton Miranchuk, Siim Luts, Marek Kaljumäe, Evgeni Kobzar (68' Andreas
Raudsepp), Rimo Hunt. Coach: Sergei Ratnikov.
Slavia Praha: Martin Berkovec, Michael Ngadeu-Ngadjui, Libor Holik, Jan Boril, Simon Deli,
Jaromir Zmrhal, Ruslan Mingazov (69' Jaroslav Mihalík), Josef Husbauer, Tomás Soucek,
Antonin Barak (61' Levan Kenia), Muris Mesanovic (78' Mick van Buren).
Coach: Dusan Uhrin.
Goals: 35' Rimo Hunt 1-0, 63' Muris Mesanovic 1-1, 67' Marcelin Gando 2-1,
90' Ilja Antonov 3-1.
Referee: Neil Doyle (IRL)   Attendance: 2,750.

14.07.16   MCH Arena, Herning: FC Midtjylland – FC Vaduz 3-0 (1-0)
FC Midtjylland: Johan Dahlin, Kian Hansen, Markus Halsti, Patrick Banggaard, Rasmus
Nissen, Jakob Poulsen, Kristoffer Olsson, Pione Sisto (87' Mikkel Duelund), Rilwan Hassan
(72' Vaclav Kadlec), Filip Novák, Martin Pusic (68' Ebere Onuachu). Coach: Jess Thorup.
FC Vaduz: Peter Jehle, Simone Grippo, Axel Borgmann, Mario Bühler, Diego Ciccone,
Moreno Costanzo, Marco Mathys (66' Ali Messaoud), Maurice Brunner (79' Marvin
Pfründer), Stjepan Kukuruzovic, Philipp Muntwiler, Gonzalo Zarate (80' Albion Avdijaj).
Coach: Giorgio Contini.
Goals: 20' Pione Sisto 1-0, 73' Ebere Onuachu 2-0, 82' Pione Sisto 3-0.
Referee: Kirill Levnikov (RUS)   Attendance: 4,455.

14.07.16   Nagyerdei, Debrecen: Debreceni VSC – Torpedo-BalAZ Zhodino 1-2 (1-1)
Debreceni VSC: Bozidar Radosevic, Norbert Meszaros, Dusan Brkovic, Mihaly Korhut, David
Holman (82' Janos Ferenczi), Jozsef Varga, Peter Szakaly, Aleksandar Jovanovic, Tibor Tisza,
Karol Meszaros (63' Ognjen Djelmic), Geoffrey Castillion (57' Tamas Takacs).
Coach: Elemer Kondas.
Torpedo-BalAZ Zhodino: Valeriy Fomichev, Artem Chelyadinski, Evgeni Klopotskiy, Aleksey
Pankovets, Terentiy Lutsevich, Vladimir Shcherbo (85' Pavel Chelyadko), Sergiy Shapoval,
Sergiy Zagynaylov (69' Denis Trapashko), Mikhail Afanasiev, Gennadiy Bliznyuk (80' Yuri
Pavlyukovets), Vadim Demidovich. Coach: Igor Kriushenko.
Goals: 2' Tibor Tisza 1-0, 23' Sergiy Zagynaylov 1-1, 88' Evgeni Klopotskiy 1-2.
Referee: Leontios Trattou (CYP)   Attendance: 6,015.

14.07.16   Netanya Stadium, Netanya: Maccabi Haifa – JK Nõmme Kalju 1-1 (0-0)
Maccabi Haifa: Ohad Levita, Marc Valiente, Eyad Abu Abaid, Gary Kagelmacher (65' Shoval
Gozlan), Eyal Meshumar (84' Ayed Habashi), Neta Lavi, Ludovic Obraniak, Gil Vermouth,
Sun Menachem, Nikita Rukavytsya, Firas Mugrabi (78' Ismail Raiyan). Coach: Roni Levy.
JK Nõmme Kalju: Vitali Teles, Maximiliano Ugge, Jorge Rodrigues, Andrei Sidorenkov,
Reginald Mbu-Alidor, Ats Purje (79' Tarmo Neemelo), Janar Toomet (68' Igor Subbotin),
Artur Valikaev, Karl Mööl, Damiano Quintieri (59' Eino Puri), Artjom Dmitrijev.
Coach: Sergey Frantsev.
Goals: 47' Janar Toomet 0-1, 70' Gil Vermouth 1-1.
Referee: Svein Edvartsen (NOR)   Attendance: 6,500.

14.07.16   Stadionul Zimbru, Chisinau: FC Zimbru – Osmanlispor FK 2-2 (1-1)
FC Zimbru: Denis Rusu, Luan, Moreira, Emerson, Ion Jardan, Diego Lima (74' Stefan
Burghiu), Amancio Fortes (89' Andrei Rusnac), Veaceslav Zagaevschii, Erick, Alex Bruno,
Ilie Damascan (85' Izaldo). Coach: Flavius Stoican.
Osmanlispor FK: Zydrunas Karcemarskas, Vaclav Prochazka, Muhammed Bayir, Numan
Cürüksu, Avdija Vrsajevic, Mehmet Güven, Raheem Lawal (64' Raul Rusescu), Papa
N'Diaye, Aminu Umar, Pierre Webo (76' Engin Bekdemir), Dzon Delarge (87' Erdal
Kilicarslan). Coach: Mustafa Akcay.
Goals: 12' Numan Cürüksu 0-1, 24' Veaceslav Zagaevschii 1-1, 62' Ilie Damascan 2-1,
77' Engin Bekdemir 2-2.
Referee: Nenad Djokic (SER)   Attendance: 4,160.

14.07.16   NV Arena, Sankt Pölten: FC Admira Wacker – FK Kapaz 1-0 (1-0)
FC Admira Wacker: Jörg Siebenhandl, Fabio Strauss, Stephan Zwierschitz, Thomas Ebner,
Markus Pavic, Markus Wostry, Markus Lackner, Maximilian Sax (58' Srdan Spiridonovic),
Christoph Knasmüllner, Eldis Bajrami, Dominik Starkl (75' Christoph Monschein).
Coach: Oliver Lederer.
FK Kapaz: Tadas Simaitis, Karim Diniyev, Vugar Baybalayev (73' Orkhan Aliyev), Dário
Júnior, Nijat Gurbanov (72' Jeyhun Javadov), Tural Akhundov, Shahriyar Aliyev, Renan
Alves, Shahriyar Rahimov, Sérginho (88' Tural Qurbatov), Julien Ebah.
Coach: Shakhin Diniyev.
Goal: 41' Dominik Strakl 1-0.
Referee: Pavle Radovanovic (MNE)   Attendance: 956.

14.07.16   Bravida Arena, Göteborg: BK Häcken – Cork City 1-1 (0-0)
BK Häcken: Peter Abrahamsson, Jasmin Sudic, Emil Wahlström, Baba Mensah, Kari Arkivuo
(78' Egzon Binaku), Rasmus Schüller, Martin Ericsson (57' Demba Savage), Mohammed
Nasiru (66' Joel Andersson), Samuel Gustafson, Paulinho, John Owoeri.
Coach: Peter Gerhardsson.
Cork City: Mark McNulty, Alan Bennett, Michael McSweeney, Kenny Browne, Greg Bolger,
Stephen Dooley, Kevin O'Connor, Gearoid Morrissey, Garry Buckley (85' Mark O'Sullivan),
Steven Beattie (75' Karl Sheppard), Sean Maguire (90+2' Colin Healy).
Coach: John Caulfield.
Goals: 64' Sean Maguire 0-1 (p), 83' John Owoeri 1-1.
Referee: Amaury Delerue (FRA)   Attendance: 2,022.
Sent off: 63' Baba Mensah.

153

14.07.16   Friends Arena, Solna: AIK Solna – Europa FC 1-0 (0-0)
AIK Solna: Patrik Carlgren, Haukur Hauksson (78' Daniel Sundgren), Per Karlsson, Jos
Hooiveld, Patrick Kpozo, Ebenezer Ofori, Stefan Ishizaki, Christos Gravius (46' Carlos
Strandberg), Amin Affane (68' Johan Blomberg), Denni Avdic, Alexander Isak.
Coach: Rikard Norling.
Europa FC: Javi Muñoz, Toni (89' Piñero), Toscano, Vazquez, Mustapha Yahaya, Ivan Moya,
Guille Roldan, Alex Quillo (75' Copi), Martin Belfortti, Alberto Merino, Pedro Carrion (66'
José Gonzalez). Coach: Juan Gallardo Fernandez.
Goal: 89' Carlos Strandberg 1-0.
Referee: Ognjen Valjic (BIH)   Attendance: 5,250.

14.07.16   Teddy Kollek Stadium, Jerusalem: Beitar Jerusalem – Omonia Nikosia 1-0 (0-0)
Beitar Jerusalem: Boris Kleiman, David Keltjens, Dan Mori, Tal Kachila, Omer Atzily, Idan
Vered (72' Kobi Moyal), Dani Preda, Claudemir, Ya'akov Berihon (64' Shimon Abuhazira),
Ori Majabi, Arsenio Valpoort (85' Itay Shechter). Coach: Ran Ben-Shimon.
Omonia Nikosia: Kostas Panayi, Carlitos, Thanasis Panteliadis, Cleyton, Amir Agajev (68'
Ibrahim Toure), Gerasimos Fylaktou, Margaça, George Florescu, Marin Orsulic, Cillian
Sheridan, Matt Derbyshire. Coach: John Carver.
Goal: 71' Shimon Abuhazira 1-0.
Referee: Marcin Borski (POL)   Attendance: 9,200.

14.07.16   Sydbank Park, Haderslev: SønderjyskE – Strømsgodset IF 2-1 (1-1)
SønderjyskE: Marin Skender, Marc Pedersen, Pierre Kanstrup, Matthias Maak, Simon Kroon,
Janus Drachmann, Troels Kløve Hallstrøm (57' Casper Olesen), Adama Guira, Marcel Rømer
(63' Mikkel Uhre), Marc Hende, Tommy Bechmann (76' Nicolaj Ritter).
Coach: Jakob Michelsen.
Strømsgodset IF: Espen Pettersen, Mounir Hamoud, Kim Madsen, Bismark Boateng, Gustav
Valsvik, Francisco Santos, Mohammed Abu, Lars-Christopher Vilsvik, Marcus Pedersen,
Flamur Kastrati (76' Jonathan Parr), Muhamed Keit. Coach: Bjørn Petter Ingebretsen.
Goals: 9' Troels Kløve Hallstrøm 1-0, 16' Marcus Pedersen 1-1, 82' Mikkel Uhre 2-1.
Referee: Georgi Kabakov (BUL)   Attendance: 4,795.

14.07.16   Stroitel, Soligorsk: Shakhter Soligorsk – NK Domzale 1-1 (1-0)
Shakhter Soligorsk: Vladimir Bushma, Aleksey Yanushkevich, Aleksandr Yurevich, Igor
Burko, Nikola Ignjatijevic, Pavel Rybak, Igor Kuzmenok, Sergiy Rudika (75' Denis Laptev),
Artem Stargorodskiy, Yuri Kovalev (66' Yevgeniy Elezarenko), Dmitriy Osipenko (55'
Nikolai Yanush). Coach: Sergey Nikiforenko.
NK Domzale: Axel Maraval, Alvaro Brachi, Dejan Trajkovski, Gaber Dobrovoljc, Kenan
Horic, Matic Crnic (70' Jan Repas), Lucas Horvat, Zan Majer (78' Marko Alvir), Luka Zinko,
Benjamin Morel (83' Juninho), Antonio Mance. Coach: Luka Elsner.
Goals: 35' Nikola Ignjatijevic 1-0, 52' Dejan Trajkovski 1-1.
Referee: Dumitru Muntean (MOL)   Attendance: 2,100.

14.07.16   Beroe, Stara Zagora: PFC Beroe – HJK Helsinki 1-1 (0-1)
PFC Beroe: Blagoj Makendzhiev, Ivo Ivanov, Ventzislav Vasilev (76' Aleksandar Vasilev),
Veselin Penev, Iliya Milanov, Kohei Kato, Nemanja Milisavljevic (89' Vasil Panayotov), Tom
(89' Alexander Kolev), Erik Pochanski, Radoslav Kirilov, Georgi Bozhilov.
Coach: Aleksandar Dimitrov.
HJK Helsinki: Thomas Dähne, Taye Taiwo, Lum Rexhepi, Ivan Tatomirovic, Ville Jalasto,
Medo (80' Anthony Annan), Atomu Tanaka, Sebastian Sorsa, Sebastian Dahlström, Nikolai
Alho (73' Obed Malolo), Alfredo Morelos. Coach: Mika Lehkosuo.
Goals: 37' Alfredo Morelos 0-1, 49' Veselin Penev 1-1.
Referee: Petr Ardeleanu (CZE)   Attendance: 4,424.

14.07.16   Karadjordje, Novi Sad: Vojvodina – Gap Connah's Quay FC 1-0 (0-0)
Vojvodina: Marko Kordic, Nikola Antic, Darko Puskaric, Aleksandar Palocevic, Ivan
Lakicevic (57' Dusan Jovancic), Sinisa Babic (57' Nikola Asceric), Filip Malbasic (82' Lazar
Zlicic), Novica Maksimovic, Nemanja Miletic, Nikola Trujic, Dejan Meleg.
Coach: Nenad Lalatovic.
Gap Connah's Quay FC: John Danby, Ian Kearney, George Horan, Callum Morris, Sean
Smith, Wes Baynes, Danny Harrison, Nathan Woolfe, Jay Owen (89' Matty Owen), Lewis
Short, Michael Wilde (81' Les Davies). Coach: Andrew Morrison.
Goal: 86' Aleksandar Palocevic 1-0.
Referee: Aleksey Nikolaev (RUS)   Attendance: 4,276.

14.07.16   Ljudski vrt, Maribor: NK Maribor – Levski Sofia 0-0
NK Maribor: Jasmin Handanovic, Adis Hodzic, Erik Janza, Marko Suler, Denis Sme, Blaz
Vrhovec (46' Dare Vrsic), Sintayehu Sallalich (46' Gregor Bajde), Dino Hotic, Marwan
Kabha, Marcos Tavares, Milivoje Novakovic (76' Sunny Omoregie). Coach: Darko Milanic.
Levski Sofia: Bojan Jorgacevic, Dimitar Pirgov, Aleksander Aleksandrov, Veselin Minev,
Sasho Aleksandrov, Jeremy de Nooijer, Roman Prochazka, Georgi Kostadinov, Francis Narh,
Añete (85' Miki Orachev), Ventsislav Hristov (71' Babatunde Adeniji).
Coach: Ljupko Petrovic.
Referee: Cristian Balaj (ROM)   Attendance: 7,345.

14.07.16   Cristal Arena, Genk: KRC Genk – FK Buducnost Podgorica 2-0 (1-0)
KRC Genk: Marco Bizot, Sebastien Dewaest, Jere Uronen, Timoty Castagne, Bennard
Kumordzi, Thomas Buffel, Onyinye Ndidi, Yoni Buyens (74' Bryan Heynen), Neeskens
Kebano (76' Nikolaos Karelis), Leon Bailey, Mbwana Samatta (88' Leandro Trossard).
Coach: Peter Maes.
FK Buducnost Podgorica: Milos Dragojević, Risto Radunović, Nikola Vukcević, Filip
Mitrović, Momcilo Raspopović, Milos Raicković (60' Velizar Janketić), Ivan Pejaković (75'
Ermin Saratlić), Deni Hocko, Luka Mirković, Milan Vusurović (85' Driton Camaj), Radomir
Djalović. Coach: Miodrag Vukotic.
Goals: 17' Neeskens Kebano 1-0 (p), 79' Mbwana Samatta 2-0.
Referee: Vilhjalmur Alvar Thorarinsson (ISL)   Attendance: 10,450.

14.07.16   Emil Alexandrescu, Iasi: CSMS Iasi – Hajduk Split 2-2 (2-0)
CSMS Iasi: Branko Grahovac, Marius Mihalache, Ionut Voica, Cosmin Frasinescu, Vasile
Gheorghe, Lukacs Bole, Milan Mitic, Alexandru Tiganasu (78' Madalin Martin), Alexandru
Ciucur (64' Madalin Ciuca), Andrei Cristea, Gianmarco Piccioni (83' Dan Roman).
Coach: Nicolo Napoli.
Hajduk Split: Dante Stipica, Jefferson, Zoran Nizic, Fran Tudor (68' Ahmed Said), Nikola
Vlasic, Josip Juranovic, Zvonimir Kozulj, Hrvoje Milic, Toma Basic (57' Tonci Mujan),
Marko Cosic, Ivan Mastelic (46' Franck Ohandza). Coach: Marijan Pusnik.
Goals: 19' Andrei Cristea 1-0, 23' Gianmarco Piccioni 2-0, 48' Franck Ohandza 2-1,
90+5' Ahmed Said 2-2.
Referee: Yuriy Mozharovsky (UKR)   Attendance: 8,004.

14.07.16   Zosimades Stadium, Ioannina: PAS Giannina – Odds BK 3-0 (2-0)
PAS Giannina: Alexandros Paschalakis, Andi Lila, Theodoros Berios, Alexandros Michail,
Nikos Karanikas, Themistoklis Tzimopoulos, Noe Acosta (90+2' Apostolos Skondras), Fonsi,
Chrysovalantis Kozoronis, Euripidis Giakos (80' Christos Donis), Dimitrios Ferfelis (77'
Pedro Conde). Coach: Giannis Petrakis.
Odds BK: Sondre Rossbach, Espen Ruud, Thomas Grøgaard, Joakim Nilsen (73' Sigurd
Haugen), Steffen Hagen, Lars-Kristian Eriksen, Oliver Berg (46' Fredrik Jensen), Ole
Halvorsen, Fredrik Nordkvelle (86' Vegard Bergan), Henrik Johansen, Bentley.
Coach: Dag-Eilev Fagermo.
Goals: 7' Alexandros Michail 1-0, 31', 68' Noe Acosta 2-0, 3-0.
Referee: Glenn Nyberg (SWE)   Attendance: 5,615.

14.07.16   Partizan Stadion, Belgrade: Partizan – Zaglebie Lubin 0-0
Partizan: Bojan Saranov, Miroslav Vulicevic, Miroslav Bogosavac, Nikola Milenkovic, Cedric
Gogoua, Darko Brasanac (76' Sasa Marjanovic), Miroslav Radovic, Everton, Marko Jankovic
(83' Alen Stevanovic), Nemanja Mihajlovic, Nikola Djurdjic (69' Valeri Bojinov).
Coach: Ivan Tomic.
Zaglebie Lubin: Martin Polacek, Maciej Dabrowski, Djordje Cotra, Aleksandar Todorovski
(73' Jakub Tosik), Lubomir Guldan, Adrian Rakowski (66' Krzysztof Piatek), Jaroslaw
Kubicki, Lukasz Piatek, Arkadiusz Wozniak, Lukasz Janoszka (82' Jan Vlasko), Michal
Papadopulos. Coach: Piotr Stokowiec.
Referee: Eitan Shemeulevitch (ISR)   Attendance: 15,870.
Sent off: 56' Michal Papadopulos.

14.07.16   Pasienky, Bratislava: Slovan Bratislava – FK Jelgava 0-0
Slovan Bratislava: Jan Mucha, Boris Sekulic, Lorenzo Burnet, Ruben Ligeon, Kornel Salata,
Vukan Savicevic (90+3' Vasilis Pliatsikas), Joeri de Kamps, Frantisek Kubik (87' Richard
Lasik), Seydouba Soumah, Adam Zrelak, Mitchell Schet. Coach: Nicky Papavasiliou.
FK Jelgava: Kaspars Ikstens, Igors Savcenkovs, Valerijs Redjko, Abdoulaye Diallo, Gints
Freimanis, Ryotaro Nakano (82' Vladislavs Sorokins), Boriss Bogdaskins, Mindaugas
Grigaravicius (62' Andrejs Kovalovs), Glebs Kluskins, Artis Lazdins, Daniils Turkovs (72'
Olegs Malasenoks). Coach: Saulius Sirmelis.
Referee: Alexandros Aretopoulos (GRE)   Attendance: 1,451.

14.07.16   Alcufer Stadion, Györ: MTK Budapest – Gabala FK 1-2 (0-1)
MTK Budapest: Lajos Hegedüs, Akos Baki, Mato Grgic, Barnabas Bese, Patrik Poor, Jozsef
Kanta, Balint Borbely (74' Lorand Szatmari), Adam Vass, Darko Nikac (65' Szabolcs Varga),
Daniel Gera (78' David Jakab), Sandor Torghelle. Coach: Vaszilisz Teodoru.
Gabala FK: Dmitro Bezotosniy, Vojislav Stankovic, Vitaliy Vernydub, Ricardinho, Räsad
Sadiqov, Nika Kvekveskiri, Magomed Mirzabekov, Filip Ozobic, Theo Weeks, Sergei Zenjov,
Bagaliy Dabo (86' Asif Mammadov). Coach: Roman Grygorchuk.
Goals: 25' Nika Kvekveskiri 0-1, 63' Filip Ozobic 0-2, 70' Sandor Torghelle 1-2.
Referee: Bojan Pandzic (SWE)   Attendance: 501.

14.07.16   Puskas Akademia Pancho Arena, Felcsut:
           Videoton FC – FK Cukaricki-Stankom 2-0 (0-0)
Videoton FC: Adam Kovacsik, Paulo Vinicius, Loïc Nego, Adam Lang, Stopira, Mate Patkai,
Adam Bodi, Roland Szolnoki, Krisztian Geresi (84' Robert Feczesin), Asmir Suljic, David
Barczi (81' Filip Oliveira). Coach: Henning Berg.
FK Cukaricki-Stankom: Nemanja Stevanovic, Lucas Piasentin, Nikola Jankovic, Djordje
Djuric, Stefan Zivkovic, Marko Docic, Asmir Kajevic (46' Igor Matic), Dusan Lagator, Stanisa
Mandic (56' Sasa Jovanovic), Ismaël Fofana, Filip Knezevic. Coach: Milan Lesnjak.
Goals: 58' Adam Bodi 1-0, 90+2' Asmir Suljic 2-0.
Referee: Mads-Kristoffer Kristoffersen (DEN)   Attendance: 1,858.
Sent off: 80' Loïc Nego.

14.07.16   Hibernians Ground, Paolo: Birkirkara FC – Heart of Midlothian 0-0
Birkirkara FC: Miroslav Kopric, Christian Bubalovic, Joseph Zerafa, Gareth Sciberras, Srdan
Dimitrov (90+2' Edinson Bilbao), Shaun Bajada (81' Frank Temile), Ryan Scicluna (90+1'
Bruno Marotti), Cain Attard, Matthew Guillaumier, Emerson, Vito Plut. Coach: Drazen Besek.
Heart of Midlothian: Jack Hamilton, Callum Paterson, Igor Rossi, Alim Öztürk, Liam Smith,
Faycal Rherras, Perry Kitchen (30' Don Cowie), Prince Buaben, Arnaud Sutchuin Djoum,
Jamie Walker (82' Sam Nicholson), Conor Sammon (74' Juanma). Coach: Robbie Neilson.
Referee: Ivaylo Stoyanov (BUL)   Attendance: 1,868.

14.07.16   Easter Road Stadium, Edinburgh: Hibernian FC – Brøndby IF 0-1 (0-1)
Hibernian FC: Otso Virtanen, David Gray, Paul Hanlon, Darren McGregor, Marvin Bartley
(65' Liam Fontaine), John McGinn, Dylan McGeouch (65' James Keatings), Lewis Stevenson,
Grant Holt, Martin Boyle (77' Alex Harris), Jason Cummings. Coach: Neil Lennon.
Brøndby IF: Frederik Rønnow, Benedikt Röcker, Martin Albrechtsen, Frederik Holst, Johan
Larsson, Patrick da Silva, Rodolph Austin (43' Andrew Hjulsager), Christian Nørgaard, Kamil
Wilczek, Christian Jakobsen (84' Jesper Juelsgård), Daniel Stückler (52' Teemu Pukki).
Coach: Alexander Zorniger.
Goal: 1' Kamil Wilczek 0-1.
Referee: Juan Martinez Munuera (ESP)   Attendance: 13,454.

14.07.16 Pittodrie Stadium, Aberdeen: Aberdeen FC – FK Ventspils 3-0 (0-0)
Aberdeen FC: Joe Lewis, Shaleum Logan, Graeme Shinnie, Andrew Considine, Ash Taylor,
Mark Reynolds, Kenny McLean (68' Jayden Stockley), Jonathan Hayes, Ryan Jack, Adam
Rooney (89' Wes Burns), Niall McGinn. Coach: Derek McInnes.
FK Ventspils: Maksims Uvarenko, Alans Sinelnikovs, Nikita Kolesovs, Nikola Boranijasevic,
Antons Jemelins, Simonas Paulius, Eduards Tidenbergs (81' Vadims Zulevs), Vitalijs
Recickis, Ritvars Rugins, Aleksey Alekseev (87' Kaspars Svarups), Girst Karlsons.
Coach: Paul Ashworth.
Goals: 72' Jayden Stockley 1-0, 76' Adam Rooney 2-0, 90+1' Wes Burns 3-0.
Referee: João Pinheiro (POR)   Attendance: 10,672.

14.07.16 Solitude, Belfast: Cliftonville FC – AEK Larnaca 2-3 (1-0)
Cliftonville FC: Jason Mooney, Levi Ives, Caoimhin Bonner, Jason McGuinness, Christopher
Curran, James Knowles, Martin Donnelly (82' Ross Lavery), Jude Winchester (88' Stephen
Garrett), Tomas Cosgrove, David McDaid (74' Daniel Hughes), Jay Donnelly.
Coach: Gerry Lyttle.
AEK Larnaca: Ruben Miño, Daniel Mojsov, Català, Elias Charalambous, Jorge Larena, Joan
Tomas, Tete (84' Nikos Englezou), Juanma Ortiz, Vincent Laban (81' Vladimir Boljevic),
André Alves (72' Costas Charalambides), Ivan Trickovski. Coach: Imanol Idiakez.
Goals: 18' Jason McGuinness 1-0, 50' Jay Donnelly 2-0, 59' Ivan Trickovski 2-1,
64' Elias Charalambous 2-2, 77' Joan Tomas 2-3.
Referee: Adrien Jaccottet (SUI)   Attendance: 1,352.

14.07.16 Stadion Piast, Gliwice: Piast Gliwice – IFK Göteborg 0-3 (0-2)
Piast Gliwice: Jakub Szmatula, Patrik Mraz, Tomasz Mokwa (46' Michal Maslowski), Hebert
Santos, Edvinas Girdvainis, Marcin Pietrowski, Radoslaw Murawski, Sasa Zivec, Bartosz
Szeliga (61' Maciej Jankowski), Martin Bukata, Josip Barisic (72' Mateusz Mak).
Coach: Radoslav Latal.
IFK Göteborg: John Alvbåge, Emil Salomonsson, Haitam Aleesami, Sebastian Eriksson,
Thomas Rogne, Mattias Bjärsmyr, Mads Albæk, Søren Rieks, Jakob Ankersen (82' Martin
Smedberg), Tobias Hysén (80' Gustav Engvall), Mikael Boman (87' Tom Pettersson).
Coach: Jörgen Lennartsson.
Goals: 2' Thomas Rogne 0-1, 35' Tobias Hysén 0-2, 86' Gustav Engvall 0-3.
Referee: Manuel Schüttengruber (AUT)   Attendance: 5,629.

14.07.16 Ernst-Happel-Stadion, Vienna: Austria Wien – FK Kukësi 1-0 (1-0)
Austria Wien: Osman Hadzikic, Petar Filipovic, Jens Stryger Larsen, Christoph Martschinko,
Lukas Rotpuller, Lucas Venuto, Tarkan Serbest, Dominik Prokop (69' Marko Kvasina),
Raphael Holzhauser, Olarenwaju Kayode (90+2' Ognjen Vukojevic), Felipe Pires (85' De
Paula). Coach: Thorsten Fink.
FK Kukësi: Enea Kolici, Ylli Shameti, Rrahman Hallaçi, Renato Malota, Sabien Lilaj, Gledi
Mici, Liridon Latifi, Besar Musolli, Jean Carioca (73' Izair Emini), Rangel (70' Sindri Guri),
Masato Fukui (81' Matija Dvornekovic). Coach: Hasan Lika.
Goal: 23' Felipe Pires 1-0.
Referee: Paolo Valeri (ITA)   Attendance: 4,312.

14.07.16   Valsvöllur, Reykjavik: KR Reykjavík – Grasshoppers Zürich 3-3 (0-2)
KR Reykjavík: Stefan Magnusson, Michael Præst Møller, Gunnar Gunnarsson, Indridi
Sigurdsson, Aron Josepsson, Morten Beck, Finnur Margeirsson, Palmi Palmason (76' Denis
Fazlagic), Óskar Hauksson (90+2' Gudmundur Andri Tryggvason), Holmbert Fridjonsson (46'
Morten Andersen), Kennie Chopart. Coach: Willum Thorsson.
Grasshoppers Zürich: Joël Mall, Alban Pnishi, Numa Lavanchy, Jan Bamert, Benjamin Lüthi,
Runar Sigurjonsson, Marko Basic, Mergim Brahimi (68' Florian Kamberi), Caio, Nikola
Gjorgjev (62' Lucas Andersen), Ridge Munsy (78' Haris Tabakovic). Coach: Pierluigi Tami.
Goals: 18' Ridge Munsy 0-1, 36' Nikola Gjorgjev 0-2, 46', 50' Morten Andersen 1-2, 2-2,
59' Caio 2-3, 77' Óskar Hauksson 3-3 (p).
Referee: Peter Kjærsgaard-Andersen (DEN)   Attendance: 767.

20.07.16   Dalga Arena, Baku: FK Kapaz – FC Admira Wacker 0-2 (0-1)
FK Kapaz: Tadas Simaitis, Karim Diniyev, Vugar Baybalayev (46' Jeyhun Javadov), Dário
Júnior, Nijat Gurbanov (69' Orkhan Aliyev), Tural Akhundov, Shahriyar Aliyev, Renan Alves,
Shahriyar Rahimov, Sérginho (82' Tural Qurbatov), Julien Ebah. Coach: Shakhin Diniyev.
FC Admira Wacker: Jörg Siebenhandl, Stephan Zwierschitz, Thomas Ebner, Markus Pavic,
Markus Wostry, Markus Lackner, Maximilian Sax (54' Ilter Ayyildiz), Christoph Knasmüllner
(75' Florian Fischerauer), Daniel Toth, Eldis Bajrami, Dominik Starkl (38' Patrick Schmidt).
Coach: Oliver Lederer.
Goals: 17' Christoph Knasmüllner 0-1, 76' Patrick Schmidt 0-2.
Referee: Vitaliy Meshkov (RUS)   Attendance: 1,500.

21.07.16   Anton Malatinsky, Trnava: Spartak Trnava – Shirak FC 2-0 (0-0)
Spartak Trnava: Adam Jakubech, Andrej Kadlec, Denis Hornik, Boris Godal, Lukas Gressak,
Martin Mikovic, Anton Sloboda, Emir Halilovic (80' Matus Paukner), Bello Babatounde, Ivan
Schranz (87' Martin Kostal), Robert Tambe (76' Erik Jirka). Coach: Miroslav Karhan.
Shirak FC: Anatoly Ayvazov, Arman Hovhannisyan (76' Aghvan Davoyan), Artyom
Mikaelyan, Gevorg Hovhannisyan, Robert Darbinyan, Rumyan Hovsepyan (65' Viulen
Ayvazyan), Solomon Udo, Mohamed Kaba, Nemanja Stoskovic (65' Ghukas Poghosyan),
Konan Kouakou, Drissa Diarrassouba. Coach: Vardan Bichakhchyan.
Goals: 57' Ivan Schranz 1-0, 61' Robert Tambe 2-0.
Referee: Arnold Hunter (NIR)   Attendance: 6,129.

21.07.16   Netanya Stadium, Netanya: Maccabi Tel Aviv – Kairat Almaty 2-1 (1-0)
Maccabi Tel Aviv: Predrag Rajkovic, Eitan Tibi, Tal Ben Haim (I), Haris Medunjanin (90'
Egor Filipenko), Gal Alberman, Avi Rikan, Nosa Igiebor, Dor Peretz (69' Elazar Dasa), Tal
Ben Haim (II) (75' Yossi Benayoun), Dor Mikha, Orlando Sá. Coach: Shota Arveladze.
Kairat Almaty: Vladimir Plotnikov, Zarko Markovic, Arzo (80' Ermek Kuantaev), Gafurzhan
Suyombaev, Mikhail Bakaev, Isael (88' Leandre Tawamba), Gerson Acevedo (46' Islambek
Kuat), Anatoliy Tymoshchuk, Gerard Gohou, Stanislav Lunin, Andrey Arshavin.
Coach: Kakhaber Tskhadadze.
Goals: 5' Tal Ben Haim (II) 1-0, 64' Gerard Gohou 1-1, 86' Gal Alberman 2-1.
Referee: Tiago Martins (POR)   Attendance: 9,832.

159

21.07.16   Richmond Park, Dublin: St Patrick's Athletic – Dinamo Minsk 0-1 (0-1)
St Patrick's Athletic: Brendan Clarke, Ger O'Brien, Ian Bermingham, Darren Dennehy, Sean
Hoare, Keith Treacy, Conan Byrne (90+1' Dinny Corcoran), Graham Kelly (69' David
Cawley), Billy Dennehy, Chris Fagan, Mark Timlin (62' Jamie McGrath).
Coach: Liam Buckley.
Dinamo Minsk: Sergey Ignatovich, Yuriy Ostroukh, Mohamed El-Mounir (90+2' Kirill
Premudrov), Aleksandr Sverchinski, Artem Bykov, Uladzimir Karytska, Valeriy Zhukovskiy
(79' Anton Shramchenko), Oleksandr Noyok, Yuriy Gabovda, Nikita Kaplenko, Gleb
Rassadkin (58' Luka Rotkovic). Coach: Sergey Borovskiy.
Goal: 18' Gleb Rassadkin 0-1.
Referee: Alan Sant (MLT)   Attendance: 2,400.
Sent off: 84' Vladimir Khvashchinskiy (unused substitute).

21.07.16   Kranjcevicevoj, Zagreb: Lokomotiva Zagreb – Rovaniemi PS 3-0 (1-0)
Lokomotiva Zagreb: Ivan Filipovic, Karlo Bartolec, Tomislav Mrcela, Dino Peric, Herdi
Prenga, Luka Capan (71' Ivan Sunjic), Ivan Fiolic, Josip Coric (85' Ivan Antunovic), Endri
Cekici (65' Petar Bockaj), Eros Grezda, Mirko Maric. Coach: Valentin Barisic.
Rovaniemi PS: Reguero, Abdou Jammeh, Janne Saksela, Juha Pirinen, Mika Mäkitalo (62'
Jean Nganbe), Robert Taylor, Eetu Muinonen, Michal Mravec (75' Jarkko Lahdenmäki), Juuso
Hämäläinen, Will John, Aleksandr Kokko (45' Antti Okkonen). Coach: Juha Malinen.
Goals: 44' Ivan Fiolic 1-0, 49', 83' Mirko Maric 2-0, 3-0.
Referee: Giorgi Kruashvili (GEO)   Attendance: 630.
Sent off: 33' Juha Pirinen, 89' Abdou Jammeh.

21.07.16   Nacionalna Arena Filip II Makedonski, Skopje:
             KF Shkëndija 79 – Neftci PFK 1-0 (1-0)
KF Shkëndija 79: Kostadin Zahov, Egzon Bejtulai, Ardijan Cuculi, Armend Alimi (90+4'
Victor Juffo), Ferhan Hasani (90+1' Sciprim Taipi), Besir Demiri, Blagoja Todorovski,
Stephan Vujcic, Besart Ibraimi (87' Artim Polozani), Marjan Radeski, Stenio Junior.
Coach: Bruno Akrapovic.
Neftci PFK: Krsevan Santini, Jairo, Vance Sikov, Magsad Isayev, Dario Melnjak, Araz
Abdullayev, Murad Agaev, Rahman Hajiyev (80' Javid Imamverdiyev), Edson Castillo,
Ruslan Qurbanov (87' Rahil Mammadov), Fahmin Muradbayli (85' Akshin Gurbanli).
Coach: Veli Kasumov.
Goal: 31' Besart Ibraimi 1-0.
Referee: Erik Lambrechts (BEL)   Attendance: 9,510.
Sent off: 70' Vance Sikov.

21.07.16   Eden Arena, Praha: Slavia Praha – FC Levadia 2-0 (1-0)
Slavia Praha: Jiri Pavlenka, Jan Mikula, Tomas Jablonsky (61' Jaroslav Mihalík), Jan Boril,
Simon Deli, Jiri Bilek (75' Michael Ngadeu-Ngadjui), Josef Husbauer, Levan Kenia, Tomás
Soucek, Milan Skoda, Gino van Kessel (71' Antonin Barak). Coach: Dusan Uhrin.
FC Levadia: Sergei Lepmets, Luc Tabi, Maksim Podholjuzin, Igor Morozov, Ilja Antonov,
Marcelin Gando, Anton Miranchuk, Siim Luts, Marek Kaljumäe (80' Alan Gatagov), Evgeni
Kobzar (80' Andreas Raudsepp), Rimo Hunt. Coach: Sergei Ratnikov.
Goals: 10' Milan Skoda 1-0, 67' Gino van Kessel 2-0.
Referee: Christos Nicolaides (CYP)   Attendance: 14,856.

21.07.16   Rheinpark, Vaduz: FC Vaduz – FC Midtjylland 2-2 (0-1)
FC Vaduz: Benjamin Siegrist, Marvin Pfründer, Simone Grippo, Matthias Strohmaier, Axel Borgmann, Diego Ciccone, Moreno Costanzo, Marco Mathys (80' Franz Burgmeier), Stjepan Kukuruzovic (65' Nicolas Hasler), Philipp Muntwiler, Gonzalo Zarate (65' Maurice Brunner). Coach: Giorgio Contini.
FC Midtjylland: Johan Dahlin, Kian Hansen (57' Kristian Riis), Markus Halsti (69' Kristoffer Olsson), Patrick Banggaard, André Rømer, Rasmus Nissen, Jakob Poulsen, Pione Sisto, Rilwan Hassan, Vaclav Kadlec, Ebere Onuachu (57' Mikkel Duelund). Coach: Jess Thorup.
Goals: 40', 68' Pione Sisto 0-1, 0-2, 82' Maurice Brunner 1-2, 86' Moreno Costanzo 2-2 (p).
Referee: Andrew Davey (NIR)   Attendance: 842.
Sent off: 45' Jakob Poulsen.

21.07.16   Torpedo, Zhodzina: Torpedo-BalAZ Zhodino – Debreceni VSC 1-0 (1-0)
Torpedo-BalAZ Zhodino: Valeriy Fomichev, Artem Chelyadinski, Evgeni Klopotskiy, Aleksey Pankovets, Terentiy Lutsevich, Sergiy Shapoval, Andrey Khachaturyan, Anton Golenkov (66' Pavel Chelyadko), Sergiy Zagynaylov (78' Denis Trapashko), Mikhail Afanasiev (87' Aleksey Belevich), Vadim Demidovich. Coach: Igor Kriushenko.
Debreceni VSC: Bozidar Radosevic, Norbert Meszaros, Dusan Brkovic, Mihaly Korhut, David Holman (59' Zsolt Horvath), Danilo Sekulic, Jozsef Varga, Peter Szakaly (65' Janos Ferenczi), Aleksandar Jovanovic, Tibor Tisza, Geoffrey Castillion (57' Tamas Takacs).
Coach: Elemer Kondas.
Goal: 25' Vadim Demidovich 1-0.
Referee: Dimitar Meckarovski (MKD)   Attendance: 2,650.

21.07.16   Kadrioru staadion, Tallinn: JK Nõmme Kalju- Maccabi Haifa 1-1 (0-1, 1-1)
JK Nõmme Kalju: Vitali Teles, Maximiliano Ugge, Jorge Rodrigues, Andrei Sidorenkov, Reginald Mbu-Alidor, Ats Purje, Janar Toomet (71' Igor Subbotin), Artur Valikaev (84' Hidetoshi Wakui), Karl Mööl, Damiano Quintieri (63' Tarmo Neemelo), Artjom Dmitrijev. Coach: Sergey Frantsev.
Maccabi Haifa: Ohad Levita, Marc Valiente, Eyad Abu Abaid, Gary Kagelmacher, Eyal Meshumar (71' Dekel Keinan), Neta Lavi, Ludovic Obraniak, Gil Vermouth (89' Amit Zenati), Sun Menachem, Nikita Rukavytsya, Firas Mugrabi (77' Shoval Gozlan). Coach: Roni Levy.
Goals: 34' Nikita Rukavytsya 0-1 (p), 90' Tarmo Neemelo 1-1.
Referee: Markus Hameter (AUT)   Attendance: 2,273.

JK Nõmme Kalju won 5-3 on penalties following extra time.

Penalties: Ugge 1-0, Obraniak 1-1, Sidorenkov 2-1, Rukavytsya 2-2, Purje 3-2, Zenati missed, Wakui 4-2, Menachem 4-3, Subbotin 5-3.

21.07.16   Osmanli Stadi, Ankara: Osmanlispor FK – FC Zimbru 5-0 (2-0)
Osmanlispor FK: Zydrunas Karcemarskas, Tiago Pinto, Vaclav Prochazka, Numan Cürüksu, Avdija Vrsajevic, Mehmet Güven, Papa N'Diaye, Aminu Umar, Musa Cagiran (14' Engin Bekdemir, 38' Erdal Kilicarslan), Pierre Webo (75' Raul Rusescu), Dzon Delarge. Coach: Mustafa Akcay.
FC Zimbru: Denis Rusu, Luan, Moreira, Emerson, Ion Jardan, Diego Lima, Amancio Fortes, Veaceslav Zagaevschii (57' Gheorghe Anton), Erick (46' Dan Spataru, 76' Daniel Jalo), Alex Bruno, Ilie Damascan. Coach: Flavius Stoican.
Goals: 16', 26', 50' Aminu Umar 1-0 (p), 2-0, 3-0, 74' Erdal Kilicarslan 4-0, 83' Raul Rusescu 5-0.
Referee: Mitja Zganec (SVN)   Attendance: 6,382.

21.07.16   Turners Cross, Cork: Cork City – BK Häcken 1-0 (1-0)
Cork City: Mark McNulty, Alan Bennett, Michael McSweeney, Kenny Browne, Greg Bolger, Stephen Dooley, Kevin O'Connor, Gearoid Morrissey (79' Gavan Holohan), Garry Buckley, Steven Beattie, Sean Maguire (90+1' Mark O'Sullivan). Coach: John Caulfield.
BK Häcken: Peter Abrahamsson, Jasmin Sudic, Emil Wahlström, Kari Arkivuo, Rasmus Schüller (64' Martin Ericsson), Mohammed Abubakari, Mohammed Nasiru (45+2' Demba Savage), Samuel Gustafson, Joal Andersson, Paulinho, John Owoeri (74' Alexander Jeremejeff). Coach: Peter Gerhardsson.
Goal: 26' Kevin O'Connor 1-0.
Referee: Carlos Xistra (POR)   Attendance: 5,334.

21.07.16   Victoria Stadium, Gibraltar: Europa FC – AIK Solna 0-1 (0-0)
Europa FC: Javi Muñoz, Toni (67' Copi), Toscano, Vazquez, Mustapha Yahaya, Ivan Moya, Guille Roldan, Alex Quillo (39' José Gonzalez), Martin Belfortti, Alberto Merino, Pedro Carrion. Coach: Juan Gallardo Fernandez.
AIK Solna: Patrik Carlgren, Haukur Hauksson, Nils-Eric Johansson, Sauli Väisänen (88' Patrick Kpozo), Jos Hooiveld, Johan Blomberg, Ebenezer Ofori, Daniel Sundgren, Anton Saletros, Amin Affane (46' Stefan Ishizaki), Eero Markkanen (78' Ahmed Yasin). Coach: Rikard Norling.
Goal: 55' Eero Markkanen 0-1.
Referee: Adam Farkas (HUN)   Attendance: 1,145.

21.07.16   Neo GSP, Nikosia: Omonia Nikosia – Beitar Jerusalem 3-2 (2-2)
Omonia Nikosia: Kostas Panayi, Bruno Nascimento, Carlitos, Cleyton, Amir Agajev (55' Ibrahim Toure), Gerasimos Fylaktou (55' Aristides Soiledis), Margaça, George Florescu, Marin Orsulic, Cillian Sheridan (65' Onisiforos Roushias), Matt Derbyshire. Coach: John Carver.
Beitar Jerusalem: Boris Kleiman, David Keltjens, Jesus Rueda, Dan Mori, Omer Atzily, Dan Einbinder, Claudemir, Kobi Moyal (64' Oz Rali), Ori Majabi, Itay Shechter (78' Shimon Abuhazira), Arsenio Valpoort (58' Idan Vered). Coach: Ran Ben-Shimon.
Goals: 17' Omer Atzili 0-1, 26' Amir Agajev 1-1, 45' Omer Atzili 1-2 (p), 45' Cillian Sheridan 2-2 (p), 81' Onisiforos Roushias 3-2.
Referee: Davide Massa (ITA)   Attendance: 14,383.

21.07.16 Marienlyst, Drammen: Strømsgodset IF – SønderjyskE 2-2 (2-0, 2-1)
Strømsgodset IF: Espen Pettersen, Mounir Hamoud, Kim Madsen, Bismark Boateng, Gustav Valsvik, Francisco Santos (72' Petter Moen), Mohammed Abu, Lars-Christopher Vilsvik, Øyvind Storflor (66' Flamur Kastrati), Marcus Pedersen, Muhamed Keit (96' Jonathan Parr). Coach: Bjørn Petter Ingebretsen.
SønderjyskE: Marin Skender, Marc Pedersen (118' Mikkel Hedegaard), Pierre Kanstrup, Matthias Maak, Simon Kroon, Janus Drachmann, Johan Absalonsen (71' Troels Kløve Hallstrøm), Adama Guira, Marcel Rømer, Marc Hende, Mikkel Uhre (80' Tommy Bechmann). Coach: Jakob Michelsen.
Goals: 17', 45' Muhamed Keita 1-0, 2-0, 69' Mik. Uhre 2-1, 120' Troels Kløve Hallstrøm 2-2.
Referee: Steven McLean (SCO)   Attendance: 3,875.

SønderjyskE won after extra time.

21.07.16 Sportni Park, Domzale: NK Domzale – Shakhter Soligorsk 2-1 (1-0)
NK Domzale: Axel Maraval, Alvaro Brachi, Gaber Dobrovoljc, Jure Balkovec, Kenan Horic, Matic Crnic (64' Jan Repas), Lucas Horvat, Zan Majer (89' Zan Zuzek), Marko Alvir, Benjamin Morel, Antonio Mance (84' Juninho). Coach: Luka Elsner.
Shakhter Soligorsk: Vladimir Bushma, Aleksandr Yurevich, Igor Burko, Nikola Ignjatijevic, Pavel Rybak (72' Dmitriy Osipenko), Igor Kuzmenok, Artem Stargorodskiy, Yevgeniy Elezarenko (77' Sergiy Rudika), Yuri Kovalev, Mikhail Shibun (46' Denis Laptev), Nikolai Yanush. Coach: Sergey Nikiforenko.
Goals: 35' Marko Alvir 1-0, 61' Denis Laptev 1-1, 69' Zan Majer 2-1.
Referee: Alain Bieri (SUI)   Attendance: 1,800.

21.07.16 Sonera Stadium, Helsinki: HJK Helsinki – PFC Beroe 1-0 (1-0)
HJK Helsinki: Thomas Dähne, Taye Taiwo (79' Sebastian Sorsa), Lum Rexhepi, Ivan Tatomirovic, Ville Jalasto, Medo (90+2' Sebastian Dahlström), Atomu Tanaka, Anthony Annan, Nnamdi Oduamadi, Nikolai Alho, Alfredo Morelos. Coach: Mika Lehkosuo.
PFC Beroe: Blagoj Makendzhiev, Ivo Ivanov, Ventzislav Vasilev, Veselin Penev, Iliya Milanov, Kohei Kato, Nemanja Milisavljevic (65' Pedro Marques), Tom (84' Alexander Kolev), Erik Pochanski, Radoslav Kirilov (84' Stanislav Dryanov), Georgi Bozhilov. Coach: Aleksandar Dimitrov.
Goal: 25' Atomu Tanaka 1-0.
Referee: Padraig Sutton (IRL)   Attendance: 3,872.

21.07.16 Belle Vue, Rhyl: Gap Connah's Quay FC – Vojvodina 1-2 (0-1)
Gap Connah's Quay FC: John Danby, John Disney (55' Les Davies), Ian Kearney, George Horan, Callum Morris, Sean Smith, Wes Baynes, Nathan Woolfe, Jay Owen (71' Matty Owen), Lewis Short, Michael Wilde (84' Ashley Ruane). Coach: Andrew Morrison.
Vojvodina: Marko Kordic, Vladimir Kovacevic, Nikola Antic, Darko Puskaric, Aleksandar Palocevic, Filip Malbasic, Novica Maksimovic, Dusan Jovancic (68' Dusan Micic), Nemanja Miletic, Nikola Trujic (74' Uros Stamenic), Dejan Meleg (82' Lazar Zlicic). Coach: Nenad Lalatovic.
Goals: 8', 49' Dejan Meleg 0-1, 0-2 (p), 65' Michael Wilde 1-2.
Referee: Peter Kralovic (SVK)   Attendance: 809.

163

21.07.16   Georgi Asparuhov, Sofia: Levski Sofia – NK Maribor 1-1 (1-0)
Levski Sofia: Bojan Jorgacevic, Dimitar Pirgov, Aleksander Aleksandrov, Veselin Minev, Sasho Aleksandrov, Jeremy de Nooijer, Roman Prochazka, Georgi Kostadinov (79' Babatunde Adeniji), Francis Narh, Añete (86' Jean Deza), Ventsislav Hristov. Coach: Ljupko Petrovic.
NK Maribor: Jasmin Handanovic, Adis Hodzic, Erik Janza, Marko Suler, Denis Sme, Blaz Vrhovec (54' Dare Vrsic), Dino Hotic (76' Ales Mertelj), Marwan Kabha, Damjan Bohar (68' Gregor Bajde), Marcos Tavares, Milivoje Novakovic. Coach: Darko Milanic.
Goals: 22' Francis Narh 1-0, 68' Marcos Tavares 1-1.
Referee: Michael Tykgaard (DEN)   Attendance: 17,600.

21.07.16   Pod Goricom, Podgorica: FK Buducnost Podgorica – KRC Genk 2-0 (2-0, 2-0)
FK Buducnost Podgorica: Milos Dragojević, Risto Radunović, Nikola Vukcević, Filip Mitrović, Momcilo Raspopović, Milos Raicković (64' Deni Hocko), Luka Mirkovic, Velizar Janketić (53' Ivan Pejaković), Milan Vusurović, Goran Vujevic (92' Milivoje Raicevic), Radomir Djalović. Coach: Miodrag Vukotic.
KRC Genk: Marco Bizot, Sebastien Dewaest, Jere Uronen, Timoty Castagne (67' Sandy Walsh), Bennard Kumordzi, Thomas Buffel, Onyinye Ndidi, Yoni Buyens (46' Bryan Heynen), Nikolaos Karelis (75' Dries Wouters), Leon Bailey, Mbwana Samatta. Coach: Peter Maes.
Goals: 1', 40' Radomir Djalovic 1-0, 2-0.
Referee: Charalambos Kalogeropoulos (GRE)   Attendance: 4,500.
Sent off: 74' Bennard Kumordzi.

KRC Genk won 4-2 on penalties following extra time.

Penalties: Radunovic 1-0, Buffel 1-1, Raspopovic missed, Heynen 1-2, Djalovic 2-2, Samatta 2-3, Mirkovic missed, Walsh 2-4.

21.07.16   Poljud, Split: Hajduk Split – CSMS Iasi 2-1 (1-1)
Hajduk Split: Dante Stipica, Jefferson (68' Maksim Beliy), Zoran Nizic, Fran Tudor, Nikola Vlasic, Josip Juranovic, Zvonimir Kozulj, Hrvoje Milic, Tino-Sven Susic (60' Toma Basic), Marko Cosic, Ahmed Said (46' Franck Ohandza). Coach: Marijan Pusnik.
CSMS Iasi: Branko Grahovac, Marius Mihalache, Ionut Voica, Cosmin Frasinescu, Vasile Gheorghe (76' Alexandru Cretu), Lukacs Bole, Milan Mitic, Alexandru Tiganasu, Alexandru Ciucur (62' Madalin Martin), Andrei Cristea (81' Dan Roman), Gianmarco Piccioni. Coach: Nicolo Napoli.
Goals: 22' Fran Tudor 1-0, 26' Alexandru Ciucur 1-1, 90' Franck Ohandza 2-1.
Referee: Frank Schneider (FRA)   Attendance: 16,798.

21.07.16   Skagerak Arena, Skien: Odds BK – PAS Giannina 3-1 (0-0, 3-0)
Odds BK: Sondre Rossbach, Espen Ruud, Thomas Grøgaard, Fredrik Semb Berge, Steffen
Hagen, Jone Samuelsen (63' Oliver Berg), Fredrik Nordkvelle (84' Zakaria Messoudi), Fredrik
Jensen (101' Joakim Nilsen), Henrik Johansen, Rafik Zekhnini, Bentley.
Coach: Dag-Eilev Fagermo.
PAS Giannina: Alexandros Paschalakis, Andi Lila, Theodoros Berios, Alexandros Michail,
Nikos Karanikas, Themistoklis Tzimopoulos, Noe Acosta, Fonsi, Chrysovalantis Kozoronis
(94' Christos Donis), Euripidis Giakos (79' Christopher Maboulou), Dimitrios Ferfelis (66'
Leonardo Koutris). Coach: Giannis Petrakis.
Goals: 55' Fredrik Nordkvelle 1-0 (p), 57' Bentley 2-0, 89' Espen Ruud 3-0,
98' Leonardo Koutris 3-1.
Referee: Tomasz Musial (POL)   Attendance: 3,184.

PAS Giannina won following extra time.

21.07.16   Stadion Zaglebie, Lubin: Zaglebie Lubin – Partizan 0-0
Zaglebie Lubin: Martin Polacek, Maciej Dabrowski, Djordje Cotra, Aleksandar Todorovski,
Lubomir Guldan, Adrian Rakowski (61' Jan Vlasko), Jaroslaw Kubicki, Lukasz Piatek,
Arkadiusz Wozniak, Lukasz Janoszka (74' Krzysztof Janus), Krzysztof Piatek (101' Jakub
Tosik). Coach: Piotr Stokowiec.
Partizan: Bojan Saranov, Miroslav Vulicevic, Miroslav Bogosavac (120' Petar Djurickovic),
Nikola Milenkovic, Cedric Gogoua, Darko Brasanac, Miroslav Radovic (91' Sasa Ilic),
Everton, Marko Jankovic, Nemanja Mihajlovic, Nikola Djurdjic (70' Dusan Vlahovic).
Coach: Ivan Tomic.
Referee: Anatoliy Abdula (UKR)   Attendance: 11,279.

Zaglebie Lubin won 4-3 on penalties following extra time.

Penalties: Brasanac missed, Janus 0-1, Ilic 1-1, Guldan 1-2, Djurickovic 2-2, Todorovski
missed, Jankovic 3-2, Wozniak 3-3, Mihajlovic missed, Vlasko 3-4.

21.07.16   Zemgalas Olimpiska Centra, Jelgava: FK Jelgava – Slovan Bratislava 3-0 (1-0)
FK Jelgava: Kaspars Ikstens, Igors Savcenkovs, Valerijs Redjko, Abdoulaye Diallo, Gints
Freimanis, Ryotaro Nakano, Boriss Bogdaskins, Mindaugas Grigaravicius (82' Andrejs
Kovalovs), Glebs Kluskins (64' Artjoms Osipovs), Artis Lazdins, Olegs Malasenoks (90+2'
Vitalijs Smirnovs). Coach: Saulius Sirmelis.
Slovan Bratislava: Jan Mucha, Boris Sekulic, Lorenzo Burnet, Ruben Ligeon, Kornel Salata,
Vukan Savicevic (72' Richard Lasik), Joeri de Kamps (72' Granwald Scott), Frantisek Kubik
(50' Tamas Priskin), Seydouba Soumah, Adam Zrelak, Mitchell Schet.
Coach: Nicky Papavasiliou.
Goals: 27' Glebs Kluskins 1-0 (p), 48' Boriss Bogdaskins 2-0, 85' Olegs Malasenoks 3-0.
Referee: Ken Johnsen (NOR)   Attendance: 1,560.
Sent off: 89' Abdoulaye Diallo.

165

21.07.16   Bakcell Arena, Baku: Gabala FK – MTK Budapest 2-0 (2-0)
Gabala FK: Dmitro Bezotosniy, Vojislav Stankovic (88' Rafael Santos), Vitaliy Vernydub,
Ricardinho, Räsad Sadiqov, Nika Kvekveskiri (79' Elvin Jamalov), Magomed Mirzabekov,
Filip Ozobic, Theo Weeks, Sergei Zenjov (77' Asif Mammadov), Bagaliy Dabo.
Coach: Roman Grygorchuk.
MTK Budapest: Lajos Hegedüs, Akos Baki, Mato Grgic, Barnabas Bese (77' Szabolcs Varga),
Daniel Vadnai, Patrik Poor, Lorand Szatmari, Jozsef Kanta (72' Balint Borbely), Adam Vass,
Darko Nikac (52' Adam Hrepka), Sandor Torghelle. Coach: Vaszilisz Teodoru.
Goals: 7' Sergei Zenjov 1-0, 37' Theo Weeks 2-0.
Referee: Mete Kalkavan (TUR)   Attendance: 5,550.

21.07.16   Cukaricki, Belgrade: FK Cukaricki-Stankom – Videoton FC 1-1 (1-0)
FK Cukaricki-Stankom: Nemanja Stevanovic, Nikola Jankovic, Djordje Djuric, Stefan
Zivkovic, Marko Tomic, Marko Docic (65' Stanisa Mandic), Igor Matic, Obeng Regan (86'
Dragoljub Srnic), Erhan Masovic, Ismaël Fofana, Alen Masovic (65' Nemanja Radonjic).
Coach: Milan Lesnjak.
Videoton FC: Adam Kovacsik, Paulo Vinicius, Adam Lang, Stopira, Mate Patkai, Adam Bodi,
Roland Szolnoki, Krisztian Geresi (79' Robert Feczesin), Asmir Suljic, David Barczi, Adam
Simon (79' Filip Oliveira). Coach: Henning Berg.
Goals: 13' Ismaël Fofana 1-0, 76' Krisztian Geresi 1-1.
Referee: Alexandre Boucaut (BEL)   Attendance: 1,653.

21.07.16   Tynecastle, Edinburgh: Heart of Midlothian – Birkirkara FC 1-2 (0-0)
Heart of Midlothian: Jack Hamilton, Callum Paterson, Igor Rossi (74' Robbie Muirhead), Alim
Öztürk, Liam Smith (57' Juanma), Faycal Rherras, Prince Buaben (81' Jordan McGhee),
Arnaud Sutchuin Djoum, Sam Nicholson, Jamie Walker, Conor Sammon.
Coach: Robbie Neilson.
Birkirkara FC: Miroslav Kopric, Christian Bubalovic, Joseph Zerafa, Gareth Sciberras, Srdan
Dimitrov (73' Matthew Guillaumier), Shaun Bajada (66' Predrag Jovic), Ryan Scicluna (90+2'
Ryan Camenzuli), Cain Attard, Edward Herrera, Emerson, Vito Plut. Coach: Drazen Besek.
Goals: 55' Christian Bubalovic 0-1, 67' Edward Herrera 0-2, 74' Conor Sammon 1-2.
Referee: Ville Nevalainen (FIN)   Attendance: 14,301.

21.07.16   Brøndby Stadion, Brøndby: Brøndby IF – Hibernian FC 0-1 (0-0, 0-1)
Brøndby IF: Frederik Rønnow, Benedikt Röcker, Martin Albrechtsen, Johan Larsson, Svenn
Crone, Lebogang Phiri (102' Rezan Corlu), Christian Nørgaard, Kamil Wilczek, Andrew
Hjulsager, Christian Jakobsen (64' Frederik Holst), Teemu Pukki (114' Daniel Stückler).
Coach: Alexander Zorniger.
Hibernian FC: Ross Laidlaw, David Gray (77' Martin Boyle), Paul Hanlon, Liam Fontaine,
Darren McGregor, Marvin Bartley (104' Jordon Forster), John McGinn, Dylan McGeouch,
Lewis Stevenson, Grant Holt, Jason Cummings (90+1' James Keatings). Coach: Neil Lennon.
Goal: 62' David Gray 0-1.
Referee: Marius Avram (ROM)   Attendance: 11,548.

Brøndby IF won 5-3 on penalties following extra time.

*Penalties: Larsson 1-0, McGinn missed, Nørgaard 2-0, Hanlon 2-1, Stückler 3-1, Holt 3-2,
Wilczek 4-2, Boyle 4-3, Holst 5-3.*

21.07.16 Ventspils Stadions, Ventspils: FK Ventspils – Aberdeen FC 0-1 (0-0)
FK Ventspils: Maksims Uvarenko, Alans Sinelnikovs (65' Eduards Tidenbergs), Nikita
Kolesovs, Nikola Boranijasevic, Antons Jemelins, Rashid Abdul Obuobi, Simonas Paulius,
Vitalijs Recickis (86' Abdullahi Alfa), Ritvars Rugins, Aleksey Alekseev (81' Kaspars
Svarups), Girst Karlsons. Coach: Paul Ashworth.
Aberdeen FC: Joe Lewis, Shaleum Logan, Graeme Shinnie, Andrew Considine, Ash Taylor,
Mark Reynolds, Kenny McLean, Jonathan Hayes (82' Miles Storey), Ryan Jack, Adam
Rooney (80' Wes Burns), Niall McGinn (71' Jayden Stockley). Coach: Derek McInnes.
Goal: 79' Adam Rooney 0-1.
Referee: Danilo Grujic (SER)   Attendance: 2,100.

21.07.16 Antonis Papadopoulos, Larnaca: AEK Larnaca – Cliftonville FC 2-0 (1-0)
AEK Larnaca: Ruben Miño, Daniel Mojsov (46' André Alves), Català, Murillo, Jorge Larena,
Joan Tomas, Tete (77' Thomas Ioannou), Vladimir Boljevic, Juanma Ortiz, Costas
Charalambides, Ivan Trickovski (69' Nikos Englezou). Coach: Imanol Idiakez.
Cliftonville FC: Jason Mooney, Jamie McGovern, Levi Ives, Caoimhin Bonner, Christopher
Curran (75' Martin Murray), James Knowles, Ryan Catney, Jude Winchester (55' Stephen
Garrett), Tomas Cosgrove, David McDaid (15' Chris Ramsey), Jay Donnelly.
Coach: Gerry Lyttle.
Goals: 45' Vladimir Boljevic 1-0, 48' Joan Tomas 2-0.
Referee: Tihomir Pejin (CRO)   Attendance: 2,112.
Sent off: 12' Caoimhin Bonner.

21.07.16 Gamla Ullevi, Göteborg: IFK Göteborg – Piast Gliwice 0-0
IFK Göteborg: John Alvbåge, Emil Salomonsson, Haitam Aleesami, Thomas Rogne, Mattias
Bjärsmyr, Mads Albæk (69' Sebastian Eriksson), Søren Rieks (63' Jakob Ankersen), Tobias
Hysén (78' Viktor Sköld), Martin Smedberg, Tom Pettersson, Gustav Engvall.
Coach: Jörgen Lennartsson.
Piast Gliwice: Dobrivoj Rusov, Marcin Flis (69' Bartosz Szeliga), Tomasz Mokwa, Aleksandar
Sedlar, Pawel Moskwik, Michal Maslowski (73' Radoslaw Murawski), Mateusz Mak, Gerard
Badia, Martin Bukata, Uros Korun, Maciej Jankowski (81' Josip Barisic).
Coach: Radoslav Latal.
Referee: Georgios Kominis (GRE)   Attendance: 7,276.

21.07.16 Elbasan Arena, Elbasan: FK Kukësi – Austria Wien 1-4 (0-1)
FK Kukësi: Enea Kolici, Ylli Shameti, Rrahman Hallaçi, Renato Malota, Sabien Lilaj, Gledi
Mici, Liridon Latifi, Besar Musolli, Jean Carioca (46' Matija Dvornekovic), Rangel (33' Izair
Emini), Masato Fukui (61' Sindri Guri). Coach: Hasan Lika.
Austria Wien: Robert Almer, Petar Filipovic, Jens Stryger Larsen, Christoph Martschinko,
Lukas Rotpuller, Lucas Venuto, Tarkan Serbest, Roi Kehat, Raphael Holzhauser (79' Ognjen
Vukojevic), Olarenwaju Kayode (70' Marko Kvasina), Felipe Pires (79' Ismael Tajouri
Shradi). Coach: Thorsten Fink.
Goals: 16', 58' Olarenwaju Kayode 0-1, 0-2, 67' Raphael Holzhauser 0-3,
78' Rrahman Hallaçi 1-3, 90+4' Christoph Martschinko 1-4.
Referee: Vilhjalmur Alvar Thorarinsson (ISL)   Attendance: 3,000.

21.07.16 Letzigrund, Zürich: Grasshoppers Zürich – KR Reykjavík 2-1 (1-0)
Grasshoppers Zürich: Joël Mall, Alban Pnishi (63' Kim Källström), Numa Lavanchy, Jan
Bamert, Benjamin Lüthi, Runar Sigurjonsson, Marko Basic, Lucas Andersen (73' Florian
Kamberi), Mergim Brahimi, Caio (66' Nikola Gjorgjev), Ridge Munsy. Coach: Pierluigi Tami.
KR Reykjavík: Stefan Magnusson, Michael Præst Møller (72' Denis Fazlagic), Gunnar
Gunnarsson, Indridi Sigurdsson, Aron Josepsson, Morten Beck, Finnur Margeirsson, Palmi
Palmason, Oskar Hauksson (81' Gudmundur Andri Tryggvason), Morten Andersen, Kennie
Chopart. Coach: Willum Thorsson.
Goals: 45' Runar Sigurjonsson 1-0, 52' Morten Andersen 1-1, 68' Runar Sigurjonsson 2-1.
Referee: Erez Papir (ISR)   Attendance: 3,940.

THIRD QUALIFYING ROUND

28.07.16 Antonis Papadopoulos, Larnaca: AEK Larnaca – Spartak Moskva 1-1 (0-1)
AEK Larnaca: Ruben Miño, Daniel Mojsov, Català, Elias Charalambous (84' Thomas
Ioannou), Jorge Larena, Joan Tomas, Tete (76' Costas Charalambides), Vladimir Boljevic,
Juanma Ortiz, André Alves, Ivan Trickovski. Coach: Imanol Idiakez.
Spartak Moskva: Artem Rebrov, Salvatore Bocchetti, Ilya Kutepov, Andrey Eshchenko, Jano
Ananidze (72' Georgi Melkadze), Denis Glushakov, Quincy Promes, Dmitriy Kombarov,
Roman Zobnin, Zé Luís, Ivelin Popov (59' Aleksandr Zuev). Coach: Dmitriy Alenichev.
Goals: 38' Jano Ananidze 0-1, 65' André Alves 1-1.
Referee: Alejandro Hernandez Hernandez (ESP)   Attendance: 4,323.

28.07.16 Nika, Aleksandriya: FC Aleksandriya – Hajduk Split 0-3 (0-0)
FC Aleksandriya: Vladyslav Levanidov, Stanislav Mikitsey, Maksim Zhichikov (77' Dmytro
Leonov), Andriy Gitchenko, Anton Shendrik, Sergiy Basov, Andriy Zaporozhan, Eugene
Banada, Stanislav Kulish (62' Roman Yaremchuk), Vitali Ponomar, Mykhaylo Kozak (73'
Vasili Gritsuk). Coach: Volodymyr Sharan.
Hajduk Split: Lovre Kalinic, Maksim Beliy (64' Toma Basic), Jefferson, Zoran Nizic, Nikola
Vlasic (71' Ante Erceg), Josip Juranovic, Zvonimir Kozulj, Hrvoje Milic, Tino-Sven Susic,
Marko Cosic, Ahmed Said (68' Franck Ohandza). Coach: Marijan Pusnik.
Goals: 53' Marko Cosic 0-1, 82' Ante Erceg 0-2, 90' Franck Ohandza 0-3.
Referee: Gediminas Mazeika (LTU)   Attendance: 6,205.

28.07.16 Polman Stadion, Almelo: Heracles Almelo – FC Arouca 1-1 (0-0)
Heracles Almelo: Bram Castro, Tim Beukers, Mike te Wierik (74' Robin Pröpper), Ramon
Zomer, Robin Gosens, Iliass Bel Hassani, Thomas Bruns, Joey Pelupessy, Paul Gladon,
Jaroslav Navratil (81' Brahim Darri), Brandley Kuwas. Coach: John Stegeman.
FC Arouca: Rafael Bracalli, Hugo Basto, Gegé, Jubal, Nelsinho, Artur (50' Nuno Valente),
Adilson Goiano (55' André Santos), Nuno Coelho, Mateus, Zéquinha (88' Crivellaro), Walter
Gonzalez. Coach: Lito Vidigal.
Goals: 53' Paul Gladon 1-0, 90' Walter Gonzalez 1-1.
Referee: Charalambos Kalogeropoulos (GRE)   Attendance: 11,617.

Coach Lito Vidigal sent to the stands (90').

28.07.16   Stade Nord Lille Métropole, Villeneuve d'Ascq: Lille OSC – Gabala FK 1-1 (0-1)
Lille OSC: Vincent Enyeama, Sebastien Corchia, Renato Civelli, Julien Palmieri, Marko Basa, Mounir Obbadi (27' Yassine Benzia), Morgan Amalfitano, Eric Bautheac, Rony Lopes, Rio Mavuba (62' Ibrahim Amadou), Ryan Mendes (76' Yves Bissouma). Coach: Frederic Antonetti.
Gabala FK: Dmitro Bezotosniy, Vojislav Stankovic (76' Rafael Santos), Vitaliy Vernydub, Ricardinho, Räsad Sadiqov, Nika Kvekveskiri, Magomed Mirzabekov, Filip Ozobic, Theo Weeks, Sergei Zenjov (81' Asif Mammadov), Bagaliy Dabo (90+3' Rashad Eyyubov). Coach: Roman Grygorchuk.
Goals: 13' Vitaliy Vernydub 0-1, 47' Ryan Mendes 1-1.
Referee: Daniel Stefanski (POL)   Attendance: 8,265.

28.07.16   Skonto Stadions, Riga: FK Jelgava – Beitar Jerusalem 1-1 (0-1)
FK Jelgava: Kaspars Ikstens, Igors Savcenkovs, Vitalijs Smirnovs, Valerijs Redjko (28' Artjoms Osipovs), Gints Freimanis, Ryotaro Nakano, Boriss Bogdaskins, Mindaugas Grigaravicius (71' Andrejs Kovalovs), Glebs Kluskins (55' Andrejs Pereplotkins), Artis Lazdins, Olegs Malasenoks. Coach: Saulius Sirmelis.
Beitar Jerusalem: Boris Kleiman, Jesus Rueda, Dan Mori, Omer Atzily, Idan Vered, Dan Einbinder, Claudemir, Lidor Cohen (73' Shimon Abuhazira), Oz Rali (69' Tal Benesh), Ori Majabi, Itay Shechter (80' Marcel Heister). Coach: Ran Ben-Shimon.
Goals: 25' Idan Vered 0-1, 70' Vitalijs Smirnovs 1-1.
Referee: Georgi Kabakov (BUL)   Attendance: 2,886.

28.07.16   Ernst-Happel-Stadion, Vienna: Austria Wien – Spartak Trnava 0-1 (0-0)
Austria Wien: Robert Almer, Petar Filipovic, Jens Stryger Larsen, Christoph Martschinko, Lukas Rotpuller, Lucas Venuto, Tarkan Serbest, Roi Kehat (61' Alexander Grünwald), Raphael Holzhauser, Olarenwaju Kayode (85' Kevin Friesenbichler), Felipe Pires (72' Ismael Tajouri Shradi). Coach: Thorsten Fink.
Spartak Trnava: Adam Jakubech, Andrej Kadlec, Denis Hornik, Boris Godal, Lukas Gressak, Martin Mikovic (88' Kouakou Privat Yao), Anton Sloboda, Emir Halilovic (61' Erik Jirka), Bello Babatounde, Ivan Schranz, Robert Tambe (72' Matus Paukner). Coach: Miroslav Karhan.
Goal: 46' Robert Tambe 0-1.
Referee: Alexandru Tudor (ROM)   Attendance: 6,835.

28.07.16   Stadion Maksimir, Zagreb: Lokomotiva Zagreb – Vorskla Poltava 0-0
Lokomotiva Zagreb: Matko Kramer, Karlo Bartolec, Sinisa Rozman, Dino Peric, Luka Capan (80' Ivan Sunjic), Ante Majstorovic, Ivan Fiolic, Luka Ivanusec, Josip Coric, Eros Grezda (89' Endri Cekici), Mirko Maric (67' Dejan Radonjic). Coach: Valentin Barisic.
Vorskla Poltava: Bogdan Shust, Sergiy Simini (72' Vadim Sapay), Igor Perduta, Volodimir Chesnakov, Oleksiy Dytyatev, Aleksandr Sklyar, Aleksandr Kobakhidze, Andriy Tkachuk, Pavlo Rebenok (66' Mladen Bartulovic), Evgen Zarichnyuk (56' Yuriy Kolomoyets), Dmytro Khlyobas. Coach: Vasil Sachko.
Referee: Erik Lambrechts (BEL)   Attendance: 355.

28.07.16   Eden Arena, Prague: Slavia Praha – Rio Ave FC 0-0
Slavia Praha: Jiri Pavlenka, Jan Mikula, Jan Boril, Simon Deli, Jiri Bilek, Josef Husbauer, Levan Kenia (81' Jasmin Scuk), Jaroslav Mihalík (60' Jaromir Zmrhal), Tomás Soucek, Milan Skoda, Gino van Kessel. Coach: Dusan Uhrin.
Rio Ave FC: Cassio, Eliseu Cassama, Roderick Miranda, Marcelo, Rafa, Filip Krovinovic (69' Guedes), João Novais, Alhassan Wakaso, Gil Dias, Ruben Ribeiro (82' Tarantini), Yazalde (59' Heldon). Coach: Capucho.
Referee: Sergey Lapochkin (RUS)   Attendance: 15,082.

28.07.16   Stadion Zaglebia, Lubin: Zaglebie Lubin – SønderjyskE 1-2 (1-2)
Zaglebie Lubin: Martin Polacek, Maciej Dabrowski, Djordje Cotra, Aleksandar Todorovski,
Lubomir Guldan, Jaroslaw Kubicki, Lukasz Piatek, Jan Vlasko (46' Filip Starzynski),
Arkadiusz Wozniak, Lukasz Janoszka (73' Krzysztof Janus), Krzysztof Piatek (79' Michal
Papadopulos). Coach: Piotr Stokowiec.
SønderjyskE: Marin Skender, Marc Pedersen, Pierre Kanstrup, Matthias Maak, Simon Kroon
(69' Troels Kløve Hallstrøm), Janus Drachmann, Johan Absalonsen, Adama Guira, Marcel
Rømer (74' Nicolai Madsen), Marc Hende, Tommy Bechmann (64' Mikkel Uhre).
Coach: Jakob Michelsen.
Goals: 19' Simon Kroon 0-1, 36' Marc Hende 0-2, 45' Lukasz Janoszka 1-2.
Referee: Robert Madley (ENG)   Attendance: 10,271.

Filip Stazynski missed a penalty kick (62').

28.07.16   Torpedo, Zhodino: Torpedo-BalAZ Zhodino – Rapid Wien 0-0
Torpedo-BalAZ Zhodino: Valeriy Fomichev, Artem Chelyadinski, Evgeni Klopotskiy, Aleksey
Pankovets, Terentiy Lutsevich, Maksym Imerekov, Sergiy Shapoval, Andrey Khachaturyan,
Sergiy Zagynaylov (71' Anton Golenkov), Mikhail Afanasiev (87' Vladimir Shcherbo), Vadim
Demidovich (90+1' Aleksey Belevich). Coach: Igor Kriushenko.
Rapid Wien: Jan Novota, Christoph Schösswendter, Thomas Schrammel, Christopher Dibon,
Mario Pavelic, Philipp Schobesberger (70' Arnor Ingvi Traustason), Stefan Schwab, Louis
Schaub, Srdan Grahovac, Thomas Murg (85' Ivan Mocinic), Joelinton. Coach: Mike Büskens.
Referee: Thorvaldur Arnason (ISL)   Attendance: 3,940.

28.07.16   Gamla Ullevi, Gothenburg: IFK Göteborg – HJK Helsinki 1-2 (0-0)
IFK Göteborg: John Alvbåge, Emil Salomonsson, Haitam Aleesami, Sebastian Eriksson,
Thomas Rogne, Mattias Bjärsmyr (46' Hjalmar Jonsson), Mads Albæk, Søren Rieks, Jakob
Ankersen, Tobias Hysén (79' Gustav Engvall), Martin Smedberg (66' Patrik Karlsson-
Lagemyr). Coach: Jörgen Lennartsson.
HJK Helsinki: Thomas Dähne, Lum Rexhepi, Ivan Tatomirovic, Ville Jalasto, Medo, Atomu
Tanaka (77' Toni Kolehmainen), Anthony Annan, Sebastian Sorsa, Nikolai Alho, Alfredo
Morelos, Richard Gadze (87' Obed Malolo). Coach: Mika Lehkosuo.
Goals: 47' Atomu Tanaka 0-1, 73' Emil Salomonsson 1-1, 75' Alfredo Morelos 1-2.
Referee: Johnny Casanova (SMR)   Attendance: 9,046.

28.07.16   Hibernians Ground, Paola: Birkirkara FC – FK Krasnodar 0-3 (0-1)
Birkirkara FC: Miroslav Kopric, Christian Bubalovic, Joseph Zerafa, Gareth Sciberras, Srdan
Dimitrov (83' Matthew Guillaumier), Shaun Bajada (62' Frank Temile), Ryan Scicluna, Cain
Attard, Emerson, Dejan Djordjevic (62' Mislav Andjelkovic), Vito Plut. Coach: Drazen Besek.
FK Krasnodar: Stanislav Kritsyuk, Stefan Strandberg, Andreas Granqvist, Artur Jedrzejczyk,
Marat Izmailov, Dmitriy Torbinskiy, Yuri Gazinskiy, Odil Akhmedov (83' Joãozinho),
Mauricio Pereyra (64' Ricardo Laborde), Ari (76' Wanderson), Fedor Smolov.
Coach: Oleg Kononov.
Goals: 45' Andreas Granqvist 0-1, 75' Fedor Smolov 0-2 (p), 89' Ricardo Laborde 0-3.
Referee: Bart Vertenten (BEL)   Attendance: 1,560.
Sent off: 87' Ryan Scicluna.

28.07.16   Fatih Terim Stadium, Istanbul: Medipol Basaksehir FK – HNK Rijeka 0-0
Medipol Basaksehir FK: Volkan Babacan, Yalcin Ayhan, Alexandru Epureanu, Mahmut
Tekdemir, Ugur Ucar, Emre Belözoglu, Edin Visca, Doka Madureira (76' Cengiz Ünder), Eren
Albayrak, Samuel Holmen (58' Marcio Mossoro), Mehmet Batdal (85' Sokol Cikalleshi).
Coach: Abdullah Avci.
HNK Rijeka: Andrej Prskalo, Stefan Ristovski, Leonard Zuta, Matej Mitrovic, Josip Elez,
Marin Tomasov (79' Josip Misic), Mate Males, Filip Bradaric, Marko Vesovic (86' Haris
Handzic), Roman Bezjak, Mario Gavranovic (61' Florentin Matei). Coach: Matjaz Kek.
Referee: Svein Edvartsen (NOR)   Attendance: 7,371.

28.07.16   kybunpark, St. Gallen: Grasshoppers Zürich – Apollon Limassol 2-1 (1-0)
Grasshoppers Zürich: Joël Mall, Nemanja Antonov, Alban Pnishi, Jan Bamert, Benjamin
Lüthi, Kim Källström, Runar Sigurjonsson, Marko Basic, Lucas Andersen (77' Mergim
Brahimi), Haris Tabakovic (46' Ridge Munsy), Florian Kamberi (71' Numa Lavanchy).
Coach: Pierluigi Tami.
Apollon Limassol: Bruno Vale, Angelis Angeli, Paulo Vinicius, Alexandre, Bedoya (90+2'
Alejandro Barbaro), João Pedro, Charis Kyriakou, Marios Stylianou, Ioannis Pittas (63'
Esteban Sachetti), Giorgos Vasiliou, Abraham Guie-Guie (83' Anton Maglica).
Coach: Pedro Emanuel.
Goals: 11' Haris Tabakovic 1-0, 76' Abraham Guie-Guie 1-1, 90+3' Numa Lavanchy 2-1.
Referee: Andris Treimanis (LAT)   Attendance: 2,230.
Sent off: 87' Esteban Sachetti.

Alexandre missed a penalty kick (10').

28.07.16   swissporarena, Luzern: FC Luzern – Sassuolo Calcio 1-1 (1-1)
FC Luzern: David Zibung, Claudio Lustenberger, Tomislav Puljic, Ricardo Costa, Jahmir
Hyka (54' Simon Grether), Jakob Jantscher, Christian Schneuwly, Nicolas Haas, Markus
Neumayr, Marco Schneuwly, Cedric Itten (63' Tomi Juric). Coach: Markus Babbel.
Sassuolo Calcio: Andrea Consigli, Federico Peluso, Francesco Acerbi, Marcello Gazzola,
Paolo Cannavaro, Francesco Magnanelli, Davide Biondini, Alfred Duncan, Gregoire Defrel
(81' Diego Falcinelli), Nicola Sansone (72' Matteo Politano), Domenico Berardi (90' Luca
Mazzitelli). Coach: Eusebio Di Francesco.
Goals: 8' Marco Schneuwly 1-0, 42' Domenico Berardi 1-1 (p).
Referee: Andreas Ekberg (SWE)   Attendance: 10,555.

Markus Neumayr missed a penalty kick (65').

28.07.16   Apostolos Nikolaidis, Athen: Panathinaikos – AIK Solna 1-0 (0-0)
Panathinaikos: Luke Steele, Georgios Koutroubis (46' Lucas Villafañez), Giandomenico
Mesto, Rodrigo Moledo, Ivan Ivanov, Victor Ibarbo (89' Robin Lod), Zeca, Mubarak Wakaso
(71' Sebastian Leto), Niklas Hult, Cristian Ledesma, Markus Berg.
Coach: Andrea Stramaccioni.
AIK Solna: Patrik Carlgren, Haukur Hauksson, Per Karlsson, Nils-Eric Johansson, Patrick
Kpozo, Johan Blomberg, Ebenezer Ofori, Daniel Sundgren, Stefan Ishizaki (65' Ahmed
Yasin), Denni Avdic (87' Anton Saletros), Eero Markkanen. Coach: Rikard Norling.
Goal: 79' Rodrigo Moledo 1-0.
Referee: Bastian Dankert (GER)   Attendance: 12,021.

28.07.16   Osmanli Stadi, Ankara: Osmanlispor FK – JK Nõmme Kalju 1-0 (0-0)
Osmanlispor FK: Zydrunas Karcemarskas, Tiago Pinto, Vaclav Prochazka, Numan Cürüksu, Avdija Vrsajevic, Mehmet Güven, Papa N'Diaye, Aminu Umar, Pierre Webo (81' Cheick Diabate), Erdal Kilicarslan (71' Raul Rusescu), Dzon Delarge (89' Raheem Lawal). Coach: Mustafa Akcay.
JK Nõmme Kalju: Vitali Teles, Maximiliano Ugge, Jorge Rodrigues, Andrei Sidorenkov, Reginald Mbu-Alidor, Ats Purje (67' Tarmo Neemelo), Janar Toomet (75' Eino Puri), Artur Valikaev, Karl Mööl, Damiano Quintieri (64' Igor Subbotin), Artjom Dmitrijev. Coach: Sergey Frantsev.
Goal: 74' Tiago Pinto 1-0.
Referee: Nikola Dabanovic (MNE)   Attendance: 8,634.

28.07.16   Stadionul Municipal, Drobeta-Turnu Severin:
          Pandurii Targu Jiu – Maccabi Tel Aviv 1-3 (1-1)
Pandurii Targu Jiu: Razvan Stanca, Gordan Bunoza, Nikola Vasiljevic, Bogdan Ungurusan, Constantin Grecu, Marian Pleasca (80' Rodemis Trifu), Claudiu Voiculet, Ioan Hora, Ovidiu Herea (62' Valentin Munteanu), Filip Mrzljak (62' Chris Obodo), Alexandru Rautu. Coach: Petre Grigoras.
Maccabi Tel Aviv: Predrag Rajkovic, Eitan Tibi, Egor Filipenko, Haris Medunjanin (68' Eliel Peretz), Gal Alberman, Avi Rikan, Nosa Igiebor (79' Barak Itzhaki), Dor Peretz, Tal Ben Haim (II), Dor Mikha, Orlando Sá (75' Eden Ben Basat). Coach: Shota Arveladze.
Goals: 7' Tal Ben Haim (II) 0-1, 30' Ovidiu Herea 1-1, 49' Nosa Igiebor 1-2, 76' Dor Mikha 1-3.
Referee: Sergey Boyko (UKR)   Attendance: 4,899.

28.07.16   Karadjordje, Novi Sad: Vojvodina – Dinamo Minsk 1-1 (1-0)
Vojvodina: Marko Kordic, Vladimir Kovacevic, Nikola Antic, Darko Puskaric, Aleksandar Palocevic (87' Lazar Zlicic), Sinisa Babic, Filip Malbasic (71' Milos Trifunovic), Novica Maksimovic, Nemanja Miletic, Nikola Trujic (79' Dusan Jovancic), Dejan Meleg. Coach: Nenad Lalatovic.
Dinamo Minsk: Sergey Ignatovich, Yuriy Ostroukh, Mohamed El-Mounir (84' Anton Shramchenko), Sergey Kontsevoy, Aleksandr Sverchinski, Artem Bykov, Uladzimir Karytska, Valeriy Zhukovskiy (64' Sergei Karpovich), Oleksandr Noyok, Yuriy Gabovda, Luka Rotkovic (64' Yevhen Budnik). Coach: Sergey Borovskiy.
Goals: 29' Sinisa Babic 1-0, 83' Artem Bykov 1-1.
Referee: Oliver Drachta (AUT)   Attendance: 8,574.

28.07.16   Luminus Arena, Genk: KRC Genk – Cork City 1-0 (1-0)
KRC Genk: Marco Bizot, Sandy Walsh, Sebastien Dewaest, Dries Wouters, Jere Uronen, Thomas Buffel, Pozuelo (82' Bryan Heynen), Onyinye Ndidi, Nikolaos Karelis (73' Neeskens Kebano), Leon Bailey, Mbwana Samatta. Coach: Peter Maes.
Cork City: Mark McNulty, Alan Bennett, Michael McSweeney, Kenny Browne, Greg Bolger, Stephen Dooley, Kevin O'Connor, Gearoid Morrissey, Garry Buckley, Steven Beattie (83' Danny Morrissey), Sean Maguire (86' Mark O'Sullivan). Coach: John Caulfield.
Goal: 31' Leon Bailey 1-0.
Referee: Clayton Pisani (MLT)   Attendance: 12,332.

28.07.16   Nacionalna Arena Filip II Makedonski, Skopje:
KF Shkëndija 79 – FK Mladá Boleslav 2-0 (0-0)
KF Shkëndija 79: Kostadin Zahov, Egzon Bejtulai, Ardijan Cuculi, Armend Alimi (66' Victor Juffo), Ferhan Hasani, Besir Demiri, Blagoja Todorovski, Stephan Vujcic, Besart Ibraimi (81' Demir Imeri), Marjan Radeski (46' Sciprim Taipi), Stenio Junior. Coach: Bruno Akrapovic.
FK Mladá Boleslav: Jakub Divis, Jiri Fleisman, Ondrej Kudela, Lukas Pauschek, Lukas Hulka, Adam Janos, Jan Kalabiska, Jakub Rada, Miljan Vukadinovic, Lukas Magera (82' Laco Takacs), Golgol Mebrahtu (46' Jan Chramosta, 59' Miroslav Kerestes). Coach: Karel Jarolim.
Goals: 69' Stenio Junior 1-0, 75' Ferhan Hasani 2-0.
Referee: Artyom Kuchin (KAZ)   Attendance: 11,717.
Sent off: 52' Lukas Hulka.

28.07.16   Friedrich-Ludwig-Jahn-Sportpark, Berlin: Hertha BSC – Brøndby IF 1-0 (1-0)
Hertha BSC: Rune Jarstein, Peter Pekarík, Sebastian Langkamp, Marvin Plattenhardt, John Anthony Brooks, Per Skjelbred, Vladimir Darida, Mitchell Weiser, Fabian Lustenberger (90' Niklas Stark), Salomon Kalou (73' Genki Haraguchi), Vedad Ibisevic (87' Julian Schieber). Coach: Pál Dárdai.
Brøndby IF: Frederik Rønnow, Benedikt Röcker, Martin Albrechtsen, Frederik Holst (58' Hany Mukhtar), Johan Larsson, Svenn Crone, Lebogang Phiri, Christian Nørgaard (78' Rodolph Austin), Kamil Wilczek (84' Christian Jakobsen), Andrew Hjulsager, Teemu Pukki. Coach: Alexander Zorniger.
Goal: 28' Vedad Ibiseciv 1-0)
Referee: Kevin Blom (HOL)   Attendance: 18,454.

28.07.16   Puskas Akademia Pancho Arena, Felcsut: Videoton FC – FC Midtjylland 0-1 (0-0)
Videoton FC: Adam Kovacsik, Paulo Vinicius, Loïc Nego, Adam Lang, Stopira, Mate Patkai, Adam Bodi (61' Filip Oliveira), Roland Szolnoki, Krisztian Geresi (83' David Barczi), Asmir Suljic, Danko Lazovic (46' Robert Feczesin). Coach: Henning Berg.
FC Midtjylland: Johan Dahlin, Kian Hansen, Markus Halsti, Patrick Banggaard, Rasmus Nissen, Kristoffer Olsson, Pione Sisto (88' Mikkel Duelund), Rilwan Hassan, Filip Novák, Vaclav Kadlec (71' André Rømer), Ebere Onuachu. Coach: Jess Thorup.
Goal: 55' Filip Novák 0-1.
Referee: Ville Nevalainen (FIN)   Attendance: 2,899.

28.07.16   GHELAMCO-arena, Gent: KAA Gent – FC Viitorul Constanta 5-0 (2-0)
KAA Gent: Jacob Rinne, Stefan Mitrovic, Lasse Nielsen, Rami Gershon, Thomas Matton (65' Danijel Milicevic), Renato Neto, Sven Kums (76' Rob Schoofs), Kenny Saief, Thomas Foket, Kalifa Coulibaly, Laurent Depoitre (69' Jeremy Perbet). Coach: Hein Vanhaezebrouck.
FC Viitorul Constanta: Victor Ramniceanu, Romario Benzar, Bogdan Tiru, Ioan Filip (46' Robert Hodorogea), Florin Tanase, Gabriel Iancu (46' Dragos Nedelcu), Razvan Marin, Cristian Ganea, Florin Purece, Catalin Carp (70' Carlos Casap), Aurelian Chitu. Coach: Gheorghe Hagi.
Goals: 16' Stefan Mitrovic 1-0, 37', 50' Kalifa Coulibaly 2-0, 3-0, 56' Laurent Depoitre 4-0, 66' Renato Neto 5-0.
Referee: Stephan Klossner (SUI)   Attendance: 12,332.

173

28.07.16   AFAS Stadion, Alkmaar: AZ Alkmaar – PAS Giannina 1-0 (1-0)
AZ Alkmaar: Sergio Rochet, Mattias Johansson, Ron Vlaar, Ridgeciano Haps, Derrick
Luckassen, Joris van Overeem (87' Mats Seuntjens), Markus Henriksen, Stijn Wuytens,
Alireza Jahanbakhsh (63' Levi Garcia), Wout Weghorst (63' Fred Friday), Dabney dos Santos.
Coach: John van den Brom.
PAS Giannina: Alexandros Paschalakis, Andi Lila, Theodoros Berios, Alexandros Michail,
Nikos Karanikas, Themistoklis Tzimopoulos, Noe Acosta, Fonsi, Chrysovalantis Kozoronis
(61' Leonardo Koutris), Euripidis Giakos (74' Christos Donis), Dimitrios Ferfelis (50'
Christopher Maboulou). Coach: Giannis Petrakis.
Goal: 36' Derrick Luckassen 1-0.
Referee: Mattias Gestranius (FIN)   Attendance: 9,156.

28.07.16   Pittodrie Stadium, Aberdeen: Aberdeen FC – NK Maribor 1-1 (0-0)
Aberdeen FC: Joe Lewis, Shaleum Logan, Graeme Shinnie (72' Wes Burns), Andrew
Considine, Ash Taylor, Mark Reynolds, Jonathan Hayes, Ryan Jack, Adam Rooney, Niall
McGinn, Jayden Stockley (72' Kenny McLean). Coach: Derek McInnes.
NK Maribor: Jasmin Handanovic, Erik Janza, Marko Suler, Rodrigo Defendi, Denis Sme, Blaz
Vrhovec (68' Aleks Pihler), Dino Hotic (46' Damjan Bohar), Dare Vrsic (84' Gregor Bajde),
Marwan Kabha, Marcos Tavares, Milivoje Novakovic. Coach: Darko Milanic.
Goals: 83' Milivoje Novakovic 0-1, 88' Jonathan Hayes 1-1.
Referee: Tore Hansen (NOR)   Attendance: 17,105.

28.07.16   Stadion Stozice, Ljubljana: NK Domzale – West Ham United 2-1 (1-1)
NK Domzale: Axel Maraval, Alvaro Brachi, Gaber Dobrovoljc, Jure Balkovec, Kenan Horic,
Matic Crnic (90+1' Juninho), Lucas Horvat, Zan Majer (86' Amedej Vetrih), Marko Alvir,
Benjamin Morel (77' Jan Repas), Antonio Mance. Coach: Luka Elsner.
West Ham United: Adrian, Winston Reid, Håvard Nordtveit, Sam Byram, Sofiane Feghouli,
Cheikhou Kouyate, Pedro Obiang, Mark Noble, Michail Antonio (80' Domingos Quina), Andy
Carroll, Enner Valencia. Coach: Slaven Bilic.
Goals: 11' Matic Crnic 1-0 (p), 18' Mark Noble 1-1 (p), 49' Matic Crnic 2-1.
Referee: Mete Kalkavan (TUR)   Attendance: 8,458.

28.07.16   Stade Geoffroy Guichard, Saint-Étienne: AS Saint-Étienne – AEK Athen 0-0
AS Saint-Étienne: Stephane Ruffier, Kevin Theophile-Catherine, Pierre-Yves Polomat,
Florentin Pogba, Loïc Perrin, Vincent Pajot (69' Bryan Dabo), Ole Selnæs, Fabien Lemoine,
Nolan Roux, Oussama Tannane (64' Robert Beric), Romain Hamouma (86' Kevin Monnet-
Paquet). Coach: Christophe Galtier.
AEK Athen: Giannis Anestis, Rodrigo Galo, Dmitro Chigrinskiy, Didac Vila, Dimitrios
Kolovetsios, Helder Barbosa, Andre Simões, Ronald Vargas (67' Konstantinos Galanpoulos),
Jakob Johansson, Petros Mantalos (82' Vangelis Platellas), Tomas Pekhart (46' Anastasios
Bakasetas). Coach: Temur Ketsbaia.
Referee: Antonio Damato (ITA)   Attendance: 30,438.

174

28.07.16   BSFZ-Arena, Maria Endersdorf: FC Admira Wacker – Slovan Liberec 1-2 (1-1)
FC Admira Wacker: Manuel Kuttin, Fabio Strauss, Stephan Zwierschitz, Thomas Ebner,
Markus Wostry, Markus Lackner, Maximilian Sax, Christoph Knasmüllner, Daniel Toth (56'
Toni Vastic), Eldis Bajrami (56' Srdan Spiridonovic), Dominik Starkl. Coach: Oliver Lederer.
Slovan Liberec: Martin Dubravka, Vladimír Coufal, David Hovorka, Lukas Pokorny, Radim
Breite, Jan Sykora, Zdenek Folprecht, Petr Sevcik, Egon Vuch (88' Jan Navratil), Daniel Bartl
(78' Milan Nitriansky), Nikolay Komlichenko (60' Milan Baros). Coach: Jindrich Trpisovsky.
Goals: 7' Christoph Knasmüllner 1-0, 11', 69' Egon Vuch 1-1, 1-2.
Referee: Halis Özkahya (TUR)   Attendance: 2,245.
Sent off: 90+2' Toni Vastic.

03.08.16   U Nisy, Liberec: Slovan Liberec – FC Admira Wien 2-0 (2-0)
Slovan Liberec: Martin Dubravka, Vladimír Coufal, David Hovorka, Lukas Pokorny, Radim
Breite, Jan Sykora, Zdenek Folprecht, Petr Sevcik (83' Filip Lesniak), Egon Vuch, Daniel
Bartl (76' Jan Navratil), Nikolay Komlichenko (62' Milan Baros). Coach: Jindrich Trpisovsky.
FC Admira Wacker: Manuel Kuttin, Fabio Strauss, Stephan Zwierschitz, Thomas Ebner,
Markus Wostry, Philipp Posch, Markus Lackner (88' Ante Roguljic), Christoph Knasmüllner,
Eldis Bajrami, Srdan Spiridonovic, Dominik Starkl (62' Lukas Grozurek).
Coach: Oliver Lederer.
Goals: 20' Vladimír Coufal 1-0, 34' Nikolay Komlichenko 2-0 (p).
Referee: Radu Petrescu (ROM)   Attendance: 6,125.

04.08.16   Kadrioru staadion, Tallinn: JK Nõmme Kalju – Osmanlispor FK 0-2 (0-2)
JK Nõmme Kalju: Vitali Teles, Maximiliano Ugge, Jorge Rodrigues, Andrei Sidorenkov,
Reginald Mbu-Alidor, Ats Purje, Janar Toomet (46' Igor Subbotin), Artur Valikaev (79'
Hidetoshi Wakui), Karl Mööl, Damiano Quintieri (63' Tarmo Neemelo), Artjom Dmitrijev.
Coach: Sergey Frantsev.
Osmanlispor FK: Zydrunas Karcemarskas, Tiago Pinto, Vaclav Prochazka, Numan Cürüksu,
Avdija Vrsajevic, Mehmet Güven, Papa N'Diaye (54' Raheem Lawal), Aminu Umar (70'
Cheick Diabate), Erdal Kilicarslan, Raul Rusescu (79' Tugay Kacar), Dzon Delarge.
Coach: Mustafa Akcay.
Goals: 4' Numan Cürüksu 0-1, 29' Dzon Delarge 0-2.
Referee: Christin Dingert (GER)   Attendance: 2,235.

04.08.16   MCH Arena, Herning: FC Midtjylland – Videoton FC 1-1 (0-0, 0-1)
FC Midtjylland: Johan Dahlin, Kian Hansen, Markus Halsti, Patrick Banggaard, André Rømer
(80' Martin Pusic), Rasmus Nissen, Kristoffer Olsson (109' Marco Larsen), Rilwan Hassan,
Filip Novák, Vaclav Kadlec (69' Mikkel Duelund), Ebere Onuachu. Coach: Jess Thorup.
Videoton FC: Adam Kovacsik, Paulo Vinicius, Loïc Nego, Adam Lang, Stopira (12' Adam
Bodi), Roland Juhasz, Istvan Kovacs (91' Asmir Suljic), Mate Patkai, Roland Szolnoki,
Krisztian Geresi (67' Robert Feczesin), David Barczi. Coach: Henning Berg.
Goals: 75' Istvan Kovacs 0-1, 103' Filip Novák 1-1.
Referee: Marco Guida (ITA)   Attendance: 6,258.
Sent off: 47' Paulo Vinicius.

FC Midtjylland won after extra time.

04.08.16   Sonera Stadium, Helsinki: HJK Helsinki – IFK Göteborg 0-2 (0-1)
HJK Helsinki: Thomas Dähne, Ivan Tatomirovic, Ville Jalasto, Aapo Halme, Medo, Anthony Annan, Sebastian Sorsa, Nnamdi Oduamadi, Nikolai Alho, Alfredo Morelos, Richard Gadze (67' Toni Kolehmainen). Coach: Mika Lehkosuo.
IFK Göteborg: John Alvbåge, Emil Salomonsson, Haitam Aleesami, Sebastian Eriksson, Thomas Rogne, Mattias Bjärsmyr, Mads Albæk, Søren Rieks, Jakob Ankersen, Martin Smedberg (86' Tom Pettersson), Mikael Boman. Coach: Jörgen Lennartsson.
Goals: 35' Mikael Boman 0-1, 82' Jakob Ankersen 0-2.
Referee: Anatoliy Zhabchenko (UKR)   Attendance: 10,107.

04.08.16   Stadion Antona Malatinskeho, Trnava:
          Spartak Trnava – Austria Wien 0-1 (0-0, 0-1)
Spartak Trnava: Adam Jakubech, Andrej Kadlec, Denis Hornik, Boris Godal, Lukas Gressak, Martin Mikovic, Anton Sloboda, Emir Halilovic (97' Erik Jirka), Bello Babatounde, Ivan Schranz, Robert Tambe (79' Ivan Hladik). Coach: Miroslav Karhan.
Austria Wien: Robert Almer, Petar Filipovic, Jens Stryger Larsen, Christoph Martschinko, Lukas Rotpuller, Alexander Grünwald, Lucas Venuto (86' Marko Kvasina), Tarkan Serbest, Raphael Holzhauser (72' Kevin Friesenbichler), Olarenwaju Kayode, Felipe Pires (71' Ismael Tajouri Shradi). Coach: Thorsten Fink.
Goal: 88' Kevin Friesenbichler 0-1.
Referee: Ivan Bebek (CRO)   Attendance: 17,152.

Austria Wien won 5-4 on penalties following extra time.

Penalties: Stryger Larsen 0-1, Godal 1-1, Tajouri Shradi 1-2, Schranz 2-2, Kvasina 2-3, Sloboda 3-3, Serbest 3-4, Jirka 4-4, Friesenbichler 4-5, Mikovic missed.

04.08.16   Otkrytije Arena, Moskva: Spartak Moskva – AEK Larnaca 0-1 (0-0)
Spartak Moskva: Artem Rebrov, Salvatore Bocchetti, Ilya Kutepov, Evgeniy Makeev, Andrey Eshchenko (90+1' Lorenzo Melgarejo), Jano Ananidze (46' Denis Glushakov), Quincy Promes, Fernando, Dmitriy Kombarov, Roman Zobnin (68' Romulo), Zé Luís.
Coach: Dmitriy Alenichev.
AEK Larnaca: Ruben Miño, Daniel Mojsov, Català, Murillo (81' Costas Charalambides), Jorge Larena, Joan Tomas, Tete (89' Nikos Englezou), Vladimir Boljevic (84' Acoran), Juanma Ortiz, André Alves, Ivan Trickovski. Coach: Imanol Idiakez.
Goal: 89' Ivan Trickovski 0-1.
Referee: Alexander Harkam (AUT)   Attendance: 24,017.

04.08.16   Stadion Kuban, Krasnodar: FK Krasnodar – Birkirkara FC 3-1 (3-0)
FK Krasnodar: Andrey Sinitsyn, Stefan Strandberg, Aleksandr Martinovich, Sergey Petrov, Dmitriy Torbinskiy (79' Mauricio Pereyra), Vladimir Bystrov, Ricardo Laborde (40' Ari), Joãozinho, Kouassi Eboue, Charles Kabore (69' Yuri Gazinskiy), Wanderson.
Coach: Oleg Kononov.
Birkirkara FC: Miroslav Kopric, Christian Bubalovic, Joseph Zerafa, Gareth Sciberras, Srdan Dimitrov (77' Dejan Djordjevic), Shaun Bajada (46' Frank Temile), Cain Attard, Mislav Andjelkovic, Edward Herrera, Emerson (46' Predrag Jovic), Vito Plut. Coach: Drazen Besek.
Goals: 15' Kouassi Eboue 1-0, 37' Joãozinho 2-0, 38' Ricardo Laborde 3-0, 61' Predrag Jovic 3-1.
Referee: Aliyar Agayev (AZE)   Attendance: 7,256.

Wanderson missed a penalty kick (90').

04.08.16   Stadion Vorskla im. Olexiy Butovskiy, Poltava:
Vorskla Poltava – Lokomotiva Zagreb 2-3 (0-1)
Vorskla Poltava: Bogdan Shust, Igor Perduta, Volodimir Chesnakov, Oleksiy Dytyatev, Aleksandr Sklyar (70' Oleg Golodyuk), Aleksandr Kobakhidze, Andriy Tkachuk, Mladen Bartulovic, Vadim Sapay (60' Pavlo Rebenok), Dmytro Khlyobas (74' Evgen Zarichnyuk), Yuriy Kolomoyets. Coach: Vasil Sachko.
Lokomotiva Zagreb: Daniel Zagorac, Karlo Bartolec, Sinisa Rozman, Dino Peric, Luka Capan, Petar Bockaj (68' Endri Cekici), Ante Majstorovic, Ivan Fiolic (81' Ivan Sunjic), Josip Coric, Eros Grezda, Mirko Maric (65' Dejan Radonjic). Coach: Tomislav Ivkovic.
Goals: 1' Petar Bockaj 0-1, 49' Dino Peric 1-1 (og), 53' Ivan Fiolic 1-2, 64' Dino Peric 1-3, 74' Volodimir Chesnakov 2-3.
Referee: Orel Grinfeld (ISR)   Attendance: 12,000.

Dmytro Khlyobas missed a penalty kick (45').

04.08.16   Estadio Municipal de Arouca, Arouca: FC Arouca – Heracles Almelo 0-0
FC Arouca: Rafael Bracalli, Hugo Basto, Anderson Luiz, Gegé, Jubal, Nuno Valente (90+1' Adilson Goiano), André Santos (78' Marlon de Jesus), Nuno Coelho, Mateus, Zéquinha, Walter Gonzalez (69' Crivellaro). Coach: Lito Vidigal.
Heracles Almelo: Bram Castro, Tim Beukers, Mike te Wierik, Ramon Zomer (46' Justin Hoogma), Robin Gosens, Iliass Bel Hassani, Thomas Bruns (82' Robin Pröpper), Joey Pelupessy, Paul Gladon, Jaroslav Navratil, Brandley Kuwas (61' Daryl van Mieghem). Coach: John Stegeman.
Referee: Adrien Jaccottet (SUI)   Attendance: 2,750.

04.08.16   Dimotiko Peristeriou, Athen: PAS Giannina – AZ Alkmaar 1-2 (1-2)
PAS Giannina: Alexandros Paschalakis, Andi Lila, Theodoros Berios, Alexandros Michail, Nikos Karanikas, Themistoklis Tzimopoulos (46' Apostolos Skondras), Noe Acosta, Fonsi, Chrysovalantis Kozoronis (78' Christos Donis), Euripidis Giakos (51' Christopher Maboulou), Pedro Conde. Coach: Giannis Petrakis.
AZ Alkmaar: Sergio Rochet, Rens van Eijden, Ron Vlaar, Ridgeciano Haps, Derrick Luckassen, Joris van Overeem (71' Guus Til), Markus Henriksen, Stijn Wuytens, Alireza Jahanbakhsh, Wout Weghorst, Dabney dos Santos (79' Levi Garcia).
Coach: John van den Brom.
Goals: 9' Pedro Conde 1-0, 29' Dabney dos Santos 1-1, 36' Derrick Luckassen 1-2.
Referee: Robert Schörgenhofer (AUT)   Attendance: 3,373.

04.08.16   Teddy Kollek Stadium, Jerusalem: Beitar Jerusalem – FK Jelgava 3-0 (2-0)
Beitar Jerusalem: Boris Kleiman, Jesus Rueda, Dan Mori, Marcel Heister (57' Ori Majabi), Omer Atzily, Idan Vered (76' Shimon Abuhazira), Dan Einbinder, Claudemir, Lidor Cohen (66' David Keltjens), Oz Rali, Itay Shechter. Coach: Ran Ben-Shimon.
FK Jelgava: Kaspars Ikstens, Igors Savcenkovs, Vitalijs Smirnovs, Gints Freimanis, Ryotaro Nakano, Boriss Bogdaskins, Mindaugas Grigaravicius (71' Mareks Labanovskis), Glebs Kluskins (63' Olegs Malasenoks), Artis Lazdins, Andrejs Pereplotkins (54' Andrejs Kovalovs), Artjoms Osipovs. Coach: Saulius Sirmelis.
Goals: 16' Omer Atzili 1-0 (p), 29' Itay Shechter 2-0, 47' Marcel Heister 3-0.
Referee: Hugo Miguel (POR)   Attendance: 16,175.

177

04.08.16   Tele2 Arena, Stockholm: AIK Solna – Panathinaikos 0-2 (0-0)
AIK Solna: Patrik Carlgren, Haukur Hauksson, Per Karlsson, Nils-Eric Johansson, Jos
Hooiveld, Johan Blomberg (61' Ahmed Yasin), Ebenezer Ofori, Daniel Sundgren, Stefan
Ishizaki (78' Anton Saletros), Amin Affane (62' Denni Avdic), Eero Markkanen.
Coach: Rikard Norling.
Panathinaikos: Luke Steele, Georgios Koutroubis, Giandomenico Mesto, Rodrigo Moledo,
Ivan Ivanov, Victor Ibarbo (70' Sebastian Leto), Zeca, Robin Lod (84' Lucas Villafañez),
Mubarak Wakaso, Cristian Ledesma (67' Nano), Markus Berg. Coach: Andrea Stramaccioni.
Goals: 46' Victor Ibarco 0-1, 73' Marcus Berg 0-2.
Referee: Tony Chapron (FRA)   Attendance: 15,175.

04.08.16   Bakcell Arena, Baku: Gabala FK – Lille OSC 1-0 (1-0)
Gabala FK: Dmitro Bezotosniy, Vojislav Stankovic, Vitaliy Vernydub, Ricardinho, Räsad
Sadiqov, Nika Kvekveskiri, Magomed Mirzabekov, Filip Ozobic (77' Asif Mammadov), Theo
Weeks, Sergei Zenjov, Bagaliy Dabo. Coach: Roman Grygorchuk.
Lille OSC: Vincent Enyeama, Sebastien Corchia, Renato Civelli, Julien Palmieri, Adama
Soumaoro, Ibrahim Amadou, Mounir Obbadi (64' Younousse Sankhare), Morgan Amalfitano
(73' Yassine Benzia), Eric Bautheac (64' Ryan Mendes), Rony Lopes, Eder.
Coach: Frederic Antonetti.
Goal: 34' Filip Ozobic 1-0.
Referee: Aleksey Eskov (RUS)   Attendance: 10,550.

04.08.16   Mestsky stadion, Mlada Boleslav: FK Mladá Boleslav – KF Shkëndija 79 1-0 (0-0)
FK Mladá Boleslav: Jakub Divis, Jiri Fleisman, Douglas Silva, Ondrej Kudela, Lukas
Pauschek (46' Golgol Mebrahtu), Adam Janos, Jan Kalabiska (61' Miroslav Kerestes), Jakub
Rada, Miljan Vukadinovic (69' Laco Takacs), Lukas Magera, Jan Chramosta.
Coach: Karel Jarolim.
KF Shkëndija 79: Kostadin Zahov, Egzon Bejtulai, Ardijan Cuculi, Armend Alimi (54' Artim
Polozani), Ferhan Hasani, Besir Demiri, Blagoja Todorovski, Stephan Vujcic, Besart Ibraimi,
Marjan Radeski (75' Sciprim Taipi), Stenio Junior (85' Besmir Bojku).
Coach: Bruno Akrapovic.
Goal: 82' Lukas Magera 1-0.
Referee: Simon Evans (WAL)   Attendance: 3,528.

04.08.16   Neo GSP, Nicosia: Apollon Limassol – Grasshoppers Zürich 3-3 (0-0, 2-1)
Apollon Limassol: Bruno Vale, Angelis Angeli, Paulo Vinicius, Alexandre, Bedoya, João
Pedro, Charis Kyriakou (68' Fotis Papoulis), Marios Stylianou, Giorgos Vasiliou (84' Dudu
Paraiba), Abraham Guie-Guie, Anton Maglica (39' Arkadiusz Piech). Coach: Pedro Emanuel.
Grasshoppers Zürich: Joël Mall, Alban Pnishi, Numa Lavanchy, Jan Bamert, Benjamin Lüthi,
Kim Källström (91' Nikola Gjorgjev), Runar Sigurjonsson (90+4' Mergim Brahimi), Marko
Basic, Lucas Andersen, Caio, Ridge Munsy (86' Haris Tabakovic). Coach: Pierluigi Tami.
Goals: 73' Paulo Vinicius 1-0, 77' Lucas Andersen 1-1, 87' Fotis Papoulis 2-1,
101' Abraham Guie-Guie 3-1, 103' Caio 3-2, 120+2' Nikola Gjorgjev 3-3.
Referee: Andre Marriner (ENG)   Attendance: 5,887.

Grasshoppers Zürich won after extra time.

04.08.16   Sydbank Park, Haderslev: SønderjyskE – Zaglebie Lubin 1-1 (0-1)
SønderjyskE: Marin Skender, Marc Pedersen, Pierre Kanstrup, Matthias Maak, Simon Kroon
(76' Troels Kløve Hallstrøm), Nicolai Madsen, Johan Absalonsen, Adama Guira, Marcel
Rømer, Marc Hende, Tommy Bechmann (81' Mikkel Uhre). Coach: Jakob Michelsen.
Zaglebie Lubin: Martin Polacek, Maciej Dabrowski, Djordje Cotra, Aleksandar Todorovski,
Lubomir Guldan, Krzysztof Janus (67' Lukasz Janoszka), Filip Starzynski, Jaroslaw Kubicki,
Lukasz Piatek, Jan Vlasko (85' Jakub Tosik), Krzysztof Piatek (72' Michal Papadopulos).
Coach: Piotr Stokowiec.
Goals: 22' Lubomir Guldan 0-1, 65' Marc Pedersen 1-1.
Referee: Tamas Bognar (HUN)   Attendance: 4,795.

04.08.16   Netanya Stadium, Netanya: Maccabi Tel Aviv – Pandurii Targu Jiu 2-1 (1-0)
Maccabi Tel Aviv: Predrag Rajkovic, Elazar Dasa, Eitan Tibi, Egor Filipenko, Haris
Medunjanin, Gal Alberman (59' Oscar Scarione), Avi Rikan, Nosa Igiebor, Yossi Benayoun
(82' Eden Ben Basat), Dor Mikha, Orlando Sá (72' Barak Itzhaki). Coach: Shota Arveladze.
Pandurii Targu Jiu: David Lazar, Gordan Bunoza, Jordy Buijs (71' Rodemis Trifu), Nikola
Vasiljevic, Marian Pleasca, Valentin Munteanu (46' Claudiu Voiculet), Ovidiu Herea, Andrei
Pitian, Filip Mrzljak, Alexandru Rautu, Adelin Pircalabu (79' Constantin Grecu).
Coach: Petre Grigoras.
Goals: 24' Nosa Igiebor 1-0, 57' Marian Pleasca 1-1, 80' Oscar Scarione 2-1.
Referee: Serge Gumienny (BEL)   Attendance: 8,126.

04.08.16   OSK Brestksy, Brest: Dinamo Minsk – Vojvodina 0-2 (0-1)
Dinamo Minsk: Sergey Ignatovich, Yuriy Ostroukh, Mohamed El-Mounir, Sergei Karpovich,
Sergey Kontsevoy, Aleksandr Sverchinski, Artem Bykov, Uladzimir Karytska (70' Valeriy
Zhukovskiy), Oleksandr Noyok, Yuriy Gabovda, Yevhen Budnik (84' Luka Rotkovic).
Coach: Sergey Borovskiy.
Vojvodina: Marko Kordic, Vladimir Kovacevic, Nikola Antic, Darko Puskaric, Aleksandar
Palocevic, Sinisa Babic (74' Milos Trifunovic), Filip Malbasic, Novica Maksimovic, Nemanja
Miletic, Nikola Trujic (84' Dusan Micic), Dejan Meleg (85' Dusan Jovancic).
Coach: Nenad Lalatovic.
Goals: 32' Sinisa Babic 0-1, 82' Nikola Antic 0-2.
Referee: Sebastien Delferiere (BEL)   Attendance: 7,500.
Sent off: 55' Mohamed El-Mounir.

04.08.16   OAKA Spiros Louis, Athen: AEK Athen – AS Saint-Étienne 0-1 (0-1)
AEK Athen: Giannis Anestis, Vassilios Lambropoulos, Rodrigo Galo, Dmitro Chigrinskiy,
Didac Vila, Dimitrios Kolovetsios, Helder Barbosa (61' Christos Aravidis), Andre Simões (67'
Hugo Almeida), Ronald Vargas (53' Vangelis Platellas), Petros Mantalos, Anastasios
Bakasetas. Coach: Temur Ketsbaia.
AS Saint-Étienne: Stephane Ruffier, Kevin Theophile-Catherine, Pierre-Yves Polomat,
Florentin Pogba, Loïc Perrin, Bryan Dabo (30' Vincent Pajot), Ole Selnæs, Fabien Lemoine
(79' Kevin Monnet-Paquet), Oussama Tannane, Romain Hamouma (84' Nolan Roux), Robert
Beric. Coach: Christophe Galtier.
Goal: 23' Robert Beric 0-1.
Referee: Alon Yefet (ISR)   Attendance: 25,004.

04.08.16   Brøndby Stadion, Brøndby: Brøndby IF – Hertha BSC 3-1 (2-1)
Brøndby IF: Frederik Rønnow, Benedikt Röcker, Martin Albrechtsen, Johan Larsson, Svenn
Crone, Hany Mukhtar (67' Christian Jakobsen), Lebogang Phiri, Christian Nørgaard (76'
Rodolph Austin), Kamil Wilczek, Andrew Hjulsager, Teemu Pukki (76' Marco Ureña).
Coach: Alexander Zorniger.
Hertha BSC: Thomas Kraft, Peter Pekarík (84' Valentin Stocker), Sebastian Langkamp,
Marvin Plattenhardt, John Anthony Brooks, Per Skjelbred (62' Niklas Stark), Vladimir Darida,
Mitchell Weiser, Fabian Lustenberger (62' Sami Allagui), Salomon Kalou, Vedad Ibisevic.
Coach: Pál Dárdai.
Goals: 3' Teemu Pukki 1-0, 30' Vedad Ibisevic 1-1, 34', 52' Teemu Pukki 2-1, 3-1.
Referee: Pawel Gil (POL)   Attendance: 17,102.

04.08.16   Stadion HNK Rijeka, Rijeka: HNK Rijeka – Medipol Basaksehir FK 2-2 (1-1)
HNK Rijeka: Andrej Prskalo, Stefan Ristovski (90+3' Dario Canadija), Leonard Zuta, Matej
Mitrovic, Josip Elez, Marin Tomasov, Mate Males, Josip Misic (83' Haris Handzic), Marko
Vesovic (67' Florentin Matei), Roman Bezjak, Mario Gavranovic. Coach: Matjaz Kek.
Medipol Basaksehir FK: Volkan Babacan, Yalcin Ayhan, Alexandru Epureanu, Mahmut
Tekdemir, Ugur Ucar (64' Cenk Alkilic), Emre Belözoglu, Edin Visca, Marcio Mossoro (84'
Samuel Holmen), Doka Madureira (64' Cengiz Ünder), Eren Albayrak, Mehmet Batdal.
Coach: Abdullah Avci.
Goals: 24' Roman Bezjak 1-0, 42' Edin Visca 1-1, 50' Roman Bezjak 2-1 (p),
74' Edin Visca 2-2.
Referee: Marius Avram (ROM)   Attendance: 5,524.

04.08.16   Stadionul Central, Ovidiu: FC Viitorul Constanta – KAA Gent 0-0
FC Viitorul Constanta: Alexandru Buzbuchi, Sorin Radoi, Dragos Nedelcu, Robert Hodorogea,
Carlos Casap (65' Razvan Marin), Gabriel Iancu (77' Doru Dumitrescu), Dani Lopez, Pablo
Brandan, Catalin Carp, Vlad Rusu (46' Florin Tanase), Alex Nimely-Tchuimeni.
Coach: Gheorghe Hagi.
KAA Gent: Yannick Thoelen, Stefan Mitrovic (46' Lasse Nielsen), Siebe Horemans, Rami
Gershon, Renato Neto (64' Lucas Schoofs), Kenny Saief, Rob Schoofs, Thomas Foket (72'
Dieumerci Ndongala), Danijel Milicevic, Emir Kujovic, Jeremy Perbet.
Coach: Hein Vanhaezebrouck.
Referee: Carlos Del Cerro Grande (ESP)   Attendance: 1,294.

04.08.16   Stadion Ljudski vrt, Maribor: NK Maribor – Aberdeen FC 1-0 (0-0)
NK Maribor: Jasmin Handanovic, Erik Janza, Marko Suler, Rodrigo Defendi, Denis Sme, Blaz
Vrhovec, Aleks Pihler (77' Marwan Kabha), Dare Vrsic (89' Sintayehu Sallalich), Damjan
Bohar (74' Gregor Bajde), Marcos Tavares, Milivoje Novakovic. Coach: Darko Milanic.
Aberdeen FC: Joe Lewis, Shaleum Logan, Graeme Shinnie, Andrew Considine, Ash Taylor,
Mark Reynolds, Kenny McLean (66' Miles Storey), Ryan Jack, Wes Burns (51' Jayden
Stockley), Adam Rooney, Niall McGinn (84' Scott Wright). Coach: Derek McInnes.
Goal: 90+4' Graeme Shinnie 1-0 (og).
Referee: Nikola Popov (BUL)   Attendance: 9,796.
Sent off: 61' Jayden Stockley.

04.08.16   MAPEI Stadium - Citta del Tricolore, Reggio Emilia:
          Sassuolo Calcio – FC Luzern 3-0 (2-0)
Sassuolo Calcio: Andrea Consigli, Federico Peluso, Francesco Acerbi, Marcello Gazzola,
Paolo Cannavaro, Francesco Magnanelli, Davide Biondini (72' Stefano Sensi), Alfred Duncan,
Gregoire Defrel (82' Diego Falcinelli), Nicola Sansone, Domenico Berardi (72' Matteo
Politano). Coach: Eusebio Di Francesco.
FC Luzern: David Zibung, Claudio Lustenberger, Tomislav Puljic (11' Sally Sarr), Ricardo
Costa, Jahmir Hyka (72' João Oliveira), Jakob Jantscher, Christian Schneuwly, Hekuran
Kryeziu, Nicolas Haas, Markus Neumayr (72' Remo Arnold), Marco Schneuwly.
Coach: Markus Babbel.
Goals: 19', 39' Domenico Berardi 1-0, 2-0 (p), 64' Gregoire Defrel 3-0.
Referee: Ali Palabiyik (TUR)   Attendance: 13,415.
Sent off: 38' Ricardo Costa.

04.08.16   Stadion Poljud, Split: Hajduk Split – FC Aleksandriya 3-1 (1-1)
Hajduk Split: Lovre Kalinic, Maksim Beliy (61' Toma Basic), Jefferson, Zoran Nizic, Nikola
Vlasic, Josip Juranovic, Zvonimir Kozulj, Hrvoje Milic, Tino-Sven Susic (77' Fran Tudor),
Marko Cosic, Ahmed Said (66' Franck Ohandza). Coach: Marijan Pusnik.
FC Aleksandriya: Andriy Novak, Stanislav Mikitsey, Pavlo Myagkov, Andriy Tsurikov,
Andriy Gitchenko, Anton Shendrik, Sergey Starenkiy (57' Yuriy Putrash), Eugene Banada,
Vitali Ponomar (46' Vasili Gritsuk), Roman Yaremchuk (73' Stanislav Kulish), Mykhaylo
Kozak. Coach: Volodymyr Sharan.
Goals: 13' Sergey Starenkly 0-1, 21' Zoran Nizic 1-1, 52', 56' Tino-Sven Susic 2-1 (p), 3-1.
Referee: John Beaton (SCO)   Attendance: 25,000.

04.08.16   Turner's Cross, Cork: Cork City – KRC Genk 1-2 (0-2)
Cork City: Mark McNulty, Alan Bennett, Michael McSweeney (46' Mark O'Sullivan), Kenny
Browne, Greg Bolger, Stephen Dooley, Kevin O'Connor, Gearoid Morrissey (46' Danny
Morrissey), Garry Buckley, Steven Beattie, Sean Maguire (56' Karl Sheppard).
Coach: John Caulfield.
KRC Genk: Marco Bizot, Sandy Walsh, Sebastien Dewaest, Dries Wouters, Jere Uronen,
Thomas Buffel (83' Holly Tshimanga), Pozuelo, Onyinye Ndidi, Neeskens Kebano, Leon
Bailey (65' Leandro Trossard), Mbwana Samatta (77' Bryan Heynen). Coach: Peter Maes.
Goals: 13' Thomas Buffel 0-1, 41' Sebastien Dewaest 0-2, 63' Alan Bennett 1-2.
Referee: Kristo Tohver (EST)   Attendance: 6,745.

Neeskens Kebano missed a penalty kick (90+2').

04.08.16   London Stadium, London: West Ham United – NK Domzale 3-0 (2-0)
West Ham United: Darren Randolph, Winston Reid, Håvard Nordtveit, Sam Byram, Reece
Oxford, Sofiane Feghouli (87' Domingos Quina), Cheikhou Kouyate (79' Pedro Obiang),
Mark Noble, Michail Antonio, Andy Carroll (90' Ashley Fletcher), Enner Valencia.
Coach: Slaven Bilic.
NK Domzale: Axel Maraval, Alvaro Brachi, Gaber Dobrovoljc, Jure Balkovec, Kenan Horic,
Matic Crnic, Lucas Horvat (62' Zeni Husmani), Zan Majer (77' Juninho), Marko Alvir,
Benjamin Morel, Antonio Mance (68' Elvis Bratanovic). Coach: Luka Elsner.
Goals: 8', 25' Cheikhou Kouyate 1-0, 2-0, 81' Sofiane Feghouli 3-0.
Referee: Fredy Fautrel (FRA)   Attendance: 53,914.

04.08.16   Estadio do Rio Ave FC, Vila Do Conde: Rio Ave FC – Slavia Praha 1-1 (0-1)
Rio Ave FC: Cassio, Eliseu Cassama, Roderick Miranda, Marcelo, Rafa, Filip Krovinovic (46'
Pedrinho), João Novais (61' Heldon), Alhassan Wakaso, Gil Dias, Ruben Ribeiro, Yazalde
(46' Tarantini). Coach: Capucho.
Slavia Praha: Jiri Pavlenka, Jan Mikula, Michael Ngadeu-Ngadjui (90+2' Antonin Barak), Jan
Boril, Simon Deli, Jiri Bilek, Jaromir Zmrhal (90+6' Jaroslav Mihalík), Josef Husbauer, Tomás
Soucek, Milan Skoda, Gino van Kessel (66' Jasmin Scuk). Coach: Dusan Uhrin.
Goals: 22' Josef Husbauer 0-1, 57' Ruben Ribeiro 1-1.
Referee: Andrew Dallas (SCO)   Attendance: 6,081.
Sent off: 45+1' Eliseu Cassama.

04.08.16   Allianz Stadion, Vienna: Rapid Wien – Torpedo-BalAZ Zhodino 3-0 (2-0)
Rapid Wien: Jan Novota, Christoph Schösswendter, Thomas Schrammel, Christopher Dibon,
Mario Pavelic, Stefan Schwab, Louis Schaub, Arnor Ingvi Traustason (68' Srdan Grahovac),
Ivan Mocinic (80' Tamas Szanto), Thomas Murg, Joelinton (71' Philipp Schobesberger).
Coach: Mike Büskens.
Torpedo-BalAZ Zhodino: Valeriy Fomichev, Artem Chelyadinski, Evgeni Klopotskiy, Aleksey
Pankovets (46' Vladimir Shcherbo), Terentiy Lutsevich, Maksym Imerekov, Sergiy Shapoval,
Andrey Khachaturyan, Sergiy Zagynaylov (57' Denis Trapashko), Mikhail Afanasiev (66'
Pavel Chelyadko), Vadim Demidovich. Coach: Igor Kriushenko.
Goals: 26' Mario Pavelic 1-0, 36' Thomas Schrammel 2-0, 90+2' Louis Schaub 3-0.
Referee: Roy Reinshreiber (ISR)   Attendance: 18,640.

PLAY-OFFS

17.08.16   Teddy Kollek Stadium, Jerusalem: Beitar Jerusalem – AS Saint-Étienne 1-2 (1-2)
Beitar Jerusalem: Boris Kleiman, Jesus Rueda, Dan Mori, Marcel Heister, Omer Atzily, Idan
Vered (82' Johan Audel), Dan Einbinder, Claudemir, Lidor Cohen (59' Shimon Abuhazira),
Oz Rali, Itay Shechter (82' David Keltjens). Coach: Ran Ben-Shimon.
AS Saint-Étienne: Stephane Ruffier, Kevin Theophile-Catherine, Pierre-Yves Polomat,
Florentin Pogba, Loïc Perrin, Vincent Pajot, Ole Selnæs, Fabien Lemoine, Romain Hamouma
(46' Nolan Roux), Kevin Monnet-Paquet, Robert Beric (78' Oussama Tannane).
Coach: Christophe Galtier.
Goals: 8' Idan Vered 1-0, 15' Fabien Lemoine 1-1, 30' Jesus Rueda (1-2) (og).
Referee: Michael Oliver (ENG)   Attendance: 25,049.

18.08.16   Astana Arena, Astana: FK Astana – BATE Borisov 2-0 (0-0)
FK Astana: Nenad Eric, Marin Anicic, Abzal Beysebekov, Sergiy Maliy, Yuriy Logvinenko,
Nemanja Maksimovic, Serikzhan Muzhikov, Roger Cañas, Agim Ibraimi (63' Azat Nurgaliev),
Patrick Twumasi (89' Askhat Tagybergen), Junior Kabananga (84' Djordje Despotovic).
Coach: Stanimir Stoilov.
BATE Borisov: Sergey Veremko, Vitaly Gayduchik, Maksim Zhavnerchik, Denis Polyakov,
Aleksandr Karnitskiy (80' Nikolay Signevich), Aleksey Rios, Mikhail Gordeychuk, Yuri
Kendysh, Valeriane Gvilia (46' Evgeni Yablonski), Aliaksandr Hleb (39' Mirko Ivanic),
Vitaliy Rodionov. Coach: Aleksandr Yermakovich.
Goals: 70' Junior Kabananga 1-0, 80' Azat Nurgaliev 2-0.
Referee: Sebastien Delferiere (BEL)   Attendance: 17,536.

18.08.16   Boris Paichadze Dinamo Arena, Tbilisi: Dinamo Tbilisi – PAOK Saloniki 0-3 (0-1)
Dinamo Tbilisi: Anthony Scribe, Ucha Lobjanidze (58' Giorgi Tevzadze), Aleksandr
Amisulashvili, Mate Tsintsadze (70' Mikel Alvaro), Vakhtang Chanturishvili, Giorgi
Papunashvili (63' Vladimir Dvalishvili), Otari Kiteishvili, Lasha Parunashvili, Rene, Jambul
Jigauri, Zaza Chelidze. Coach: Juraj Jarabek.
PAOK Saloniki: Panagiotis Glykos, Leo Matos, Marin Leovac, Angel Crespo, Giorgos
Tzavellas, Charilaos Charisis (46' Cañas), Gojko Cimirot, Garry Rodrigues, Yevhen Shakhov
(68' Diego Biseswar), Djalma (81' Facundo Pereyra), Stefanos Athanasiadis.
Coach: Vladimir Ivic.
Goals: 20' Leo Matos 0-1, 71' Angel Crespo 0-2, 83' Facundo Pereyra 0-3.
Referee: Liran Liany (ISR)   Attendance: 12,006.

18.08.16   Sydbank Park, Haderslev: SønderjyskE – Sparta Praha 0-0
SønderjyskE: Marin Skender, Marc Pedersen, Pierre Kanstrup, Matthias Maak, Janus
Drachmann, Nicolai Madsen, Johan Absalonsen, Adama Guira, Marcel Rømer (73' Simon
Kroon), Marc Hende, Mikkel Uhre (74' Troels Kløve Hallstrøm). Coach: Jakob Michelsen.
Sparta Praha: Tomas Koubek, Ondrej Mazuch, Michal Kadlec, Costa Nhamoinesu, Ondrej
Zahustel, Lukas Vacha, Borek Dockal, Lukas Marecek, Daniel Holzer (46' Martin Frydek),
Josef Sural (80' Matej Pulkrab), Lukas Julis. Coach: Zdenek Scasny.
Referee: Hüseyin Göcek (TUR)   Attendance: 4,795.

18.08.16   MCH Arena, Herning: FC Midtjylland – Osmanlispor FK 0-1 (0-1)
FC Midtjylland: Johan Dahlin, Kian Hansen, Markus Halsti (61' André Rømer), Patrick
Banggaard, Rasmus Nissen, Jakob Poulsen, Kristoffer Olsson (53' Martin Pusic), Rilwan
Hassan, Filip Novák, Vaclav Kadlec, Ebere Onuachu (78' Mikkel Duelund).
Coach: Jess Thorup.
Osmanlispor FK: Zydrunas Karcemarskas, Tiago Pinto, Vaclav Prochazka, Numan Cürüksu,
Avdija Vrsajevic, Mehmet Güven, Raheem Lawal (61' Musa Cagiran), Papa N'Diaye, Pierre
Webo (77' Muhammed Bayir), Erdal Kilicarslan (77' Raul Rusescu), Dzon Delarge.
Coach: Mustafa Akcay.
Goal: 20' Patrick Banggaard 0-1 (og).
Referee: Istvan Kovacs (ROM)   Attendance: 7,003.

18.08.16   Stadion Kuban, Krasnodar: FK Krasnodar – FK Partizani 4-0 (3-0)
FK Krasnodar: Stanislav Kritsyuk, Aleksandr Martinovich, Andreas Granqvist, Vitaliy
Kaleshin, Artur Jedrzejczyk, Odil Akhmedov (66' Kouassi Eboue), Joãozinho, Mauricio
Pereyra (61' Yuri Gazinskiy), Charles Kabore, Ari, Fedor Smolov (76' Dmitriy Torbinskiy).
Coach: Oleg Kononov.
FK Partizani: Alban Hoxha, Gëzim Krasniqi, Labinot Ibrahimi (64' Arbnor Fejzullahu),
Renato Arapi, Idriz Batha, Jurgen Bardhi (64' Realdo Fili), Ylber Ramadani, Lorenc Trashi,
Emiljano Vila, Agustin Torassa, Caleb Ekuban. Coach: Adolfo Sormani.
Goals: 18' Joãozinho 1-0 (p), 27' Fedor Smolov 2-0, 45' Artur Jedrzejczyk 3-0,
73' Gezim Krasniqi 4-0 (og).
Referee: Gediminas Mazeika (LTU)   Attendance: 11,575.

183

18.08.16   Dalga Arena, Baku: Gabala FK – NK Maribor 3-1 (1-1)
Gabala FK: Dmitro Bezotosniy, Vojislav Stankovic, Vitaliy Vernydub (90' Elvin Jamalov),
Ricardinho, Rafael Santos, Nika Kvekveskiri, Magomed Mirzabekov, Filip Ozobic (81' Asif
Mammadov), Theo Weeks (90+2' Rashad Eyyubov), Sergei Zenjov, Bagaliy Dabo.
Coach: Roman Grygorchuk.
NK Maribor: Jasmin Handanovic, Erik Janza, Marko Suler, Rodrigo Defendi, Denis Sme, Blaz
Vrhovec, Aleks Pihler, Dare Vrsic (72' Gregor Bajde), Damjan Bohar (72' Sintayehu
Sallalich), Marcos Tavares (81' Sunny Omoregie), Milivoje Novakovic.
Coach: Darko Milanic.
Goals: 18' Marcos Tavares 0-1, 38' Sergei Zenjov 1-1, 51', 52' Bagaliy Dabo 2-1, 3-1.
Referee: Aleksey Kulbakov (BLS)   Attendance: 4,723.

18.08.16   Eden Arena, Prague: Slavia Praha – RSC Anderlecht 0-3 (0-0)
Slavia Praha: Jiri Pavlenka, Jan Mikula (9' Michal Frydrych), Michael Ngadeu-Ngadjui, Jan
Boril, Simon Deli, Jiri Bilek, Levan Kenia (78' Muris Mesanovic), Antonin Barak (67' Ruslan
Mingazov), Dusan Svento, Milan Skoda, Gino van Kessel. Coach: Dusan Uhrin.
RSC Anderlecht: Davy Roef, Dennis Appiah (73' Michaël Heylen), Bram Nuytinck, Dennis
Praet (68' Stephane Badji), Alexandru Chipciu, Frank Acheampong, Youri Tielemans, Leander
Dendoncker, Sofiane Hanni, Idrissa Sylla (78' Capel), Lukasz Teodorczyk.
Coach: Rene Weiler.
Goals: 49' Idrissa Sylla 0-1, 60' Lukasz Teodorczyk 0-2, 71' Sofiane Hanni 0-3.
Referee: Martin Strömbergsson (SWE)   Attendance: 16,096.

18.08.16   Antonis Papadopoulos, Larnaca: AEK Larnaca – Slovan Liberec 0-1 (0-1)
AEK Larnaca: Ruben Miño, Truyols (34' Elias Charalambous), Daniel Mojsov, Murillo, Jorge
Larena, Joan Tomas, Tete (82' Acoran), Vladimir Boljevic, Juanma Ortiz, André Alves (75'
Costas Charalambides), Ivan Trickovski. Coach: Imanol Idiakez.
Slovan Liberec: Martin Dubravka, Vladimír Coufal, David Hovorka, Lukas Bartosak (70' Igor
Sukennik), Lukas Pokorny, Radim Breite (85' Ilia Kubyshkin), Jan Sykora, Zdenek Folprecht,
Egon Vuch (60' Jan Navratil), Daniel Bartl, Nikolay Komlichenko.
Coach: Jindrich Trpisovsky.
Goal: 29' Vladimír Coufal 0-1.
Referee: Ruddy Buquet (FRA)   Attendance: 4,645.
Sent off: 65' Juanma Ortiz.

18.08.16   Ernst-Happel-Stadion, Vienna: Austria Wien – Rosenborg BK 2-1 (0-0)
Austria Wien: Robert Almer, Petar Filipovic, Jens Stryger Larsen, Christoph Martschinko,
Lukas Rotpuller, Alexander Grünwald (81' Richard Windbichler), Lucas Venuto (84' De
Paula), Tarkan Serbest, Raphael Holzhauser, Olarenwaju Kayode (90' Kevin Friesenbichler),
Felipe Pires. Coach: Thorsten Fink.
Rosenborg BK: Adam Kwarasey, Jonas Svensson, Tore Reginiussen, Holmar Eyjolfsson,
Jørgen Skjelvik (71' Elbasan Rashani), Mike Jensen, Anders Konradsen, Alex Gersbach,
Fredrik Midtsjø (77' Matthias Vilhjalmsson), Pål Helland, Christian Gytkjær.
Coach: Kåre Ingebrigtsen.
Goals: 51' Alexander Grünwald 1-0, 53' Felipe Pires 2-0, 90+2' Tore Reginiussen 2-1.
Referee: Benoit Bastien (FRA)   Attendance: 6,090.

184

18.08.16   Gamla Ullevi, Gothenburg: IFK Göteborg – Qarabag FK 1-0 (0-0)
IFK Göteborg: John Alvbåge, Emil Salomonsson, Scott Jamieson, Thomas Rogne, Mattias
Bjärsmyr, Mads Albæk, Søren Rieks (88' Billy Nordström), Jakob Ankersen, Tobias Hysen
(83' Martin Smedberg), Mikael Boman, Tom Pettersson. Coach: Jörgen Lennartsson.
Qarabag FK: Ibrahim Sehic, Qara Qarayev, Maksim Medvedev, Rashad Sadygov, Ansi Agolli,
Badavi Guseynov, Michel, Reynaldo, Muarem Muarem (72' Namig Alasgarov), Dani
Quintana, Richard. Coach: Gurban Gurbanov.
Goal: 56' Mads Albæk 1-0.
Referee: Pawel Raczkowski (POL)   Attendance: 11,458.

18.08.16   Netanya Municipal Stadium, Netahya: Maccabi Tel Aviv – Hajduk Split 2-1 (1-0)
Maccabi Tel Aviv: Predrag Rajkovic, Eitan Tibi, Egor Filipenko, Haris Medunjanin, Oscar
Scarione (84' Yossi Benayoun), Gal Alberman (68' Eden Ben Basat), Avi Rikan, Nosa Igiebor,
Dor Peretz (63' Elazar Dasa), Tal Ben Haim (II), Dor Mikha. Coach: Shota Arveladze.
Hajduk Split: Lovre Kalinic, Jefferson, Zoran Nizic, Hysen Memolla, Ardian Ismajli, Nikola
Vlasic, Zvonimir Kozulj (73' Maksim Beliy), Tino-Sven Susic, Marko Cosic, Savvas
Gentsoglou (87' Toma Basic), Ahmed Said (62' Franck Ohandza). Coach: Marijan Pusnik.
Goals: 9' Gal Alberman 1-0, 56' Ahmed Said 1-1, 77' Oscar Scarione 2-1.
Referee: Jesus Gil Manzano (ESP)   Attendance: 9,932.

18.08.16   Fatih Terim Stadium, Istanbul:
            Medipol Basaksehir FK – Shakhtar Donetsk 1-2 (0-2)
Medipol Basaksehir FK: Volkan Babacan, Yalcin Ayhan, Ferhat Öztorun, Alexandru
Epureanu, Mahmut Tekdemir, Emre Belözoglu (75' Samuel Holmen), Edin Visca, Marcio
Mossoro, Doka Madureira (46' Cengiz Ünder), Cenk Alkilic (72' Cheikhou Dieng), Sokol
Cikalleshi. Coach: Abdullah Avci.
Shakhtar Donetsk: Andriy Pyatov, Oleksandr Kucher, Ismaily, Darijo Srna, Yaroslav
Rakitskiy, Taras Stepanenko, Fred, Marlos, Viktor Kovalenko (87' Maksym Malyshev),
Facundo Ferreyra (71' Eduardo), Taison (80' Wellington Nem). Coach: Paulo Fonseca.
Goals: 24' Sokol Cikalleshi 0-1 (og), 41' Viktor Kovalenko 0-2, 56' Emre Belözoglu 1-2 (p).
Referee: Javier Estrada Fernandez (ESP)   Attendance: 3,016.

18.08.16   Sükrü Saracoglu, Istanbul: Fenerbahçe – Grasshoppers Zürich 3-0 (1-0)
Fenerbahçe: Volkan Demirel, Hasan-Ali Kaldirim, Gregory van der Wiel, Martin Skrtel,
Mehmet Topal, Ozan Tufan, Roman Neustädter, Salih Ucan, Aatif Chahechouhe (68' Robin
van Persie), Fernandão (68' Miroslav Stoch), Emmanuel Emenike. Coach: Dick Advocaat.
Grasshoppers Zürich: Vaso Vasic, Alban Pnishi, Numa Lavanchy, Jan Bamert, Benjamin
Lüthi, Kim Källström, Runar Sigurjonsson (84' Mergim Brahimi), Marko Basic, Caio (74'
Florian Kamberi), Nikola Gjorgjev (64' Lucas Andersen), Ridge Munsy.
Coach: Pierluigi Tami.
Goals: 4' Aatif Chahechouhe 1-0, 72', 90+2' Miroslav Stoch 2-0, 3-0.
Referee: Robert Schörgenhofer (AUT)   Attendance: 16,280.

185

18.08.16   Apostolos Nikolaidis, Athen: Panathinaikos – Brøndby IF 3-0 (1-0)
Panathinaikos: Luke Steele, Georgios Koutroubis (58' Sebastian Leto), Giandomenico Mesto,
Rodrigo Moledo, Ivan Ivanov, Victor Ibarbo, Zeca, Mubarak Wakaso (74' Lucas Villafañez),
Niklas Hult, Cristian Ledesma, Markus Berg (86' Lautaro Rinaldi).
Coach: Andrea Stramaccioni.
Brøndby IF: Frederik Rønnow, Benedikt Röcker, Martin Albrechtsen, Johan Larsson, Svenn
Crone, Hany Mukhtar (46' Jesper Juelsgård), Lebogang Phiri, Christian Nørgaard, Kamil
Wilczek (72' Hjörtur Hermannsson), Andrew Hjulsager, Teemu Pukki (53' Mads Toppel
goalkeeper). Coach: Alexander Zorniger.
Goals: 45' Markus Berg 1-0, 54' Cristian Ledesma 2-0 (p), 82' Markus Berg 3-0.
Referee: Istvan Vad (HUN)   Attendance: 11,072.
Sent off: 33' Svenn Crone, 50' Frederik Rønnow.

18.08.16   Karadjordje, Novi Sad: Vojvodina – AZ Alkmaar 0-3 (0-2)
Vojvodina: Marko Kordic, Vladimir Kovacevic, Nikola Antic, Darko Puskaric, Aleksandar
Palocevic (77' Lazar Zlicic), Sinisa Babic (46' Dusan Jovancic), Filip Malbasic, Novica
Maksimovic, Nemanja Miletic, Nikola Trujic (61' Milos Trifunovic), Dejan Meleg.
Coach: Nenad Lalatovic.
AZ Alkmaar: Sergio Rochet, Mattias Johansson, Rens van Eijden, Ron Vlaar, Ridgeciano
Haps, Derrick Luckassen, Markus Henriksen, Stijn Wuytens (83' Guus Til), Alireza
Jahanbakhsh, Fred Friday (77' Wout Weghorst), Levi Garcia (70' Dabney dos Santos).
Coach: John van den Brom.
Goals: 32' Stijn Wuytens 0-1, 45' Fred Friday 0-2, 80' Stijn Wuytens 0-3.
Referee: Paolo Tagliavento (ITA)   Attendance: 10,473.

18.08.16   Stadion Maksimir, Zagreb: Lokomotiva Zagreb – KRC Genk 2-2 (0-1)
Lokomotiva Zagreb: Daniel Zagorac, Karlo Bartolec, Sinisa Rozman, Dino Peric, Petar Bockaj
(87' Endri Cekici), Ante Majstorovic, Ivan Fiolic, Josip Coric (46' Luka Ivanusec), Eros
Grezda, Ivan Sunjic, Mirko Maric. Coach: Tomislav Ivkovic.
KRC Genk: Marco Bizot, Omar Colley, Sandy Walsh, Sebastien Dewaest, Jere Uronen,
Thomas Buffel (42' Leandro Trossard), Pozuelo, Onyinye Ndidi, Bryan Heynen, Leon Bailey,
Mbwana Samatta (83' Nikolaos Karelis). Coach: Peter Maes.
Goals: 35' Leon Bailey 0-1 (p), 47' Mbwana Samatta 0-2, 52' Mirko Maric 1-2 (p),
59' Ivan Fiolic 2-2.
Referee: Tamas Bognar (HUN)   Attendance: 1,700.

18.08.16   Stadionul Marin Anastasovici, Giurgiu: Astra Giurgiu – West Ham United 1-1 (0-1)
Astra Giurgiu: Silviu Lung Jr., Geraldo Alves, Fabricio, Junior Maranhão, Cristian Sapunaru,
Kristi Vangjeli (58' Denis Alibec), Takayuki Seto, Florin Lovin, Alexandru Ionita (85' Daniel
Florea), Filipe Teixeira (90+4' Silviu Balaure), Daniel Niculae. Coach: Marius Sumudica.
West Ham United: Darren Randolph, Angelo Ogbonna, Sam Byram, Reece Burke, Reece
Oxford, Pedro Obiang, Mark Noble, Gökhan Töre (75' Marcus Browne), Michail Antonio,
Enner Valencia (63' James Collins), Jonathan Calleri (63' Andy Carroll). Coach: Slaven Bilic.
Goals: 45' Mark Noble 0-1 (p), 83' Denis Alibec 1-1.
Referee: Artur Soares Dias (POR)   Attendance: 3,360.

186

18.08.16   Ghelamco Arena, Gent: KAA Gent – KF Shkëndija 79 2-1 (1-1)
KAA Gent: Jacob Rinne, Stefan Mitrovic, Lasse Nielsen, Rami Gershon (85' Jeremy Perbet),
Thomas Matton (73' Moses Simon), Renato Neto, Sven Kums, Kenny Saief, Thomas Foket,
Kalifa Coulibaly, Emir Kujovic (64' Danijel Milicevic). Coach: Hein Vanhaezebrouck.
KF Shkëndija 79: Kostadin Zahov, Egzon Bejtulai, Ardijan Cuculi, Armend Alimi (82'
Sciprim Taipi), Ferhan Hasani, Besir Demiri, Artim Polozani, Blagoja Todorovski, Stephan
Vujcic, Besart Ibraimi (90+3' Demir Imeri), Stenio Junior. Coach: Bruno Akrapovic.
Goals: 9' Besart Ibraimi 0-1, 45' Thomas Matton 1-1, 90+2' Kalifa Coulibaly 2-1.
Referee: Sergey Boyko (UKR)   Attendance: 13,416.

18.08.16   MAPEI Stadium - Citta del Tricolore, Reggio Emilia:
           Sassuolo Calcio – Crvena Zvezda 3-0 (2-0)
Sassuolo Calcio: Andrea Consigli, Federico Peluso, Francesco Acerbi, Marcello Gazzola,
Paolo Cannavaro, Francesco Magnanelli, Davide Biondini, Matteo Politano (84' Stefano
Sensi), Alfred Duncan, Gregoire Defrel (76' Marcello Trotta), Domenico Berardi (69' Diego
Falcinelli). Coach: Eusebio Di Francesco.
Crvena Zvezda: Damir Kahriman, Milos Cvetkovic, Thomas Phibel, Damien Le Tallec,
Mitchell Donald, Hugo Vieira (84' Predrag Sikimic), Mihailo Ristic, Marko Poletanovic, John
Ruiz (58' Srdan Plavsic), Aleksandar Katai, Pablo Mouche (71' Slavoljub Srnic),
Coach: Miodrag Bozovic.
Goals: 17' Domenico Berardi 1-0, 41' Matteo Politano 2-0, 69' Gregoire Defrel 3-0.
Referee: Serdar Gözübüyük (HOL)   Attendance: 6,861.

18.08.16   Estadio Municipal de Arouca, Arouca: FC Arouca – Olympiakos Piraeus 0-1 (0-1)
FC Arouca: Rafael Bracalli, Hugo Basto, Anderson Luiz, Thiago Carleto (59' Marlon de
Jesus), Jubal, Artur (68' André Santos), Adilson Goiano (75' Crivellaro), Nuno Valente, Nuno
Coelho, Mateus, Walter Gonzalez. Coach: Lito Vidigal.
Olympiakos Piraeus: Stefanos Kapino, Alberto Botia, Manuel Da Costa, De la Bella, Diogo,
Luka Milivojevic, Esteban Cambiasso, Felipe Pardo (90' Sasa Zdjelar), Alejandro Dominguez
(72' Athanasios Androutsos), Seba (88' Jimmy Durmaz), Brown Ideye. Coach: Paulo Bento.
Goal: 27' Seba 0-1.
Referee: Slavko Vincic (SVN)   Attendance: 1,950.

18.08.16   Stadion pod Dubnom, Zilina: FK AS Trencin – Rapid Wien 0-4 (0-1)
FK AS Trencin: Adrian Chovan, Martin Sulek, Christopher Udeh, Peter Klescik, Jamie
Lawrence (80' Jeffrey Ket), Jakub Paur, Jakub Holubek, Denis Janco (62' Ibrahim Rabiu),
Aliko Bala (63' Erik Prekop), Rangelo Janga, Samuel Kalu. Coach: Martin Sevela.
Rapid Wien: Jan Novota, Christoph Schösswendter, Thomas Schrammel, Christopher Dibon,
Mario Pavelic, Philipp Schobesberger (50' Thomas Murg), Stefan Schwab, Louis Schaub (85'
Stephan Auer), Srdan Grahovac, Ivan Mocinic, Joelinton (84' Maximilian Entrup).
Coach: Mike Büskens.
Goals: 32', 54' Louis Schaub 0-1, 0-2, 73' Stefan Schwab 0-3, 83' Louis Schaub 0-4.
Referee: Stefan Johannesson (SWE)   Attendance: 4,065.

187

25.08.16   Tofig Bahramov Republican stadium, Baku: Qarabag FK – IFK Göteborg 3-0 (2-0)
Qarabag FK: Ibrahim Sehic, Qara Qarayev, Maksim Medvedev, Rashad Sadygov, Ansi Agolli,
Elvin Yunuszade, Michel, Reynaldo (90' Namig Alasgarov), Muarem Muarem (84' Dino
Ndlovu), Dani Quintana, Richard (88' Rahid Amirguliyev). Coach: Gurban Gurbanov.
IFK Göteborg: John Alvbåge, Emil Salomonsson, Scott Jamieson, Sebastian Eriksson (83'
Martin Smedberg), Thomas Rogne, Mattias Bjärsmyr, Mads Albæk, Søren Rieks, Jakob
Ankersen, Tobias Hysen (72' Elias Mar Omarsson), Mikael Boman (72' Tom Pettersson).
Coach: Jörgen Lennartsson.
Goals: 19' Rashad Sadygov 1-0, 26' Muarem Muarem 2-0, 51' Dani Quintana 3-0.
Referee: Vladislav Bezborodov (RUS)   Attendance: 25,500.

25.08.16   Stadion Letzigrund, Zürich: Grasshoppers Zürich – Fenerbahçe 0-2 (0-0)
Grasshoppers Zürich: Joël Mall, Nemaja Antonov, Alban Pnishi, Jean-Pierre Rhyner,
Benjamin Lüthi, Runar Sigurjonsson, Lucas Andersen (81' Harun Alpsoy), Mergim Brahimi,
Nikola Gjorgjev, Haris Tabakovic, Sherko Gubari (68' Florian Kamberi).
Coach: Pierluigi Tami.
Fenerbahçe: Volkan Demirel, Hasan-Ali Kaldirim (73' Ismail Köybasi), Simon Kjær, Gregory
van der Wiel, Martin Skrtel, Mehmet Topal, Alper Potuk, Ozan Tufan, Salih Ucan (53' Aatif
Chahechouhe), Robin van Persie (68' Fernandão), Miroslav Stoch. Coach: Dick Advocaat.
Goals: 77' Fernandão 0-1, 84' Miroslav Stoch 0-2.
Referee: Danny Makkelie (HOL)   Attendance: 14,400.

25.08.16   Brøndby Stadium, Brøndby: Brøndby IF – Panathinaikos 1-1 (1-0)
Brøndby IF: Mads Toppel, Benedikt Röcker, Hjörtur Hermannsson, Frederik Holst (67' Marco
Ureña), Johan Larsson, Hany Mukhtar, Lebogang Phiri (75' Rezan Corlu), Christian Nørgaard,
Kamil Wilczek, Andrew Hjulsager, Teemu Pukki (83' Christian Jakobsen).
Coach: Alexander Zorniger.
Panathinaikos: Luke Steele, Georgios Koutroubis, Giandomenico Mesto, Rodrigo Moledo,
Ivan Ivanov, Victor Ibarbo (46' Sebastian Leto), Zeca, Mubarak Wakaso, Niklas Hult (85'
Lucas Villafañez), Cristian Ledesma (59' Robin Lod), Markus Berg.
Coach: Andrea Stramaccioni.
Goals: 35' Hany Mukhtar 1-0, 66' Ivan Ivanov 1-1.
Referee: Oliver Drachta (AUT)   Attendance: 13,521.

25.08.16   U Nisy, Liberec: Slovan Liberec – AEK Larnaca 3-0 (3-0)
Slovan Liberec: Martin Dubravka, Vladimír Coufal, David Hovorka, Lukas Bartosak, Lukas
Pokorny, Radim Breite, Jan Sykora, Zdenek Folprecht, Egon Vuch (89' Igor Sukennik), Daniel
Bartl (79' Jan Navratil), Milan Baros (83' Nikolay Komlichenko). Coach: Jindrich Trpisovsky.
AEK Larnaca: Ruben Miño, Daniel Mojsov, Murillo, Elias Charalambous (46' Acoran),
Constantinos Mintikkis (46' Costas Charalambides), Jorge Larena, Joan Tomas, Tete (59'
Nikos Englezou), Vladimir Boljevic, André Alves, Ivan Trickovski. Coach: Imanol Idiakez.
Goals: 8', 15', 41' Jan Sykora 1-0, 2-0, 3-0.
Referee: Ivan Bebek (CRO)   Attendance: 7,570.
Sent off: 90' Murillo.

Joan Tomas missed a penalty kick (88').

25.08.16 Lerkendal Stadion, Trondheim: Rosenborg BK – Austria Wien 1-2 (0-0)
Rosenborg BK: Adam Kwarasey, Jonas Svensson, Tore Reginiussen, Holmar Eyjolfsson,
Jørgen Skjelvik (70' Alex Gersbach), Mike Jensen, Anders Konradsen, Fredrik Midtsjø, Pål
Helland (24' Matthias Vilhjalmsson), Christian Gytkjær, Elbasan Rashani.
Coach: Kåre Ingebrigtsen.
Austria Wien: Robert Almer, Petar Filipovic, Jens Stryger Larsen (89' Ismael Tajouri Shradi),
Christoph Martschinko, Lukas Rotpuller, Alexander Grünwald, Lucas Venuto (76' De Paula),
Tarkan Serbest, Raphael Holzhauser, Olarenwaju Kayode (78' Kevin Friesenbichler), Felipe
Pires. Coach: Thorsten Fink.
Goals: 57' Alexander Grünwald 0-1, 59' Christian Gytkjær 1-1 (p),
69' Olarenwaju Kayode 1-2.
Referee: Martin Atkinson (ENG)   Attendance: 11,692.

25.08.16 Elbasan Arena, Elbasan: FK Partizani – FK Krasnodar 0-0
FK Partizani: Alban Hoxha, Gëzim Krasniqi, Labinot Ibrahimi, Arbnor Fejzullahu (64' Jurgen
Bardhi), Sodiq Atanda, Idriz Batha, Ylber Ramadani (22' Luca Bertoni), Lorenc Trashi (74'
Jurgen Vatnikaj), Emiljano Vila, Agustin Torassa, Caleb Ekuban. Coach: Adolfo Sormani.
FK Krasnodar: Andrey Sinitsyn, Aleksandr Martinovich, Andreas Granqvist, Sergey Petrov,
Dmitriy Torbinskiy, Vyacheslav Podberezkin (46' Artur Jedrzejczyk), Vladimir Bystrov,
Joãozinho, Mauricio Pereyra (46' Odil Akhmedov), Kouassi Eboue, Ari (64' Dmitri
Vorobyev). Coach: Oleg Kononov.
Referee: Jakob Kehlet (DEN)   Attendance: 1,550.

25.08.16 Constant Vanden Stock Stadium, Brussels:
          RSC Anderlecht – Slavia Praha 3-0 (2-0)
RSC Anderlecht: Davy Roef, Bram Nuytinck, Michaël Heylen, Stephane Badji, Alexandru
Chipciu, Capel, Frank Acheampong, Youri Tielemans (62' Idrissa Doumbia), Leander
Dendoncker, Sofiane Hanni (70' Emmanuel Adjei), Lukasz Teodorczyk (56' Idrissa Sylla).
Coach: Rene Weiler.
Slavia Praha: Martin Berkovec, Jan Mikula, Tomas Jablonsky, Michael Ngadeu-Ngadjui,
Michal Frydrych, Jaromir Zmrhal, Josef Husbauer (89' Jiri Bilek), Tomás Soucek, Antonin
Barak (46' Jaroslav Mihalík), Muris Mesanovic (46' Mick van Buren), Gino van Kessel.
Coach: Dusan Uhrin.
Goals: 22' Youri Tielemans 1-0 (p), 40' Lukasz Teodorczyk 2-0 (p), 61' Michaël Heylen 3-0.
Referee: Anthony Taylor (ENG); 13.075.

25.08.16 Generali Arena, Prague: Sparta Praha – SønderjyskE 3-2 (1-2)
Sparta Praha: Tomas Koubek, Michal Kadlec, Vyacheslav Karavaev (85' Jakub Brabec), Mario
Holek, Costa Nhamoinesu, Lukas Vacha, Lukas Marecek (46' Lukas Julis), Martin Frydek,
Josef Sural, David Lafata, Matej Pulkrab (82' Ondrej Zahustel). Coach: Zdenek Scasny.
SønderjyskE: Marin Skender, Marc Pedersen, Pierre Kanstrup, Matthias Maak, Janus
Drachmann, Nicolai Madsen, Johan Absalonsen (87' Kees Luijckx), Troels Kløve Hallstrøm
(76' Simon Kroon), Marcel Rømer (83' Sakari Mattila), Marc Hende, Mikkel Uhre.
Coach: Jakob Michelsen.
Goals: 35' Mikkel Uhre 0-1, 40' Troels Kløve Hallstrøm 0-2, 44' David Lafata 1-2,
69' Josef Sural 2-2, 85' Jakub Brabec 3-2.
Referee: Bobby Madden (SCO)   Attendance: 13,685.

25.08.16   Borisov Arena, Borisov: BATE Borisov – FK Astana 2-2 (1-0)
BATE Borisov: Artem Soroko, Vitaly Gayduchik, Maksim Zhavnerchik, Denis Polyakov, Maksim Volodko (55' Nikolay Signevich), Mirko Ivanic, Aleksey Rios, Igor Stasevich, Mikhail Gordeychuk (73' Dmitriy Mozolevskiy), Yuri Kendysh, Vitaliy Rodionov (86' Artur Pikk). Coach: Aleksandr Yermakovich.
FK Astana: Aleksandr Mokin, Marin Anicic, Igor Shitov, Yuriy Logvinenko (46' Abzal Beysebekov), Dmitriy Shomko, Nemanja Maksimovic, Serikzhan Muzhikov (85' Askhat Tagybergen), Azat Nurgaliev (46' Sergiy Maliy), Roger Cañas, Patrick Twumasi, Junior Kabananga. Coach: Stanimir Stoilov.
Goals: 27' Mikhail Gordeychuk 1-0, 50' Nemanja Maksimovic 1-1, 76' Patrick Twumasi 1-2, 89' Igor Stasevich 2-2 (p).
Referee: Tony Chapron (FRA)   Attendance: 9,516.
Sent off: 82' Aleksey Rios.

25.08.16   AFAS Stadion, Alkmaar: AZ Alkmaar – Vojvodina 0-0
AZ Alkmaar: Sergio Rochet, Mattias Johansson, Rens van Eijden, Ron Vlaar, Ridgeciano Haps, Derrick Luckassen, Markus Henriksen, Stijn Wuytens, Alireza Jahanbakhsh (76' Joris van Overeem), Fred Friday (70' Wout Weghorst), Levi Garcia (65' Dabney dos Santos). Coach: John van den Brom.
Vojvodina: Marko Kordic, Bogdan Planic, Nikola Antic, Dusan Micic, Darko Puskaric, Aleksandar Palocevic, Filip Malbasic (78' Milos Trifunovic), Novica Maksimovic (71' Marko Vukasovic), Nemanja Miletic, Dejan Meleg, Nikola Asceric (60' Sinisa Babic). Coach: Nenad Lalatovic.
Referee: Tobias Stieler (GER)   Attendance: 8,401.

25.08.16   Stadio Toumb, Saloniki: PAOK Saloniki – Dinamo Tbilisi 2-0 (2-0)
PAOK Saloniki: Panagiotis Glykos, Leo Matos, Marin Leovac (65' Stelios Kitsiou), Angel Crespo (76' Fernando Varela), Giorgos Tzavellas, Gojko Cimirot, Garry Rodrigues, Yevhen Shakhov (57' Diego Biseswar), Cañas, Djalma, Facundo Pereyra. Coach: Vladimir Ivic.
Dinamo Tbilisi: Anthony Scribe, Ucha Lobjanidze, Aleksandr Amisulashvili, Mate Tsintsadze (74' Stefan Velev), Giorgi Papunashvili, Otari Kiteishvili (62' Vakhtang Chanturishvili), Lasha Parunashvili, Mikel Alvaro, Rene, Matija Spicic, Vladimir Dvalishvili (77' Beka Mikeltadze). Coach: Juraj Jarabek.
Goals: 5' Garry Rodrigues 1-0, 45' Giorgos Tzavellas 2-0.
Referee: Harald Lechner (AUT)   Attendance: 14,821.

25.08.16   Osmanli Stadi, Ankara: Osmanlispor FK – FC Midtjylland 2-0 (1-0)
Osmanlispor FK: Zydrunas Karcemarskas, Koray Altinay (82' Muhammed Bayir), Tiago Pinto, Vaclav Prochazka, Numan Cürüksu, Raheem Lawal, Papa N'Diaye, Aminu Umar, Musa Cagiran, Pierre Webo (66' Cheick Diabate), Dzon Delarge (75' Erdal Kilicarslan). Coach: Mustafa Akcay.
FC Midtjylland: Johan Dahlin, Kian Hansen, Markus Halsti, Patrick Banggaard, André Rømer, Rasmus Nissen, Jakob Poulsen (55' Martin Pusic), Kristoffer Olsson, Rilwan Hassan, Filip Novák (62' Mikkel Duelund), Vaclav Kadlec (72' Rafael van der Vaart). Coach: Jess Thorup.
Goals: 20', 50' Tiago Pinto 1-0, 2-0.
Referee: Evgen Aranovskiy (UKR)   Attendance: 12,116.

25.08.16   Luminus Arena, Genk: KRC Genk – Lokomotiva Zagreb 2-0 (1-0)
KRC Genk: Marco Bizot, Omar Colley, Sandy Walsh, Sebastien Dewaest, Jere Uronen, Leandro Trossard, Pozuelo (82' Bennard Kumordzi), Onyinye Ndidi, Bryan Heynen, Leon Bailey (74' Neeskens Kebano), Mbwana Samatta (80' Nikolaos Karelis). Coach: Peter Maes.
Lokomotiva Zagreb: Daniel Zagorac, Karlo Bartolec, Sinisa Rozman, Dino Peric, Luka Capan (66' Luka Ivanusec), Petar Bockaj (72' Endri Cekici), Ante Majstorovic, Ivan Fiolic, Eros Grezda (46' Josip Coric), Ivan Sunjic, Mirko Maric. Coach: Tomislav Ivkovic.
Goals: 2' Mbwana Samatta 1-0, 50' Leon Bailey 2-0.
Referee: John Beaton (SCO)   Attendance: 8,166.

25.08.16   Nacionalna Arena Filip II Makedonski, Skopje:
          KF Shkëndija 79 – KAA Gent 0-4 (0-0)
KF Shkëndija 79: Kostadin Zahov, Egzon Bejtulai, Ardijan Cuculi, Armend Alimi (74' Ennur Totre), Ferhan Hasani, Besir Demiri, Sciprim Taipi (40' Marjan Radeski), Artim Polozani, Blagoja Todorovski, Besart Ibraimi, Stenio Junior (66' Victor Juffo). Coach: Bruno Akrapovic.
KAA Gent: Jacob Rinne, Stefan Mitrovic, Lasse Nielsen (46' Nana Asare), Rami Gershon, Renato Neto, Sven Kums, Kenny Saief, Thomas Foket, Danijel Milicevic (71' Thomas Matton), Kalifa Coulibaly (75' Jeremy Perbet), Moses Simon. Coach: Hein Vanhaezebrouck.
Goals: 60', 69' Kalifa Coulibaly 0-1, 0-2, 81' Jeremy Perbet 0-3, 86' Renato Neto 0-4.
Referee: Luca Banti (ITA)   Attendance: 30,252.

25.08.16   Stadion Ljudski vrt., Maribor: NK Maribor – Gabala FK 1-0 (0-0)
NK Maribor: Jasmin Handanovic, Erik Janza, Marko Suler, Rodrigo Defendi (85' Gregor Bajde), Denis Sme, Blaz Vrhovec (46' Marwan Kabha), Aleks Pihler (63' Sintayehu Sallalich), Dare Vrsic, Damjan Bohar, Marcos Tavares, Milivoje Novakovic. Coach: Darko Milanic.
Gabala FK: Dmitro Bezotosniy, Vojislav Stankovic, Vitaliy Vernydub, Ricardinho, Rafael Santos, Nika Kvekveskiri, Magomed Mirzabekov, Filip Ozobic, Theo Weeks, Sergei Zenjov (86' Asif Mammadov), Bagaliy Dabo (90+6' Rashad Eyyubov). Coach: Roman Grygorchuk.
Goal: 66' Marcos Tavares 1-0.
Referee: Viktor Kassai (HUN)   Attendance: 9,000.
Sent off: 69' Theo Weeks.

25.08.16   Stadion Rajko Mitic, Belgrade: Crvena Zvezda – Sassuolo Calcio 1-1 (0-1)
Crvena Zvezda: Damir Kahriman, Milos Cvetkovic, Thomas Phibel, Damien Le Tallec (57' Zoran Rendulic), Mitchell Donald, Hugo Vieira, Mihailo Ristic, Marko Poletanovic, John Ruiz (85' Slavoljub Srnic), Aleksandar Katai, Pablo Mouche (80' David Babunski).
Coach: Miodrag Bozovic.
Sassuolo Calcio: Andrea Consigli, Federico Peluso, Francesco Acerbi, Por Lirola, Paolo Cannavaro, Francesco Magnanelli, Davide Biondini, Matteo Politano (62' Diego Falcinelli), Alfred Duncan, Alessandro Matri (83' Marcello Trotta), Domenico Berardi (72' Timo Letschert). Coach: Eusebio Di Francesco.
Goals: 28' Domenico Berardi 0-1, 54' Aleksandar Katai 1-1.
Referee: David Fernandez Borbalan (ESP)   Attendance: 22,314.

25.08.16   Stadion Poljud, Split: Hajduk Split – Maccabi Tel Aviv 2-1 (1-0, 2-1)
Hajduk Split: Lovre Kalinic, Lorenco Simic, Jefferson, Hysen Memolla, Ardian Ismajli, Nikola
Vlasic, Zvonimir Kozulj (69' Fran Tudor), Tino-Sven Susic, Marko Cosic, Savvas Gentsoglou,
Ahmed Said (63' Franck Ohandza). Coach: Marijan Pusnik.
Maccabi Tel Aviv: Predrag Rajkovic, Elazar Dasa, Eitan Tibi, Omri Ben Harush, Tal Ben
Haim (I), Haris Medunjanin, Oscar Scarione, Nosa Igiebor, Yossi Benayoun (81' Orlando Sa),
Eden Ben Basat (106' Avi Rikan), Dor Mikha (114' Barak Itzhaki). Coach: Shota Arveladze.
Goals: 40' Marko Cosic 1-0, 52' Oscar Scarione 1-1, 59' Marko Cosic 2-1.
Referee: Felix Zwayer (GER)   Attendance: 21,102.

Maccabi Tel Aviv won 4-3 on penalties following extra time.
Penalties: Vlasic 1-0, Itzhaki 1-1, Tudor missed, Ben Haim missed, Gentsoglou 2-1
Ohandza missed, Scarione missed, Sa 2-2, Susic 3-2, Medunjanin 3-3, Cosic missed, Rikan 3-4

25.08.16   London Stadium, London: West Ham United – Astra Giurgiu 0-1 (0-1)
West Ham United: Darren Randolph, Winston Reid, Håvard Nordtveit (46' Enner Valencia),
Angelo Ogbonna, Sam Byram, Reece Burke (88' James Collins), Cheikhou Kouyate, Pedro
Obiang, Gökhan Töre, Michail Antonio, Jonathan Calleri (61' Ashley Fletcher).
Coach: Slaven Bilic.
Astra Giurgiu: Silviu Lung Jr., Geraldo Alves, Fabricio, Junior Maranhão, Cristian Sapunaru,
Takayuki Seto, Florin Lovin (88' Daniel Florea), Alexandru Ionita (75' Alexandru Stan), Filipe
Teixeira, Denis Alibec, Daniel Niculae (57' Cristian Oros). Coach: Marius Sumudica.
Goal: 45' Filipe Teixeira 0-1.
Referee: Manuel Gräfe (GER)   Attendance: 56,932.

25.08.16   Stadio Georgios Karaiskakis, Piraeus:
            Olympiakos Piraeus – FC Arouca 2-1 (0-0, 0-1)
Olympiakos Piraeus: Stefanos Kapino, Alberto Botia, Manuel Da Costa, De la Bella,
Panagiotis Retsos, Luka Milivojevic, Kostas Fortounis (72' Andre Martins), Esteban
Cambiasso (91' Alejandro Dominguez), Felipe Pardo (99' Georgios Manthatis), Seba, Brown
Ideye. Coach: Paulo Bento.
FC Arouca: Rafael Bracalli, Hugo Basto, Jose Velazquez, Gege (112' Bruno Lopes), Jubal,
Artur (90+4' Nuno Valente), André Santos, Crivellaro, Marlon de Jesus, Zéquinha (77'
Mateus), Walter Gonzalez. Coach: Lito Vidigal.
Goals: 80' Gege 0-1, 94' Alejandro Dominguez 1-1, 113' Brown Ideye 2-1.
Referee: Aleksey Eskov (RUS)   Attendance: 18,348.

Olympiakos Piraeus won after extra time.

25.08.16   Stade Geoffroy Guichard, Saint-Étienne: AS Saint-Étienne – Beitar Jerusalem 0-0
AS Saint-Étienne: Stephane Ruffier, Kevin Theophile-Catherine, Florentin Pogba, Loïc Perrin,
Kevin Malcuit, Ole Selnæs, Fabien Lemoine, Nolan Roux (87' Vincent Pajot), Kevin Monnet-
Paquet (53' Oussama Tannane), Robert Beric, Dylan Saint-Louis (45' Jessy Moulin
goalkeeper). Coach: Christophe Galtier.
Beitar Jerusalem: Boris Kleiman, David Keltjens (46' Omer Atzily), Jesus Rueda, Dan Mori,
Marcel Heister, Idan Vered, Dan Einbinder, Claudemir, Lidor Cohen (69' Johan Audel), Oz
Rali (59' Tal Benesh), Itay Shechter. Coach: Ran Ben-Shimon.
Referee: Matej Jug (SVN)   Attendance: 20,354.
Sent off: 45' Stephane Ruffier.

25.08.16   Arena Lviv, Lviv: Shakhtar Donetsk – Medipol Basaksehir FK 2-0 (1-0)
Shakhtar Donetsk: Andriy Pyatov, Oleksandr Kucher, Ismaily, Darijo Srna, Yaroslav
Rakitskiy, Taras Stepanenko, Fred (72' Maksym Malyshev), Marlos, Viktor Kovalenko (83'
Wellington Nem), Facundo Ferreyra (77' Eduardo), Taison. Coach: Paulo Fonseca.
Medipol Basaksehir FK: Volkan Babacan, Ferhat Öztorun, Alexandru Epureanu, Rajko
Rotman, Emre Belözoglu (28' Samuel Holmen), Eren Albayrak, Joseph Attamah, Cengiz
Ünder, Hakan Özmert (78' Marcio Mossoro), Cenk Alkilic (46' Ugur Ucar), Sokol Cikalleshi.
Coach: Abdullah Avci.
Goals: 22' Joseph Attamah 1-0 (og), 71' Marlos 2-0 (p).
Referee: Ivan Kruzliak (SVK)   Attendance: 7,014.

25.08.16   Allianz Stadion, Vienna: Rapid Wien – FK AS Trencin 0-2 (0-2)
Rapid Wien: Jan Novota, Christopher Dibon, Maximilian Hofmann, Mario Pavelic, Stephan
Auer, Louis Schaub (90+2' Steffen Hofmann), Srdan Grahovac, Arnor Ingvi Traustason (83'
Thomas Schrammel), Ivan Mocinic, Thomas Murg (46' Stefan Schwab), Joelinton.
Coach: Mike Büskens.
FK AS Trencin: Igor Semrinec, Jeffrey Ket (64' Kingsley Madu), Martin Sulek, Christopher
Udeh, Peter Klescik, Jamie Lawrence, Jakub Paur, Jakub Holubek (84' Filip Halgos), Denis
Janco, Aliko Bala (79' Erik Prekop), Rangelo Janga. Coach: Martin Sevela.
Goals: 12' Jamie Lawrence 0-1, 35' Jakub Paur 0-2.
Referee: Aleksandar Stavrev (MKD)   Attendance: 21,200.
Sent off: 53' Denis Janco.

GROUP STAGE

GROUP A

Fenerbahçe	6	4	1	1	8 - 6	13
Manchester United	6	4	0	2	12 - 4	12
Feyenoord	6	2	1	3	3 - 7	7
Zorya Luhansk	6	0	2	4	2 - 8	2

GROUP B

APOEL Nicosia	6	4	0	2	8 - 6	12
Olympiakos Piraeus	6	2	2	2	7 - 6	8
BSC Young Boys	6	2	2	2	7 - 4	8
FK Astana	6	1	2	3	5 - 11	5

GROUP C

AS Saint-Étienne	6	3	3	0	8 - 5	12
RSC Anderlecht	6	3	2	1	16 - 8	11
1. FSV Mainz 05	6	2	3	1	8 - 10	9
Gabala FK	6	0	0	6	5 - 14	0

GROUP D

Zenit St.Petersburg	6	5	0	1	17 - 8	15
AZ Alkmaar	6	2	2	2	6 - 10	8
Maccabi Tel Aviv	6	2	1	3	7 - 9	7
Dundalk FC	6	1	1	4	5 - 8	4

GROUP E

AS Roma	6	3	3	0	16 - 7	12
Astra Giurgiu	6	2	2	2	7 - 10	8
Viktoria Plzen	6	1	3	2	7 - 10	6
Austria Wien	6	1	2	3	11 - 14	5

GROUP F

KRC Genk	6	4	0	2	13 - 9	12
Athletic Bilbao	6	3	1	2	10 - 11	10
Rapid Wien	6	1	3	2	7 - 8	6
Sassuolo Calcio	6	1	2	3	9 - 11	5

GROUP G

AFC Ajax	6	4	2	0	11 - 6	14
Celta de Vigo	6	2	3	1	10 - 7	9
Standard Liège	6	1	4	1	8 - 6	7
Panathinaikos	6	0	1	5	3 - 13	1

GROUP H

Shakhtar Donetsk	6	6	0	0	21 - 5	18
KAA Gent	6	2	2	2	9 - 13	8
Sporting Braga	6	1	3	2	9 - 11	6
Atiker Konyaspor	6	0	1	5	2 - 12	1

GROUP I

FC Schalke 04	6	5	0	1	9 - 3	15
FK Krasnodar	6	2	1	3	8 - 8	7
Red Bull Salzburg	6	2	1	3	6 - 6	7
OGC Nice	6	2	0	4	5 - 11	6

GROUP J

ACF Fiorentina	6	4	1	1	15 - 6	13
PAOK Saloniki	6	3	1	2	7 - 6	10
Qarabag FK	6	2	1	3	7 - 12	7
Slovan Liberec	6	1	1	4	7 - 12	4

GROUP K

Sparta Praha	6	4	0	2	8 - 6	12
Hapoel Be'er Sheva	6	2	2	2	6 - 6	8
Southampton FC	6	2	2	2	6 - 4	8
Internazionale	6	2	0	4	7 - 11	6

GROUP L

Osmanlispor FK	6	3	1	2	10 - 7	10
Villarreal CF	6	2	3	1	9 - 8	9
FC Zürich	6	1	3	2	5 - 7	6
Steaua Bucuresti	6	1	3	2	5 - 7	6

The top 2 teams in each group advanced to the knockout phase of the competition.

GROUP STAGE – GROUP A

15.09.16   De Kuip, Rotterdam: Feyenoord – Manchester United 1-0 (0-0)
Feyenoord: Brad Jones, Rick Karsdorp (90+1' Bart Nieuwkoop), Terence Kongolo, Jan-Arie
van der Heijden, Eric Botteghin, Karim El Ahmadi, Tonny Vilhena, Jens Toornstra, Dirk Kuyt,
Nicolai Jørgensen, Steven Berghuis (68' Bilal Basaçikoglu).
Coach: Giovanni van Bronckhorst.
Manchester United: De Gea, Eric Bailly, Marcos Rojo, Chris Smalling, Matteo Darmian, Paul
Pogba, Mata (63' Ashley Young), Ander Herrera, Morgan Schneiderlin, Anthony Martial (63'
Memphis Depay), Marcus Rashford (63' Zlatan Ibrahimovic). Coach: José Mourinho.
Goal: 79' Tonny Vilhena 1-0.
Referee: Jesús Gil Manzano (ESP)   Attendance: 31,000.

15.09.16   Chernomorets Stadium, Odesa: Zorya Luhansk – Fenerbahçe 1-1 (0-0)
Zorya Luhansk: Oleksiy Shevchenko, Nikita Kamenyuka, Rafael Forster, Eduard Sobol,
Mikhail Sivakov, Igor Chaykovskiy, Ivan Petryak (73' Paulo Victor), Oleksandr Karavayev,
Zeljko Ljubenovic (83' Evgeniy Opanasenko), Dmytro Grechyshkin, Vladislav Kulach (87'
Artem Gordienko). Coach: Yuriy Vernydub.
Fenerbahçe: Volkan Demirel, Hasan-Ali Kaldirim, Simon Kjær, Sener Özbayrakli, Martin
Skrtel, Mehmet Topal, Souza, Alper Potuk (73' Emmanuel Emenike), Salih Uçan (46' Ozan
Tufan), Moussa Sow, Miroslav Stoch (58' Robin van Persie). Coach: Dick Advocaat.
Goals: 52' Dmytro Grechyshkin 1-0, 90' Simon Kjær 1-1.
Referee: István Kovács (ROM)   Attendance: 16,000.

29.09.16   Sükrü Saracoglu Stadium, Istanbul: Fenerbahçe – Feyenoord 1-0 (1-0)
Fenerbahçe: Volkan Demirel, Hasan-Ali Kaldirim (76' Ismail Köybasi), Simon Kjær, Gregory
van der Wiel, Martin Skrtel, Mehmet Topal, Souza, Ozan Tufan, Moussa Sow, Emmanuel
Emenike (77' Robin van Persie), Jeremain Lens (85' Alper Potuk). Coach: Dick Advocaat.
Feyenoord: Brad Jones, Rick Karsdorp, Terence Kongolo, Jan-Arie van der Heijden, Eric
Botteghin (82' Michiel Kramer), Karim El Ahmadi, Tonny Vilhena, Jens Toornstra, Dirk Kuyt,
Nicolai Jørgensen, Steven Berghuis (57' Bilal Basaçikoglu).
Coach: Giovanni van Bronckhorst.
Goal: 18' Emmanuel Emenike 1-0.
Referee: Jonas Eriksson (SWE)   Attendance: 16,500.

29.09.16   Old Trafford, Manchester: Manchester United – Zorya Luhansk 1-0 (0-0)
Manchester United: Sergio Romero, Eric Bailly, Marcos Rojo, Chris Smalling, Timothy Fosu-
Mensah (74' Ashley Young), Paul Pogba, Mata (74' Anthony Martial), Jesse Lingard (67'
Wayne Rooney), Marouane Fellaini, Zlatan Ibrahimovic, Marcus Rashford.
Coach: José Mourinho.
Zorya Luhansk: Oleksiy Shevchenko, Nikita Kamenyuka, Rafael Forster, Eduard Sobol,
Mikhail Sivakov, Igor Chaykovskiy (80' Artem Gordienko), Ivan Petryak, Oleksandr
Karavayev, Zeljko Ljubenovic (76' Jaba Lipartia), Dmytro Grechyshkin, Vladislav Kulach
(60' Paulo Victor). Coach: Yuriy Vernydub.
Goal: 69' Zlatan Ibrahimovic 1-0.
Referee: Orel Grinfeld (ISR)   Attendance: 58,179.

20.10.16   Old Trafford, Manchester: Manchester United – Fenerbahçe 4-1 (3-0)
Manchester United: De Gea, Eric Bailly, Chris Smalling (46' Marcos Rojo), Luke Shaw,
Matteo Darmian, Paul Pogba (75' Timothy Fosu-Mensah), Mata, Jesse Lingard (66' Memphis
Depay), Michael Carrick, Wayne Rooney, Anthony Martial. Coach: José Mourinho.
Fenerbahçe: Volkan Demirel, Hasan-Ali Kaldirim, Simon Kjær (46' Emmanuel Emenike),
Sener Özbayrakli, Martin Skrtel, Mehmet Topal, Souza, Alper Potuk, Roman Neustädter,
Robin van Persie, Volkan Sen (69' Ismail Köybasi). Coach: Dick Advocaat.
Goals: 31' Paul Pogba 1-0 (p), 34' Anthony Martial 2-0 (p), 45' Paul Pogba 3-0,
48' Jesse Lingard 4-0, 83' Robin van Persie 4-1.
Referee: Benoît Bastien (FRA)   Attendance: 73.063

20.10.16   De Kuip, Rotterdam: Feyenoord – Zorya Luhansk 1-0 (0-0)
Feyenoord: Brad Jones, Rick Karsdorp, Terence Kongolo, Jan-Arie van der Heijden, Eric
Botteghin, Karim El Ahmadi, Tonny Vilhena, Renato Tapia, Jens Toornstra, Nicolai Jørgensen
(81' Michiel Kramer), Bilal Basaçikoglu. Coach: Giovanni van Bronckhorst.
Zorya Luhansk: Oleksiy Shevchenko, Nikita Kamenyuka, Rafael Forster, Eduard Sobol,
Mikhail Sivakov, Artem Gordienko (65' Igor Kharatin), Ivan Petryak (58' Paulo Victor),
Oleksandr Karavayev, Dmytro Grechyshkin, Vladislav Kulach (46' Zeljko Ljubenovic), Jaba
Lipartia. Coach: Yuriy Vernydub.
Goal: 55' Nicolai Jørgensen 1-0.
Referee: Andris Treimanis (LAT)   Attendance: 35,000.

03.11.16   Sükrü Saracoglu Stadium, Istanbul: Fenerbahçe – Manchester United 2-1 (1-0)
Fenerbahçe: Volkan Demirel, Hasan-Ali Kaldirim, Simon Kjær, Sener Özbayrakli, Martin
Skrtel, Mehmet Topal, Souza, Alper Potuk (82' Roman Neustädter), Moussa Sow (86' Ismail
Köybasi), Volkan Sen (68' Emmanuel Emenike), Jeremain Lens. Coach: Dick Advocaat.
Manchester United: De Gea, Marcos Rojo, Daley Blind, Luke Shaw, Matteo Darmian, Paul
Pogba (30' Zlatan Ibrahimovic), Ander Herrera, Morgan Schneiderlin (46' Mata), Wayne
Rooney, Anthony Martial, Marcus Rashford (61' Henrikh Mkhitaryan). Coach: José Mourinho.
Goals: 2' Moussa Sow 1-0, 59' Jeremain Lens 2-0, 89' Wayne Rooney 2-1.
Referee: Milorad Mazic (SER)   Attendance: 35,378.

03.11.16   Chornomorets Stadium, Odessa: Zorya Luhansk – Feyenoord 1-1 (1-1)
Zorya Luhansk: Oleksiy Shevchenko, Rafael Forster, Evgeniy Opanasenko (30' Nikita
Kamenyuka), Eduard Sobol, Igor Chaykovskiy, Ivan Petryak, Igor Kharatin, Oleksandr
Karavayev, Zeljko Ljubenovic (63' Paulo Victor), Dmytro Grechyshkin, Emmanuel
Bonaventure (55' Vladislav Kulach). Coach: Yuriy Vernydub.
Feyenoord: Brad Jones, Rick Karsdorp, Terence Kongolo, Jan-Arie van der Heijden, Eric
Botteghin, Marko Vejinovic, Renato Tapia, Jens Toornstra (81' Bart Nieuwkoop), Dirk Kuyt
(70' Bilal Basaçikoglu), Nicolai Jørgensen (46' Miquel Nelom), Eljero Elia.
Coach: Giovanni van Bronckhorst.
Goals: 15' Nicolai Jørgensen 0-1, 44' Rafael Forster 1-1.
Referee: Jakob Kehlet (DEN)   Attendance: 16,855.
Sent off: 43' Eric Botteghin.

Rafael Forster missed a penalty kick (44').

*(Zorya Luhansk played their home matches at Chronomorets Stadium, Odessa instead of their
regular stadium, Avanhard Stadium, Luhansk, due to the ongoing conflict in Eastern Ukraine)*

197

24.11.16　Sükrü Saracoglu Stadium, Istanbul: Fenerbahçe – Zorya Luhansk 2-0 (0-0)
Fenerbahçe: Volkan Demirel, Hasan-Ali Kaldirim, Simon Kjær, Sener Özbayrakli, Martin
Skrtel, Mehmet Topal, Souza, Alper Potuk, Moussa Sow (86' Salih Uçan), Volkan Sen (73'
Roman Neustädter), Emmanuel Emenike (46' Miroslav Stoch). Coach: Dick Advocaat.
Zorya Luhansk: Oleksiy Shevchenko, Nikita Kamenyuka (35' Evgeniy Opanasenko), Rafael
Forster, Eduard Sobol, Mikhail Sivakov, Igor Chaykovskiy, Ivan Petryak (57' Emmanuel
Bonaventure), Igor Kharatin, Oleksandr Karavayev, Dmytro Grechyshkin, Vladislav Kulach
(69' Paulo Victor). Coach: Yuriy Vernydub.
Goals: 59' Miroslav Stoch 1-0, 67' Simon Kjær 2-0.
Referee: Harald Lechner (AUT)　　Attendance: 16,145.
Sent off: 90' Eduard Sobol.

24.11.16　Old Trafford, Manchester: Manchester United – Feyenoord 4-0 (1-0)
Manchester United: Sergio Romero, Phil Jones, Daley Blind, Luke Shaw, Antonio Valencia,
Paul Pogba, Mata (70' Marcus Rashford), Michael Carrick, Henrikh Mkhitaryan (82' Jesse
Lingard), Zlatan Ibrahimovic, Wayne Rooney (82' Memphis Depay). Coach: José Mourinho.
Feyenoord: Brad Jones, Rick Karsdorp, Jan-Arie van der Heijden, Miquel Nelom, Wessel
Dammers, Tonny Vilhena, Renato Tapia, Jens Toornstra (78' Bilal Basaçikoglu), Dirk Kuyt
(61' Steven Berghuis), Nicolai Jørgensen (73' Michiel Kramer), Eljero Elia.
Coach: Giovanni van Bronckhorst.
Goals: 35' Wayne Rooney 1-0, 69' Mata 2-0, 75' Brad Jones 3-0 (og), 90' Jesse Lingard 4-0.
Referee: Manuel Gräfe (GER)　　Attendance: 64,628.

08.12.16　De Kuip, Rotterdam: Feyenoord – Fenerbahçe 0-1 (0-1)
Feyenoord: Brad Jones, Rick Karsdorp, Jan-Arie van der Heijden, Miquel Nelom, Eric
Botteghin, Karim El Ahmadi, Tonny Vilhena (75' Michiel Kramer), Jens Toornstra (46' Bilal
Basaçikoglu), Dirk Kuyt, Nicolai Jørgensen, Eljero Elia. Coach: Giovanni van Bronckhorst.
Fenerbahçe: Volkan Demirel, Hasan-Ali Kaldirim, Simon Kjær, Sener Özbayrakli, Martin
Skrtel, Mehmet Topal (86' Roman Neustädter), Souza, Alper Potuk, Robin van Persie (75'
Emmanuel Emenike), Moussa Sow, Jeremain Lens (70' Volkan Sen). Coach: Dick Advocaat.
Goal: 22' Moussa Sow 0-1.
Referee: David Fernández Borbalán (ESP)　　Attendance: 32,000.

08.12.16　Chornomorets Stadium, Odessa: Zorya Luhansk – Manchester United 0-2 (0-0)
Zorya Luhansk: Igor Levchenko, Artem Sukhotsky, Rafael Forster, Evgeniy Opanasenko,
Mikhail Sivakov, Igor Chaykovskiy, Ivan Petryak, Igor Kharatin (57' Dmytro Grechyshkin),
Oleksandr Karavayev, Zeljko Ljubenovic (72' Jaba Lipartia), Denys Bezborodko (54'
Emmanuel Bonaventure). Coach: Yuriy Vernydub.
Manchester United: Sergio Romero, Eric Bailly, Marcos Rojo, Daley Blind, Paul Pogba, Mata
(65' Jesse Lingard), Ashley Young, Ander Herrera, Henrikh Mkhitaryan (85' Timothy Fosu-
Mensah), Zlatan Ibrahimovic, Wayne Rooney (70' Marouane Fellaini). Coach: José Mourinho.
Goals: 48' Henrikh Mkhitaryan 0-1, 88' Zlatan Ibrahimovic 0-2.
Referee: Tamás Bognár (HUN)　　Attendance: 25,900.

GROUP B

15.09.16   Stade de Suisse, Bern: BSC Young Boys – Olympiakos Piraeus 0-1 (0-1)
BSC Young Boys: Yvon Mvogo, Steve von Bergen, Jan Lecjaks, Alain Rochat, Scott Sutter, Leonardo Bertone, Denis Zakaria, Miralem Sulejmani, Yoric Ravet (86' Kwadwo Duah), Michael Frey (78' Thorsten Schick), Yüya Kubo. Coach: Adi Hütter.
Olympiakos Piraeus: Nicola Leali, Alberto Botía, Manuel Da Costa, De La Bella, Diogo, Luka Milivojevic, Marko Marin (63' André Martins), Tarik Elyounoussi (90' Alaixys Romao), Esteban Cambiasso, Sebá, Brown Ideye (82' Óscar Cardozo). Coach: Paulo Bento.
Goal: 42' Esteban Cambiasso 0-1.
Referee: Sergey Boyko (UKR)   Attendance: 11,132.

15.09.16   Neo GSP Stadium, Nicosia: APOEL Nicosia – FK Astana 2-1 (0-1)
APOEL Nicosia: Boy Waterman, Roberto Lago, Carlão, Zhivko Milanov, Astiz, Nuno Morais, Giorgos Efrem (70' Igor de Camargo), Andrea Orlandi (56' Facundo Bertoglio), Vinicius, Pieros Sotiriou, Giannis Gianniotas (78' Vander). Coach: Thomas Christiansen.
FK Astana: Nenad Eric, Marin Anicic, Igor Shitov, Abzal Beysebekov, Sergiy Maliy, Dmitriy Shomko, Nemanja Maksimovic, Serikzhan Muzhikov (77' Askhat Tagybergen), Roger Cañas, Djordje Despotovic (57' Patrick Twumasi), Junior Kabananga (70' Tanat Nuserbaev). Coach: Stanimir Stoilov.
Goals: 45' Nemanja Maksimovic 0-1, 75' Vinicius 1-1, 87' Igor de Camargo 2-1.
Referee: Aleksandar Stavrev (MKD)   Attendance: 12,008.

29.09.16   Astana Arena, Astana: FK Astana – BSC Young Boys 0-0
FK Astana: Nenad Eric, Marin Anicic, Igor Shitov, Abzal Beysebekov, Sergiy Maliy, Dmitriy Shomko, Nemanja Maksimovic, Serikzhan Muzhikov (84' Azat Nurgaliev), Roger Cañas, Djordje Despotovic (75' Tanat Nuserbaev), Junior Kabananga (85' Askhat Tagybergen). Coach: Stanimir Stoilov.
BSC Young Boys: Yvon Mvogo, Steve von Bergen, Jan Lecjaks, Scott Sutter, Kasim Nuhu, Leonardo Bertone, Denis Zakaria, Miralem Sulejmani (82' Thorsten Schick), Yoric Ravet, Michael Frey (81' Kwadwo Duah), Yüya Kubo (90' Michel Aebischer). Coach: Adi Hütter.
Referee: Simon Lee Evans (WAL)   Attendance: 21,328.

29.09.16   Georgios Karaiskakis Stadium, Piraeus:
          Olympiakos Piraeus – APOEL Nicosia 0-1 (0-1)
Olympiakos Piraeus: Nicola Leali, Alberto Botía, Manuel Da Costa, De La Bella, Diogo, Luka Milivojevic, Kostas Fortounis (64' Tarik Elyounoussi), Marko Marin (78' Óscar Cardozo), Esteban Cambiasso (79' André Martins), Sebá, Brown Ideye. Coach: Paulo Bento.
APOEL Nicosia: Boy Waterman, Roberto Lago, Carlão, Zhivko Milanov, Nuno Morais, Giorgios Merkis, Facundo Bertoglio (65' Kostakis Artymatas), Vinicius, Vander (68' Giorgos Efrem), Pieros Sotiriou, Giannis Gianniotas (82' Astiz). Coach: Thomas Christiansen.
Goal: 10' Pieros Sotiriou 0-1.
Referee: Pawel Gil (POL)   Attendance: 24,378.

20.10.16   Georgios Karaiskakis Stadium, Piraeus: Olympiakos Piraeus – FK Astana 4-1 (3-0)
Olympiakos Piraeus: Nicola Leali, Alberto Botía, Manuel Da Costa, Panagiotis Retsos, Diogo,
Luka Milivojevic (73' Esteban Cambiasso), Kostas Fortounis (79' Andreas Bouchalakis),
Tarik Elyounoussi (69' Georgios Manthatis), André Martins, Óscar Cardozo, Sebá.
Coach: Paulo Bento.
FK Astana: Nenad Eric, Marin Anicic, Abzal Beysebekov, Sergiy Maliy, Yuriy Logvinenko,
Dmitriy Shomko, Askhat Tagybergen (63' Serikzhan Muzhikov), Roger Cañas, Tanat
Nuserbaev (59' Igor Shitov), Patrick Twumasi, Junior Kabananga (72' Djordje Despotovic).
Coach: Stanimir Stoilov.
Goals: 25' Diogo 1-0, 33' Tarik Elyounoussi 2-0, 34' Sebá (34'), 54' Junior Kabananga 3-1,
65' Sebá (65').
Referee: Tobias Stieler (GER)   Attendance: 21,480.
Sent off: 58' Roger Cañas.

20.10.16   Stade de Suisse, Bern: BSC Young Boys – APOEL Nicosia 3-1 (1-1)
BSC Young Boys: Yvon Mvogo, Steve von Bergen, Jan Lecjaks, Scott Sutter, Kasim Nuhu,
Thorsten Schick (80' Leonardo Bertone), Denis Zakaria, Sékou Sanogo, Yoric Ravet (88'
Kwadwo Duah), Yūya Kubo, Guillaume Hoarau (84' Michael Frey). Coach: Adi Hütter.
APOEL Nicosia: Boy Waterman, Roberto Lago, Carlão (50' Giorgios Merkis), Zhivko
Milanov, Astiz, Nuno Morais, Giorgos Efrem, Facundo Bertoglio (78' Renan Bressan),
Vinicius, Vander (68' Giannis Gianniotas), Pieros Sotiriou. Coach: Thomas Christiansen.
Goals: 14' Giorgos Efrem 0-1, 18', 52', 82' Guillaume Hoarau 1-1, 2-1, 3-1 (p).
Referee: Tobias Welz (GER)   Attendance: 9,553.

Guillaume Hoarau missed a penalty kick (52').

03.11.16   Astana Arena, Astana: FK Astana – Olympiakos Piraeus 1-1 (1-1)
FK Astana: Nenad Eric, Igor Shitov, Abzal Beysebekov, Sergiy Maliy, Yuriy Logvinenko,
Dmitriy Shomko, Nemanja Maksimovic, Serikzhan Muzhikov, Djordje Despotovic (82'
Birzhan Kulbekov), Patrick Twumasi (90' Gevorg Najaryan), Junior Kabananga.
Coach: Stanimir Stoilov.
Olympiakos Piraeus: Nicola Leali, Alberto Botía, Omar Elabdellaoui, Bruno Viana, Panagiotis
Retsos, Andreas Bouchalakis, Esteban Cambiasso (81' Alaixys Romao), André Martins (90'
Athanasios Androutsos), Georgios Manthatis (64' Tarik Elyounoussi), Óscar Cardozo, Sebá.
Coach: Paulo Bento.
Goals: 8' Djordje Despotovic 1-0, 30' Sebá 1-1.
Referee: Orel Grinfeeld (ISR)   Attendance: 12,158.

03.11.16   Neo GSP Stadium, Nicosia: APOEL Nicosia – BSC YoungBoys 1-0 (0-0)
APOEL Nicosia: Boy Waterman, Roberto Lago, Carlão, Zhivko Milanov, Astiz, Nuno Morais,
Giorgos Efrem, Vinicius, Renan Bressan (59' Facundo Bertoglio), Pieros Sotiriou (84' Igor de
Camargo), Efstathios Aloneftis (67' Giannis Gianniotas). Coach: Thomas Christiansen.
BSC Young Boys: Yvon Mvogo, Steve von Bergen, Jan Lecjaks, Scott Sutter, Kasim Nuhu,
Thorsten Schick, Denis Zakaria (80' Leonardo Bertone), Sékou Sanogo, Yoric Ravet (65'
Kevin Mbabu), Yūya Kubo (80' Michael Frey), Guillaume Hoarau. Coach: Adi Hütter.
Goal: 69' Pieros Sotiriou 1-0.
Referee: Sébastien Delferière (BEL)   Attendance: 12,761.
Sent off: 67' Kevin Mbabu.

200

24.11.16   Astana Arena, Astana: FK Astana – APOEL Nicosia 2-1 (0-1)
FK Astana: Nenad Eric, Marin Anicic, Igor Shitov (77' Tanat Nuserbaev), Abzal Beysebekov, Yuriy Logvinenko, Dmitriy Shomko, Nemanja Maksimovic, Serikzhan Muzhikov (81' Azat Nurgaliev), Roger Cañas, Djordje Despotovic, Junior Kabananga (90' Sergiy Maliy).
Coach: Stanimir Stoilov.
APOEL Nicosia: Boy Waterman, Roberto Lago, Carlão, Zhivko Milanov, Astiz, Nuno Morais, Giorgos Efrem (81' Giannis Gianniotas), Vinicius, Igor de Camargo (63' Vander), Pieros Sotiriou, Efstathios Aloneftis (35' Kostakis Artymatas). Coach: Thomas Christiansen.
Goals: 31' Giorgos Efrem 0-1, 59' Marin Anicic 1-1, 84' Djordje Despotovic 2-1.
Referee: Kevin Blom (HOL)   Attendance: 9,143.
Sent off: 33' Astiz.

24.11.16   Georgios Karaiskakis Stadium, Piraeus:
Olympiakos Piraeus – BSC Young Boys 1-1 (0-0)
Olympiakos Piraeus: Nicola Leali, Alberto Botía, Manuel Da Costa, Panagiotis Retsos, Diogo, Luka Milivojevic, Kostas Fortounis, Tarik Elyounoussi (84' Georgios Manthatis), André Martins, Sebá, Brown Ideye. Coach: Paulo Bento.
BSC Young Boys: Yvon Mvogo, Steve von Bergen, Jan Lecjaks, Scott Sutter, Loris Benito, Leonardo Bertone, Thorsten Schick (88' Michael Frey), Denis Zakaria, Sékou Sanogo (77' Kwadwo Duah), Miralem Sulejmani (58' Alexander Gerndt), Guillaume Hoarau.
Coach: Adi Hütter.
Goals: 48' Kostas Fortounis 1-0, 58' Guillaume Hoarau 1-1.
Referee: Miroslav Zelinka (CZE)   Attendance: 24,131.

08.12.16   Stade de Suisse, Bern: BSC Young Boys – FK Astana 3-0 (0-0)
BSC Young Boys: Yvon Mvogo, Steve von Bergen, Scott Sutter, Kasim Nuhu, Linus Obexer (67' Loris Benito), Leonardo Bertone, Thorsten Schick, Sékou Sanogo, Michel Aebischer (61' Michael Frey), Alexander Gerndt, Guillaume Hoarau (78' Kwadwo Duah). Coach: Adi Hütter.
FK Astana: Nenad Eric, Igor Shitov, Abzal Beysebekov, Yuriy Logvinenko (55' Sergiy Maliy), Dmitriy Shomko, Nemanja Maksimovic, Serikzhan Muzhikov (87' Abay Zhunussov), Roger Cañas, Djordje Despotovic (77' Gevorg Najaryan), Patrick Twumasi, Junior Kabananga.
Coach: Stanimir Stoilov.
Goals: 63' Michael Frey 1-0, 66' Guillaume Hoarau 2-0, 81' Thorsten Schick 3-0.
Referee: Clayton Pisani (MLT)   Attendance: 7,616.

08.12.16   Neo GSP Stadium, Nicosia: APOEL Nicosia – Olympiakos Piraeus 2-0 (1-0)
APOEL Nicosia: Boy Waterman, Carlão, Zhivko Milanov, Nuno Morais, Giorgios Merkis, Giorgos Efrem (59' Giannis Gianniotas), Facundo Bertoglio (67' Andrea Orlandi), Vinicius, Nektarios Alexandrou, Pieros Sotiriou (80' Igor de Camargo), Efstathios Aloneftis.
Coach: Thomas Christiansen.
Olympiakos Piraeus: Nicola Leali, Manuel Da Costa, De la Bella (76' Georgios Manthatis), Bruno Viana, Diogo, Alaixys Romao, Kostas Fortounis (76' Alejandro Domínguez), Tarik Elyounoussi, André Martins (66' Athanasios Androutsos), Sebá, Brown Ideye.
Coach: Paulo Bento.
Goals: 19' Manuel Da Costa 1-0 (og), 83' Igor de Camargo 2-0.
Referee: Carlos Del Cerro Grande (ESP)   Attendance: 14,779.

GROUP C

15.09.16   Opel Arena, Mainz: 1. FSV Mainz 05 – AS Saint-Étienne 1-1 (0-0)
1. FSV Mainz 05: Jonas Lössl, Giulio Donati, Stefan Bell, Gaëtan Bussmann, Jean-Philippe
Gbamin, Niko Bungert, Yunus Malli, Christian Clemens (84' Levin Öztunali), Pablo de Blasis,
Suat Serdar (72' Fabian Frei), Yoshinori Muto (69' Jhon Córdoba). Coach: Martin Schmidt.
AS Saint-Étienne: Jessy Moulin, Kévin Théophile-Catherine, Florentin Pogba, Loïc Perrin,
Kévin Malcuit, Bryan Dabo (57' Oussama Tannane), Henri Saivet (80' Alexander Søderlund),
Ole Selnæs, Fabien Lemoine (67' Jordan Veretout), Romain Hamouma, Robert Beríc.
Coach: Christophe Galtier.
Goals: 57' Niko Bungert 1-0, 88' Robert Beríc 1-1.
Referee: Svein Oddvar Moen (NOR)   Attendance: 20,275.

15.09.16   Constant Vanden Stock Stadium, Brussels: RSC Anderlecht – Gabala FK 3-1 (2-1)
RSC Anderlecht: Davy Roef, Serigne Mbodj, Uros Spajic, Bram Nuytinck, Alexandru Chipciu
(73' Capel), Frank Acheampong, Youri Tielemans (18' Stephane Badji), Leander Dendoncker,
Nicolae Stanciu, Sofiane Hanni, Lukasz Teodorczyk (80' Hamdi Harbaoui).
Coach: René Weiler.
Gabala FK: Dmitro Bezotosniy, Vojislav Stankovic, Vitaliy Vernydub (59' Petar Franjic),
Ricardinho, Rafael Santos, Räsad Sadiqov, Magomed Mirzabekov, Filip Ozobic, Sergei Zenjov
(90' Rashad Eyyubov), Ruslan Qurbanov (46' Asif Mammadov), Bagaliy Dabo.
Coach: Roman Grygorchuk.
Goals: 14' Lukasz Teodorczyk 1-0, 20' Bagaliy Dabo 1-1, 41' Rafael Santos 2-1 (og),
77' Capel 3-1.
Referee: Harald Lechner (AUT)   Attendance: 11,638.

29.09.16   Bakcell Arena, Baku: Gabala FK – 1. FSV Mainz 05 2-3 (0-1)
Gabala FK: Dmitro Bezotosniy, Vojislav Stankovic, Vitaliy Vernydub (86' Elvin Jamalov),
Ricardinho, Rafael Santos, Räsad Sadiqov (81' Asif Mammadov), Magomed Mirzabekov,
Filip Ozobic, Sergei Zenjov, Ruslan Qurbanov (81' Petar Franjic), Bagaliy Dabo.
Coach: Roman Grygorchuk.
1. FSV Mainz 05: Jonas Lössl, Stefan Bell, Daniel Brosinski, Gaëtan Bussmann, Alexander
Hack, José Rodríguez (67' Jhon Córdoba), Yunus Malli, Fabian Frei, Christian Clemens (67'
Levin Öztunali), Pablo de Blasis, Yoshinori Muto (84' Suat Serdar). Coach: Martin Schmidt.
Goals: 41' Yoshinori Muto 0-1, 57' Ruslan Qurbanov 1-1 (p), 62' Sergei Zenjov 2-1,
68' Jhon Córdoba 2-2, 78' Levin Öztunali 2-3.
Referee: Gediminas Mazeika (LTU)   Attendance: 6,500.

29.09.16   Stade Geoffroy-Guichard, Saint-Étienne:
            AS Saint-Étienne – RSC Anderlecht 1-1 (0-0)
AS Saint-Étienne: Jessy Moulin, Léo Lacroix, Kévin Malcuit, Benjamin Kantie Karamoko,
Vincent Pajot (76' Alexander Søderlund), Jérémy Clément (86' Benjamin Corgnet), Bryan
Dabo (77' Oussama Tannane), Jordan Veretout, Nolan Roux, Romain Hamouma, Kévin
Monnet-Paquet. Coach: Christophe Galtier.
RSC Anderlecht: Davy Roef, Serigne Mbodj, Uros Spajic, Bram Nuytinck, Alexandru Chipciu,
Frank Acheampong, Youri Tielemans, Leander Dendoncker, Nicolae Stanciu (82' Capel),
Sofiane Hanni (75' Stephane Badji), Lukasz Teodorczyk (69' Hamdi Harbaoui).
Coach: René Weiler.
Goals: 62' Youri Tielemans 0-1 (p), 90' Nolan Roux 1-1.
Referee: Vladislav Bezborodov (RUS)   Attendance: 23,258.

20.10.16   Stade Geoffroy-Guichard, Saint-Étienne: AS Saint-Étienne – Gabala FK 1-0 (0-0)
AS Saint-Étienne: Jessy Moulin, Kévin Théophile-Catherine, Cheikh M'Bengue, Florentin
Pogba, Loïc Perrin, Henri Saivet (90' Vincent Pajot), Jordan Veretout, Ole Selnæs, Nolan
Roux, Oussama Tannane (62' Robert Beric), Kévin Monnet-Paquet. Coach: Christophe Galtier.
Gabala FK: Dmitro Bezotosniy, Vojislav Stankovic, Vitaliy Vernydub, Ricardinho, Urfan
Abbasov, Magomed Mirzabekov, Filip Ozobic, Theo Weeks, Sergei Zenjov (81' Petar Franjic),
Ruslan Qurbanov, Asif Mammadov (81' Rashad Eyyubov). Coach: Roman Grygorchuk.
Goal: 70' Ricardinho 1-0 (og).
Referee: Ali Palabiyik (TUR)   Attendance: 22,855.

20.10.16   Opel Arena, Mainz: 1. FSV Mainz 05 – RSC Anderlecht 1-1 (1-0)
1. FSV Mainz 05: Jonas Lössl, Giulio Donati, Stefan Bell, Gaëtan Bussmann, Jean-Philippe
Gbamin, Niko Bungert, Yunus Malli, Pablo de Blasis (76' Jairo), Suat Serdar (59' Daniel
Brosinski), Jhon Córdoba, Karim Onisiwo (80' Levin Öztunali). Coach: Martin Schmidt.
RSC Anderlecht: Davy Roef, Olivier Deschacht, Serigne Mbodj, Bram Nuytinck, Emmanuel
Adjei (82' Massimo Bruno), Frank Acheampong, Youri Tielemans, Leander Dendoncker,
Nicolae Stanciu (60' Capel), Sofiane Hanni, Lukasz Teodorczyk (76' Stephane Badji).
Coach: René Weiler.
Goals: 10' Yunus Malli 1-0 (p), 65' Lukasz Teodorczyk 1-1.
Referee: Jesús Gil Manzano (ESP)   Attendance: 21,317.

03.11.16   Bakcell Arena, Baku: Gabala FK – AS Saint-Étienne 1-2 (1-1)
Gabala FK: Dmitro Bezotosniy, Vojislav Stankovic, Vitaliy Vernydub, Ricardinho, Räsad
Sadiqov (84' Nika Kvekveskiri), Magomed Mirzabekov, Filip Ozobic, Theo Weeks, Sergei
Zenjov (61' Asif Mammadov), Ruslan Qurbanov, Rashad Eyyubov (65' Petar Franjic).
Coach: Roman Grygorchuk.
AS Saint-Étienne: Stéphane Ruffier, Cheikh M'Bengue, Florentin Pogba, Loïc Perrin, Kévin
Malcuit, Henri Saivet (74' Vincent Pajot), Jordan Veretout, Ole Selnæs, Oussama Tannane
(84' Nolan Roux), Kévin Monnet-Paquet, Robert Beric (62' Alexander Søderlund).
Coach: Christophe Galtier.
Goals: 39' Ruslan Qurbanov 1-0, 45' Oussama Tannane 1-1, 53' Robert Beric 1-2.
Referee: Carlos Del Cerro Grande (ESP)   Attendance: 5,600.

03.11.16   Constant Vanden Stock Stadium, Brussels:
            RSC Anderlecht – 1. FSV Mainz 05 6-1 (2-1)
RSC Anderlecht: Davy Roef, Olivier Deschacht, Serigne Mbodj, Emmanuel Adjei, Alexandru
Chipciu (56' Capel), Frank Acheampong, Youri Tielemans (89' Massimo Bruno), Leander
Dendoncker, Nicolae Stanciu (67' Stephane Badji), Sofiane Hanni, Lukasz Teodorczyk.
Coach: René Weiler.
1. FSV Mainz 05: Jonas Lössl, Giulio Donati (79' Levin Öztunali), Leon Balogun, Stefan Bell,
Daniel Brosinski, Jean-Philippe Gbamin, Yunus Malli, Pablo de Blasis, Suat Serdar (67' Jairo),
Jhon Córdoba, Karim Onisiwo. Coach: Martin Schmidt.
Goals: 9' Nicolae Stanciu 1-0, 15' Pablo de Blasis 1-1, 41' Nicolae Stanciu 2-1,
62' Youri Tielemans 3-1, 89' Lukasz Teodorczyk 4-1, 90+2' Massimo Bruno 5-1,
90+4' Lukasz Teodorczyk 6-1 (p).
Referee: Andreas Ekberg (SWE)   Attendance: 13,275.

24.11.16   Bakcell Arena, Baku: Gabala FK – RSC Anderlecht 1-3 (1-1)
Gabala FK: Dmitro Bezotosniy, Vitaliy Vernydub, Ricardinho, Urfan Abbasov, Rafael Santos, Nika Kvekveskiri, Filip Ozobic, Theo Weeks, Asif Mammadov, Bagaliy Dabo (52' Ruslan Qurbanov), Rashad Eyyubov. Coach: Roman Grygorchuk.
RSC Anderlecht: Frank Boeckx, Uros Spajic, Bram Nuytinck, Ivan Obradovic, Emmanuel Adjei, Capel (60' Massimo Bruno), Frank Acheampong (90' Idrissa Doumbia), Youri Tielemans, Leander Dendoncker, Nicolae Stanciu (70' Sofiane Hanni), Lukasz Teodorczyk. Coach: René Weiler.
Goals: 11' Youri Tielemans 0-1, 15' Ricardinho 1-1 (p), 90' Massimo Bruno 1-2, 90+4' Lukasz Teodorczyk 1-3.
Referee: Evgen Aranovskiy (UKR)   Attendance: 4,500.
Sent off: 89' Rashad Eyyubov.

24.11.16   Stade Geoffroy-Guichard, Saint-Étienne: AS Saint-Étienne – 1. FSV Mainz 05 0-0
AS Saint-Étienne: Stéphane Ruffier, Kévin Théophile-Catherine, Pierre-Yves Polomat, Florentin Pogba, Loïc Perrin, Henri Saivet, Jordan Veretout (90' Léo Lacroix), Ole Selnæs, Nolan Roux (83' Vincent Pajot), Oussama Tannane, Kévin Monnet-Paquet (59' Arnaud Nordin). Coach: Christophe Galtier.
1. FSV Mainz 05: Jonas Lössl, Leon Balogun, Stefan Bell, Daniel Brosinski, Gaëtan Bussmann (83' Jairo), Jean-Philippe Gbamin (83' Aaron Seydel), Levin Öztunali, Yunus Malli, André Ramalho (65' Fabian Frei), Jhon Córdoba, Karim Onisiwo. Coach: Martin Schmidt.
Referee: Bas Nijhuis (HOL)   Attendance: 21,750.

08.12.16   Opel Arena, Mainz: 1. FSV Mainz 05 – Gabala FK 2-0 (2-0)
1. FSV Mainz 05: Jannik Huth, Giulio Donati, Stefan Bell, Gaëtan Bussmann, Jean-Philippe Gbamin (69' Yunus Malli), Alexander Hack, Jairo, Fabian Frei, André Ramalho, Pablo de Blasis (86' Gerrit Holtmann), Jhon Córdoba (81' Aaron Seydel). Coach: Martin Schmidt.
Gabala FK: Dmitro Bezotosniy, Vojislav Stankovic, Vitaliy Vernydub, Ricardinho, Urfan Abbasov, Räsad Sadiqov (46' Ruslan Qurbanov), Nika Kvekveskiri, Filip Ozobic, Theo Weeks (86' Elvin Jamalov), Sergei Zenjov (77' Roman Huseynov), Asif Mammadov.
Coach: Roman Grygorchuk.
Goals: 30' Alexander Hack 1-0, 40' Pablo de Blasis 2-0.
Referee: Simon Lee Evans (WAL)   Attendance: 12,860.

08.12.16   Constant Vanden Stock Stadium, Brussels:
                   RSC Anderlecht – AS Saint-Étienne 2-3 (2-0)
RSC Anderlecht: Davy Roef, Uros Spajic, Bram Nuytinck, Ivan Obradovic, Emmanuel Adjei, Stéphane Badji, Alexandru Chipciu (60' Andy Najar), Frank Acheampong (66' Sofiane Hanni), Leander Dendoncker, Nicolae Stanciu, Jorn Vancamp (60' Lukasz Teodorczyk). Coach: René Weiler.
AS Saint-Étienne: Stéphane Ruffier, Kévin Théophile-Catherine, Pierre-Yves Polomat, Léo Lacroix, Florentin Pogba, Kévin Malcuit, Bryan Dabo, Henri Saivet (63' Vincent Pajot), Kévin Monnet-Paquet, Alexander Søderlund (76' Oussama Tannane), Arnaud Nordin (63' Romain Hamouma). Coach: Christophe Galtier.
Goals: 21' Alexandru Chipciu 1-0, 31' Nicolae Stanciu 2-0, 62', 67' Alexander Søderlund 1-2, 2-2, 74' Kévin Monnet-Paquet 2-3.
Referee: István Kovács (ROM)   Attendance: 13,583.

204

GROUP D

15.09.16   AFAS Stadion, Alkmaar: AZ Alkmaar – Dundalk FC 1-1 (0-0)
AZ Alkmaar: Sergio Rochet, Mattias Johansson, Rens van Eijden, Ron Vlaar, Ridgeciano Haps, Derrick Luckassen, Joris van Overeem, Stijn Wuytens (65' Ben Rienstra), Alireza Jahanbakhsh (75' Iliass Bel Hassani), Dabney dos Santos, Fred Friday (55' Wout Weghorst). Coach: John van den Brom.
Dundalk FC: Gary Rogers, Sean Gannon, Brian Gartland, Andrew Boyle, Dane Massey, Stephen O'Donnell, Daryl Horgan, John Mountney (77' Robbie Benson), Ronan Finn, David McMillan (75' Chris Shields), Patrick McEleney (84' Ciarán Kilduff). Coach: Stephen Kenny.
Goals: 61' Stijn Wuytens 1-0, 89' Ciarán Kilduff 1-1.
Referee: Clayton Pisani (MLT)   Attendance: 10,003.
Sent off: 71' Stephen O'Donnell.

15.09.16   Netanya Stadium, Netanya: Maccabi Tel Aviv – Zenit St.Petersburg 3-4 (1-0)
Maccabi Tel Aviv: Predrag Rajkovic, Elazar Dasa, Omri Ben Harush, Egor Filipenko, Tal Ben Haim (I), Haris Medunjanin, Gal Alberman, Nosa Igiebor, Yossi Benayoun (79' Dor Mikha), Tal Ben Haim (II) (85' Dor Peretz), Vidar Kjartansson (74' Eden Ben Basat). Coach: Shota Arveladze.
Zenit St.Petersburg: Yuriy Lodygin, Domenico Criscito, Neto, Igor Smolnikov, Javi García (71' Maurício), Axel Witsel, Yuriy Zhirkov (90' Ivan Novoseltsev), Giuliano, Aleksandr Kokorin, Aleksandr Kerzhakov (61' Luka Djordjevic), Róbert Mak. Coach: Mircea Lucescu.
Goals: 26' Haris Medunjanin 1-0, 50' Vidar Kjartansson 2-0, 70' Haris Medunjanin 3-0, 77' Aleksandr Kokorin 3-1, 84' Maurício 3-2, 86' Giuliano 3-3, 90+2' Luka Djordjevic 3-4.
Referee: Ivan Kruzliak (SVK)   Attendance: 10,855.
Sent off: 81' Elazar Dasa.

(Maccabi Tel Aviv played their home matches at Netanya Stadium, Netanya instead of their regular stadium, Bloomfield Stadium, Tel Aviv)

29.09.16   Petrovsky Stadium, Saint Petersburg: Zenit St.Petersburg – AZ Alkmaar 5-0 (1-0)
Zenit St.Petersburg: Yuriy Lodygin, Domenico Criscito, Nicolas Lombaerts, Neto, Igor Smolnikov, Javi García (63' Maurício), Axel Witsel, Giuliano, Aleksandr Kokorin, Artem Dzyuba (64' Oleg Shatov), Róbert Mak (69' Luka Djordjevic). Coach: Mircea Lucescu.
AZ Alkmaar: Sergio Rochet, Rens van Eijden, Ron Vlaar (57' Ben Rienstra), Ridgeciano Haps, Derrick Luckassen, Fernando Lewis, Joris van Overeem, Stijn Wuytens, Wout Weghorst (27' Mats Seuntjens), Dabney dos Santos (73' Iliass Bel Hassani), Fred Friday. Coach: John van den Brom.
Goals: 26' Aleksandr Kokorin 1-0, 48' Giuliano 2-0, 59' Aleksandr Kokorin 3-0, 66' Domenico Criscito 4-0 (p), 80' Oleg Shatov 5-0.
Referee: Xavier Estrada Fernández (ESP)   Attendance: 15,275.

29.09.16   Tallaght Stadium, Dubin: Dundalk FC – Maccabi Tel Aviv 1-0 (0-0)
Dundalk FC: Gary Rogers, Sean Gannon, Brian Gartland, Andrew Boyle, Dane Massey, Chris
Shields, Daryl Horgan, Ronan Finn, David McMillan (65' Ciarán Kilduff), Patrick McEleney
(75' John Mountney), Robbie Benson (85' Dean Shiels). Coach: Stephen Kenny.
Maccabi Tel Aviv: Predrag Rajkovic, Eitan Tibi, Omri Ben Harush, Tal Ben Haim (I), Haris
Medunjanin, Oscar Scarione, Gal Alberman (76' Barak Itzhaki), Nosa Igiebor (60' Dor
Mikha), Dor Peretz, Tal Ben Haim (II) (82' Yossi Benayoun), Vidar Kjartansson.
Coach: Shota Arveladze.
Goal: 72' Ciarán Kilduff.
Referee: Andris Treimanis (LAT)   Attendance: 5,543.

*(Dundalk FC played their home matches at Tallaght Stadium, Dublin instead of their regular
stadium, Oriel Park, Dublin)*

20.10.16   Tallaght Stadium, Dubin: Dundalk FC – Zenit St.Petersburg 1-2 (0-0)
Dundalk FC: Gabriel Sava, Sean Gannon, Brian Gartland, Andrew Boyle, Dane Massey, Chris
Shields (86' Dean Shiels), Daryl Horgan, Ronan Finn, David McMillan (72' Ciarán Kilduff),
Patrick McEleney, Robbie Benson (79' John Mountney). Coach: Stephen Kenny.
Zenit St.Petersburg: Yuriy Lodygin, Aleksandr Anyukov, Domenico Criscito, Nicolas
Lombaerts, Neto, Oleg Shatov (62' Aleksandr Kokorin), Javi García (71' Maurício), Axel
Witsel, Giuliano, Artem Dzyuba, Róbert Mak (78' Luka Djordjevic), Coach: Mircea Lucescu.
Goals: 52' Robbie Benson1-0, 71' Róbert Mak 1-1, 77' Giuliano 1-2.
Referee: Miroslav Zelinka (CZE)   Attendance: 5,500.

Maurício missed a penalty kick (90').

20.10.16   AFAS Stadium, Alkmaar: AZ Alkmaar – Maccabi Tel Aviv 1-2 (0-1)
AZ Alkmaar: Sergio Rochet, Mattias Johansson, Rens van Eijden, Ridgeciano Haps, Derrick
Luckassen (84' Wout Weghorst), Ben Rienstra (57' Guus Til), Joris van Overeem (61' Levi
García), Iliass Bel Hassani, Stijn Wuytens, Robert Mühren, Fred Friday.
Coach: John van den Brom.
Maccabi Tel Aviv: Predrag Rajkovic, Elazar Dasa, Eitan Tibi, Omri Ben Harush, Tal Ben
Haim (I), Haris Medunjanin, Oscar Scarione (84' Egor Filipenko), Gal Alberman (79' Nosa
Igiebor), Eyal Golasa, Tal Ben Haim (II) (69' Dor Mikha), Vidar Kjartansson.
Coach: Shota Arveladze.
Goals: 24' Oscar Scarione 0-1, 72' Robert Mühren 1-1, 82' Eyal Golasa 1-2.
Referee: István Kovács (ROM)   Attendance: 12,016.

03.11.16   Petrovsky Stadium, Saint Petersburg: Zenit St.Petersburg – Dundalk FC 2-1 (1-0)
Zenit St.Petersburg: Mikhail Kerzhakov, Aleksandr Anyukov, Domenico Criscito, Nicolas
Lombaerts (89' Yuriy Zhirkov), Neto, Maurício, Oleg Shatov (68' Róbert Mak), Axel Witsel,
Giuliano, Aleksandr Kokorin, Aleksandr Kerzhakov (90' Luka Djordjevic).
Coach: Mircea Lucescu.
Dundalk FC: Gary Rogers, Sean Gannon, Brian Gartland, Andrew Boyle, Dane Massey, Chris
Shields, Daryl Horgan, John Mountney (46' Stephen O'Donnell), Ronan Finn, David
McMillan (65' Ciarán Kilduff), Patrick McEleney (83' Dean Shiels). Coach: Stephen Kenny.
Goals: 42' Giuliano 1-0, 52' Daryl Horgan 1-1, 78' Giuliano 2-1.
Referee: Luca Banti (ITA)   Attendance: 17,723.

03.11.16   Netanya Stadium, Netanya: Maccabi Tel Aviv – AZ Alkmaar 0-0
Maccabi Tel Aviv: Predrag Rajkovic, Elazar Dasa, Eitan Tibi, Omri Ben Harush (71' Avi
Rikan), Tal Ben Haim (I), Haris Medunjanin, Oscar Scarione, Gal Alberman, Tal Ben Haim
(II), Dor Mikha (81' Yossi Benayoun), Vidar Kjartansson (72' Nosa Igiebor).
Coach: Shota Arveladze.
AZ Alkmaar: Sergio Rochet, Mattias Johansson, Rens van Eijden (55' Robert Mühren), Ron
Vlaar, Ridgeciano Haps, Derrick Luckassen, Ben Rienstra, Iliass Bel Hassani (61' Dabney dos
Santos), Stijn Wuytens, Wout Weghorst (77' Fred Friday), Levi García.
Coach: John van den Brom.
Referee: Davide Massa (ITA)   Attendance: 11,356.

24.11.16   Petrovsky Stadium, Saint Petersburg:
          Zenit St.Petersburg – Maccabi Tel Aviv 2-0 (1-0)
Zenit St.Petersburg: Yuriy Lodygin, Ivan Novoseltsev, Domenico Criscito, Neto, Javi García,
Axel Witsel, Yuriy Zhirkov (75' Nicolas Lombaerts), Giuliano, Aleksandr Kokorin (66'
Aleksandr Kerzhakov), Róbert Mak, Luka Djordjevic (46' Artem Dzyuba).
Coach: Mircea Lucescu.
Maccabi Tel Aviv: Predrag Rajkovic, Elazar Dasa, Eitan Tibi, Omri Ben Harush, Egor
Filipenko, Haris Medunjanin (82' Eliel Peretz), Oscar Scarione (46' Yossi Benayoun), Eyal
Golasa, Nosa Igiebor, Eden Ben Basat, Tal Ben Haim (II) (46' Sagiv Yehezkel).
Coach: Shota Arveladze.
Goals: 44' Aleksandr Kokorin 1-0, 90+1' Aleksandr Kerzhakov 2-0.
Referee: Aleksandar Stavrev (MKD)   Attendance: 15,843.

24.11.16   Tallaght Stadium, Dublin: Dundalk FC – AZ Alkmaar 0-1 (0-1)
Dundalk FC: Gary Rogers, Sean Gannon, Brian Gartland, Andrew Boyle, Dane Massey,
Stephen O'Donnell (42' John Mountney), Daryl Horgan, Ronan Finn, Patrick McEleney (80'
Dean Shiels), Ciarán Kilduff (77' David McMillan), Robbie Benson. Coach: Stephen Kenny.
AZ Alkmaar: Sergio Rochet, Mattias Johansson, Ron Vlaar, Ridgeciano Haps, Derrick
Luckassen, Ben Rienstra, Mats Seuntjens, Stijn Wuytens, Alireza Jahanbakhsh (75' Dabney
dos Santos), Wout Weghorst (87' Fred Friday), Muamer Tankovic (79' Thomas Ouwejan).
Coach: John van den Brom.
Goal: 9' Wout Weghorst 0-1.
Referee: István Vad (HUN)   Attendance: 5,500.

08.12.16   AFAS Stadion, Alkmaar: AZ Alkmaar – Zenit St.Petersburg 3-2 (2-0)
AZ Alkmaar: Sergio Rochet, Mattias Johansson, Ridgeciano Haps, Derrick Luckassen, Ben
Rienstra, Iliass Bel Hassani (69' Alireza Jahanbakhsh), Mats Seuntjens (73' Joris van
Overeem), Stijn Wuytens, Wout Weghorst, Muamer Tankovic (69' Dabney dos Santos),
Robert Mühren. Coach: John van den Brom.
Zenit St.Petersburg: Yuriy Lodygin, Aleksandr Anyukov, Ivan Novoseltsev, Nicolas
Lombaerts, Javi García (60' Artur Yusupov), Axel Witsel, Yuriy Zhirkov, Giuliano, Artem
Dzyuba, Róbert Mak, Luka Djordjevic (46' Aleksandr Kokorin). Coach: Mircea Lucescu.
Goals: 7' Ben Rienstra 1-0, 43' Ridgeciano Haps 2-0, 58' Giuliano 2-1,
68' Muamer Tankovic 3-1, 80' Stijn Wuytens 3-2 (og).
Referee: Svein Oddvar Moen (NOR)   Attendance: 13,713.

08.12.16   Netanya Stadium, Netanya: Maccabi Tel Aviv – Dundalk FC 2-1 (2-1)
Maccabi Tel Aviv: Predrag Rajkovic, Elazar Dasa, Eitan Tibi, Omri Ben Harush, Tal Ben
Haim (I), Haris Medunjanin, Eyal Golasa (82' Gal Alberman), Nosa Igiebor (84' Yossi
Benayoun), Tal Ben Haim (II) (88' Eden Ben Basat), Dor Mikha, Vidar Kjartansson.
Coach: Shota Arveladze.
Dundalk FC: Gary Rogers, Sean Gannon (68' Stephen O'Donnell), Brian Gartland (46' Patrick
Barrett), Andrew Boyle, Dane Massey, Chris Shields, Daryl Horgan, Ronan Finn, David
McMillan, Patrick McEleney (80' Ciarán Kilduff), Robbie Benson. Coach: Stephen Kenny.
Goals: 21' Tal Ben Haim (II) 1-0 (p), 27' Elazar Dasa 1-1 (og), 38' Dor Mikha 2-1.
Referee: Robert Schörgenhofer (AUT)   Attendance: 9,891.

GROUP E

15.09.16   Doosan Arena, Plzen: Viktoria Plzen – AS Roma 1-1 (1-1)
Viktoria Plzen: Petr Bolek, Lukás Hejda, Ales Mateju, Roman Hubník, David Limbersky,
Tomás Horava, Martin Zeman (72' Milan Petrzela), Jan Kopic, Ergis Kaçe, Michal Duris (78'
Michal Krmencík), Marek Bakos (85' Tomás Poznar). Coach: Roman Pivarník.
AS Roma: Alisson, Juan Jesus, Bruno Peres, Federico Fazio, Kostas Manolas, Radja
Nainggolan, Leandro Paredes, Diego Perotti, Gerson (46' Edin Dzeko), Juan Iturbe (71'
Alessandro Florenzi), Stephan El Shaarawy (72' Francesco Totti). Coach: Luciano Spalletti.
Goals: 4' Diego Perotti 0-1 (p), 11' Marek Bakos 1-1.
Referee: Ruddy Buquet (FRA)   Attendance: 10,326.

15.09.16   Arena Nationala, Bucharest: Astra Giurgiu – Austria Wien 2-3 (1-2)
Astra Giurgiu: Silviu Lung Jr., Geraldo Alves, Fabricio, Junior Maranhão, Cristian Sapunaru,
Florin Lovin (46' Viorel Nicoara), Damien Boudjemaa (76' Daniel Florea), Filipe Teixeira,
Denis Alibec, Constantin Budescu, Daniel Niculae (46' Takayuki Seto).
Coach: Marius Sumudica.
Austria Wien: Osman Hadzikic, Petar Filipovic, Lukas Rotpuller, Ismael Tajouri Shradi,
Alexander Grünwald, Tarkan Serbest, De Paula (37' Jens Stryger Larsen), Thomas Salamon,
Raphael Holzhauser, Kevin Friesenbichler (81' Olarenwaju Kayode), Felipe Pires (62' Lucas
Venuto). Coach: Thorsten Fink.
Goals: 16' Raphael Holzhauser 0-1 (p), 18' Denis Alibec 1-1, 33' Kevin Friesenbichler 1-2,
58' Alexander Grünwald 1-3, 74' Cristian Sapunaru 2-3.
Referee: Andreas Ekberg (SWE)   Attendance: 3,300.
Sent off: 79' Lukas Rotpuller.

*(Astra Giurgiu played their home matches at Arena Nationala, Bucharest instead of their
regular stadium, Stadionul Marin Anastasovici, Giurgiu)*

29.09.16   Ernst-Happel-Stadion, Vienna: Austria Wien – Viktoria Plzen 0-0
Austria Wien: Robert Almer, Petar Filipovic, Jens Stryger Larsen, Patrizio Stronati, Christoph Martschinko, Alexander Grünwald, Lucas Venuto (79' Ismael Tajouri Shradi), Tarkan Serbest, Raphael Holzhauser, Olarenwaju Kayode (86' Kevin Friesenbichler), Felipe Pires.
Coach: Thorsten Fink.
Viktoria Plzen: Matús Kozácik, Lukás Hejda, Ales Mateju, Roman Hubník, David Limbersky, Tomás Horava, Martin Zeman, Milan Petrzela (58' Jan Kopic), Ergis Kaçe (90' Jakub Hromada), Tomás Poznar, Marek Bakos (66' Michal Krmencík). Coach: Roman Pivarník.
Referee: John Beaton (SCO)   Attendance: 16,509.

(Austria Wien played their home matches at Ernst-Happel-Stadion, Vienna instead of their regular stadium, Franz Horr Stadium, Vienna)

29.09.16   Stadio Olimpico, Rome: AS Roma – Astra Giurgiu 4-0 (2-0)
AS Roma: Alisson, Juan Jesus, Bruno Peres (63' Alessandro Florenzi), Federico Fazio, Kostas Manolas, Leandro Paredes, Kevin Strootman (69' Gerson), Diego Perotti, Mohamed Salah (57' Radja Nainggolan), Juan Iturbe, Francesco Totti. Coach: Luciano Spalletti.
Astra Giurgiu: Silviu Lung Jr., Geraldo Alves, Fabricio, Vlatko Lazic (61' Daniel Niculae), Junior Maranhão, Cristian Sapunaru, Takayuki Seto, Viorel Nicoara (61' Constantin Budescu), Boubacar Mansaly (46' Florin Lovin), Filipe Teixeira, Denis Alibec. Coach: Marius Sumudica.
Goals: 15' Kevin Strootman 1-0, 45+2' Federico Fazio 2-0, 47' Fabricio 3-0 (og), 55' Mohamed Salah 4-0.
Referee: Aliyar Aghayev (AZE)   Attendance: 13,509.

20.10.16   Stadio Olimpico, Rome: AS Roma – Austria Wien 3-3 (2-1)
AS Roma: Alisson, Juan Jesus, Federico Fazio, Kostas Manolas, Radja Nainggolan, Leandro Paredes, Alessandro Florenzi (76' Emerson), Gerson, Juan Iturbe (81' Edin Dzeko), Francesco Totti, Stephan El Shaarawy (65' Mohamed Salah). Coach: Luciano Spalletti.
Austria Wien: Robert Almer (25' Osman Hadzikic), Petar Filipovic, Jens Stryger Larsen, Patrizio Stronati, Christoph Martschinko, Alexander Grünwald (78' Dominik Prokop), Lucas Venuto (76' Ismael Tajouri Shradi), Tarkan Serbest, Raphael Holzhauser, Olarenwaju Kayode, Felipe Pires. Coach: Thorsten Fink.
Goals: 16' Raphael Holzhauser 0-1, 19', 34' Stephan El Shaarawy 1-1, 2-1, 69' Alessandro Florenzi 3-1, 82' Dominik Prokop 3-2, 84' Olarenwaju Kayode 3-3.
Referee: Vladislav Bezborodov (RUS)   Attendance: 16,478.

20.10.16   Doosan Arena, Plzen: Viktoria Plzen – Astra Giurgiu 1-2 (0-1)
Viktoria Plzen: Matús Kozácik, Lukás Hejda, David Limbersky, Radim Rezník, Jan Baránek, Tomás Horava, Martin Zeman (76' Jan Kovarík), Milan Petrzela, Ergis Kaçe, Michal Duris (53' Tomás Poznar), Marek Bakos (65' Michal Krmencík). Coach: Roman Pivarník.
Astra Giurgiu: Silviu Lung Jr., Geraldo Alves, Fabricio, Vlatko Lazic, Junior Maranhão, Cristian Sapunaru, Takayuki Seto, Boubacar Mansaly, Florin Lovin (90' Cristian Oros), Denis Alibec (90' Daniel Florea), Constantin Budescu (84' Alexandru Ionita).
Coach: Marius Sumudica.
Goals: 41' Denis Alibec 0-1, 64', 86' Tomás Horava 0-2 (og), 1-2.
Referee: Aleksey Eskov (RUS)   Attendance: 9,440.

Tomás Horava missed a penalty kick (86').

03.11.16 Ernst-Happel-Stadion, Vienna: Austria Wien – AS Roma 2-4 (1-2)
Austria Wien: Osman Hadzikic, Petar Filipovic, Jens Stryger Larsen, Christoph Martschinko, Lukas Rotpuller, Alexander Grünwald, Lucas Venuto (86' Ismael Tajouri Shradi), Tarkan Serbest (84' Dominik Prokop), Raphael Holzhauser, Olarenwaju Kayode (71' Kevin Friesenbichler), Felipe Pires. Coach: Thorsten Fink.
AS Roma: Alisson, Antonio Rüdiger, Juan Jesus, Bruno Peres, Radja Nainggolan, Leandro Paredes, Kevin Strootman, Diego Perotti (84' Juan Iturbe), Daniele De Rossi, Edin Dzeko, Stephan El Shaarawy (70' Gerson). Coach: Luciano Spalletti.
Goals: 2' Olarenwaju Kayode 1-0, 5' Edin Dzeko 1-1, 15' Daniele De Rossi 1-2, 65' Edin Dzeko 1-3, 78' Radja Nainggolan 1-4, 89' Alexander Grünwald 2-4.
Referee: Xavier Estrada Fernández (ESP)   Attendance: 32,751.

03.11.16 Arena Nationala, Bucharest: Astra Giurgiu – Viktoria Plzen 1-1 (1-1)
Astra Giurgiu: Silviu Lung Jr., Geraldo Alves, Junior Maranhão, Cristian Oros, Cristian Sapunaru, Takayuki Seto, Boubacar Mansaly, Florin Lovin (55' Viorel Nicoara), Alexandru Stan, Filipe Teixeira (88'Alexandru Ionita), Constantin Budescu (75' Daniel Niculae). Coach: Marius Sumudica.
Viktoria Plzen: Matús Kozácik, Lukás Hejda, Roman Hubník, David Limbersky, Radim Rezník, Milan Petrzela, Patrik Hrosovsky, Jan Kovarík (67' Jan Kopic), Ergis Kaçe (62' Tomás Horava), Jakub Hromada (87' Marek Bakos), Michal Krmencík. Coach: Roman Pivarník.
Goals: 19' Alexandru Stan 1-0, 25' Michal Krmencík 1-1.
Referee: Alon Yefet (ISR)   Attendance: 1,450.

24.11.16 Stadio Olimpico, Rome: AS Roma – Viktoria Plzen 4-1 (1-1)
AS Roma: Alisson, Antonio Rüdiger, Bruno Peres, Federico Fazio, Emerson, Radja Nainggolan, Leandro Paredes, Kevin Strootman (89' Gerson), Mohamed Salah (82' Daniele De Rossi), Juan Iturbe (62' Diego Perotti), Edin Dzeko. Coach: Luciano Spalletti.
Viktoria Plzen: Matús Kozácik, Lukás Hejda, Ales Mateju, David Limbersky, Martin Zeman, Jan Kopic (63' Michal Duris), Milan Petrzela, Patrik Hrosovsky, Jan Kovarík, Jakub Hromada, Michal Krmencík (75' Marek Bakos). Coach: Roman Pivarník.
Goals: 10' Edin Dzeko 1-0, 18' Martin Zeman 1-1, 61' Edin Dzeko 2-1, 82' Ales Mateju 3-1 (og), 88' Edin Dzeko 4-1.
Referee: Tobias Stieler (GER)   Attendance: 13,789.

24.11.16 Ernst-Happel-Stadion, Vienna: Austria Wien – Astra Giurgiu 1-2 (0-0)
Austria Wien: Osman Hadzikic, Petar Filipovic, Jens Stryger Larsen, Christoph Martschinko, Lukas Rotpuller, Alexander Grünwald, Lucas Venuto (90' Ismael Tajouri Shradi), Tarkan Serbest, Raphael Holzhauser, Olarenwaju Kayode (90' Kevin Friesenbichler), Felipe Pires. Coach: Thorsten Fink.
Astra Giurgiu: Silviu Lung Jr., Geraldo Alves, Junior Maranhão, Cristian Oros (61' Daniel Florea), Cristian Sapunaru, Takayuki Seto, Boubacar Mansaly (71' Florin Lovin), Alexandru Stan, Filipe Teixeira, Denis Alibec, Constantin Budescu (90' Viorel Nicoara). Coach: Marius Sumudica.
Goals: 57' Lukas Rotpuller 1-0, 79' Daniel Florea 1-1, 88' Constantin Budescu 1-2 (p).
Referee: Pawel Raczkowski (POL)   Attendance: 14,127.
Sent off: 65' Alexander Grünwald.

210

08.12.16   Doosan Arena, Plzen: Viktoria Plzen – Austria Wien 3-2 (1-2)
Viktoria Plzen: Matús Kozácik, Lukás Hejda, Radim Rezník, Tomás Horava (90' Tomás
Poznar), Martin Zeman, Jan Kopic (83' Marek Bakos), Milan Petrzela, Patrik Hrosovsky, Jan
Kovarík, Jakub Hromada, Michal Krmencík (58' Michal Duris). Coach: Roman Pivarník.
Austria Wien: Osman Hadzikic, Petar Filipovic, Jens Stryger Larsen, Christoph Martschinko,
Lukas Rotpuller, Lucas Venuto (85' Marko Kvasina), Tarkan Serbest, Dominík Prokop (70'
Kevin Friesenbichler), Raphael Holzhauser, Olarenwaju Kayode, Felipe Pires (77' Ismael
Tajouri Shradi). Coach: Thorsten Fink.
Goals: 19' Raphael Holzhauser 0-1 (p), 40' Lukas Rotpuller 0-2, 44' Tomás Horava 1-2,
72, 84' Michal Duris 2-2, 3-2.
Referee: Sergey Boyko (UKR)   Attendance: 9,117.
Sent off: 19' Lukás Hejda.

08.12.16   Arena Nationala, Bucharest: Astra Giurgiu – AS Roma 0-0
Astra Giurgiu: Silviu Lung Jr., Fabrício (72' Daniel Florea), Cristian Oros, Cristian Sapunaru,
Takayuki Seto, Viorel Nicoara, Florin Lovin, Alexandru Stan, Filipe Teixeira, Denis Alibec
(90' Daniel Niculae), Constantin Budescu (88' Boubacar Mansaly). Coach: Marius Sumudica.
AS Roma: Alisson, Juan Jesus, Bruno Peres, Thomas Vermaelen, Moustapha Seck, Emerson
(89' Riccardo Marchizza), Kevin Strootman (70' Radja Nainggolan), Gerson, Juan Iturbe,
Francesco Totti, Stephan El Shaarawy (70' Edin Dzeko). Coach: Luciano Spalletti.
Referee: Hüseyin Göçek (TUR)   Attendance: 7,100.

GROUP F

15.09.16   Allianz Stadion, Vienna: Rapid Wien – KRC Genk 3-2 (0-1)
Rapid Wien: Richard Strebinger, Christoph Schösswendter, Thomas Schrammel, Christopher
Dibon, Mario Pavelic, Stefan Schwab, Louis Schaub, Tamás Szántó (63' Steffen Hofmann),
Arnór Ingvi Traustason (79' Thomas Murg), Ivan Mocinic, Joelinton (87' Giorgi Kvilitaia).
Coach: Mike Büskens.
KRC Genk: Marco Bizot, Omar Colley, Sandy Walsh, Sebastien Dewaest, Jere Uronen,
Thomas Buffel (66' Leandro Trossard), Pozuelo, Onyinye Wilfred Ndidi, Bryan Heynen (78'
Nikolaos Karelis), Leon Bailey, Mbwana Samatta (78' Tino-Sven Susic). Coach: Peter Maes.
Goals: 29' Leon Bailey 0-1, 51' Stefan Schaub 1-1, 59' Joelinton 2-1,
60' Omar Colley 3-1 (og), 90' Leon Bailey 3-2 (p).
Referee: Kevin Blom (HOL)   Attendance: 21,800.

15.09.16   MAPEI Stadium – Città del Tricolore, Reggio nell'Emilia:
            Sassuolo Calcio – Athletic Bilbao 3-0 (0-0)
Sassuolo Calcio: Andrea Consigli, Francesco Acerbi, Por Lirola, Paolo Cannavaro, Timo
Letschert, Francesco Magnanelli, Davide Biondini, Matteo Politano, Luca Mazzitelli (74'
Alfred Duncan), Federico Ricci (55' Antonino Ragusa), Gregoire Defrel (84' Alessandro
Matri). Coach: Eusebio Di Francesco.
Athletic Bilbao: Iago Herrerín, Aymeric Laporte, San José, De Marcos, Balenziaga (78'
Lekue), Yeray, Beñat, Raúl García, Williams (56' Aduriz), Sabin, Muniain (56' Susaeta).
Coach: Valverde.
Goals: 60' Por Lirola (60'), 75' Gregoire Defrel 2-0, 82' Matteo Politano 3-0.
Referee: Pawel Raczkowski (POL)   Attendance: 7,032.

29.09.16   San Mamés Barria, Bilbao: Athletic Bilbao – Rapid Wien 1-0 (0-0)
Athletic Bilbao: Iago Herrerín, Aymeric Laporte, De Marcos, Balenziaga, Yeray, Beñat (80'
Mikel Rico), Iturraspe (59' San José), Susaeta (59' Muniain), Raúl García, Williams, Aduriz.
Coach: Valverde.
Rapid Wien: Richard Strebinger, Christoph Schösswendter, Thomas Schrammel, Christopher
Dibon, Mario Pavelic, Stefan Schwab, Louis Schaub, Srdan Grahovac, Arnór Ingvi Traustason
(72' Tamás Szántó), Ivan Mocinic (67' Steffen Hofmann), Joelinton (84' Giorgi Kvilitaia).
Coach: Mike Büskens.
Goal: 59' Beñat 1-0.
Referee: Tony Chapron (FRA)   Attendance: 34,039.

29.09.16   Luminas Arena, Genk: KRC Genk – Sassuolo Calcio 3-1 (2-0)
KRC Genk: Marco Bizot, Jakub Brabec, Bojan Nastic, Omar Colley, Sandy Walsh, Tino-Sven
Susic (82' Bennard Kumordzi), Thomas Buffel (87' Leandro Trossard), Pozuelo, Onyinye
Wilfred Ndidi, Leon Bailey, Nikolaos Karelis (75' Mbwana Samatta). Coach: Peter Maes.
Sassuolo Calcio: Andrea Consigli, Federico Peluso, Francesco Acerbi, Por Lirola, Timo
Letschert, Francesco Magnanelli, Lorenzo Pellegrini (66' Luca Mazzitelli), Davide Biondini
(59' Antonino Ragusa), Matteo Politano, Federico Ricci (79' Simone Caputo), Gregoire
Defrel. Coach: Eusebio Di Francesco.
Goals: 8' Nikolaos Karelis 1-0, 25' Leon Bailey 2-0, 61' Thomas Buffel 3-0,
65' Matteo Politano 3-1.
Referee: Liran Liany (ISR)   Attendance: 9,134.

20.10.16   Luminus Arena, Genk: KRC Genk – Athletic Bilbao 2-0 (1-0)
KRC Genk: Marco Bizot, Jakub Brabec, Bojan Nastic, Omar Colley, Timoty Castagne, Tino-
Sven Susic (77' Bryan Heynen), Thomas Buffel (56' Mbwana Samatta), Pozuelo, Onyinye
Wilfred Ndidi, Leon Bailey, Nikolaos Karelis (85' Leandro Trossard). Coach: Peter Maes.
Athletic Bilbao: Iago Herrerín, Aymeric Laporte, San José (79' Elustondo), Balenziaga (46'
Saborit), Yeray, Iturraspe, Lekue, Raúl García, Williams (79' Susaeta), Muniain, Aduriz.
Coach: Valverde.
Goals: 40' Jakub Brabec 1-0, 83' Onyinye Wilfred Ndidi 2-0.
Referee: Stefan Johannesson (SWE)   Attendance: 10,238.

20.10.16   Allianz Stadion, Vienna: Rapid Wien – Sassuolo Calcio 1-1 (1-0)
Rapid Wien: Richard Strebinger, Christoph Schösswendter, Thomas Schrammel, Christopher
Dibon (46' Maximilian Hofmann), Mario Pavelic, Stefan Schwab, Louis Schaub, Arnór Ingvi
Traustason (73' Matej Jelic), Ivan Mocinic, Thomas Murg (64' Srdan Grahovac), Joelinton.
Coach: Mike Büskens.
Sassuolo Calcio: Andrea Consigli, Luca Antei, Federico Peluso, Francesco Acerbi, Por Lirola,
Francesco Magnanelli, Lorenzo Pellegrini, Matteo Politano (87' Claud Adjapong), Luca
Mazzitelli, Alessandro Matri (78' Federico Ricci), Antonino Ragusa (58' Gregoire Defrel).
Coach: Eusebio Di Francesco.
Goals: 7' Louis Schaub 1-0, 66' Thomas Schrammel 1-1 (og).
Referee: Hugo Miguel (POR)   Attendance: 22,200.

03.11.16   San Mamés Barria, Bilbao: Athletic Bilbao – KRC Genk 5-3 (3-1)
Athletic Bilbao: Iago Herrerín, Aymeric Laporte, De Marcos, Balenziaga, Yeray, Iturraspe,
Susaeta (75' Williams), Mikel Rico, Raúl García (88' Eraso), Muniain (83' Sabin), Aduriz.
Coach: Valverde.
KRC Genk: Marco Bizot, Jakub Brabec, Bojan Nastic (75' Sandy Walsh), Omar Colley,
Timoty Castagne, Tino-Sven Susic, Thomas Buffel (75' Leandro Trossard), Pozuelo, Onyinye
Wilfred Ndidi, Leon Bailey, Mbwana Samatta (83' Nikolaos Karelis). Coach: Peter Maes.
Goals: 8', 24' Aduriz 1-0, 2-0 (p), 28' Leon Bailey 2-1, 44' Aduriz 3-1 (p), 51' Onyinye
Wilfred Ndidi 3-2, 74' Aduriz 4-2, 80' Tino-Sven Susic 4-3, 90+4' Aduriz 5-3 (p).
Referee: Martin Atkinson (ENG)   Attendance: 33,417.

03.11.16   MAPEI Stadium – Città del Tricolore, Reggio nell'Emilia:
           Saccuolo Calcio – Rapid Wien 2-2 (2-0)
Sassuolo Calcio: Andrea Consigli, Federico Peluso, Francesco Acerbi, Por Lirola, Marcello
Gazzola, Claud Adjapong, Lorenzo Pellegrini, Davide Biondini, Alessandro Matri (64' Matteo
Politano), Gregoire Defrel (90' Simone Franchini), Antonino Ragusa (81' Federico Ricci).
Coach: Eusebio Di Francesco.
Rapid Wien: Richard Strebinger, Thomas Schrammel, Mario Sonnleitner, Maximilian
Hofmann, Manuel Thurnwald, Louis Schaub, Srdan Grahovac, Arnór Ingvi Traustason, Ivan
Mocinic (85' Tamás Szántó), Thomas Murg (61' Matej Jelic), Joelinton (61' Giorgi Kvilitaia).
Coach: Mike Büskens.
Goals: 34' Gregoire Defrel 1-0, 45+2' Lorenzo Pellegrini 2-0, 86' Matej Jelic 2-1,
90' Giorgi Kvilitaia 2-2.
Referee: Craig Pawson (ENG)   Attendance: 7,838.

24.11.16   Luminus Arena, Genk: KRC Genk – Rapid Wien 1-0 (1-0)
KRC Genk: Marco Bizot, Jakub Brabec, Bojan Nastic, Omar Colley, Timoty Castagne, Tino-
Sven Susic (79' Bryan Heynen), Thomas Buffel (90' Leandro Trossard), Pozuelo, Onyinye
Wilfred Ndidi, Leon Bailey, Nikolaos Karelis (84' Mbwana Samatta). Coach: Peter Maes.
Rapid Wien: Ján Novota, Christoph Schösswendter, Thomas Schrammel, Mario Sonnleitner,
Christopher Dibon, Manuel Thurnwald (72' Giorgi Kvilitaia), Maximilian Wöber, Louis
Schaub (84' Matej Jelic), Srdan Grahovac, Arnór Ingvi Traustason, Joelinton (63' Philipp
Schobesberger). Coach: Damir Canadi.
Goal: 11' Nikolaos Karelis 1-0.
Referee: Ivan Kruzliak (SVK)   Attendance: 9,406.

24.11.16   San Mamés Barria, Bilbao: Athletic Bilbao – Sassuolo Calcio 3-2 (1-1)
Athletic Bilbao: Iago Herrerín, Aymeric Laporte, San José, Balenziaga, Yeray, Beñat, Lekue,
Raúl García, Williams (61' Eneko Bóveda), Muniain (72' Mikel Rico), Aduriz (88' Sabin).
Coach: Valverde.
Sassuolo Calcio: Andrea Consigli, Francesco Acerbi, Por Lirola, Marcello Gazzola, Paolo
Cannavaro, Francesco Magnanelli, Lorenzo Pellegrini (70' Simone Missiroli), Davide Biondini
(71' Alessandro Matri), Federico Ricci, Gregoire Defrel (77' Matteo Politano), Antonino
Ragusa. Coach: Eusebio Di Francesco.
Goals: 2' Balenziaga 0-1 (og), 10' Raúl García 1-1, 58' Aduriz 2-1, 79' Lekue 3-1,
83' Antonino Ragusa 3-2.
Referee: Viktor Kassai (HUN)   Attendance: 37,806.

08-12-16   Allianz Stadion, Vienna: Rapid Wien – Athletic Bilbao 1-1 (0-0)
Rapid Wien: Tobias Knoflach, Thomas Schrammel, Mario Sonnleitner, Christopher Dibon (69'
Louis Schaub), Maximilian Hofmann, Stephan Auer, Maximilian Wöber, Srdan Grahovac,
Philipp Malicsek, Matej Jelic (57' Giorgi Kvilitaia), Tomi (57' Joelinton).
Coach: Damir Canadi.
Athletic Bilbao: Iraizoz, Etxeita, Saborit, Yeray, Eraso (74' Susaeta), Mikel Vesga, Lekue,
Mikel Rico (64' Beñat), Williams, Muniain, Sabin (77' Villalibre). Coach: Valverde.
Goals: 72' Joelinton 1-0, 84' Saborit 1-1.
Referee: Serdar Gözübüyük (HOL)   Attendance: 22,800.

09-12-16   MAPEI Stadium – Città del Tricolore, Reggio Nell'Emilia:
          Sassuolo Calcio – KRC Genk 0-2 (0-0)
Sassuolo Calcio: Gianluca Pegolo, Luca Antei, Francesco Acerbi, Por Lirola, Paolo Cannavaro,
Claud Adjapong, Luca Mazzitelli, Simone Missiroli (46' Lorenzo Pellegrini), Alessandro
Matri, Simone Caputo (74' Francesco Magnanelli), Antonino Ragusa (46' Federico Ricci).
Coach: Eusebio Di Francesco.
KRC Genk: Nordin Jackers, Jakub Brabec, Sandy Walsh, Sebastien Dewaest, Timoty
Castagne, Leandro Trossard, Onyinye Wilfred Ndidi, Bryan Heynen (89' Bennard Kumordzi),
Leon Bailey (81' Thomas Buffel), Nikolaos Karelis (90' Paolo Sabak), Mbwana Samatta.
Coach: Peter Maes.
Goals: 58' Bryan Heynen 0-1, 80' Leandro Trossard 0-2.
Referee: Orel Grinfeld (ISR)   Attendance: 1,154.

GROUP G

15.09.16   Stade Maurice Dufrasne, Liège: Standard Liège – Celta de Vigo 1-1 (1-1)
Standard Liège: Jean-François Gillet, Elderson Echiéjilé (86' Corentin Fiore), Alexander
Scholz, Collins Fai, Kostas Laifis, Mathieu Dossevi, Eyong Enoh, Edmilson, Adrien Trebel,
Benito Raman (68' Isaac Mbenza), Ishak Belfodil (82' Orlando Sá).
Coach: Aleksandar Jankovic.
Celta de Vigo: Sergio Álvarez, David Costas, Jonny, Sergi Gómez, Gustavo Cabral, Nemanja
Radoja, Pablo Hernández, Pione Sisto (82' Théo Bongonda), Lemos, Naranja (71' Daniel
Wass), Giuseppe Rossi (86' Iago Aspas). Coach: Eduardo Berizzo.
Goals: 3' Mathieu Dossevi 1-0, 13' Giuseppe Rossi 1-1.
Referee: Hüseyin Göçek (TUR)   Attendance: 10,723.

15.09.16   Apostolos Nikolaidis Stadium, Athen: Panathinaikos – AFC Ajax 1-2 (1-1)
Panathinaikos: Luke Steele, Georgios Koutroubis (68' Lucas Villafáñez), Giandomenico
Mesto, Rodrigo Moledo, Ivan Ivanov, Zeca, Robin Lod (73' Christopher Samba), Mubarak
Wakaso, Niklas Hult, Cristian Ledesma (65' Sebastián Leto), Markus Berg.
Coach: Andrea Stramaccioni.
AFC Ajax: André Onana, Joël Veltman, Davinson Sánchez, Nick Viergever, Mitchell Dijks,
Jaïro Riedewald, Davy Klaassen (89' Lasse Schöne), Hakim Ziyech, Nemanja Gudelj,
Bertrand Traoré (73' Kasper Dolberg), Amin Younes (87' Daley Sinkgraven).
Coach: Peter Bosz.
Goals: 5' Markus Berg 1-0, 33 Bertrand Traoré 1-1, 67' Jaïro Riedewald 1-2.
Referee: Andre Marriner (ENG)   Attendance: 13,019.
Sent off: 69' Ivan Ivanov, 79' Hakim Ziyech, 90' Mubarak Wakaso.

Davy Klaassen missed a penalty kick (67').

214

29.09.16   Amsterdam ArenA, Amsterdam: AFC Ajax – Standard Liège 1-0 (1-0)
AFC Ajax: André Onana, Joël Veltman, Davinson Sánchez, Nick Viergever, Daley
Sinkgraven, Davy Klaassen, Lasse Schöne (62' Jaïro Riedewald), Nemanja Gudelj, Bertrand
Traoré, Amin Younes (86' Anwar El Ghazi), Kasper Dolberg (69' Mateo Cassierra).
Coach: Peter Bosz.
Standard Liège: Jean-François Gillet, Alexander Scholz, Darwin Andrade, Collins Fai, Kostas
Laifis, Mathieu Dossevi (80' Jonathan Legear), Eyong Enoh, Edmilson (69' Isaac Mbenza),
Adrien Trebel, Benito Raman (69' Jean-Luc Dompé), Ishak Belfodil.
Coach: Aleksandar Jankovic.
Goal: 28' Kasper Dolberg 1-0.
Referee: Paolo Mazzoleni (ITA)   Attendance: 31,352.

29.09.16   Municipal de Balaídos, Vigo: Celta de Vigo – Panathinaikos 2-0 (0-0)
Celta de Vigo: Sergio Álvarez, Hugo Mallo, Fontàs, Jonny, Gustavo Cabral, Marcelo Díaz,
Pablo Hernández, Señé (71' Daniel Wass), John Guidetti, Naranja (60' Pione Sisto), Giuseppe
Rossi (79' Iago Aspas). Coach: Eduardo Berizzo.
Panathinaikos: Luke Steele, Georgios Koutroubis (88' Paul Mpoku), Christopher Samba,
Rodrigo Moledo, Ousmane Coulibaly, Víctor Ibarbo, Zeca, Robin Lod, Cristian Ledesma,
Markus Berg, Lucas Villafáñez. Coach: Andrea Stramaccioni.
Goals: 84' John Guidetti 1-0, 89' Daniel Wass 2-0.
Referee: Luca Banti (ITA)   Attendance: 15,726.

20.10.16   Municipal de Balaídos, Vigo: Celta de Vigo – AFC Ajax 2-2 (1-1)
Celta de Vigo: Rubén Blanco, Fontàs, Sergi Gómez, Carles Planas, Facundo Roncaglia,
Nemanja Radoja, Pablo Hernández (76' Daniel Wass), Pione Sisto, Lemos (63' Fabián
Orellana), Señé, John Guidetti (73' Giuseppe Rossi). Coach: Eduardo Berizzo.
AFC Ajax: André Onana, Joël Veltman, Davinson Sánchez, Daley Sinkgraven, Nick
Viergever, Davy Klaassen, Hakim Ziyech (77' Riechedly Bazoer), Nemanja Gudelj, Bertrand
Traoré, Amin Younes (77' Mateo Cassierra), Kasper Dolberg. Coach: Peter Bosz.
Goals: 22' Hakim Ziyech 0-1, 29' Fontàs 1-1, 71' Amin Younes 1-2, 82' Fabián Orellana 2-2.
Referee: Ivan Kruzliak (SVK)   Attendance: 18,397.

20.10.16   Stade Maurice Dufrasne, Liège: Standard Liège – Panathinaikos 2-2 (1-2)
Standard Liège: Jean-François Gillet, Alexander Scholz, Darwin Andrade, Collins Fai, Kostas
Laifis, Ibrahima Cissé (72' Eyong Enoh), Mathieu Dossevi (63' Isaac Mbenza), Edmilson,
Adrien Trebel, Orlando Sá, Ishak Belfodil. Coach: Aleksandar Jankovic.
Panathinaikos: Luke Steele, Georgios Koutroubis, Christopher Samba (46' Ivan Ivanov),
Rodrigo Moledo, Ousmane Coulibaly, Víctor Ibarbo, Zeca (78' Paul Mpoku), Sebastián Leto
(74' Robin Lod), Niklas Hult, Cristian Ledesma, Lucas Villafáñez.
Coach: Andrea Stramaccioni.
Goals: 12', 36' Víctor Ibarbo 0-1, 0-2, 45+1' Edmilson 1-2 (p), 82' Ishak Belfodil 2-2.
Referee: Daniel Stefanski (POL)   Attendance: 14,463.

215

03.11.16   Amsterdam ArenA, Amsterdam: AFC Ajax – Celta de Vigo 3-2 (1-0)
AFC Ajax: André Onana, Joël Veltman, Davinson Sánchez, Daley Sinkgraven, Jaïro
Riedewald, Davy Klaassen, Lasse Schöne, Hakim Ziech (78' Nemanja Gudelj), Bertrand
Traoré, Amin Younes, Kasper Dolberg (83' Mateo Cassierra). Coach: Peter Bosz.
Celta de Vigo: Rubén Blanco, Hugo Mallo, Fontàs, Sergi Gómez, Carles Planas, Marcelo Díaz,
Nemanja Radoja, Lemos (54' Daniel Wass), Señé (71' Iago Aspas), Théo Bongonda, Giuseppe
Rossi (78' John Guidetti). Coach: Eduardo Berizzo.
Goals: 41' Kasper Dolberg 1-0, 68' Hakim Ziech 2-0, 71' Amin Younes 3-0,
79' John Guidetti 3-1, 86' Iago Aspas 3-2.
Referee: Pawel Raczkowski (POL)   Attendance: 44,545.

03.11.16   Apostolos Nikolaidis Stadium, Athen: Panathinaikos – Standard Liège 0-3 (0-0)
Panathinaikos: Luke Steele, Diamantis Chouchoumis, Georgios Koutroubis, Giandomenico
Mesto (77' Anastasios Chatzigiovannis), Rodrigo Moledo, Ivan Ivanov, Ousmane Coulibaly,
Víctor Ibarbo (86' Lautaro Rinaldi), Robin Lod, Paul Mpoku, Markus Berg (30' Sebastián
Leto). Coach: Andrea Stramaccioni.
Standard Liège: Guillaume Hubert, Elderson Echiéjilé (46' Corentin Fiore), Alexander Scholz,
Collins Fai, Kostas Laifis, Ibrahima Cissé, Edmilson (88' Isaac Mbenza), Adrien Trebel,
Benito Raman (62' Beni Badibanga), Orlando Sá, Ishak Belfodil. Coach: Aleksandar Jankovic.
Goals: 62' Ibrahima Cissé 0-1, 76, 90+3' Ishak Belfodil 0-2, 0-3.
Referee: Sergey Boyko (UKR)   Attendance: 10,837.
Sent off: 77' Paul Mpoku.

24.11.16   Municipal de Balaídos, Vigo: Celta de Vigo – Standard Liège 1-1 (1-0)
Celta de Vigo: Rubén Blanco, Hugo Mallo, Jonny (82' Sergi Gómez), Gustavo Cabral,
Facundo Roncaglia, Marcelo Díaz (62' Nemanja Radoja), Pablo Hernández, Pione Sisto,
Daniel Wass (84' Giuseppe Rossi), John Guidetti, Iago Aspas. Coach: Eduardo Berizzo.
Standard Liège: Guillaume Hubert, Alexander Scholz, Corentin Fiore, Collins Fai, Kostas
Laifis, Ibrahima Cissé, Edmilson (62' Isaac Mbenza), Adrien Trebel, Benito Raman (89' Beni
Badibanga), Orlando Sá, Ishak Belfodil. Coach: Aleksandar Jankovic.
Goals: 8' Iago Aspas 1-0, 81' Kostas Laifis 1-1.
Referee: Benoît Bastien (FRA)   Attendance: 16,470.
Sent off: 90' Iago Aspas.

24.11.16   Amsterdam ArenA, Amsterdam: AFC Ajax – Panathinaikos 2-0 (1-0)
AFC Ajax: André Onana, Kenny Tete, Heiko Westermann, Mitchell Dijks, Matthijs de Ligt,
Lasse Schöne (68' Frenkie de Jong), Donny van de Beek, Abdelhak Nouri, Amin Younes (62'
Pelle Clement), Vaclav Cerny, Mateo Cassierra. Coach: Peter Bosz.
Panathinaikos: Luke Steele, Georgios Koutroubis, Christopher Samba (57' Ivan Ivanov),
Rodrigo Moledo, Ousmane Coulibaly, Víctor Ibarbo (75' Lautaro Rinaldi), Zeca, Robin Lod,
Mubarak Wakaso, Niklas Hult, Lucas Villafáñez (62' Cristian Ledesma).
Coach: Andrea Stramaccioni.
Goals: 39' Lasse Schöne 1-0, 50' Kenny Tete 2-0.
Referee: Aleksey Eskov (RUS)   Attendance: 41,011.

216

08.12.16   Stade Maurice Dufrasne, Liège: Standard Liège – AFC Ajax 1-1 (0-1)
Standard Liège: Guillaume Hubert, Réginal Goreux, Alexander Scholz, Corentin Fiore (57'
Elderson Echiéjilé), Kostas Laifis, Eyong Enoh, Edmilson (66' Beni Badibanga), Adrien
Trebel, Jean-Luc Dompé (57' Benito Raman), Isaac Mbenza, Orlando Sá.
Coach: Aleksandar Jankovic.
AFC Ajax: Diederik Boer, Kenny Tete, Mitchell Dijks, Matthijs de Ligt, Jaïro Riedewald,
Davy Klaassen, Donny van de Beek, Abdelhak Nouri (79' Hakim Ziyech), Anwar El Ghazi,
Amin Younes (66' Kasper Dolberg), Mateo Cassierra. Coach: Peter Bosz.
Goals: 27' Anwar El Ghazi 0-1, 85' Benito Raman 1-1.
Referee: Bobby Madden (SCO)   Attendance: 20,344.

08.12.16   Apostolos Nikolaidis Stadium, Athen: Panathinaikos – Celta de Vigo 0-2 (0-1)
Panathinaikos: Luke Steele, Diamantis Chouchoumis, Giandomenico Mesto, Rodrigo Moledo,
Ivan Ivanov, Zeca, Robin Lod (83' Georgios Koutroubis), Mubarak Wakaso, Paul Mpoku,
Lucas Villafáñez (70' Sebastián Leto), Lautaro Rinaldi (60' Víctor Ibarbo).
Coach: Marinos Ouzounidis.
Celta de Vigo: Rubén Blanco, Hugo Mallo, Jonny, Gustavo Cabral, Facundo Roncaglia,
Nemanja Radoja, Pablo Hernández, Daniel Wass (63' Marcelo Díaz), Théo Bongonda, John
Guidetti (90' Sergi Gómez), Fabián Orellana (82' Pione Sisto). Coach: Eduardo Berizzo.
Goals: 4' John Guidetti 0-1, 76' Fabián Orellana 0-2 (p).
Referee: Andris Treimanis (LAT)   Attendance: 4,005.

GROUP H

15.09.16   Konya Büyüksehir Stadyumu, Konya:
           Atiker Konyaspor – Shakhtar Donetsk 0-1 (0-0)
Atiker Konyaspor: Serkan Kirintili, Barry Douglas, Ali Turan, Jens Jønsson (85' Halil
Sönmez), Jagos Vukovic, Nejc Skubic, Ömer Sahiner, Ali Çamdali, Deni Milosevic (76' Alban
Meha), Amir Hadziahmetovic, Rijad Bajic (70' Ioan Hora). Coach: Aykut Kocaman.
Shakhtar Donetsk: Andriy Pyatov, Bogdan Butko, Oleksandr Kucher, Ismaily, Yaroslav
Rakitskiy, Taras Stepanenko, Fred, Bernard (67' Taison), Marlos, Viktor Kovalenko (90'
Maksym Malyshev), Facundo Ferreyra (90' Eduardo). Coach: Paulo Fonseca.
Goal: 76' Facundo Ferreyra 0-1.
Referee: Robert Schörgenhofer (AUT)   Attendance: 26,860.

15.09.16   Estádio Municipal de Braga, Braga: Sporting Braga – KAA Gent 1-1 (1-1)
Sporting Braga: Matheus Magalhães, Lazar Rosic, André Pinto, Baiano, Marcelo Goiano,
Marko Bakic (73' Nikola Vuksevic), Pedro Santos (76' Nikola Stojiljkovic), Petro Tiba,
Mauro, Wilson Eduardo (84' Alan), Ahmed Hassan. Coach: José Peseiro.
KAA Gent: Jacob Rinne, Stefan Mitrovic, Nana Asare, Rami Gershon, Renato Neto, Kenny
Saief, Thomas Foket, Anderson Esiti, Danijel Milicevic, Jérémy Perbet (70' Ofir Davidadze),
Moses Simon (40' Kalifa Coulibaly). Coach: Hein Vanhaezebrouck.
Goals: 6' Danijel Milicevic 0-1, 24' André Pinto 1-1.
Referee: Benoît Bastien (FRA)   Attendance: 8,903.

29.09.16   Ghelamco Arena, Ghent: KAA Gent – Atiker Konyaspor 2-0 (2-0)
KAA Gent: Jacob Rinne, Stefan Mitrovic, Nana Asare, Lasse Nielsen, Rami Gershon, Renato Neto, Kenny Saief (89' Ofir Davidadze), Hannes Van Der Bruggen, Danijel Milicevic (46' Jérémy Perbet), Kalifa Coulibaly, Dieumerci Ndongala (72' Anderson Esiti).
Coach: Hein Vanhaezebrouck.
Atiker Konyaspor: Serkan Kirintili, Barry Douglas, Ali Turan, Jens Jønsson (41' Volkan Findikli), Jagos Vukovic, Nejc Skubic, Ömer Sahiner, Ali Çamdali, Deni Milosevic (81' Halil Sönmez), Amir Hadziahmetovic (65' Alban Meha), Rijad Bajic. Coach: Aykut Kocaman.
Goals: 17' Kenny Saief 1-0, 33' Renato Neto 2-0.
Referee: István Vad (HUN)   Attendance: 15,873.

29.09.16   Arena Lviv, Lviv: Shakhtar Donetsk – Sporting Braga 2-0 (1-0)
Shakhtar Donetsk: Andriy Pyatov, Bogdan Butko, Oleksandr Kucher, Ivan Ordets, Ismaily, Taras Stepanenko, Fred, Bernard, Marlos (74' Taison), Viktor Kovalenko (90' Maksym Malyshev), Facundo Ferreyra (85' Dentinho). Coach: Paulo Fonseca.
Sporting Braga: Marafona, Lazar Rosic, Baiano, Artur Jorge, Marcelo Goiano, Pedro Santos (67' Marko Bakic), Nikola Vuksevic, Mauro, Wilson Eduardo (67' Tomás Martínez), Ahmed Hassan, Ricardo Horta (58' Nikola Stojiljkovic). Coach: José Peseiro.
Goals: 5' Taras Stepanenko 1-0, 56' Viktor Kovalenko 2-0.
Referee: Tobias Stieler (GER)   Attendance: 11,938.
Sent off: 47' Fred.

(Shakhtar Donetsk played their home matches at Arena Lviv, Lviv instead of their regular stadium, Donbass Arena, Donetsk due to the ongoing conflict in Eastern Ukraine)

20.10.16   Arena Lviv, Lviv: Shakhtar Donetsk – KAA Gent 5-0 (2-0)
Shakhtar Donetsk: Andriy Pyatov, Oleksandr Kucher, Maksym Malyshev, Ismaily, Darijo Srna, Yaroslav Rakitskiy, Taras Stepanenko, Bernard (74' Taison), Marlos, Viktor Kovalenko (37' Dentinho), Facundo Ferreyra (81' Eduardo). Coach: Paulo Fonseca.
KAA Gent: Jacob Rinne, Stefan Mitrovic, Nana Asare, Rami Gershon, Renato Neto, Kenny Saief, Hannes Van Der Bruggen (64' Ibrahim Rabiu), Thomas Foket, Danijel Milicevic (72' Brecht Dejaegere), Jérémy Perbet (46' Kalifa Coulibaly), Moses Simon.
Coach: Hein Vanhaezebrouck.
Goals: 12' Viktor Kovalenko 1-0, 30' Facundo Ferreyra 2-0, 46' Bernard 3-0, 75' Taison 4-0, 85' Maksym Malyshev 5-0.
Referee: Anthony Taylor (ENG)   Attendance: 10,505.

20.10.16   Konya Büyüksehir Stadyumu, Konya: Atiker Konyaspor – Sporting Braga 1-1 (1-0)
Atiker Konyaspor: Serkan Kirintili, Volkan Findikli, Barry Douglas, Ali Turan, Jagos Vukovic, Nejc Skubic, Ömer Sahiner (46' Alban Meha), Ali Çamdali, Deni Milosevic, Amir Hadziahmetovic (82' Halil Sönmez), Rijad Bajic. Coach: Aykut Kocaman.
Sporting Braga: Matheus Magalhães, Emiliano Velázquez, Lazar Rosic, Baiano, Marcelo Goiano, Pedro Santos, Nikola Vuksevic, Mauro, Wilson Eduardo (67' Ricardo Horta), Ahmed Hassan (75' Nikola Stojiljkovic), Alan (75' Rui Fonte). Coach: José Peseiro.
Goals: 9' Deni Milosevic 1-0, 55' Ahmed Hassan 1-1.
Referee: Aliyar Aghayev (AZE)   Attendance: 24,968.

218

03.11.16   Ghelamco Arena, Ghent: KAA Gent – Shakhtar Donetsk 3-5 (1-3)
KAA Gent: Jacob Rinne, Nana Asare, Lasse Nielsen, Rami Gershon, Renato Neto, Brecht
Dejaegere (70' Kenny Saief), Thomas Foket, Anderson Esiti, Danijel Milicevic, Kalifa
Coulibaly (74' Jérémy Perbet), Moses Simon (77' Dieumerci Ndongala).
Coach: Hein Vanhaezebrouck.
Shakhtar Donetsk: Andriy Pyatov, Oleksandr Kucher, Ismaily, Darijo Srna, Yaroslav Rakitskiy
(78' Ivan Ordets), Taras Stepanenko (72' Maksym Malyshev), Fred, Bernard, Marlos, Facundo
Ferreyra, Taison (71' Dentinho). Coach: Paulo Fonseca.
Goals: 1' Kalifa Coulibaly 1-0, 36' Marlos 1-1 (p), 41' Taison 1-2, 45+3' T. Stepanenko 1-3,
68' Fred 1-4, 83' Jérémy Perbet 2-4, 87' Facundo Ferreyra 2-5, 89' Danijel Milicevic 3-5.
Referee: Aleksey Kulbakov (BLS)   Attendance: 14,526.

03.11.16   Estádio Municipal de Braga, Braga: Sporting Braga – Atiker Konyaspor 3-1 (2-1)
Sporting Braga: Matheus Magalhães, Emiliano Velázquez (73' Alan), Lazar Rosic, Baiano,
Marcelo Goiano, Nikola Vuksevic, Mauro, Wilson Eduardo (70' Pedro Santos), Ahmed
Hassan, Rui Fonte (43' Pedro Tiba), Ricardo Horta. Coach: José Peseiro.
Atiker Konyaspor: Serkan Kirintili, Volkan Findikli, Ali Turan (46' Ali Çamdali), Jens
Jønsson, Abdülkerim Bardakçi, Mehmet Uslu, Nejc Skubic, Deni Milosevic, Amir
Hadziahmetovic (46' Ömer Sahiner), Alban Meha, Dimitar Rangelov (76' Rijad Bajic).
Coach: Aykut Kocaman.
Goals: 30' Dimitar Rangelov 0-1, 34' Emiliano Velázquez 1-1, 45+1' Wilson Eduardo 2-1,
90+7' Ricardo Horta 3-1.
Referee: Alexandru Tudor (ROM)   Attendance: 7,729.
Sent off: 38' Mauro, 54' Nejc Skubic.

24.11.16   Arena Lviv, Lviv: Shakhtar Donetsk – Atiker Konyaspor 4-0 (2-0)
Shakhtar Donetsk: Nikita Shevchenko, Maksym Malyshev, Ivan Ordets, Mykola Matvienko,
Darijo Srna, Sergiy Krivtsov, Bernard, Viktor Kovalenko (46' Vyacheslav Tankovski),
Dentinho, Taison (64' Eduardo), Andriy Boryachuk (79' Taras Stepanenko).
Coach: Paulo Fonseca.
Atiker Konyaspor: Serkan Kirintili, Volkan Findikli, Selim Ay, Abdülkerim Bardakçi, Mehmet
Uslu, Ömer Sahiner, Ali Çamdali (16' Alban Meha), Deni Milosevic (63' Halil Sönmez), Marc
Mbamba, Amir Hadziahmetovic, Ioan Hora (83' Rijad Bajic). Coach: Aykut Kocaman.
Goals: 11' Abdülkerim Bardakçi 1-0 (og), 36' Dentinho 2-0, 66' Eduardo 3-0, 74' Bernard 4-0.
Referee: Kevin Clancy (SCO)   Attendance: 10,021.

24.11.16   Ghelamco Arena, Ghent: KAA Gent – Sporting Braga 2-2 (2-2)
KAA Gent: Yannick Thoelen, Stefan Mitrovic, Nana Asare, Lasse Nielsen, Renato Neto,
Kenny Saief (90' Thomas Matton), Thomas Foket, Anderson Esiti (85' Jérémy Perbet), Danijel
Milicevic, Kalifa Coulibaly, Moses Simon (70' Brecht Dejaegere).
Coach: Hein Vanhaezebrouck.
Sporting Braga: Matheus Magalhães, Lazar Rosic, André Pinto (65' Artur Jorge), Baiano,
Marcelo Goiano, Pedro Tiba, Nikola Vuksevic, Wilson Eduardo, Ahmed Hassan (76' Rui
Fonte), Nikola Stojiljkovic, Ricardo Horta (89' Pedro Santos). Coach: José Peseiro.
Goals: 14' Nikola Stojiljkovic 0-1, 32' Kalifa Coulibaly 1-1, 36' Ahmed Hassan 1-2,
40' Danijel Milicevic 2-2.
Referee: Vladislav Bezborodov (RUS)   Attendance: 19,650.

08.12.16   Konya Büyükşehir Stadyumu, Konya: Atiker Konyaspor – KAA Gent 0-1 (0-0)
Atiker Konyaspor: Serkan Kirintili, Volkan Findikli, Barry Douglas, Selim Ay, Jens Jønsson,
Jagos Vukovic, Nejc Skubic, Ömer Sahiner (73' Deni Milosevic), Marc Mbamba, Alban Meha
(87' Amir Hadziahmetovic), Ioan Hora (66' Rijad Bajic). Coach: Aykut Kocaman.
KAA Gent: Jacob Rinne, Stefan Mitrovic, Lasse Nielsen, Rami Gershon, Thomas Matton (66'
Brecht Dejaegere), Renato Neto (69' Anderson Esiti), Kenny Saief, Hannes Van Der Bruggen,
Thomas Foket, Danijel Milicevic, Jérémy Perbet (67' Kalifa Coulibaly).
Coach: Hein Vanhaezebrouck.
Goal: 90+4' Kalifa Coulibaly 0-1.
Referee: Jakob Kehlet (DEN)   Attendance: 10,720.

08.12.16   Estádio Municipal de Braga, Braga: Sporting Braga – Shakhtar Donetsk 2-3 (1-2)
Sporting Braga: Marafona, Lazar Rosic, André Pinto, Baiano, Marcelo Goiano, Pedro Tiba,
Nikola Vuksevic, Wilson Eduardo (66' Óscar Benítez), Rui Fonte (58' Ahmed Hassan), Nikola
Stojiljkovic (70' Alan), Ricardo Horta. Coach: José Peseiro.
Shakhtar Donetsk: Nikita Shevchenko, Bogdan Butko, Maksym Malyshev, Ivan Ordets,
Mykola Matvienko, Sergiy Krivtsov, Marlos (58' Bernard), Vyacheslav Tankovski (61' Fred),
Dentinho, Taison, Andriy Boryachuk (69' Facundo Ferreyra). Coach: Paulo Fonseca.
Goals: 22' Sergiy Krivtsov 0-1, 39' Taison 0-2, 43' Nikola Stojiljkovic 1-2,
62' Sergiy Krivtsov 1-3, 66' Taison 1-4, 89' Nikola Vuksevic 2-4.
Referee: Ali Palabiyik (TUR)   Attendance: 15,084.

GROUP I

15.09.16   Red Bull Arena, Wals-Siezenheim: Red Bull Salzburg – FK Krasnodar 0-1 (0-1)
Red Bull Salzburg: Alexander Walke, Paulo Miranda, Dayot Upamecano, Duje Caleta-Car,
Andreas Ulmer, Andre Wisdom (30' Stefan Lainer, 80' Wanderson), Diadie Samassekou (73'
Munas Dabbur), Valentino Lazaro, Valon Berisha, Takumi Minamino, Jonathan Soriano.
Coach: Óscar.
FK Krasnodar: Stanislav Kritsyuk, Naldo, Andreas Granqvist, Artur Jedrzejczyk, Sergey
Petrov, Odil Akhmedov (62' Yuri Gazinskiy), Vyacheslav Podberezkin (60' Ricardo Laborde),
Joãozinho (74' Vitaliy Kaleshin), Kouassi Eboue, Charles Kaboré, Fedor Smolov.
Coach: Igor Shalimov.
Goal: 37' Joãozinho 0-1.
Referee: Miroslav Zelinka (CZE)   Attendance: 6,507.
Sent off: 71' Sergey Petrov.

15.09.16   Allianz Riviera, Nice: OGC Nice – FC Schalke 04 0-1 (0-0)
OGC Nice: Yoan Cardinale, Paul Baysse, Ricardo Pereira, Dalbert (81' Younès Belhanda),
Dante, Malang Sarr, Jean Michaël Seri, Wylan Cyprien, Vincent Koziello (67' Mathieu
Bodmer), Mario Balotelli, Alassane Pléa. Coach: Lucien Favre.
FC Schalke 04: Ralf Fährmann, Benedikt Höwedes, Abdul Rahman Baba, Naldo, Matija
Nastasic, Leon Goretzka (90' Sead Kolasinac), Nabil Bentaleb, Benjamin Stambouli (58' Max
Meyer), Alessandro Schöpf (53' Yevhen Konoplyanka), Eric Maxim Choupo-Moting, Breel
Embolo. Coach: Markus Weinzierl.
Goal: 75' Abdul Rahman Baba 0-1.
Referee: Alberto Undiano Mallenco (ESP)   Attendance: 21,378.

29.09.16   VELTINS-Arena, Gelsenkirchen: FC Schalke 04 – Red Bull Salzburg 3-1 (1-0)
FC Schalke 04: Ralf Fährmann, Benedikt Höwedes, Sead Kolasinac (80' Abdul Rahman
Baba), Naldo, Matija Nastasic, Johannes Geis, Max Meyer (89' Benjamin Stambouli), Leon
Goretzka (67' Yevhen Konoplyanka), Nabil Bentaleb, Alessandro Schöpf, Breel Embolo.
Coach: Markus Weinzierl.
Red Bull Salzburg: Alexander Walke, Paulo Miranda, Dayot Upamecano, Duje Caleta-Car,
Andreas Ulmer, Stefan Lainer, Valentino Lazaro (65' Takumi Minamino), Valon Berisha,
Konrad Laimer (65' Josip Radosevic), Wanderson (89' Marc Rzatkowski), Jonathan Soriano.
Coach: Óscar.
Goals: 15' Leon Goretzka 1-0, 47' Duje Caleta-Car 2-0 (og), 58' Benedikt Höwedes 3-0,
72' Jonathan Soriano 3-1.
Referee: Serdar Gözübüyük (HOL)   Attendance: 48,374.

29.09.16   Kuban Stadium, Krasnodar: FK Krasnodar – OGC Nice 5-2 (2-1)
FK Krasnodar: Stanislav Kritsyuk, Naldo, Andreas Granqvist, Artur Jedrzejczyk, Dmitriy
Torbinskiy, Odil Akhmedov (59' Yuri Gazinskiy), Vyacheslav Podberezkin (74' Ricardo
Laborde), Joãozinho, Kouassi Eboue, Charles Kaboré, Fedor Smolov (29' Ari).
Coach: Igor Shalimov.
OGC Nice: Yoan Cardinale, Paul Baysse, Ricardo Pereira, Dalbert (66' Wylan Cyprien),
Dante, Malang Sarr, Younès Belhanda, Jean Michaël Seri, Valentin Eysseric, Vincent Koziello
(79' Rémi Walter), Mario Balotelli (46' Alassane Pléa). Coach: Lucien Favre.
Goals: 22' Fedor Smolov 1-0, 33' Joãozinho 2-0, 43' Mario Balotelli 2-1,
65' Joãozinho 3-1 (p), 71' Wylan Cyprien 3-2, 86', 90+3' Ari 4-2, 5-2.
Referee: Ivan Bebek (CRO)   Attendance: 10,750.

20.10.16   Krasnodar Stadium, Krasnodar: FK Krasnodar – FC Schalke 04 0-1 (0-1)
FK Krasnodar: Stanislav Kritsyuk, Aleksandr Martinovich, Andreas Granqvist, Artur
Jedrzejczyk, Sergey Petrov, Odil Akhmedov (75' Pavel Mamaev), Vyacheslav Podberezkin
(67' Ricardo Laborde), Joãozinho, Kouassi Eboue (55' Yuri Gazinskiy), Charles Kaboré, Ari.
Coach: Igor Shalimov.
FC Schalke 04: Ralf Fährmann, Junior Caiçara, Benedikt Höwedes, Abdul Rahman Baba,
Naldo, Matija Nastasic, Max Meyer (77' Klas-Jan Huntelaar), Yevhen Konoplyanka (67'
Alessandro Schöpf), Dennis Aogo, Benjamin Stambouli, Franco Di Santo (90' Thilo Kehrer).
Coach: Markus Weinzierl.
Goal: 11' Yevhen Konoplyanka 0-1.
Referee: Mark Clattenburg (ENG)   Attendance: 33,550.

20.10.16   Red Bull Arena, Wals-Siezenheim: Red Bull Salzburg – OGC Nice 0-1 (0-1)
Red Bull Salzburg: Alexander Walke, Paulo Miranda, Andreas Ulmer, Stefan Lainer, Andre
Wisdom, Valentino Lazaro (80' Takumi Minamino), Marc Rzatkowski, Josip Radosevic,
Konrad Laimer, Fredrik Gulbrandsen (83' Munas Dabbur), Jonathan Soriano (83' Hee-chan
Hwang). Coach: Óscar.
OGC Nice: Yoan Cardinale, Paul Baysse, Ricardo Pereira, Mathieu Bodmer (73' Jean Michaël
Seri), Dalbert (76' Younès Belhanda), Dante, Malang Sarr, Valentin Eysseric, Rémi Walter,
Vincent Koziello (74' Wylan Cyprien), Alassane Pléa. Coach: Lucien Favre.
Goal: 13' Alassane Pléa 1-0.
Referee: Evgen Aranovskiy (UKR)   Attendance: 9,473.

221

03.11.16   VELTINS-Arena, Gelsenkirchen: FC Schalke 04 – FK Krasnodar 2-0 (2-0)
FC Schalke 04: Ralf Fährmann, Junior Caiçara, Benedikt Höwedes, Abdul Rahman Baba (69'
Sead Kolasinac), Naldo, Matija Nastasic, Nabil Bentaleb (58' Leon Goretzka), Yevhen
Konoplyanka (82' Alessandro Schöpf), Dennis Aogo, Benjamin Stambouli, Eric Maxim
Choupo-Moting. Coach: Markus Weinzierl.
FK Krasnodar: Stanislav Kritsyuk, Naldo, Andreas Granqvist, Artur Jedrzejczyk (75' Vitaliy
Kaleshin), Sergey Petrov, Odil Akhmedov (62' Marat Izmailov), Vyacheslav Podberezkin (12'
Ricardo Laborde), Joãozinho, Mauricio Pereyra, Kouassi Eboue, Charles Kaboré.
Coach: Igor Shalimov.
Goals: 25' Junior Caiçara 1-0, 28' Nabil Bentaleb 2-0.
Referee: Slavko Vincic (SVN)   Attendance: 42,210.

03.11.16   Allianz Riviera, Nice: OGC Nice – Red Bull Salzburg 0-2 (0-0)
OGC Nice: Yoan Cardinale, Arnaud Souquet, Ricardo Pereira, Dante, Malang Sarr, Younès
Belhanda, Jean Michaël Seri (76' Rémi Walter), Wylan Cyprien (79' Anastasios Donis),
Vincent Koziello, Mario Balotelli, Alassane Pléa (71' Valentin Eysseric).
Coach: Lucien Favre.
Red Bull Salzburg: Alexander Walke, Paulo Miranda, Dayot Upamecano, Andreas Ulmer,
Andre Wisdom, Valentino Lazaro, Marc Rzatkowski (76' Stefan Lainer), Josip Radosevic,
Konrad Laimer, Munas Dabbur (83' Jonathan Soriano), Fredrik Gulbrandsen (62' Hee-chan
Hwang). Coach: Óscar.
Goals: 72', 73' Hee-chan Hwang 0-1, 0-2.
Referee: Hüseyin Göçek (TUR)   Attendance: 17,582.

24.11.16   Krasnodar Stadium, Krasnodar: FK Krasnodar – Red Bull Salzburg 1-1 (0-1)
FK Krasnodar: Stanislav Kritsyuk, Naldo, Andreas Granqvist, Vitaliy Kaleshin, Dmitriy
Torbinskiy, Odil Akhmedov, Joãozinho (73' Marat Izmailov), Mauricio Pereyra (58' Ricardo
Laborde), Kouassi Eboue (46' Yuri Gazinskiy), Charles Kaboré, Fedor Smolov.
Coach: Igor Shalimov.
Red Bull Salzburg: Alexander Walke, Paulo Miranda, Dayot Upamecano, Andreas Ulmer,
Andre Wisdom, Diadie Samassekou, Valentino Lazaro, Valon Berisha (88' Xaver Schlager),
Josip Radosevic, Munas Dabbur, Fredrik Gulbrandsen (73' Hee-chan Hwang). Coach: Óscar.
Goals: 37' Munas Dabbur 0-1, 85' Fedor Smolov 1-1.
Referee: Liran Liany (ISR)   Attendance: 19,150.

24.11.16   VELTINS-Arena, Gelsenkirchen: FC Schalke 04 – OGC Nice 2-0 (1-0)
FC Schalke 04: Ralf Fährmann, Junior Caiçara, Abdul Rahman Baba, Thilo Kehrer, Sascha
Riether, Naldo, Max Meyer (46' Fabian Reese), Yevhen Konoplyanka (61' Nabil Bentaleb, 81'
Donis Avdijaj), Dennis Aogo, Benjamin Stambouli, Bernard Tekpetey.
Coach: Markus Weinzierl.
OGC Nice: Yoan Cardinale, Arnaud Souquet, Ricardo Pereira (66' Alassane Pléa), Mathieu
Bodmer, Olivier Boscagli, Dalbert, Dante, Younès Belhanda (65' Valentin Eysseric), Rémi
Walter (69' Vincent Marcel), Vincent Koziello, Anastasios Donis. Coach: Lucien Favre.
Goals: 14' Yevhen Konoplyanka 1-0 80' Dennis Aogo 2-0 (p).
Referee: Aliyar Aghayev (AZE)   Attendance: 51,504.
Sent off: 90' Bernard Tekpetey.

222

08.12.16   Red Bull Arena, Wals-Siezenheim: Red Bull Salzburg – FC Schalke 04 2-0 (1-0)
Red Bull Salzburg: Cican Stankovic, Duje Caleta-Car, Christian Schwegler, Stefan Lainer, Andre Wisdom, Valentino Lazaro (75' Hannes Wolf), Marc Rzatkowski, Josip Radosevic, Konrad Laimer (60' Diadie Samassekou), Xaver Schlager (86' Reinhold Yabo), Takumi Minamino. Coach: Óscar.
FC Schalke 04: Fabian Giefer, Junior Caiçara, Benedikt Höwedes, Abdul Rahman Baba, Thilo Kehrer, Sascha Riether (83' Atsuto Uchida), Yevhen Konoplyanka (75' Sidney Sam), Dennis Aogo, Benjamin Stambouli, Donis Avdijaj, Fabian Reese (58' Alessandro Schöpf). Coach: Markus Weinzierl.
Goals: 22' Xaver Schlager 1-0, 90+4' Josip Radosevic 2-0.
Referee: Radu Petrescu (ROM)   Attendance: 23,133.

08.12.16   Allianz Riviera, Nice: OGC Nice – FK Krasnodar 2-1 (0-0)
OGC Nice: Walter Benítez, Arnaud Souquet (74' Albert Rafetraniaina), Maxime Le Marchand, Mathieu Bodmer, Olivier Boscagli, Patrick Burner, Arnaud Lusamba, Vincent Marcel, Romain Perraud, Mario Balotelli (46' Alexy Bosetti), Anastasios Donis (68' Hicham Mahou). Coach: Lucien Favre.
FK Krasnodar: Andrey Sinitsyn, Naldo, Aleksandr Martinovich, Andreas Granqvist, Artur Jedrzejczyk, Dmitriy Torbinskiy (65' Vitaliy Kaleshin), Yuri Gazinskiy, Odil Akhmedov, Joãozinho, Kouassi Eboue, Fedor Smolov. Coach: Igor Shalimov.
Goals: 52' Fedor Smolov 0-1, 64' Alexy Bosetti 1-1 (p), 77' Maxime Le Marchand 2-1.
Referee: Sandro Schärer (SUI)   Attendance: 12,722.
Sent off: 61' Andreas Granqvist.

GROUP J

15.09.16   Dalga Arena, Baku: Qarabag FK – Slovan Liberec 2-2 (1-1)
Qarabag FK: Ibrahim Sehic, Qara Qarayev (76' Afran Ismayilov), Maksim Medvedev, Rashad Sadygov, Ansi Agolli (86' Mahir Madatov), Elvin Yunuszade, Michel, Reynaldo, Dani Quintana, Dino Ndlovu (66' Muarem Muarem), Richard. Coach: Gurban Gurbanov.
Slovan Liberec: Martin Dúbravka, Vladimír Coufal, David Hovorka, Lukás Bartosák, Martin Latka, Radim Breite, Jan Sykora (86' Milan Nitriansky), Zdenek Folprecht, Egon Vuch, Daniel Bartl (65' Ondrej Karafiát), Milan Baros (75' Igor Súkennik). Coach: Jindrich Trpisovsky.
Goals: 1' Jan Sykora 0-1, 7' Michel 1-1, 68' Milan Baros 1-2, 90+4' Rashad Sadygov 2-2.
Referee: Stephen Klossner (SUI)   Attendance: 6,200.

(Qarabag FK played their home match on matchday 1 at Dalga Arena, Baku, and played their home matches on matchday 3 and matchday 6 at Tofiq Bahramov Republican stadium, Baku instead of their regular stadium, Azersun Arena, Baku)

15.09.16   Toumba Stadium, Thessaloniki: PAOK Saloniki – ACF Fiorentina 0-0
PAOK Saloniki: Panagiotis Glykos, Léo Matos, Marin Leovac, Giorgos Tzavellas, Fernando Varela, Gojko Cimirot, Garry Rodrigues, Dimitrios Pelkas (57' Yevhen Shakhov), Cañas, Djalma (58' Ángel Crespo), Stefanos Athanasiadis (79' Mame Thiam). Coach: Vladimir Ivic.
ACF Fiorentina: Ciprian Tatarusanu, Gonzalo Rodríguez, Davide Astori, Maximiliano Olivera, Carlos Salcedo (74' Federico Bernardeschi), Nenad Tomovic, Milan Badelj, Borja Valero, Josip Ilicic (63' Carlos Sánchez), Nikola Kalinic, Khouma Babacar (76' Cristian Tello). Coach: Paulo Sousa.
Referee: Slavko Vincic (SVN)   Attendance: 20,904.

29.09.16   Stadio Artemio Franchi, Florence: ACF Fiorentina – Qarabag FK 5-1 (3-0)
ACF Fiorentina: Ciprian Tatarusanu, Sebastien De Maio, Maximiliano Olivera, Carlos
Salcedo, Nenad Tomovic, Carlos Sánchez (46' Matías Vecino), Sebastián Cristóforo, Nikola
Kalinic (61' Mauro Zárate), Federico Bernardeschi (61' Federico Chiesa), Cristian Tello,
Khouma Babacar. Coach: Paulo Sousa.
Qarabag FK: Ibrahim Sehic, Maksim Medvedev, Rashad Sadygov, Ansi Agolli, Elvin
Yunuszade, Michel, Reynaldo (84' Dino Ndlovu), Rahid Amirguliyev, Afran Ismayilov (61'
Muarem Muarem), Dani Quintana (46' Badavi Guseynov), Richard. Coach: Gurban Gurbanov.
Goals: 39' Khouma Babacar 1-0, 43' Nikola Kalinic 2-0, 45+2' Khouma Babacar 3-0,
63, 78' Mauro Zárate 4-0, 5-0, 90+2' Dino Ndlovu 5-1.
Referee: Oliver Drachta (AUT)   Attendance: 14,145.
Sent off: 30' Elvin Yunuszade.

29.09.16   Stadion u Nisy, Liberec: Slovan Liberec – PAOK Saloniki 1-2 (1-1)
Slovan Liberec: Martin Dúbravka, Vladimír Coufal, David Hovorka, Lukás Bartosák (79'
Milan Baros), Martin Latka, Radim Breite, Jan Sykora, Zdenek Folprecht (73' Ondrej
Karafiát), Egon Vuch, Daniel Bartl (46' Ubong Moses Ekpai), Nikolay Komlichenko.
Coach: Jindrich Trpisovsky.
PAOK Saloniki: Panagiotis Glykos, Léo Matos, Marin Leovac, Giorgos Tzavellas, Fernando
Varela, Gojko Cimirot, Garry Rodrigues, Yevhen Shakhov (73' Mame Thiam), Cañas, Djalma
(59' Ioannis Mystakidis), Stefanos Athanasiadis (86' Ángel Crespo). Coach: Vladimir Ivic.
Goals: 1' Nikolay Komlichenko 1-0, 10, 82' Stefanos Athanasiadis 1-1 (p), 1-2.
Referee: Tamás Bognár (HUN)   Attendance: 8,883.

20.10.16   Stadion u Nisy, Liberec: Slovan Liberec – ACF Fiorentina 1-3 (0-2)
Slovan Liberec: Martin Dúbravka, Ondrej Karafiát, Vladimír Coufal, David Hovorka, Radim
Breite, Jan Sykora (68' Lukás Bartosák), Jan Navrátil (72' Daniel Bartl), Zdenek Folprecht,
Petr Sevcík, Egon Vuch, Nikolay Komlichenko (78' Miroslav Markovic).
Coach: Jindrich Trpisovsky.
ACF Fiorentina: Ciprian Tatarusanu, Gonzalo Rodríguez, Davide Astori, Maximiliano Olivera,
Nenad Tomovic, Milan Badelj, Matías Vecino, Sebastián Cristóforo (62' Federico
Bernardeschi), Borja Valero, Nikola Kalinic (53' Cristian Tello), Khouma Babacar (79' Carlos
Sánchez). Coach: Paulo Sousa.
Goals: 8', 23' Nikola Kalinic 0-1, 0-2, 58' Petr Sevcík 1-2, 70' Khouma Babacar 1-3.
Referee: Serdar Gözübüyük (HOL)   Attendance: 9,037.
Sent off: 84' Radim Breite.

20.10.16   Tofiq Bahramow Republican Stadium, Baku:
Qarabag FK – PAOK Saloniki 2-0 (0-0)
Qarabag FK: Ibrahim Sehic, Qara Qarayev, Maksim Medvedev, Rashad Sadygov, Ansi Agolli,
Badavi Guseynov, Muarem Muarem (90' Vüqar Nadirov), Rahid Amirguliyev, Dani Quintana
(90' Namig Alasgarov), Dino Ndlovu (76' Mahir Madatov), Richard.
Coach: Gurban Gurbanov.
PAOK Saloniki: Panagiotis Glykos, Léo Matos, Marin Leovac, Ángel Crespo, Fernando
Varela, Gojko Cimirot, Garry Rodrigues, Yevhen Shakhov, Cañas (59' Diego Biseswar),
Mame Thiam (66' Facundo Pereyra), Djalma (76' Efthimios Koulouris). Coach: Vladimir Ivic.
Goals: 56' Dani Quintana, 87' Rahid Amirguliyev 2-0.
Referee: Alon Yefet (ISR)   Attendance: 26,784.

03.11.16   Stadio Artemio Franchi, Florence: ACF Fiorentina – Slovan Liberec 3-0 (2-0)
ACF Fiorentina: Ciprian Tatarusanu, Gonzalo Rodríguez, Sebastien De Maio, Nenad Tomovic,
Carlos Sánchez, Sebastián Cristóforo, Borja Valero (79' Khouma Babacar), Hrvoje Milic,
Josip Ilicic (69' Matías Vecino), Nikola Kalinic (86' Federico Bernardeschi), Federico Chiesa.
Coach: Paulo Sousa.
Slovan Liberec: Václav Hladky, Vladimír Coufal, David Hovorka (17' Milan Nitriansky),
Lukás Bartosák, Jan Sykora (79' Jan Navrátil), Zdenek Folprecht, Igor Súkenník, Petr Sevcík,
Egon Vuch, Daniel Bartl, Miroslav Markovic (59' Nikolay Komlichenko).
Coach: Jindrich Trpisovsky.
Goals: 30' Josip Ilicic 1-0 (p), 43' Nikola Kalinic 2-0, 73' Sebastián Cristóforo 3-0.
Referee: Aleksandar Stavrev (MKD)   Attendance: 11,583.

03.11.16   Toumba Stadium, Thessaloniki: PAOK Saloniki – Qarabag FK 0-1 (0-0)
PAOK Saloniki: Panagiotis Glykos, Léo Matos, Marin Leovac, Giorgos Tzavellas, Fernando
Varela, Gojko Cimirot (81' Yevhen Shakhov), Diego Biseswar (73' Mame Thiam), Garry
Rodrigues, Cañas, Ioannis Mystakidis (61' Facundo Pereyra), Stefanos Athanasiadis.
Coach: Vladimir Ivic.
Qarabag FK: Ibrahim Sehic, Qara Qarayev, Maksim Medvedev, Rashad Sadygov, Ansi Agolli,
Badavi Guseynov, Muarem Muarem (88' Afran Ismayilov), Rahid Amirguliyev (64' Míchel),
Dani Quintana, Dino Ndlovu (76' Reynaldo), Richard. Coach: Gurban Gurbanov.
Goal: 69' Míchel 0-1.
Referee: John Beaton (SCO)   Attendance: 11,476.

24.11.16   Stadion u Nisy, Liberec: Slovan Liberec – Qarabag FK 3-0 (1-0)
Slovan Liberec: Martin Dúbravka, Ondrej Karafiát, Vladimír Coufal, Lukás Bartosák, Lukás
Pokorny, Radim Breite, Zdenek Folprecht, Petr Sevcík (80' Jan Navrátil), Egon Vuch (90'
Ondrej Bláha), Ubong Moses Ekpai, Nikolay Komlichenko (86' Daniel Bartl).
Coach: Jindrich Trpisovsky.
Qarabag FK: Ibrahim Sehic, Qara Qarayev, Maksim Medvedev, Ansi Agolli, Badavi
Guseynov, Míchel (52' Afran Ismayilov), Muarem Muarem (60' Reynaldo), Arif
Dashdemirov, Dani Quintana, Dino Ndlovu, Richard. Coach: Gurban Gurbanov.
Goals: 11' Egon Vuch 1-0, 57, 63' Nikolay Komlichenko 2-0 (p), 3-0.
Referee: Stefan Johannesson (SWE)   Attendance: 4,942.

24.11.16   Stadio Artemio Franchi, Florence: ACF Fiorentina – PAOK Saloniki 2-3 (1-2)
ACF Fiorentina: Luca Lezzerini, Gonzalo Rodríguez, Davide Astori, Nenad Tomovic, Milan
Badelj, Matías Vecino, Sebastián Cristóforo (66' Carlos Sánchez), Hrvoje Milic (51' Federico
Chiesa), Federico Bernardeschi, Cristian Tello (83' Josip Ilicic), Khouma Babacar.
Coach: Paulo Sousa.
PAOK Saloniki: Zeljko Brkic, Léo Matos, Marin Leovac, Ángel Crespo, Fernando Varela,
Gojko Cimirot, Garry Rodrigues, Yevhen Shakhov (83' Ioannis Mystakidis), Cañas, Djalma
(71' Dimitrios Pelkas), Efthimios Koulouris (61' Mame Thiam). Coach: Vladimir Ivic.
Goals: 5' Yevhen Shakhov 0-1, 26' Djalma 0-2, 33' Federico Bernardeschi 1-2,
50' Khouma Babacar 2-2, 90+3' Garry Rodrigues 2-3.
Referee: Stephan Klossner (SUI)   Attendance: 12,793.

08.12.16   Tofiq Bahramow Republican Stadium, Baku:
Qarabag FK – ACF Fiorentina 1-2 (0-0)
Qarabag FK: Ibrahim Sehic, Qara Qarayev, Rashad Sadygov, Ansi Agolli, Badavi Guseynov, Muarem Muarem (46' Afran Ismayilov), Rahid Amirguliyev (62' Reynaldo), Dani Quintana, Dino Ndlovu (71' Mahir Madatov), Ilgar Gurbanov, Richard. Coach: Gurban Gurbanov.
ACF Fiorentina: Ciprian Tatarusanu, Gonzalo Rodríguez, Davide Astori, Maximiliano Olivera, Nenad Tomovic, Milan Badelj, Matías Vecino, Sebastián Cristóforo (61' Borja Valero), Federico Bernardeschi (83' Carlos Sánchez), Federico Chiesa, Khouma Babacar (51' Nikola Kalinic). Coach: Paulo Sousa.
Goals: 60' Matías Vecino 0-1, 73' Reynaldo 1-1, 76' Federico Chiesa 1-2.
Referee: Ivan Bebek (CRO)   Attendance: 21,750.
Sent off: 84' Federico Chiesa.

08.12.16   Toumba Stadium, Thessaloniki: PAOK Saloniki – Slovan Liberec 2-0 (1-0)
PAOK Saloniki: Panagiotis Glykos, Léo Matos, Marin Leovac (82' Stelios Malezas), Ángel Crespo, Fernando Varela, Gojko Cimirot, Garry Rodrigues, Dimitrios Pelkas (80' Yevhen Shakhov), Cañas, Djalma, Stefanos Athanasiadis (71' Efthimios Koulouris).
Coach: Vladimir Ivic.
Slovan Liberec: Martin Dúbravka, Ondrej Karafiát (46' Daniel Bartl), Vladimír Coufal, Lukás Bartosák, Lukás Pokorny, Radim Breite, Zdenek Folprecht (80' Ilia Kubyshkin), Petr Sevcík, Egon Vuch, Ubong Moses Ekpai (65' Jan Sykora), Nikolay Komlichenko.
Coach: Jindrich Trpisovsky.
Goals: 29' Garry Rodrigues 1-0, 67' Dimitrios Pelkas 2-0.
Referee: Andre Marriner (ENG)   Attendance: 11,463.

GROUP K

15.09.16   Stadio Giuseppe Meazza, Milan: Internazionale – Hapoel Be'er Sheva 0-2 (0-0)
Internazionale: Samir Handanovic, Andrea Ranocchia, Jeison Murillo, Danilo D'Ambrosio, Yuto Nagatomo, Felipe Melo (74' Mauro Icardi), Gary Medel, Marcelo Brozovic (46' Éver Banega), Rodrigo Palacio, Jonathan Biabiany (58' Antonio Candreva), Éder.
Coach: Frank de Boer.
Hapoel Be'er Sheva: David Goresh, Ben Biton, Miguel Vítor, Shir Tzedek, Loai Taha, Mihály Korhut (85' Ben Turgeman), Maor Buzaglo (77' Ben Sahar), Ovidiu Hoban, John Ogu, Anthony Nuatuzor, Lucio Maranhão (67' Maor Melikson). Coach: Barak Bakhar.
Goals: 54' Miguel Vítor 0-1, 69' Maor Buzaglo 0-2.
Referee: Jakob Kehlet (DEN)   Attendance: 16,778.

15.09.16   Saint Mary's Stadium, Southampton: Southampton FC – Sparta Praha 3-0 (2-0)
Southampton FC: Fraser Forster, Maya Yoshida, Cuco Martina, Virgil van Dijk, Matt Targett, Oriol Romeu (83' Steven Davis), James Ward-Prowse, Pierre-Emile Højbjerg, Shane Long, Charlie Austin (77' Jay Rodriguez), Dusan Tadic (70' Nathan Redmond). Coach: Claude Puel.
Sparta Praha: Tomás Koubek, Michal Kadlec, Vyacheslav Karavaev, Mario Holek, Costa Nhamoinesu, Lukás Vácha (64' Lukás Marecek), Martin Frydek, Michal Sácek, Josef Sural (75' Matej Pulkrab), Lukás Julis (46' David Lafata), Václav Kadlec. Coach: Zdenek Scasny.
Goals: 5, 27' Charlie Austin 1-0 (p), 2-0, 90+2' Jay Rodriguez 3-0.
Referee: Manuel Gräfe (GER)   Attendance: 25,125.

29.09.16   Generali Arena, Prague: Sparta Praha – Internazionale 3-1 (2-0)
Sparta Praha: Tomás Koubek, Ondrej Mazuch, Michal Kadlec (74' Matej Pulkrab), Vyacheslav
Karavaev, Mario Holek, Borek Dockal, Martin Frydek (66' Lukás Julis), Michal Sácek, Ales
Cermák (88' David Lafata), Daniel Holzer, Václav Kadlec. Coach: David Holoubek.
Internazionale: Samir Handanovic, Andrea Ranocchia, Jeison Murillo, Danilo D'Ambrosio
(56' Cristian Ansaldi), Senna Miangue, Felipe Melo, Éver Banega, Assane Gnoukouri (70'
Mauro Icardi), Antonio Candreva (63' Ivan Perisic), Rodrigo Palacio, Éder.
Coach: Frank de Boer.
Goals: 7', 25' Václav Kadlec 1-0, 2-0, 71' Rodrigo Palacio 2-1, 76' Mario Holek 3-1.
Referee: Artur Soares Dias (POR)   Attendance: 14,651.
Sent off: 75' Andrea Ranocchia.

29.09.16   Yaakov Turner Toto Stadium, Beer Sheva:
            Hapoel Be'er Sheva – Southampton FC 0-0
Hapoel Be'er Sheva: David Goresh, Ben Biton, Miguel Vítor, Shir Tzedek, Loai Taha, Mihály
Korhut, Maharan Radi (80' Ovidiu Hoban), Maor Melikson (70' Maor Buzaglo), John Ogu,
Anthony Nuatuzor, Lucio Maranhão (63' Ben Sahar). Coach: Barak Bakhar.
Southampton FC: Fraser Forster, Maya Yoshida, Cuco Martina, Virgil van Dijk, Matt Targett,
Jordy Clasie, Oriol Romeu, James Ward-Prowse, Nathan Redmond (85' Pierre-Emile
Højbjerg), Jake Hesketh (35' Dusan Tadic), Shane Long. Coach: Claude Puel.
Referee: Stefan Johannesson (SWE)   Attendance: 16,138.

20.10.16   Yaakov Turner Toto Stadium, Beer Sheva:
            Hapoel Be'er Sheva – Sparta Praha 0-1 (0-0)
Hapoel Be'er Sheva: David Goresh, Ben Biton, Miguel Vítor, Shir Tzedek, Mihály Korhut,
Maharan Radi (86' Maor Buzaglo), Ovidiu Hoban (73' Ben Sahar), Maor Melikson, John Ogu,
Anthony Nuatuzor, Lucio Maranhão (82' Mohammad Ghadir). Coach: Barak Bakhar.
Sparta Praha: Tomás Koubek, Ondrej Mazuch, Michal Kadlec, Vyacheslav Karavaev, Mario
Holek, Ondrej Zahustel, Borek Dockal, Lukás Marecek, Daniel Holzer (46' Matej Pulkrab),
Lukás Julis (77' David Lafata), Václav Kadlec (90' Václav Dudl). Coach: David Holoubek.
Goal: 71' Matej Pulkrab 0-1.
Referee: Ivan Bebek (CRO)   Attendance: 15,607.

20.10.16   Stadio Giuseppe Meazza, Milan: Internazionale – Southampton FC 1-0 (0-0)
Internazionale: Samir Handanovic, Davide Santon, Jeison Murillo, Miranda, Yuto Nagatomo
(90' Danilo D'Ambrosio), Gary Medel, Assane Gnoukouri, Marcelo Brozovic, Antonio
Candreva (80' Cristian Ansaldi), Mauro Icardi, Éder (86' Ivan Perisic). Coach: Frank de Boer.
Southampton FC: Fraser Forster, Maya Yoshida, Cuco Martina, Virgil van Dijk, Samuel
McQueen, Oriol Romeu, James Ward-Prowse, Pierre-Emile Højbjerg, Shane Long (48' Charlie
Austin), Jay Rodriguez (78' Steven Davis), Dusan Tadic (73' Sofiane Boufal).
Coach: Claude Puel.
Goal: 67' Antonio Candreva 1-0.
Referee: Gediminas Mazeika (LTU)   Attendance: 26,719.
Sent off: 77' Marcelo Brozovic.

03.11.16 Generali Arena, Prague: Sparta Praha – Hapoel Be'er Sheva 2-0 (2-0)
Sparta Praha: Tomás Koubek, Ondrej Mazuch, Michal Kadlec, Vyacheslav Karavaev, Mario Holek, Costa Nhamoinesu, Borek Dockal, Lukás Marecek, Daniel Holzer (90' Milan Kadlec), David Lafata (80' Matej Pulkrab), Lukás Julis (72' Václav Dudl). Coach: David Holoubek.
Hapoel Be'er Sheva: David Goresh, Ben Biton, Miguel Vítor (46' Yuval Shabtai), Shir Tzedek, Loai Taha, Mihály Korhut, Maharan Radi, Maor Buzaglo (62' Mohammad Ghadir), Ovidiu Hoban, Maor Melikson, Lucio Maranhão (73' Ben Sahar). Coach: Barak Bakhar.
Goals: 23' Ben Biton 1-0 (og), 38' David Lafata 2-0.
Referee: István Vad (HUN)   Attendance: 12,891.

03.11.16 Saint Mary's Stadium, Southampton: Southampton FC – Internazionale 2-1 (0-1)
Southampton FC: Fraser Forster, Maya Yoshida, Cuco Martina, Virgil van Dijk, Samuel McQueen, Oriol Romeu, James Ward-Prowse, Nathan Redmond, Pierre-Emile Højbjerg, Jay Rodriguez (59' Charlie Austin), Dusan Tadic (77' Steven Davis). Coach: Claude Puel.
Internazionale: Samir Handanovic, Andrea Ranocchia, Miranda, Danilo D'Ambrosio, Yuto Nagatomo, Gary Medel (74' Éder), Éver Banega, Assane Gnoukouri (82' Felipe Melo), Ivan Perisic, Antonio Candreva (89' Jonathan Biabiany), Mauro Icardi. Coach: Stefano Vecchi.
Goals: 33' Mauro Icardi 0-1, 64' Virgil van Dijk 1-1, 69' Yuto Nagatomo 2-1 (og).
Referee: Pawel Gil (POL)   Attendance: 30,389.

Dusan Tadic missed a penalty kick (45').

24.11.16 Yaakov Turner Toto Stadium, Beer Sheva:
Hapoel Be'er Sheva – Internazionale 3-2 (0-2)
Hapoel Be'er Sheva: David Goresh, Ben Biton, Miguel Vítor, Shir Tzedek, Loai Taha (36' Maharan Radi), Mihály Korhut, Maor Buzaglo, Ovidiu Hoban (81' Mohammad Ghadir), John Ogu, Anthony Nuatuzor, Lucio Maranhão (75' Ben Sahar). Coach: Barak Bakhar.
Internazionale: Samir Handanovic, Jeison Murillo, Miranda, Danilo D'Ambrosio, Yuto Nagatomo, Felipe Melo (62' Assane Gnoukouri), Éver Banega (70' Juan Carrizo *goalkeeper*), Marcelo Brozovic, Antonio Candreva, Mauro Icardi, Éder (60' Ivan Perisic).
Coach: Stefano Pioli.
Goals: 13' Mauro Icardi 0-1, 25' Marcelo Brozovic 0-2, 58' Lucio Maranhão 1-2,
71' Anthony Nuatuzor 2-2 (p), 90+3' Ben Sahar 3-2.
Referee: Xavier Estrada Fernández (ESP)   Attendance: 15,973.
Sent off: 69' Samir Handanovic.

24.11.16 Generali Arena, Prague: Sparta Praha – Southampton FC 1-0 (1-0)
Sparta Praha: Tomás Koubek, Ondrej Mazuch, Michal Kadlec, Vyacheslav Karavaev, Mario Holek, Costa Nhamoinesu, Borek Dockal, Lukás Marecek, Daniel Holzer (90' Václav Dudl), David Lafata (88' Filip Havelka), Lukás Julis (90' Daniel Köstl). Coach: David Holoubek.
Southampton FC: Fraser Forster, Maya Yoshida, Cuco Martina, Virgil van Dijk, Samuel McQueen, Jordy Clasie (72' Charlie Austin), James Ward-Prowse, Nathan Redmond, Pierre-Emile Højbjerg (55' Oriol Romeu), Shane Long, Jay Rodriguez (55' Sofiane Boufal).
Coach: Claude Puel.
Goal: 11' Costa Nhamoinesu 1-0.
Referee: Jesús Gil Manzano (ESP)   Attendance: 17,429.

228

08.12.16   Stadio Giuseppe Meazza, Milan: Internazionale – Sparta Praha 2-1 (1-0)
Internazionale: Juan Carrizo, Marco Andreolli, Andrea Ranocchia, Cristian Ansaldi, Jeison
Murillo, Senna Miangue, Felipe Melo, Rodrigo Palacio (46' Ivan Perisic), Jonathan Biabiany,
Éder, Andrea Pinamonti (80' Axel Mohamed Bakayoko). Coach: Stefano Pioli.
Sparta Praha: Tomás Koubek, Ondrej Mazuch, Michal Kadlec, Vyacheslav Karavaev, Mario
Holek, Costa Nhamoinesu, Borek Dockal, Lukás Marecek, Ales Cermák (78' Michal Sácek),
David Lafata (74' Matej Pulkrab), Lukás Julis (89' Václav Dudl). Coach: David Holoubek.
Goals: 23' Éder 1-0, 54' Lukás Marecek 1-1, 90' Éder 2-1.
Referee: Bart Vertenten (BEL)   Attendance: 6,449.

08.12.16   Saint Mary's Stadium, Southampton:
           Southampton FC – Hapoel Be'er Sheva 1-1 (0-0)
Southampton FC: Fraser Forster, Cédric Soares, Maya Yoshida, Virgil van Dijk, Ryan
Bertrand, Steve Davis, Oriol Romeu, Nathan Redmond, Pierre-Emile Højbjerg (82' James
Ward-Prowse), Charlie Austin (39' Shane Long), Josh Sims (59' Dusan Tadic).
Coach: Claude Puel.
Hapoel Be'er Sheva: David Goresh, Ben Biton, Miguel Vítor, Shir Tzedek, Mihály Korhut (77'
Yuval Shabtai), Maharan Radi, Maor Buzaglo, Ovidiu Hoban (56' Mohammad Ghadir), John
Ogu, Anthony Nuatuzor, Ben Sahar (68' Lucio Maranhão). Coach: Barak Bakhar.
Goals: 79' Maor Buzaglo 0-1, 90+1' Virgil van Dijk 1-1.
Referee: Paolo Tagliavento (ITA)   Attendance: 30,416.

GROUP L

15.09.16   Osmanli Stadyumu, Ankara: Osmanlispor FK – Steaua Bucuresti 2-0 (0-0)
Osmanlispor FK: Zydrūnas Karcemarskas, Koray Altinay, Aykut Demir, Tiago Pinto, Numan
Çürüksu, Raheem Lawal, Papa N'Diaye, Adrien Regattin, Aminu Umar (75' Dzon Delarge),
Musa Çagiran (83' Adam Maher), Cheick Diabaté (78' Raul Rusescu). Coach: Mustafa Akçay.
Steaua Bucuresti: Florin Nita, Gabriel Tamas, Alin Tosca, Adnan Aganovic, Wilfred Moke,
Rick (61' Florin Tanase), Gabriel Enache, Alexandru Bourceanu, Adrian Popa, Bojan
Golubovic (46' Bogdan Mitrea), William Amorim (67' Antonio Jakolis).
Coach: Laurentiu Reghecampf.
Goals: 64' Cheick Diabaté 1-0 (p), 74' Aminu Umar 2-0.
Referee: Tobias Welz (GER)   Attendance: 11,807.
Sent off: 45'Gabriel Enache.

15.09.16   El Madrigal, Villarreal: Villarreal CF – FC Zürich 2-1 (2-1)
Villarreal CF: Andrés Fernández, José Ángel, Víctor Ruiz, Álvaro González, Antonio
Rukavina, Alfred N'Diaye, Jonathan Dos Santos (72' Samu Castillejo), Bruno Soriano, Denis
Cheryshev (81' Roberto Soriano), Alexandre Pato, Rafael Borré (67' Nicola Sansone).
Coach: Fran Escribá.
FC Zürich: Andris Vanins, Alain Nef, Umaru Bangura, Ivan Kecojevic, Kay Voser, Adrian
Winter (65' Marco Schönbächler), Burim Kukeli, Cédric Brunner, Sangoné Sarr (58' Gilles
Yapi-Yapo), Roberto Rodríguez (83' Dzengis Cavusevic), Armando Sadiku. Coach: Uli Forte.
Goals: 2' Armando Sadiku 0-1, 28 Alexandre Pato 1-1, 44' Jonathan Dos Santos 2-1.
Referee: Sébastien Delferière (BEL)   Attendance: 16,384.

29.09.16 Letzigrund, Zürich: FC Zürich – Osmanlispor FK 2-1 (1-0)
FC Zürich: Andris Vanins, Alain Nef, Ivan Kecojevic, Kay Voser, Oliver Buff (88' Gilles
Yapi-Yapo), Burim Kukeli, Cédric Brunner, Marco Schönbächler (70' Adrian Winter),
Sangoné Sarr, Moussa Koné (55' Roberto Rodríguez), Dzengis Cavusevic. Coach: Uli Forte.
Osmanlispor FK: Zydrūnas Karcemarskas, Aykut Demir, Tiago Pinto, Numan Çürüksu, Avdija
Vrsajevic, Raheem Lawal, Papa N'Diaye, Adrien Regattin, Musa Çagiran (61' Adam Maher),
Raul Rusescu (72' Cheick Diabaté), Dzon Delarge (67' Aminu Umar). Coach: Mustafa Akçay.
Goals: 45+1' Marco Schönbächler 1-0, 73' Adam Maher 1-1, 79' Dzengis Cavusevic 2-1.
Referee: Aleksey Eskov (RUS)   Attendance: 7,473.

29.09.16 Arena Nationala, Bucharest: Steaua Bucuresti – Villarreal CF 1-1 (1-1)
Steaua Bucuresti: Florin Nita, Gabriel Tamas, Alin Tosca, Marko Momcilovic, Sulley Muniru,
Wilfred Moke, Rick, Alexandru Bourceanu, Adrian Popa (77' Florin Tanase), Bojan
Golubovic (77' Antonio Jakolis), William Amorim (89' Ovidiu Popescu).
Coach: Laurentiu Reghecampf.
Villarreal CF: Andrés Fernández, José Ángel, Mateo Musacchio, Antonio Rukavina, Daniele
Bonera, Alfred N'Diaye, Jonathan Dos Santos, Bruno Soriano, Denis Cheryshev (73' Roberto
Soriano), Alexandre Pato (63' Samu Castillejo), Rafael Borré (82' Cédric Bakambu).
Coach: Fran Escribá.
Goals: 9' Rafael Borré 0-1, 19' Sulley Muniru 1-1.
Referee: Evgen Aranovskiy (UKR)   Attendance: 13,231.

20.10.16 Arena Nationala, Bucharest: Steaua Bucuresti – FC Zürich 1-1 (0-0)
Steaua Bucuresti: Florin Nita, Gabriel Tamas, Alin Tosca, Marko Momcilovic, Sulley Muniru
(83' Antonio Jakolis), Ovidiu Popescu, Rick, Alexandru Bourceanu, Adrian Popa, Bojan
Golubovic (79' Alexandru Tudorie), William Amorim. Coach: Laurentiu Reghecampf.
FC Zürich: Andris Vanins, Alain Nef, Ivan Kecojevic, Kay Voser, Adrian Winter (73' Marco
Schönbächler), Oliver Buff, Cédric Brunner (84' Antonio Marchesano), Sangoné Sarr (78'
Dzengis Cavusevic), Roberto Rodríguez, Gilles Yapi-Yapo, Moussa Koné. Coach: Uli Forte.
Goals: 63' Bojan Golubovic 1-0, 86' Moussa Koné 1-1.
Referee: Tamás Bognár (HUN)   Attendance: 13,154.

20.10.16 Osmanli Stadyumu, Ankara: Osmanlispor FK – Villarreal CF 2-2 (2-0)
Osmanlispor FK: Hakan Arikan, Aykut Demir, Tiago Pinto, Numan Çürüksu, Avdija
Vrsajevic, Raheem Lawal (39' Mehmet Güven), Papa N'Diaye, Aminu Umar, Adam Maher
(57' Václav Procházka), Raul Rusescu (80' Adrien Regattin), Dzon Delarge.
Coach: Mustafa Akçay.
Villarreal CF: Andrés Fernández, José Ángel, Álvaro González, Antonio Rukavina, Daniele
Bonera, Alfred N'Diaye (82' Nicola Sansone), Jonathan Dos Santos (70' Roberto Soriano),
Bruno Soriano, Alexandre Pato, Samu Castillejo, Rafael Borré (65' Cédric Bakambu).
Coach: Fran Escribá.
Goals: 23', 24' Raul Rusescu 1-0, 2-0, 56' Alfred N'Diaye 2-1, 74' Alexandre Pato 2-2.
Referee: Liran Liany (ISR)   Attendance: 11,692.
Sent off: 53' Mehmet Güven.

Bruno Soriano missed a penalty kick (55').

230

03.11.16 Letzigrund, Zürich: FC Zürich – Steaua Bucuresti 0-0
FC Zürich: Andris Vanins, Alain Nef, Ivan Kecojevic, Kay Voser (29' Nicolas Stettler),
Adrian Winter (65' Moussa Koné), Oliver Buff (75' Marco Schönbächler), Burim Kukeli,
Cédric Brunner, Sangoné Sarr, Roberto Rodríguez, Dzengis Cavusevic. Coach: Uli Forte.
Steaua Bucuresti: Florin Nita, Gabriel Tamas, Alin Tosca, Marko Momcilovic, Sulley Muniru
(85' Alexandru Tudorie), Wilfred Moke, Rick, Alexandru Bourceanu (63' Adnan Aganovic),
Adrian Popa, Bojan Golubovic (72' Vlad Achim), William Amorim.
Coach: Laurentiu Reghecampf.
Referee: Robert Schörgenhofer (AUT)   Attendance: 8,060.

03.11.16 El Madrigal, Villarreal: Villarreal CF – Osmanlispor FK 1-2 (0-1)
Villarreal CF: Andrés Fernández, José Ángel, Víctor Ruiz, Álvaro González, Antonio
Rukavina, Jonathan Dos Santos (80' Nicola Sansone), Rodri, Bruno Soriano, Denis Cheryshev
(69' Samu Castillejo), Cédric Bakambu, Rafael Borré (63' Alexandre Pato).
Coach: Fran Escribá.
Osmanlispor FK: Hakan Arikan, Tiago Pinto, Václav Procházka, Muhammed Bayir, Numan
Çürüksu, Papa N'Diaye, Aminu Umar, Musa Çagiran (86' Aykut Demir), Adam Maher, Pierre
Webó (73' Raul Rusescu), Dzon Delarge (67' Adrien Regattin). Coach: Mustafa Akçay.
Goals: 8' Pierre Webó 0-1, 48' Rodri 1-1, 75' Raul Rusescu 1-2.
Referee: Harald Lechner (AUT)   Attendance: 15,386.

24.11.16 Arena Nationala, Bucharest: Steaua Bucuresti – Osmanlispor FK 2-1 (0-1)
Steaua Bucuresti: Florin Nita, Gabriel Tamas, Alin Tosca, Marko Momcilovic, Mihai Pintilii
(46' Alexandru Bourceanu), Sulley Muniru (63' Vlad Achim), Wilfred Moke, Rick, Gabriel
Enache (46' Bojan Golubovic), Adrian Popa, William Amorim. Coach: Laurentiu Reghecampf.
Osmanlispor FK: Zydrūnas Karcemarskas, Tiago Pinto, Václav Procházka, Numan Çürüksu,
Avdija Vrsajevic (75' Muhammed Bayir), Papa N'Diaye, Adrien Regattin, Musa Çagiran,
Adam Maher (61' Raheem Lawal), Raul Rusescu, Dzon Delarge (69' Erdal Kiliçaslan).
Coach: Mustafa Akçay.
Goals: 30' Papa N'Diaye 0-1, 68' Marko Momcilovic 1-1, 86' Gabriel Tamas 2-1.
Referee: Paolo Mazzoleni (ITA)   Attendance: 6,020.

24.11.16 Letzigrund, Zürich: FC Zürich – Villarreal CF 1-1 (0-1)
FC Zürich: Andris Vanins, Alain Nef, Umaru Bangura, Ivan Kecojevic, Kay Voser (69' Adrian
Winter), Antonio Marchesano, Burim Kukeli (79' Armando Sadiku), Cédric Brunner (69'
Roberto Rodríguez), Marco Schönbächler, Sangoné Sarr, Moussa Koné. Coach: Uli Forte.
Villarreal CF: Asenjo, José Ángel, Mateo Musacchio, Víctor Ruiz, Antonio Rukavina,
Jonathan Dos Santos, Trigueros, Bruno Soriano, Denis Cheryshev (70' Samu Castillejo),
Alexandre Pato (78' Nicola Sansone), Cédric Bakambu (82' Rodri). Coach: Fran Escribá.
Goals: 14' Bruno Soriano 0-1, 87' Roberto Rodríguez 1-1 (p).
Referee: Davide Massa (ITA)   Attendance: 10,069.

231

08.12.16   Osmanli Stadyumu, Ankara: Osmalispor FK – FC Zürich 2-0 (0-0)
Osmanlispor FK: Zydrūnas Karcemarskas, Tiago Pinto, Václav Procházka, Numan Çürüksu,
Avdija Vrsajevic, Mehmet Güven, Papa N'Diaye, Adrien Regattin (87' Erdal Kiliçaslan),
Adam Maher, Pierre Webó (78' Raul Rusescu), Dzon Delarge (74' Aminu Umar).
Coach: Mustafa Akçay.
FC Zürich: Andris Vanins, Alain Nef, Umaru Bangura, Ivan Kecojevic, Kay Voser (77'
Moussa Koné), Adrian Winter, Burim Kukeli, Cédric Brunner (60' Armando Sadiku), Sangoné
Sarr, Roberto Rodríguez, Dzengis Cavusevic (67' Marco Schönbächler). Coach: Uli Forte.
Goals: 73' Dzon Delarge 1-0, 89' Erdal Kiliçaslan 2-0.
Referee: Matej Jug (SVN)   Attendance: 10,250.

08.12.16   El Madrigal, Villarreal: Villarreal CF – Steaua Bucuresti 2-1 (1-0)
Villarreal CF: Asenjo, Mario, Mateo Musacchio (39' Álvaro González), Víctor Ruiz, Jaume
Costa, Jonathan Dos Santos, Trigueros, Roberto Soriano, Bruno Soriano, Cédric Bakambu (85'
Rodri), Nicola Sansone (80' Rafael Borré). Coach: Fran Escribá.
Steaua Bucuresti: Florin Nita, Gabriel Tamas, Alin Tosca, Marko Momcilovic, Mihai Pintilii
(54' Vlad Achim), Wilfred Moke, Rick (76' Ovidiu Popescu), Gabriel Enache (46' Bojan
Golubovic), Alexandru Bourceanu, Adrian Popa, William Amorim.
Coach: Laurentiu Reghecampf.
Goals: 16' Nicola Sansone 1-0, 55' Vlad Achim 1-1, 88' Trigueros 2-1.
Referee: Manuel Gräfe (GER)   Attendance: 19,471.
Sent off: 79' Gabriel Tamas.

ROUND OF 32

*FC København, Olympique Lyon, Tottenham Hotspur, Besiktas, FK Rostov, Borussia
Mönchengladbach, Legia Warszawa and PFC Ludogorets Razgrad entered the UEFA Europa
League after finishing in third-place in their respective UEFA Champions League groups.*

16.02.17   Krasnodar Stadium, Krasnodar: FK Krasnodar – Fenerbahçe 1-0 (1-0)
FK Krasnodar: Stanislav Kritsyuk, Naldo, Aleksandr Martinovich, Cristian Ramírez, Vitaliy
Kaleshin, Yuri Gazinskiy, Vyacheslav Podberezkin (70' Mauricio Pereyra), Víctor Claession,
Charles Kaboré, Wanderson (65' Ricardo Laborde), Fedor Smolov. Coach: Igor Shalimov.
Fenerbahçe: Volkan Demirel, Hasan-Ali Kaldirim, Simon Kjær, Sener Özbayrakli, Mehmet
Topal, Souza, Alper Potuk, Roman Neustädter, Moussa Sow (72' Ozan Tufan), Emmanuel
Emenike (72' Fernandão), Jeremain Lens. Coach: Dick Advocaat.
Goal: 4' Víctor Claesson 1-0.
Referee: Ivan Kruzliak (SVK)   Attendance: 32,460.

16.02.17   Stadionul Marin Anastasovici, Giurgiu: Astra Giurgiu – KRC Genk 2-2 (1-1)
Astra Giurgiu: Silviu Lung Jr., Geraldo Alves, Fabrício, Junior Maranhão, Cristian Sapunaru,
Takayuki Seto, Constantin Budescu, Alexandru Ionita (64' Sergiu Bus, 80' Viorel Nicoara),
Alexandru Stan, Filipe Teixeira, Daniel Niculae (64' Daniel Florea). Coach: Marius Sumudica.
KRC Genk: Mathew Ryan, Jakub Brabec, Omar Colley, Jere Uronen, Timoty Castagne,
Bennard Kumordzi (64' Sander Berge), Pozuelo (75' Jean-Paul Boëtius), Bryan Heynen,
Leandro Trossard (88' Thomas Buffel), Siebe Schrijvers, Mbwana Samatta.
Coach: Albert Stuivenberg.
Goals: 25' Timoty Castagne 0-1, 43' Constantin Budescu 1-1, 83' Leandro Trossard 1-2,
90' Takayuki Seto 2-2.
Referee: Svein Moen (NOR)   Attendance: 3,775.

16.02.17   Stadion Vasil Levski, Sofia: PFC Ludogorets Razgrad – FC København 1-2 (0-1)
PFC Ludogorets Razgrad: Vladislav Stoyanov, José Palomino, Natanael Pimienta, Jordan
Minev, Cosmin Moti, Svetoslav Dyakov, Marcelinho, Wanderson (80' João Paulo), Anicet
Andrianantenaina, Jonathan Cafú, Virgil Misidjan (62' Claudiu Keserü).
Coach: Georgi Dermendjiev.
FC København: Robin Olsen, Ludwig Augustinsson, Erik Johansson, Peter Ankersen, Mathias
Jørgensen, William Kvist, Uros Matic, Andreas Cornelius, Federico Santander (71' Andrija
Pavlovic), Youssef Toutouh (90' Tom Høgli), Rasmus Falk (72' Ján Gregus).
Coach: Ståle Solbakken.
Goals: 2' Anicet Andrianantenaina 0-1 (og), 53' Youssef Toutouh 0-2, 81' Claudiu Keserü 1-2.
Referee: Ivan Bebek (CRO)   Attendance: 14,257.
Sent off: 90+6' Ján Gregus.

16.02.17   Municipal de Balaídos, Vigo: Celta de Vigo – Shakhtar Donetsk 0-1 (0-1)
Celta de Vigo: Sergio Álvarez, Hugo Mallo, Jonny, Gustavo Cabral, Facundo Roncaglia,
Nemanja Radoja (74' Jozabed), Pablo Hernández, Daniel Wass, Théo Bongonda (58' Pione
Sisto), John Guidetti (84' Giuseppe Rossi), Iago Aspas. Coach: Eduardo Berizzo.
Shakhtar Donetsk: Andriy Pyatov, Maksym Malyshev, Ivan Ordets, Ismaily, Darijo Srna,
Yaroslav Rakitskiy, Fred, Marlos (90+3' Márcio Azevedo), Dentinho (46' Viktor Kovalenko),
Taison (84' Bernard), Gustavo Blanco Leschuk. Coach: Paulo Fonseca.
Goal: 26' Gustavo Blanco Leschuk 0-1.
Referee: Gediminas Mazeika (LTU)   Attendance: 18,318.

16.02.17   Georgios Karaiskakis, Piraeus: Olympiakos Piraeus – Osmanlispor FK 0-0
Olympiakos Piraeus: Nicola Leali, Alberto Botía, Aly Cissokho, Bruno Viana, Panagiotis
Retsos, Diogo, Kostas Fortounis (71' Georgios Manthatis), André Martins (88' Karim
Ansarifard), Athanasios Androutsos, Óscar Cardozo (76' Alaixys Romao), Sebá.
Coach: Paulo Bento.
Osmanlispor FK: Zydrūnas Karcemarskas, Tiago Pinto, Václav Procházka, Numan Çürüksu,
Avdija Vrsajevic, Papa N'Diaye, Adrien Regattin, Luíz Carlos (87' Adam Maher), Musa
Çagiran, Dzon Delarge (81' Raul Rusescu), Thievy Bifouma (90+4' Mehmet Güven).
Coach: Mustafa Akçay.
Referee: Ruddy Buquet (FRA)   Attendance: 24,478.
Sent off: 74' Bruno Viana.

16.02.17   GHELAMCO-arena, Gent: KAA Gent – Tottenham Hotspur 1-0 (0-0)
KAA Gent: Lovre Kalinic, Stefan Mitrovic, Nana Asare (80' Rami Gershon), Samuel Gigot,
Kenny Saief, Brecht Dejaegere, Thomas Foket, Anderson Esiti, Danijel Milicevic, Jérémy
Perbet (75' Kalifa Coulibaly), Moses Simon (74' Samuel Kalu). Coach: Hein Vanhaezebrouck.
Tottenham Hotspur: Hugo Lloris, Kyle Walker, Toby Alderweireld, Ben Davies, Victor
Wanyama, Eric Dier, Moussa Sissoko (72' Georges-Kévin N'Koudou), Mousa Dembélé (68'
Heung-min Son), Dele Alli, Harry Winks (80' Christian Eriksen), Harry Kane.
Coach: Mauricio Pochettino.
Goal: 59' Jérémy Perbet 1-0.
Referee: Benoît Bastien (FRA)   Attendance: 19,267.

233

16.02.17   Stadion Olimp 2, Rostov: FK Rostov – Sparta Praha 4-0 (3-0)
FK Rostov: Nikita Medvedev, Vladimir Granat, Miha Mevlja, Fedor Kudryashov, César
Navas, Tsimafei Kalachev, Christian Noboa, Alexandru Gatcan, Aleksandr Erokhin (83'
Andrei Prepelita), Dmitriy Poloz (75' Marko Devic), Aleksandr Bukharov (67' Sardar
Azmoun). Coach: Ivan Daniliants.
Sparta Praha: Tomás Koubek, Ondrej Mazuch, Michal Kadlec, Vyacheslav Karavaev, Costa
Nhamoinesu, Lukás Vácha (80' Mario Holek), Borek Dockal (87' David Lafata), Michal
Sácek, Tiémoko Konaté, Albiach Roger (76' Matej Hybs), Lukás Julis. Coach: Tomás Pozár.
Goals: 15' Miha Mevlja 1-0, 38' Dmitriy Poloz 2-0, 40' Christian Noboa 3-0,
68' Sardar Azmoun 4-0.
Referee: Bas Nijhuis (HOL)   Attendance: 6,160.
Sent off: 32' Tiémoko Konaté.

16.02.17   Borussia-Park, Mönchengladbach:
           Borussia Mönchengladbach – ACF Fiorentina 0-1 (0-1)
Borussia Mönchengladbach: Yann Sommer, Andreas Christensen, Jannik Vestergaard, Oscar
Wendt, Tony Jantschke (64' Josip Drmic), Christoph Kramer, Patrick Herrmann (77' André
Hahn), Mahmoud Dahoud, Fabian Johnson (77' Julian Korb), Thorgan Hazard, Lars Stindl.
Coach: Dieter Hecking.
ACF Fiorentina: Ciprian Tatarusanu, Gonzalo Rodríguez, Davide Astori, Maximiliano Olivera,
Milan Badelj, Carlos Sánchez, Matías Vecino, Borja Valero, Nikola Kalinic (77' Khouma
Babacar), Federico Bernardeschi (64' Sebastián Cristóforo), Cristian Tello (86' Nenad
Tomovic). Coach: Paulo Sousa.
Goal: 44' Federico Bernardeschi 0-1.
Referee: Jesús Gil Manzano (ESP)   Attendance: 41,863.

16.02.17   AFAS Stadion, Alkmaar: AZ Alkmaar – Olympique Lyon 1-4 (0-2)
AZ Alkmaar: Tim Krul, Rens van Eijden, Ridgeciano Haps, Derrick Luckassen, Ben Rienstra,
Iliass Bel Hassani, Mats Seuntjens (74' Joris van Overeem), Stijn Wuytens, Alireza
Jahanbakhsh, Wout Weghorst (65' Fred Friday), Muamer Tankovic (65' Levi García).
Coach: John van den Brom.
Olympique Lyon: Anthony Lopes, Emanuel Mammana, Mouctar Diakhaby, Christophe Jallet,
Maciej Rybus, Corentin Tolisso, Sergi Darder (84' Houssem Aouar), Maxime Gonalons, Lucas
Tousart (67' Jordan Ferri), Alexandre Lacazette (66' Maxwell Cornet), Nabil Fekir.
Coach: Bruno Génésio.
Goals: 26' Lucas Tousart 0-1, 45+2', 57' Alexandre Lacazette 0-2, 0-3,
68' Alireza Jahanbakhsh 1-3 (p), 90+5' Jordan Ferri 1-4.
Referee: Bobby Madden (SCO)   Attendance: 16,098.

16.02.17   San Mamés Barria, Bilbao: Athletic Bilbao – APOEL Nicosia 3-2 (1-1)
Athletic Bilbao: Iraizoz, Aymeric Laporte, De Marcos, Balenziaga (56' Lekue), Yeray, Beñat,
Iturraspe (56' San José), Raúl García, Muniain, Williams (77' Susaeta), Aduriz.
Coach: Valverde.
APOEL Nicosia: Boy Waterman, Zhivko Milanov, Nuno Morais, Giorgios Merkis, Nicholas
Ioannou, Cédric Yamberé, Giorgos Efrem (73' Efstathios Aloneftis), Facundo Bertoglio (59'
Igor de Camargo), Vinicius, Pieros Sotiriou (76' Astiz), Giannis Gianniotas.
Coach: Thomas Christiansen.
Goals: 36' Giorgos Efrem 0-1, 38' Giogios Merkis 1-1 (og), 61' Aduriz 2-1, 71' Williams 3-1,
88' Giannis Gianniotas 3-2.
Referee: Jonas Eriksson (SWE)   Attendance: 32,675.

16.02.17　Wojska Polskiego, Warszawa: Legia Warszawa – AFC Ajax 0-0
Legia Warszawa: Arkadiusz Malarz, Michal Pazdan, Maciej Dabrowski, Adam Hlousek,
Lukasz Broz, Tomasz Jodlowiec, Vadis Odjidja-Ofoe (82' Kasper Hämäläinen), Valeri
Qazaishvili (59' Guilherme), Michal Kopczynski, Miroslav Radovic, Tomás Necid (58' Michal
Kucharczyk). Coach: Jacek Magiera.
AFC Ajax: André Onana, Kenny Tete, Davinson Sánchez, Daley Sinkgraven, Nick Viergever,
Davy Klaassen, Lasse Schöne, Hakim Ziyech (81' Donny van de Beek), Bertrand Traoré (73'
Justin Kluivert, 86' Heiko Westermann), Amin Younes, Kasper Dolberg. Coach: Peter Bosz.
Referee: David Fernández Borbolán (ESP)　Attendance: 28,742.
Sent off: 84' Kenny Tete.

16.02.17　Constant Vanden Stock, Brussels: RSC Anderlecht – Zenit St.Petersburg 2-0 (2-0)
RSC Anderlecht: Rubén, Olivier Deschacht, Uros Spajic, Ivan Obradovic, Andy Najar,
Massimo Bruno, Frank Acheampong (60' Alexandru Chipciu), Youri Tielemans, Leander
Dendoncker, Nicolae Stanciu (74' Sofiane Hanni), Isaac Thelin (80' Lukasz Teodorczyk).
Coach: René Weiler.
Zenit St.Petersburg: Yuriy Lodygin, Domenico Criscito, Neto, Branislav Ivanovic, Oleg
Shatov (65' Róbert Mak), Javi García, Hernani, Yuriy Zhirkov, Giuliano (80' Artur Yusupov),
Aleksandr Kokorin (71' Danny), Artem Dzyuba. Coach: Mircea Lucescu.
Goals: 5', 31' Frank Acheampong 1-0, 2-0.
Referee: Michael Oliver (ENG)　Attendance: 13,415.

16.02.17　Old Trafford, Manchester: Manchester United – AS Saint-Étienne 3-0 (1-0)
Manchester United: Sergio Romero, Eric Bailly, Chris Smalling, Daley Blind, Antonio
Valencia, Paul Pogba, Mata (70' Marcus Rashford), Ander Herrera, Marouane Fellaini (46'
Jesse Lingard), Zlatan Ibrahimovic, Anthony Martial (85' Ashley Young).
Coach: José Mourinho.
AS Saint-Étienne: Stéphane Ruffier, Kévin Théophile-Catherine, Florentin Pogba (79' Robert
Beric), Loïc Perrin, Kévin Malcuit, Vincent Pajot (72' Ole Selnæs), Henri Saivet, Jordan
Veretout, Jorginho (65' Nolan Roux), Romain Hamouma, Kévin Monnet-Paquet.
Coach: Christophe Galtier.
Goals: 15', 75', 88' Zlatan Ibrahimovic 1-0, 2-0, 3-0 (p).
Referee: Pavel Královec (CZE)　Attendance: 67,192.

16.02.17　Estadio de la Cerámica, Villarreal: Villarreal CF – AS Roma 0-4 (0-1)
Villarreal CF: Asenjo, Mario, Mateo Musacchio, Víctor Ruiz, Jaume Costa, Jonathan Dos
Santos, Trigueros, Samu Castillejo (67' Denis Cheryshev), Bruno Soriano, Cédric Bakambu
(66' Adrián), Nicola Sansone (81' Rafael Borré). Coach: Fran Escribá.
AS Roma: Alisson, Antonio Rüdiger (71' Juan Jesus), Bruno Peres, Federico Fazio, Emerson,
Kostas Manolas, Radja Nainggolan (90' Leandro Paredes), Kevin Strootman, Daniele De
Rossi, Edin Dzeko, Stephan El Shaarawy (62' Mohamed Salah). Coach: Luciano Spalletti.
Goals: 32' Emerson 0-1, 65', 79', 87' Edin Dzeko 0-2, 0-3, 0-4.
Referee: Danny Makkelie (HOL)　Attendance: 17,960.

235

16.02.17   Yaakov Turner Toto Stadium, Beer Sheva: Hapoel Be'er Sheva – Besiktas 1-3 (1-1)
Hapoel Be'er Sheva: David Goresh, Ben Biton, Ben Turgeman, Shir Tzedek, Maharan Radi,
Ovidiu Hoban (67' Michael Ohana), Maor Melikson (58' Mohammad Ghadir), William
Soares, John Ogu, Anthony Nuatuzor, Elyaniv Barda (79' Ben Sahar). Coach: Barak Bakhar.
Besiktas: Fabricio, Matej Mitrovic, Dusko Tosic, Marcelo, Gökhan Gönül, Atiba Hutchinson,
Tolgay Arslan (74' Anderson Talisca), Necip Uysal, Ricardo Quaresma (90' Gökhan Inler),
Cenk Tosun (90+2' Ömer Sismanoglu), Ryan Babel. Coach: Senol Günes.
Goals: 42' William Soares 0-1 (og), 44' Elyaniv Barda 1-1, 60' Cenk Tosun 1-2,
90+3' Atiba Hutchinson 1-3.
Referee: Martin Atkinson (ENG)   Attendance: 15,347.

16.02.17   Toumba Stadium, Thessaloniki: PAOK Saloniki – FC Schalke 04 0-3 (0-1)
PAOK Saloniki: Panagiotis Glykos, Léo Matos, Marin Leovac, Stelios Malezas, Ángel Crespo,
Fernando Varela, Gojko Cimirot, Diego Biseswar (77' Pedro Henrique), Yevhen Shakhov,
Ioannis Mystakidis (55' Djalma), Stefanos Athanasiadis (85' Amr Warda).
Coach: Vladimir Ivic.
FC Schalke 04: Ralf Fährmann, Benedikt Höwedes, Sead Kolasinac, Naldo, Matija Nastasic,
Max Meyer, Leon Goretzka, Benjamin Stambouli, Daniel Caligiuri (79' Yevhen
Konoplyanka), Alessandro Schöpf (46' Thilo Kehrer), Guido Burgstaller (84' Klaas-Jan
Huntelaar). Coach: Markus Weinzierl.
Goals: 27' Guigo Burgstaller 0-1, 82' Max Meyer 0-2, 90' Klaas-Jan Huntelaar 0-3.
Referee: Javier Estrada Fernández (ESP)   Attendance: 25,593.

22.02.17   Sükrü Saracoglu, Istanbul: Fenerbahçe – FK Krasnodar 1-1 (1-1)
Fenerbahçe: Volkan Demirel (71' Fabiano), Simon Kjær, Sener Özbayrakli (71' Volkan Sen),
Ismail Köybasi, Martin Skrtel, Mehmet Topal, Souza, Alper Potuk, Robin van Persie, Moussa
Sow (71' Fernandão), Jeremain Lens. Coach: Dick Advocaat.
FK Krasnodar: Stanislav Kritsyuk, Naldo, Andreas Granqvist, Cristian Ramírez, Vitaliy
Kaleshin, Yuri Gazinskiy, Vyacheslav Podberezkin (79' Mauricio Pereyra), Víctor Claessson,
Charles Kaboré, Wanderson (64' Ricardo Laborde), Fedor Smolov. Coach: Igor Shalimov.
Goals: 7' Fedor Smolov 0-1, 41' Souza 1-1.
Referee: Pawel Raczkowski (POL)   Attendance: 21,788.

22.02.17   Stade Geoffroy Guichard, Saint-Étienne:
             AS Saint-Étienne – Manchester United 0-1 (0-1)
AS Saint-Étienne: Stéphane Ruffier, Kévin Théophile-Catherine, Florentin Pogba, Loïc Perrin,
Kévin Malcuit, Vincent Pajot, Henri Saivet (53' Jorginho), Jordan Veretout (68' Fabien
Lemoine), Romain Hamouma, Kévin Monnet-Paquet, Robert Beric (59' Nolan Roux).
Coach: Christophe Galtier.
Manchester United: Sergio Romero, Eric Bailly, Chris Smalling, Daley Blind, Paul Pogba,
Mata (64' Marcos Rojo), Michael Carrick (62' Bastian Schweinsteiger), Ashley Young,
Henrikh Mkhitaryan (25' Marcus Rashford), Marouane Fellaini, Zlatan Ibrahimovic.
Coach: José Mourinho.
Goal: 16' Henrikh Mkhitaryan 0-1.
Referee: Deniz Aytekin (GER)   Attendance: 41,492.
Sent off: 63' Eric Bailly.

236

22.02.17 VELTINS-Arena, Gelsenkirchen: FC Schalke 04 – PAOK Saloniki 1-1 (1-1)
FC Schalke 04: Ralf Fährmann, Benedikt Höwedes, Sead Kolasinac, Naldo (72' Holger Badstuber), Matija Nastasic, Johannes Geis, Max Meyer, Nabil Bentaleb (84' Thilo Kehrer), Alessandro Schöpf, Eric Maxim Choupo-Moting (56' Leon Goretzka), Klaas-Jan Huntelaar. Coach: Markus Weinzierl.
PAOK Saloniki: Panagiotis Glykos, Stelios Malezas, Ángel Crespo, Achilleas Poungouras, Gojko Cimirot, Yevhen Shakhov, Stelios Kitsiou, Amr Warda (69' Diego Biseswar), Djalma (78' Dimitrios Pelkas), Efthimios Koulouris, Ioannis Mystakidis (63' Pedro Henrique). Coach: Vladimir Ivic.
Goals: 23' Alessandro Schöpf 1-0, 25' Matija Nastasic 1-1 (og).
Referee: Luca Banti (ITA)   Attendance: 50,619.

23.02.17 Luminus Arena, Genk: KRC Genk – Astra Giurgiu 1-0 (0-0)
KRC Genk: Mathew Ryan, Jakub Brabec, Omar Colley, Jere Uronen, Timoty Castagne, Ruslan Malinovskiy (90' Jean-Paul Boëtius), Pozuelo (89' Bennard Kumordzi), Sander Berge, Leandro Trossard, Siebe Schrijvers (77' Thomas Buffel), Mbwana Samatta. Coach: Albert Stuivenberg.
Astra Giurgiu: Silviu Lung Jr., Geraldo Alves, Junior Maranhão, Cristian Sapunaru, Takayuki Seto (82' Alexandru Ionita (II)), Constantin Budescu, Boubacar Mansaly, Florin Lovin (67' Daniel Florea), Alexandru Stan, Filipe Teixeira, Daniel Niculae (70' Sergiu Bus). Coach: Marius Sumudica.
Goal: 67' Pozuelo 1-0.
Referee: Serdar Gözübüyük (HOL)   Attendance: 8,804.

23.02.17 Telia Parken, København: FC København – PFC Ludogorets Razgrad 0-0
FC København: Robin Olsen, Ludwig Augustinsson, Erik Johansson, Peter Ankersen, Mathias Jørgensen, Aboubakar Keita (66' Kasper Kusk), Uros Matic, Andreas Cornelius, Federico Santander (80' Andrija Pavlovic), Youssef Toutouh, Rasmus Falk (89' Nicolai Boilesen). Coach: Ståle Solbakken.
PFC Ludogorets Razgrad: Vladislav Stoyanov, José Palomino, Natanael Pimienta, Jordan Minev, Cosmin Moti, Svetoslav Dyakov, Marcelinho, Wanderson (83' João Paulo), Anicet Andrianantenaina (65' Juninho Quixadá), Jonathan Cafú (75' Virgil Misidjan), Claudiu Keserü. Coach: Georgi Dermendjiev.
Referee: Miroslav Zelinka (CZE)   Attendance: 17,064.

23.02.17 Metalist, Kharkiv: Shakhtar Donetsk – Celta de Vifo 0-2 (0-0, 0-1)
Shakhtar Donetsk: Andriy Pyatov, Maksym Malyshev (112' Andriy Boryachuk), Ivan Ordets, Ismaily, Darijo Srna, Yaroslav Rakitskiy, Fred, Marlos, Viktor Kovalenko (73' Taras Stepanenko), Taison (83' Bernard), Gustavo Blanco Leschuk. Coach: Paulo Fonseca.
Celta de Vigo: Sergio Álvarez, Hugo Mallo, Fontàs, Jonny, Gustavo Cabral, Facundo Roncaglia (58' Jozabed), Pablo Hernández, Pione Sisto (85' Giuseppe Rossi), Daniel Wass (80' Théo Bongonda), John Guidetti, Iago Aspas. Coach: Eduardo Berizzo.
Goals: 90+1' Iago Aspas 0-1 (p), 108' Gustavo Cabral 0-2.
Referee: Slavko Vincic (SVN)   Attendance: 33,117.

Celta de Vigo won after extra time.

237

23.02.17   Osmanli Stadi, Ankara: Osmanlispor FK – Olympiakos Piraeus 0-3 (0-0)
Osmanlispor FK: Zydrūnas Karcemarskas, Tiago Pinto (66' Muhammed Bayir), Václav
Procházka, Numan Çürüksu, Avdija Vrsajevic, Papa N'Diaye, Adrien Regattin (75' Dzon
Delarge), Musa Çagiran (74' Mehmet Güven), Adam Maher, Pierre Webó, Thievy Bifouma.
Coach: Mustafa Akçay.
Olympiakos Piraeus: Nicola Leali, Alberto Botía, Manuel Da Costa, Aly Cissokho, Panagiotis
Retsos, Diogo, Kostas Fortounis (85' Alaixys Romao), Tarik Elyounoussi (81' Georgios
Manthatis), André Martins (65' Athanasios Androutsos), Karim Ansarifard, Sebá.
Coach: Paulo Bento.
Goals: 47' Karim Ansarifard 0-1, 60' Tarik Elyounoussi 0-2, 86' Karim Ansarifard 0-3.
Referee: István Vad (HUN)   Attendance: 17,541.

23.02.17   Wembley National Stadium, London: Tottenham Hotspur – KAA Gent 2-2 (1-1)
Tottenham Hotspur: Hugo Lloris, Kyle Walker, Toby Alderweireld, Jan Vertonghen, Ben
Davies (58' Heung-min Son), Victor Wanyama, Eric Dier (89' Vincent Janssen), Mousa
Dembélé (75' Harry Winks), Dele Alli, Christian Eriksen, Harry Kane.
Coach: Mauricio Pochettino.
KAA Gent: Lovre Kalinic, Stefan Mitrovic, Samuel Gigot, Rami Gershon, Kenny Saief, Brecht
Dejaegere (56' Louis Verstraete), Thomas Foket, Anderson Esiti, Danijel Milicevic (46'
Thomas Matton), Kalifa Coulibaly, Moses Simon (75' Jérémy Perbet).
Coach: Hein Vanhaezebrouck.
Goals: 10' Christian Eriksen 1-0, 20' Harry Kane 1-1 (og), 61' Victor Wanyama 2-1,
82' Jérémy Perbet 2-2.
Referee: Jorge Sousa (POR)   Attendance: 80.465.
Sent off: 39' Dele Alli.

23.02.17   Generali Arena, Praha: Sparta Praha – FK Rostov 1-1 (0-1)
Sparta Praha: Tomás Koubek, Ondrej Mazuch (46' Filip Havelka), Michal Kadlec, Vyacheslav
Karavaev, Mario Holek, Costa Nhamoinesu, Michal Sácek, Ales Cermák, Albiach Roger (70'
Matej Hybs), Matej Pulkrab (40' Josef Sural), Lukás Julis. Coach: Tomás Pozár.
FK Rostov: Nikita Medvedev, Vladimir Granat (70' Denis Terentyev), Miha Mevlja, Fedor
Kudryashov, César Navas, Tsimafei Kalachev, Christian Noboa, Alexandru Gatcan (46'
Andrei Prepelita), Aleksandr Erokhin, Dmitriy Poloz, Aleksandr Bukharov (46' Sardar
Azmoun). Coach: Ivan Daniliants.
Goals: 13' Dmitriy Poloz 0-1, 83' Vyacheslav Karavaev 1-1.
Referee: Hüseyin Göçek (TUR)   Attendance: 13,413
Sent off: 66' Costa Nhamoinesu.

23.02.17   Artemio Franchi, Firenze: ACF Fiorentina – Borussia Mönchengladbach 2-4 (2-1)
ACF Fiorentina: Ciprian Tatarusanu, Gonzalo Rodríguez, Davide Astori, Maximiliano Olivera,
Milan Badelj (63' Khouma Babacar), Carlos Sánchez, Matías Vecino, Borja Valero, Nikola
Kalinic, Federico Bernardeschi (63' Josip Ilicic), Federico Chiesa. Coach: Paulo Sousa.
Borussia Mönchengladbach: Yann Sommer, Andreas Christensen, Jannik Vestergaard, Oscar
Wendt, Tony Jantschke, Christoph Kramer, Patrick Herrmann, Mahmoud Dahoud (80' Tobias
Strobl), Jonas Hofmann (73' Fabian Johnson), Thorgan Hazard (27' Josip Drmic), Lars Stindl.
Coach: Dieter Hecking.
Goals: 16' Nikola Kalinic 1-0, 29' Borja Valero 2-0, 44', 47', 55' Lars Stindl 2-1 (p), 2-2, 2-3,
60' Andreas Christensen 2-4.
Referee: Artur Soares Dias (POR)   Attendance: 24,712.

238

23.02.17   Stade des Lumières, Lyon: Olympique Lyon – AZ Alkmaar 7-1 (4-1)
Olympique Lyon: Anthony Lopes, Mapou Yanga-Mbiwa, Mouctar Diakhaby, Christophe
Jallet, Jérémy Morel, Jordan Ferri, Sergi Darder, Lucas Tousart (81' Corentin Tolisso), Rachid
Ghezzal (76' Alexandre Lacazette), Nabil Fekir, Maxwell Cornet (64' Houssem Aouar).
Coach: Bruno Génésio.
AZ Alkmaar: Tim Krul, Mattias Johansson, Ron Vlaar (46' Rens van Eijden), Ridgeciano
Haps, Derrick Luckassen, Ben Rienstra, Iliass Bel Hassani, Stijn Wuytens, Alireza
Jahanbakhsh (72' Mats Seuntjens), Fred Friday (77' Wout Weghorst), Levi García.
Coach: John van den Brom.
Goals: 4' Nabil Fekir 1-0, 17' Maxwel Cornet 2-0, 26' Levi García 2-1, 27' Nabil Fekir 3-1,
34' Sergi Darder 4-1, 78' Nabil Fekir 5-1, 86' Houssem Aouar 6-1, 89' Mouctar Diakhaby 7-1.
Referee: Aleksey Kulbakov (BLS)   Attendance: 25,743.

23.02.17   Neo GSP, Nicosia: APOEL Nicosia – Athletic Bilbao 2-0 (0-0)
APOEL Nicosia: Boy Waterman, Zhivko Milanov, Astiz, Nuno Morais, Giorgios Merkis,
Nicholas Ioannou, Giorgos Efrem (71' Vander), Vinicius (76' Lorenzo Ebecilio), Barral (61'
Igor de Camargo), Pieros Sotiriou, Giannis Gianniotas. Coach: Thomas Christiansen.
Athletic Bilbao: Iraizoz, San José, Etxeita (70' Iturraspe), De Marcos (79' Sabin), Balenziaga,
Yeray, Beñat, Susaeta (57' Villalibre), Raúl García, Muniain, Williams. Coach: Valverde.
Goals: 46' Pieros Sotiriou 1-0, 54' Giannis Gianniotas 2-0 (p).
Referee: Vladislav Bezborodov (RUS)   Attendance: 15,275.
Sent off: 65' Pieros Sotiriou, 90' Iturraspe.

23.02.17   Amsterdam ArenA, Amsterdam: AFC Ajax – Legia Warszawa 1-0 (0-0)
AFC Ajax: André Onana, Joël Veltman, Jaïro Riedewald, Davinson Sánchez, Nick Viergever,
Davy Klaassen, Lasse Schöne, Hakim Ziyech, Bertrand Traoré, Amin Younes, Kasper Dolberg
(81' Abdelhak Nouri). Coach: Peter Bosz.
Legia Warszawa: Arkadiusz Malarz, Michal Pazdan, Maciej Dabrowski, Adam Hlousek,
Lukasz Broz, Tomasz Jodlowiec (57' Thibault Moulin), Guilherme (73' Tomás Necid), Vadis
Odjidja-Ofoe, Valeri Qazaishvili, Michal Kopczynski (82' Daniel Chukwu), Michal
Kucharczyk. Coach: Jacek Magiera.
Goal: 49' Nick Viergever 1-0.
Referee: Anthony Taylor (ENG)   Attendance: 52,286.

23.02.17   Petrovskiy, St.Petersburg: Zenit St.Petersburg – RSC Anderlecht 3-1 (1-0)
Zenit St.Petersburg: Yuriy Lodygin, Aleksandr Anyukov, Domenico Criscito, Neto, Mauricio,
Javi García, Yuriy Zhirkov, Giuliano, Aleksandr Kokorin, Danny (89' Róbert Mak), Artem
Dzyuba. Coach: Mircea Lucescu.
RSC Anderlecht: Rubén, Olivier Deschacht, Uros Spajic, Ivan Obradovic, Andy Najar,
Alexandru Chipciu (84' Bram Nuytinck), Frank Acheampong (89' Capel), Youri Tielemans,
Leander Dendoncker, Nicolae Stanciu (73' Massimo Bruno), Isaac Thelin.
Coach: René Weiler.
Goals: 24' Giuliano 1-0, 72' Artem Dzyuba 2-0, 78' Giuliano 3-0, 90' Isaac Thelin 3-1.
Referee: Anastasios Sidiropoulos (GRE)   Attendance: 17,992.

RSC Anderlecht won on away goals.

239

23.02.17   Stadio Olimpico, Roma: AS Roma – Villarreal CF 0-1 (0-1)
AS Roma: Alisson, Juan Jesus, Bruno Peres (84' Federico Fazio), Thomas Vermaelen, Mário
Rui, Kostas Manolas (46' Antonio Rüdiger), Leandro Paredes, Diego Perotti, Daniele De Rossi
(76' Radja Nainggolan), Edin Dzeko, Francesco Totti. Coach: Luciano Spalletti.
Villarreal CF: Andrés Fernández, José Ángel, Álvaro González, Antonio Rukavina, Bruno
Soriano, Rodri, Roberto Soriano, Bruno Soriano (77' Jonathan Dos Santos), Denis Cheryshev
(73' Cédric Bakambu), Soldado (66' Adrián), Rafael Borré. Coach: Fran Escribá.
Goal: 15' Rafael Borré 0-1.
Referee: Felix Zwayer (GER)   Attendance: 19,495.
Sent off: 81' Antonio Rüdiger.

23.02.17   Vodafone Arena, Istanbul: Besiktas – Hapoel Be'er Sheva 2-1 (1-0)
Besiktas: Fabricio, Dusko Tosic, Marcelo, Andreas Beck, Atinç Nukan, Necip Uysal (72'
Oguzhan Özyakup), Gökhan Inler, Anderson Talisca, Ricardo Quaresma (61' Tolgay Arslan),
Vincent Aboubakar (79' Cenk Tosun), Ryan Babel. Coach: Senol Günes.
Hapoel Be'er Sheva: David Goresh, Ben Turgeman, Shir Tzedek, Matan Ohayon, Ovidiu
Hoban, William Soares, John Ogu, Mohammad Ghadir (64' Maor Melikson), Anthony
Nuatuzor, Ben Sahar (70' Elyaniv Barda), Vladimir Broun (57' Maor Buzaglo).
Coach: Barak Bakhar.
Goals: 17' Vincent Aboubakar 1-0, 64' Anthony Nuatuzor 1-1, 87' Cenk Tosun 2-1.
Referee: Matej Jug (SVN)   Attendance: 27,982.

ROUND OF 16

09.03.17   Neo GSP, Nicosia: APOEL Nicosia – RSC Anderlecht 0-1 (0-1)
APOEL Nicosia: Boy Waterman, Zhivko Milanov, Astiz (40' Roberto Lago), Nuno Morais,
Giorgios Merkis, Nicholas Ioannou, Lorenzo Ebecilio (72' Kostakis Artymatas), Giorgos
Efrem (55' Vander), Igor de Camargo, Barral, Giannis Gianniotas.
Coach: Thomas Christiansen.
RSC Anderlecht: Rubén, Uros Spajic, Dennis Appiah, Bram Nuytinck, Andy Najar, Alexandru
Chipciu (88' Massimo Bruno), Youri Tielemans, Leander Dendoncker, Nicolae Stanciu (80'
Frank Acheampong), Sofiane Hanni, Lukasz Teodorczyk (60' Isaac Thelin).
Coach: René Weiler.
Goal: 29' Nicolae Stanciu 0-1.
Referee: Jorge Sousa (POR)   Attendance: 19,327.

09.03.17   Stadion Olimp 2, Rostov: FK Rostov – Manchester United 1-1 (0-1)
FK Rostov: Nikita Medvedev, Vladimir Granat (18' Denis Terentyev), Miha Mevlja, Fedor
Kudryashov, César Navas, Tsimafei Kalachev, Christian Noboa, Alexandru Gatcan, Aleksandr
Erokhin, Dmitriy Poloz, Aleksandr Bukharov (74' Sardar Azmoun). Coach: Ivan Daniliants.
Manchester United: Sergio Romero, Phil Jones, Marcos Rojo, Chris Smalling, Daley Blind
(90+2' Antonio Valencia), Paul Pogba, Ashley Young, Ander Herrera (90+2' Michael
Carrick), Henrikh Mkhitaryan (67' Anthony Martial), Marouane Fellaini, Zlatan Ibrahimovic.
Coach: José Mourinho.
Goals: 35' Henrikh Mkhitaryan 0-1, 53' Aleksandr Bukharov 1-1.
Referee: Felix Zwayer (GER)   Attendance: 14,223.

09.03.17   Telia Parken, København: FC København – AFC Ajax 2-1 (1-1)
FC København: Robin Olsen, Ludwig Augustinsson, Erik Johansson, Peter Ankersen, Mathias Jørgensen, William Kvist, Uros Matic, Andreas Cornelius, Federico Santander (63' Andrija Pavlovic), Youssef Toutouh, Rasmus Falk. Coach: Ståle Solbakken.
AFC Ajax: André Onana, Kenny Tete, Daley Sinkgraven, Nick Viergever, Matthijs de Ligt, Davy Klaassen, Lasse Schöne, Donny van de Beek (77' Hakim Ziyech), Bertrand Traoré (77' David Neres), Amin Younes, Kasper Dolberg. Coach: Peter Bosz.
Goals: 1' Rasmus Falk 1-0, 32' Kasper Dolberg 1-1, 59' Andreas Cornelius 2-1.
Referee: Artur Soares Dias (POR)   Attendance: 31,189.

09.03.17   Municipal de Balaidos, Vigo: Celta de Vigo – FK Krasnodar 2-1 (0-0)
Celta de Vigo: Sergio Álvarez, Hugo Mallo, Fontàs, Jonny, Gustavo Cabral, Marcelo Díaz, Nemanja Radoja, Pione Sisto, Daniel Wass (69' Jozabed), John Guidetti (77' Claudio Beauvue), Iago Aspas. Coach: Eduardo Berizzo.
FK Krasnodar: Stanislav Kritsyuk, Naldo, Aleksandr Martinovich, Andreas Granqvist, Cristian Ramírez, Yuri Gazinskiy, Vyacheslav Podberezkin (75' Pavel Mamaev), Ilya Zhigulev (83' Dmitriy Torbinskiy), Víctor Claessson, Mauricio Pereyra, Wanderson (78' Ricardo Laborde). Coach: Igor Shalimov.
Goals: 50' Daniel Wass 1-0, 55' Victor Claesson 1-1, 90' Claudio Beauvue 2-1.
Referee: Craig Thomson (SCO)   Attendance: 18,414.

09.03.17   VELTINS-Arena, Gelsenkirchen:
             FC Schalke 04 – Borussia Mönchengladbach 1-1 (1-1)
FC Schalke 04: Ralf Fährmann, Benedikt Höwedes, Sead Kolasinac, Thilo Kehrer, Matija Nastasic, Johannes Geis, Leon Goretzka, Benjamin Stambouli (55' Nabil Bentaleb), Daniel Caligiuri, Alessandro Schöpf (72' Eric Maxim Choupo-Moting), Guido Burgstaller (84' Franco Di Santo). Coach: Markus Weinzierl.
Borussia Mönchengladbach: Yann Sommer, Jannik Vestergaard, Oscar Wendt, Tony Jantschke, Timothée Kolodziejczak, Tobias Strobl, Mahmoud Dahoud, Fabian Johnson (65' André Hahn), Jonas Hofmann (84' Nico Schulz), Raffael (79' Patrick Herrmann), Lars Stindl. Coach: Dieter Hecking.
Goals: 15' Jonas Hofmann 0-1, 25' Guido Burgstaller 1-1.
Referee: Björn Kuipers (HOL)   Attendance: 52,412.

09.03.17   Stade des Lumières, Lyon: Olympique Lyon – AS Roma 4-2 (1-2)
Olympique Lyon: Anthony Lopes, Emanuel Mammana (71' Nabil Fekir), Mouctar Diakhaby, Jérémy Morel, Rafael (46' Christophe Jallet), Corentin Tolisso, Maxime Gonalons, Mathieu Valbuena, Lucas Tousart, Alexandre Lacazette, Rachid Ghezzal (76' Maxwell Cornet). Coach: Bruno Génésio.
AS Roma: Alisson, Juan Jesus, Bruno Peres, Federico Fazio, Emerson, Kostas Manolas, Radja Nainggolan (85' Diego Perotti), Kevin Strootman, Mohamed Salah, Daniele De Rossi (82' Leandro Paredes), Edin Dzeko (90+3' Stephan El Shaarawy). Coach: Luciano Spalletti.
Goals: 8' Mouctar Diakhaby 1-0, 20' Mohamed Salah 1-1, 33' Federico Fazio 1-2, 47' Corentin Tolisso 2-2, 74' Nabil Fekir 3-2, 90+2' Alexandre Lacazette 4-2.
Referee: Anthony Taylor (ENG)   Attendance: 50,588.

09.03.17   Georgios Karaiskakis, Piraeus: Olympiakos Piraeus – Besiktas 1-1 (1-0)
Olympiakos Piraeus: Nicola Leali, Alberto Botía (64' Manuel Da Costa), Aly Cissokho,
Panagiotis Retsos, Diogo, Alaixys Romao, Kostas Fortounis (73' Marko Marin), Tarik
Elyounoussi, Esteban Cambiasso (70' André Martins), Georgios Manthatis, Karim Ansarifard.
Coach: Vasilis Vouzas.
Besiktas: Fabricio, Adriano, Dusko Tosic, Marcelo, Gökhan Gönül, Atiba Hutchinson, Tolgay
Arslan (46' Oguzhan Özyakup), Anderson Talisca (90+3' Gökhan Inler), Ricardo Quaresma,
Vincent Aboubakar (82' Cenk Tosun), Ryan Babel. Coach: Senol Günes.
Goals: 36' Esteban Cambiasso 1-0, 53' Vincent Aboubakar 1-1.
Referee: Danny Makkelie (HOL)   Attendance: 25,515.

09.03.17   GHELAMCO-arena, Gent: KAA Gent – KRC Genk 2-5 (1-4)
KAA Gent: Lovre Kalinic, Stefan Mitrovic, Samuel Gigot, Rami Gershon, Thomas Matton,
Kenny Saief (76' Moses Simon), Louis Verstraete (46' Ibrahim Rabiu), Anderson Esiti, Kalifa
Coulibaly, Samuel Kalu, Jérémy Perbet (76' Thomas Foket). Coach: Hein Vanhaezebrouck.
KRC Genk: Mathew Ryan, Jakub Brabec, Omar Colley, Jere Uronen, Timoty Castagne, Ruslan
Malinovskiy (81' Bryan Heynen), Pozuelo, Sander Berge, Jean-Paul Boëtius (46' Thomas
Buffel), Siebe Schrijvers (90' Leandro Trossard), Mbwana Samatta.
Coach: Albert Stuivenberg.
Goals: 21' Ruslan Malinovskiy 0-1, 27' Samuel Kalu 1-1, 33' Omar Colley 1-2,
41' Mbwana Samatta 1-3, 45+1' Jere Uronen 1-4, 61' Kalifa Coulibaly 2-4,
72' Mbwana Samatta 2-5.
Referee: Paolo Tagliavento (ITA)   Attendance: 17,112.
Sent off: 84' Anderson Esiti.

Jérémy Perbet missed a penalty kick (68').

16.03.17   Constant Vanden Stock, Brussels: RSC Anderlecht – APOEL Nicosia 1-0 (0-0)
RSC Anderlecht: Rubén, Serigne Mbodj, Uros Spajic, Dennis Appiah, Andy Najar, Alexandru
Chipciu (89' Massimo Bruno), Youri Tielemans, Leander Dendoncker, Nicolae Stanciu (64'
Frank Acheampong), Sofiane Hanni, Lukasz Teodorczyk (75' Isaac Thelin).
Coach: René Weiler.
APOEL Nicosia: Boy Waterman, Roberto Lago, Zhivko Milanov, Giorgios Merkis, Nicholas
Ioannou, Kostakis Artymatas, Lorenzo Ebecilio (57' Cédric Yamberé), Igor de Camargo (72'
Facundo Bertoglio), Barral (77' Vander), Pieros Sotiriou, Giannis Gianniotas.
Coach: Thomas Christiansen.
Goal: 65' Frank Acheampong 1-0.
Referee: Aleksey Kulbakov (BLS)   Attendance: 15,662.

16.03.17   Old Trafford, Manchester: Manchester United – FK Rostov 1-0 (0-0)
Manchester United: Sergio Romero, Eric Bailly, Marcos Rojo, Chris Smalling, Daley Blind
(64' Phil Jones), Antonio Valencia, Paul Pogba (48' Marouane Fellaini), Mata, Ander Herrera,
Henrikh Mkhitaryan, Zlatan Ibrahimovic. Coach: José Mourinho.
FK Rostov: Nikita Medvedev, Denis Terentyev, Miha Mevlja, Fedor Kudryashov, César
Navas, Christian Noboa, Khoren Bairamyan (81' Igor Kireev), Andrei Prepelita (79' Marko
Devic), Aleksandr Erokhin, Dmitriy Poloz, Sardar Azmoun (61' Aleksandr Bukharov).
Coach: Ivan Daniliants.
Goal: 70' Mata 1-0.
Referee: Gediminas Mazeika (LTU)   Attendance: 64,361.

16.03.17   Amsterdam ArenA, Amsterdam: AFC Ajax – FK København 2-0 (2-0)
AFC Ajax: André Onana, Joël Veltman (20' Kenny Tete), Davinson Sánchez, Nick Viergever, Matthijs de Ligt, Lasse Schöne, Hakim Ziyech, Donny van de Beek (75' Frenkie de Jong), Bertrand Traoré (81' Justin Kluivert), Amin Younes, Kasper Dolberg. Coach: Peter Bosz.
FC København: Robin Olsen, Ludwig Augustinsson, Erik Johansson, Peter Ankersen, Jores Okore (46' Nicolai Boilesen), William Kvist, Uros Matic, Ján Gregus (57' Benjamin Verbic), Andreas Cornelius, Federico Santander, Youssef Toutouh (77' Kasper Kusk).
Coach: Ståle Solbakken.
Goals: 23' Bertrand Traoré 1-0, 45+3' Kasper Dolberg 2-0 (p).
Referee: Ivan Kruzliak (SVK)   Attendance: 52,270.

16.03.17   Krasnodar Stadium, Krasnodar: FK Krasnodar – Celta de Vigo 0-2 (0-0)
FK Krasnodar: Andrey Sinitsyn, Naldo, Aleksandr Martinovich, Andreas Granqvist, Sergey Petrov, Yuri Gazinskiy, Vyacheslav Podberezkin (46' Pavel Mamaev), Víctor Claessson (60' Joãozinho), Mauricio Pereyra (70' Ricardo Laborde), Charles Kaboré, Wanderson.
Coach: Igor Shalimov.
Celta de Vigo: Sergio Álvarez, Hugo Mallo, Fontàs, Jonny, Gustavo Cabral, Nemanja Radoja, Pablo Hernández (86' Claudio Beauvue), Pione Sisto, Daniel Wass (74' Jozabed), John Guidetti, Iago Aspas (82' Facundo Roncaglia). Coach: Eduardo Berizzo.
Goals: 52' Hugo Mallo 0-1, 80' Iago Aspas 0-2.
Referee: Ruddy Buquet (FRA)   Attendance: 28,931.
Sent off: 86' Charles Kaboré.

16.03.17   Borussia-Park, Mönchengladbach:
           Borussia Mönchengladbach – FC Schalke 04 2-2 (2-0)
Borussia Mönchengladbach: Yann Sommer, Andreas Christensen, Jannik Vestergaard, Oscar Wendt, Tony Jantschke, Christoph Kramer (46' Tobias Strobl), Patrick Herrmann, Mahmoud Dahoud, Fabian Johnson (16' Jonas Hofmann), Josip Drmic (83' André Hahn), Raffael.
Coach: Dieter Hecking.
FC Schalke 04: Ralf Fährmann, Benedikt Höwedes, Sead Kolasinac, Thilo Kehrer, Matija Nastasic, Johannes Geis (46' Max Meyer), Leon Goretzka, Nabil Bentaleb (79' Benjamin Stambouli), Daniel Caligiuri (88' Alessandro Schöpf), Eric Maxim Choupo-Moting, Guido Burgstaller. Coach: Markus Weinzierl.
Goals: 26' Andreas Christensen 1-0, 45+2' Mahmoud Dahoud 2-0, 54' Leon Goretzka 2-1, 68' Nabil Bentaleb 2-2 (p).
Referee: Mark Clattenburg (ENG)   Attendance: 46,283.

FC Schalke 04 won on away goals.

16.03.17   Stadio Olimpico, Roma: AS Roma – Olympique Lyon 2-1 (1-1)
AS Roma: Alisson, Antonio Rüdiger, Bruno Peres (59' Stephan El Shaarawy), Federico Fazio, Mário Rui (76' Diego Perotti), Kostas Manolas, Radja Nainggolan, Kevin Strootman, Mohamed Salah, Daniele De Rossi (84' Francesco Totti), Edin Dzeko.
Coach: Luciano Spalletti.
Olympique Lyon: Anthony Lopes, Emanuel Mammana (78' Mapou Yanga-Mbiwa), Mouctar Diakhaby, Christophe Jallet, Jérémy Morel, Corentin Tolisso, Maxime Gonalons, Mathieu Valbuena (90+1' Rafael), Lucas Tousart, Alexandre Lacazette (84' Nabil Fekir), Maxwell Cornet. Coach: Bruno Génésio.
Goals: 16' Mouctar Diakhaby 0-1, 17' Kevin Strootman 1-1, 60' Lucas Tousart 2-1 (og).
Referee: Viktor Kassai (HUN)   Attendance: 46,453.

243

16.03.17   Vodafone Arena, Istanbul: Besiktas – Olympiakos Piraeus 4-1 (2-1)
Besiktas: Fabricio, Matej Mitrovic, Adriano, Dusko Tosic, Gökhan Gönül, Atiba Hutchinson,
Oguzhan Özyakup (60' Necip Uysal), Anderson Talisca (90+1' Gökhan Inler), Ricardo
Quaresma (83' Cenk Tosun), Vincent Aboubakar, Ryan Babel. Coach: Senol Günes.
Olympiakos Piraeus: Nicola Leali, Manuel Da Costa, Aly Cissokho, Panagiotis Retsos, Diogo,
Alaixys Romao (76' André Martins), Kostas Fortounis, Tarik Elyounoussi, Esteban Cambiasso
(68' Marko Marin), Georgios Manthatis (56' Sebá), Karim Ansarifard. Coach: Vasilis Vouzas.
Goals: 10' Vincent Aboubakar 1-0, 22' Ryan Babel 2-0, 31' Tarik Elyounoussi 2-1,
75' Ryan Babel 3-1, 84' Cenk Tosun 4-1.
Referee: Michael Oliver (ENG)   Attendance: 37,966.
Sent off: 39' Vincent Aboubakar.

16.03.17   Luminus Arena, Genk: KRC Genk – KAA Gent 1-1 (1-0)
KRC Genk: Mathew Ryan, Jakub Brabec, Omar Colley, Jere Uronen (81' Christophe
Janssens), Timoty Castagne, Ruslan Malinovskiy, Thomas Buffel (74' Leandro Trossard),
Pozuelo (46' Siebe Schrijvers), Sander Berge, Jean-Paul Boëtius, Mbwana Samatta.
Coach: Albert Stuivenberg.
KAA Gent: Lovre Kalinic, Stefan Mitrovic, Samuel Gigot, Thibault De Smet, Brecht
Dejaegere, Thomas Foket, Ibrahim Rabiu, Kalifa Coulibaly, Samuel Kalu, Jérémy Perbet (62'
Louis Verstraete), Moses Simon. Coach: Hein Vanhaezebrouck.
Goals: 20' Timoty Castagne 1-0, 84' Louis Verstraete 1-1.
Referee: Alberto Undiano Mallenco (ESP)   Attendance: 16,028.

QUARTER-FINALS

13.04.17   Constant Vanden Stock, Brussels: RSC Anderlecht – Manchester United 1-1 (0-1)
RSC Anderlecht: Rubén, Serigne Mbodj, Dennis Appiah, Bram Nuytinck, Ivan Obradovic,
Massimo Bruno (58' Alexandru Chipciu), Frank Acheampong, Youri Tielemans, Leander
Dendoncker, Nicolae Stanciu (65' Sofiane Hanni), Isaac Thelin (75' Lukasz Teodorczyk).
Coach: René Weiler.
Manchester United: Sergio Romero, Eric Bailly, Marcos Rojo, Antonio Valencia, Matteo
Darmian, Paul Pogba, Jesse Lingard (62' Anthony Martial), Michael Carrick, Henrikh
Mkhitaryan (90+1' Timothy Fosu-Mensah), Zlatan Ibrahimovic, Marcus Rashford (75'
Marouane Fellaini). Coach: José Mourinho.
Goals: 36' Henrikh Mkhitaryan 0-1, 86' Leander Dendoncker 1-1.
Referee: Dr. Felix Brych (GER)   Attendance: 20,060.

13.04.17   Municipal de Balaidos, Vigo: Celta de Vigo – KRC Genk 3-2 (3-1)
Celta de Vigo: Sergio Álvarez, Hugo Mallo, Fontàs, Jonny, Gustavo Cabral, Nemanja Radoja,
Pablo Hernández, Pione Sisto, Daniel Wass (78' Jozabed), John Guidetti (67' Claudio
Beauvue), Iago Aspas. Coach: Eduardo Berizzo.
KRC Genk: Mathew Ryan, Jakub Brabec, Omar Colley, Jere Uronen, Timoty Castagne, Ruslan
Malinovskiy (90+2' Bryan Heynen), Pozuelo, Sander Berge, Jean-Paul Boëtius (62' Thomas
Buffel), Leandro Trossard (82' Siebe Schrijvers), Mbwana Samatta.
Coach: Albert Stuivenberg.
Goals: 10' Jean-Paul Boëtius 0-1, 15' Pione Sisto 1-1, 17' Iago Aspas 2-1,
38' John Guidetti 3-1, 67' Thomas Buffel 3-2.
Referee: Clément Turpin (FRA)   Attendance: 21,608.

13.04.17   Amsterdam ArenA, Amsterdam: AFC Ajax – FC Schalke 04 2-0 (1-0)
AFC Ajax: André Onana, Joël Veltman, Davinson Sánchez, Daley Sinkgraven (46' Matthijs de Ligt), Nick Viergever, Davy Klaassen, Hakim Ziyech, Donny van de Beek (88' Frenkie de Jong), Bertrand Traoré, Amin Younes, Justin Kluivert (74' David Neres). Coach: Peter Bosz.
FC Schalke 04: Ralf Fährmann, Benedikt Höwedes, Thilo Kehrer, Matija Nastasic, Max Meyer (59' Benjamin Stambouli), Leon Goretzka, Nabil Bentaleb, Dennis Aogo, Daniel Caligiuri (83' Yevhen Konoplyanka), Alessandro Schöpf (71' Klaas-Jan Huntelaar), Guido Burgstaller. Coach: Markus Weinzierl.
Goals: 23', 52' Davy Klaassen 1-0 (p), 2-0.
Referee: Sergey Karsev (RUS)   Attendance: 52,384.

13.04.17   Stade des Lumières, Lyon: Olympique Lyon – Besiktas 2-1 (0-1)
Olympique Lyon: Anthony Lopes, Emanuel Mammana, Mouctar Diakhaby, Jérémy Morel, Rafael (52' Christophe Jallet), Corentin Tolisso, Mathieu Valbuena, Lucas Tousart, Alexandre Lacazette, Rachid Ghezzal (52' Maxwell Cornet), Nabil Fekir. Coach: Bruno Génésio.
Besiktas: Fabricio, Matej Mitrovic (64' Necip Uysal), Adriano, Dusko Tosic, Marcelo, Gökhan Gönül, Atiba Hutchinson, Oguzhan Özyakup (74' Tolgay Arslan), Anderson Talisca, Cenk Tosun (86' Gökhan Inler), Ryan Babel. Coach: Senol Günes.
Goals: 15' Ryan Babel 0-1, 83' Corentin Tolisso 1-1, 84' Jérémy Morel 2-1.
Referee: Antonio Mateu Lahoz (ESP)   Attendance: 55,452.

20.04.17   Old Trafford, Manchester: Manchester United – RSC Anderlecht 2-1 (1-1, 1-1)
Manchester United: Sergio Romero, Eric Bailly, Marcos Rojo (23' Daley Blind), Luke Shaw, Antonio Valencia, Paul Pogba, Jesse Lingard (60' Marouane Fellaini), Michael Carrick, Henrikh Mkhitaryan, Zlatan Ibrahimovic (91' Anthony Martial), Marcus Rashford. Coach: José Mourinho.
RSC Anderlecht: Rubén, Serigne Mbodj, Uros Spajic, Dennis Appiah, Ivan Obradovic, Alexandru Chipciu (64' Massimo Bruno), Frank Acheampong, Youri Tielemans, Leander Dendoncker, Sofiane Hanni (64' Nicolae Stanciu), Lukasz Teodorczyk (79' Isaac Thelin). Coach: René Weiler.
Goals: 10' Henrikh Mkhitaryan 1-0, 32' Sofiane Hanni 1-1, 107' Marcus Rashford 2-1.
Referee: Alberto Undiano Mallenco (ESP)   Attendance: 71,496.

Manchester United won after extra time.

20.04.17   Luminus Arena, Genk: KRC Genk – Celta de Vigo 1-1 (0-0)
KRC Genk: Mathew Ryan, Jakub Brabec (81' Sebastien Dewaest), Omar Colley, Jere Uronen, Timoty Castagne, Ruslan Malinovskiy (72' Jean-Paul Boëtius), Thomas Buffel (72' Siebe Schrijvers), Pozuelo, Sander Berge, Leandro Trossard, Mbwana Samatta. Coach: Albert Stuivenberg.
Celta de Vigo: Sergio Álvarez, Hugo Mallo, Fontàs, Jonny, Gustavo Cabral, Nemanja Radoja, Pablo Hernández, Pione Sisto, Daniel Wass (80' Jozabed), John Guidetti (42' Claudio Beauvue, 90+1' Facundo Roncaglia), Iago Aspas. Coach: Eduardo Berizzo.
Goals: 63' Pione Sisto 0-1, 67' Leandro Trossard 1-1.
Referee: William Collum (SCO)   Attendance: 18,833.

20.04.17   VELTINS-Arena, Gelsenkirchen: FC Schalke 04 – AFC Ajax 3-2 (0-0,2-0)
FC Schalke 04: Ralf Fährmann, Benedikt Höwedes, Sead Kolasinac, Sascha Riether (112'
Donis Avdijaj), Matija Nastasic, Max Meyer, Leon Goretzka (84' Johannes Geis), Nabil
Bentaleb, Benjamin Stambouli (53' Klaas-Jan Huntelaar), Daniel Caligiuri, Guido Burgstaller.
Coach: Markus Weinzierl.
AFC Ajax: André Onana, Joël Veltman, Davinson Sánchez, Nick Viergever, Matthijs de Ligt,
Davy Klaassen, Lasse Schöne (74' Donny van de Beek), Hakim Ziyech, Bertrand Traoré (82'
Kenny Tete), Amin Younes, Justin Kluivert (16' Kasper Dolberg). Coach: Peter Bosz.
Goals: 53' Leon Goretzka 1-0, 56' Guido Burgstaller 2-0, 101' Daniel Caligiuri 3-0,
111' Nick Viergever 3-1, 120' Amin Younes 3-2.
Referee: Ovidiu Hategan (ROM)   Attendance: 53,701.
Sent off: 80' Joël Veltman.

AFC Ajax won after extra time.

20.04.17   Vodafone Arena, Istanbul: Besiktas – Olympique Lyon 2-1 (1-1,2-1)
Besiktas: Fabricio, Matej Mitrovic, Adriano (77' Andreas Beck), Dusko Tosic, Gökhan Gönül,
Atiba Hutchinson, Oguzhan Özyakup (94' Necip Uysal), Anderson Talisca, Ricardo Quaresma
(117' Tolgay Arslan), Cenk Tosun, Ryan Babel. Coach: Senol Günes.
Olympique Lyon: Anthony Lopes, Nicolas N'Koulou, Mouctar Diakhaby, Christophe Jallet,
Jérémy Morel (120+2' Maciej Rybus), Corentin Tolisso, Maxime Gonalons, Mathieu
Valbuena, Lucas Tousart, Alexandre Lacazette (91' Rachid Ghezzal), Maxwell Cornet (77'
Nabil Fekir). Coach: Bruno Génésio.
Goals: 27' Anderson Talisca 1-0, 34' Alexandre Lacazette 1-1, 58' Anderson Talisca 2-1.
Referee: Milorad Mazic (SER)   Attendance: 39,623.

Olympique Lyon won 7-6 on penalties following extra time.

Penalties: Babel 1-0, Fekir 1-1, Tosun 2-1, Tolisso 2-2, Hutchinson 3-2, Ghezzal 3-3,
*   Arslan 4-3, Rybus 4-4, Talisca 5-4, Valbuena 5-5, Uysal 6-5, Diakhaby 6-6,*
*   Tosic missed, Jallet missed, Mitrovic missed, Gonalons 6-7.*

SEMI-FINALS

03.05.17   Amsterdam ArenA, Amsterdam: AFC Ajax – Olympique Lyon 4-1 (2-0)
AFC Ajax: André Onana, Kenny Tete, Jaïro Riedewald, Davinson Sánchez, Matthijs de Ligt,
Davy Klaassen, Lasse Schöne (71' Donny van de Beek), Hakim Ziyech, Bertrand Traoré,
Amin Younes (79' Justin Kluivert), Kasper Dolberg (88' David Neres). Coach: Peter Bosz.
Olympique Lyon: Anthony Lopes, Nicolas N'Koulou, Mouctar Diakhaby, Christophe Jallet
(69' Rafael), Jérémy Morel, Corentin Tolisso, Maxime Gonalons, Mathieu Valbuena, Lucas
Tousart (58' Rachid Ghezzal), Nabil Fekir, Maxwell Cornet (76' Alexandre Lacazette).
Coach: Bruno Génésio.
Goals: 25' Bertrand Traoré 1-0, 34' Kasper Dolberg 2-0, 49' Amin Younes 3-0,
66' Mathieu Valbuena 3-1, 71' Bertrand Traoré 4-1.
Referee: Gianluca Rocchi (ITA)   Attendance: 54,033.

04.05.17   Municipal de Balaidos, Vigo: Celta de Vigo – Manchester United 0-1 (0-0)
Celta de Vigo: Sergio Álvarez, Hugo Mallo (90+1' Claudio Beauvue), Jonny, Gustavo Cabral,
Facundo Roncaglia, Nemanja Radoja, Pablo Hernández, Pione Sisto, Daniel Wass (74'
Jozabed), John Guidetti, Iago Aspas. Coach: Eduardo Berizzo.
Manchester United: Sergio Romero, Eric Bailly, Daley Blind, Antonio Valencia, Matteo
Darmian, Paul Pogba, Jesse Lingard, Ander Herrera, Henrikh Mkhitaryan (78' Ashley Young,
89' Chris Smalling), Marouane Fellaini, Marcus Rashford (80' Anthony Martial).
Coach: José Mourinho.
Goal: 67' Marcus Rashford 0-1.
Referee: Sergey Karasev (RUS)   Attendance: 26,202.

11.05.17   Stade des Lumières, Lyon: Olympique Lyon – AFC Ajax 3-1 (2-1)
Olympique Lyon: Anthony Lopes, Nicolas N'Koulou, Mouctar Diakhaby, Jérémy Morel (75'
Maciej Rybus), Rafael, Corentin Tolisso, Maxime Gonalons, Mathieu Valbuena (77' Rachid
Ghezzal), Alexandre Lacazette, Nabil Fekir, Maxwell Cornet. Coach: Bruno Génésio.
AFC Ajax: André Onana, Joël Veltman (64' Kenny Tete), Davinson Sánchez, Nick Viergever,
Matthijs de Ligt, Davy Klaassen, Lasse Schöne (58' Donny van de Beek), Hakim Ziyech,
Bertrand Traoré, Amin Younes (82' Justin Kluivert), Kasper Dolberg. Coach: Peter Bosz.
Goals: 27' Kasper Dolberg 0-1, 45', 45+1' Alexandre Lacazette 1-1 (p), 2-1,
81' Rachid Ghezzal 3-1.
Referee: Szymon Marciniak (POL)   Attendance: 53,810.
Sent off: 84' Nick Viergever.

11.05.17   Old Trafford, Manchester: Manchester United – Celta de Vigo 1-1 (1-0)
Manchester United: Sergio Romero, Eric Bailly, Daley Blind, Antonio Valencia, Matteo
Darmian, Paul Pogba, Jesse Lingard (86' Wayne Rooney), Ander Herrera, Henrikh Mkhitaryan
(77' Michael Carrick), Marouane Fellaini, Marcus Rashford (89' Chris Smalling).
Coach: José Mourinho.
Celta de Vigo: Sergio Álvarez, Hugo Mallo, Jonny, Gustavo Cabral, Facundo Roncaglia,
Nemanja Radoja (68' Théo Bongonda), Pablo Hernández, Pione Sisto (80' Claudio Beauvue),
Daniel Wass (46' Jozabed), John Guidetti, Iago Aspas. Coach: Eduardo Berizzo.
Goals: 17' Marouane Fellaini 1-0, 85' Facundo Roncaglia 1-1.
Referee: Ovidiu Hategan (ROM)   Attendance: 75,138.
Sent off: 87' Eric Bailly, 88' Facundo Roncaglia.

FINAL

24.05.17   Friends Arena, Solna (SWE): AFC Ajax – Manchester United 0-2 (0-1)
AFC Ajax: André Onana, Joël Veltman, Jaïro Riedewald (82' Frenkie de Jong), Davinson
Sánchez, Matthijs de Ligt, Davy Klaassen, Lasse Schöne (70' Donny van de Beek), Hakim
Ziyech, Bertrand Traoré, Amin Younes, Kasper Dolberg (62' David Neres).
Coach: Peter Bosz.
Manchester United: Sergio Romero, Chris Smalling, Daley Blind, Antonio Valencia, Matteo
Darmian, Paul Pogba, Mata (90' Wayne Rooney), Ander Herrera, Henrikh Mkhitaryan (74'
Jesse Lingard), Marouane Fellaini, Marcus Rashford (84' Anthony Martial).
Coach: José Mourinho.
Goals: 18' Paul Pogba 0-1, 48' Henrikh Mkhitaryan 0-2.
Referee: Damir Skomina (SVN)   Attendance: 46,961.

247

TOP SCORERS 2016-2017

Edin Dzeko	AS Roma	8
Giuliano	Zenit St.Petersburg	8
Aduriz	Athletic Bilbao	7
Alexandre Lacazette	Olympique Lyon	6
Henrikh Mkhitaryan	Manchester United	6
Kasper Dolberg	AFC Ajax	6
Guillaume Hoarau	BSC Young Boys	5
Nikola Kalinic	ACF Fiorentina	5
Lukasz Teodorczyk	RSC Anderlecht	5
Iago Aspas	Celta de Vigo	5
Zlatan Ibrahimovic	Manchester United	5

Goal scorer statistics exclude the qualifying rounds and play-off round.

UEFA EUROPA LEAGUE 2017-2018

FIRST QUALIFYING ROUND

29.06.17   Gyumri City Stadium, Gyumri: Shirak FC – ND Gorica 0-2 (0-1)
Shirak FC: Anatoly Ayvazov, Artyom Mikailyan, Edward Kpodo, Robert Darbinyan, Solomon Udo, Aghvan Davoyan, Mohamed Kaba, Aleksandar Ilic (54' Oumarou Kaina), Kyrian Nwabueze (74' Aram Muradyan), Vahan Bichakhchyan, Moussa Bakayoko (74' Igor Stanojevic). Coach: Vardan Bichakhchyan.
ND Gorica: Grega Sorcan, Uros Celcer, Miha Gregoric, Tine Kavcic, Matija Boben, Rifet Kapic (90+2' Jan Hulmar), Jaka Kolenc, Rok Grudina, Dejan Zigon (88' Leon Marinic), Andrija Filipovic (79' Tilen Nagode), Bede Osuji. Coach: Miran Srebrnic.
Goals: 15', 69' Rifet Kapic 0-1, 0-2.
Referee: Mikhail Vilkov (RUS)   Attendance: 2,100.

29.06.17   Tsentralniy, Pavlodar: Irtysh Pavlodar – FC Dunav Ruse 1-0 (1-0)
Irtysh Pavlodar: David Loriya, Aleksandr Kislitsyn, Rodrigo Antônio, Damir Dautov, Stefan Zivkovic, Mario Maslac, Aslan Darabaev (90+1' Nurbol Zhumaskaliev), Ismaël Fofana (64' Kazbek Geteriev), Franck Dja Djédjé (64' Ilya Kalinin), Carlos Fonseca, Igor Bugaev.
Coach: Dimitar Dimitrov.
FC Dunav Ruse: Stanislav Antonov, Mario Petkov, Petar Patev, Mihail Milchev, Hristofor Hubchev, Samir Ayass (65' Krasimir Stanoev), Vasil Shopov (87' Dimitar Georgiev), Diyan Dimov, Birsent Karagaren (72' Yulian Nenov), Miroslav Budinov, Branimir Kostadinov.
Coach: Plamen Donev.
Goal: 5' Igor Bugaev 1-0.
Referee: Arnold Hunter (NIR)   Attendance: 8,000.

29.06.17   Tsentralniy, Almaty: FK Kairat – FK Atlantas 6-0 (4-0)
FK Kairat: Vladimir Plotnikov, Gafurzhan Suyombaev, César Arzo, Yan Vorogovskiy, Islambek Kuat, Mikhail Bakaev, Isael, Georgiy Zhukov (30' Ivo Ilicevic), Ákos Elek, Gerard Gohou (74' Chuma Anene), Andrey Arshavin (66' Bauyrzhan Turysbek).
Coach: Kakhaber Tskhadadze.
FK Atlantas: Deividas Mikelionis, Vytas Gaspuitis (69' Mantas Fridrikas), Justas Raziūnas, Edgaras Zarskis, Donatas Kazlauskas (88' Skirmantas Rakauskas), Domantas Simkus, Markas Beneta, Andrei Ciofu (60' Rokas Gedminas), David Andronic, Yuriy Vereshchak, Tadas Labukas. Coach: Sergey Savchenkov.
Goals: 21' Gerard Gohou 1-0, 26' Andrey Arshavin 2-0 (p), 30' Ivo Ilicevic 3-0, 42' Andrey Arshavin 4-0, 50' Gerard Gohou 5-0 (p), 73' Ivo Ilicevic 6-0.
Referee: Omar Pashayev (AZE)   Attendance: 15,000.

29.06.17   Ventspils Stadions, Ventspils: FK Ventspils – Valur Reykjavik 0-0
FK Ventspils: Andrejs Pavlovs, Nikita Kolesovs, Nikola Boranijasevic, Antons Jemelins, Vadims Zulevs, Ritvars Rugins (17' Adeleke Akinola Akinyemi, 89' Girts Karlsons), Eduards Tidenbergs, Abdullahi Alfa, Tosin Aiyegun, Simonas Paulius, Vitalijs Recickis (75' Jurijs Zigajevs). Coach: Paul Ashworth.
Valur Reykjavik: Anton Ari Einarsson, Sigurdur Lárusson, Bjarni Eiríksson, Eidur Sigurbjörnsson, Einar Karl Ingvarsson, Sindri Björnsson, Haukur Sigurdsson (78' Gudjón Lydsson), Kristinn Halldórsson (89' Sveinn Gudjohnsen), Orri Ómarsson, Arnar Geirsson, Dion Jeremy Acoff. Coach: Ólafur Jóhannesson.
Referee: Rahim Hasanov (AZE)   Attendance: 1,933.

29.06.17   Stadiumi Selman Stërmasi, Tirana: FK Partizani – Botev Plovdiv 1-3 (1-1)
FK Partizani: Alban Bekim Hoxha, Blerim Kotobelli, Labinot Ibrahimi, Arbnor Fejzullahu,
Sodiq Atanda, Idriz Batha, Lorenc Trashi, Mentor Mazrekaj (63' Realdo Fili), Xhevair Sukaj,
Gerhard Progni (54' Jurgen Bardhi), Emiljano Vila (74' Moustapha Djidjiwa).
Coach: Sulejman Starova.
Botev Plovdiv: Ivan Cvorovic, Tsvetomir Panov, Victor Genev, Meledje Omnibes, Jordan
Minev, Krum Stoyanov (84' Lazar Marin), Plamen Dimov, Felipe Brisola (80' Toni Tasev),
Todor Nedelev (90+2' Serkan Yusein), Lachezar Baltanov, Omar Kossoko.
Coach: Nikolai Kirov.
Goals: 5' Xhevair Sukaj 1-0, 27' Omar Kossoko 1-1, 62' Todor Nedelev 1-2,
88' Omar Kossoko 1-3.
Referee: Bryn Markham-Jones (WAL)   Attendance: 2,000.

29.06.17   Vazgen Sargsyan Republican Stadium, Yerevan:
           Pyunik FC – Slovan Bratislava 1-4 (1-1)
Pyunik FC: Valeriy Voskonyan, Serob Grigoryan, Artur Kartashyan, Aram Shakhnazaryan,
Armen Manucharyan, Robert Hakobyan (82' Hovhannes Nazaryan), Narek Aslanyan (72'
Hovhannes Poghosyan), Petros Avetisyan, Alik Arakelyan, Hovhannes Harutyunyan (76' Erik
Vardanyan), Vardan Poghosyan. Coach: Armen Gyulbudaghyants.
Slovan Bratislava: Dominik Greif, Boris Sekulic, Milan Rundic, Ruben Ligeon, Kornel Saláta,
Vukan Savicevic (76' Róbert Vittek), Joeri de Kamps, Uros Damnjanovic, Jakub Mares (84'
Samuel Sefcík), Filip Holosko, Mitchell Schet (60' Lesly de Sa). Coach: Ivan Vukomanovic.
Goals: 7' Petros Avetisyan 1-0 (p), 22' Filip Holosko 1-1, 62' Vukan Savicevic 1-2,
68' Filip Holosko 1-3, 75' Aram Shakhnazaryan 1-4 (og).
Referee: Ádam Farkas (HUN)   Attendance: 1,800.

29.06.17   Stadión na Sihoti, Trenčín: FK AS Trenčín – Torpedo Kutaisi 5-1 (2-1)
FK AS Trenčín: Adrián Chovan, Lukás Skovajsa, Martin Sulek, Peter Klescík, Abdul Zubairu,
Jamie Lawrence, Jakub Paur (84' Achraf El Mahdioui), Desley Ubbink, Giorgi Beridze,
Hillary Gong (65' Milan Kvocera), Antonio Mance (73' Hamza Catakovic).
Coach: Martin Sevela.
Torpedo Kutaisi: Roin Kvaskhvadze, Anri Chichinadze, Davit Khurtsilava, Oleg Mamasakhlisi
(46' Shota Babunashvili), Giorgi Guruli, Giorgi Kimadze, Tornike Kapanadze, Giorgi
Kukhianidze (82' David Khurtsidze), Grigol Dolidze, Merab Gigauri, Beka Tughushi (67'
Mate Kvirkvia). Coach: Kakha Shkhetiani.
Goals: 10' Giorgi Guruli 0-1, 36', 40' Antonio Mance 1-1, 2-1, 75' Hamza Catakovic 3-1,
81' Jakub Paur 4-1, 87' Giogi Beridze 5-1.
Referee: Timothy Marshall (NIR)   Attendance: 2,915.

29.06.17   Pärnu Rannastaadion, Pärnu: FC Levadia – Cork City 0-2 (0-1)
FC Levadia: Sergei Lepmets, Luc Tabi, Igor Dudarev, Maksim Podholjuzin, Pavel Marin (71'
Nikita Andreev), Marcelin Gando, Evgeni Kobzar (88' Ingemar Teever), João Morelli, Josip
Krznaric, Rimo Hunt, Mark Oliver Roosnupp (43' Artjom Artjunin). Coach: Igor Prins.
Cork City: Mark McNulty, Ryan Delaney, Kevin O'Connor, Greb Bolger, Conor McCormack,
Stephen Dooley (80' Shane Griffin), Gearóid Morrissey, Garry Buckley (74' Achille
Campion), Jimmy Keohane, Karl Sheppard (67' Steven Beattie), Seán Maguire.
Coach: John Caulfield.
Goals: 43' Garry Buckley 0-1, 82' Steven Beattie 0-2.
Referee: Jørgen Burchardt (DEN)   Attendance: 1,500.
Sent off: 42' Luc Tabi.

250

29.06.17   Stadyen Traktar, Minsk: Dinamo Minsk – NSÍ Runavík 2-1 (1-0)
Dinamo Minsk: Andrey Klimovich, Igor Kuzmenok, Maksim Shvetsov, Nino Galovic, Yuriy
Ostroukh, Artem Bykov, Uros Nikolic, Oleksandr Noyok, Nikola Lukic (63' Nikola Lekovic),
Anton Saroka, Vadim Demidovich (55' Artem Kiyko). Coach: Sergei Gurenko.
NSÍ Runavík: Símun Rógvi Hansen, Per Langgaard, Jens Joensen, Einar Tróndargjógv Hansen,
Pól Justinussen, Tobias Olesen (71' Jann Benjaminsen), Karl Løkin, Árni Frederiksberg (88'
Jónleif Højgaard), Bárdur Jógvansson-Hansen, Betuel Hansen (61' Petur Knudsen), Klæmint
Olsen. Coach: Anders Gerber.
Goals: 42' Yuriy Ostroukh 1-0, 52' Oleksandr Noyok 2-0, 86' Petur Knudsen 2-1.
Referee: Oleksandr Derdo (UKR)   Attendance: 3,480.

29.06.17   Stadyen Budaunik Stroitel, Soligorsk: Shakhter Soligorsk – FK Sūduva 0-0
Shakhter Soligorsk: Vladimir Bushma, Siarhei Matveichyk, Aleksey Yanushkevich, Igor
Burko, Pavel Rybak, Edgar Olekhnovich, Aleksandr Selyava, Ilya Aleksievich (46' Drazen
Bagaric), Denis Laptev (76' Nikolai Yanush), Pyry Soiri (46' Yuri Kovalev), Vitaly
Lisakovich. Coach: Oleg Kubarev.
FK Sūduva: Ivan Kardum, Radanfah Abu Bakr, Algis Jankauskas, Henri Ndong (54' Marius
Cinikas), Povilas Leimonas, Ernestas Veliulis (74' Robertas Vezevicius), Andro Svrljuga,
Paulius Janusauskas (81' Giedrius Matulevicius), Vaidas Slavickas, Ovidijus Verbickas,
Karolis Laukzemis. Coach: Vladimir Cheburin.
Referee: Aleksandr Aliyev (KAZ)   Attendance: 3,100.

29.06.17   Boris Paichadze Dinamo Arena, Tbilisi:
Chikhura Sachkhere – SCR Altach 0-1 (0-1)
Chikhura Sachkhere: Dino Hamzic, Levan Kakubava, Lasha Chikvaidze, Shota Kashia,
Tornike Gorgiashvili (83' Giorgi Gabedava), Giorgi Ganugrava, Giorgi Koripadze, Zaza
Chelidze (67' Papuna Poniava), Mikheil Sardalishvili, Dimitri Tatanashvili, Nikoloz Gelashvili
(71' Besik Dekanoidze). Coach: Soso Pruidze.
SCR Altach: Martin Kobras, Lucas Galvão, Philipp Netzer, Emanuel Sakic, Benedikt Zech,
Christian Gebauer (64' Nicolas Ngamaleu), Patrick Salomon, Simon Piesinger, Stefan Nutz
(83' Kristijan Dobras), Louis N'Gwat-Mahop, Hannes Aigner (74' Adrian Grbic).
Coach: Klaus Schmidt.
Goal: 3' Louis N'Gwat-Mahop 0-1.
Referee: Erez Papir (ISR)   Attendance: 1,700.

29.06.17   Elisa Stadion, Vaasa: Vaasan PS – Olimpija Ljubljana 1-0 (1-0)
Vaasan PS: Marko Meerits, Timi Lahti, Mikko Viitikko, Veli Lampi (90+1' Ville Koskimaa),
Jesper Engström, Jerry Voutilainen, Juho Lähde, Jonas Levänen, Joonas Vahtera (82' Andre
Clennon), Juha Hakola, Steven Morrissey (70' Ebrima Sohna). Coach: Petri Vuorinen.
Olimpija Ljubljana: Nejc Vidmar, Aris Zarifovic, Branko Ilic, Nemanja Mitrovic, Dino Stiglec,
Goran Brkic, Danijel Miskic (78' Alexandru Cretu), Tomislav Tomic, Nathan Oduwa (80'
Blessing Eleke), Issah Abass, Leon Benko (67' Luka Gajic). Coach: Igor Biscan.
Goal: 12' Joonas Vahtera 1-0.
Referee: Petr Ardeleánu (CZE)   Attendance: 3,989.

251

29.06.17   Stadion Mladost, Strumica: KF Shkëndija 79 – Dacia Chisinau 3-0 (2-0)
KF Shkëndija 79: Kostadin Zahov, Egzon Bejtulai, Ardijan Cuculi, Ivan Celikovic (62'
Mevlan Murati), Armend Alimi, Ferhan Hasani (78' Besart Abdurahimi), Stephan Vujcic,
Blagoja Todorovski, Besart Ibraimi, Marjan Radeski, Stênio Júnior (87' Ennur Totre).
Coach: Qatip Osmani.
Dacia Chisinau: Dorian Railean, Diego Seoane, Abdoul Mamah, Stefan Draskovic, Aleksandr
Pascenco, Maksim Gavrilenko, Amâncio Fortes, Zaurbek Olisaev (54' Alexandru Bejan),
Cristian Jalba (69' Oleg Andronic), Bratislav Punosevac, Cheick Alan Diarra (59' Denis
Ilescu). Coach: Viorel Frunza.
Goals: 7' Besart Ibraimi 1-0 (p), 10', 75' Marjan Radeski 2-0, 3-0.
Referee: Krzysztof Jakubik (POL)   Attendance: 1,950.

29.06.17   Givi Kiladze Stadium, Kutaisi: Dinamo Batumi – Jagiellonia Bialystok 0-1 (0-0)
Dinamo Batumi: Anatoliy Timofeev, Mirza Partenadze, Valerian Tevdoradze (65' Archil
Tvildiani), Anzor Sukhiashvili, Dato Kvirkvelia, Boris Makharadze, Giorgi Kavtaradze (78'
Mikhail Gorelishvili, Temur Shonia, Elguja Grigalashvili (82' Otari Martsvaladze), Tornike
Tarkhnishvili, Jaroslav Kvasov. Coach: Konstantin Frolov.
Jagiellonia Bialystok: Marián Kelemen, Lukasz Burliga, Guti, Ivan Runje, Jacek Góralski,
Taras Romanchuk, Dmytro Khomchenovskiy, Piotr Tomasik (50' Guilherme), Arvydas
Novikovas (75' Lukasz Sekulski), Fiodor Cernych (83' Przemyslaw Mystkowski), Cillian
Sheridan. Coaches: Michal Probierz & Ireneusz Mamrot.
Goal: 49' Cilian Sheridan 0-1.
Referee: Erik Lambrechts (BEL)   Attendance: 4,000.

29.06.17   A. Le Coq Arena, Tallinn: JK Nõmme Kalju – B36 Tórshavn 2-1 (1-0)
JK Nõmme Kalju: Vitali Teles, Maximiliano Uggè, Andrei Sidorenkov, Deniss Tjapkin,
Nikolai Masitsev (61' Réginald Mbu-Alidor), Janar Toomet (9' Igor Subbotin), Artur
Valikaev, Karl Mööl, Artjom Dmitrijev, Robert Kirss, Tarmo Neemelo.
Coach: Sergey Frantsev.
B36 Tórshavn: Tórdur Thomsen, Odmar Færø (58' Hannes Agnarsson), Gestur Dam, Bjarni
Petersen, Erlendur Magnussen, Andrias Eriksen, Eli Nielsen, Róaldur Jakobsen, Benjamin
Heinesen (75' Christian Mouritsen), Patrik Johannesen, Lukasz Cieslewicz.
Coach: Jákup á Borg.
Goals: 13' Deniss Tjapkin 1-0, 49' Patrik Johannesen 1-1, 79' Artjom Dmitrijev 2-1.
Referee: Leontios Trattou (CYP)   Attendance: 580.

29.06.17   Lyngby Stadion, Lyngby: Lyngby BK – Bangor City 1-0 (1-0)
Lyngby BK: Mikkel Andersen, Thomas Christensen, Michael Lumb, Hallgrímur Jónasson,
Martin Ørnskov, Jesper Christjansen (46' Mathias Hebo Rasmussen), Mikkel Rygaard Jensen
(46' David Boysen), Jeppe Brandrup, Bror Blume, Kristoffer Larsen, Kim Ojo (68' Jeppe
Kjær). Coach: David Nielsen.
Bangor City: Connor Roberts, Tom Kennedy, Laurence Wilson, Paul Connolly, Gary Roberts,
Gary Taylor-Fletcher, Damien Allen, Danny Gosset, Steven Hewitt, Daniel Nardiello (60'
Dean Rittenberg), Brayden Shaw. Coach: Kevin Nicholson.
Goal: 13' Brot Blume 1-0.
Referee: Stavros Mantalos (GRE)   Attendance: 2,574.
Sent off: 87' Hallgrímur Jónasson.

29.06.17   HaMoshava Stadium, Petach Tikva: Beitar Jerusalem – Budapesti Vasas 4-3 (1-2)
Beitar Jerusalem: Boris Kleyman, Antoine Conte (69' Tal Kachila), David Keltjens, Dan Mori,
Marcel Heister, Idan Vered, Georginho (72' Ya'akov Berihon), Claudemir (57' Yossi
Benayoun), Hen Ezra, Erik Sabo, Itay Shechter. Coach: Sharon Mimer.
Budapesti Vasas: Gergely Nagy, Kire Ristevski, Szilveszter Hangya, Felix Burmeister, Donát
Szivacski, Mohamed Remili (55' Mahir Saglik), Márk Kleisz, Máté Vida, Tamás Kulcsár (67'
Martin Ádám), Evgen Pavlov (78' Botond Király), Benedek Murka. Coach: Michael Oenning.
Goals: 19' Georginho 1-0, 36', 43' Evgen Pavlov 1-1, 1-2, 52' Tamás Kulcsár 1-3,
88' Yossi Benayoun 2-3, 90+1' Idan Vered 3-3, 90+3' Erik Sabo 4-3.
Referee: Nenad Djokic (SER)   Attendance: 100.

29.06.17   Groupama Aréna, Budapest: Ferencvárosi TC – FK Jelgava 2-0 (1-0)
Ferencvárosi TC: Dénes Dibusz, Endre Botka, Kenneth Otigba (82' Julian Koch), András Radó
(65' Lukász Böle), Leandro de Almeida, Zoltán Gera, Fernando Gorriarán, Amadou Moutari,
Gergö Lovrencsics, Tamás Priskin (65' Balász Lovrencsics), Roland Varga.
Coach: Thomas Doll.
FK Jelgava: Kaspars Ikstens, Endijs Slampe, Valērijs Redjko, Dmitrijs Klimasevics, Ante
Bakmaz, Mārcis Oss, Valdo Alhinho (70' Kevin Kauber), Mindaugas Grigaravicius, Glebs
Kluskins (77' Andrejs Pereplotkins), Artis Jaudzems, Rafael Ledesma Gaúcho (84' Evaldas
Razulis). Coach: Alexandru Curtianu.
Goals: 11', 69' Roland Varga 1-0, 2-0.
Referee: Vasilis Dimitriou (CYP)   Attendance: 7,133.

29.06.17   Vivacom Arena - Georgi Asparuhov, Sofia: Levski Sofia – FK Sutjeska 3-1 (3-0)
Levski Sofia: Bozhidar Mitrev, Dimitar Pirgov, Ivan Goranov, Milos Cvetkovic, David
Jablonsky, Antonio Vutov (75' Sergiu Bus), Roman Procházka, Vasil Panayotov, Francis
Narh, Junior Mpia Mapuku (80' Georgi Angelov), Babatunde Adeniji (90+3' Aleks
Borimirov). Coach: Nikolai Mitov.
FK Sutjeska: Suad Licina, Mirko Radisic, Milos Bakrac, Stevan Kovacevic (69' Vladan
Bubanja), Stefan Loncar, Nikola Stijepovic, Milos Vucic, Veljko Vukovic, Stefan Denkovic,
Bozo Markovic (90' Nemanja Nedic), Dejan Zarubica (85' Marko Vucic).
Coach: Nikola Rakojevic.
Goals: 1', 21' Junior Mpia Mapuku 1-0, 2-0, 45+1' Roman Procházka 3-0,
79' Bozo Markovic 3-1.
Referee: Martin Lundby (NOR)   Attendance: 6,456.
Sent off: 89' Mirko Radisic.

29.06.17   Skagerak Arena, Skien: Odds BK – Ballymena United 3-0 (1-0)
Odds BK: Viljar Myhra, Espen Ruud, Vegard Bergan, Fredrik Semb Berge, Joakim Våge
Nilsen, Martin Broberg, Jone Samuelsen (62' Fredrik Nordkvelle), Stefan Mladenovic (77'
Sigurd Haugen), Fredrik Oldrup Jensen, Olivier Occéan, Pape Pate Diouf (46' Rafik Zekhnini).
Coach: Dag-Eilev Fagermo.
Ballymena United: Ross Glendinning, Tony Kane (79' William Faulkner), Kyle Owens (58'
Emmet Friars), Johnny Flynn, Jim Ervin, Michael Gault, Cathair Friel (72' Jonathan
McMurray), Conor McCloskey, Leroy Millar, Kevin Braniff, Joe McKinney.
Coach: David Jeffrey.
Goals: 1' Stefan Mladenovic 1-0, 53' Martin Broberg 2-0, 90+2' Sigurd Haugen 3-0.
Referee: Edin Jakupovic (BIH)   Attendance: 2,969.

29.06.17   Estadi Comunal, Andorra la Vella: UE Santa Coloma – NK Osijek 0-2 (0-0)
UE Santa Coloma: Iván Periánez, David Maneiro, Jordi Rubio (69' Boris Antón Codina),
Pedro Muñoz, Miguel Ruiz, Cristian Orosa, Sandro Gutiérrez (83' Alberto Molina), Juan
Salomó, Víctor Bernat (81' Txus Rubio), Gerard Aloy, Juli Sánchez. Coach: Emilio Gomez.
NK Osijek: Marko Malenica, Borna Barisic, Mateo Barac (59' Petar Bockaj), Mile Skoric,
Andrej Lukic, Benedik Mioc, Josip Knezevic (85 Domagoj Pusic), Gabrijel Boban (59' Zoran
Lesjak), Muzafer Ejupi, Eros Grezda, Tomislav Sorsa. Coach: Zoran Zekic.
Goals: 81' Benedik Mioc 0-1, 90+6' Andrej Lukic 0-2.
Referee: Trustin Farrugia Cann (MLT)   Attendance: 600.

29.06.17   Stadionul Zimbru, Chisinau: FC Zaria – FK Sarajevo 2-1 (2-0)
FC Zaria: Serghei Pascenco, Victor Golovatenco, Andrey Novicov, Maxim Focsa, Sergiy
Zagynaylov (76' Gheorghe Boghiu), Vadim Rata, Igor Tigîrlas (72' Andrii Slinkin), Oleg
Ermak, Rubén Gómez (85' Ion Cararus), Georgi Ovsyannikov, Maxim Mihaliov.
Coach: Vlad Goian.
FK Sarajevo: Bojan Pavlovic, Dusan Hodzic (46' Advan Kadusic), Sasa Novakovic, Marko
Mihojevic, Almir Bekic, Perica Ivetic (46' Amar Rahmanovic), Elvis Saric, Nermin Crnkic,
Anel Hebibovic, Samir Radovac, Mersudin Ahmetovic (72' Mico Kuzmanovic).
Coach: Mehmed Janjos.
Goals: 7' Sergiy Zagynaylov 1-0, 33' Rubén Gómez 2-0, 73' Marko Mihojevic 2-1.
Referee: Alexandros Aretopoulos (GRE)   Attendance: 2,500.

29.06.17   Dalga Arena, Baku: Zira FK – FC Differdange 03 2-0 (1-0)
Zira FK: Anar Nazirov, Josef Boum, Gabriel Matei (81' Adil Naghiyev), Tamkin Khalilzade,
Jovan Krneta, Orkhan Aliyev (46' Rashad Sadiqov), Milan Djuric, David Manga, Viktor
Ibekoyi (61' Vugar Mustafayev), Kervens Belfort, Richard Gadze. Coach: Aykhan Abbasov.
FC Differdange 03: Julien Weber, André Rodrigues, David Vandenbroeck, Mathias Jänisch,
Geoffrey Franzoni, Yannick Bastos (61' Chadli Amri), David Fleurival, Jordann Yéyé, Dwayn
Holter, Mounir Hamzaoui (79' Farid Ikene), Gauthier Caron (70' Nicolas Perez).
Coach: Pascal Carzaniga.
Goals: 22' Richard Gadze 2-0, 80' Kervens Belfort 2-0.
Referee: Daniyar Sakhi (KAZ)   Attendance: 4,416.

29.06.17   AEK Arena, Larnaca: AEK Larnaca – Lincoln Red Imps 5-0 (1-0)
AEK Larnaca: Juan Pablo, Marios Antoniades, Català, Carles Soria, Jorge Larena (78'
Vladimir Boljevic), Joan Tomás, Tete (68' Elvir Maloku), Hector Hevel, Vincent Laban, Ivan
Trickovski, Florian Taulemesse (71' Nestoras Mitidis). Coach: Imanol Idiakez.
Lincoln Red Imps: Raúl Navas, Jean Garcia, Joseph Chipolina, Bernardo Lopes, Roy
Chipolina, Castells, Anthony Bardon, Kyle Casciaro (29' Anthony Hernandez), Calderón (37'
Pibe), Lee Casciaro (68' Falu Aranda), Diego. Coach: Julio Ribas.
Goals: 22' Florian Taulemesse 1-0, 52', 65' Joan Tomás 2-0, 3-0, 68' Florian Taulemesse 4-0,
77' Ivan Trickovski 5-0 (p).
Referee: Nikolaj Hänni (SUI)   Attendance: 3,496.

254

29.06.17   Haugesund Stadion, Haugesund: FK Haugesund – Coleraine FC 7-0 (3-0)
FK Haugesund: Helge Sandvik, Fredrik Knudsen, Vegard Skjerve, Kristoffer Haraldseid, Filip
Kiss, Liban Abdi, Sondre Tronstad, Alexander Stølås (46' Sverre Bjørkkjær), Haris
Hajradinovic (62' Johnny Buduson), Anthony Ikedi, Shuaibu Ibrahim (54' Erik Huseklepp).
Coach: Eirik Horneland.
Coleraine FC: Michael Doherty, Gareth McConaghie, Stephen O'Donnell, Ciaron Harkin (82'
Matthew Kirk), Darren McCauley, Josh Carson (82' Ian Parkhill), Aaron Traynor, Jamie
McGonigle (72' James McLaughlin), Adam Mullan, Eoin Bradley, Bradley Lyons.
Coach: Oran Kearney.
Goals: 8' Sondre Tronstad 1-0, 33' Liban Abdi 2-0, 42' Haris Hajradinovic 3-0,
49' Anthony Ikedi 4-0, 52' Shuaibu Ibrahim 5-0, 61' Erik Huseklepp 6-0,
71' Johnny Buduson 7-0.
Referee: Alexandru Tean (MOL)   Attendance: 2,523.

29.06.17   Stade Émile Mayrisch, Esch-sur-Alzette: CS FOLA Esch – FC Milsami 2-1 (1-0)
CS FOLA Esch: Thomas Hym, Tom Laterza, Mehdi Kirch, Ryan Klapp (67' Alexander
Cvetkovic), Julien Klein, Peter Chrappan, Veldin Muharemovic, Jakob Dallevedove, Corentin
Koçur (86' Michel Bechtold), Enis Saiti (61' Stefano Bensi), Samir Hadji. Coach: Jeff Strasser.
FC Milsami: Radu Mîtu, Artur Craciun, Constantin Bogdan, Dinu Graur, Eugen Celeadnic (86'
Daniel Ciobanu), Vladimir Rassulov (84' Andrei Rusnac), Alexandru Antoniuc, Andrei
Cojocari, Alexandru Dulghier (76' Vasile Jardan), Maxim Antoniuc, Sergiu Platica.
Coach: Veaceslav Rusnac.
Goals: 4' Jakob Dallevedove 1-0, 80' Samir Hadji 2-0, 81' Sergiu Platica 2-1.
Referee: Dennis Antamo (FIN)   Attendance: 989.

29.06.17   Netanya Stadium, Netanya: Maccabi Tel Aviv – KF Tiranë 2-0 (1-0)
Maccabi Tel Aviv: Predrag Rajkovic, Eli Dasa, Eitan Tibi, Ofir Davidzade, Omer Atzili (72'
Barak Itzhaki), Sheran Yeini, Shlomy Azulay, Eyal Golasa (65' Eliel Peretz), Vidar
Kjartansson (78' Aaron Schoenfeld), Tal Ben Haim, Yonathan Cohen. Coach: Jordi Cruijff.
KF Tiranë: Ilion Lika, Dorian Kërçiku (76' Rei Qilimi), Erion Hoxhallari, Marvin Turtulli,
David Domgjoni, Albi Doka, Erando Karabeci, Elvi Berisha (67' Fjoralb Deliaj), Merveil
Ndockyt, Reuben Acquah, Yunus Sentamu. Coach: Zé Maria.
Goals: 27' Yonatan Cohen 1-0, 64' Eli Dasa 2-0.
Referee: Tihomir Pejin (CRO)   Attendance: 7,098.

29.06.17   Corbetts Sports Stadium, Rhyl: Bala Town – FC Vaduz 1-2 (0-2)
Bala Town: Ashley Morris, Anthony Stephens, Stuart Jones Sr., Stuart Jones Jr., Les Davies
(86' Mike Hayes), Lee Owens, Nathan Burke, Ian Sheridan, Chris Venables, David Thompson,
Kieran Smith. Coach: Colin Caton.
FC Vaduz: Peter Jehle, Tomislav Puljic, Nils von Niederhäusern, Axel Borgmann, Mario
Bühler (46' Thomas Konrad), Diego Ciccone, Marco Mathys, Maurice Brunner (90+2' Franz
Burgmeier), Philipp Muntwiler, Aldin Turkes, Gonzalo Zárate (73' Robin Kamber).
Coach: Roland Vrabec.
Goals: 21' Gonzalo Zárate 0-1, 29' Maurice Brunner 0-2, 46' Chris Venables 1-2.
Referee: Alain Durieux (LUX)   Attendance: 803.

29.06.17   Bangor University Stadium, Bangor:
Gap Connah's Quay FC – HJK Helsinki 1-0 (1-0)
Gap Connah's Quay FC: John Danby, Kai Edwards, George Horan, Danny Harrison, Sean
Smith, Mike Pearson, Declan Poole (77' Ryan Wignall), Callum Morris, Nathan Woolfe, Jay
Owen, Michael Wilde. Coach: Andrew Morrison.
HJK Helsinki: Markus Uusitalo, Hannu Patronen, Rafinha, Ville Jalasto, Faith Obilor, Vincent
Onovo, Anthony Annan (83' Lassi Lappalainen), Moshtagh Yaghoubi, Demba Savage, Akseli
Pelvas, Evans Mensah (61' Ousman Jallow). Coach: Mika Lehkosuo.
Goal: 40' Nathan Woolfe 1-0.
Referee: Catalin Gaman (ROM)   Attendance: 472.

29.06.17   Stadion Karadjordje, Novi Sad: Vojvodina – MFK Ruzomberok 2-1 (2-0)
Vojvodina: Emil Rockov, Bogdan Planic, Dzenan Burekovic, Nikola Kovacevic, Ivan
Lakicevic, Aleksandar Mesarovic (74' Milan Bubalo), Nemanja Subotic (83' Stefan
Mihajlovic), Filip Malbasic, Marko Vukasovic, Dusan Jovancic, Nikola Trujic.
Coach: Radoslav Batak.
MFK Ruzomberok: Matús Macík, Ján Maslo, Simon Kupec, Peter Maslo, Jozef Menich, Kristi
Qose (60' Dalibor Takác), Peter Gál-Andrezly, Matej Kochan, Erik Daniel, Marek Sapara (76'
Tomás Dubek), Milos Lacny (69' Stefan Gerec). Coach: Norbert Hrncár.
Goals: 8', 21' Filip Malbasic 1-0, 2-0, 81' Erik Daniel 2-1.
Referee: Halil Meler (TUR)   Attendance: 5,093.

29.06.17   MCH Arena, Herning: FC Midtjylland – Derry City 6-1 (3-0)
FC Midtjylland: Jesper Hansen, Zsolt Korcsmár, Marc Hende, Kristian Riis, André Rømer,
Tim Sparv, Jakob Poulsen, Janus Drachmann (46' Gustav Wikheim), Simon Kroon, Rilwan
Hassan (72' Bozhidar Kraev), Ebere Onuachu (57' Alexander Sørloth). Coach: Jess Thorup.
Derry City: Gerard Doherty, Dean Jarvis, Aaron Barry, Aaron McEneff, Nicky Low, Harry
Monaghan (62' Lukas Schubert), Ben Doherty, Ronan Curtis, Rory Patterson (74' Joshua
Daniels), Rory Holden, Nathan Boyle (84' Mark Timlin). Coach: Kenny Shiels.
Goals: 4' Marc Hende 1-0, 15' Kristian Riis 2-0, 44' Jakob Poulsen 3-0 (p),
59', 61' Simon Kroon 4-0, 5-0, 66' Ronan Curtis 5-1, 84' Bozhidar Kraev 6-1.
Referee: Markus Hameter (AUT)   Attendance: 5,122.

29.06.17   Stadiumi Skënderbeu, Korçë: KF Skënderbeu – UE Sant Julià 1-0 (0-0)
KF Skënderbeu: Orges Shehi, Gledi Mici, Bajram Jashanica, Tefik Osmani, Kristi Vangjeli,
Marko Radas, Enis Gavazaj (62' Afrim Taku), Liridon Latifi, Sabien Lilaj, Goran Vujovic (69'
Sebino Plaku), Segun Adeniyi (79' Donjet Shkodra). Coach: Ilir Daja.
UE Sant Julià: Manuel Vidal Rodriguez, Mateo Rodriguez Firpo, Iván Vigo, Jamal Zarioh
Taouil, Francisco Rodriguez Girau, Luis Blanco, Eric Rodríguez Barcelo, Nikola Zugic, José
Villanueva (71' Leonel Alves), Fábio Serra Alves (76' Christian Cellay), Noah Baffoe (88'
João López Leita). Coach: Luis Blanco.
Goal: 69' Liridon Latifi 1-0.
Referee: Robert Hennessey (IRL)   Attendance: 2,700.

256

29.06.17   Östgötaporten, Norrköping: IFK Norrköping – Prishtina KF 5-0 (5-0)
IFK Norrköping: Michael Langer, Jón Fjóluson, Linus Wahlqvist (78' Eric Smith), Andreas Johansson, Christopher Telo, Daniel Sjölund (64' Gudmundur Thórarinsson), Niclas Eliasson, Filip Dagerstål, David Moberg-Karlsson, Kall Holmberg (56' Simon Skrabb), Sebastian Andersson. Coach: Jens Gustafsson.
Prishtina KF: Alban Muçiqi, Armend Dallku, Debatik Çurri (72' Liridon Fetahaj), Liridon Leci, Laurit Boshnjaku, Endritt Krasniqi (42' Mërgim Pefqeli), Lorik Maxhuni, Mergim Neziri, Shend Kelmendi (46' Diar Miftaraj), Gauthier Mankenda, Khalid Abdul Basit. Coach: Arsim Thaçi.
Goals: 10' David Moberg-Karlsson 1-0, 24' Sebastian Andersson 2-0, 26' Niclas Eliasson 3-0, 31', 40' Kalle Holmberg 4-0, 5-0.
Referee: Aleksandrs Golubevs (LTU)   Attendance: 6,540.

29.06.17   Gundadalur, Tórshavn: KÍ Klaksvík – AIK Solna 0-0
KÍ Klaksvík: Meinhardt Joensen, Ísak Simonsen, Jonas Rasmussen, Ahmed Mujdragic, Ólavur Niclasen, Albert Adu, Hørdur Askham, Jákup Andreasen, Semir Hadzibulic, Jóannes Bjartalíd (76' Hjalgrím Elttør), Páll Klettskard. Coach: Mikkjal Thomassen.
AIK Solna: Oscar Linnér, Nils-Eric Johansson, Jesper Nyholm, Sauli Väisänen, Simon Thern (68' Henok Goitom), Johan Blomberg (69' Kristoffer Olsson), Daniel Sundgren, Stefan Ishizaki, Anton Jönsson Salétros, Amin Affane, Eero Markkanen. Coach: Rikard Norling.
Referee: Michal Ocenás (SVK)   Attendance: 1,374.

29.06.17   Stadion Pecara, Siroki Brijeg: Siroki Brijeg – FK Ordabasy 2-0 (2-0)
Siroki Brijeg: Luka Bilobrk, Josip Barisic, Dino Coric, Slavko Bralic, Stipo Markovic, Josip Coric (79' Josip Corluka), Stjepan Loncar (81' Luka Grubisic), Luka Begonja, Dejan Cabraja, Luka Menalo (89' Danijel Kozul), Ivan Krstanovic. Coach: Denis Coric.
FK Ordabasy: Almat Bekbaev, Samat Smakov, Pablo Fontanello, Temirlan Yerlanov, Aleksandar Simcevic, Kyrylo Kovalchuk, Azat Nurgaliev, Mardan Tolebek (53' Nikita Bocharov), Abdoulaye Diakhaté, Tanat Nuserbayev, Yerkebulan Tunggyshbayev (78' Vitali Li). Coach: Aleksei Petrushin.
Goals: 37', 45' Ivan Krstenovic 1-0 (p), 2-0.
Referee: Ferenc Karakó (HUN)   Attendance: 3,100.

29.06.17   Stadion Rajko Mitic, Beograd: Crvena Zvezda – Floriana FC 3-0 (1-0)
Crvena Zvezda: Filip Manojlovic, Abraham Frimpong, Filip Stojkovic, Dusan Andjelkovic, Vujadin Savic, Damien Le Tallec, Mitchell Donald, Slavoljub Srnic, Richmond Boakye (90+1' Milan Pavkov), Nemanja Milic (68' Nenad Milijas), Ricardinho (81' Luka Adzic). Coach: Vladan Milojevic.
Floriana FC: Justin Haber, Enrico Pepe, Enzo Ruiz, Arthur Henrique, James Baldacchino, Sebastián Nayar, Maurizio Vella, Stephen Pisani, Ignacio Varela (66' Júninho), Nicolas Hernan Chiesa (46' Noël Nyason), Mario Fontanella (62' Clyde Borg). Coach: Giovanni Tedesco.
Goals: 45+5' Richmond Boakye 1-0 (p), 78' Slavoljub Srnic 2-0, 89' Richmond Boakye 3-0.
Referee: Mattias Gestranius (FIN)   Attendance: 19,823.
Sent off: 45+4' Enzo Ruiz.

29.06.17   Stadion Mladosti u Lucanima, Lucani: Mladost Lucani – Inter Baku 0-3 (0-2)
Mladost Lucani: Nemanja Krznaric, Ivan Milosevic, Nikola Andric, Bogdan Milosevic, Sasa
Jovanovic, Aleksandr Pejovic, Vladimir Radivojevic (84' Nenad Gavric), Milos Satara, Milos
Trifunovic, Obiora Odita (69' Ivan Markovic), Nenad Marinkovic (54' Janko Tumbasevic).
Coach: Nenad Milovanovic.
Inter Baku: Sälahät Agayev, Dênis, Slavik Alkhasov, Ilkin Qirtimov, Adrian Scarlatache,
Tarlan Guliyev, Nizami Hajiyev (89' Mirsayib Abbasov), Elnur Abdullayev (88' Mirhuseyn
Seyidov), Fuad Bayramov, Pardis Fardjad-Azad (83' Samir Zargarov), Rauf Aliyev.
Coach: Zaur Svanadze.
Goals: 23', 41' Adrian Scarlatache 0-1, 0-2, 75' Rauf Aliyev 0-3.
Referee: Alexey Matyanin (RUS)   Attendance: 1,950.

29.06.17   Stadio Olimpico di Serravalle, Serravalle: SP Tre Penne – FK Rabotnicki 0-1 (0-0)
SP Tre Penne: Mattia Migani, Dario Merendino, Andrea Rossi, Stefano Fraternali (84' Lorenzo
Capicchioni), Luca Patregnani, Alex Gasperoni, Nicola Gai, Mirko Palazzi, Riccardo Santini
(72' Pietro Calzolari), Andrea Moretti (62' Marco Martini), Michele Simoncelli.
Coach: Luigi Bizzotto.
FK Rabotnicki: Damjan Siskovski, Dejan Mitrev, Sebastián Herrera, Tomislav Iliev, Moncilo
Raso, Suad Sahiti (73' Emir Sahiti), Filip Duranski, Bojan Najdenov (81' Mario Stankovski),
Florian Kadriu, Dusko Trajcevski, Kire Markoski. Coach: Viktor Trenevski.
Goal: 90' Dejan Mitrev 0-1.
Referee: Jason Lee Barcelo (GIB)   Attendance: 294.

29.06.17   Arena Petrol, Celje: NK Domzale – FC Flora 2-0 (0-0)
NK Domzale: Dejan Milic, Matija Sirok, Miha Blazic, Gaber Dobrovoljc, Jure Balkovec,
Amedej Vetrih, Jan Repas (85' Alen Ozbolt), Jure Matjasic (81' Luka Volaric), Zeni Husmani,
Ivan Firer, Lovro Bizjak (67' Zan Zuzek). Coach: Simon Rozman.
FC Flora: Mait Toom, Märten Kuusk, Madis Vihmann, Joonas Tamm, Martin Miller (83'
Maksim Gussev), Brent Lepistu, Rauno Sappinen, Mihkel Ainsalu, Joseph Saliste, Zakaria
Beglarishvili, Rauno Alliku. Coach: Arno Pijpers.
Goals: 77' Jan Repas 1-0, 90' Zan Zuzek 2-0.
Referee: João Pinheiro (POR)   Attendance: 724.

29.06.17   Stadion Pod Goricom, Podgorica: FK Mladost Podgorica – Gandzasar FC 1-0 (0-0)
FK Mladost Podgorica: Damir Ljuljanovic, Ivan Novovic, Stefan Cicmil, Nikola Vukcevic,
Milos Krkotic (90+4' Ognjen Stijepovic), Milan Djurisic, Marko Cetkovic, Andrija
Kaludjerovic, Stefan Bukorac, Ivan Knezevic (73' Boris Kopitovic), Zoran Petrovic (80'
Marko Burzanovic). Coach: Dejan Vukicevic.
Gandzasar FC: Grigor Meliksetyan, Alex Júnior, Damir Memovic, Hayk Ishkhanyan,
Vaspurak Minasyan, Wbeymar Angulo (85' Vardan Bakalyan), Lubambo Musonda,
Christopher Mandiangu (68' Sargis Shahinyan), Wal (83' Ashot Karapetyan), Artur
Yuspashyan, Claudir. Coach: Ashot Barseghyan.
Goal: 58' Milan Djurisic 1-0 (p).
Referee: Paul McLaughlin (IRL)   Attendance: 2,369.

29.06.17   Hibernians Ground, Paola: Valletta FC – SS Folgore/Falciano 2-0 (1-0)
Valletta FC: Henry Bonello, Steve Borg, Ryan Camilleri, Juan Gill, Joseph Zerafa, Romeu, Claudio Pani (90' Roderick Briffa), Santiago Malano, Michael Mifsud, Maximiliano Velasco (64' Kyrian Nwoko), Uchenna Umeh (81' Jean Borg). Coach: Zoran Popovic.
SS Folgore/Falciano: Luca Bianchi, Alberto Semprini, Andrea Nucci, Christofer Genestreti, Francesco Sartori (84' Manuel Iuzzolino), Cristian Brolli, Luca Bezzi, Luca Paradisi, Lago Ramiro, Alessandro Bianchi (77' Nicolò Venerucci), Marco Bernardi (83' Stefano Sacco). Coach: Oscar Lasagni.
Goals: 41' Steve Borg 1-0, 48' Maximiliano Velasco 2-0.
Referee: Denis Scherbakov (BLS)   Attendance: 1,141.

29.06.17   McDiarmid Park, Perth: St. Johnstone FC – FK Trakai 1-2 (1-2)
St. Johnstone FC: Zander Clark, Joe Shaughnessy, Ricky Foster, Brian Easton, Blair Alston, David Wotherspoon (62' Stefan Scougall), Paul Paton (63' Chris Millar), Liam Craig (84' Chris Kane), Steven MacLean, Ally Gilchrist, Graham Cummins. Coach: Tommy Wright.
FK Trakai: Ignas Plūkas, Justinas Janusevskis, Alma Wakili (81' Svajūnas Cyzas), Mychailo Shyshka, Arūnas Klimavicius, Valdemars Borovskis, Modestas Vorobjovas, Oscar Dorley (90' Pavel Kruk), Vaidas Silénas, Aleksandr Bychenok, Maksim Maksimov (90+3' Deividas Cesnauskis). Coach: Oleg Vasilenko.
Goals: 14' Maksim Maksimov 0-1, 32' Joe Shaughnessy 1-1, 36' Vaidas Silénas 1-2.
Referee: Fran Jovic (CRO)   Attendance: 5,636.
Sent off: 82' Vaidas Silénas.

29.06.17   Ibrox Stadium, Glasgow: Rangers FC – Progrès Niedercorn 1-0 (1-0)
Rangers FC: Wesley Foderingham, James Tavernier, Fábio Cardoso, Lee Wallace, David Bates, Ryan Jack, Niko Kranjcar (69' Jordan Rossiter), Jason Holt (77' Candeias), Dálcio, Kenny Miller, Martyn Waghorn (77' Alfredo Morelos). Coach: Pedro Caixinha.
Progrès Niedercorn: Sebastian Flauss, Adrien Ferino, Metin Karayer, Yann Matias Marques, Oliver Thill (81' Ben Vogel), Maximilian Watzka, Alexis Lafon, Sébastien Thill, Mike Schneider (90' Alessandro Fiorani), Emmanuel Françoise, Alexander Karapetyan (86' Théo Sully). Coach: Paolo Amodio.
Goal: 37' Kenny Miller 1-0.
Referee: Mohammed Al Hakim (SWE)   Attendance: 48,681.

29.06.17   Seaview, Belfast: Crusaders FC – FK Liepāja 3-1 (2-0)
Crusaders FC: Brian Jensen, Billy Joe Burns, Colin Coates, Sean Ward, Rodney Brown, Philip Lowry (73' Jamie Glackin), Jordan Forsythe, Matthew Snoddy, Michael Carvill (86' Howard Beverland), Jordan Owens, Paul Heatley (83' Gavin Whyte). Coach: Stephen Baxter.
FK Liepāja: Pāvels Dorosevs, Oskars Klava, Deniss Ivanovs, Dario Tomic (72' Mārtins Kigurs), Leonel Strumia, Dmitrijs Hmizs, Raivis Jurkovskis, Valerijs Afanasjevs (60' Marks Kurtiss), Cristian Torres, Artūrs Karasausks, Kristaps Grebis. Coach: Tamaz Pertia.
Goals: 28' Philip Lowry 1-0, 35' Michael Carvill 2-0, 55' Jordan Owens 3-0,
61' Artūrs Karasausks 3-1.
Referee: Anders Poulsen (DEN)   Attendance: 1,375.

29.06.17   Stadion Grbavica, Sarajevo: Zeljeznicar Sarajevo – FK Zeta 1-0 (0-0)
Zeljeznicar Sarajevo: Vedran Kjosevski, Sinisa Stevanovic, Danijel Graovac, Jadranko
Bogicevic, Jovan Blagojevic, Srdan Stanic, Goran Zakaric, Zajko Zeba (77' Denis Zeric),
Ugljesa Radinovic (70' Darko Markovic), Asim Zec, Ivan Lendric (90+2' Stevo Nikolic).
Coach: Slavko Petrovic.
FK Zeta: Marko Novovic, Nemanja Cavnic, Igor Vujacic (83' Bozidar Djukic), Goran Milojko
(64' Vladislav Rogosic), Vasko Kalezic, Aldin Adzovic, Nemanja Sekulic, Filip Kukulicic,
Nikola Krstovic (68' Stefan Vukcevic), Pjeter Ljuljdjuraj, Perisa Pesukic.
Coach: Dusan Vlaisavljevic.
Goal: 48' Ivan Lendric 1-0.
Referee: Kirill Levnikov (RUS)   Attendance: 8,858.

29.06.17   INEA stadion, Poznan: Lech Poznan – FK Pelister 4-0 (3-0)
Lech Poznan: Matús Putnocky, Robert Gumny, Lasse Nielsen, Volodymyr Kostevych, Emir
Dilaver, Abdul Tetteh, Darko Jevtic (76' Maciej Gajos), Maciej Makuszewski (71' Nicklas
Bärkroth), Radoslaw Majewski, Mario Situm, Nicki Bille Nielsen (70' Marcin Robak).
Coach: Nenad Bjelica.
FK Pelister: Ilce Petrovski, Kristijan Tosevski, Radenko Bojovic (46' Filip Petrov), Blagojce
Ljamcevski, Martin Kovachev, Goce Todorovski, Riste Markoski (62' Fernando Silva), Oliver
Peev, Dimitar Iliev (77' Matej Cvetanoski), Baze Ilijoski, Lucas. Coach: Naci Sensoy.
Goals: 28' Nicki Bille Nielsen 1-0 (p), 30' Mario Situm 2-0, 38' Radoslaw Majewski 3-0,
57' Mario Situm 4-0.
Referee: Luis Godinho (POR)   Attendance: 18,215.

29.06.17   Puskás Akadémia Pancho Aréna, Felcsút: Videoton FC – Balzan Youths 2-0 (0-0)
Videoton FC: Ádam Kovácsik, András Fejes, Loïc Négo, Stopira, Roland Juhász, Anel Hadzic,
Ádám Bódi (63' Krisztián Géresi), József Varga (54' Máté Pátkai), Asmir Suljic, Danko
Lazovic, Marko Scepovic. Coach: Marko Nikolic.
Balzan Youths: Ivan Janjusevic, Steven Bezzina, Uros Ljubomirac (77' Lecão), Elkin Serrano,
Milan Savic, Bruno Oliveira, Ryan Fenech, Paul Fenech, Cadú (83' Milos Lepovic), Alfred
Effiong (90+2' Dylan Grima), Bojan Kaljevic. Coach: Marko Micovic.
Goals: 79' Marko Scepovic 1-0, 90+4' Danko Lazovic 2-0.
Referee: Dejan Jakimovski (MCD)   Attendance: 2,188.

29.06.17   Estádio Do Algarve, Faro-Loulé (POR): St. Joseph's FC – AEL Limassol 0-4 (0-1)
St. Joseph's FC: Jose Félix Romero, Mané, Samuel Fernández, Esteban Montes, Iván Lobato,
Borja Gómez (65' Jaime Contreras Robles), Ángel Guirado, Juan Carlos Villalba (65'
Domingo Ferrer), José Miguel, John-Paul Duarte (76' Antonio Ortega), Boro.
Coach: Raúl Procopio.
AEL Limassol: Vózinha, Kevin Lafrance, Marco Airosa, Bogdan Mitrea, Aly Savane (66'
Dani Benítez), Mários Nikolaou, Ismail Sassi, Marco Soares, Andreas Avraam, Mikel
Arruabarrena (73' Marios Elia), Mesca (76' Yiannis Mavrou). Coach: Bruno Baltazar.
Goals: 4' Mikel Arruabarrena 0-1, 51' Mesca 0-2, 64', 71' Kevin Lafrance 0-3, 0-4.
Referee: Petur Reinert (FAR)   Attendance: 163.

29.06.17   Alvogenvöllurinn, Reykjavík: KR Reykjavík – SJK Seinäjoki 0-0
KR Reykjavík: Beitir Ólafsson, Arnór Adalsteinsson, Gunnar Thor Gunnarsson, Skúli Jón Fridgeirsson, Aron Jósepsson, Morten Beck, Finnur Margeirsson (76' Gardar Jóhannsson), Pálmi Pálmason, Óskar Hauksson, Tobias Thomsen, Kennie Chopart (80' Gudmundur Andri Tryggvason). Coach: Willum Thórsson.
SJK Seinäjoki: Mihkel Aksalu, Dani Hatakka, Jarkko Hurme, Marc Vales, Timo Tahvanainen, Johannes Laaksonen, Tomas Hradecky (80' Obed Malolo), Matti Klinga (80' Jesse Sarajärvi), Mehmet Hetemaj, Billy Ions, Elias Ahde (64' Erfan Zeneli).
Coaches: José Roca & Sixten Boström.
Referee: Zbynek Proske (CZE)   Attendance: 531.

29.06.17   Samsung völlurinn, Gardabær: UMF Stjarnan – Shamrock Rovers 0-1 (0-1)
UMF Stjarnan: Haraldur Björnsson, Brynjar Gudjónsson, Jósef Kristinn Jósefsson, Jóhann Laxdal (87' Heidar Ægisson), Daníel Laxdal, Baldur Sigurdsson, Eyjólfur Hédinsson, Alex Thór Hauksson, Gudjón Baldvinsson, Hilmar Árni Halldórsson, Hólmbert Fridjónsson (82' Ólafur Finsen). Coaches: Rúnar Sigmundsson & Brynjar Gunnarsson.
Shamrock Rovers: Tomer Chencinski, Luke Byrne, David Webster, Roberto Lopes, Simon Madden, Trevor Clarke, Ryan Connolly (74' Sam Bone), Ronan Finn, Brandon Miele, Gary Shaw (87' Michael O'Connor), Graham Burke (82' David McAllister).
Coach: Stephen Bradley.
Goal: 38' Gary Shaw 0-1.
Referee: Tomasz Musial (POL)   Attendance: 1,020.

04.07.17   Hibernians Ground, Paola: Balzan Youths – Videoton FC 3-3 (1-2)
Balzan Youths: Ivan Janjusevic, Steven Bezzina, Uros Ljubomirac, Elkin Serrano, Milan Savic (72' Lecão), Bruno Oliveira, Ryan Fenech (85' Jamie Zerafa), Paul Fenech, Cadú (74' Lydon Micallef), Alfred Effiong, Bojan Kaljevic. Coach: Marko Micovic.
Videoton FC: Ádam Kovácsik, Paulo Vinícius, Loïc Négo, Stopira, Roland Juhász, Anel Hadzic (85' József Varga), Máté Pátkai, Asmir Suljic, Danko Lazovic (81' Mirko Maric), Marko Scepovic, Krisztián Géresi (60' István Kovács). Coach: Marko Nikolic.
Goals: 3' Bojan Kaljevic 1-0, 15' Krisztián Géresi 1-1, 23' Marko Scepovic 1-2, 56' Alfred Effiong 2-2, 80' Roland Juhász 2-3, 86' Bojan Kaljevic 3-3 (p).
Referee: Filip Glova (SVK)   Attendance: 550.

04.07.17   Stade Josy Barthel, Luxembourg: Progrès Niedercorn – Rangers FC 2-0 (0-0)
Progrès Niedercorn: Sebastian Flauss (33' Charly Schinker), Adrien Ferino, Metin Karayer, Yann Matias Marques, Oliver Thill (79' Ben Vogel), Maximilian Watzka, Alexis Lafon, Sébastien Thill, Mike Schneider, Emmanuel Françoise, Alexander Karapetyan (84' Alessandro Fiorani). Coach: Paolo Amodio.
Rangers FC: Wesley Foderingham, James Tavernier, Fábio Cardoso, Lee Wallace, David Bates, Ryan Jack, Jordan Rossiter (78' Eduardo Herrera), Niko Kranjcar, Kenny Miller, Alfredo Morelos (46' Dálcio), Candeias (59' Josh Windass). Coach: Pedro Caixinha.
Goals: 66' Emmanuel Françoise 1-0, 75' Sébastien Thill 2-0.
Referee: Vilhjálmur Alvar Thórarinsson (ISL)   Attendance: 5,505.

06.07.17   Stadionul Moldova, Speia: Dacia Chisinau – KF Shkëndija 79 0-4 (0-2)
Dacia Chisinau: Dorian Railean, Diego Seoane (57' Denis Ilescu), Abdoul Mamah, Stefan
Draskovic, Aleksandr Pascenco, Maksim Gavrilenko, Amâncio Fortes, Cristian Jalba, Oleg
Andronic, Bratislav Punosevac (73' Maxim Cojocaru), Alexandru Bejan (58' Andrei
Marandici). Coach: Viorel Frunza.
KF Shkëndija 79: Kostadin Zahov, Egzon Bejtulai, Ardijan Cuculi, Mevlan Murati, Armend
Alimi (77' Arbin Zejnulai), Ferhan Hasani, Stephan Vujcic, Blagoja Todorovski, Besart
Ibraimi, Marjan Radeski (69 Olsi Teqja), Stênio Júnior (77' Ennur Totre).
Coach: Qatip Osmani.
Goals: 32' Armend Alimi 0-1, 44' Stênio Júnior 0-2, 81' Arbin Zejnulai 0-3,
88' Ferhan Hasani 0-4 (p)
Referee: Peter Kralovic (SVK)   Attendance: 200
Sent off: 37' Oleg Andronic.

06.07.17   Tsirion Athlítiko Kentro, Limassol: AEL Limassol – St. Joseph's FC 6-0 (3-0)
AEL Limassol: Vózinha, Kevin Lafrance, Bogdan Mitrea (46' Andreas Kyriakou),
Charalambos Kyriakou, Fidelis Irhene, Aly Savane, Mários Nikolaou (59' Giannis
Gerolemou), Dani Benítez, Andreas Avraam, Mesca, Marios Elia (61' Yiannis Mavrou).
Coach: Bruno Baltazar.
St. Joseph's FC: Jamie Robba, Jaime Contreras Robles, Mané, Samuel Fernández, Esteban
Montes, Iván Lobato, Borja Gómez (46' Juan Carlos Villalba), Ángel Guirado, José Miguel
(61' Carlos Pomares), John-Paul Duarte (46' Antonio Ortega), Boro. Coach: Raúl Procopio.
Goals: 2' Andreas Avraam 1-0, 37, 45+6' Marios Elia 2-0, 3-0, 52' Dani Benítez 4-0,
89' Andreas Kyriakou 5-0, 90+2' Yiannis Mavrou 6-0.
Referee: Luis Teixeira (POR)   Attendance: 1,774.

06.07.17   Arvi Futbolo Arena, Marijampólè: FK Sūduva – Shakhter Soligorsk 2-1 (1-1)
FK Sūduva: Ivan Kardum, Radanfah Abu Bakr, Semir Kerla (55' Marijan Altiparmakovski),
Algis Jankauskas, Povilas Leimonas, Ernestas Veliulis (79' Sergei Amirzian), Andro Svrljuga,
Paulius Janusauskas (70' Giedrius Matulevicius), Vaidas Slavickas, Ovidijus Verbickas,
Karolis Laukzemis. Coach: Vladimir Cheburin.
Shakhter Soligorsk: Ivan Karadzhov, Siarhei Matveichyk, Aleksey Yanushkevich, Igor Burko,
Pavel Rybak, Edgar Olekhnovich, Aleksandr Selyava, Drazen Bagaric (46' Ljuban Crepulja),
Yuri Kovalev, Denis Laptev (78' Nikolai Yanush), Vitaly Lisakovich (46' Alexandr Poznyak).
Coach: Oleg Kubarev.
Goals: 34' Povilas Leimonas 1-0, 38' Yuri Kovalev 1-1, 90+1' Algis Jankauskas 2-1.
Referee: Don Robertson (SCO)   Attendance: 2,000.
Sent off: 43' Siarhei Matveichyk.

06.07.17   Complexul Sportiv Raional, Orhei: FC Milsami – CS FOLA Esch 1-1 (1-0)
FC Milsami: Radu Mîtu, Artur Craciun, Constantin Bogdan (75' Vasile Jardan), Dinu Graur,
Eugen Celeadnic (67' Alexandru Dulghier), Gheorghe Andronic (32' Vladimir Rassulov),
Alexandru Antoniuc, Andrei Cojocari, Maxim Antoniuc, Yero Bello, Sergiu Platica.
Coach: Veaceslav Rusnac.
CS FOLA Esch: Thomas Hym, Tom Laterza, Mehdi Kirch, Ryan Klapp (87' Stefano Bensi),
Julien Klein, Peter Chrappan, Veldin Muharemovic, Jakob Dallevedove, Corentin Koçur (76'
Michel Bechtold), Enis Saiti (70' Ken Corral), Samir Hadji. Coach: Jeff Strasser.
Goals: 37' Alexandru Antoniuc 1-0, 58' Jakob Dallevedove 1-1.
Referee: Roomer Tarajev (EST)   Attendance: 2,800.
Sent off: 86' Dinu Graur.

06.07.17   Stadiumi Selman Stërmasi, Tirana: KF Tiranë – Maccabi Tel Aviv 0-3 (0-0)
KF Tiranë: Ilion Lika, Marvin Turtulli, Albi Doka, Erion Hoxhallari, Rei Qilimi (64' Fjoralb Deliaj), Erando Karabeci, Asion Daja, Wellyson (79' Elvi Berisha), Reuben Acquah, Yunus Sentamu, Merveil Ndockyt. Coach: Zé Maria.
Maccabi Tel Aviv: Predrag Rajkovic, Eli Dasa (62' Yuval Shpungin), Eitan Tibi, Tal Ben Haim, Ofir Davidzade, Omer Atzili, Sheran Yeini (73' Barak Itzhaki), Eyal Golasa, Dor Peretz, Yonathan Cohen (62' Avi Rikan), Aaron Schoenfeld. Coach: Jordi Cruijff.
Goals: 50' Aaron Schoenfeld 0-1, 80' Barak Itzhaki 0-2, 86' Avi Rikan 0-3.
Referee: Sándor Andó-Szabó (HUN)   Attendance: 400.
Sent off: 44' Yunus Sentamu.

06.07.17   Ortaliq Stadion, Almaty: FK Ordabasy – Siroki Brijeg 0-0
FK Ordabasy: Almat Bekbaev, Samat Smakov (58' Temirlan Yerlanov), Pablo Fontanello, Aleksandar Simcevic, Kyrylo Kovalchuk (83' Sanat Zhumakanov), Azat Nurgaliev, Mardan Tolebek, Abdoulaye Diakhaté, Nikita Bocharov, Vitali Li (65' Preslav Yordanov), Yerkebulan Tunggyshbayev. Coach: Aleksei Petrushin.
Siroki Brijeg: Luka Bilobrk, Josip Barisic, Dino Coric, Slavko Bralic, Stipo Markovic, Josip Coric (59' Danijel Kozul), Stjepan Loncar (69' Josip Corluka), Luka Begonja, Dejan Cabraja (90+4' Toni Nikic), Luka Menalo, Ivan Krstanovic. Coach: Denis Coric.
Referee: Zaven Hovhannisyan (ARM)   Attendance: 1,820.

06.07.17   Stadion Mladost, Strumica: FK Pelister – Lech Poznan 0-3 (0-1)
FK Pelister: Marko Jovanovski, Kristijan Tosevski, Blagojce Ljamcevski, Martin Kovachev, Goce Todorovski (46' Lucas), Riste Markoski (60' Matej Cvetanoski), Oliver Peev, Dimitar Iliev, Fernando Silva, Baze Ilijoski, Filip Petrov (76' Ive Trifunovski). Coach: Naci Sensoy.
Lech Poznan: Jasmin Buric, Robert Gumny, Lasse Nielsen, Volodymyr Kostevych, Abdul Tetteh, Lukasz Tralka, Radoslaw Majewski (64' Darko Jevtic), Maciej Gajos, Nicki Bille Nielsen (70' Kamil Józwiak), Mario Situm (46' Maciej Makuszewski), Nicklas Bärkroth. Coach: Nenad Bjelica.
Goals: 39' Lukasz Tralka 0-1, 66' Darko Jevtic 0-2, 77' Kamil Józwiak 0-3.
Referee: François Letexier (FRA)   Attendance: 750.

06.07.17   Zemgalas Olimpiskā Centra, Jelgava: FK Jelgava – Ferencvárosi TC 0-1 (0-1)
FK Jelgava: Kaspars Ikstens, Endijs Slampe, Valērijs Redjko, Dmitrijs Klimasevics, Ante Bakmaz (69' Evaldas Razulis), Mārcis Oss, Valdo Alhinho (88' Artis Lazdins), Glebs Kluskins, Kevin Kauber, Artis Jaudzems (57' Mindaugas Grigaravicius), Rafael Ledesma Gaúcho. Coach: Alexandru Curtianu.
Ferencvárosi TC: Dénes Dibusz, Julian Koch, Endre Botka (75' Tamás Hajnal), Leandro de Almeida, Zoltán Gera (75' Kornél Csernik), Fernando Gorriarán, Amadou Moutari, Gergö Lovrencsics, Lukász Böle, Tamás Priskin, Roland Varga (71' Rui Pedro). Coach: Thomas Doll.
Goal: 37' Tamás Priskin 0-1.
Referee: Dumitru Muntean (MOL)   Attendance: 1,400.

06.07.17   Trening centar Petar Milosevski, Skopje: FK Rabotnicki – SP Tre Penne 6-0 (2-0)
FK Rabotnicki: Damjan Siskovski, Dejan Mitrev, Sebastián Herrera, Vance Sikov, Moncilo
Raso (61' Tomislav Iliev), Suad Sahiti (80' Florian Kadriu), Filip Duranski (69' Emir Sahiti),
Bojan Najdenov, Dusko Trajcevski, Stojanco Velinov, Kire Markoski.
Coach: Viktor Trenevski.
SP Tre Penne: Mattia Migani, Dario Merendino (82' Davide Succi), Davide Cesarini, Andrea
Rossi, Stefano Fraternali, Luca Patregnani, Nicola Gai, Mirko Palazzi, Andrea Moretti (65'
Riccardo Santini), Michele Simoncelli (73' Pietro Calzolari), Marco Martini.
Coach: Luigi Bizzotto.
Goals: 28' Suad Sahiti 1-0, 43', 59' Bojan Najdenov 2-0, 3-0, 71' Kire Markoski 4-0,
82', 83' Stojanco Velinov 5-0, 6-0.
Referee: Manfredas Lukjancukas (LTU)   Attendance: 500.

06.07.17   Klaipédosmiesto Centrinis, Klaipeda: FK Atlantas – FK Kairat 1-2 (1-2)
FK Atlantas: Deividas Mikelionis, Justas Raziūnas, Mantas Fridrikas, Edgaras Zarskis,
Domantas Simkus (82' Dovydas Norvilas), Rokas Gedminas (79' Skirmantas Rakauskas),
Markas Beneta, Andrei Ciofu, David Andronic, Yuriy Vereshchak (68' Donatas Kazlauskas),
Tadas Labukas. Coaches: Konstantin Sarsaniya & Sergey Savchenkov.
FK Kairat: Vladimir Plotnikov, Timur Rudosselskiy, Eldos Akhmetov, Gafurzhan Suyombaev,
Islambek Kuat, Mikhail Bakaev, Ivo Ilicevic (46' Isael), Ákos Elek, Gerard Gohou (46' Chuma
Anene), Bauyrzhan Turysbek, Andrey Arshavin (82' Aybol Abiken).
Coach: Kakhaber Tskhadadze.
Goals: 12' Andrei Ciofu 1-0, 35' Ivo Ilicevic 1-1 (p), 39' Gerard Gohou 1-2.
Referee: Nicolas Laforge (BEL)   Attendance: 1,450.

06.07.17   Telia 5G-areena, Helsinki: HJK Helsinki – Gap Connah's Quay FC 3-0 (2-0)
HJK Helsinki: Thomas Dähne, Hannu Patronen, Juha Pirinen, Rafinha, Aapo Halme, Sebastian
Dahlström (81' Vincent Onovo), Anthony Annan, Moshtagh Yaghoubi, Demba Savage,
Ousman Jallow (85' Evans Mensah), Akseli Pelvas (90+2' Lucas Lingman).
Coach: Mika Lehkosuo.
Gap Connah's Quay FC: John Danby, Kai Edwards, George Horan, Danny Harrison, Sean
Smith, Mike Pearson, Declan Poole (60' Ryan Wignall), Callum Morris (83' Matthew
Williams), Nathan Woolfe, Jay Owen (71' Jake Phillips), Michael Wilde.
Coach: Andrew Morrison.
Goals: 11' Moshtagh Yaghoubi 1-0, 31', 55' Akseli Pelvas 2-0, 3-0.
Referee: Furkat Atazhanov (KAZ)   Attendance: 6,103.

06.07.17   A. Le Coq Arena, Tallinn: FC Flora – NK Domzale 2-3 (2-1)
FC Flora: Mait Toom, Märten Kuusk, Madis Vihmann, Joonas Tamm (78' Maksim Gussev),
Martin Miller, Brent Lepistu, Rauno Sappinen (63' Roman Sobtsenko), Mihkel Ainsalu,
Joseph Saliste, Zakaria Beglarishvili (67' Mark Anders Lepik), Rauno Alliku.
Coach: Arno Pijpers.
NK Domzale: Dejan Milic, Matija Sirok, Miha Blazic, Gaber Dobrovoljc, Jure Balkovec,
Amedej Vetrih, Jan Repas, Jure Matjasic (69' Luka Volaric), Zeni Husmani, Ivan Firer (81'
Zan Zuzek), Lovro Bizjak (53' Senijad Ibricic). Coach: Simon Rozman.
Goals: 1' Zakaria Beglarishvili 1-0, 22' Mihkel Ainsalu 2-0, 40' Ivan Firer 2-1,
86' Senijad Ibricic 2-2 (p), 89' Jure Balkovec 2-3.
Referee: Horatiu Fesnic (ROM)   Attendance: 818.

06.07.17   Vazgen Sargsyan anvan Hanrapetakan, Yerevan:
Gandzasar FC – FK Mladost Podgorica 0-3 (0-0)
Gandzasar FC: Grigor Meliksetyan, Alex Júnior, Damir Memovic, Hayk Ishkhanyan,
Vaspurak Minasyan, Wbeymar Angulo (62' Gegham Harutyunyan), Lubambo Musonda,
Christopher Mandiangu (72' Sargis Shahinyan), Wal, Artur Yuspashyan, Claudir (81' Vardan
Bakalyan). Coach: Ashot Barseghyan.
FK Mladost Podgorica: Damir Ljuljanovic, Ivan Novovic, Stefan Cicmil, Nikola Vukcevic,
Milos Krkotic (90' Marko Burzanovic), Stefan Bukorac (62' Mirko Raicevic), Milan Djurisic,
Andrija Kaludjerovic, Marko Cetkovic, Ivan Knezevic, Zoran Petrovic (82' Ognjen
Stijepovic). Coach: Dejan Vukicevic.
Goals: 68' Zoran Petrovic 0-1, 90+2' Andrija Kaludjerovic 0-2, 90+4' Mirko Raicevic 0-3.
Referee: Sascha Amhof (SUI)   Attendance: 2,470.

06.07.17   Vilniaus LFF stadionas, Vilnius: FK Trakai – St. Johnstone FC 1-0 (0-0)
FK Trakai: Ignas Plūkas, Justinas Janusevskis, Alma Wakili, Mychailo Shyshka, Arūnas
Klimavicius, Valdemars Borovskis (81' Svajūnas Cyzas), Modestas Vorobjovas, Deividas
Cesnauskis (60' Pavel Kruk), Oscar Dorley, Aleksandr Bychenok, Maksim Maksimov (90+4'
Lajo Traore). Coach: Oleg Vasilenko.
St. Johnstone FC: Zander Clark, Scott Tanser, Joe Shaughnessy, Ricky Foster, Ally Gilchrist,
Blair Alston (76' Graham Cummins), Chris Millar (63' Steven MacLean), Murray Davidson,
Stefan Scougall (74' David Wotherspoon), Liam Craig, Chris Kane. Coach: Tommy Wright.
Goal: 88' Maksim Maksimov 1-0.
Referee: Stanislav Todorov (BUL)   Attendance: 2,000.
Sent off: 57' Arūnas Klimavicius.

06.07.17   OmaSp Stadion, Seinäjoki: SJK Seinäjoki – KR Reykjavík 0-2 (0-0)
SJK Seinäjoki: Mihkel Aksalu, Dani Hatakka, Jarkko Hurme, Marc Vales (78' Obed Malolo),
Timo Tahvanainen, Johannes Laaksonen, Tomas Hradecky (58' Aristote Mboma), Facundo
Guichón (73' Matti Klinga), Mehmet Hetemaj, Erfan Zeneli, Billy Ions.
Coaches: José Roca & Sixten Boström.
KR Reykjavík: Stefán Magnússon, Arnór Adalsteinsson, Gunnar Thor Gunnarsson, Skúli Jón
Fridgeirsson (90+2' Óliver Dagur Thorlacius), Aron Jósepsson, Morten Beck, Finnur
Margeirsson, Pálmi Pálmason, Óskar Hauksson, Tobias Thomsen (84' Gudmundur Andri
Tryggvason), Kennie Chopart (80' Robert Sandnes). Coach: Willum Thórsson.
Goals: 51' Pálmi Pálmason 0-1, 83' Tobias Thomsen 0-2.
Referee: Irfan Peljto (BIH)   Attendance: 4,511.

06.07.17 ` Stadions Daugava, Liepāja: FK Liepāja – Crusaders FC 2-0 (1-0)
FK Liepāja: Valentīns Ralkevics, Sady Guèye, Stanislav Lebamba, Dario Tomic (70' Kristaps
Grebis), Leonel Strumia, Dmitrijs Hmizs (60' Valerijs Afanasjevs), Cristian Torres, Giorgi
Eristavi, Marks Kurtiss (67' Mārtins Kigurs), Artūrs Karasausks, Seydina Keita.
Coach: Tamaz Pertia.
Crusaders FC: Brian Jensen, Billy Joe Burns, Howard Beverland, Colin Coates, Sean Ward,
Declan Caddell (59' Jordan Forsythe), Rodney Brown, Matthew Snoddy, Michael Carvill (46'
Gavin Whyte), Jordan Owens, Paul Heatley. Coach: Stephen Baxter.
Goals: 33' Giorgi Eristavi 1-0 (p), 90+4' Artūrs Karasausks 2-0.
Referee: Suren Baliyan (ARM)   Attendance: 2,310.

FK Liepāja won on away goals.

265

06.07.17   Gradski stadion, Ruse: FC Dunav Ruse – Irtysh Pavlodar 0-2 (0-1)
FC Dunav Ruse: Stanislav Antonov, Mario Petkov, Petar Patev, Mihail Milchev, Hristofor
Hubchev, Samir Ayass (71' Andreas Vasev), Vasil Shopov (50' Dimitar Georgiev), Diyan
Dimov, Birsent Karagaren (56' Yulian Nenov), Miroslav Budinov, Branimir Kostadinov.
Coach: Plamen Donev.
Irtysh Pavlodar: David Loriya, Aleksandr Kislitsyn, Rodrigo Antônio, Damir Dautov (76'
Ruslan Esimov), Stefan Zivkovic, Mario Maslac, Aslan Darabaev, Kazbek Geteriev, Ismaël
Fofana (60' Milos Stamenkovic), Carlos Fonseca, Igor Bugaev (90+1' Franck Dja Djédjé).
Coach: Dimitar Dimitrov.
Goals: 6' Mario Maslac 0-1, 88' Aslan Darabaev 0-2.
Referee: Jovan Kaludjerovic (MNE)   Attendance: 5,100.

06.07.17   Stadion Lazur, Burgas: Botev Plovdiv – FK Partizani 1-0 (1-0)
Botev Plovdiv: Ivan Cvorovic, Tsvetomir Panov, Victor Genev, Meledje Omnibes (88' Serkan
Yusein), Jordan Minev, Plamen Dimov, Felipe Brisola (78' Álvaro), Todor Nedelev, Toni
Tasev (64' Krum Stoyanov), Lachezar Baltanov, Omar Kossoko. Coach: Nikolai Kirov.
FK Partizani: Alban Bekim Hoxha, Gëzim Krasniqi, Blerim Kotobelli, Labinot Ibrahimi,
Arbnor Fejzullahu, Sodiq Atanda, Idriz Batha (65' Mentor Mazrekaj), Lorenc Trashi (75'
Renaldo Kalari), Realdo Fili (81' Xhevair Sukaj), Gerhard Progni, Emiljano Vila.
Coach: Sulejman Starova.
Goal: 22' Felipe Brisola 1-0.
Referee: Alper Ulusoy (TUR)   Attendance: 3,560.

06.07.17   Stadión Pasienky, Bratislava: Slovan Bratislava – Pyunik FC 5-0 (2-0)
Slovan Bratislava: Dominik Greif, Boris Sekulic, Milan Rundic, Kornel Saláta, Vukan
Savicevic, Joeri de Kamps, Frantisek Kubík, Samuel Sefcík (63' Mitchell Schet), Jakub Mares
(71' Uros Damnjanovic), Filip Holosko, Aleksandar Cavric (63' Róbert Vittek).
Coach: Ivan Vukomanovic.
Pyunik FC: Gor Manukyan, Serob Grigoryan, Artur Kartashyan, Aram Shakhnazaryan, Armen
Manucharyan, Robert Hakobyan (80' Hovhannes Nazaryan), Narek Aslanyan, Petros
Avetisyan, Alik Arakelyan, Hovhannes Harutyunyan (27' Vahagn Hayrapetyan), Vardan
Poghosyan (71' Hovhannes Poghosyan). Coach: Armen Gyulbudaghyants.
Goals: 10', 23' Jakub Mares 1-0, 2-0, 62' Joeri de Kamps 3-0, 64' Jakub Mares 4-0,
66' Boris Sekulic 5-0.
Referee: Bojan Nikolic (SER)   Attendance: 1,602.

06.07.17   Givi Kiladze Stadium, Kutaisi: Torpedo Kutaisi – FK AS Trenčín 0-3 (0-1)
Torpedo Kutaisi: Roin Kvaskhvadze, Vazha Tabatadze, Davit Khurtsilava (65' Guram
Adamadze), Giorgi Guruli, Giorgi Kimadze, Tornike Kapanadze, Giorgi Kukhianidze, Grigol
Dolidze, Merab Gigauri, David Khurtsidze (46' Oleg Mamasakhlisi), Beka Tughushi (57' Mate
Kvirkvia). Coach: Kakha Shkhetiani.
FK AS Trenčín: Adrián Chovan, Lukás Skovajsa, Rodney Klooster (76' Martin Sulek), Peter
Klescík, Abdul Zubairu, Jamie Lawrence (81' Keston Julien), Desley Ubbink, Achraf El
Mahdioui, Giorgi Beridze, Hillary Gong, Antonio Mance (68' Hamza Catakovic).
Coach: Martin Sevela.
Goals: 21' Hillary Gong 0-1, 49' Giorgi Beridze 0-2, 64' Hillary Gong 0-3.
Referee: Mario Zebec (CRO)   Attendance: 4,221.

266

06.07.17   Stade de la Ville de Differdange, Differdange:
FC Differdange 03 – Zira FK 1-2 (1-0)
FC Differdange 03: Julien Weber, Tom Siebenaler (84' Gilles Bettmer), David Vandenbroeck, Mathias Jänisch, Geoffrey Franzoni, David Fleurival, Jordann Yéyé, Mounir Hamzaoui (71' Yannick Bastos), Chadli Amri (60' Dwayn Holter), Nicolas Perez, Gauthier Caron. Coach: Pascal Carzaniga.
Zira FK: Anar Nazirov, Josef Boum, Adil Naghiyev, Gabriel Matei, Jovan Krneta, Tamkin Khalilzade, Vugar Mustafayev, Rashad Sadiqov (60' Milan Djuric), David Manga, Kervens Belfort (80' Aleksandr Shemonayev), Richard Gadze (76' Nijat Gurbanov). Coach: Aykhan Abbasov.
Goals: 10' David Vandenbroeck 1-0, 64' David Manga 1-1, 68' Richard Gadze 1-2.
Referee: Boris Marhefka (SVK)   Attendance: 1,626.

06.07.17   Rheinpark Stadion, Vaduz: FC Vaduz – Bala Town 3-0 (3-0)
FC Vaduz: Peter Jehle, Thomas Konrad, Tomislav Puljic, Nils von Niederhäusern, Axel Borgmann, Diego Ciccone, Marco Mathys, Robin Kamber, Maurice Brunner (60' Yones Felfel), Philipp Muntwiler (67' Maximilian Göppel), Aldin Turkes (46' Franz Burgmeier). Coach: Roland Vrabec.
Bala Town: Ashley Morris, Anthony Stephens, Stuart Jones Sr. (43' Will Bell), Stuart Jones Jr., Lee Owens, Nathan Burke, Ian Sheridan (76' Mike Hayes), Chris Venables, David Thompson, Kieran Smith, Les Davies (60' Ryan Wade). Coach: Colin Caton.
Goals: 22', 39' Aldin Turkes 1-0, 2-0, 43' Marco Mathys 3-0.
Referee: Jari Järvinen (FIN)   Attendance: 621.

06.07.17   Futbalovy stadión MFK Ruzomberok, Ruzomberok:
MFK Ruzomberok – Vojvodina 2-0 (0-0)
MFK Ruzomberok: Matús Macík, Ján Maslo, Simon Kupec, Peter Maslo, Jozef Menich, Kristi Qose, Peter Gál-Andrezly, Matej Kochan, Erik Daniel (90+1' Dominik Kruzliak), Marek Sapara (58' Dalibor Takác), Milos Lacny (81' Stefan Gerec). Coach: Norbert Hrncár.
Vojvodina: Emil Rockov, Bogdan Planic, Dzenan Burekovic, Nikola Kovacevic, Ivan Lakicevic, Aleksandar Mesarovic (86' Milan Spremo), Nemanja Subotic (71' Kristijan Zivkovic), Filip Malbasic, Marko Vukasovic, Dusan Jovancic (73' Milan Mirosavljev), Nikola Trujic. Coach: Nenad Vanic.
Goals: 67' Nikola Kovacevic 1-0 (og), 87' Ján Maslo 2-0.
Referee: Dennis Higler (HOL)   Attendance: 4,486.

06.07.17   Friends Arena, Solna: AIK Solna – KÍ Klaksvík 5-0 (5-0)
AIK Solna: Oscar Linnér, Per Karlsson (64' Sauli Väisänen), Nils-Eric Johansson, Jesper Nyholm, Kristoffer Olsson, Daniel Sundgren, Stefan Ishizaki (46' Nebiyou Perry), Anton Jönsson Salétros, Amin Affane, Denni Avdic, Eero Markkanen (86' Daniel Mushitu Mwinkeu). Coach: Rikard Norling.
KÍ Klaksvík: Meinhardt Joensen, Ísak Simonsen (81' Hjalgrím Elttør), Jonas Rasmussen, Ahmed Mujdragic, Ólavur Niclasen, Albert Adu (90+1' Steinbjørn Olsen), Hørdur Askham, Jákup Andreasen, Semir Hadzibulic, Jóannes Bjartalíd, Páll Klettskard. Coach: Mikkjal Thomassen.
Goals: 3', 6' Eero Markkanen 1-0, 2-0, 16' Stefan Ishizaki 3-0, 24' Kristoffer Olsson 4-0, 42' Eero Markkanen 5-0.
Referee: Laurent Kopriwa (LUX)   Attendance: 6,257.

06.07.17   Dalga Arena, Baku: Inter Baku – Mladost Lucani 2-0 (1-0)
Inter Baku: Sälahät Agayev, Dênis, Slavik Alkhasov (90+1' Sertan Taskin), Ilkin Qirtimov,
Adrian Scarlatache, Tarlan Guliyev, Nizami Hajiyev, Elnur Abdullayev (80' Mirhuseyn
Seyidov), Fuad Bayramov, Pardis Fardjad-Azad (85' Samir Zargarov), Rauf Aliyev.
Coach: Zaur Svanadze.
Mladost Lucani: Nemanja Krznaric, Ivan Milosevic (39' Ivan Pesic), Nikola Andric, Bogdan
Milosevic, Sasa Jovanovic, Nenad Gavric (46' Nenad Marinkovic), Aleksandr Pejovic,
Vladimir Radivojevic, Janko Tumbasevic, Milos Satara, Milos Trifunovic (70' Ivan
Markovic). Coach: Nenad Milovanovic.
Goals: 23' Dênis 1-0, 74' Nizami Hajiyev 2-0.
Referee: Mikola Balakin (UKR)   Attendance: 3,150.
Sent off: 45+3' Aleksandr Pejovic.

06.07.17   Svangaskard, Toftir: NSÍ Runavík – Dinamo Minsk 0-2 (0-1)
NSÍ Runavík: Símun Rógvi Hansen, Per Langgaard, Jens Joensen (70' Jan Ellingsgaard), Einar
Tróndargjógv Hansen, Pól Justinussen, Karl Løkin (78' Jónleif Højgaard), Árni Frederiksberg,
Jann Benjaminsen, Bárdur Jógvansson-Hansen, Betuel Hansen, Klæmint Olsen (53' Petur
Knudsen). Coach: Anders Gerber.
Dinamo Minsk: Andrey Klimovich, Igor Kuzmenok, Nino Galovic, Aleksandr Sachivko,
Roman Begunov, Nikola Lekovic (90+2' Vadim Demidovich), Artem Bykov, Oleksandr
Noyok, Nikola Lukic (16' Yuriy Ostroukh), Anton Saroka, Vladimir Khvashchinskiy (89'
Uros Nikolic). Coach: Sergei Gurenko.
Goals: 32', 90+5' Anton Saroka 0-1, 0-2 (p).
Referee: Iwan Griffith (WAL)   Attendance: 557
Sent off: 7' Artem Bykov.

06.07.17   Nantporth, Bangor: Bangor City – Lyngby BK 0-3 (0-3)
Bangor City: Connor Roberts, Tom Kennedy, Anthony Miley, Laurence Wilson, Paul
Connolly (25' Luke Wall), Gary Taylor-Fletcher, Damien Allen, Danny Gosset, Steven Hewitt,
Dean Rittenberg (73' David Henry), Brayden Shaw (73' Sion Edwards).
Coach: Kevin Nicholson.
Lyngby BK: Mikkel Andersen, Thomas Christensen, Michael Lumb (46' Casper Højer
Nielsen), Thomas Sørensen, Martin Ørnskov (43' Mathias Hebo Rasmussen), Jesper
Christjansen, Lasse Fosgaard, Mikkel Rygaard Jensen, Jeppe Brandrup, Jeppe Kjær, Kristoffer
Larsen (46' David Boysen). Coach: David Nielsen.
Goals: 3' Kristoffer Larsen 0-1, 37' Jeppe Kjær 0-2, 44' Kristoffer Larsen 0-3.
Referee: Donatas Rumsas (LTU)   Attendance: 1,089.

06.07.17   Gundadalur, Tórshavn: B36 Tórshavn – JK Nõmme Kalju 1-2 (0-1)
B36 Tórshavn: Tórdur Thomsen, Odmar Færø, Gestur Dam (65' Alex Mellemgaard), Erlendur
Magnussen (87' Bjarni Petersen), Andrias Eriksen, Eli Nielsen, Hannes Agnarsson (77'
Christian Mouritsen), Róaldur Jakobsen, Benjamin Heinesen, Patrik Johannesen, Lukasz
Cieslewicz. Coach: Jákup á Borg.
JK Nõmme Kalju: Vitali Teles, Maximiliano Uggè, Andrei Sidorenkov, Deniss Tjapkin,
Réginald Mbu-Alidor, Artur Valikaev, Igor Subbotin (90+5' Nikolai Masitsev), Karl Mööl,
Artjom Dmitrijev, Liliu (71' Tarmo Neemelo), Robert Kirss (90+2' Trevor Elhi).
Coach: Sergey Frantsev.
Goals: 18 Liliu 0-1, 52' Benjamin Heinesen 1-1, 88' Artur Valikaev 1-2.
Referee: Espen Eskås (NOR)   Attendance: 1,725.

06.07.17   Asim Ferhatovic Hase, Sarajevo: FK Sarajevo – FC Zaria 2-1 (2-0,2-1)
FK Sarajevo: Bojan Pavlovic, Sasa Novakovic, Marko Mihojevic, Almir Bekic, Advan
Kadusic (58' Dusan Hodzic), Nermin Crnkic, Elvis Saric, Amar Rahmanovic (73' Nemanja
Andusic), Anel Hebibovic (87' Perica Ivetic), Samir Radovac, Mico Kuzmanovic.
Coach: Mehmed Janjos.
FC Zaria: Serghei Pascenco, Victor Golovatenco, Andrey Novicov, Maxim Focsa, Sergiy
Zagynaylov, Vadim Rata, Igor Tigîrlas (46' Alexandru Suvorov), Oleg Ermak, Rubén Gómez
(91' Tihomir Trifonov), Georgi Ovsyannikov (73' Andrii Slinkin), Maxim Mihaliov.
Coach: Vlad Goian.
Goals: 13' Anel Hebibovic 1-0, 35' Advan Kadusic 2-0 (p), 60' Sergiy Zagynaylov 2-1.
Referee: Aleksandrs Anufrijevs (LAT)   Attendance: 12,000.
Sent off: 90' Andrey Novicov.

FC Zaria won 6-5 on penalties following extra time.

Penalties: Hodzic 1-0, Slinkin 1-1, Ivetic 2-1, Suvorov 2-2, Mihojevic missed, Golovatenco
2-3, Bekic 3-3, Zaynaylov 3-4, Saric 4-4, Ermak missed, Andusic 5-4, Mihaliov
5-5, Kuzmanovic missed, Focsa 5-6.

06.07.17   Stadiumi Olimpik Adem Jashari, Mitrovica:
Prishtina KF – IFK Norrköping 0-1 (0-0)
Prishtina KF: Alban Muçiqi, Armend Dallku, Debatik Çurri, Liridon Leci, Diar Miftaraj, Laurit
Boshnjaku, Lorik Maxhuni (74' Bleon Sekiraqa), Mërgim Pefqeli (68' Blend Baftiu), Liridon
Fetahaj (59' Përparim Osmani), Gauthier Mankenda, Khalid Abdul Basit. Coach: Arsim Thaçi.
IFK Norrköping: Michael Langer, Jón Fjóluson, Linus Wahlqvist, Nikola Tkalcic, Andreas
Johansson, Simon Skrabb, Eric Smith, Gudmundur Thórarinsson (71' Andreas Hadenius),
Niclas Eliasson (59' Alfons Sampsted), Filip Dagerstål, Sebastian Andersson.
Coach: Jens Gustafsson.
Goal: 71' Sebastian Andersson 0-1.
Referee: Jens Maae (DEN)   Attendance: 3,358.

06.07.17   Stadion Stozice, Ljubljana: Olimpija Ljubljana – Vaasan PS 0-1 (0-0)
Olimpija Ljubljana: Nejc Vidmar, Alexandru Cretu, Branko Ilic (76' Danijel Miskic), Nemanja
Mitrovic, Dino Stiglec, Goran Brkic (70' Luka Gajic), Kenan Bajric, Tomislav Tomic, Nathan
Oduwa, Issah Abass, Leon Benko (63' Blessing Eleke). Coach: Igor Biscan.
Vaasan PS: Marko Meerits, Timi Lahti, Mikko Viitikko, Veli Lampi, Jesper Engström (75'
Markus Jürgenson), Jerry Voutilainen, Juho Lähde (46' Ebrima Sohna), Jonas Levänen, Joonas
Vahtera (65' Sebastian Strandvall), Juha Hakola, Steven Morrissey. Coach: Petri Vuorinen.
Goal: 66' Sebastian Strandvall 0-1.
Referee: Georgios Kominis (GRE)   Attendance: 4,700.

06.07.17   Sportni Park, Nova Gorica: ND Gorica – Shirak FC 2-2 (1-1)
ND Gorica: Grega Sorcan, Uros Celcer, Miha Gregoric, Tine Kavcic, Alen Jogan, Rifet Kapic
(87' Leon Marinic), Jaka Kolenc (73' Jan Hulmar), Rok Grudina, Dejan Zigon, Andrija
Filipovic (74' Tilen Nagode), Bede Osuji. Coach: Miran Srebrnic.
Shirak FC: Anatoly Ayvazov, Edward Kpodo, Marko Prljevic (35' Artyom Mikailyan), Robert
Darbinyan, Solomon Udo, Oumarou Kaina (74' Gagik Poghosyan), Igor Stanojevic (59'
Aleksandar Ilic), Aghvan Davoyan, Mohamed Kaba, Kyrian Nwabueze, Vahan Bichakhchyan.
Coach: Vardan Bichakhchyan.
Goals: 13' Marko Prljevic 1-0 (og), 34' Mohamed Kaba 1-1, 56' Vahan Bichakhchyan 1-2,
90+2' Bede Osuji 2-2.
Referee: Peter Kjærsgaard-Andersen (DEN)   Attendance: 1,200.
Sent off: 89' Robert Darbinyan, 90+3' Aghvan Davoyan.

Marko Prljevic missed a penalty kick (13').

06.07.17   CASHPOINT Arena, Altach: SCR Altach – Chikhura Sachkhere 1-1 (1-0)
SCR Altach: Martin Kobras, Lucas Galvão, Philipp Netzer, Emanuel Sakic, Benedikt Zech,
Christian Gebauer (69' Kristijan Dobras), Patrick Salomon, Simon Piesinger, Stefan Nutz,
Louis N'Gwat-Mahop (84' Emanuel Schreiner), Hannes Aigner (66' Adrian Grbic).
Coach: Klaus Schmidt.
Chikhura Sachkhere: Dino Hamzic, Levan Kakubava, Lasha Chikvaidze, Shota Kashia,
Tornike Gorgiashvili (61' George Ivanishvili), Giorgi Ganugrava (82' Besik Dekanoidze),
Giorgi Koripadze, Zaza Chelidze, Mikheil Sardalishvili, Dimitri Tatanashvili, Nikoloz
Gelashvili (77' Papuna Poniava). Coach: Soso Pruidze.
Goals: 29' Stefan Nutz 1-0, 56' Dimitri Tatanashvili 1-1.
Referee: Veaceslav Banari (MOL)   Attendance: 3,335.

06.07.17   Stadion Miejski, Bialystok: Jagiellonia Bialystok – Dinamo Batumi 4-0 (0-0)
Jagiellonia Bialystok: Marián Kelemen, Lukasz Burliga, Guilherme, Guti, Ivan Runje, Jacek
Góralski (82' Damian Szymanski), Taras Romanchuk, Dmytro Khomchenovskiy, Arvydas
Novikovas (74' Przemyslaw Mystkowski), Fiodor Cernych, Cillian Sheridan (85' Lukasz
Sekulski). Coach: Ireneusz Mamrot.
Dinamo Batumi: Anatoliy Timofeev, Anzor Sukhiashvili, Dato Kvirkvelia, Archil Tvildiani
(87' Beka Varshanidze), Nica Mgeladze, Boris Makharadze, Giorgi Kavtaradze (62' Otari
Martsvaladze), Temur Shonia, Elguja Grigalashvili (78' Mirza Partenadze), Tornike
Tarkhnishvili, Jaroslav Kvasov. Coach: Konstantin Frolov.
Goals: 58' Guti 1-0, 81' Fiodor Cernych 2-0, 88' Ivan Runje 3-0, 90+3' Lukasz Sekulski 4-0.
Referee: Vuriy Mozharovsky (UKR)   Attendance: 13,538.
Sent off: 75' Tornike Tarkhnishvili.

06.07.17   Szusza Ferenc Stadion, Budapest: Budapesti Vasas – Beitar Jerusalem 0-3 (0-1)
Budapesti Vasas: Gergely Nagy, Kire Ristevski, Szilveszter Hangya, Felix Burmeister, Tamás
Vaskó, Mohamed Remili (72' Martin Ádám), Márk Kleisz, Máté Vida, Tamás Kulcsár, Evgen
Pavlov, Benedek Murka (68' Donát Szivacski). Coach: Michael Oenning.
Beitar Jerusalem: Boris Kleyman, Antoine Conte, David Keltjens, Dan Mori, Tal Kachila,
Marcel Heister, Idan Vered (82' Gaëtan Varenne), Claudemir, Hen Ezra (62' Georginho), Erik
Sabo, Itay Shechter (74' Yossi Benayoun). Coach: Sharon Mimer.
Goals: 10', 61' Hen Ezra 0-1, 0-2, 90+1' Gaëtan Varenne 0-3.
Referee: Fábio Veríssimo (POR)   Attendance: 4,016.

270

06.07.17   Stadion Kraj Bistrice, Niksic: FK Sutjeska – Levski Sofia 0-0
FK Sutjeska: Vladan Giljen, Nemanja Nedic, Milos Bakrac, Stevan Kovacevic (61' Bojan Bozovic), Stefan Loncar (87' Igor Pocek), Nikola Stijepovic, Milos Vucic, Veljko Vukovic, Stefan Denkovic, Bozo Markovic, Dejan Zarubica (73' Vladan Bubanja).
Coach: Nikola Rakojevic.
Levski Sofia: Bozhidar Mitrev, Dimitar Pirgov, Ivan Goranov, Milos Cvetkovic, David Jablonsky, Roman Procházka, Georgi Angelov, Vasil Panayotov, Francis Narh (90+3' Aleks Borimirov), Junior Mpia Mapuku (77' Sergiu Bus), Babatunde Adeniji (82' Miki Orachev).
Coach: Nikolai Mitov.
Referee: Demetrios Masias (CYP)   Attendance: 3,500.

06.07.17   Estadi Comunal d'Andorra la Vella, Andorra la Vella:
UE Sant Julià – KF Skënderbeu 0-5 (0-2)
UE Sant Julià: Manuel Vidal Rodriguez, Mateo Rodriguez Firpo (74' Leonel Alves), Iván Vigo, Jamal Zarioh Taouil, Francisco Rodriguez Girau, Luis Blanco, Eric Rodríguez Barcelo, Nikola Zugic (46' Rafael Brito), José Villanueva (46' Luigi San Nicolas), Fábio Serra Alves, Noah Baffoe. Coach: Luis Blanco.
KF Skënderbeu: Orges Shehi, Gledi Mici, Bajram Jashanica, Tefik Osmani (51' Bakary Nimaga), Kristi Vangjeli, Marko Radas, Enis Gavazaj (62' Donjet Shkodra), Liridon Latifi, Sabien Lilaj, Goran Vujovic (46' Gjergj Muzaka), Segun Adeniyi. Coach: Ilir Daja.
Goals: 2' Goran Vujovic 0-1, 38' Segun Adeniyi 0-2, 79' Liridon Latifi 0-3, 90+1' Kristi Vangjeli 0-4, 90+3' Liridon Latifi 0-5.
Referee: Kai Steen (NOR)   Attendance: 700.

06.07.17   Hibernians Ground, Paola: Floriana FC – Crvena Zvezda 3-3 (1-1)
Floriana FC: Matthew Grech, Enrico Pepe (37' Noël Nyason), Arthur Henrique, James Baldacchino, Clyde Borg (81' Nicolas Hernan Chiesa), Sebastián Nayar, Maurizio Vella (90+2' Daniel Agius), Stephen Pisani, Ignacio Varela, Júninho, Mario Fontanella.
Coach: Giovanni Tedesco.
Crvena Zvezda: Filip Manojlovic, Abraham Frimpong, Filip Stojkovic, Dusan Andjelkovic, Vujadin Savic, Damien Le Tallec, Uros Racic, Slavoljub Srnic (90+1' Luka Ilic), Richmond Boakye, Nemanja Milic (64' Nenad Milijas), Ricardinho (73' Marko Gobeljic).
Coach: Vladan Milojevic.
Goals: 12' Richmond Boakye 0-1, 45+3' Stephen Pisani 1-1 (p), 70' Richmond Boakye 1-2, 76' Nenad Milijas 1-3, 78' Maurizio Vella 2-3, 84' Ignacio Varela 3-3.
Referee: Georgios Kyzas (GRE)   Attendance: 1,176.
Sent off: 80' Marko Gobeljic, 85' Ignacio Varela.

06.07.17   Stadio Olimpico di Serravalle, Serravalle:
SS Folgore/Falciano – Valletta FC 0-1 (0-0)
SS Folgore/Falciano: Luca Bianchi, Alberto Semprini, Andrea Nucci, Marco Bernardi, Francesco Sartori, Cristian Brolli, Stefano Sacco (62' Luca Bonifazi), Luca Bezzi, Luca Paradisi, Lago Ramiro (87' Luca Rossi), Marco Bernardi (81' Nicolò Venerucci).
Coach: Oscar Lasagni.
Valletta FC: Henry Bonello, Steve Borg, Ryan Camilleri (69' Jean Borg), Juan Gill (81' Kyrian Nwoko), Joseph Zerafa, Romeu (61' Roderick Briffa), Claudio Pani, Santiago Malano, Michael Mifsud, Maximiliano Velasco, Uchenna Umeh. Coach: Zoran Popovic.
Goal: 65' Santiago Malano 0-1.
Referee: Genc Nuza (KOS)   Attendance: 437.

271

06.07.17   Stadion Pod Goricom, Podgorica: FK Zeta – Zeljeznicar Sarajevo 2-2 (1-1)
FK Zeta: Marko Novovic, Igor Vujacic (83' Bojan Aligrudic), Goran Milojko, Bozidar Djukic,
Vasko Kalezic, Aldin Adzovic (72' Balsa Bozovic), Stefan Vukcevic, Nemanja Sekulic, Filip
Kukulicic (66' Nikola Krstovic), Pjeter Ljuljdjuraj, Perisa Pesukic.
Coach: Dusan Vlaisavljevic.
Zeljeznicar Sarajevo: Vedran Kjosevski, Sinisa Stevanovic, Danijel Graovac, Jadranko
Bogicevic, Jovan Blagojevic, Srdan Stanic, Goran Zakaric, Zajko Zeba (85' Denis Zeric),
Ugljesa Radinovic (70' Darko Markovic), Asim Zec, Ivan Lendric (79' Stevo Nikolic).
Coach: Slavko Petrovic.
Goals: 29' Filip Kukulicic 1-0, 32' Goran Zakaric 1-1, 61' Ivan Lendric 1-2,
76' Nikola Krstovic 2-2.
Referee: Tiago Martins (POR)   Attendance: 2,500.

06.07.17   Turner's Cross, Cork: Cork City – FC Levadia 4-2 (1-2)
Cork City: Mark McNulty, Ryan Delaney, Kevin O'Connor, Greb Bolger (85' Achille
Campion), Conor McCormack, Stephen Dooley (78' Shane Griffin), Gearóid Morrissey, Garry
Buckley, Jimmy Keohane, Karl Sheppard (69' Steven Beattie), Seán Maguire.
Coach: John Caulfield.
FC Levadia: Sergei Lepmets, Artjom Artjunin, Igor Dudarev, Maksim Podholjuzin, Marcelin
Gando, Evgeni Kobzar (60' Pavel Marin), João Morelli, Josip Krznaric, Nikita Andreev (87'
Ingemar Teever), Rimo Hunt, Mark Oliver Roosnupp. Coach: Igor Prins.
Goals: 15' Evgeni Kobzar 0-1, 28' Karl Sheppard 1-1, 32' Nikita Andreev 1-2,
46', 86', 90' Seán Maguire 2-2, 3-2, 4-2.
Referee: Gunnar Jarl Jónsson (ISL)   Attendance: 6,314.

06.07.17   Seaview, Belfast: Ballymena United – Odds BK 0-2 (0-0)
Ballymena United: Ross Glendinning (89' Timothy Allen), Tony Kane, Emmet Friars, Johnny
Flynn, Andrew Burns, Michael Gault, Cathair Friel (72' Jonathan McMurray), Conor
McCloskey (85' Neil Lowry), Leroy Millar, Kevin Braniff, Joe McKinney.
Coach: David Jeffrey.
Odds BK: Sondre Lovseth Rossbach, Espen Ruud, Fredrik Semb Berge, Steffen Hagen, John
Kitelano, Martin Broberg (77' Sigurd Haugen), Jone Samuelsen, Fredrik Nordkvelle, Fredrik
Oldrup Jensen, Olivier Occéan (81' Torbjørn Agdestein), Pape Pate Diouf (63' Riku Riski).
Coach: Dag-Eilev Fagermo.
Goals: 79' Leroy Millar 0-1 (og), 88' Sigurd Haugen 0-2.
Referee: Radek Príhoda (CZE)   Attendance: 1,792.

06.07.17   Stadion Gradski vrt, Osijek: NK Osijek – UE Santa Coloma 4-0 (2-0)
NK Osijek: Marko Malenica, Borna Barisic, Mateo Barac, Petar Bockaj (71' Domagoj Pusic),
Mile Skoric, Andrej Lukic, Dmitriy Lepa, Gabrijel Boban (62' Antonio Perosevic), Muzafer
Ejupi, Eros Grezda, Tomislav Sorsa (63' Alen Grgic). Coach: Zoran Zekic.
UE Santa Coloma: José Escalante, Txus Rubio (83' Juan Salomó), David Maneiro, Miguel
Ruiz, Walid Bousenine (57' Jordi Rubio), Cristian Orosa, Sandro Gutiérrez, Boris Antón
Codina, Pedro Reis (68' Víctor Bernat), Gerard Aloy, Sergi Crespo. Coach: Emilio Gomez.
Goals: 8' Muzafer Ejupi 1-0, 40' Borna Barisic 2-0 (p), 56, 62' Petar Bockaj 3-0, 4-0.
Referee: Keith Kennedy (NIR)   Attendance: 4,682.

06.07.17   The Showgrounds, Coleraine: Coleraine FC – FK Haugesund 0-0
Coleraine FC: Christopher Johns, Steven Douglas, Stephen O'Donnell, Ciaron Harkin, Darren McCauley, Josh Carson, Aaron Traynor (83' Matthew Kirk), Jamie McGonigle (80' Ian Parkhill), Adam Mullan, Eoin Bradley (81' James McLaughlin), Bradley Lyons.
Coach: Oran Kearney.
FK Haugesund: Helge Sandvik, Vegard Skjerve, Sverre Bjørkkjær, Filip Kiss (76' Sondre Tronstad), Liban Abdi, Frederik Gytkjær, Tor Andreassen, Alexander Stølås (77' Bruno Leite), Anthony Ikedi, Erik Huseklepp, Johnny Buduson (77' Shuaibu Ibrahim).
Coach: Eirik Horneland.
Referee: Carlos Xista (POR)   Attendance: 944.

06.07.17   The Showgrounds, Sligo: Derry City – FC Midtjylland 1-4 (1-2)
Derry City: Gerard Doherty, Dean Jarvis, Scott Whiteside (72' Sam Todd), Lukas Schubert, Aaron McEneff, Nicky Low, Harry Monaghan, Ben Doherty, Ronan Curtis, Rory Holden (76' Mark Timlin), Nathan Boyle (63' Rory Patterson). Coach: Kenny Shiels.
FC Midtjylland: Jesper Hansen, Zsolt Korcsmár, Marc Hende, Kristian Riis (46' Kian Hansen), André Rømer (70' Rasmus Nissen Kristensen), Tim Sparv, Jakob Poulsen, Janus Drachmann, Simon Kroon (58' Gustav Wikheim), Rilwan Hassan, Ebere Onuachu. Coach: Jess Thorup.
Goals: 7', 38' Ebere Onuachu 0-1, 0-2, 41' Aaron McEneff 1-2, 58' Gustav Wikheim 1-3, 69' Ebere Onuachu 1-4.
Referee: Rade Obrenovic (SVN)   Attendance: 467.

06.07.17   Tallaght Stadium, Dublin: Shamrock Rovers – UMF Stjarnan 1-0 (1-0)
Shamrock Rovers: Tomer Chencinski, Luke Byrne, David Webster, Roberto Lopes, Simon Madden, Trevor Clarke, Ryan Connolly (87' Aaron Bolger), Ronan Finn, Brandon Miele, Gary Shaw (69' Michael O'Connor), Graham Burke (78' David McAllister).
Coach: Stephen Bradley.
UMF Stjarnan: Haraldur Björnsson, Brynjar Gudjónsson, Jósef Kristinn Jósefsson, Jóhann Laxdal, Daníel Laxdal, Baldur Sigurdsson (78' Heidar Ægisson), Eyjólfur Hédinsson, Alex Thór Hauksson (49' Ólafur Finsen), Gudjón Baldvinsson, Hilmar Árni Halldórsson, Hólmbert Fridjónsson (90+3' Máni Hilmarsson). Coaches: Rúnar Sigmundsson & Brynjar Gunnarsson.
Goal: 20' Graham Burke 1-0.
Referee: Glenn Nyberg (SWE)   Attendance: 3,352.

06.07.17   Valsvöllur, Reykjavík: Valur Reykjavík – FK Ventspils 1-0 (0-0)
Valur Reykjavík: Anton Ari Einarsson, Sigurdur Lárusson, Bjarni Eiríksson, Eidur Sigurbjörnsson, Einar Karl Ingvarsson, Haukur Sigurdsson, Kristinn Halldórsson (87' Sveinn Gudjohnsen), Gudjón Lydsson (83' Sindri Björnsson), Orri Ómarsson, Arnar Geirsson, Dion Jeremy Acoff. Coach: Ólafur Jóhannesson.
FK Ventspils: Andrejs Pavlovs, Nikita Kolesovs, Nikola Boranijasevic, Antons Jemelins (47' Rashid Abdul Obuobi), Vadims Zulevs, Jurijs Zigajevs (56' Vitalijs Recickis), Abdullahi Alfa (77' Maksims Uvarenko goalkeeper), Artiom Vaskov, Tosin Aiyegun, Simonas Paulius, Girts Karlsons. Coach: Paul Ashworth.
Goal: 71' Sigurdur Lárusson 1-0.
Referee: Robert Harvey (IRL)   Attendance: 1,129.
Sent off: 76' Andrejs Pavlovs.

273

06.07.17   Estádio Do Algarve, Faro-Loulé (POR):
Lincoln Red Imps – AEK Larnaca 1-1 (1-0)
Lincoln Red Imps: Raúl Navas, Joseph Chipolina, Bernardo Lopes, Roy Chipolina, Fernando
Andrada (60' Jean Garcia), Anthony Bardon, Felix Lopez, Lee Casciaro, Anthony Hernandez
(85' Alain Pons), Pibe (75' Falu Aranda), Diego. Coach: Julio Ribas.
AEK Larnaca: Juan Pablo, Marios Antoniades, Truyols, Català, Carles Soria, Joan Tomás,
Hector Hevel (71' Tete), Vladimir Boljevic, Vincent Laban (46' Jorge Larena), Elvir Maloku,
Nestoras Mitidis (62' Onisiforos Roushias). Coach: Imanol Idiakez.
Goals: 42' Anthony Bardon 1-0, 78' Jorge Larena 1-1 (p).
Referee: Pavel Orel (CZE)   Attendance: 127.

SECOND QUALIFYING ROUND

12.07.17   Dalga Arena, Baku: Inter Baku – CS FOLA Esch 1-0 (0-0)
Inter Baku: Sälahät Agayev, Dênis, Slavik Alkhasov, Ilkin Qirtimov (87' Samir Zargarov),
Adrian Scarlatache, Tarlan Guliyev, Nizami Hajiyev, Elnur Abdullayev (84' Mirhuseyn
Seyidov), Fuad Bayramov, Pardis Fardjad-Azad (79' Mirsayib Abbasov), Rauf Aliyev.
Coach: Zaur Svanadze.
CS FOLA Esch: Thomas Hym, Tom Laterza, Mehdi Kirch, Ryan Klapp (52' Ken Corral),
Julien Klein, Peter Chrappan, Veldin Muharemovic, Jakob Dallevedove, Michel Bechtold
(90+2' Christophe Martín-Suárez), Enis Saiti (71' Stefano Bensi), Samir Hadji.
Coach: Jeff Strasser.
Goal: 89' Mirhuseyn Seyidov 1-0.
Referee: Eitan Shmeulevitch (ISR)   Attendance: 2,407.

13.07.17   Ortaliq Stadion, Pavlodar: Irtysh Pavlodar – Crvena Zvezda 1-1 (0-0)
Irtysh Pavlodar: David Loriya, Aleksandr Kislitsyn (85' Pavel Shabalin), Rodrigo Antônio,
Damir Dautov, Stefan Zivkovic, Milos Stamenkovic, Mario Maslac, Ilya Kalinin (77' Aslan
Darabaev), Kazbek Geteriev, Carlos Fonseca, Igor Bugaev (78' Ismaël Fofana).
Coach: Dimitar Dimitrov.
Crvena Zvezda: Filip Manojlovic, Filip Stojkovic, Dusan Andjelkovic, Vujadin Savic, Branko
Jovicic, Damien Le Tallec, Guélor Kanga (63' Nenad Milijas), Mitchell Donald, Slavoljub
Srnic, Richmond Boakye (90' Uros Racic), Ricardinho (84' John Ruiz).
Coach: Vladan Milojevic.
Goals: 52' Richmond Boakye 0-1 (p), 90+3' Stefan Zivkovic 1-1 (p).
Referee: Marius Avram (ROM)   Attendance: 8,500.

13.07.17   Ortaliq Stadion, Almaty: FK Kairat – KF Skënderbeu 1-1 (1-0)
FK Kairat: Stas Pokatilov, Eldos Akhmetov, Gafurzhan Suyombaev, Sheldon Bateau, Islambek
Kuat, Mikhail Bakaev, Bauyrzhan Islamkhan (84' Bauyrzhan Turysbek), Isael (90' Chuma
Anene), Ákos Elek, Gerard Gohou, Andrey Arshavin. Coach: Kakhaber Tskhadadze.
KF Skënderbeu: Orges Shehi, Gledi Mici, Bajram Jashanica, Tefik Osmani, Kristi Vangjeli,
Marko Radas, Bakary Nimaga, Afrim Taku (80' Enis Gavazaj), Liridon Latifi, Sabien Lilaj,
Segun Adeniyi (90+2' Gjergj Muzaka). Coach: Ilir Daja.
Goals: 9' Gerard Gohou 1-0, 72' Bakary Nimaga 1-1.
Referee: Leontios Trattou (CYP)   Attendance: 7,054.

13.07.17   Netanya Stadium, Netanya: Maccabi Tel Aviv – KR Reykjavik 3-1 (0-0)
Maccabi Tel Aviv: Predrag Rajkovic, Eli Dasa, Eitan Tibi, Tal Ben Haim, Ofir Davidzade,
Omer Atzili (87' Eliel Peretz), Sheran Yeini, Shlomy Azulay (61' Aaron Schoenfeld), Avi
Rikan (61' Barak Itzhaki), Eyal Golasa, Vidar Kjartansson. Coach: Jordi Cruijff.
KR Reykjavík: Stefán Magnússon, Arnór Adalsteinsson, Gunnar Thor Gunnarsson, Skúli Jón
Fridgeirsson, Aron Jósepsson, Morten Beck, Finnur Margeirsson, Pálmi Pálmason (69' Robert
Sandnes), Óskar Hauksson, Tobias Thomsen (84' Gudmundur Andri Tryggvason), Kennie
Chopart (88' Ástbjörn Thórdarson). Coach: Willum Thórsson.
Goals: 58' Pálmi Pálmason 0-1, 65' Aaron Schoenfeld 1-1, 78' Vidar Kjartansson 2-1,
82' Omer Atzili 3-1.
Referee: Anastasios Papapetrou (GRE)   Attendance: 6,923.

13.07.17   Trening centar Petar Milosevski, Skopje: FK Rabotnicki – Dinamo Minsk 1-1 (0-0)
FK Rabotnicki: Damjan Siskovski, Dejan Mitrev, Sebastián Herrera, Tomislav Iliev (55' Amir
Bilali), Moncilo Raso, Suad Sahiti (67' Florian Kadriu), Filip Duranski (59' Emir Sahiti),
Bojan Najdenov, Dusko Trajcevski, Stojanco Velinov, Kire Markoski.
Coach: Viktor Trenevski.
Dinamo Minsk: Andrey Klimovich, Igor Kuzmenok, Nino Galovic, Yuriy Ostroukh, Aleksandr
Sachivko, Roman Begunov, Nikola Lekovic, Oleksandr Noyok, Nikola Lukic (69' Uros
Nikolic), Anton Saroka, Vladimir Khvashchinskiy (85' Sergei Karpovich).
Coach: Sergei Gurenko.
Goals: 53' Vladimir Khvashchinskiy 0-1, 90+2' Bojan Najdenov 1-1 (p).
Referee: Arnold Hunter (NIR)   Attendance: 510.
Sent off: 82' Emir Sahiti.

13.07.17   Futbalovy stadión MFK Ruzomberok, Ruzomberok:
              MFK Ruzomberok – SK Brann 0-1 (0-0)
MFK Ruzomberok: Matús Macík, Dominik Kruzliak, Ján Maslo, Simon Kupec (86' Stefan
Gerec), Peter Maslo, Kristi Qose, Peter Gál-Andrezly, Dalibor Takác (62' Marek Sapara),
Matej Kochan (74' Tihomir Kostadinov), Erik Daniel, Nermin Haskic. Coach: Norbert Hrncár.
SK Brann: Piotr Leciejewski, Vito Wormgoor, Bismark Acosta, Gilli Rólantsson Sørensen,
Ruben Kristiansen, Amin Nouri, Fredrik Haugen, Sivert Nilsen, Kristoffer Barmen (79' Peter
Larsen), Jakob Orlov (87' Azar Karadas), Steffen Skålevik (74' Kasper Skaanes).
Coach: Lars Nilsen.
Goal: 47' Bismark Acosta 0-1.
Referee: Kevin Clancy (SCO)   Attendance: 4,487.

13.07.17   Stadion, Mladost, Strumica: KF Shkëndija 79 – HJK Helsinki 3-1 (1-1)
KF Shkëndija 79: Kostadin Zahov, Egzon Bejtulai, Ardijan Cuculi, Mevlan Murati (25' Ivan
Celikovic), Armend Alimi (83' Ennur Totre), Ferhan Hasani, Stephan Vujcic, Blagoja
Todorovski, Besart Ibraimi, Marjan Radeski (75' Besart Abdurahimi), Stênio Júnior.
Coach: Qatip Osmani.
HJK Helsinki: Thomas Dähne, Hannu Patronen, Juha Pirinen, Rafinha, Ville Jalasto, Sebastian
Dahlström (67' Faith Obilor), Vincent Onovo, Anthony Annan, Demba Savage (78' Filip
Valencic), Ousman Jallow, Akseli Pelvas (75' Evans Mensah). Coach: Mika Lehkosuo.
Goals: 35' Ousman Jallow 0-1, 45', 59', 64' Besart Ibraimi 1-1 (p), 2-1, 3-1 (p).
Referee: Markus Hameter (AUT)   Attendance: 1,492.
Sent off: 63' Hannu Patronen.

13.07.17   Kadrioru staadion, Tallinn: JK Nõmme Kalju – Videoton FC 0-3 (0-1)
JK Nõmme Kalju: Vitali Teles, Maximiliano Uggè, Andrei Sidorenkov, Deniss Tjapkin,
Réginald Mbu-Alidor, Artur Valikaev, Igor Subbotin, Karl Mööl, Artjom Dmitrijev, Liliu (60'
Tarmo Neemelo), Robert Kirss (69' Carlos Geovane Santos). Coach: Sergey Frantsev.
Videoton FC: Ádam Kovácsik, Paulo Vinícius, Loïc Négo, Stopira, Roland Juhász, Anel
Hadzic, Máté Pátkai, Roland Szolnoki, Asmir Suljic (82' Mirko Maric), Danko Lazovic (77'
Dávid Barczi), Marko Scepovic (74' Krisztián Géresi). Coach: Marko Nikolic.
Goals: 8' Máté Pátkai 0-1, 47', 74' Marko Scepovic 0-2 (p), 0-3 (p).
Referee: João Capela (POR)   Attendance: 760.

13.07.17   Brøndby Stadion, Brøndby: Brøndby IF – Vaasan PS 2-0 (2-0)
Brøndby IF: Frederik Rønnow, Benedikt Röcker, Gregor Sikosek, Hjörtur Hermannsson, Johan
Larsson, Kasper Fisker (82' Zsolt Kalmár), Hany Mukhtar, Kevin Mensah, Christian Nørgaard,
Kamil Wilczek (64' Besar Halimi), Teemu Pukki (73' Jan Kliment).
Coach: Alexander Zorniger.
Vaasan PS: Marko Meerits, Timi Lahti, Mikko Viitikko, Veli Lampi, Jesper Engström, Jerry
Voutilainen (67' Juho Lähde), Jonas Levänen, Joonas Vahtera (78' Kim Böling), Ebrima
Sohna, Juha Hakola, Steven Morrissey (70' Sebastian Strandvall). Coach: Petri Vuorinen.
Goals: 17' Teemu Pukki 1-0, 29' Kasper Fisker 2-0.
Referee: Bart Vertenten (BEL)   Attendance: 8,533.

13.07.17   CASHPOINT Arena, Altach: SCR Altach – Dinamo Brest 1-1 (0-0)
SCR Altach: Martin Kobras, Lucas Galvão, Philipp Netzer, Emanuel Sakic, Benedikt Zech,
Christian Gebauer, Patrick Salomon, Simon Piesinger, Stefan Nutz, Louis N'Gwat-Mahop (76'
Kristijan Dobras), Hannes Aigner (70' Adrian Grbic). Coach: Klaus Schmidt.
Dinamo Brest: Jérémy Malherbe, Andrey Lebedev, Maksim Vitus, Dmitriy Aliseyko, Oleg
Veretilo, Adrian Avramia, Kirill Premudrov (62' Pavel Sedko), Leandro Torres, Aleksey
Legchilin, Nivaldo (85' Joel Fameyeh), Aleksandar Vujacic (86' Artem Milevskiy).
Coach: Vladimir Zhuravel.
Goals: 49' Stefan Nutz 1-0, 74' Pavel Sedko 1-1.
Referee: Barbeno Luca (SMR)   Attendance: 2,811.
Sent off: 88' Dmitriy Aliseyko.

13.07.17   Stadions Daugava, Liepāja: FK Liepāja – FK Sūduva 0-2 (0-1)
FK Liepāja: Valentīns Ralkevics, Mihailo Tomkovic, Sady Guèye, Stanislav Lebamba (78'
Valerijs Afanasjevs), Dario Tomic, Leonel Strumia, Dmitrijs Hmizs (69' Kristaps Grebis),
Cristian Torres, Giorgi Eristavi, Artūrs Karasausks, Seydina Keita. Coach: Tamaz Pertia.
FK Sūduva: Ivan Kardum, Radanfah Abu Bakr, Semir Kerla, Algis Jankauskas, Povilas
Leimonas, Andro Svrljuga, Paulius Janusauskas (69' Giedrius Matulevicius), Vaidas Slavickas,
Ovidijus Verbickas (80' Sergei Amirzian), Marijan Altiparmakovski (57' Ernestas Veliulis),
Karolis Laukzemis. Coach: Vladimir Cheburin.
Goals: 18' Ovidijus Verbickas 0-1, 74' Karolis Laukzemis 0-2.
Referee: Erez Papir (ISR)   Attendance: 2,798.

13.07.17 Haugesund Stadion, Haugesund: FK Haugesund – Lech Poznan 3-2 (1-0)
FK Haugesund: Per Bråtveit, Fredrik Knudsen, Vegard Skjerve, Kristoffer Haraldseid, Filip Kiss, Liban Abdi (72' Tor Andreassen), Sondre Tronstad, Bruno Leite, Alexander Stølås, Haris Hajradinovic (79' Frederik Gytkjær), Shuaibu Ibrahim (82' Erik Huseklepp). Coach: Eirik Horneland.
Lech Poznan: Matús Putnocky, Robert Gumny, Lasse Nielsen, Volodymyr Kostevych, Abdul Tetteh, Lukasz Tralka, Darko Jevtic, Maciej Makuszewski (79' Nicklas Bärkroth), Radoslaw Majewski, Maciej Gajos (84' Mihai Radut), Christian Gytkjær (79' Deniss Rakels). Coach: Nenad Bjelica.
Goals: 24' Liban Abdi 1-0, 71' Haris Hajradinovic 2-0, 73' Shuaibu Ibrahim 3-0, 75' Radoslaw Majewski 3-1, 90+3' Darko Jevtic 3-2 (p).
Referee: Alain Bieri (SUI)   Attendance: 4,011.

13.07.17 AEK Arena – George Karapatakis, Larnaca: Apollon Limassol – FC Zaria 3-0 (3-0)
Apollon Limassol: Bruno Vale, Jander, Valentin Roberge, Héctor Yuste, Esteban Sachetti, Alex da Silva (86' Marios Stylianou), João Pedro, Charis Kyriakou, Emilio Zelaya (60' Jason Silva), André Schembri (77' Ioannis Pittas), Anton Maglica. Coach: Sofronis Avgousti.
FC Zaria: Serghei Pascenco, Victor Golovatenco, Andrii Slinkin (54' Igor Tigîrlas), Maxim Focsa, Tihomir Trifonov, Sergiy Zagynaylov (64' Gheorghe Boghiu), Vadim Rata, Alexandru Suvorov, Rubén Gómez (82' Vadim Gulceac), Georgi Ovsyannikov, Maxim Mihaliov. Coach: Vlad Goian.
Goals: 10' André Schembri 1-0, 21' Alex da Silva 2-0 (p), 28' João Pedro 3-0.
Referee: Ádam Farkas (HUN)   Attendance: 4,450.

13.07.17 Rheinpark Stadion, Vaduz: FC Vaduz – Odds BK 0-1 (0-1)
FC Vaduz: Peter Jehle, Tomislav Puljic, Nils von Niederhäusern, Axel Borgmann, Mario Bühler, Diego Ciccone (46' Milan Gajic), Mohamed Coulibaly, Marco Mathys, Maurice Brunner (74' Enrico Schirinzi), Philipp Muntwiler, Aldin Turkes (66' Robin Kamber). Coach: Roland Vrabec.
Odds BK: Sondre Lovseth Rossbach, Espen Ruud, Fredrik Semb Berge, Joakim Nilsen, Steffen Hagen, Jone Samuelsen (79' Oliver Berg), Fredrik Nordkvelle, Fredrik Oldrup Jensen, Riku Riski, Olivier Occéan, Rafik Zekhnini. Coach: Dag-Eilev Fagermo.
Goal: 42' Olivier Occéan 0-1.
Referee: Antti Munukka (FIN)   Attendance: 1,043.

13.07.17 Bakcell Arena, Baku: Gabala FK – Jagiellonia Bialystok 1-1 (0-1)
Gabala FK: Dmitro Bezotosniy, Vojislav Stankovic, Vitaliy Vernydub, Urfan Abbasov, Elvin Mammadov (46' Famoussa Koné), Andy Halliday, Ilgar Gurbanov (84' Dave Bulthuis), Filip Ozobic, Javi Hernández (68' Asif Mammadov), Steeven Joseph-Monrose, Javid Hüseynov. Coach: Roman Grygorchuk.
Jagiellonia Bialystok: Marián Kelemen, Lukasz Burliga, Guilherme, Guti, Ivan Runje, Jacek Góralski (53' Damian Szymanski), Taras Romanchuk, Arvydas Novikovas (85' Lukasz Sekulski), Fiodor Cernych, Przemyslaw Mystkowski (58' Martin Pospísil), Cillian Sheridan. Coach: Ireneusz Mamrot.
Goals: 15' Taras Romanchuk 0-1, 47' Steeven Joseph-Monrose 1-1.
Referee: Marco Fritz (GER)   Attendance: 6,500.

13.07.17 Jämtkraft Arena, Östersund: Östersunds FK – Galatasaray 2-0 (0-0)
Östersunds FK: Aly Keita, Sotirios Papagiannopoulos, Dennis Widgren, Ronald Mukiibi (76'
Doug Bergqvist), Samuel Laryeal Mensah, Tom Pettersson, Ken Sema (88' Gabriel Somi),
Fouad Bachirou, Brwa Nouri, Saman Ghoddos, Alhaji Gero (81' Jamie Hopcutt).
Coach: Graham Potter.
Galatasaray: Fernando Muslera, Maicon, Ahmet Çalik, Martin Linnes, Lionel Carole, Tolga
Cigerci, Yasin Öztekin, Selçuk Inan, Garry Rodrigues, Sinan Gümüs (87' Emrah Bassan),
Bafétimbi Gomis (69' Eren Derdiyok). Coach: Igor Tudor.
Goals: 68' Saman Ghoddos 1-0, 90+2' Jamie Hopcutt 2-0.
Referee: Juan Martínez Munuera (ESP)   Attendance: 5,407.

13.07.17 Stadionul Marin Anastasovici, Giurgiu: Astra Giurgiu – Zira FK 3-1 (1-1)
Astra Giurgiu: Plamen Iliev, Florin Bejan, Claudiu Belu, Erico, Alexandru Dandea (63' Robert
Vâlceanu), Marquinhos Carioca, Alexandru Ionita (II), Viorel Nicoara (78' Silviu Balaure),
Filip Mrzljak, Alexandru Stan, Bogdan Chipirliu (46' Anthony Le Tallec).
Coach: Eduard Iordanescu.
Zira FK: Anar Nazirov, Josef Boum, Aleksandr Shemonayev (56' Tamkin Khalilzade), Gabriel
Matei, Jovan Krneta, Vugar Mustafayev, Rashad Sadiqov (77' Viktor Ibekoyi), Orkhan Aliyev
(65' Richard Gadze), Milan Djuric, David Manga, Kervens Belfort. Coach: Aykhan Abbasov.
Goals: 31' Alexandru Ionita (II) 1-0, 34' Rashad Sadiqov 1-1, 55' Alexandru Dandea 2-1,
74' Anthony Le Tallec 3-1.
Referee: Sergey Tsinkevich (BLS)   Attendance: 1,730.

13.07.17 Hibernians Ground, Paola: Valletta FC – FC Utrecht 0-0
Valletta FC: Henry Bonello, Steve Borg, Ryan Camilleri, Juan Gill, Joseph Zerafa, Romeu (69'
Kyrian Nwoko), Claudio Pani, Santiago Malano, Michael Mifsud (89' Roderick Briffa),
Maximiliano Velasco (73' Jean Borg), Uchenna Umeh. Coach: Zoran Popovic.
FC Utrecht: David Jensen, Mark van der Maarel, Jeff Hardeveld (80' Urby Emanuelson),
Willem Janssen, Sean Klaiber, Edson Braafheid, Yassin Ayoub, Zakaria Labyad, Sander van
de Streek, Gyrano Kerk (88' Bilal Ould-Chikh), Simon Makienok. Coach: Erik ten Hag.
Referee: Ognjen Valjic (BIH)   Attendance: 1,795.

13.07.17 Stade Parc des Sports, Differdange: Progrès Niedercorn – AEL Limassol 0-1 (0-0)
Progrès Niedercorn: Charly Schinker, Adrien Ferino, Metin Karayer, Yann Matias Marques,
Oliver Thill, Maximilian Watzka (75' Ben Vogel), Alexis Lafon (76' David Soares), Sébastien
Thill, Mike Schneider, Emmanuel Françoise, Alexander Karapetyan (86' Théo Sully).
Coach: Paolo Amodio.
AEL Limassol: Vózinha, Kevin Lafrance, Marco Airosa, Bogdan Mitrea, Mários Nikolaou,
Ismail Sassi, Marco Soares, Dani Benítez (80' Mesca), Arthur (70' Fidelis Irhene), Andreas
Avraam, Mikel Arruabarrena (88' Marios Elia). Coach: Bruno Baltazar.
Goal: 66' Mikel Arruabarrena 0-1.
Referee: Massimiliano Irrati (ITA)   Attendance: 1,929.

13.07.17 HaMoshava Stadium, Petach Tikva: Beitar Jerusalem – Botev Plovdiv 1-1 (1-0)
Beitar Jerusalem: Boris Kleyman, Antoine Conte, David Keltjens (74' Georginho), Dan Mori,
Tal Kachila, Marcel Heister, Idan Vered, Claudemir, Hen Ezra (67' Yossi Benayoun), Erik
Sabo, Itay Shechter (82' Gaëtan Varenne). Coach: Sharon Mimer.
Botev Plovdiv: Ivan Cvorovic, Tsvetomir Panov, Victor Genev, Meledje Omnibes (69'
Álvaro), Jordan Minev, Krum Stoyanov (90+3' Lazar Marin), Plamen Dimov, Felipe Brisola
(57' Toni Tasev), Todor Nedelev, Serkan Yusein, Omar Kossoko. Coach: Nikolai Kirov.
Goals: 11' Tal Kachila 1-0, 73' Serkan Yusein 1-1.
Referee: Bartosz Frankowski (POL)   Attendance: 9,450.

278

13.07.17   Östgötaporten, Norrköping: IFK Norrköping – FK Trakai 2-1 (1-0)
IFK Norrköping: David Mitov-Nilsson, Jón Fjóluson, Linus Wahlqvist, Andreas Johansson, Christophèr Telo, Gudmundur Thórarinsson (78' Simon Skrabb), Daniel Sjölund, Niclas Eliasson (84' Eric Smith), Filip Dagerstål, Kalle Holmberg (65' David Moberg-Karlsson), Sebastian Andersson. Coach: Jens Gustafsson.
FK Trakai: Tymofey Sheremeta, Justinas Janusevskis, Alma Wakili (88' Lajo Traore), Mychailo Shyshka, Valdemars Borovskis, Modestas Vorobjovas, Oscar Dorley, Vaidas Silenas, Pavel Kruk, Aleksandr Bychenok (83' Svajūnas Cyzas), Maksim Maksimov. Coach: Oleg Vasilenko.
Goals: 32' Sebastian Andersson 1-0, 61' Kalle Holmberg 2-0, 66' Maksim Maksimov 2-1.
Referee: Amaury Delerue (FRA)   Attendance: 5,133.

13.07.17   Stadión Pasienky, Bratislava: Slovan Bratislava – Lyngby BK 0-1 (0-0)
Slovan Bratislava: Dominik Greif, Boris Sekulic, Milan Rundic, Kornel Saláta, Vukan Savicevic, Joeri de Kamps, Frantisek Kubík, Jakub Mares, Filip Holosko (71' Róbert Vittek), Aleksandar Cavric, Mitchell Schet (71' Samuel Sefcík). Coach: Ivan Vukomanovic.
Lyngby BK: Mikkel Andersen, Michael Lumb, Thomas Sørensen, Hallgrímur Jónasson, Martin Ørnskov, Jesper Christjansen, Lasse Fosgaard (65' Jeppe Kjær), Jeppe Brandrup, Bror Blume, Kristoffer Larsen (46' Mikkel Rygaard Jensen), Kim Ojo (61' David Boysen). Coach: David Nielsen.
Goal: 75' Jeppe Kjær 0-1.
Referee: Nenad Djokic (SER)   Attendance: 3,817.

13.07.17   Stadion Hrvatski vitezovi, Dugopolje: Hajduk Split – Levski Sofia 1-0 (1-0)
Hajduk Split: Dante Stipica, Borja López, Zoran Nizic, Hysen Memolla, Hamza Barry, Nikola Vlasic (86' Ivan Pesic), Josip Radosevic, Ante Erceg (88' Franck Ohandza), Savvas Gentsoglou (66' Zvonimir Kozulj), Márkó Futács, Fran Tudor. Coach: Joan Carrillo.
Levski Sofia: Bozhidar Mitrev, Dimitar Pirgov, Ivan Goranov, Milos Cvetkovic, David Jablonsky, Antonio Vutov (69' Jordi Gómez), Roman Procházka, Nelut Rosu, Vasil Panayotov (83' Babatunde Adeniji), Francis Narh, Junior Mpia Mapuku (67' Sergiu Bus). Coach: Nikolai Mitov.
Goal: 24' Márkó Futács 1-0 (p).
Referee: Mohammed Al Hakim (SWE)   Attendance: 5,000.

13.07.17   Merkur Arena, Graz: Sturm Graz – FK Mladost Podgorica 0-1 (0-1)
Sturm Graz: Jörg Siebenhandl, Charalampos Lykogiannis, Christian Schulz (80' Fabian Schubert), Fabian Koch, Dario Maresic, Sandi Lovric, Peter Zulj (70' Philipp Huspek), Stefan Hierländer, Thorsten Röcher (64' Marc Andre Schmerböck), Deni Alar, Philipp Zulechner. Coach: Franco Foda.
FK Mladost Podgorica: Damir Ljuljanovic, Ivan Novovic, Stefan Cicmil, Nikola Vukcevic, Mirko Raicevic (76' Ognjen Stijepovic), Milos Krkotic (63' Stefan Bukorac), Milan Djurisic, Andrija Kaludjerovic, Marko Cetkovic (87' Nedeljko Vlahovic), Ivan Knezevic, Zoran Petrovic. Coach: Dejan Vukicevic.
Goal: 2' Milos Krkotic 0-1 (p).
Referee: Mattias Gestranius (FIN)   Attendance: 7,109.
Sent off: 90+2' Andrija Kaludjerovic.

13.07.17   Futbalovy stadión Spartak Myjava, Myjava:
FK AS Trencín – Bnei Yehuda Tel Aviv 1-1 (0-1)
FK AS Trencín: Adrián Chovan, Lukás Skovajsa, Rodney Klooster, Peter Klescík, Keston Julien, Jakub Paur, Desley Ubbink, Achraf El Mahdioui, Giorgi Beridze, Hillary Gong (57' Milan Kvocera), Antonio Mance (79' Hamza Catakovic). Coach: Martin Sevela.
Bnei Yehuda Tel Aviv: Emilius Zubas, Ben Turgeman, Ayed Habashi, Itzhak Azouz, Maor Kandil, Paz Ben Ari, Roei Gordana, Stav Finish, Matan Hozez (70' Shay Konstantini), Daniel Avital (63' Mavis Tchibota), Nerijus Valskis (82' Yuval Ashkenazi). Coach: Yossi Abuksis.
Goals: 3' Nerijus Valskis 0-1, 59' Jakub Paur 1-1.
Referee: José Sánchez Martínez (ESP)   Attendance: 2,365.
Sent off: 80' Maor Kandil.

13.07.17   Stadion Grbavica, Sarajevo: Zeljeznicar Sarajevo – AIK Solna 0-0
Zeljeznicar Sarajevo: Vedran Kjosevski, Sinisa Stevanovic, Danijel Graovac, Jadranko Bogicevic, Jovan Blagojevic, Srdan Stanic, Goran Zakaric, Zajko Zeba, Ugljesa Radinovic (85' Darko Markovic), Asim Zec (68' Josip Projic), Stevo Nikolic (76' Dzenis Beganovic). Coach: Slavko Petrovic.
AIK Solna: Oscar Linnér, Per Karlsson, Jesper Nyholm, Sauli Väisänen, Simon Thern (82' Stefan Ishizaki), Kristoffer Olsson, Johan Blomberg, Daniel Sundgren, Anton Jönsson Salétros, Denni Avdic (74' Henok Goitom), Eero Markkanen. Coach: Rikard Norling.
Referee: Adrien Jaccottet (SUI)   Attendance: 11,870.

13.07.17   Turner's Cross, Cork: Cork City – AEK Larnaca 0-1 (0-0)
Cork City: Mark McNulty, Ryan Delaney, Kevin O'Connor, Greb Bolger (75' Achille Campion), Conor McCormack, Steven Beattie, Stephen Dooley (62' Kieran Sadlier), Gearóid Morrissey, Garry Buckley, Karl Sheppard (79' Shane Griffin), Seán Maguire.
Coach: John Caulfield.
AEK Larnaca: Juan Pablo, Marios Antoniades, Truyols, Daniel Mojsov, Català, Jorge Larena (90' Onisiforos Roushias), Joan Tomás (76' Tete), Hector Hevel, Vincent Laban, Ivan Trickovski (85' Vladimir Boljevic), Florian Taulemesse. Coach: Imanol Idiakez.
Goal: 70' Truyols 0-1.
Referee: François Letexier (FRA)   Attendance: 6,441.

13.07.17   Pittodrie Stadium, Aberdeen: Aberdeen FC – Siroki Brijeg 1-1 (1-0)
Aberdeen FC: Joe Lewis, Shaleum Logan, Graeme Shinnie, Andrew Considine, Anthony O'Connor, Mark Reynolds, Kenny McLean (73' Greg Stewart), Gary Mackay-Steven (63' Nicky Maynard), Greg Tansey, Ryan Christie, Adam Rooney (89' Miles Storey).
Coach: Derek McInnes.
Siroki Brijeg: Luka Bilobrk, Josip Barisic, Dino Coric (83' Josip Corluka), Slavko Bralic, Stipo Markovic, Bernardo Matic, Stjepan Loncar (74' Josip Coric), Luka Begonja, Dejan Cabraja, Luka Menalo (89' Danijel Kozul), Ivan Krstanovic. Coach: Denis Coric.
Goals: 17' Ryan Christie 1-0, 69' Stipo Markovic 1-1.
Referee: Erik Lambrechts (BEL)   Attendance: 17,067.

13.07.17   Stadion Gradski vrt, Osijek: NK Osijek – FC Luzern 2-0 (0-0)
NK Osijek: Marko Malenica, Borna Barisic, Mateo Barac, Petar Bockaj (89' Antonio Perosevic), Mile Skoric, Benedik Mioc, Robert Mudrazija, Dmitriy Lepa (82' Andrej Lukic), Muzafer Ejupi, Eros Grezda (85' Gabrijel Boban), Tomislav Sorsa. Coach: Zoran Zekic.
FC Luzern: Jonas Omlin, Remo Arnold (18' Yannick Schmid), Claudio Lustenberger, Christian Schwegler, Stefan Knezevic, Olivier Custodio, Pascal Schürpf, Hekuran Kryeziu, Filip Ugrinic (68' Christian Schneuwly), Francisco Rodríguez, Cedric Itten.
Coach: Markus Babbel.
Goals: 66' Muzafer Ejupi 1-0, 79' Eros Grezda 2-0.
Referee: Marco Guida (ITA)   Attendance: 7,452.

13.07.17   Stadio Néas Smyrnis, Athen: Panionios GSS – ND Gorica 2-0 (1-0)
Panionios GSS: Matic Kotnik, Vangelis Ikonomou, Ehsan Hajsafi, Yaya Banana, Valentinos Vlachos, Panagiotis Korbos, Giorgos Masouras, Masoud Shojaei (78' Fiorin Durmishaj), Kyriakos Savvidis, Lazaros Lamprou (90+2' Giorgos Saramantas), Samed Yesil (82' Kevin Tapoko). Coach: Michalis Grigoriou.
ND Gorica: Grega Sorcan, Uros Celcer, Miha Gregoric, Tine Kavcic, Alen Jogan, Rifet Kapic, Jaka Kolenc (46' Leon Marinic), Rok Grudina, Dejan Zigon, Andrija Filipovic (46' Jani Curk), Bede Osuji. Coach: Miran Srebrnic.
Goals: 12, 47' Samed Yesil 1-0, 2-0.
Referee: Hugo Miguel (POR)   Attendance: 3,298.
Sent off: 45' Tine Kavcic.

13.07.17   Tallaght Stadium, Dublin: Shamrock Rovers – FK Mladá Boleslav 2-3 (0-1)
Shamrock Rovers: Tomer Chencinski, Luke Byrne, David Webster, Roberto Lopes, Simon Madden, Trevor Clarke, Ryan Connolly, Ronan Finn, Brandon Miele (83' David McAllister), Gary Shaw, Graham Burke. Coach: Stephen Bradley.
FK Mladá Boleslav: Jakub Divis, Jirí Fleisman, Patrizio Stronati, Petr Mares (73' Tomás Fabián), Lukás Pauschek, Pavel Cmovs, Marek Matejovsky (90' Lukás Magera), Tomás Príkryl, Jakub Rada, Jan Chramosta, Golgol Mebrahtu (90+1' Adam János).
Coach: Dusan Uhrin.
Goals: 35' Golgol Mebrahtu 0-1, 48' Graham Burke 1-1, 63' Golgol Mebrahtu 1-2, 88' Jan Chramosta 1-3, 90+2' Graham Burke 2-3.
Referee: Bojan Pandzic (SWE)   Attendance: 3,160.

13.07.17   Groupama Aréna, Budapest: Ferencvárosi TC – FC Midtjylland 2-4 (2-1)
Ferencvárosi TC: Dénes Dibusz, Julian Koch, Leandro de Almeida, Zoltán Gera, Fernando Gorriarán, Amadou Moutari (70' Lukász Böle), Gergö Lovrencsics, Tamás Priskin (77' Balász Lovrencsics), Rui Pedro (46' Bence Batik), Roland Varga. Coach: Thomas Doll.
FC Midtjylland: Jesper Hansen, Kian Hansen (74' Kristian Riis), Zsolt Korcsmár, Marc Hende, Rasmus Nissen Kristensen, Tim Sparv, Jakob Poulsen, Janus Drachmann (64' Mikkel Duelund), Rilwan Hassan, Ebere Onuachu, Gustav Wikheim (73' Simon Kroon).
Coach: Jess Thorup.
Goals: 22' Endre Botka 1-0, 42' Roland Varga 2-0, 45+1', 61', 67' Jakob Poulsen 2-1 (p), 2-2, 2-3 (p), 90' Ebere Onuachu 2-4.
Referee: Sandro Schärer (SUI)   Attendance: 8,034.
Sent off: 45+1' Julian Koch.

281

13.07.17   Vodafoneavöllurinn, Reykjavík: Valur Reykjavík – NK Domzale 1-2 (1-1)
Valur Reykjavík: Anton Ari Einarsson, Sigurdur Lárusson (77' Andri Adolphsson), Bjarni
Eiríksson, Eidur Sigurbjörnsson, Einar Karl Ingvarsson, Haukur Sigurdsson, Kristinn
Halldórsson (65' Sveinn Gudjohnsen), Gudjón Lydsson (74' Nicolas Bøgild), Orri Ómarsson,
Arnar Geirsson, Dion Jeremy Acoff. Coach: Ólafur Jóhannesson.
NK Domzale: Dejan Milic, Matija Sirok, Miha Blazic, Gaber Dobrovoljc, Jure Balkovec,
Amedej Vetrih, Jan Repas, Jure Matjasic (68' Alen Ozbolt), Zeni Husmani, Ivan Firer (86'
Tilen Klemencic), Lovro Bizjak (55' Senijad Ibricic). Coach: Simon Rozman.
Goals: 22' Jan Repas 0-1, 36' Sigurdur Lárusson 1-1 (p), 73' Senijad Ibricic 1-2 (p).
Referee: Tore Hansen (NOR)   Attendance: 794.

20.07.17   Stadyen Traktar, Minsk: Dinamo Minsk – FK Rabotnicki 3-0 (1-0)
Dinamo Minsk: Andrey Klimovich, Igor Kuzmenok, Nino Galovic, Yuriy Ostroukh, Aleksandr
Sachivko, Roman Begunov (71' Sergei Karpovich), Nikola Lekovic, Oleksandr Noyok, Nikola
Lukic (78' Uros Nikolic), Anton Saroka, Vladimir Khvashchinskiy (86' Artem Kiyko).
Coach: Sergei Gurenko.
FK Rabotnicki: Damjan Siskovski, Leon Najdovski (30' Suad Sahiti), Dejan Mitrev, Sebastián
Herrera (69' Florian Kadriu), Amir Bilali, Moncilo Raso, Filip Duranski (82' Mario
Stankovski), Bojan Najdenov, Dusko Trajcevski, Stojanco Velinov, Kire Markoski.
Coach: Viktor Trenevski.
Goals: 21' Oleksandr Noyok 1-0, 70' Nino Galovic 2-0, 84' Anton Saroka 3-0.
Referee: Nicolas Rainville (FRA)   Attendance: 3,500.

20.07.17   Lyngby Stadion, Lyngby: Lyngby BK – Slovan Bratislava 2-1 (2-0)
Lyngby BK: Mikkel Andersen, Michael Lumb, Thomas Sørensen, Hallgrímur Jónasson,
Martin Ørnskov, Jesper Christjansen, Lasse Fosgaard, Mikkel Rygaard Jensen (63' Mathias
Hebo Rasmussen), Jeppe Brandrup (69' Oliver Lund), Bror Blume, Jeppe Kjær (74' Kim Ojo).
Coach: David Nielsen.
Slovan Bratislava: Dominik Greif, Boris Sekulic, Milan Rundic, Kornel Saláta, Vukan
Savicevic, Joeri de Kamps, Frantisek Kubík, Jakub Mares (61' Mitchell Schet), Filip Holosko
(85' Filip Orsula), Róbert Vittek, Aleksandar Cavric (74' Lesly de Sa).
Coach: Ivan Vukomanovic.
Goals: 19' Mikkel Rygaard Jensen 1-0 (p), 30' Martin Ørnskov 2-0, 89' Filip Orsula 2-1.
Referee: Vilhjálmur Alvar Thórarinsson (ISL)   Attendance: 2,286.

20.07.17   Telia 5G-areena, Helsinki: HJK Helsinki – KF Shkëndija 79 1-1 (1-0)
HJK Helsinki: Thomas Dähne, Juha Pirinen, Rafinha, Ville Jalasto, Faith Obilor, Vincent
Onovo, Anthony Annan, Moshtagh Yaghoubi (79' Sebastian Dahlström), Demba Savage,
Ousman Jallow (64' Filip Valencic), Akseli Pelvas (73' Evans Mensah).
Coach: Mika Lehkosuo.
KF Shkëndija 79: Kostadin Zahov, Egzon Bejtulai, Ardijan Cuculi, Ivan Celikovic, Armend
Alimi, Ferhan Hasani, Stephan Vujcic (79' Besmir Bojku), Blagoja Todorovski, Besart
Ibraimi, Marjan Radeski (90+5' Olsi Teqja), Besart Abdurahimi (66' Ennur Totre).
Coach: Qatip Osmani.
Goals: 28' Marjan Radeski 1-0 (og), 71' Ivan Celikovic 1-1.
Referee: Gunnar Jarl Jónsson (ISL)   Attendance: 5,326.

20.07.17   Elisa Stadion, Vaasa: Vaasan PS – Brøndby IF 2-1 (2-1)
Vaasan PS: Marko Meerits, Timi Lahti, Mikko Viitikko, Veli Lampi (21' Ville Koskimaa, 61' Steven Morrissey), Jesper Engström, Jerry Voutilainen, Sebastian Strandvall, Jonas Levänen, Joonas Vahtera, Ebrima Sohna, Juha Hakola (70' Kim Böling). Coach: Petri Vuorinen.
Brøndby IF: Benjamin Bellot, Gregor Sikosek (46' Svenn Crone), Hjörtur Hermannsson, Johan Larsson, Paulus Arajuuri, Kasper Fisker, Hany Mukhtar, Zsolt Kalmár (46' Benedikt Röcker), Besar Halimi (69' Teemu Pukki), Kamil Wilczek, Jan Kliment. Coach: Alexander Zorniger.
Goals: 11' Jerry Voutilainen 1-0, 16' Marko Meerits 1-1 (og), 40' Ebrima Sohna 2-1.
Referee: Paolo Valeri (ITA)   Attendance: 4,385.
Sent off: 51' Jan Kliment.

20.07.17   ARVI futbolo arena, Marijampolè: FK Sūduva – FK Liepāja 0-1 (0-0)
FK Sūduva: Ivan Kardum, Radanfah Abu Bakr, Semir Kerla, Algis Jankauskas, Povilas Leimonas (35' Giedrius Matulevicius), Ernestas Veliulis (72' Marijan Altiparmakovski), Andro Svrljuga, Paulius Janusauskas, Vaidas Slavickas, Ovidijus Verbickas, Karolis Laukzemis (82' Robertas Vezevicius). Coach: Vladimir Cheburin.
FK Liepāja: Valentīns Ralkevics, Mihailo Tomkovic (66' Valerijs Afanasjevs), Sady Guèye, Stanislav Lebamba (87' Oskars Klava), Dario Tomic, Leonel Strumia, Cristian Torres, Giorgi Eristavi (74' Dmitrijs Hmizs), Artūrs Karasausks, Kristaps Grebis, Seydina Keita.
Coach: Tamaz Pertia.
Goal: 57' Seydina Keita 0-1.
Referee: Laurent Kopriwa (LUX)   Attendance: 2,632.

20.07.17   Vilniais LFF stadionas, Vilnius: FK Trakai – IFK Norrköping 2-1 (2-0,2-1)
FK Trakai: Ignas Plūkas, Justinas Janusevskis, Alma Wakili, Mychailo Shyshka, Arūnas Klimavicius, Valdemars Borovskis, Modestas Vorobjovas, Oscar Dorley, Vaidas Silenas (84' Svajūnas Cyzas), Aleksandr Bychenok (116' Yuriy Mamaev), Maksim Maksimov (87' Deividas Cesnauskis). Coach: Oleg Vasilenko.
IFK Norrköping: David Mitov-Nilsson, Jón Fjóluson, Linus Wahlqvist, Andreas Johansson, Christopher Telo, Gudmundur Thórarinsson (46' Simon Skrabb), Daniel Sjölund (74' Eric Smith), Filip Dagerstål, David Moberg-Karlsson, Kalle Holmberg (46' Niclas Eliasson), Sebastian Andersson. Coach: Jens Gustafsson.
Goals: 11', 35' Maksim Maksimov 1-0, 2-0, 86' Simon Skrabb 2-1.
Referee: Dennis Higler (HOL)   Attendance: 2,750.

FK Trakai won 5-3 on penalties following extra time.

Penalties: Klimavicius 1-0, Wahlqvist 1-1, Vorobjovas 2-1, Smith missed, Cyzas 3-1, Eliasson
     3-2, Shyshka 4-2, Skrabb 4-3, Janusevskis 5-3.

20.07.17   Mestsky stadion, Mladá Boleslav: FK Mladá Boleslav – Shamrock Rovers 2-0 (2-0)
FK Mladá Boleslav: Jakub Divis, Jirí Fleisman, Douglas Silva, Petr Mares (77' Adam János), Lukás Pauschek, Pavel Cmovs, Marek Matejovsky (83' Lukás Magera), Tomás Príkryl, Jakub Rada, Jan Chramosta (64' Tomás Fabián), Golgol Mebrahtu. Coach: Dusan Uhrin.
Shamrock Rovers: Tomer Chencinski, Luke Byrne (67' Sam Bone), David Webster, Roberto Lopes, Simon Madden, Trevor Clarke, Ronan Finn, Brandon Miele (72' Sean Boyd), David McAllister (75' Ryan Connolly), Gary Shaw, Graham Burke. Coach: Stephen Bradley.
Goals: 9' Jan Chramosta 1-0, 31' Golgol Mebrahtu 2-0.
Referee: Giorgi Kruashvili (GEO)   Attendance: 4,727.

283

20.07.17   Stadyen DASK Brestski, Brest: Dinamo Brest – SCR Altach 0-3 (0-2)
Dinamo Brest: Jérémy Malherbe, Andrey Lebedev (69' Aleksei Ivanov), Maksim Vitus, Oleg
Veretilo, Adrian Avramia, Kirill Premudrov, Leandro Torres, Aleksey Legchilin (65' Pavel
Sedko), Chidi Osuchukwu, Artem Milevskiy (46' Joel Fameyeh), Nivaldo.
Coach: Vladimir Zhuravel.
SCR Altach: Martin Kobras, Lucas Galvão, Philipp Netzer (73' Jan Zwischenbrugger),
Andreas Lienhart, Benedikt Zech, Patrick Salomon, Simon Piesinger, Stefan Nutz (77'
Emanuel Schreiner), Louis N'Gwat-Mahop, Kristijan Dobras, Nicolas Ngamaleu (59' Christian
Gebauer). Coach: Klaus Schmidt.
Goals: 8' Nicolas Ngamaleu 0-1, 44' Stefan Nutz 0-2, 52' Philipp Netzer 0-3.
Referee: Keith Kennedy (NIR)   Attendance: 10,168.

20.07.17   Brann Stadion, Bergen: SK Brann – MFK Ruzomberok 0-2 (0-0)
SK Brann: Alex Horwath, Vito Wormgoor, Bismark Acosta, Gilli Rólantsson Sørensen, Ruben
Kristiansen, Amin Nouri (82' Steffen Skålevik), Fredrik Haugen, Kasper Skaanes, Sivert
Nilsen, Kristoffer Barmen (65' Peter Larsen), Jakob Orlov (81' Azar Karadas).
Coach: Lars Nilsen.
MFK Ruzomberok: Matús Macík, Dominik Kruzliak, Ján Maslo, Simon Kupec (46' Stefan
Gerec), Peter Maslo, Kristi Qose, Peter Gál-Andrezly (84' Jozef Menich), Dalibor Takác,
Matej Kochan, Erik Daniel (90' Tihomir Kostadinov), Nermin Haskic. Coach: Norbert Hrncár.
Goals: 64' Kristi Qose 0-1, 78' Dominik Kruzliak 0-2 (p).
Referee: Artyom Kuchin (KAZ)   Attendance: 4,688.

20.07.17   Stadionul Zimbru, Chisinau: FC Zaria – Apollon Limassol 1-2 (0-1)
FC Zaria: Serghei Pascenco, Victor Golovatenco, Maxim Focsa, Tihomir Trifonov, Sergiy
Zagynaylov (73' Gheorghe Boghiu), Vadim Rata, Igor Tigîrlas, Rubén Gómez (65' Alexandru
Suvorov), Georgi Ovsyannikov, Vadim Gulceac (81' Andrii Slinkin), Maxim Mihaliov.
Coach: Vlad Goian.
Apollon Limassol: Bruno Vale, Jander (59' Giorgos Vasiliou), Valentin Roberge, Marios
Stylianou (70' Emilio Zelaya), Héctor Yuste (78' Alef), Esteban Sachetti, Alex da Silva, João
Pedro, Charis Kyriakou, André Schembri, Anton Maglica. Coach: Sofronis Avgousti.
Goals: 44' Alex da Silva 0-1 (p), 47' Maxim Focsa 1-1, 80' André Schembri 1-2.
Referee: Alexandre Boucaut (BEL)   Attendance: 2,191.
Sent off: 76' Vadim Rata.

20.07.17   Skagerak Arena, Skien: Odds BK – FC Vaduz 1-0 (0-0)
Odds BK: Sondre Lovseth Rossbach, Espen Ruud, Thomas Grøgaard (72' Joakim Nilsen),
Fredrik Semb Berge, Steffen Hagen, Jone Samuelsen, Fredrik Nordkvelle (84' Martin
Broberg), Fredrik Oldrup Jensen, Riku Riski, Olivier Occéan, Pape Diouf (72' Stefan
Mladenovic). Coach: Dag-Eilev Fagermo.
FC Vaduz: Peter Jehle, Tomislav Puljic, Nils von Niederhäusern, Axel Borgmann, Mario
Bühler, Enrico Schirinzi (68' Diego Ciccone), Milan Gajic (78' Franz Burgmeier), Marco
Mathys, Robin Kamber (46' Aldin Turkes), Maurice Brunner, Philipp Muntwiler.
Coach: Roland Vrabec.
Goal: 82' Stefan Mladenovic 1-0.
Referee: Aleksandar Vasic (SER)   Attendance: 2,492.

20.07.17   Dalga Arena, Baku: Zira FK – Astra Giurgiu 0-0
Zira FK: Anar Nazirov, Josef Boum, Gabriel Matei (84' Sadig Guliyev), Jovan Krneta, Tamkin
Khalilzade, Rashad Sadiqov (72' Orkhan Aliyev), Milan Djuric, David Manga, Viktor Ibekoyi
(60' Nijat Gurbanov), Kervens Belfort, Richard Gadze. Coach: Aykhan Abbasov.
Astra Giurgiu: Plamen Iliev, Claudiu Belu, Erico, Piotr Polczak, Alexandru Dandea,
Marquinhos Carioca (79' Andrei Pitian), Alexandru Ionita (II) (69' Silviu Balaure), Viorel
Nicoara, Filip Mrzljak, Alexandru Stan, Bogdan Chipirliu (58' Anthony Le Tallec).
Coach: Eduard Iordanescu.
Referee: George Vadachkoria (GEO)   Attendance: 4,200.

20.07.17   Vivacom Arena - Georgi Asparuhov, Sofia: Levski Sofia – Hajduk Split 1-2 (0-0)
Levski Sofia: Bozhidar Mitrev, Dimitar Pirgov, Ivan Goranov, Milos Cvetkovic, David
Jablonsky, Jordi Gómez, Roman Procházka, Nelut Rosu (83' Aleks Borimirov), Vasil
Panayotov (46' Babatunde Adeniji), Francis Narh (57' Sergiu Bus), Junior Mpia Mapuku.
Coach: Nikolai Mitov.
Hajduk Split: Dante Stipica, Borja López, Zoran Nizic, Hysen Memolla, Hamza Barry (84'
Zvonimir Kozulj), Nikola Vlasic (78' Franck Ohandza), Josip Radosevic, Ante Erceg (87'
Ahmed Said), Savvas Gentsoglou, Márkó Futács, Fran Tudor. Coach: Joan Carrillo.
Goals: 69' Sergiu Bus 1-0, 80' Franck Ohandza 1-1, 86' Ante Erceg 1-2.
Referee: Ali Palabiyik (TUR)

Match was played behind closed doors.

20.07.17   HaMoshava Stadium, Petach Tikva:
              Bnei Yehuda Tel Aviv – FK AS Trencín 2-0 (0-0)
Bnei Yehuda Tel Aviv: Emilius Zubas, Ben Turgeman, Ayed Habashi, Shay Konstantini,
Itzhak Azouz, Paz Ben Ari, Roei Gordana, Stav Finish, Matan Hozez (73' Yuval Ashkenazi),
Mavis Tchibota (61' Almog Buzaglo), Nerijus Valskis (81' Daniel Avital).
Coach: Yossi Abuksis.
FK AS Trencín: Adrián Chovan, Lukás Skovajsa, Rodney Klooster, Peter Klescík, Keston
Julien (54' Hillary Gong), Jakub Paur, Desley Ubbink, Achraf El Mahdioui, Giorgi Beridze
(88' Milton Klooster), Milan Kvocera (55' Hamza Catakovic), Antonio Mance.
Coach: Martin Sevela.
Goals: 49' Mavis Tchibota 1-0, 85' Yuval Ashkenazi 2-0.
Referee: Tomasz Musial (POL)   Attendance: 1,700.

20.07.17   Friends Arena, Solna: AIK Solna – Zeljeznicar Sarajevo 2-0 (0-0)
AIK Solna: Oscar Linnér, Per Karlsson, Nils-Eric Johansson, Jesper Nyholm (90' Sauli
Väisänen), Kristoffer Olsson, Johan Blomberg, Daniel Sundgren, Stefan Ishizaki, Anton
Jönsson Salétros (57' Simon Thern), Eero Markkanen (80' Denni Avdic), Henok Goitom.
Coach: Rikard Norling.
Zeljeznicar Sarajevo: Vedran Kjosevski, Sinisa Stevanovic (81' Srdan Stanic), Danijel
Graovac, Jadranko Bogicevic, Josip Projic, Jovan Blagojevic (76' Dzenis Beganovic), Goran
Zakaric, Zajko Zeba (68' Sinan Ramovic), Ugljesa Radinovic, Asim Zec, Stevo Nikolic.
Coach: Slavko Petrovic.
Goals: 48' Nils-Eric Johansson 1-0, 85' Henok Goitom 2-0.
Referee: Georgios Kominis (GRE)   Attendance: 9,126.

285

20.07.17   AEK Arena – George Karapatakis, Larnaca: AEK Larnaca – Cork City 1-0 (1-0)
AEK Larnaca: Juan Pablo, Marios Antoniades, Truyols, Daniel Mojsov, Català, Jorge Larena,
Joan Tomás (72' Tete), Hector Hevel, Vincent Laban, Ivan Trickovski (88' Vladimir Boljevic),
Florian Taulemesse (80' Nestoras Mitidis). Coach: Imanol Idiakez.
Cork City: Mark McNulty, Ryan Delaney, Kevin O'Connor, Greb Bolger, Conor McCormack,
Steven Beattie, Stephen Dooley (61' Kieran Sadlier), Gearóid Morrissey, Garry Buckley (61'
Achille Campion), Jimmy Keohane (67' Karl Sheppard), Seán Maguire.
Coach: John Caulfield.
Goal: 33' Florian Taulemesse 1-0.
Referee: Pavle Radovanovic (MNE)   Attendance: 3,771.

20.07.17   MCH Arena, Herning: FC Midtjylland – Ferencvárosi TC 3-1 (1-0)
FC Midtjylland: Jesper Hansen, Kian Hansen, Marc Hende, Markus Halsti, Rasmus Nissen
Kristensen, Tim Sparv, Jakob Poulsen, Janus Drachmann (78' Mikkel Duelund), Rilwan
Hassan, Ebere Onuachu (46' Alexander Sørloth), Gustav Wikheim (63' Simon Kroon).
Coach: Jess Thorup.
Ferencvárosi TC: Dénes Dibusz, Bence Batik, Kornél Csernik, Zoltán Gera, Fernando
Gorriarán, Amadou Moutari, Gergö Lovrencsics, Lukász Böle (44' Norbert Kundrák), Tamás
Priskin (87' András Csonka), Rui Pedro, Balász Lovrencsics. Coach: Thomas Doll.
Goals: 34' Gustav Wikheim 1-0, 64' Rui Pedro 1-1, 71' Rasmus Nissen Kristensen 2-1,
81' Alexander Sørloth 3-1.
Referee: Alper Ulusoy (TUR)   Attendance: 5,413.

20.07.17   Stade Émile Mayrisch, Esch-sur-Alzette: CS FOLA Esch – Inter Baku 4-1 (2-0)
CS FOLA Esch: Thomas Hym, Tom Laterza, Mehdi Kirch, Julien Klein, Peter Chrappan,
Veldin Muharemovic, Jakob Dallevedove (82' Corentin Koçur), Michel Bechtold, Enis Saiti
(67' Stefano Bensi), Ken Corral (77' Cédric Sacras), Samir Hadji. Coach: Jeff Strasser.
Inter Baku: Sälahät Agayev, Dênis, Slavik Alkhasov (61' Pardis Fardjad-Azad), Ilkin
Qirtimov, Adrian Scarlatache, Tarlan Guliyev, Mirsayib Abbasov (71' Samir Zargarov),
Nizami Hajiyev, Elnur Abdullayev (46' Mirhuseyn Seyidov), Fuad Bayramov, Rauf Aliyev.
Coach: Zaur Svanadze.
Goals: 21' Samir Hadji 1-0, 32' Enis Saiti 2-0, 59' Tom Laterza 3-0,
70' Pardis Fardjad-Azad 3-1, 90+3' Cédric Sacras 4-1.
Referee: Donatas Rumsas (LTU)   Attendance: 1,250.

20.07.17   Türk Telekom Stadyumu, Istanbul: Galatasaray – Östersunds FK 1-1 (0-0)
Galatasaray: Fernando Muslera, Maicon, Ahmet Çalik, Martin Linnes, Lionel Carole (56' Eren
Derdiyok), Tolga Cigerci, Yasin Öztekin (69' Garry Rodrigues), Selçuk Inan, Younès
Belhanda, Sinan Gümüs, Bafétimbi Gomis. Coach: Igor Tudor.
Östersunds FK: Aly Keita, Sotirios Papagiannopoulos, Dennis Widgren, Ronald Mukiibi (65'
Doug Bergqvist), Samuel Laryeal Mensah, Tom Pettersson, Ken Sema (81' Jamie Hopcutt),
Fouad Bachirou, Brwa Nouri, Saman Ghoddos (66' Curtis Edwards), Alhaji Gero.
Coach: Graham Potter.
Goals: 60' Brwa Nouri 0-1 (p), 69' Ahmet Çalik 1-1.
Referee: Bastian Dankert (GER)   Attendance: 33,646.

20.07.17   Mandemakers Stadion, Waalwijk: FC Utrecht – Valletta FC 3-1 (1-0)
FC Utrecht: David Jensen, Mark van der Maarel, Willem Janssen, Sean Klaiber, Edson
Braafheid (86' Urby Emanuelson), Yassin Ayoub, Zakaria Labyad, Sander van de Streek,
Wout Brama (85' Ramon Leeuwin), Gyrano Kerk (62' Cyriel Dessers), Simon Makienok.
Coach: Erik ten Hag.
Valletta FC: Henry Bonello, Steve Borg, Ryan Camilleri, Juan Gill, Joseph Zerafa (87' Jean
Borg), Romeu (58' Roderick Briffa), Claudio Pani, Santiago Malano, Michael Mifsud (71'
Kyrian Nwoko), Maximiliano Velasco, Uchenna Umeh. Coach: Zoran Popovic.
Goals: 18' Sean Klaiber 1-0, 76' Willem Janssen 2-0, 83' Zakaria Labyad 3-0,
88' Santiago Malano 3-1.
Referee: Ian McNabb (NIR)   Attendance: 5,550.

20.07.17   Stadion Lazur, Burgas: Botev Plovdiv – Beitar Jerusalem 4-0 (2-0)
Botev Plovdiv: Ivan Cvorovic, Tsvetomir Panov, Victor Genev, Meledje Omnibes, Jordan
Minev, Krum Stoyanov (79' Lazar Marin), Plamen Dimov, Todor Nedelev, Lachezar Baltanov
(73' Serkan Yusein), Fernando Viana (83' Felipe Brisola), Omar Kossoko.
Coach: Nikolai Kirov.
Beitar Jerusalem: Boris Kleyman, Antoine Conte, David Keltjens (39' Georginho), Dan Mori,
Michael Siroshtein, Marcel Heister, Idan Vered, Yossi Benayoun (53' Claudemir), Hen Ezra,
Erik Sabo, Itay Shechter (68' Gaëtan Varenne). Coach: Sharon Mimer.
Goals: 10' Plamen Dimov 1-0, 32' Fernando Viana 2-0, 47' Lachezar Baltanov 3-0,
90' Felipe Brisola 4-0.
Referee: Kirill Levnikov (RUS)   Attendance: 6,400.
Sent off: 76' Marcel Heister.

20.07.17   swissporarena, Luzern: FC Luzern – NK Osijek 2-1 (1-0)
FC Luzern: Jonas Omlin, Claudio Lustenberger, Yannick Schmid, Christian Schwegler, Stefan
Knezevic, Olivier Custodio, Christian Schneuwly, João De Oliveira (61' Pascal Schürpf),
Francisco Rodríguez (77' Il-gwan Jong), Tomi Juric, Cedric Itten (77' Shkelqim Demhasaj).
Coach: Markus Babbel.
NK Osijek: Marko Malenica, Borna Barisic, Mateo Barac, Petar Bockaj, Mile Skoric, Benedik
Mioc (60' Zoran Lesjak), Robert Mudrazija, Dmitriy Lepa (60' Andrej Lukic), Muzafer Ejupi,
Eros Grezda (78' Gabrijel Boban), Tomislav Sorsa. Coach: Zoran Zekic.
Goals: 19', 62' Tomi Juric 1-0, 2-0, 72' Muzafer Ejupi 2-1.
Referee: Martin Lundby (NOR)   Attendance: 8,443.

20.07.17   Stadiumi Skënderbeu, Korçë: KF Skënderbeu – FK Kairat 2-0 (0-0)
KF Skënderbeu: Orges Shehi, Gledi Mici, Bajram Jashanica, Tefik Osmani (71' Gjergj
Muzaka), Kristi Vangjeli, Marko Radas, Bakary Nimaga, Afrim Taku (90' Bruno Dita),
Liridon Latifi, Sabien Lilaj, Segun Adeniyi (46' Sebino Plaku). Coach: Ilir Daja.
FK Kairat: Stas Pokatilov, Eldos Akhmetov (69' Ivo Ilicevic), Gafurzhan Suyombaev, César
Arzo, Sheldon Bateau, Islambek Kuat, Bauyrzhan Islamkhan, Isael (78' Chuma Anene), Ákos
Elek, Gerard Gohou, Andrey Arshavin. Coach: Kakhaber Tskhadadze.
Goals: 50' Sabien Lilaj 1-0, 83' Sebino Plaku 2-0.
Referee: Jens Maae (DEN)   Attendance: 4,800.
Sent off: 75' Sabien Lilaj, 86' César Arzo.

20.07.17 INEA stadion, Poznan: Lech Poznan – FK Haugesund 2-0 (1-0)
Lech Poznan: Matús Putnocky, Robert Gumny, Lasse Nielsen, Volodymyr Kostevych, Emir Dilaver, Lukasz Tralka, Darko Jevtic (46' Mihai Radut), Maciej Makuszewski (85' Deniss Rakels), Maciej Gajos, Mario Situm, Christian Gytkjær (71' Nicki Bille Nielsen).
Coach: Nenad Bjelica.
FK Haugesund: Per Bråtveit, Fredrik Knudsen, Vegard Skjerve, Kristoffer Haraldseid, Filip Kiss, Liban Abdi, Sondre Tronstad (72' Frederik Gytkjær), Bruno Leite, Alexander Stølås, Haris Hajradinovic (82' Erik Huseklepp), Shuaibu Ibrahim (60' Tor Andreassen).
Coach: Eirik Horneland.
Goals: 32' Darko Jevtic 1-0, 90+3' Nicki Bille Nielsen 2-0.
Referee: Alexander Harkam (AUT)   Attendance: 21,968.
Sent off: 76' Liban Abdi.

20.07.17 Stadio Antonis Papadopoulos, Larnaca:
AEL Limassol – Progrès Niedercorn 2-1 (0-0)
AEL Limassol: Vózinha, Kevin Lafrance, Marco Airosa, Bogdan Mitrea, Mários Nikolaou (52' Fidelis Irhene), Ismail Sassi, Marco Soares, Arthur, Andreas Avraam, Mikel Arruabarrena (79' Marios Elia), Mesca (67' Aldair). Coach: Bruno Baltazar.
Progrès Niedercorn: Charly Schinker, Ben Vogel (69' Oliver Thill), David Soares (76' Théo Sully), Adrien Ferino, Metin Karayer, Yann Matias Marques, Maximilian Watzka, Sébastien Thill, Mike Schneider (62' Alexis Lafon), Emmanuel Françoise, Alexander Karapetyan.
Coach: Paolo Amodio.
Goals: 70' Fidelis Irhene 1-0, 83' Emmanuel Françoise 1-1, 88' Kevin Lafrance 2-1.
Referee: Frank Schneider (FRA)   Attendance: 3,740.
Sent off: 79' Metin Karayer.

20.07.17 Sportni Park, Domzale: NK Domzale – Valur Reykjavík 3-2 (1-2)
NK Domzale: Dejan Milic, Matija Sirok, Miha Blazic, Gaber Dobrovoljc, Jure Balkovec, Amedej Vetrih (55' Senijad Ibricic), Jan Repas, Jure Matjasic (83' Zan Zuzek), Zeni Husmani, Ivan Firer, Lovro Bizjak (64' Petar Franjic). Coach: Simon Rozman.
Valur Reykjavík: Anton Ari Einarsson, Rasmus Christiansen, Eidur Sigurbjörnsson, Einar Karl Ingvarsson, Sindri Björnsson, Kristinn Halldórsson, Gudjón Lydsson, Orri Ómarsson, Andri Stefánsson, Nicolas Bøgild (69' Dion Jeremy Acoff), Andri Adolphsson (75' Sigurdur Lárusson). Coach: Ólafur Jóhannesson.
Goals: 3' Gudjón Lydsson 0-1 (p), 25' Ivan Firer 1-1 (p), 43' Nicolas Bøglid 1-2, 69' Jure Balkovec 2-2, 71' Senijad Ibricic 3-2.
Referee: Dimitar Meckarovski (MKD)   Attendance: 1,900.

20.07.17 Stadion Rajko Mitic, Beograd: Crvena Zvezda – Irtysh Pavlodar 2-0 (1-0)
Crvena Zvezda: Filip Manojlovic, Filip Stojkovic, Dusan Andjelkovic, Vujadin Savic, Branko Jovicic, Damien Le Tallec, Guélor Kanga, Mitchell Donald (90+1' Uros Racic), Slavoljub Srnic (81' Aleksandar Pesic), Richmond Boakye, Ricardinho (72' John Ruiz).
Coach: Vladan Milojevic.
Irtysh Pavlodar: David Loriya, Aleksandr Kislitsyn (66' Aslan Darabaev), Rodrigo Antônio, Damir Dautov, Stefan Zivkovic, Milos Stamenkovic, Mario Maslac, Ilya Kalinin, Kazbek Geteriev (82' Ismaël Fofana), Carlos Fonseca (84' Artem Popov), Igor Bugaev.
Coach: Dimitar Dimitrov.
Goals: 10' Mitchell Donald 1-0, 76' Slavoljub Srnic 2-0.
Referee: Fedayi San (SUI)   Attendance: 22,414.

20.07.17   Stadion Miejski, Bialystok: Jagiellonia Bialystok – Gabala FK 0-2 (0-1)
Jagiellonia Bialystok: Marián Kelemen, Lukasz Burliga (77' Karol Swiderski), Guilherme (84'
Lukasz Sekulski), Guti, Ivan Runje, Taras Romanchuk, Rafal Grzyb, Arvydas Novikovas,
Fiodor Cernych, Przemyslaw Mystkowski (34' Martin Pospísil), Cillian Sheridan.
Coach: Ireneusz Mamrot.
Gabala FK: Dmitro Bezotosniy, Vojislav Stankovic, Vitaliy Vernydub, Dave Bulthuis, Andy
Halliday (78' Elvin Jamalov), Dion Malone, Ilgar Gurbanov, Filip Ozobic, Steeven Joseph-
Monrose, Javid Hüseynov (90+1' Elvin Mammadov), Famoussa Koné (72' Asif Mammadov).
Coach: Roman Grygorchuk.
Goals: 18' Ilgar Gurbanov 0-1, 89' Filip Ozobic 0-2.
Referee: Sebastian Coltescu (ROM)   Attendance: 13,326.

20.07.17   Stadion Pod Goricom, Podgorica: FK Mlados Podgorica – Sturm Graz 0-3 (0-2)
FK Mladost Podgorica: Damir Ljuljanovic, Ivan Novovic, Stefan Cicmil, Nikola Vukcevic,
Mirko Raicevic (72' Marko Burzanovic), Milos Krkotic (58' Nedeljko Vlahovic), Stefan
Bukorac, Milan Djurisic, Marko Cetkovic, Ivan Knezevic, Zoran Petrovic (46' Ognjen
Stijepovic). Coach: Dejan Vukicevic.
Sturm Graz: Jörg Siebenhandl, Charalampos Lykogiannis, Marvin Potzmann, Fabian Koch,
Dario Maresic, Sandi Lovric, Peter Zulj (73' James Jeggo), Stefan Hierländer, Thorsten Röcher
(55' Marc Andre Schmerböck), Deni Alar, Philipp Zulechner (86' Philipp Huspek).
Coach: Franco Foda.
Goals: 33' Thorsten Röcher 0-1, 39' Phlipp Zulecher 0-2, 46' Deni Alar 0-3.
Referee: Nikola Popov (BUL)   Attendance: 5,500.

Deni Alar missed a penalty kick (67').

20.07.17   Stadion Pecara, Siroki Brijeg: Siroki Brijeg – Aberdeen FC 0-2 (0-0)
Siroki Brijeg: Luka Bilobrk, Josip Barisic, Dino Coric, Slavko Bralic, Stipo Markovic (78'
Luka Grubisic), Bernardo Matic, Josip Coric (51' Stjepan Loncar), Luka Begonja, Dejan
Cabraja (67' Josip Corluka), Luka Menalo, Ivan Krstanovic. Coach: Denis Coric.
Aberdeen FC: Joe Lewis, Shaleum Logan, Graeme Shinnie, Andrew Considine, Anthony
O'Connor, Mark Reynolds, Kenny McLean, Gary Mackay-Steven (79' Adam Rooney), Ryan
Christie, Greg Stewart (75' Greg Tansey), Jayden Stockley (68' Nicky Maynard).
Coach: Derek McInnes.
Goals: 72' Greg Stewart 0-1, 78' Gary Mackay-Steven 0-2.
Referee: Michael Tykgaard (DEN)   Attendance: 4,800.

20.07.17   Sportni Park, Nova Gorica: ND Gorica – Panionios GSS 2-3 (1-3)
ND Gorica: Grega Sorcan, Uros Celcer, Matija Skarabot, Miha Gregoric, Jani Curk, Rifet
Kapic, Jaka Kolenc (81' Jan Hulmar), Rok Grudina, Dejan Zigon (68' Tilen Nagode), Andrija
Filipovic (56' Leon Marinic), Bede Osuji. Coach: Miran Srebrnic.
Panionios GSS: Matic Kotnik, Vangelis Ikonomou, Ehsan Hajsafi, Yaya Banana (60' Kevin
Tapoko), Valentinos Vlachos, Panagiotis Korbos, Giorgos Masouras (68' Giorgos
Saramantas), Masoud Shojaei, Kyriakos Savvidis, Lazaros Lamprou (80' Jérôme Guihoata),
Samed Yesil. Coach: Michalis Grigoriou.
Goals: 11' Giorgos Masouras 0-1, 15' Rifet Kapic 1-1 (p), 16' Samed Yesil 1-2,
23' Lazaros Lamprou 1-3, 67' Rifet Kapic 2-3 (p).
Referee: Anatoliy Abdula (UKR)   Attendance: 1,400.

20.07.17 Puskás Akadémia Pancho Aréna, Felcsút:
Videoton FC – JK Nõmme Kalju 1-1 (1-0)
Videoton FC: Ádam Kovácsik, Paulo Vinícius (24' András Fejes), Loïc Négo, Stopira (61'
Bence Szabó), Roland Juhász, Anel Hadzic, Roland Szolnoki, József Varga, Asmir Suljic,
Danko Lazovic (58' Krisztián Géresi), Mirko Maric. Coach: Marko Nikolic.
JK Nõmme Kalju: Pavel Londak (46' Vitali Teles), Maximiliano Uggè, Andrei Sidorenkov,
Deniss Tjapkin, Réginald Mbu-Alidor, Artur Valikaev, Igor Subbotin, Karl Mööl, Artjom
Dmitrijev, Liliu (75' Tarmo Neemelo), Robert Kirss (68' Carlos Geovane Santos).
Coach: Sergey Frantsev.
Goals: 37' Danko Lazovic 1-0, 50' Artjom Dmitrijev 1-1 (p).
Referee: Mario Zebec (CRO)   Attendance: 2,612.

20.07.17 Alvogenvöllurinn, Reykjavík: KR Reykjavík – Maccabi Tel Aviv 0-2 (0-0)
KR Reykjavík: Beitir Ólafsson, Arnór Adalsteinsson, Gunnar Thor Gunnarsson, Skúli Jón
Fridgeirsson (87' Robert Sandnes), Aron Jósepsson, Morten Beck, Pálmi Pálmason, Atli
Sigurjónsson, Óskar Hauksson (74' Ástbjörn Thórdarson), Gudmundur Andri Tryggvason,
Gardar Jóhannsson (66' Tobias Thomsen). Coach: Willum Thórsson.
Maccabi Tel Aviv: Predrag Rajkovic, Yuval Shpungin, Eitan Tibi, Tal Ben Haim, Ofir
Davidzade, Omer Atzili, Sheran Yeini, Avi Rikan (64' Dor Peretz), Eyal Golasa (68' Cristian
Battocchio), Vidar Kjartansson, Aaron Schoenfeld (75' Yonathan Cohen). Coach: Jordi Cruijff.
Goals: 57' Omer Atzili 0-1, 66' Dor Peretz 0-2.
Referee: Ivaylo Stoyanov (BUL)   Attendance: 609.

THIRD QUALIFYING ROUND

27.07.17 Mestsky stadion, Mladá Boleslav: FK Mladá Boleslav – KF Skënderbeu 2-1 (1-0)
FK Mladá Boleslav: Jakub Divis, Jirí Fleisman, Douglas Silva, Tomás Fabián, Petr Mares,
Pavel Cmovs, Marek Matejovsky, Tomás Príkryl (78' Adam János), Jakub Rada, Jan
Chramosta (68' Lukás Magera), Golgol Mebrahtu (87' Nikolay Komlichenko).
Coach: Dusan Uhrin.
KF Skënderbeu: Orges Shehi, Gledi Mici, Bajram Jashanica, Tefik Osmani (88' Bruno Dita),
Kristi Vangjeli, Marko Radas, Bakary Nimaga, Gjergj Muzaka (78' Donjet Shkodra), Afrim
Taku (67' Enis Gavazaj), Liridon Latifi, Sebino Plaku. Coach: Ilir Daja.
Goals: 42' Jan Chramosta 1-0, 86' Pavel Cmovs 1-1 (og), 87' Adam János 2-1.
Referee: Alan Sant (MLT)   Attendance: 4,487.

27.07.17 Vilniais LFF stadionas, Vilnius: FK Trakai – KF Shkëndija 79 2-1 (1-1)
FK Trakai: Ignas Plūkas, Justinas Janusevskis, Alma Wakili (84' Lajo Traore), Mychailo
Shyshka (80' Valentin Jeriomenko), Arūnas Klimavicius, Valdemars Borovskis, Modestas
Vorobjovas, Oscar Dorley, Vaidas Silenas, Aleksandr Bychenok, Maksim Maksimov.
Coach: Oleg Vasilenko.
KF Shkëndija 79: Kostadin Zahov, Egzon Bejtulai, Ardijan Cuculi, Ivan Celikovic, Armend
Alimi, Ennur Totre, Ferhan Hasani (90+4' Mevlan Murati), Blagoja Todorovski, Besart
Ibraimi (72' Besmir Bojku), Marjan Radeski (64' Olsi Teqja), Stênio Júnior.
Coach: Qatip Osmani.
Goals: 2' Maksim Maksimov 1-0, 39' Stênio Júnior 1-1, 52' Maksim Maksimov 2-1.
Referee: Neil Doyle (IRL)   Attendance: 3,580.
Sent off: 57' Stênio Júnior, 62' Ardijan Cuculi.

27.07.17   Stadion Dynoamo im. Valery Lobanovsky, Kiev:
Olimpik Donetsk – PAOK Saloniki 1-1 (0-0)
Olimpik Donetsk: Zauri Makharadze, Pavlo Lukyanchuk, Artem Shabanov, Dmitriy
Nemchaninov, Evgeniy Tsymbalyuk, Anton Kravchenko, Sergiy Shestakov, Vladyslav
Khomutov (69' Ilya Mikhalev), Andrey Bogdanov, Mohammed Rhasalla (64' Oleksandr
Migunov), Stanislav Bilenkyi (78' Ivan Sondey). Coach: Roman Sanzhar.
PAOK Saloniki: Rodrigo Rey, Léo Matos, Marin Leovac, José Ángel Crespo, Fernando
Varela, Gojko Cimirot, Yevhen Shakhov (55' Diego Biseswar), Cañas, Aleksandar Prijovic,
Djalma (55' Pedro Henrique), Róbert Mak (81' Dimitrios Pelkas).
Coach: Aleksandar Stanojevic.
Goals: 49' Stanislav Bilenkyi 1-0, 59' Pedro Henrique 1-1.
Referee: Alain Bieri (SUI)   Attendance: 2,632.

27.07.17   Netanya Stadium, Netanya: Maccabi Tel Aviv – Panionios GSS 1-0 (0-0)
Maccabi Tel Aviv: Predrag Rajkovic, Yuval Shpungin, Eitan Tibi, Tal Ben Haim, Ofir
Davidzade, Omer Atzili (74' Barak Itzhaki), Sheran Yeini (82' Dor Peretz), Eyal Golasa,
Cristian Battocchio, Vidar Kjartansson (85' Avi Rikan), Aaron Schoenfeld.
Coach: Jordi Cruijff.
Panionios GSS: Matic Kotnik, Vangelis Ikonomou, Yaya Banana, Giorgos Saramantas,
Valentinos Vlachos, Panagiotis Korbos, Giorgos Masouras, Kevin Tapoko (83' Fiorin
Durmishaj), Kyriakos Savvidis (72' Athanasios Papageorgiou), Lazaros Lamprou, Samed
Yesil (90+2' Spyridon Glinos). Coach: Michalis Grigoriou.
Goal: 48' Vidar Kjartansson 1-0.
Referee: Bart Vertenten (BEL)   Attendance: 7,862.

27.07.17   Philips Stadion, Eindhoven: PSV Eindhoven – NK Osijek 0-1 (0-0)
PSV Eindhoven: Jeroen Zoet, Nicolas Isimat-Mirin, Santiago Arias, Daniel Schwaab (79'
Davy Pröpper), Joshua Brenet, Jorrit Hendrix, Marco van Ginkel, Bart Ramselaar (62' Gastón
Pereiro), Luuk de Jong, Steven Bergwijn, Jürgen Locadia (62' Hirving Lozano).
Coach: Phillip Cocu.
NK Osijek: Marko Malenica, Borna Barisic, Mateo Barac, Petar Bockaj (90' Domagoj Pusic),
Mile Skoric, Benedik Mioc, Robert Mudrazija (81' Zoran Lesjak), Dmitriy Lepa (66' Andrej
Lukic), Muzafer Ejupi, Eros Grezda, Tomislav Sorsa. Coach: Zoran Zekic.
Goal: 57' Borna Barisic 0-1 (p).
Referee: Andrew Dallas (SCO)   Attendance: 31,983.

27.07.17   Stadion FK Krasnodar, Krasnodar: FK Krasnodar – Lyngby BK 2-1 (0-0)
FK Krasnodar: Andrey Sinitsyn, Aleksandr Martinovich, Andreas Granqvist, Roman Shishkin
(81' Magomed Suleymanov), Renat Yanbaev, Wanderson, Victor Claesson, João dos Santos
(63' Ilya Zhigulev), Mihailo Ristic, Mauricio Pereyra, Ivan Ignatyev (46' Cristian Ramírez).
Coach: Igor Shalimov.
Lyngby BK: Mikkel Andersen, Thomas Christensen, Michael Lumb, Oliver Lund, Martin
Ørnskov, Jesper Christjansen (84' Mathias Hebo Rasmussen), Mikkel Rygaard Jensen, Jeppe
Brandrup, Bror Blume (86' Lasse Fosgaard), Jeppe Kjær (80' Kristoffer Larsen), David
Boysen. Coach: David Nielsen.
Goals: 64' Jeppe Kjær 0-1, 67' Victor Claesson 1-1, 90+3' Magomed Suleymanov 2-1.
Referee: Christos Nicolaides (CYP)   Attendance: 20,239.

27.07.17   Merkur Arena, Graz: Sturm Graz – Fenerbahçe 1-2 (1-2)
Sturm Graz: Jörg Siebenhandl, Charalampos Lykogiannis, Marvin Potzmann, Fabian Koch,
Dario Maresic, Sandi Lovric (75' Romano Schmid), Peter Zulj, Stefan Hierländer, Thorsten
Röcher (84' Fabian Schubert), Deni Alar, Philipp Zulechner (16' Philipp Huspek).
Coach: Franco Foda.
Fenerbahçe: Volkan Demirel, Hasan-Ali Kaldirim, Nabil Dirar (74' Mehmet Topal), Sener
Özbayrakli, Martin Skrtel, Alper Potuk (89' Aatif Chahechouhe), Ozan Tufan, Mathieu
Valbuena, Roman Neustädter, Ahmethan Köse (76' Mauricio Isla), Souza.
Coach: Aykut Kocaman.
Goals: 10' Stefan Hierländer 1-0, 29' Dario Maresic 1-1 (og), 35' Roman Neustädter 1-2.
Referee: Ola Nilsen (NOR)   Attendance: 15,323.

27.07.17   Jämtkraft Arena, Östersund: Östersunds FK – CS FOLA Esch 1-0 (0-0)
Östersunds FK: Aly Keita, Sotirios Papagiannopoulos, Dennis Widgren, Ronald Mukiibi (62'
Samuel Laryeal Mensah), Tom Pettersson, Ken Sema (70' Johan Bertilsson), Curtis Edwards,
Fouad Bachirou, Brwa Nouri, Alhaji Gero (46' Jamie Hopcutt), Hosam Aiesh.
Coach: Graham Potter.
CS FOLA Esch: Thomas Hym, Tom Laterza, Mehdi Kirch, Julien Klein, Peter Chrappan,
Veldin Muharemovic, Jakob Dallevedove (81' Cédric Sacras), Michel Bechtold, Enis Saiti (64'
Stefano Bensi), Ken Corral (77' Gérard Mersch), Samir Hadji. Coach: Jeff Strasser.
Goal: 50' Fouad Bachirou 1-0.
Referee: Evgen Aranovskiy (UKR)   Attendance: 6,061.
Sent off: 79' Mehdi Kirch.

27.07.17   Stadion Galgenwaard, Utrecht: FC Utrecht – Lech Poznan 0-0
FC Utrecht: David Jensen, Mark van der Maarel (85' Robin van der Meer), Willem Janssen,
Sean Klaiber, Edson Braafheid, Zakaria Labyad, Urby Emanuelson, Sander van de Streek,
Wout Brama (75' Giovanni Troupée), Gyrano Kerk, Cyriel Dessers (75' Ramon Leeuwin).
Coach: Erik ten Hag.
Lech Poznan: Matús Putnocky, Nikola Vujadinovic, Volodymyr Kostevych, Rafal Janicki,
Emir Dilaver, Lukasz Tralka, Maciej Makuszewski (77' Robert Gumny), Radoslaw Majewski
(85' Mihai Radut), Maciej Gajos, Mario Situm, Christian Gytkjær (69' Nicki Bille Nielsen).
Coach: Nenad Bjelica.
Referee: Aleksandar Stavrev (MKD)   Attendance: 13,817.

27.07.17   AEK Arena – George Karapatakis, Larnaca:
AEK Larnaca – Dinamo Minsk 2-0 (1-0)
AEK Larnaca: Juan Pablo, Marios Antoniades, Truyols, Daniel Mojsov, Català, Jorge Larena,
Tete (78' Acorán), Hector Hevel (73' Joan Tomás), Vincent Laban, Ivan Trickovski, Florian
Taulemesse (90+1' Nestoras Mitidis). Coach: Imanol Idiakez.
Dinamo Minsk: Andrey Klimovich, Igor Kuzmenok, Nino Galovic, Yuriy Ostroukh, Aleksandr
Sachivko, Roman Begunov (46' Sergei Karpovich), Nikola Lekovic, Oleksandr Noyok, Nikola
Lukic (73' Uros Nikolic), Anton Saroka, Vladimir Khvashchinskiy (68' Dmytro Khlyobas).
Coach: Sergei Gurenko.
Goals: 42' Tete 1-0, 70' Hector Hevel 2-0.
Referee: Petr Ardeleánu (CZE)   Attendance: 4,050.

27.07.17   Friends Arena, Solna: AIK Solna – Sporting Braga 1-1 (1-1)
AIK Solna: Oscar Linnér, Per Karlsson, Nils-Eric Johansson, Jesper Nyholm, Kristoffer
Olsson, Johan Blomberg, Rasmus Lindkvist, Daniel Sundgren, Nicolás Marcelo Stefanelli (81'
Denni Avdic), Stefan Ishizaki, Henok Goitom (89' Eero Markkanen). Coach: Rikard Norling.
Sporting Braga: Matheus Magalhães, Lazar Rosic, Jefferson, Raúl Silva, Ricardo Esgaio,
Danilo Barbosa, Pedro Santos (84' Bruno Xadas), Fransérgio, Rui Fonte, Nikola Stojiljkovic
(66' Ahmed Hassan Koka), Fábio Martins (73' Wilson Eduardo). Coach: Abel Ferreira.
Goals: 1-0' Raúl Silva 0-1, 18' Daniel Sundgren 1-1 (p).
Referee: Marius Avram (ROM)   Attendance: 12,456.

27.07.17   Arvi Futbolo Arena, Marijampólè: FK Sūduva – FC Sion 3-0 (2-0)
FK Sūduva: Ivan Kardum, Radanfah Abu Bakr, Semir Kerla, Algis Jankauskas, Ernestas
Veliulis (77' Marijan Altiparmakovski), Andro Svrljuga, Paulius Janusauskas (75' Karolis
Chvedukas), Giedrius Matulevicius (66' Povilas Leimonas), Vaidas Slavickas, Ovidijus
Verbickas, Karolis Laukzemis. Coach: Vladimir Cheburin.
FC Sion: Anton Mitryushkin, Paulo Ricardo, Elsad Zverotic, Quentin Maceiras (69' Nicolas
Lüchinger), Bruno Morgado, Birama N'Doye, Joaquim Adão, Gregory Karlen, Moussa
Konaté, Matheus Cunha (58' Marco Schneuwly), Adryan (59' Bastien Toma).
Coach: Paolo Tramezzani.
Goals: 3' Paulo Ricardo 1-0 (og), 9' Paulius Janusauskas 2-0, 90' Karolis Laukzemis 3-0.
Referee: Alexander Harkam (AUT)   Attendance: 3,818.

27.07.17   HaMoshava Stadium, Petach Tikva:
              Bnei Yehuda Tel Aviv – Zenit St.Petersburg 0-2 (0-0)
Bnei Yehuda Tel Aviv: Emilius Zubas, Ben Turgeman, Ayed Habashi, Itzhak Azouz, Maor
Kandil, Paz Ben Ari, Roei Gordana, Stav Finish (87' Yuval Ashkenazi), Mavis Tchibota (81'
Dovev Gabay), Nerijus Valskis, Almog Buzaglo (71' Matan Hozez). Coach: Yossi Abuksis.
Zenit St.Petersburg: Andrei Lunev, Aleksandr Anyukov, Domenico Criscito, Neto, Branislav
Ivanovic, Javi García, Yuriy Zhirkov (71' Leandro Paredes), Aleksandr Erokhin, Dmitriy
Poloz (75' Artem Dzyuba), Aleksandr Kokorin, Giuliano (58' Sebastián Driussi).
Coach: Roberto Mancini.
Goals: 59' Domenico Criscito 0-1, 90' Aleksandr Kokorin 0-2.
Referee: Nikola Dabanovic (MNE)   Attendance: 3,200.

27.07.17   Stadionul Marin Anastasovici, Giurgiu: Astra Giurgiu – FC Aleksandriya 0-0
Astra Giurgiu: Plamen Iliev, Florin Bejan, Claudiu Belu, Valentin Gheorghe (52' Marquinhos
Carioca), Piotr Polczak, Alexandru Dandea, Alexandru Ionita (II) (77' Silviu Balaure), Viorel
Nicoara, Filip Mrzljak, Alexandru Stan, Bogdan Chipirliu (55' Anthony Le Tallec).
Coach: Eduard Iordanescu.
FC Aleksandriya: Yuri Pankiv, Sergiy Chebotaev, Andriy Gitchenko, Andriy Batsula, Sergiy
Basov, Artem Polyarus (71' Andriy Tsurikov), Andriy Zaporozhan, Artem Sitalo, Vasili
Gritsuk (66' Vitali Ponomar), Sergey Starenkiy (80' Valeriy Bondarenko), Eugene Banada.
Coach: Volodymyr Sharan.
Referee: Dimitar Meckarovski (MKD)   Attendance: 1,482.
Sent off: 78' Sergiy Basov.

27.07.17   Arena Nationala, Bucuresti: Dinamo Bucuresti – Athletic Bilbao 1-1 (0-1)
Dinamo Bucuresti: Jaime Penedo, Giorgios Katsikas, Ionut Nedelcearu, Romera, Sergiu
Hanca, Azer Busuladzic (46' Rivaldinho), Steliano Filip, May Mahlangu, Filipe Nascimento
(84' Paul Anton), Adam Nemec (67' Juan Albín), Diogo Salomão. Coach: Cosmin Contra.
Athletic Bilbao: Iago Herrerín, Aymeric Laporte, Etxeita, De Marcos, Balenziaga, Beñat (81'
Mikel Rico), Susaeta (68' Lekue), Mikel Vesga, Raúl García (90' Sabin Merino), Muniain,
Aduriz. Coach: José Ángel Ziganda.
Goals: 21' Aymeric Laporte 0-1, 54' Rivaldinho 1-1.
Referee: Tore Hansen (NOR)   Attendance: 26,783.

27.07.17   Stadion Lazur, Burgas: Botev Plovdiv – CS Marítimo 0-0
Botev Plovdiv: Ivan Cvorovic, Tsvetomir Panov, Victor Genev, Meledje Omnibes (77' Serkan
Yusein), Jordan Minev, Krum Stoyanov (66' Felipe Brisola), Plamen Dimov, Todor Nedelev
(83' Toni Tasev), Lachezar Baltanov, Fernando Viana, Omar Kossoko. Coach: Nikolai Kirov.
CS Marítimo: Charles, Maurício Antônio, Zainadine Junior, Luís Martins, Bebeto, Erdem Sen,
Éber Bessa (82' Jean Cleber), Gamboa, Rodrigo Pinho (86' Viktor Lundberg), Piqueti (72'
Edgar Costa), Ricardo Valente. Coach: Daniel Ramos.
Referee: Bojan Pandzic (SWE)   Attendance: 6,335.

27.07.17   Stadionul Municipal, Drobeta-Turnu Severin:
           CS Universitatea Craiova – AC Milan 0-1 (0-1)
CS Universitatea Craiova: Nicolae Calancea, Marius Briceag, Renato Kelic, Radoslav
Dimitrov (81' Mihai Roman), Hrvoje Spahija, Alexandru Baluta, Nicusor Bancu, Fausto Rossi
(74' Alexandru Mateiu), Hristo Zlatinski, Alexandru Mitrita (67' Cristian Barbut), Gustavo Di
Mauro. Coach: Devis Mangia.
AC Milan: Gianluigi Donnarumma, Cristián Zapata, Ignazio Abate (73' Andrea Conti), Mateo
Musacchio, Ricardo Rodríguez, Giacomo Bonaventura, Riccardo Montolivo, Franck Kessié,
Fabio Borini (66' André Silva), Patrick Cutrone (81' Luca Antonelli), M'Baye Niang.
Coach: Vincenzo Montella.
Goal: 44' Ricardo Rodríguez 0-1.
Referee: Halis Özkahya (TUR)   Attendance: 14,438.

27.07.17   Stadion GOSiR, Gdynia: Arka Gdynia – FC Midtjylland 3-2 (2-2)
Arka Gdynia: Pāvels Steinbors, Tadeusz Socha, Krzysztof Sobieraj, Dawid Soldecki, Adam
Marciniak, Marcin Warcholak, Michal Marcjanik, Grzegorz Piesio, Yannick Kakoko (84'
Michal Nalepa), Patryk Kun (57' Rafal Siemaszko), Marcus Vinícius (70' Luka Zarandia).
Coach: Leszek Ojrzynski.
FC Midtjylland: Jesper Hansen, Kian Hansen, Marc Hende, Markus Halsti, Rasmus Nissen
Kristensen, Tim Sparv, Jakob Poulsen, Janus Drachmann (72' Simon Kroon), Rilwan Hassan,
Ebere Onuachu (90' Alexander Sørloth), Gustav Wikheim (79' Jonas Borring).
Coach: Jess Thorup.
Goals: 31' Marcus Vinícius 1-0, 33' Rilwan Hassan 1-1, 36' Marc Hende 1-2,
39' Marcus Vinícius 2-2 (p), 90+2' Rafal Siemaszko 3-2.
Referee: Enea Jorgji (ALB)   Attendance: 14,037.

27.07.17   Brøndby Stadion, Brøndby: Brøndby IF – Hajduk Split 0-0
Brøndby IF: Frederik Rønnow, Benedikt Röcker, Johan Larsson, Paulus Arajuuri, Svenn
Crone, Kasper Fisker, Hany Mukhtar, Kevin Mensah (62' Kamil Wilczek), Christian Nørgaard,
Lasse Christensen (75' Besar Halimi), Teemu Pukki (90+4' Hjörtur Hermannsson).
Coach: Alexander Zorniger.
Hajduk Split: Dante Stipica, Borja López, Zoran Nizic, Hysen Memolla, Hamza Barry, Nikola
Vlasic (86' Ivan Pesic), Josip Radosevic, Ante Erceg (74' Franck Ohandza), Savvas
Gentsoglou, Márkó Futács, Fran Tudor (70' Josip Juranovic). Coach: Joan Carrillo.
Referee: Kevin Clancy (SCO)   Attendance: 12,535.
Sent off: 90+3' Paulus Arajuuri.

27.07.17   Apostolos Nikolaidis Stadium, Athen: Panathinaikos – Gabala FK 1-0 (1-0)
Panathinaikos: Odisseas Vlachodimos, Dimitrios Kolovetsios, Rodrigo Moledo, Ousmane
Coulibaly, Omri Altman (87' Christos Donis), Zeca, Robin Lod, Dimitrios Kourbelis, Niklas
Hult, Guillermo Molins (70' Luciano), Anastasios Chatzigiovannis (70' Bryan Cabezas).
Coach: Marinos Ouzounidis.
Gabala FK: Dmitro Bezotosniy, Vojislav Stankovic, Vitaliy Vernydub, Dave Bulthuis, Andy
Halliday, Dion Malone (76' Famoussa Koné), Ilgar Gurbanov, Filip Ozobic, Steeven Joseph-
Monrose, Bagaliy Dabo, Javid Hüseynov. Coach: Roman Grygorchuk.
Goal: 37' Guillermo Molins 1-0 (p).
Referee: Juan Martínez Munuera (ESP)   Attendance: 11,237.

27.07.17   GHELAMCO-arena, Gent: KAA Gent – SCR Altach 1-1 (0-1)
KAA Gent: Lovre Kalinic, Samuel Gigot, Stefan Mitrovic, Nana Asare, Birger Verstraete (46'
Samuel Kalu), Brecht Dejaegere, Damien Marcq (66' Kalifa Coulibaly), Danijel Milicevic,
Mamadou Sylla, Moses Simon, Yūya Kubo. Coach: Hein Vanhaezebrouck.
SCR Altach: Martin Kobras, Lucas Galvão, Philipp Netzer, Andreas Lienhart (13' Emanuel
Sakic), Benedikt Zech, Patrick Salomon, Simon Piesinger, Stefan Nutz (84' Christian
Gebauer), Louis N'Gwat-Mahop (65' Hannes Aigner), Kristijan Dobras, Nicolas Ngamaleu.
Coach: Klaus Schmidt.
Goals: 5' Louis N'Gwat-Mahop 0-1, 76' Kalifa Coulibaly 1-1.
Referee: Adrien Jaccottet (SUI)   Attendance: 13,745.

27.07.17   Stade Matmut-Atlantique, Bordeaux: Girondins Bordeaux – Videoton FC 2-1 (2-1)
Girondins Bordeaux: Benoît Costil, Diego Contento, Igor Lewczuk, Youssouf Sabaly, Mauro
Arambarri, Younousse Sankharé (86' Jaroslav Plasil), Jérémy Toulalan, Lukas Lerager,
Malcom, François Kamano, Gaëtan Laborde (77' Alexandre Mendy).
Coach: Jocelyn Gourvennec.
Videoton FC: Ádam Kovácsik, András Fejes, Loïc Négo, Stopira, Roland Juhász, Anel Hadzic,
Máté Pátkai (86' Mirko Maric), József Varga (57' Roland Szolnoki), Asmir Suljic, Danko
Lazovic, Marko Scepovic (79' Ezekiel Henty). Coach: Marko Nikolic.
Goals: 18' Younousse Sankharé 1-0, 23' Marko Scepovic 1-1, 33' Younousse Sankharé 2-1.
Referee: Bartosz Frankowski (POL)   Attendance: 21,337.

27.07.17   Stadion Rajko Mitic, Beograd: Crvena Zvezda – Sparta Praha 2-0 (1-0)
Crvena Zvezda: Milan Borjan, Milan Rodic, Filip Stojkovic, Vujadin Savic, Branko Jovicic,
Damien Le Tallec, Guélor Kanga, Mitchell Donald, Richmond Boakye (87' Aleksandar Pesic),
Nemanja Milic (74' Marko Gobeljic), Ricardinho (61' Nemanja Radonjic).
Coach: Vladan Milojevic.
Sparta Praha: Martin Dúbravka, Semih Kaya, Lukás Stetina, Vyacheslav Karavaev, Bogdan
Vatajelu (46' Eldar Civic), Lukás Marecek, Georges Mandjeck, Martin Frydek, Srdan Plavsic
(77' Tal Ben Haim), Lukás Julis (46' David Lafata), Marc Janko. Coach: Andrea Stramaccioni.
Goals: 13' Richmond Boakye 1-0, 65' Guélor Kanga 2-0.
Referee: Sergey Lapochkin (RUS)   Attendance: 32,816.

27.07.17   Stade Vélodrome, Marseille: Olympique Marseille – KV Oostende 4-2 (2-1)
Olympique Marseille: Steve Mandanda, Hiroki Sakai, Rolando, Patrice Evra (75' Tomás
Hubocan), Adil Rami, Morgan Sanson, Dimitri Payet, Luiz Gustavo, Florian Thauvin (58'
Lucas Ocampos), Maxime Lopez, Valère Germain (85' Grégory Sertic). Coach: Rudi García.
KV Oostende: Silvio Proto, David Rozehnal, Ramin Rezaeian, Brecht Capon, Zarko
Tomasevic, Antonio Milic, Sébastien Siani, Franck Berrier (71' Emmanuel Banda), Andile
Jali, Knowledge Musona (79' Fernando Canesin Matos), Joseph Akpala (64' Richairo
Zivkovic). Coach: Yves Vanderhaeghe.
Goals: 2' Valère Germain 1-0, 26' Sébastien Siani 1-1 (p), 32' Morgan Sanson 2-1,
57' Valère Germain 3-1, 69' Knowledge Musona 3-2, 82' Valère Germain 4-2.
Referee: Mete Kalkavan (TUR)   Attendance: 46,519.

27.07.17   Stadion Maksimir, Zagreb: Dinamo Zagreb – Odds BK 2-1 (2-1)
Dinamo Zagreb: Dominik Livakovic, Jan Lecjaks, Leonardo Sigali, Petar Stojanovic, Marko
Leskovic, Domagoj Antolic, Ante Coric (68' Amer Gojak), Nikola Moro, El Arbi Soudani,
Armin Hodzic (80' Ángelo Henríquez), Junior Fernándes. Coach: Mario Cvitanovic.
Odds BK: Sondre Lovseth Rossbach, Espen Ruud, Thomas Grøgaard, Fredrik Semb Berge,
Joakim Nilsen, Steffen Hagen, Martin Broberg (46' Oliver Berg), Jone Samuelsen, Stefan
Mladenovic (87' John Kitelano), Riku Riski (72' Pape Diouf), Olivier Occéan.
Coach: Dag-Eilev Fagermo.
Goals: 20' Stefan Mladenovic 0-1, 31' Armin Hodzic 1-1, 41' Junior Fernándes 2-1.
Referee: Manuel Schüttengruber (AUT)   Attendance: 7,080.

27.07.17   Pittodrie Stadium, Aberdeen: Aberdeen FC – Apollon Limassol 2-1 (1-0)
Aberdeen FC: Joe Lewis, Shaleum Logan, Graeme Shinnie, Andrew Considine, Anthony
O'Connor, Mark Reynolds (76' Scott Wright), Kenny McLean, Gary Mackay-Steven (61' Kári
Árnason), Ryan Christie, Greg Stewart, Nicky Maynard (60' Jayden Stockley).
Coach: Derek McInnes.
Apollon Limassol: Bruno Vale, Jander, Valentin Roberge, Héctor Yuste, Esteban Sachetti,
Alex da Silva (46' Antonio Jakolis), João Pedro, Charis Kyriakou, André Schembri (70' Alef),
Adrián Sardinero (81' Giorgos Vasiliou), Anton Maglica. Coach: Sofronis Avgousti.
Goals: 4' Ryan Christie 1-0, 59' Jander 1-1, 78' Graeme Shinnie 2-1.
Referee: Mattias Gestranius (FIN)   Attendance: 20,085.
Sent off: 71' Esteban Sachetti.

27.07.17   Ernst-Happel-Stadion, Wien: Austria Wien – AEL Limassol 0-0
Austria Wien: Osman Hadzikic, Petar Filipovic, Jens Stryger Larsen (61' David De Paula),
Heiko Westermann, Christoph Martschinko, Ismael Tajouri Shradi (85' Dominík Prokop),
Alexander Grünwald, Tarkan Serbest, Raphael Holzhauser, Kevin Friesenbichler (81'
Christoph Monschein), Felipe Pires. Coach: Thorsten Fink.
AEL Limassol: Vózinha, Kevin Lafrance, Marco Airosa, Bogdan Mitrea, Fidelis Irhene, Ismail
Sassi (90+3' Marios Elia), Marco Soares, Arthur (89' Aly Savane), Andreas Avraam, Mikel
Arruabarrena (78' Aldair), Mesca. Coach: Bruno Baltazar.
Referee: Antti Munukka (FIN)   Attendance: 5,892.

27.07.17   Goodison Park, Liverpool: Everton FC – MFK Ruzomberok 1-0 (0-0)
Everton FC: Maarten Stekelenburg, Leighton Baines, Michael Keane, Ashley Williams, Cuco
Martina, Morgan Schneiderlin, Idrissa Gueye, Davy Klaassen (86' Tom Davies), Wayne
Rooney, Kevin Mirallas (82' Ademola Lookman), Dominic Calvert-Lewin (61' Sandro
Ramírez). Coach: Ronald Koeman.
MFK Ruzomberok: Matús Macík, Dominik Kruzliak, Ján Maslo, Simon Kupec, Peter Maslo,
Kristi Qose, Peter Gál-Andrezly (88' Stefan Gerec), Dalibor Takác (72' Tihomir Kostadinov),
Matej Kochan, Erik Daniel, Nermin Haskic (83' Milos Lacny). Coach: Norbert Hrncár.
Goal: 65' Leighton Baines 1-0.
Referee: Georgi Kabakov (BUL)   Attendance: 32,124.

27.07.17   Schwarzwald-Stadion, Freiburg im Breisgau: SC Freiburg – NK Domzale 1-0 (1-0)
SC Freiburg: Alexander Schwolow, Philipp Lienhart, Çaglar Söyüncü, Pascal Stenzel,
Christian Günter, Amir Abrashi, Mike Frantz (87' Mohamed Dräger), Nicolas Höfler, Florian
Niederlechner, Nils Petersen, Tim Kleindienst (60' Janik Haberer).
Coaches: Christian Streich & Florian Bruns.
NK Domzale: Dejan Milic, Matija Sirok, Miha Blazic, Gaber Dobrovoljc, Jure Balkovec,
Amedej Vetrih, Jan Repas, Senijad Ibricic (74' Nermin Hodzic), Zeni Husmani, Ivan Firer (89'
Zan Zuzek), Lovro Bizjak (58' Petar Franjic). Coach: Simon Rozman.
Goal: 20' Nils Petersen 1-0.
Referee: Anatoliy Zhabchenko (UKR)   Attendance: 14,000.

Nils Petersen missed a penalty kick (24').

02.08.17   Stade de Genève, Lancy: FC Sion – FK Sūduva 1-1 (0-0)
FC Sion: Anton Mitryushkin, Ivan Lurati, Paulo Ricardo, Kévin Constant, Elsad Zverotic,
Nicolas Lüchinger (57' Matheus Cunha), Quentin Maceiras (46' Adryan), Birama N'Doye (67'
Joaquim Adão), Gregory Karlen, Moussa Konaté, Marco Schneuwly.
Coach: Paolo Tramezzani.
FK Sūduva: Ivan Kardum, Radanfah Abu Bakr, Semir Kerla, Algis Jankauskas, Povilas
Leimonas, Ernestas Veliulis (66' Robertas Vezevicius), Andro Svrljuga, Paulius Janusauskas
(57' Giedrius Matulevicius), Vaidas Slavickas, Ovidijus Verbickas, Karolis Laukzemis (88'
Karolis Chvedukas). Coach: Vladimir Cheburin.
Goals: 54' Moussa Konaté 1-0, 80' Robertas Vezevicius 1-1.
Referee: Antony Gautier (FRA)   Attendance: 410.

02.08.17   Stadio Antonis Papadopoulos, Larnaca: AEL Limassol – Austria Wien 1-2 (0-1)
AEL Limassol: Vózinha, Kevin Lafrance, Marco Airosa, Bogdan Mitrea, Fidelis Irhene, Ismail
Sassi, Marco Soares, Arthur (46' Aldair), Andreas Avraam, Mikel Arruabarrena (34'
Charalambos Kyriakou), Mesca (73' Dani Benítez). Coach: Bruno Baltazar.
Austria Wien: Osman Hadzikic, Petar Filipovic, Jens Stryger Larsen, Heiko Westermann,
Christoph Martschinko, Ismael Tajouri Shradi (66' David De Paula), Alexander Grünwald,
Tarkan Serbest, Raphael Holzhauser (90+3' Abdul Kadiri Mohammed), Christoph Monschein
(83' Kevin Friesenbichler), Felipe Pires. Coach: Thorsten Fink.
Goals: 34' Raphael Holzhauser 0-1 (p), 60' Aldair 1-1, 90' Felipe Pires 1-2.
Referee: Artyom Kuchin (KAZ)   Attendance: 3,450.
Sent off: 27' Marco Airosa.

03.08.17   Stadion Mladost, Strumica: KF Shkëndija 79 – FK Trakai 3-0 (2-0)
KF Shkëndija 79: Kostadin Zahov, Egzon Bejtulai, Ivan Celikovic, Armend Alimi, Ennur
Totre, Ferhan Hasani (90+3' Arbin Zejnulai), Besmir Bojku, Blagoja Todorovski, Besart
Ibraimi, Marjan Radeski (90' Enis Fazlagikj), Besart Andurahimi (82' Shefit Shefiti).
Coach: Qatip Osmani.
FK Trakai: Ignas Plūkas, Justinas Janusevskis, Alma Wakili, Mychailo Shyshka (88' Yuriy
Mamaev), Arūnas Klimavicius, Valdemars Borovskis, Modestas Vorobjovas, Oscar Dorley,
Vaidas Silenas (81' Svajūnas Cyzas), Aleksandr Bychenok (46' Valentin Jeriomenko),
Maksim Maksimov. Coach: Oleg Vasilenko.
Goals: 29' Besart Ibraimi 1-0, 42', 88' Ferhan Hasani 2-0, 3-0.
Referee: Clayton Pisani (MLT)   Attendance: 2,057.
Sent off: 72' Arūnas Klimavicius.

03.08.17   Stadyen Traktar, Minsk: Dinamo Minsk – AEK Larnaca 1-1 (0-0)
Dinamo Minsk: Sergey Ignatovich, Igor Kuzmenok, Nino Galovic, Yuriy Ostroukh, Sergei
Karpovich, Nikola Lekovic (77' Aleksandr Sachivko), Artem Bykov, Oleksandr Noyok, Anton
Saroka, Dmytro Khlyobas (70' Uros Nikolic), Vladimir Khvashchinskiy (46' Nikola Lukic).
Coach: Sergei Gurenko.
AEK Larnaca: Juan Pablo, Marios Antoniades, Truyols, Daniel Mojsov, Català, Jorge Larena,
Tete (73' Acorán), Hector Hevel (62' Joan Tomás), Vincent Laban, Ivan Trickovski (83'
Ander Murillo), Florian Taulemesse. Coach: Imanol Idiakez.
Goals: 47' Anton Saroka 1-0 (p), 90+3' Acorán 1-1.
Referee: Simon Evans (WAL)   Attendance: 3,670.
Sent off: 85' Artem Bykov.

03.08.17   Skagerak Arena, Skien: Odds BK – Dinamo Zagreb 0-0
Odds BK: Sondre Lovseth Rossbach, Espen Ruud, Thomas Grøgaard, Fredrik Semb Berge,
Joakim Nilsen, Steffen Hagen, Oliver Berg, Jone Samuelsen (64' Martin Broberg), Stefan
Mladenovic (76' Pape Diouf), Riku Riski (82' Sigurd Haugen), Olivier Occéan.
Coach: Dag-Eilev Fagermo.
Dinamo Zagreb: Dominik Livakovic, Jan Lecjaks, Leonardo Sigali, Filip Benkovic, Petar
Stojanovic, Domagoj Antolic, Ante Coric (75' Daniel Olmo), Nikola Moro, El Arbi Soudani
(90+1' Amir Rrahmani), Armin Hodzic (65' Amer Gojak), Junior Fernándes.
Coach: Mario Cvitanovic.
Referee: Anatoliy Abdula (UKR)   Attendance: 4,270.
Sent off: 86' Daniel Olmo.

03.08.17   Stadion Krestovskyi, St.Petersburg:
           Zenit St.Petersburg – Bnei Yehuda Tel Aviv 0-1 (0-0)
Zenit St.Petersburg: Yuriy Lodygin, Aleksandr Anyukov (73' Aleksandr Kokorin), Denis
Terentyev, Neto, Javi García (80' Branislav Ivanovic), Christian Noboa, Yuriy Zhirkov,
Hernani, Dmitriy Poloz, Giuliano (78' Sebastián Driussi), Artem Dzyuba.
Coach: Roberto Mancini.
Bnei Yehuda Tel Aviv: Emilius Zubas, Ben Turgeman, Ayed Habashi, Itzhak Azouz, Maor
Kandil (88' Dovev Gabay), Paz Ben Ari, Roei Gordana, Stav Finish (90' Yuval Ashkenazi),
Mavis Tchibota, Nerijus Valskis (61' Matan Hozez), Almog Buzaglo. Coach: Yossi Abuksis.
Goal: 67' Almog Buzaglo 0-1.
Referee: Ali Palabiyik (TUR)   Attendance: 45,670.

03.08.17   KSK Nika, Aleksandriya: FC Aleksandriya – Astra Giurgiu 1-0 (1-0)
FC Aleksandriya: Yuri Pankiv, Sergiy Chebotaev, Valeriy Bondarenko, Andriy Tsurikov,
Andriy Gitchenko, Andriy Batsula, Andriy Zaporozhan, Artem Sitalo (69' Stanislav Kulish),
Vasili Gritsuk (78' Maksim Kalenchuk), Sergey Starenkiy (57' Vitali Ponomar), Eugene
Banada. Coach: Volodymyr Sharan.
Astra Giurgiu: Plamen Iliev, Claudiu Belu, Piotr Polczak, Alexandru Dandea, Marquinhos
Carioca, Mateo Poljak (52' Romario Moise), Alexandru Ionita (II), Viorel Nicoara (65' Silviu
Balaure), Filip Mrzljak (85' Bogdan Chipirliu), Alexandru Stan, Anthony Le Tallec.
Coach: Eduard Iordanescu.
Goal: 43' Andriy Zaporozhan 1-0 (p).
Referee: Oliver Drachta (AUT)   Attendance: 4,820.

03.08.17   Bakcell Arena, Baku: Gabala FK – Panathinaikos 1-2 (0-0)
Gabala FK: Dmitro Bezotosniy, Vojislav Stankovic, Vitaliy Vernydub, Dave Bulthuis, Andy
Halliday, Dion Malone (79' Elvin Mammadov), Ilgar Gurbanov, Filip Ozobic, Steeven Joseph-
Monrose, Bagaliy Dabo (74' Famoussa Koné), Javid Hüseynov (74' Asif Mammadov).
Coach: Roman Grygorchuk.
Panathinaikos: Odisseas Vlachodimos, Dimitrios Kolovetsios, Rodrigo Moledo, Ousmane
Coulibaly, Omri Altman (56' Luciano), Zeca, Robin Lod, Dimitrios Kourbelis, Niklas Hult,
Guillermo Molins (79' Nuno Reis), Anastasios Chatzigiovannis (61' Bryan Cabezas).
Coach: Marinos Ouzounidis.
Goals: 52' Rodrigo Moledo 1-0 (og), 63' Robin Lod 1-1, 67' Bryan Cabezas 1-2.
Referee: Craig Pawson (ENG)   Attendance: 11,000.

03.08.17   Puskás Akadémia Pancho Aréna, Felcsút:
           Videoton FC – Girondins Bordeaux 1-0 (1-0)
Videoton FC: Ádám Kovácsik, Attila Fiola, Loïc Négo, Stopira, Roland Juhász, Máté Pátkai,
Roland Szolnoki, József Varga, Asmir Suljic (88' Krisztián Tamás), Ezekiel Henty (90+5'
Bence Szabó), Marko Scepovic (46' Danko Lazovic). Coach: Marko Nikolic.
Girondins Bordeaux: Benoît Costil, Milan Gajic, Igor Lewczuk, Youssouf Sabaly, Younousse
Sankharé, Jérémy Toulalan, Jaroslav Plasil (78' Thomas Touré), Valentín Vada (46' Alexandre
Mendy), Malcom, François Kamano, Gaëtan Laborde (49' Diego Contento).
Coach: Jocelyn Gourvennec.
Goal: 45+5' Stopira 1-0.
Referee: Christian Dingert (GER)   Attendance: 3,537.
Sent off: 47' Youssouf Sabaly, 69' József Varga.

Videoton FC won on away goals.

299

03.08.17   Generali Arena, Praha: Sparta Praha – Crvena Zvezda 0-1 (0-1)
Sparta Praha: Martin Dúbravka, Michal Kadlec, Lukás Stetina, Vyacheslav Karavaev, Lukás
Marecek, Georges Mandjeck, Martin Frydek, Srdan Plavsic, Rio Mavuba (66' Tomás
Rosicky), Václav Kadlec (46' Tal Ben Haim), Marc Janko (61' David Lafata).
Coach: Andrea Stramaccioni.
Crvena Zvezda: Milan Borjan, Milan Rodic, Filip Stojkovic, Vujadin Savic, Branko Jovicic,
Damien Le Tallec, Guélor Kanga, Mitchell Donald, Slavoljub Srnic (70' Nemanja Radonjic),
Richmond Boakye (80' Aleksandar Pesic), Nemanja Milic (90' Marko Gobeljic).
Coach: Vladan Milojevic.
Goal: 19' Richmond Boakye 0-1.
Referee: Tony Chapron (FRA)   Attendance: 16,808.

03.08.17   AEK Arena – George Karapatakis, Larnaca:
          Apollon Limassol – Aberdeen FC 2-0 (1-0)
Apollon Limassol: Bruno Vale, Jander, Valentin Roberge, Héctor Yuste, Alex da Silva (84'
Emilio Zelaya), João Pedro, Charis Kyriakou, Alef, André Schembri (65' Adrián Sardinero),
Antonio Jakolis (73' Marios Stylianou), Anton Maglica. Coach: Sofronis Avgousti.
Aberdeen FC: Joe Lewis, Shaleum Logan, Graeme Shinnie, Andrew Considine, Anthony
O'Connor, Mark Reynolds (78' Scott Wright), Kenny McLean, Gary Mackay-Steven, Ryan
Christie, Greg Stewart (64' Greg Tansey), Jayden Stockley (54' Nicky Maynard).
Coach: Derek McInnes.
Goals: 17' André Schembri 1-0, 86' Emilio Zelaya 2-0.
Referee: Stephan Klossner (SUI)   Attendance: 6,250.

03.08.17   Sükrü Saracoglustadion, Istanbul: Fenerbahçe – Sturm Graz 1-1 (1-0)
Fenerbahçe: Volkan Demirel, Hasan-Ali Kaldirim, Nabil Dirar, Sener Özbayrakli, Martin
Skrtel, Alper Potuk, Ozan Tufan (83' Mehmet Topal), Mathieu Valbuena (90+3' Mauricio
Isla), Roman Neustädter, Ahmethan Köse (63' Robin van Persie), Souza.
Coach: Aykut Kocaman.
Sturm Graz: Jörg Siebenhandl, Charalampos Lykogiannis, Marvin Potzmann, Fabian Koch,
Dario Maresic, James Jeggo (82' Romano Schmid), Peter Zulj, Philipp Huspek, Stefan
Hierländer, Thorsten Röcher (46' Philipp Zulechner), Deni Alar (63' Fabian Schubert).
Coach: Franco Foda.
Goals: 32' Nabil Dirar 1-0, 66' Philipp Huspek 1-1.
Referee: Bobby Madley (ENG)   Attendance: 37,701.

03.08.17   Stade Émile Mayrisch, Esch-sur-Alzette: CS FOLA Esch – Östersunds FK 1-2 (0-0)
CS FOLA Esch: Thomas Hym, Cédric Sacras, Tom Laterza, Julien Klein, Peter Chrappan,
Veldin Muharemovic, Michel Bechtold (66' Ken Corral), Enis Saiti (81' Gérard Mersch),
Alexander Cvetkovic (75' Stefan Lopes Rocha), Samir Hadji, Stefano Bensi.
Coach: Jeff Strasser.
Östersunds FK: Aly Keita, Sotirios Papagiannopoulos, Tim Björkström (46' Saman Ghoddos),
Dennis Widgren, Gabriel Somi (85' Bobo Sollander), Samuel Laryeal Mensah, Tom
Pettersson, Jamie Hopcutt (80' Ronald Mukiibi), Fouad Bachirou, Brwa Nouri, Alhaji Gero.
Coach: Graham Potter.
Goals: 53' Stefano Bensi 1-0, 59' Gabriel Somi 1-1, 66' Tom Pettersson 1-2.
Referee: Kristo Tohver (EST)   Attendance: 1,590.

03.08.17   Lyngby Stadion, Lyngby: Lyngby BK – FK Krasnodar 1-3 (1-2)
Lyngby BK: Mikkel Andersen, Thomas Christensen, Michael Lumb, Thomas Sørensen (81'
Kevin Tshiembe), Oliver Lund, Martin Ørnskov, Jesper Christjansen, Mikkel Rygaard Jensen
(72' Kim Ojo), Bror Blume (59' Kristoffer Larsen), Jeppe Kjær, David Boysen.
Coach: David Nielsen.
FK Krasnodar: Andrey Sinitsyn, Aleksandr Martinovich, Andreas Granqvist, Cristian Ramírez,
Roman Shishkin (64' Yuri Gazinskiy), Wanderson (86' Magomed Suleymanov), Víctor
Claessson, Pavel Mamaev, Mihailo Ristic, Mauricio Pereyra (80' Ilya Zhigulev), Charles
Kaboré. Coach: Igor Shalimov.
Goals: 9', 22' Mauricio Pereyra 0-1, 0-2, 28' Mikkel Rygaard Jensen 1-2,
89' Pavel Mamaev 1-3 (p).
Referee: Sebastian Coltescu (ROM)   Attendance: 2,887.

03.08.17   Elbasan Arena, Elbasan: KF Skënderbeu – FK Mladá Boleslav 2-1 (0-1,2-1)
KF Skënderbeu: Orges Shehi, Gledi Mici, Bajram Jashanica, Tefik Osmani (80' Sebino Plaku),
Kristi Vangjeli, Marko Radas, Enis Gavazaj (74' Gjergj Muzaka), Bakary Nimaga, Liridon
Latifi, Sabien Lilaj, Segun Adeniyi (68' Donjet Shkodra). Coach: Ilir Daja.
FK Mladá Boleslav: Jakub Divis, Jirí Fleisman, Douglas Silva, Tomás Fabián (71' Petr Mares),
Patrizio Stronati, Lukás Pauschek, Adam János (111' Lukás Magera), Marek Matejovsky,
Tomás Príkryl, Jakub Rada, Nikolay Komlichenko (60' Golgol Mebrahtu).
Coach: Dusan Uhrin.
Goals: 19' Adam János 0-1, 55' Sabien Lilaj 1-1 (p), 83' Sebino Plaku 2-1.
Referee: Sergey Boyko (UKR)   Attendance: 4,850.

KF Skënderbeu won 4-2 on penalties following extra time.
Penalties: Shehi 1-0, Mares 1-1, Latifi 2-1, Príkryl 2-2, Muzaka 3-2, Rada missed, Lilaj 4-2,
Mebrahtu missed.

03.08.17   Stadio Toumbas, Saloniki: PAOK Saloniki – Olimpik Donetsk 2-0 (2-0)
PAOK Saloniki: Rodrigo Rey, Léo Matos, Marin Leovac, José Ángel Crespo, Fernando
Varela, Gojko Cimirot, Diego Biseswar (66' Pedro Henrique), Cañas (72' Yevhen Shakhov),
Aleksandar Prijovic, Djalma (81' Dimitrios Pelkas), Róbert Mak.
Coach: Aleksandar Stanojevic.
Olimpik Donetsk: Zauri Makharadze, Pavlo Lukyanchuk (46' Oleksandr Migunov), Artem
Shabanov, Dmitriy Nemchaninov, Evgeniy Tsymbalyuk, Anton Kravchenko, Sergiy
Shestakov, Vladyslav Khomutov (60' Ivan Sondey), Andrey Bogdanov, Mohammed Rhasalla,
Stanislav Bilenkyi (71' Ilya Mikhalev). Coach: Roman Sanzhar.
Goals: 24' Róbert Mak 1-0, 45+1' Gojko Cimirot 2-0.
Referee: Ivaylo Stoyanov (BUL)   Attendance: 13,960.

03.08.17   Estádio dos Barreiros, Funchal: CD Marítimo – Botev Plovdiv 2-0 (1-0)
CS Marítimo: Charles, Pablo, Zainadine Junior, Luís Martins, Bebeto, Erdem Sen, Éber Bessa
(69' Jean Cleber), Gamboa, Rodrigo Pinho (84' Viktor Lundberg), Edgar Costa, Ricardo
Valente (76' Piqueti). Coach: Daniel Ramos.
Botev Plovdiv: Ivan Cvorovic, Tsvetomir Panov, Victor Genev, Meledje Omnibes (46' Felipe
Brisola), Jordan Minev (82' Lazar Marin), Krum Stoyanov (61' Toni Tasev), Plamen Dimov,
Serkan Yusein, Lachezar Baltanov, Fernando Viana, Omar Kossoko. Coach: Nikolai Kirov.
Goals: 34' Rodrigo Pinho 1-0 (p), 49' Ricardo Valente 2-0.
Referee: Srdan Jovanovic (SER)   Attendance: 6,143.

03.08.17   INEA stadion, Poznan: Lech Poznan – FC Utrecht 2-2 (1-1)
Lech Poznan: Matús Putnocky, Nikola Vujadinovic, Volodymyr Kostevych, Rafal Janicki,
Emir Dilaver (81' Deniss Rakels), Abdul Tetteh (85' Nicki Bille Nielsen), Lukasz Tralka,
Maciej Makuszewski, Radoslaw Majewski, Mario Situm (71' Nicklas Bärkroth), Christian
Gytkjær. Coach: Nenad Bjelica.
FC Utrecht: David Jensen, Mark van der Maarel, Ramon Leeuwin, Willem Janssen, Sean
Klaiber, Edson Braafheid (69' Robin van der Meer), Zakaria Labyad, Urby Emanuelson (46'
Yassin Ayoub), Sander van de Streek, Gyrano Kerk (74' Giovanni Troupée), Cyriel Dessers.
Coach: Erik ten Hag.
Goals: 1' Gyrano Kerk 0-1, 26' Christian Gytkjær 1-1, 89' Cyriel Dessers 1-2,
90+4' Christian Gytkjær 2-2.
Referee: Mads-Kristoffer Kristoffersen (DEN)   Attendance: 33,446.
Sent off: 70' Ramon Leeuwin.

FC Utrecht won on away goals.

03.08.17   MCH Arena, Herning: FC Midtjylland – Arka Gdynia 2-1 (0-0)
FC Midtjylland: Jesper Hansen, Kian Hansen, Zsolt Korcsmár, Marc Hende (69' Filip Novák),
Rasmus Nissen Kristensen, Tim Sparv (75' Bozhidar Kraev), Jakob Poulsen, Jonas Borring
(57' Alexander Sørloth), Rilwan Hassan, Ebere Onuachu, Gustav Wikheim.
Coach: Jess Thorup.
Arka Gdynia: Pāvels Steinbors, Tadeusz Socha, Krzysztof Sobieraj, Dawid Soldecki, Adam
Marciniak, Marcin Warcholak, Michal Marcjanik, Grzegorz Piesio, Yannick Kakoko, Patryk
Kun (56' Rafal Siemaszko), Marcus Vinícius (75' Álvaro Rey). Coach: Leszek Ojrzynski.
Goals: 59' Dawid Soldecki 0-1, 77' Tadeusz Socha 1-1 (og), 90+3' Alexander Sørloth 2-1.
Referee: Eitan Shmeulevitch (ISR)   Attendance: 8,138.

FC Midtjylland won on away goals.

03.08.17   Stadion Poljud, Split: Hajduk Split – Brøndby IF 2-0 (0-0)
Hajduk Split: Dante Stipica, Borja López, Josip Juranovic, Zoran Nizic, Hysen Memolla,
Hamza Barry, Nikola Vlasic, Zvonimir Kozulj (75' Edin Sehic), Ante Erceg (83' Ahmed Said),
Savvas Gentsoglou, Márkó Futács (90+1' Ivan Pesic). Coach: Joan Carrillo.
Brøndby IF: Frederik Rønnow, Benedikt Röcker, Hjörtur Hermannsson, Johan Larsson, Svenn
Crone, Kasper Fisker (65' Simon Tibbling), Hany Mukhtar, Besar Halimi (62' Kevin Mensah),
Christian Nørgaard, Kamil Wilczek (65' Zsolt Kalmár), Lasse Christensen.
Coach: Alexander Zorniger.
Goals: 59', 63' Ante Erceg 1-0, 2-0.
Referee: Orel Grinfeld (ISR)   Attendance: 30,204.

03.08.17   Tivoli Stadion Tirol, Innsbruck: SCR Altach – KAA Gent 3-1 (1-1)
SCR Altach: Martin Kobras, Lucas Galvão, Philipp Netzer, Emanuel Sakic, Benedikt Zech,
Patrick Salomon, Simon Piesinger (26' Christian Gebauer), Stefan Nutz (86' Jan
Zwischenbrugger), Kristijan Dobras, Nicolas Ngamaleu, Hannes Aigner (80' Adrian Grbic).
Coach: Klaus Schmidt.
KAA Gent: Jacob Rinne, Samuel Gigot, Stefan Mitrovic, Nana Asare, Brecht Dejaegere,
Franko Andrijasevic (68' Mamadou Sylla), Damien Marcq, Anderson Esiti (39' Samuel Kalu),
Danijel Milicevic (80' Yūya Kubo), Kalifa Coulibaly, Moses Simon.
Coach: Hein Vanhaezebrouck.
Goals: 11' Nicolas Ngamaleu 1-0, 44' Danijel Milicevic 1-1 (p), 76' Stefan Nutz 2-1,
88' Kristijan Dobras 3-1.
Referee: Nicolas Rainville (FRA)   Attendance: 3,852.
Sent off: 49' Stefan Mitrovic.

302

03.08.17   Stadion Gradski vrt, Osijek: NK Osijek – PSV Eindhoven 1-0 (1-0)
NK Osijek: Marko Malenica, Borna Barisic, Mateo Barac, Petar Bockaj, Mile Skoric, Benedik Mioc (88' Zoran Lesjak), Robert Mudrazija, Dmitriy Lepa (78' Aljosa Vojnovic), Muzafer Ejupi, Eros Grezda (90+1' Alen Grgic), Tomislav Sorsa. Coach: Zoran Zekic.
PSV Eindhoven: Jeroen Zoet, Nicolas Isimat-Mirin, Derrick Luckassen, Santiago Arias, Joshua Brenet (64' Gastón Pereiro), Davy Pröpper (76' Sam Lammers), Jorrit Hendrix, Marco van Ginkel, Hirving Lozano, Steven Bergwijn (64' Luuk de Jong), Jürgen Locadia.
Coach: Phillip Cocu.
Goal: 25' Petar Bockaj 1-0.
Referee: Hugo Miguel (POR)   Attendance: 15,000.

03.08.17   San Mamés Barria, Bilbao: Athletic Bilbao – Dinamo Bucuresti 3-0 (2-0)
Athletic Bilbao: Iago Herrerín, Aymeric Laporte, Etxeita, De Marcos, Balenziaga, Beñat (80' Iñaki Williams), Susaeta, Mikel Vesga, Raúl García (70' San José), Muniain, Aduriz (88' Ager Aketxe). Coach: José Ángel Ziganda.
Dinamo Bucuresti: Jaime Penedo, Giorgios Katsikas, Ionut Nedelcearu, Romera, Sergiu Hanca (55' Valentin Costache), Steliano Filip, May Mahlangu, Filipe Nascimento (72' Paul Anton), Rivaldinho, Adam Nemec (66' Juan Albín), Diogo Salomão. Coach: Cosmin Contra.
Goals: 24', 29' Raúl García 1-0, 2-0, 86' Aduriz 3-0.
Referee: Pavle Radovanovic (MNE)   Attendance: 41,845.

03.08.17   Stadio Giuseppe Meazza, Milano: AC Milan – CS Universitatea Craiova 2-0 (1-0)
AC Milan: Gianluigi Donnarumma, Andrea Conti, Cristián Zapata, Mateo Musacchio, Ricardo Rodríguez, Giacomo Bonaventura (81' Fabio Borini), Manuel Locatelli, Franck Kessié, Suso (65' Hakan Çalhanoglu), Patrick Cutrone (71' André Silva), M'Baye Niang.
Coach: Vincenzo Montella.
CS Universitatea Craiova: Nicolae Calancea, Tiago Ferreira, Renato Kelic, Radoslav Dimitrov, Hrvoje Spahija, Alexandru Baluta (65' Mihai Roman), Nicusor Bancu, Fausto Rossi (46' Alexandru Mateiu), Hristo Zlatinski, Alexandru Mitrita (83' Cristian Barbut), Gustavo Di Mauro. Coach: Devis Mangia.
Goals: 9' Giacomo Bonaventura 1-0, 51' Patrick Cutrone 2-0.
Referee: Nikola Popov (BUL)   Attendance: 65,763.

03.08.17   Versluys Arena, Oostende: KV Oostende – Olympique Marseille 0-0
KV Oostende: Silvio Proto, David Rozehnal, Ramin Rezaeian (46' Yassine El Ghanassy), Brecht Capon, Zarko Tomasevic, Antonio Milic, Sébastien Siani, Franck Berrier (76' Fernando Canesin Matos), Andile Jali, Knowledge Musona, Joseph Akpala (69' Richairo Zivkovic). Coach: Yves Vanderhaeghe.
Olympique Marseille: Steve Mandanda, Hiroki Sakai, Rolando, Tomás Hubocan, Adil Rami, Lucas Ocampos, Morgan Sanson, Dimitri Payet (88' Dória), Luiz Gustavo, Maxime Lopez (60' Grégory Sertic), Valère Germain (73' Clinton N'Jie). Coach: Rudi García.
Referee: Marco Guida (ITA)   Attendance: 7,900.

03.08.17   Futbalovy stadión MFK Ruzomberok, Ruzomberok:
MFK Ruzomberok – Everton FC 0-1 (0-0)
MFK Ruzomberok: Matús Macík, Dominik Kruzliak, Ján Maslo, Peter Maslo, Jozef Menich
(46' Milos Lacny), Kristi Qose, Peter Gál-Andrezly, Dalibor Takác (71' Marek Sapara), Matej
Kochan, Erik Daniel, Nermin Haskic (80' Stefan Gerec). Coach: Norbert Hrncár.
Everton FC: Jordan Pickford, Leighton Baines, Michael Keane, Ashley Williams, Phil
Jagielka, Morgan Schneiderlin (81' Gareth Barry), Idrissa Gueye, Davy Klaassen, Tom Davies,
Sandro Ramírez (69' Dominic Calvert-Lewin), Wayne Rooney (86' Kevin Mirallas).
Coach: Ronald Koeman.
Goal: 80' Dominic Calvert-Lewin 0-1.
Referee: Michael Tykgaard (DEN)   Attendance: 4,752.

03.08.17   Stadio Néas Smírnis, Athen: Panionios GSS – Maccabi Tel Aviv 0-1 (0-0)
Panionios GSS: Matic Kotnik, Vangelis Ikonomou (12' Dimitris Stavropoulos), Ehsan Hajsafi,
Yaya Banana, Valentinos Vlachos, Panagiotis Korbos, Giorgos Masouras, Masoud Shojaei,
Kyriakos Savvidis (86' Spyridon Glinos), Lazaros Lamprou (73' Fiorin Durmishaj), Samed
Yesil. Coach: Michalis Grigoriou.
Maccabi Tel Aviv: Predrag Rajkovic, Yuval Shpungin, Eitan Tibi, Tal Ben Haim, Ofir
Davidzade, Omer Atzili, Sheran Yeini, Eyal Golasa (87' Avi Rikan), Cristian Battocchio (76'
Dor Mikha), Vidar Kjartansson (83' Dor Peretz), Aaron Schoenfeld. Coach: Jordi Cruijff.
Goal: 79' Panagiotis Korbos 0-1 (og).
Referee: Ville Nevalainen (FIN)   Attendance: 3,167.

03.08.17   Stadion Stozice, Ljubljana: NK Domzale – SC Freiburg 2-0 (0-0)
NK Domzale: Dejan Milic, Tilen Klemencic, Matija Sirok, Miha Blazic, Gaber Dobrovoljc,
Jure Balkovec, Amedej Vetrih, Senijad Ibricic (90' Adam Gneza Cerin), Zeni Husmani, Ivan
Firer (71' Zan Zuzek), Lovro Bizjak (78' Alen Ozbolt). Coach: Simon Rozman.
SC Freiburg: Alexander Schwolow, Aleksandar Ignjovski (56' Janik Haberer), Philipp
Lienhart, Çaglar Söyüncü (62' Marc Oliver Kempf), Pascal Stenzel, Christian Günter, Amir
Abrashi, Mike Frantz (85' Tim Kleindienst), Nicolas Höfler, Florian Niederlechner, Nils
Petersen. Coaches: Christian Streich & Florian Bruns.
Goals: 50' Senijad Ibricic 1-0 (p), 59' Lovro Bizjak 2-0.
Referee: Alexander Boucaut (BEL)   Attendance: 5,136.

03.08.17   Estádio Municipal de Braga, Braga: Sporting Braga – AIK Solna 2-1 (0-1,1-1)
Sporting Braga: Matheus Magalhães, Lazar Rosic, Jefferson, Raúl Silva, Ricardo Esgaio,
Fransérgio, Danilo Barbosa (68' Nikola Vukcevic), Rui Fonte, Wilson Eduardo (105' Ricardo
Horta), Pedro Santos (46' Bruno Xadas), Ahmed Hassan Koka. Coach: Abel Ferreira.
AIK Solna: Oscar Linnér, Per Karlsson, Nils-Eric Johansson, Jesper Nyholm, Kristoffer
Olsson, Johan Blomberg, Rasmus Lindkvist, Daniel Sundgren, Stefan Ishizaki (76' Anton
Jönsson Salétros), Henok Goitom, Chinedu Obasi (68' Nicolás Marcelo Stefanelli).
Coach: Rikard Norling.
Goals: 13' Chinedu Obasi 0-1, 74' Rui Fonte 1-1, 120+1' Raúl Silva 2-1.
Referee: Frank Schneider (FRA)   Attendance: 13,851.

Sporting Braga through after extra time.

304

PLAY-OFFS

16.08.17   Stadion Galgenwaard, Utrecht: FC Utrecht – Zenit St.Petersburg 1-0 (0-0)
FC Utrecht: David Jensen, Mark van der Maarel, Robin van der Meer (78' Giovanni Troupée), Sean Klaiber, Edson Braafheid (89' Dario Dumic), Yassin Ayoub, Zakaria Labyad, Urby Emanuelson, Sander van de Streek, Gyrano Kerk (79' Lukas Görtler), Cyriel Dessers. Coach: Erik ten Hag.
Zenit St.Petersburg: Andrei Lunev, Domenico Criscito, Igor Smolnikov, Emanuel Mammana, Branislav Ivanovic, Leandro Paredes, Matías Kranevitter (84' Daler Kuzyaev), Yuriy Zhirkov, Aleksandr Erokhin, Aleksandr Kokorin (89' Artem Dzyuba), Sebastián Driussi (57' Dmitriy Poloz). Coach: Roberto Mancini.
Goal: 76' Zakaria Labyad 1-0.
Referee: Slavko Vincic (SVN)   Attendance: 19,370.

17.08.17   AEK Arena – George Karapatakis, Larnaca:
           Apollon Limassol – FC Midtjylland 3-2 (1-1)
Apollon Limassol: Bruno Vale, Jander, Valentin Roberge, Héctor Yuste, Esteban Sachetti, Alex da Silva (67' Emilio Zelaya), João Pedro, Charis Kyriakou, André Schembri (81' Ioannis Pittas), Adrián Sardinero (57' Antonio Jakolis), Anton Maglica. Coach: Sofronis Avgousti.
FC Midtjylland: Jesper Hansen, Kian Hansen, Zsolt Korcsmár, Marc Hende, Rasmus Nissen Kristensen, Tim Sparv, Jakob Poulsen, Janus Drachmann (81' Gustav Wikheim), Jonas Borring (64' Filip Novák), Rilwan Hassan (69' André Rømer), Alexander Sørloth. Coach: Jess Thorup.
Goals: 15' Charis Kyriakou 1-0, 38' Alexander Sørloth 1-1, 69' Jander 2-1, 74' Alexander Sørloth 2-2, 90+1' Ioannis Pittas 3-2.
Referee: Michael Oliver (ENG)   Attendance: 5,250.

17.08.17   Stadion FK Krasnodar, Krasnodar: FK Krasnodar – Crvena Zvezda 3-2 (1-0)
FK Krasnodar: Andrey Sinitsyn, Aleksandr Martinovich, Andreas Granqvist, Cristian Ramírez, Sergey Petrov, Wanderson, Yuri Gazinskiy, Victor Claessson (78' Magomed Suleymanov), Pavel Mamaev (72' Ilya Zhigulev), Mihailo Ristic, Ivan Ignatyev (66' Fedor Smolov). Coach: Igor Shalimov.
Crvena Zvezda: Milan Borjan, Srdan Babic (70' Aleksandar Pesic), Filip Stojkovic, Dusan Andjelkovic (78' Marko Gobeljic), Vujadin Savic, Damien Le Tallec, Guélor Kanga, Mitchell Donald, Slavoljub Srnic, Richmond Boakye, Nemanja Radonjic (66' Nemanja Milic). Coach: Vladan Milojevic.
Goals: 20' Ivan Ignatyev 1-0, 46' Victor Claesson 2-0, 57' Slavoljub Srnic 2-1, 66' Sergey Petrov 3-1, 71' Aleksandar Pesic 3-2.
Referee: Gediminas Mazeika (LTU)   Attendance: 24,587.

17.08.17   Borisov Arena, Borisov: BATE Borisov – FC Aleksandriya 1-1 (1-1)
BATE Borisov: Denis Scherbitski, Jurica Buljat, Nemanja Milunovic, Maksim Volodko, Aleksandr Volodko (59' Nikolay Signevich), Mirko Ivanic, Stanislav Dragun, Igor Stasevich, Dmitriy Baga, Vitaliy Rodionov (83' Jasse Tuominen), Mikhail Gordeychuk (77' Yuri Kendysh). Coach: Aleksandr Yermakovich.
FC Aleksandriya: Yuri Pankiv, Sergiy Chebotaev, Andriy Tsurikov, Andriy Gitchenko, Andriy Batsula, Sergiy Basov, Artem Polyarus (77' Sergey Starenkiy), Andriy Zaporozhan (63' Maksim Kalenchuk), Artem Sitalo, Vasili Gritsuk (69' Vitali Ponomar), Eugene Banada. Coach: Volodymyr Sharan.
Goals: 8' Mirko Ivanic 1-0, 20' Eugene Banada 1-1.
Referee: Tamás Bognar (HUN)   Attendance: 11,467.

17.08.17   Stadion Maksimir, Zagreb: Dinamo Zagreb – KF Skënderbeu 1-1 (0-1)
Dinamo Zagreb: Dominik Livakovic, Jan Lecjaks, Leonardo Sigali, Filip Benkovic, Petar
Stojanovic, Tongo Doumbia (81' Ivan Fiolic), Ante Coric (36' Domagoj Pavicic), Amer
Gojak, Nikola Moro, Armin Hodzic (77' Ángelo Henríquez), Junior Fernándes.
Coach: Mario Cvitanovic.
KF Skënderbeu: Orges Shehi, Gledi Mici, Bajram Jashanica, Tefik Osmani (69' Segun
Adeniyi), Kristi Vangjeli, Marko Radas, Enis Gavazaj (81' Gjergj Muzaka), Bakary Nimaga,
Liridon Latifi, Sabien Lilaj, Ali Sowe (88' Bruno Dita). Coach: Ilir Daja.
Goals: 37' Liridon Latifi 0-1, 90+4' Ángelo Henríquez 1-1.
Referee: Andris Treimanis (LAT)   Attendance: 9,369.

17.08.17   Kaplakrikavöllur, Hafnarfjördur: FH Hafnarfjördur – Sporting Braga 1-2 (1-0)
FH Hafnarfjördur: Gunnar Nielsen, Cédric D'Ulivo, Pétur Vidarsson (70' Emil Pálsson),
Kassim Doumbia, Bödvar Bödvarsson, Bergsveinn Ólafsson, Robbie Crawford (75' Thórarinn
Valdimarsson), David Vidarsson, Steven Lennon, Atli Gudnason, Halldór Björnsson (87' Atli
Björnsson). Coach: Heimir Gudjónsson.
Sporting Braga: Matheus Magalhães, Jefferson, Raúl Silva, Bruno Viana, Ricardo Esgaio,
Bruno Xadas (77' Fábio Martins), Fransérgio, Nikola Vukcevic, Ahmed Hassan Koka (59'
Nikola Stojiljkovic), Paulinho (84' Danilo Barbosa), Ricardo Horta. Coach: Abel Ferreira.
Goals: 39' Halldór Björnsson 1-0, 62' Paulinho 1-1, 79' Nikola Stojiljkovic 1-2.
Referee: Kevin Blom (HOL)   Attendance: 1,432.

17.08.17   Filip II Makedonski, Skopje: Vardar Skopje – Fenerbahçe 2-0 (1-0)
Vardar Skopje: Filip Gacevski, Boban Hambardzumyan, Evgen Novak,
Stefan Spirovski, Dejan Blazevic (85' Nikola Gligorov), Damir Kojasevic (67' Jambul
Jigauri), Tigran Barseghyan, Boban Nikolov, Besir Demiri (46' Vladica Brdarovski), Juan
Felipe Alves. Coaches: Goce Sedloski & Cedomir Janevski.
Fenerbahçe: Carlos Kameni, Hasan-Ali Kaldirim, Nabil Dirar, Sener Özbayrakli (71' Aatif
Chahechouhe), Martin Skrtel, Mehmet Topal, Alper Potuk, Ozan Tufan (82' Mauricio Isla),
Mathieu Valbuena, Ahmethan Köse (64' Soldado), Souza. Coach: Aykut Kocaman.
Goals: 20' Tigran Barseghyan 1-0, 90+2' Mehmet Topal 2-0 (og).
Referee: Luca Banti (ITA)   Attendance: 20,863.
Sent off: 89' Boban Grncarov, 90+3' Souza.

17.08.17   Stadio Toumbas, Saloniki: PAOK Saloniki – Östersunds FK 3-1 (1-1)
PAOK Saloniki: Rodrigo Rey, Léo Matos, Marin Leovac, José Ángel Crespo, Fernando
Varela, Gojko Cimirot, Diego Biseswar (74' Pedro Henrique), Yevhen Shakhov (63' Dimitrios
Pelkas), Aleksandar Prijovic, Djalma, Róbert Mak (81' Stefanos Athanasiadis).
Coach: Razvan Lucescu.
Östersunds FK: Aly Keita, Sotirios Papagiannopoulos, Dennis Widgren, Samuel Laryeal
Mensah, Ronald Mukiibi (72' Doug Bergqvist), Tom Pettersson, Ken Sema (71' Alhaji Gero),
Fouad Bachirou, Brwa Nouri, Saman Ghoddos (81' Tim Björkström), Hosam Aiesh.
Coach: Graham Potter.
Goals: 21' Brwa Nouri 0-1 (p), 38' Léo Matos 1-1, 77', 88' Aleksandar Prijovic 2-1, 3-1 (p).
Referee: Bas Nijhuis (HOL)   Attendance: 16,743.

306

17.08.17   Doosan Aréna, Plzen: Viktoria Plzen – AEK Larnaca 3-1 (2-1)
Viktoria Plzen: Ales Hruska, Roman Hubník, David Limbersky, Radim Rezník, Tomás Hajek, Václav Pilar (63' Jan Kopic), Tomás Horava, Martin Zeman (84' Ales Cermák), Patrik Hrosovsky, Daniel Kolár, Marek Bakos (77' Jakub Reznícek). Coach: Pavel Vrba.
AEK Larnaca: Juan Pablo, Marios Antoniades (74' Tete), Truyols, Daniel Mojsov, Català, Ander Murillo, Jorge Larena, Joan Tomás (86' Nestoras Mitidis), Vincent Laban (82' Hector Hevel), Acorán, Ivan Trickovski. Coach: Imanol Idiakez.
Goals: 8' Acorán 0-1, 29' Marek Bakos 1-1, 36' Daniel Kolár 2-1, 75' Marek Bakos 3-1 (p).
Referee: Matej Jug (SVN)   Attendance: 10,031.

17.08.17   Stadio Apóstolos Nikolaidis, Athen: Panathinaikos – Athletic Bilbao 2-3 (1-0)
Panathinaikos: Odisseas Vlachodimos, Georgios Koutroubis, Nuno Reis, Rodrigo Moledo, Omri Altman (51' Luciano), Zeca, Bryan Cabezas (84' Christos Donis), Robin Lod, Dimitrios Kourbelis, Niklas Hult, Guillermo Molins (72' Anastasios Chatzigiovannis). Coach: Marinos Ouzounidis.
Athletic Bilbao: Iago Herrerín, Aymeric Laporte, Etxeita, De Marcos, Balenziaga, Beñat (77' San José), Lekue (57' Iñaki Williams), Mikel Vesga, Raúl García, Muniain (84' Susaeta), Aduriz. Coach: José Ángel Ziganda.
Goals: 29' Robin Lod 1-0, 55' Bryan Cabezas 2-0, 68' Aduriz 2-1, 71' De Marcos 2-2, 74' Aduriz 2-3 (p).
Referee: Jorge Sousa (POR)   Attendance: 15,000.

17.08.17   Tivoli Stadion Tirol, Innsbruck: SCR Altach – Maccabi Tel Aviv 0-1 (0-0)
SCR Altach: Martin Kobras, Lucas Galvão, Philipp Netzer, Andreas Lienhart, Jan Zwischenbrugger, Benedikt Zech, Christian Gebauer (71' Adrian Grbic), Patrick Salomon, Stefan Nutz, Kristijan Dobras, Nicolas Ngamaleu. Coach: Klaus Schmidt.
Maccabi Tel Aviv: Predrag Rajkovic, Yuval Shpungin, Eitan Tibi, Tal Ben Haim, Ofir Davidzade, Omer Atzili (65' Dor Mikha), Sheran Yeini, Avi Rikan, Cristian Battocchio (85' Egor Filipenko), Vidar Kjartansson, Aaron Schoenfeld (73' Dor Peretz). Coach: Jordi Cruijff.
Goal: 67' Vidar Kjartansson 0-1.
Referee: Aleksey Kulbakov (BLS)   Attendance: 5,269.

17.08.17   Ludogorets Arena, Razgrad: PFC Ludogorets Razgrad – FK Sūduva 2-0 (0-0)
PFC Ludogorets Razgrad: Renan, Cicinho, Natanael Pimienta, Cosmin Moti, Lucas Sasha, Svetoslav Dyakov, Igor Plastun, Wanderson (90+4' Gustavo Campanharo), Anicet Andrianantenaina, Claudiu Keserü (88' João Paulo), Virgil Misidjan (78' Jody Lukoki). Coach: Dimitar Dimitrov.
FK Sūduva: Ivan Kardum, Marius Cinikas, Radanfah Abu Bakr, Semir Kerla, Algis Jankauskas, Povilas Leimonas, Karolis Chvedukas (54' Ernestas Veliulis), Paulius Janusauskas (68' Jérémy Manzorro), Vaidas Slavickas, Ovidijus Verbickas, Robertas Vezevicius (80' Deividas Sesplaukis). Coach: Vladimir Cheburin.
Goals: 61' Cosmin Moti 1-0, 76' Virgil Misidjan 2-0.
Referee: Sebastien Delferière (BEL)   Attendance: 5,428.

17.08.17   Stadio Giuseppe Meazza, Milano: AC Milan – KF Shkëndija 79 6-0 (3-0)
AC Milan: Gianluigi Donnarumma, Andrea Conti (69' Ignazio Abate), Cristián Zapata,
Leonardo Bonucci, Luca Antonelli, Hakan Çalhanoglu (61' Giacomo Bonaventura), Riccardo
Montolivo, Franck Kessié, Suso (75' Patrick Cutrone), André Silva, Fabio Borini.
Coach: Vincenzo Montella.
KF Shkëndija 79: Kostadin Zahov, Egzon Bejtulai, Ardijan Cuculi, Ivan Celikovic (64' Olsi
Teqja), Armend Alimi, Ennur Totre, Ferhan Hasani, Blagoja Todorovski, Besart Ibraimi,
Marjan Radeski (82' Shefit Shefiti), Besart Abdurahimi (70' Besmir Bojku).
Coach: Qatip Osmani.
Goals: 13' André Silva 1-0, 25' Riccardo Montolivo 2-0, 27' André Silva 3-0,
67' Fabio Borini 4-0, 68' Luca Antonelli 5-0, 85' Riccardo Montolivo 6-0.
Referee: Harald Lechner (AUT)   Attendance: 40,613.

17.08.17   Stadion Gradski vrt, Osijek: NK Osijek – Austria Wien 1-2 (1-1)
NK Osijek: Marko Malenica, Borna Barisic, Petar Bockaj, Zoran Lesjak, Mile Skoric, Benedik
Mioc (73' Nikola Jambor), Milovan Petrovikj (46' Domagoj Pusic), Dmitriy Lepa, Muzafer
Ejupi, Eros Grezda (72' Antonio Perosevic), Tomislav Sorsa. Coach: Zoran Zekic.
Austria Wien: Osman Hadzikic, Abdul Kadiri Mohammed, Jens Stryger Larsen, Heiko
Westermann, Christoph Martschinko, Tarkan Serbest, Dominik Prokop (86' Ismael Tajouri
Shradi), David De Paula (90+1' David Cancola), Raphael Holzhauser, Christoph Monschein
(78' Kevin Friesenbichler), Felipe Pires. Coach: Thorsten Fink.
Goals: 15' Muzafer Ejupi 1-0, 26' Christoph Monschein 1-1, 60' Raphael Holzhauser 1-2.
Referee: Deniz Aytekin (GER)   Attendance: 15,000.

Borna Barisic missed a penalty kick (19').

17.08.17   Amsterdam ArenA, Amsterdam: AFC Ajax – Rosenborg BK 0-1 (0-0)
AFC Ajax: André Onana, Joël Veltman, Matthijs de Ligt, Nick Viergever, Mitchell Dijks,
Donny van de Beek, Hakim Ziyech, Lasse Schöne, David Neres (61' Justin Kluivert), Amin
Younes, Kasper Dolberg (66' Klaas-Jan Huntelaar). Coach: Marcel Keizer.
Rosenborg BK: André Hansen, Vegar Hedenstad (72' Matthías Vilhjálmsson), Birger Meling,
Johan Bjørdal, Jørgen Skjelvik, Mike Jensen, Anders Konradsen, Fredrik Midtsjø, Nicklas
Bendtner, Yann-Erik De Lanlay (69' Samuel Adegbenro), Milan Jevtovic (90+2' Alex
Gersbach). Coach: Kåre Ingebrigtsen.
Goal: 0-1 77' Samuel Adegbenro 0-1.
Referee: Craig Thomson (SCO)   Attendance: 50,717.

17.08.17   Jan Breydelstadion, Brugge: Club Brugge KV – AEK Athen 0-0
Club Brugge KV: Ethan Horvath, Helibelton Palacios (72' Lior Refaelov), Stefano Denswil,
Brandon Mechele, Timmy Simons, Hans Vanaken, Ruud Volmer, Marvelous Nakamba, Jelle
Vossen (57' Wesley), Anthony Limbombe, Emmanuel Bonaventure Dennis (80' Abdoulaye
Diaby). Coach: Ivan Leko.
AEK Athen: Giannis Anestis, Michalis Bakakis, Hélder Lopes, Ognjen Vranjes, Uros Cosic,
Dmitro Chigrinskiy, André Simões (86' Astrit Ajdarevic), Petros Mantalos (73' Jakob
Johansson), Konstantinos Galanopoulos, Viktor Klonaridis (58' Lazaros Christodoulopoulos),
Marko Livaja. Coach: Manolo Jiménez.
Referee: Viktor Kassai (HUN)   Attendance: 27,115.
Sent off: 59' Marko Livaja.

17.08.17   Stadion Stozice, Ljubljana: NK Domzale – Olympique Marseille 1-1 (1-0)
NK Domzale: Dejan Milic, Tilen Klemencic, Matija Sirok, Miha Blazic, Jure Balkovec,
Amedej Vetrih, Jan Repas, Senijad Ibricic (90' Zan Zuzek), Zeni Husmani, Ivan Firer (73'
Petar Franjic), Lovro Bizjak (88' Alen Ozbolt). Coach: Simon Rozman.
Olympique Marseille: Steve Mandanda, Hiroki Sakai, Patrice Evra, Adil Rami, Lucas
Ocampos, Morgan Sanson, Luiz Gustavo, Grégory Sertic, Florian Thauvin (75' Clinton N'Jie),
Maxime Lopez (84' André Zambo Anguissa), Valère Germain (87' Rémy Cabella).
Coach: Rudi García.
Goals: 12' Amedej Vetrih 1-0, 63' Morgan Sanson 1-1.
Referee: Bobby Madden (SCO)   Attendance: 10,543.

17.08.17   Stadion Wojska Polskiego, Warszawa: Legia Warszawa – FC Sheriff 1-1 (0-0)
Legia Warszawa: Arkadiusz Malarz, Michal Pazdan, Maciej Dabrowski, Adam Hlousek, Artur
Jedrzejczyk, Guilherme (24' Michal Kucharczyk), Dominik Nagy (72' Hildeberto Pereira),
Krzysztof Maczynski, Sebastian Szymanski, Thibault Moulin, Armando Sadiku (56' Kasper
Hämäläinen). Coach: Jacek Magiera.
FC Sheriff: Zvonimir Mikulic, Cristiano, Ante Kulusic, Mateo Susic, Veaceslav Posmac,
Jeremy de Nooijer (87' Wilfried Balima), Gheorghe Anton, Josip Brezovec (84' Vitalie
Damascan), Zlatko Tripic (64' Jairo), Cyrille Bayala, Ziguy Badibanga.
Coach: Roberto Bordin.
Goals: 76' Kasper Hämäläinen 1-0, 87' Cyrille Bayala 1-1.
Referee: Aleksandar Stavrev (MKD)   Attendance: 17,732.

17.08.17   Stadionul Central, Ovidiu: FC Viitorul Constanta – Red Bull Salzburg 1-3 (1-3)
FC Viitorul Constanta: Victor Râmniceanu, Marius Constantin, Sebastian Mladen, Bogdan
Tîru (46' Robert Hodorogea), Kévin Boli, Dani Lopez, Cristian Ganea, Alexandru Cicâldau
(51' Florinel Coman), George Tucudean, Aurelian Chitu (71' Eric de Oliveira), Ionut Vîna.
Coach: Gheorghe Hagi.
Red Bull Salzburg: Cican Stankovic, Paulo Miranda, Duje Caleta-Car, Andreas Ulmer, Stefan
Lainer, Diadie Samassekou, Marc Rzatkowski (70' Amadou Haïdara), Valon Berisha, Munas
Dabbur, Hannes Wolf (81' Takumi Minamino), Hee-chan Hwang (75' Fredrik Gulbrandsen).
Coach: Marco Rose.
Goals: 2' Hee-chan Hwang 0-1, 7' George Tucudean 1-1, 28' Hannes Wolf 1-2,
31' Munas Dabbur 1-3.
Referee: Anthony Taylor (ENG)   Attendance: 3,338.

17.08.17   Stadion Partizana, Beograd: Partizan – Videoton FC 0-0
Partizan: Vladimir Stojkovic, Miroslav Vulicevic, Bojan Ostojic, Nemanja G.Miletic (II),
Nemanja Miletic (I), Marko Jankovic (78' Petar Djurickovic), Seydouba Soumah (66' Sasa
Ilic), Marko Jevtovic, Milán Rádin, Léandro Tawamba Kana, Uros Djurdjevic (80' Djordje
Jovanovic). Coach: Miroslav Djukic.
Videoton FC: Ádám Kovácsik, Attila Fiola, Loïc Négo, Stopira, Roland Juhász, Anel Hadzic
(33' Krisztián Géresi), Máté Pátkai, Roland Szolnoki, Danko Lazovic, Ezekiel Henty (77'
Mirko Maric), Marko Scepovic (43' Bence Szabó). Coach: Marko Nikolic.
Referee: John Beaton (SCO).

Match was played behind closed doors.

17.08.17　Goodison Park, Liverpool: Everton FC – Hajduk Split 2-0 (2-0)
Everton FC: Jordan Pickford, Leighton Baines, Michael Keane, Ashley Williams, Cuco
Martina, Morgan Schneiderlin (46' Tom Davies), Idrissa Gueye, Davy Klaassen (63' Dominic
Calvert-Lewin), Wayne Rooney, Kevin Mirallas (76' Muhamed Besic), Ademola Lookman.
Coach: Ronald Koeman.
Hajduk Split: Dante Stipica, Gustavo Carbonieri, Josip Juranovic, Zoran Nizic, Hysen
Memolla, Hamza Barry, Nikola Vlasic, Josip Radosevic, Zvonimir Kozulj (66' Ante Erceg),
Savvas Gentsoglou (85' Toma Basic), Franck Ohandza (66' Ahmed Said).
Coach: Joan Carrillo.
Goals: 30' Michael Keane 1-0, 45' Idrissa Gueye 2-0.
Referee: Ivan Kruzliak (SVK)　　Attendance: 34,977.

17.08.17　Estádio dos Barreiros, Funchal: CS Marítimo – Dinamo Kiev 0-0
CS Marítimo: Charles, Pablo, Zainadine Junior, Luís Martins, Bebeto, Erdem Sen, Éber Bessa,
Gamboa (81' Jean Cleber), Piqueti (73' Ibson), Ricardo Valente, Everton (67' Rodrigo Pinho).
Coach: Daniel Ramos.
Dinamo Kiev: Maksim Koval, Domagoj Vida, Evgen Khacheridi, Tamás Kádár, Mikola
Morozyuk, Sergiy Sydorchuk, Denys Garmash (87' Artem Kravets), Vitaliy Buyalskiy (87'
Volodymyr Shepeliev), Andrey Yarmolenko, Derlis González (72' Viktor Tsygankov),
Dieumerci Mbokani. Coach: Aleksandr Khatskevich.
Referee: Jakob Kehlet (DEN)　　Attendance: 8,764.
Sent off: 89' Evgen Khacheridi.

24.08.17　AEK Arena – George Karapatakis, Larnaca: AEK Larnaca – Viktoria Plzen 0-0
AEK Larnaca: Juan Pablo, Truyols (75' Nestoras Mitidis), Daniel Mojsov, Català, Ander
Murillo, Jorge Larena, Joan Tomás (66' Hector Hevel), Tete, Acorán, Ivan Trickovski (83'
Onisiforos Roushias), Florian Taulemesse. Coach: Imanol Idiakez.
Viktoria Plzen: Ales Hruska, Lukás Hejda, Roman Hubník, David Limbersky, Radim Rezník,
Martin Zeman, Jan Kopic (57' Milan Petrzela), Patrik Hrosovsky, Ales Cermák, Daniel Kolár
(78' Diego Zivulic), Marek Bakos (70' Jakub Reznícek). Coach: Pavel Vrba.
Referee: Artur Soares Dias (POR)　　Attendance: 5,300.

24.08.17　NSK Olimpiyskyi, Kiev: Dinamo Kiev – CS Marítimo 3-1 (2-0)
Dinamo Kiev: Maksim Koval, Domagoj Vida, Tamás Kádár, Tomasz Kedziora, Mikola
Morozyuk, Sergiy Sydorchuk, Denys Garmash (77' Volodymyr Shepeliev), Vitaliy Buyalskiy
(85' Júnior Moraes), Andrey Yarmolenko, Derlis González, Dieumerci Mbokani (90+2' Artem
Kravets). Coach: Aleksandr Khatskevich.
CS Marítimo: Charles, Pablo, Zainadine Junior, Luís Martins, Bebeto, Erdem Sen (69' Viktor
Lundberg), Éber Bessa (46' Jean Cleber), Gamboa, Gildo (46' Ibson), Ricardo Valente,
Everton. Coach: Daniel Ramos.
Goals: 33' Denys Garmash 1-0, 35' Mikola Morozyuk 2-0, 61' Derlis González 3-0,
68' Erdem Sen 3-1.
Referee: Liran Liany (ISR)　　Attendance: 23,194.

24.08.17   Stadion Krestovskyi, St.Petersburg: Zenit St.Petersburg – FC Utrecht 2-0 (1-0,1-0)
Zenit St.Petersburg: Andrei Lunev, Domenico Criscito, Igor Smolnikov, Emanuel Mammana,
Branislav Ivanovic, Leandro Paredes, Daler Kuzyaev, Oleg Shatov (90' Matías Kranevitter),
Aleksandr Erokhin, Aleksandr Kokorin (107' Artem Dzyuba), Sebastián Driussi (73' Dmitriy
Poloz). Coach: Roberto Mancini.
FC Utrecht: David Jensen, Ramon Leeuwin (106' Jean-Christophe Bahebeck), Willem Janssen,
Sean Klaiber, Edson Braafheid (76' Mark van der Maarel), Yassin Ayoub, Zakaria Labyad,
Urby Emanuelson, Sander van de Streek, Gyrano Kerk (89' Lukas Görtler), Cyriel Dessers.
Coach: Erik ten Hag.
Goals: 9', 105' Aleksandr Kokorin 1-0, 2-0.
Referee: Carlos Del Cerro Grande (ESP)   Attendance: 49,237.

Zenit St.Petersburg through after extra time.

24.08.17   KSK Nika, Aleksandriya: FC Aleksandriya – BATE Borisov 1-2 (1-0)
FC Aleksandriya: Yuri Pankiv, Sergiy Chebotaev, Valeriy Bondarenko, Andriy Tsurikov,
Andriy Gitchenko (64' Vitali Ponomar), Andriy Batsula, Maksim Kalenchuk, Artem Sitalo
(87' Stanislav Kulish), Vasili Gritsuk, Sergey Starenkiy (77' Artem Chorniy), Eugene Banada.
Coach: Volodymyr Sharan.
BATE Borisov: Denis Scherbitski, Jurica Buljat, Nemanja Milunovic, Denis Polyakov,
Aleksandr Volodko (65' Nikolay Signevich), Mirko Ivanic, Aleksey Rios (78' Maksim
Volodko), Stanislav Dragun, Igor Stasevich, Vitaliy Rodionov (89' Evgeni Yablonski),
Mikhail Gordeychuk. Coach: Aleksandr Yermakovich.
Goals: 34' Vasili Gritsuk 1-0 (p), 69', 73' Mirko Ivanic 1-1, 1-2.
Referee: Miroslav Zelinka (CZE)   Attendance: 6,900.

24.08.17   Jämtkraft Arena, Östersund: Östersunds FK – PAOK Saloniki 2-0 (0-0)
Östersunds FK: Aly Keita, Sotirios Papagiannopoulos, Gabriel Somi (60' Ken Sema), Ronald
Mukiibi (67' Dennis Widgren), Tom Pettersson, Jamie Hopcutt (90' Samuel Laryeal Mensah),
Curtis Edwards, Fouad Bachirou, Brwa Nouri, Saman Ghoddos, Hosam Aiesh.
Coach: Graham Potter.
PAOK Saloniki: Rodrigo Rey, Léo Matos, Marin Leovac, José Ángel Crespo, Fernando
Varela, Gojko Cimirot (81' Efthimios Koulouris), Diego Biseswar (60' Pedro Henrique),
Yevhen Shakhov, Aleksandar Prijovic, Djalma, Róbert Mak (86' Dimitris Limnios).
Coach: Razvan Lucescu.
Goals: 70', 77' Saman Ghoddos 1-0, 2-0.
Referee: Pawel Raczkowski (POL)   Attendance: 5,697.

Östersunds FK won on away goals.

24.08.17   Netanya Stadium, Netanya: Maccabi Tel Aviv – SCR Altach 2-2 (1-1)
Maccabi Tel Aviv: Predrag Rajkovic, Yuval Shpungin (66' Omer Atzili), Eitan Tibi, Tal Ben
Haim, Ofir Davidzade, Sheran Yeini, Avi Rikan (73' Tino-Sven Susic), Cristian Battocchio,
Vidar Kjartansson, Dor Mikha (86' Egor Filipenko), Aaron Schoenfeld. Coach: Jordi Cruijff.
SCR Altach: Martin Kobras, Philipp Netzer, Andreas Lienhart, Emanuel Schreiner, Benedikt
Zech, Patrick Salomon, Simon Piesinger (84' Jan Zwischenbrugger), Stefan Nutz (74'
Christian Gebauer), Kristijan Dobras, Nicolas Ngamaleu, Hannes Aigner (89' Adrian Grbic).
Coach: Klaus Schmidt.
Goals: 20' Hannes Aigner 0-1, 41' Vidar Kjartansson 1-1, 59' Philipp Netzer 1-2,
73' Sheran Yeini 2-2.
Referee: Aleksey Eskov (RUS)   Attendance: 10,637.

311

24.08.17   Boshaya Sportivnaya Arena, Tiraspol: FC Sheriff – Legia Warszawa 0-0
FC Sheriff: Zvonimir Mikulic, Cristiano, Ante Kulusic, Mateo Susic, Veaceslav Posmac,
Jeremy de Nooijer, Gheorghe Anton, Josip Brezovec (65' Wilfried Balima), Zlatko Tripic (77'
Victor), Cyrille Bayala, Ziguy Badibanga (60' Jairo). Coach: Roberto Bordin.
Legia Warszawa: Arkadiusz Malarz, Michal Pazdan, Maciej Dabrowski, Adam Hlousek, Artur
Jedrzejczyk, Tomasz Jodlowiec (76' Armando Sadiku), Dominik Nagy (65' Hildeberto
Pereira), Kasper Hämäläinen, Krzysztof Maczynski, Thibault Moulin, Michal Kucharczyk (84'
Sebastian Szymanski). Coach: Jacek Magiera.
Referee: Ivan Bebek (CRO)   Attendance: 6,237.
Sent off: 39' Michal Pazdan.

24.08.17   Red Bull Arena, Wals-Siezenheim:
Red Bull Salzburg – FC Viitorul Constanta 4-0 (2-0)
Red Bull Salzburg: Alexander Walke, Duje Caleta-Car, Andreas Ulmer, Stefan Lainer, Marin
Pongracic, Reinhold Yabo, Diadie Samassekou, Valon Berisha (65' Amadou Haïdara), Munas
Dabbur, Hannes Wolf (46' Marc Rzatkowski), Fredrik Gulbrandsen (56' Patson Daka).
Coach: Marco Rose.
FC Viitorul Constanta: Alexandru Buzbuchi, Andrei Dumitras, Sorin Radoi, Marius Constantin
(46' Dani Lopez), Tudor Baluta, Bogdan Tîru, Robert Hodorogea, Ovidiu Herea, Florin
Cioabla (58' Aurelian Chitu), George Tucudean (24' Denis Dragus), Ionut Vîna.
Coach: Gheorghe Hagi.
Goals: 7' Munas Dabbur 1-0, 38' Fredrik Gulbrandsen 2-0, 52' Valon Berisha 3-0 (p),
88' Amadou Haïdara 4-0.
Referee: Stefan Johannesson (SWE)   Attendance: 6,606.

24.08.17   Sükrü Saracoglustadion, Istanbul: Fenerbahçe – Vardar Skopje 1-2 (0-0)
Fenerbahçe: Carlos Kameni, Ismail Köybasi, Nabil Dirar, Martin Skrtel, Mauricio Isla,
Mehmet Topal (75' Ahmethan Köse), Alper Potuk (44' Aatif Chahechouhe), Ozan Tufan,
Mathieu Valbuena, Roman Neustädter, Robin van Persie (59' Soldado).
Coach: Aykut Kocaman.
Vardar Skopje: Filip Gacevski, Darko Velkoski (74' Nikola Gligorov), Hovhannes
Hambardzumyan, Evgen Novak, Vladica Brdarovski, Jambul Jigauri (84' Damir Kojasevic),
Stefan Spirovski, Dejan Blazevski (62' Visar Musliu), Tigran Barseghyan, Boban Nikolov,
Juan Felipe Alves. Coaches: Goce Sedloski & Cedomir Janevski.
Goals: 61' Roman Neustädter 1-0, 68' Jambul Jigauri 1-1, 90+1' Nikola Gligorov 1-2.
Referee: Daniel Stedanski (POL)   Attendance: 32,480.

24.08.17   Arvi Futbolo Arena, Marijampólè: FK Sūduva – PFC Ludogorets Razgrad 0-0
FK Sūduva: Ivan Kardum, Semir Kerla, Aleksandar Zivanovic, Algis Jankauskas, Andro
Svrljuga, Karolis Chvedukas (75' Povilas Leimonas), Jérémy Manzorro (60' Marijan
Altiparmakovski), Paulius Janusauskas, Giedrius Matulevicius, Vaidas Slavickas, Karolis
Laukzemis (68' Robertas Vezevicius). Coach: Vladimir Cheburin.
PFC Ludogorets Razgrad: Jorge Broun, Cicinho, Georgi Terziev, Natanael Pimienta, Lucas
Sasha (90+1' Gustavo Campanharo), Svetoslav Dyakov, Igor Plastun, Wanderson (88' Claudiu
Keserü), Anicet Andrianantenaina, Jody Lukoki (79' João Paulo), Virgil Misidjan.
Coach: Dimitar Dimitrov.
Referee: Halis Özkahya (TUR)   Attendance: 4,312.

24.08.17   MCH Arena, Herning: FC Midtjylland – Apollon Liamssol 1-1 (1-0)
FC Midtjylland: Jesper Hansen, Kian Hansen, Zsolt Korcsmár (90+1' Mikkel Duelund), André
Rømer (77' Gustav Wikheim), Rasmus Nissen Kristensen, Filip Novák, Tim Sparv, Jakob
Poulsen, Jonas Borring, Rilwan Hassan (63' Bozhidar Kraev), Alexander Sørloth.
Coach: Jess Thorup.
Apollon Limassol: Bruno Vale, Jander, Valentin Roberge, Héctor Yuste, Esteban Sachetti,
Alex da Silva (90' Ioannis Pittas), João Pedro, Charis Kyriakou, André Schembri, Antonio
Jakolis (73' Adrián Sardinero), Anton Maglica (77' Emilio Zelaya). Coach: Sofronis Avgousti.
Goals: 10' Rilwan Hassan 1-0, 50' André Schembri 1-1.
Referee: Robert Schörgenhofer (AUT)   Attendance: 9,022.

Alex da Silva missed a penalty kick (82').

24.08.17   Skënderbeu, Korça: KF Skënderbeu – Dinamo Zagreb 0-0
KF Skënderbeu: Orges Shehi, Gledi Mici, Bajram Jashanica, Tefik Osmani (90+2' Gjergj
Muzaka), Kristi Vangjeli, Marko Radas, Enis Gavazaj (73' Segun Adeniyi), Bakary Nimaga,
Liridon Latifi, Sabien Lilaj, Ali Sowe (86' Bruno Dita). Coach: Ilir Daja.
Dinamo Zagreb: Dominik Livakovic, Jan Lecjaks (85' Armin Hodzic), Amir Rrahmani,
Leonardo Sigali, Petar Stojanovic, Tongo Doumbia, Nikola Moro (57' Amer Gojak), El Arbi
Soudani, Ángelo Henríquez (67' Ivan Fiolic), Daniel Olmo, Junior Fernándes.
Coach: Mario Cvitanovic.
Referee: István Vad (HUN)   Attendance: 11,230.
Sent off: 78' Bakary Nimaga.

KF Skënderbeu won on away goals.

24.08.17   Olympiako Stadio Spyros Louis, Athen: AEK Athen – Club Brugge KV 3-0 (2-0)
AEK Athen: Giannis Anestis, Michalis Bakakis, Hélder Lopes (61' Jakob Johansson), Ognjen
Vranjes, Uros Cosic, Dmitro Chigrinskiy, André Simões, Petros Mantalos, Konstantinos
Galanopoulos, Viktor Klonaridis (67' Hugo Almeida), Lazaros Christodoulopoulos (78'
Rodrigo Galo). Coach: Manolo Jiménez.
Club Brugge KV: Ethan Horvath, Björn Engels, Helibelton Palacios (46' Dion Cools), Stefano
Denswil, Laurens De Bock, Hans Vanaken, Ruud Volmer, Marvelous Nakamba, Jelle Vossen
(46' Lior Refaelov), Abdoulaye Diaby, Emmanuel Bonaventure Dennis (59' Anthony
Limbombe). Coach: Ivan Leko.
Goals: 27' Lazaros Christodoulopoulos 1-0 (p), 39', 90+1' André Simões 2-0, 3-0.
Referee: Jesús Gil Manzano (ESP)   Attendance: 14,275.

24.08.17   Puskás Akadémia Pancho Aréna, Felcsút: Videoton FC – Partizan 0-4 (0-3)
Videoton FC: Ádam Kovácsik, Attila Fiola, Loïc Négo, Stopira, Roland Juhász, Anel Hadzic,
Máté Pátkai, Asmir Suljic (77' Bence Szabó), Danko Lazovic, Ezekiel Henty (46' Krisztián
Géresi), Marko Scepovic (62' Mirko Maric). Coach: Marko Nikolic.
Partizan: Vladimir Stojkovic, Miroslav Vulicevic, Bojan Ostojic, Nemanja G.Miletic (II),
Nemanja Miletic (I), Marko Jankovic (77' Danilo Pantic), Seydouba Soumah (64' Sasa Ilic),
Everton Luiz, Milán Rádin, Léandro Tawamba Kana (70' Petar Djurickovic), Uros Djurdjevic.
Coach: Miroslav Djukic.
Goals: 6' Léandre Tawamba Kana 0-1, 24' Seydouba Soumah 0-2,
35', 87' Uros Djurdjevic 0-3, 0-4.
Referee: Andre Marriner (ENG)   Attendance: 3,485.
Sent off: 47' Roland Juhász.

313

24.08.17   Estádio Municipal de Braga, Braga: Sporting Braga – FH Hafnarfjördur 3-2 (1-1)
Sporting Braga: Matheus Magalhães, Jefferson, Raúl Silva, Bruno Viana, Ricardo Esgaio,
Bruno Xadas (90' Fransérgio), Danilo Barbosa, Nikola Vukcevic, Nikola Stojiljkovic (71'
Dyego Sousa), Paulinho, Ricardo Horta (78' Fábio Martins). Coach: Abel Ferreira.
FH Hafnarfjördur: Gunnar Nielsen, Pétur Vidarsson, Kassim Doumbia, Bödvar Bödvarsson,
Robbie Crawford (87' Bjarni Vidarsson), Emil Pálsson, David Vidarsson, Gudmundur Karl
Gudmundsson, Steven Lennon, Atli Gudnason (87' Thórarinn Valdimarsson), Halldór
Björnsson (67' Matija Dvornekovic). Coach: Heimir Gudjónsson.
Goals: 16' Bödvar Bödvarsson 0-1, 39' Paulinho 1-1, 51' Bödvar Bödvarsson 1-2,
80' Paulinho 2-2, 90+3' Dyego Sousa 3-2.
Referee: Pawel Gil (POL)   Attendance: 10,937.

24.08.17   San Mamés Barria, Bilbao: Athletic Bilbao – Panathinaikos 1-0 (1-0)
Athletic Bilbao: Iago Herrerín, Aymeric Laporte, San José, Etxeita, Balenziaga, Beñat (74'
Mikel Rico), Susaeta (65' Iñaki Williams), Lekue, Iñigo Córdoba, Muniain (80' Ager Aketxe),
Aduriz. Coach: José Ángel Ziganda.
Panathinaikos: Odisseas Vlachodimos, Mattias Johansson, Georgios Koutroubis, Dimitrios
Kolovetsios, Zeca, Bryan Cabezas (67' Guillermo Molins), Robin Lod (66' Omri Altman),
Dimitrios Kourbelis, Niklas Hult, Andrés Chávez (74' Christos Donis), Luciano.
Coach: Marinos Ouzounidis.
Goal: 22' Muniain 1-0.
Referee: Benoît Bastien (FRA)   Attendance: 42,747.

24.08.17   Filip II Makedonski, Skopje: KF Shkëndija 79 – AC Milan 0-1 (0-1)
KF Shkëndija 79: Kostadin Zahov, Egzon Bejtulai, Ardijan Cuculi, Ivan Celikovic, Olsi Teqja,
Armend Alimi, Ennur Totre (88' Enis Fazlagikj), Ferhan Hasani, Blagoja Todorovski (79'
Mevlan Murati), Besart Ibraimi, Marjan Radeski (73' Besart Abdurahimi).
Coach: Qatip Osmani.
AC Milan: Marco Storari, Davide Calabria, Alessio Romagnoli (46' Ignazio Abate), Cristián
Zapata, Leonardo Bonucci, Luca Antonelli, José Mauri, Niccolò Zanellato, Manuel Locatelli
(73' Matteo Gabbia), André Silva, Patrick Cutrone (58' Suso). Coach: Vincenzo Montella.
Goal: 13' Patrick Cutrone 0-1.
Referee: István Kovács (ROM)   Attendance: 25,600.

24.08.17   Lerkendal Stadion, Trondheim: Rosenborg BK – AFC Ajax 3-2 (1-0)
Rosenborg BK: André Hansen, Birger Meling, Johan Bjørdal, Jørgen Skjelvik, Mike Jensen,
Anders Konradsen, Fredrik Midtsjø, Marius Lundemo (58' Matthías Vilhjálmsson), Nicklas
Bendtner, Yann-Erik De Lanlay, Milan Jevtovic (68' Samuel Adegbenro).
Coach: Kåre Ingebrigtsen.
AFC Ajax: André Onana, Joël Veltman, Matthijs de Ligt, Nick Viergever, Mitchell Dijks,
Donny van de Beek (46' Klaas-Jan Huntelaar), Hakim Ziyech, Lasse Schöne, Amin Younes,
Kasper Dolberg (78' Deyovaisio Zeefuik), Justin Kluivert (38' Vaclav Cerny).
Coach: Marcel Keizer.
Goals: 25' Niclas Bendtner 1-0, 60' Amin Younes 1-1, 61' Lasse Schöne 1-2,
80', 89' Samuel Adegbenro 2-2, 3-2.
Referee: Ruddy Buquet (FRA)   Attendance: 21,211.

314

24.08.17   Stade Vélodrome, Marseille: Olympique Marseille – NK Domzale 3-0 (1-0)
Olympique Marseille: Steve Mandanda, Hiroki Sakai, Rolando, Patrice Evra, Adil Rami (25'
Grégory Sertic), Lucas Ocampos (82' Dória), Morgan Sanson, Luiz Gustavo, Florian Thauvin,
Maxime Lopez (63' André Zambo Anguissa), Valère Germain. Coach: Rudi García.
NK Domzale: Dejan Milic, Tilen Klemencic, Matija Sirok, Miha Blazic, Jure Balkovec,
Amedej Vetrih (83' Adam Gnezda Cerin), Jan Repas, Senijad Ibricic, Zeni Husmani, Ivan Firer
(75' Alen Ozbolt), Lovro Bizjak (65' Zan Zuzek). Coach: Simon Rozman.
Goals: 28', 56' Valère Germain 1-0, 2-0, 85' Florian Thauvin 3-0.
Referee: Orel Grinfeld (ISR)   Attendance: 47,352.

24.08.17   Stadion Rajko Mitic, Beograd: Crvena Zvezda – FK Krasnodar 2-1 (1-0)
Crvena Zvezda: Milan Borjan, Abraham Frimpong, Milan Rodic (51' Marko Gobeljic), Filip
Stojkovic, Vujadin Savic, Guélor Kanga, Mitchell Donald, Slavoljub Srnic, Richmond Boakye,
Nemanja Milic (70' Uros Racic), Nemanja Radonjic (77' Aleksandar Pesic).
Coach: Vladan Milojevic.
FK Krasnodar: Andrey Sinitsyn, Aleksandr Martinovich, Andreas Granqvist, Cristian Ramírez,
Sergey Petrov, Wanderson, Yuri Gazinskiy, Victor Claesson, Pavel Mamaev (59' Mauricio
Pereyra), Charles Kaboré (46' Ilya Zhigulev), Fedor Smolov (65' Andrei Ivan).
Coach: Igor Shalimov.
Goals: 7' Nemanja Radonjic 1-0, 46' Guélor Kanga 2-0, 82' Andreas Granqvist 2-1 (p).
Referee: Tobias Stieler (GER)   Attendance: 50,720.

Crvena Zvezda won on away goals.

24.08.17   Stadion Poljud, Split: Hajduk Split – Everton FC 1-1 (1-0)
Hajduk Split: Dante Stipica, Borja López, Josip Juranovic, Zoran Nizic, Hysen Memolla,
Hamza Barry (85' Franko Kovacevic), Nikola Vlasic (84' Zvonimir Kozulj), Josip Radosevic,
Ante Erceg, Savvas Gentsoglou, Ahmed Said (74' Fran Tudor). Coach: Joan Carrillo.
Everton FC: Jordan Pickford, Leighton Baines, Michael Keane, Ashley Williams, Cuco
Martina, Morgan Schneiderlin, Gylfi Sigurdsson, Muhamed Besic, Wayne Rooney, Dominic
Calvert-Lewin (72' Tom Davies), Ademola Lookman (46' Aaron Lennon).
Coach: Ronald Koeman.
Goals: 43' Josip Radosevic 1-0, 46' Gylfi Sigurdsson 1-1.
Referee: Sergey Karasev (RUS)   Attendance: 31,645.

Ahmed Said missed a penalty kick (65').

24.08.17   NV ARENA, Sankt Pölten: Austria Wien – NK Osijek 0-1 (0-0)
Austria Wien: Osman Hadzikic, Abdul Kadiri Mohammed, Heiko Westermann, Christoph
Martschinko, Ismael Tajouri Shradi, Tarkan Serbest (79' Thomas Salamon), Dominik Prokop
(90' Alexandar Borkovic), David De Paula, Raphael Holzhauser, Christoph Monschein (68'
Kevin Friesenbichler), Felipe Pires. Coach: Thorsten Fink.
NK Osijek: Marko Malenica, Borna Barisic, Mateo Barac, Petar Bockaj, Mile Skoric, Benedik
Mioc, Robert Mudrazija (83' Andrej Simunec), Domagoj Pusic (46' Gabrijel Boban), Muzafer
Ejupi, Eros Grezda (69' Alen Grgic), Tomislav Sorsa. Coach: Zoran Zekic.
Goal: 62' Gabrijel Boban 0-1.
Referee: Vladislav Bezborodov (RUS)   Attendance: 7,400.

GROUP STAGE

GROUP A

Villarreal CF	6	3	2	1	10 - 6	11
FK Astana	6	3	1	2	10 - 7	10
Slavia Praha	6	2	2	2	6 - 6	8
Maccabi Tel Aviv	6	1	1	4	1 - 8	4

GROUP B

Dinamo Kiev	6	4	1	1	15 - 9	13
Partizan	6	2	2	2	8 - 9	8
BSC Young Boys	6	1	3	2	7 - 8	6
KF Skënderbeu	6	1	2	3	6 - 10	5

GROUP C

Sporting Braga	6	3	1	2	9 - 8	10
PFC Ludogorets Razgrad	6	2	3	1	7 - 5	9
Istanbul Basaksehir F.K.	6	2	2	2	7 - 8	8
1899 Hoffenheim	6	1	2	3	8 - 10	5

GROUP D

AC Milan	6	3	2	1	13 - 6	11
AEK Athen	6	1	5	0	6 - 5	8
HNK Rijeka	6	2	1	3	11 - 12	7
Austria Wien	6	1	2	3	9 - 16	5

GROUP E

Atalanta	6	4	2	0	14 - 4	14
Olympique Lyon	6	3	2	1	11 - 7	11
Everton FC	6	1	1	4	7 - 15	4
Apollon Limassol	6	0	3	3	5 - 14	3

GROUP F

Lokomotiv Moskva	6	3	2	1	9 - 4	11
FC København	6	2	3	1	7 - 3	9
FC Sheriff	6	2	3	1	4 - 4	9
FC FASTAV Zlín	6	0	2	4	1 - 10	2

GROUP G

Viktoria Plzen	6	4	0	2	13 - 8	12
Steaua Bucuresti	6	3	1	2	9 - 7	10
FC Lugano	6	3	0	3	9 - 11	9
Hapoel Be'er Sheva	6	1	1	4	5 - 10	4

GROUP H

Arsenal FC	6	4	1	1	14 - 4	13
Crvena Zvezda	6	2	3	1	3 - 2	9
1. FC Köln	6	2	0	4	7 - 8	6
BATE Borisov	6	1	2	3	6 - 16	5

GROUP I

Red Bull Salzburg	6	3	3	0	7 - 1	12
Olympique Marseille	6	2	2	2	4 - 4	8
Atiker Konyaspor	6	1	3	2	4 - 6	6
Vitória Guimarães	6	1	2	3	5 - 9	5

GROUP J

Athletic Bilbao	6	3	2	1	8 - 5	11
Östersunds FK	6	3	2	1	8 - 4	11
Zorya Lugansk	6	2	0	4	3 - 9	6
Hertha BSC	6	1	2	3	6 - 7	5

GROUP K

Lazio Roma	6	4	1	1	12 - 7	13
OGC Nice	6	3	0	3	12 - 7	9
SV Zulte Waregem	6	2	1	3	8 - 13	7
Vitesse	6	1	2	3	5 - 10	5

GROUP L

Zenit St.Petersburg	6	5	1	0	17 - 5	16
Real Sociedad	6	4	0	2	16 - 6	12
Rosenborg BK	6	1	2	3	6 - 11	5
Vardar Skopje	6	0	1	5	3 - 20	1

The top 2 teams in each group advanced to the knockout phase of the competition.

GROUP STAGE – GROUP A

14.09.17 Estadio de la Cerámica, Villarreal: Villarreal CF – FK Astana 3-1 1-0)
Villarreal CF: Mariano Barbosa, Daniele Bonera, Mario Gaspar, Jaume Costa, Rúben Semedo, Trigueros, Samu Castillejo (87' Leonardo Suárez), Rodri Hernández, Pablo Fornals (74' Denis Cheryshev), Nicola Sansone (70' Cédric Bakambu), Enes Ünal. Coach: Fran Escribá.
FK Astana: Nenad Eric, Yuriy Logvinenko, Marin Anicic, Dmitriy Shomko, Abzal Beysebekov (87' Askhat Tagybergen), Evgeni Postnikov, Ivan Maevski, Srdan Grahovac, Serikzhan Muzhikov (83' Igor Shitov), Patrick Twumasi, Roman Murtazaev (67' Marin Tomasov). Coach: Stanimir Stoilov.
Goals: 16' Nicola Sansone 1-0, 68' Yuriy Logvinenko 1-1, 75' Cédric Bakambu 2-1, 77' Denis Cheryshev 3-1.
Referee: Srdan Jovanovic (SER)   Attendance: 18,144.

14.09.17 Eden Aréna, Praha: Slavia Praha – Maccabi Tel Aviv 1-0 (1-0)
Slavia Praha: Premysl Kovár, Michal Frydrych, Jakub Jugas, Eduard Sobol, Simon Deli, Miroslav Stoch, Jan Sykora (64' Josef Husbauer), Jaromir Zmrhal (66' Mick van Buren), Jakub Hromada (81' Michael Ngadeu-Ngadjui), Tomás Soucek, Tomás Necid.
Coach: Jaroslav Silhavy.
Maccabi Tel Aviv: Predrag Rajkovic, Tal Ben Haim, Egor Filipenko (67' Nick Blackman), Jean-Sylvain Babin (72' Avi Rikan), Ofir Davidzade, Sheran Yeini, Tino-Sven Susic, Dor Mikha (80' Omer Atzili), Cristian Battocchio, Vidar Kjartansson, Eliran Atar.
Coach: Jordi Cruijff.
Goal: 12' Tomás Necid 1-0.
Referee: Robert Schörgenhofer (AUT)   Attendance: 13,035.

28.09.17 Astana Arena, Astana: FK Astana – Slavia Praha 1-1 (1-1)
FK Astana: Nenad Eric, Yuriy Logvinenko, Igor Shitov, Dmitriy Shomko, Abzal Beysebekov, Evgeni Postnikov, Marin Tomasov (82' Roman Murtazaev), Ivan Maevski, Serikzhan Muzhikov (87' Askhat Tagybergen), Junior Kabananga, Patrick Twumasi.
Coach: Stanimir Stoilov.
Slavia Praha: Premysl Kovár, Jan Boril, Jakub Jugas, Eduard Sobol, Michael Ngadeu-Ngadjui, Simon Deli, Ruslan Rotan, Miroslav Stoch, Jan Sykora (87' Mick van Buren), Jaromir Zmrhal (62' Jakub Hromada), Tomás Necid (72' Milan Skoda). Coach: Jaroslav Silhavy.
Goals: 18' Michael Ngadeu-Ngadjui 0-1, 42' Marin Tomasov 1-1.
Referee: Andreas Ekberg (SWE)   Attendance: 17,215.

28.09.17 Netanya Stadium, Netanya: Maccabi Tel Aviv – Villarreal CF 0-0
Maccabi Tel Aviv: Predrag Rajkovic, Tal Ben Haim, Jean-Sylvain Babin, Ofir Davidzade, Yuval Shpungin, Sheran Yeini, Tino-Sven Susic (63' Dor Peretz), Cristian Battocchio, Vidar Kjartansson (87' Barak Itzhaki), Nick Blackman, Eliran Atar (65' Omer Atzili).
Coach: Jordi Cruijff.
Villarreal CF: Mariano Barbosa, Daniele Bonera, Mario Gaspar, Jaume Costa, Víctor Ruiz, Roberto Soriano (68' Samu Castillejo), Trigueros (82' Rodri Hernández), Ramiro Guerra, Pablo Fornals, Carlos Bacca (75' Enes Ünal), Cédric Bakambu. Coach: Javi Calleja.
Referee: Craig Pawson (ENG)   Attendance: 11,865.

19.10.17 Astana Arena, Astana: FK Astana – Maccabi Tel Aviv 4-0 (2-0)
FK Astana: Nenad Eric, Yuriy Logvinenko, Marin Anicic, Igor Shitov, Dmitriy Shomko, Abzal Beysebekov (85' Askhat Tagybergen), Ivan Maevski, Serikzhan Muzhikov (69' Srdan Grahovac), Junior Kabananga, Patrick Twumasi, Roman Murtazaev (74' Marin Tomasov). Coach: Stanimir Stoilov.
Maccabi Tel Aviv: Predrag Rajkovic, Tal Ben Haim, Jean-Sylvain Babin, Ofir Davidzade, Yuval Shpungin, Sheran Yeini, Tino-Sven Susic (46' Eliran Atar), Cristian Battocchio, Dor Peretz (46' Avi Rikan), Vidar Kjartansson (75' Eitan Tibi), Nick Blackman. Coach: Jordi Cruijff.
Goals: 33', 42' Patrick Twumasi 1-0 (p), 2-0, 47', 52' Junior Kabananga 3-0, 4-0.
Referee: Sergey Boyko (UKR)   Attendance: 10,350.

19.10.17 Estadio de la Cerámica, Villarreal: Villarreal CF – Slavia Praha 2-2 (2-2)
Villarreal CF: Mariano Barbosa, Daniele Bonera, Antonio Rukavina, Jaume Costa, Víctor Ruiz, Roberto Soriano (46' Denis Cheryshev), Trigueros, Ramiro Guerra, Pablo Fornals (77' Samu Castillejo), Carlos Bacca, Enes Ünal (60' Cédric Bakambu). Coach: Javi Calleja.
Slavia Praha: Jan Lastuvka, Michal Frydrych, Jakub Jugas, Eduard Sobol, Simon Deli (46' Jan Boril), Danny, Jan Sykora (84' Miroslav Stoch), Jaromir Zmrhal (70' Mick van Buren), Jakub Hromada, Tomás Soucek, Tomás Necid. Coach: Jaroslav Silhavy.
Goals: 18' Tomás Necid 0-1, 30' Danny 0-2, 41' Trigueros 1-2), 44' Carlos Bacca 2-2.
Referee: Svein Moen (NOR)   Attendance: 15,634.

02.11.17 Netanya Stadium, Netanya: Maccabi Tel Aviv – FK Astana 0-1 (0-0)
Maccabi Tel Aviv: Predrag Rajkovic, Jean-Sylvain Babin, Eitan Tibi, Avi Rikan, Ofir Davidzade, Sheran Yeini, Cristian Battocchio, Vidar Kjartansson, Nick Blackman (77' Omer Atzili), Eliran Atar (65' Aaron Schoenfeld), Eli Dasa (65' Dor Micha). Coach: Jordi Cruijff.
FK Astana: Nenad Eric, Igor Shitov (88' Marin Anicic), Dmitriy Shomko, Sergiy Maliy, Abzal Beysebekov, Evgeni Postnikov, Marin Tomasov (75' Roman Murtazaev), Ivan Maevski, Askhat Tagybergen (73' Serikzhan Muzhikov), Junior Kabananga, Patrick Twumasi. Coach: Stanimir Stoilov.
Goal: 57' Patrick Twumasi 0-1.
Referee: Pawel Raczkowski (POL)   Attendance: 7,934.

02.11.17 Eden Aréna, Praha: Slavia Praha – Villarreal CF 0-2 (0-1)
Slavia Praha: Jan Lastuvka, Jan Boril, Jakub Jugas, Eduard Sobol, Simon Deli, Danny (63' Mick van Buren), Miroslav Stoch, Jan Sykora (80' Milan Skoda), Jakub Hromada (46' Michael Ngadeu-Ngadjui), Tomás Soucek, Tomás Necid. Coach: Jaroslav Silhavy.
Villarreal CF: Mariano Barbosa, Mario Gaspar, Víctor Ruiz, Álvaro González, Adrián Marín, Roberto Soriano (82' Nicola Sansone), Trigueros, Rodri Hernández, Pablo Fornals (67' Denis Cheryshev), Carlos Bacca (72' Chuca), Cédric Bakambu. Coach: Javi Calleja.
Goals: 15' Carlos Bacca 0-1, 89' Simon Deli 0-2 (og).
Referee: Bobby Madden (SCO)   Attendance: 18,403.

23.11.17   Astana Arena, Astana: FK Astana – Villarreal CF 2-3 (1-1)
FK Astana: Nenad Eric, Yuriy Logvinenko (82' Djordje Despotovic), Marin Anicic, Igor
Shitov, Dmitriy Shomko, Abzal Beysebekov (68' Srdan Grahovac), Evgeni Postnikov, Ivan
Maevski, Serikzhan Muzhikov (71' Marin Tomasov), Junior Kabananga, Patrick Twumasi.
Coach: Stanimir Stoilov.
Villarreal CF: Mariano Barbosa, Daniele Bonera, Antonio Rukavina, Víctor Ruiz, Adrián
Marín, Trigueros, Rodri Hernández, Pablo Fornals (60' Cédric Bakambu), Carlos Bacca (67'
Roberto Soriano), Nicola Sansone, Dani Raba (77' Ramiro Guerra). Coach: Javi Calleja.
Goals: 22' Junior Kabananga 1-0, 39' Dani Raba 1-1, 65' 83' Cédric Bakambu 1-2, 1-3,
88' Patrick Twumasi 2-3.
Referee: Gediminas Mazeika (LTU)   Attendance: 29,800.

23.11.17   Netanya Stadium, Netanya: Maccabi Tel Aviv – Slavia Praha 0-2 (0-1)
Maccabi Tel Aviv: Predrag Rajkovic, Tal Ben Haim, Eitan Tibi, Avi Rikan (60' Eyal Golasa),
Ofir Davidzade, Sheran Yeini, Dor Micha, Cristian Battocchio (75' Tino-Sven Susic), Dor
Peretz, Vidar Kjartansson, Aaron Schoenfeld (60' Eliran Atar). Coach: Jordi Cruijff.
Slavia Praha: Jan Lastuvka, Michal Frydrych, Jakub Jugas, Eduard Sobol, Michael Ngadeu-
Ngadjui, Simon Deli, Josef Husbauer (88' Danny), Miroslav Stoch (79' Mick van Buren),
Jaromír Zmrhal, Tomás Soucek, Tomás Necid (69' Milan Skoda). Coach: Jaroslav Silhavy.
Goals: 45+1', 54' Josef Husbauer 0-1, 0-2.
Referee: István Kovács (ROM)   Attendance: 6,874.

07.12.17   Eden Aréna, Praha: Slavia Praha – FK Astana 0-1 (0-1)
Slavia Praha: Jan Lastuvka, Michal Frydrych, Jakub Jugas, Eduard Sobol, Michael Ngadeu-
Ngadjui, Ruslan Rotan (68' Mick van Buren), Danny, Miroslav Stoch, Jaromír Zmrhal (76' Jan
Sykora), Tomás Soucek, Milan Skoda (17' Tomás Necid). Coach: Jaroslav Silhavy.
FK Astana: Nenad Eric, Yuriy Logvinenko, Marin Anicic, Igor Shitov, Dmitriy Shomko,
Marin Tomasov (68' Roman Murtazaev), Ivan Maevski, Srdan Grahovac, Serikzhan Muzhikov
(84' Sergiy Maliy), Junior Kabananga, Patrick Twumasi (90+3' Djordje Despotovic).
Coach: Stanimir Stoilov.
Goal: 38' Marin Anicic 0-1.
Referee: Davide Massa (ITA)   Attendance: 14,198

07.12.17   Estadio de la Cerámica, Villarreal: Villarreal CF – Maccabi Tel Aviv 0-1 (0-0)
Villarreal CF: Mariano Barbosa, Antonio Rukavina, Adrián Marín, Pau Torres, Genís
Montolio, Roberto Soriano (62' Pedro Martínez), Ramiro Guerra (82' Dani Raba), Manu
Morlanes (76' Sergio Lozano), Chuca, Mario González, Darío Poveda. Coach: Javi Calleja.
Maccabi Tel Aviv: Predrag Rajkovic, Jean-Sylvain Babin, Eitan Tibi, Avi Rikan (83' Cristian
Battocchio), Ofir Davidzade, Yuval Shpungin, Eyal Golasa, Dor Micha (72' Eli Dasa), Dor
Peretz, Nick Blackman (90' Eliran Atar), Aaron Schoenfeld. Coach: Jordi Cruijff.
Goal: 60' Nick Blackman 0-1.
Referee: Mads-Kristoffer Kristoffersen (DEN)   Attendance: 12,613

GROUP B

14.09.17   Stade de Suisse, Bern: BSC Young Boys – Partizan 1-1 (1-1)
BSC Young Boys: David von Ballmoos, Steve von Bergen, Kevin Mbabu, Kasim Nuhu,
Jordan Lotomba, Miralem Sulejmani (84' Thorsten Schick), Sékou Sanogo, Djibril Sow, Jean
Pierre Nsamé, Roger Assalé (68' Nicolas Ngamaleu), Christian Fassnacht. Coach: Adi Hütter.
Partizan: Vladimir Stojkovic, Miroslav Vulicevic, Bojan Ostojic, Nemanja Miletic (I), Everton
Luiz, Zoran Tosic (89' Danilo Pantic), Marko Jevtovic, Marko Jankovic, Nemanja G.Miletic
(II), Ognjen Ozegovic (64' Theophilus Solomon),Léandro Tawamba Kana.
Coach: Miroslav Djukic.
Goals: 11' Marko Jankovic 0-1, 14' Christian Fassnacht 1-1.
Referee: István Kovács (ROM)   Attendance: 13,004.

14.09.17   NSK Olimpiyskyi, Kiev: Dinamo Kiev – KF Skënderbeu 3-1 (0-1)
Dinamo Kiev: Maksim Koval, Domagoj Vida, Josip Pivaric, Evgen Khacheridi, Tamás Kádár,
Sergiy Sydorchuk, Denys Garmash (46' Júnior Moraes), Derlis González (82' Oleg Gusev),
Vitaliy Buyalskiy, Viktor Tsygankov (70' Mikola Morozyuk), Dieumerci Mbokani.
Coach: Aleksandr Khatskevich.
KF Skënderbeu: Orges Shehi, Kristi Vangjeli, Marko Radas, Tefik Osmani (60' Enis Gavazaj),
Gledi Mici, Bajram Jashanica (68' Fidan Aliti), Gjergj Muzaka, Sabien Lilaj, Bruno Dita, Ali
Sowe, Segun Adeniyi (76' Suad Sahiti). Coach: Ilir Daja.
Goals: 39' Gjergj Muzaka 0-1, 47' Sergiy Sydorchuk 1-1, 50' Júnior Moraes 2-1,
65' Dieumerci Mbokani 3-1 (p).
Referee: Bart Vertenten (BEL)   Attendance: 24,893

28.09.17   Elbasan Arena, Elbasan: KF Skënderbeu – BSC Young Boys 1-1 (0-0)
KF Skënderbeu: Orges Shehi, Kristi Vangjeli, Gledi Mici, Fidan Aliti, Bajram Jashanica,
Gjergj Muzaka (77' Bruno Dita), Sabien Lilaj, Enis Gavazaj (20' Afrim Taku), Suad Sahiti
(67' Bakary Nimaga), Ali Sowe, Segun Adeniyi. Coach: Ilir Daja.
BSC Young Boys: David von Ballmoos, Steve von Bergen, Marco Bürki, Gregory Wüthrich,
Sven Joss (76' Kevin Mbabu), Miralem Sulejmani (70' Jean Pierre Nsamé), Thorsten Schick
(70' Christian Fassnacht), Sékou Sanogo, Nicolas Ngamaleu, Michel Aebischer, Roger Assalé.
Coach: Adi Hütter.
Goals: 65' Ali Sowe 1-0, 72' Roger Assalé 1-1.
Referee: Kevin Blom (HOL)   Attendance: 3,300.

28.09.17   Stadion Partizana, Beograd: Partizan – Dinamo Kiev 2-3 (2-0)
Partizan: Vladimir Stojkovic, Miroslav Vulicevic, Bojan Ostojic, Nemanja Miletic (I), Everton
Luiz, Seydouba Soumah (75' Danilo Pantic), Marko Jankovic, Milán Rádin, Nemanja
G.Miletic (II), Ognjen Ozegovic (79' Djordje Jovanovic), Léandro Tawamba Kana.
Coach: Miroslav Djukic.
Dinamo Kiev: Maksim Koval, Domagoj Vida, Josip Pivaric, Tamás Kádár, Tomasz Kedziora,
Sergiy Sydorchuk, Denys Garmash, Derlis González (90+1' Mikola Morozyuk), Vitaliy
Buyalskiy, Viktor Tsygankov (46' Júnior Moraes), Artem Kravets (46' Artem Besedin).
Coach: Aleksandr Khatskevich.
Goals: 34' Ognjen Ozegovic 1-0, 42' Léandre Tawamba Kana 2-0, 54' Júnior Moraes 2-1 (p),
68' Vitaliy Buyalskiy 2-2, 84' Júnior Moraes 2-3.
Referee: Svein Moen (NOR).

Match was played behind closed doors.

19.10.17 NSK Olimpiyskyi, Kiev: Dinamo Kiev – BSC Young Boys 2-2 (1-2)
Dinamo Kiev: Maksim Koval, Domagoj Vida (79' Aleksandar Pantic), Josip Pivaric, Tamás
Kádár, Tomasz Kedziora, Mikola Morozyuk, Sergiy Sydorchuk (64' Denys Garmash), Derlis
González, Vitaliy Buyalskiy, Júnior Moraes, Dieumerci Mbokani (90+2' Artem Besedin).
Coach: Aleksandr Khatskevich.
BSC Young Boys: David von Ballmoos, Steve von Bergen, Kevin Mbabu, Kasim Nuhu,
Jordan Lotomba, Miralem Sulejmani, Sékou Sanogo, Nicolas Ngamaleu (85' Thorsten Schick),
Djibril Sow (76' Michel Aebischer), Roger Assalé (89' Jean Pierre Nsamé), Christian
Fassnacht. Coach: Adi Hütter.
Goals: 17' Roger Assalé 0-1, 34' Dieumerci Mbokani 1-1, 40' Roger Assalé 1-2,
49' Mikola Morozyuk 2-2.
Referee: Mattias Gestranius (FIN)   Attendance: 21,789.
Sent off: 82' Sékou Sanogo.

19.10.17 Elbasan Arena, Elbasan: KF Skënderbeu – Partizan 0-0
KF Skënderbeu: Orges Shehi, Kristi Vangjeli, Marko Radas (33' Fidan Aliti), Gledi Mici,
Bajram Jashanica, Gjergj Muzaka (90+2' Tefik Osmani), Sabien Lilaj, Afrim Taku, Bruno Dita
(80' Donjet Shkodra), Ali Sowe, Segun Adeniyi. Coach: Ilir Daja.
Partizan: Vladimir Stojkovic, Miroslav Vulicevic, Milan Mitrovic, Nemanja Miletic (I),
Everton Luiz, Zoran Tosic, Marko Jevtovic, Seydouba Soumah, Marko Jankovic (87' Sasa
Ilic), Nemanja G.Miletic (II), Léandro Tawamba Kana (66' Ognjen Ozegovic).
Coach: Miroslav Djukic.
Referee: Daniel Stefanski (POL)   Attendance: 6,300.

02.11.17 Stade de Suisse, Bern: BSC Young Boys – Dinamo Kiev 0-1 (0-0)
BSC Young Boys: David von Ballmoos, Steve von Bergen, Kevin Mbabu, Kasim Nuhu,
Jordan Lotomba, Miralem Sulejmani, Djibril Sow, Michel Aebischer, Jean Pierre Nsamé (73'
Nicolas Ngamaleu), Roger Assalé, Christian Fassnacht (79' Thorsten Schick).
Coach: Adi Hütter.
Dinamo Kiev: Georgiy Bushchan, Domagoj Vida, Josip Pivaric, Evgen Khacheridi, Tomasz
Kedziora (46' Artem Kravets), Mikola Morozyuk, Denys Garmash, Derlis González, Vitaliy
Buyalskiy (86' Volodymyr Shepeliev), Nikita Korzun, Júnior Moraes.
Coach: Aleksandr Khatskevich.
Goal: 70' Vitaliy Buyalskiy 0-1.
Referee: Tony Chapron (FRA)   Attendance: 10,077

02.11.17 Stadion Partizana, Beograd: Partizan – KF Skënderbeu 2-0 (1-0)
Partizan: Vladimir Stojkovic, Miroslav Vulicevic, Milan Mitrovic, Nemanja Miletic (I),
Everton Luiz, Zoran Tosic (82' Danilo Pantic), Marko Jevtovic, Marko Jankovic, Nemanja
G.Miletic (II), Ognjen Ozegovic (74' Milán Rádin), Léandro Tawamba Kana (88' Djordje
Jovanovic). Coach: Miroslav Djukic.
KF Skënderbeu: Orges Shehi, Kristi Vangjeli, Marko Radas, Gledi Mici (65' Fidan Aliti),
Bajram Jashanica, Gjergj Muzaka, Sabien Lilaj, Afrim Taku (89' Suad Sahiti), Enis Gavazaj
(68' Martin Nespor), Ali Sowe, Segun Adeniyi. Coach: Ilir Daja.
Goals: 39' Zoran Tosic 1-0, 66' Lénadre Tawamba Kana 2-0.
Referee: Carlos Del Cerro Grande (ESP)   Attendance: 12,659.

23.11.17   Stadion Partizana, Beograd: Partizan – BSC Young Boys 2-1 (1-1)
Partizan: Vladimir Stojkovic, Miroslav Vulicevic, Milan Mitrovic, Nemanja Miletic (I),
Everton Luiz, Marko Jevtovic, Marko Jankovic, Danilo Pantic (82' Sasa Ilic), Nemanja
G.Miletic (II), Ognjen Ozegovic (79' Milán Rádin), Léandro Tawamba Kana (89' Bojan
Ostojic). Coach: Miroslav Djukic.
BSC Young Boys: David von Ballmoos, Loris Benito, Kevin Mbabu, Gregory Wüthrich (83'
Christian Fassnacht), Kasim Nuhu, Miralem Sulejmani, Nicolas Ngamaleu, Djibril Sow,
Michel Aebischer, Jean Pierre Nsamé (66' Guillaume Hoarau), Roger Assalé.
Coach: Adi Hütter.
Goals: 12' Léandre Tawamba Kana 1-0, 25' Nicolas Ngamaleu 1-1, 53' Ognjen Ozegovic 2-1.
Referee: Tamás Bognar (HUN)   Attendance: 20,568.

23.11.17   Elbasan Arena, Elbasan: KF Skënderbeu – Dinamo Kiev 3-2 (1-1)
KF Skënderbeu: Orges Shehi, Kristi Vangjeli, Marko Radas, Tefik Osmani (70' Bakary
Nimaga), Gledi Mici, Fidan Aliti, Gjergj Muzaka, Sabien Lilaj, Enis Gavazaj (72' Afrim
Taku), Ali Sowe (90' Bruno Dita), Segun Adeniyi. Coach: Ilir Daja.
Dinamo Kiev: Georgiy Bushchan, Josip Pivaric, Evgen Khacheridi, Tamás Kádár, Tomasz
Kedziora (71' Nazariy Rusyn), Mikola Morozyuk, Nikita Korzun (60' Mykola Shaparenko),
Viktor Tsygankov, Volodymyr Shepeliev, Júnior Moraes, Artem Besedin.
Coach: Aleksandr Khatskevich.
Goals: 16' Viktor Tsygankov 0-1, 18' Sabien Lilaj 1-1, 52' Segun Adeniyi 2-1,
56' Ali Sowe 3-1, 90+1' Nazariy Rusyn 3-2.
Referee: Oliver Drachta (AUT)   Attendance: 100

07.12.17   Stade de Suisse, Bern: BSC Young Boys – KF Skënderbeu 2-1 (0-0)
BSC Young Boys: Marco Wölfli, Kevin Mbabu, Marco Bürki, Gregory Wüthrich, Sven Joss,
Thorsten Schick, Nicolas Ngamaleu, Pedro Teixeira, Michel Aebischer (71' Leonardo
Bertone), Guillaume Hoarau (81' Roger Assalé), Jean Pierre Nsamé. Coach: Adi Hütter.
KF Skënderbeu: Orges Shehi, Kristi Vangjeli, Gledi Mici, Fidan Aliti, Bajram Jashanica,
Gjergj Muzaka, Sabien Lilaj, Enis Gavazaj, Bakary Nimaga, Suad Sahiti (72' Tefik Osmani),
Binyam Belay Demte (75' Afrim Taku). Coach: Ilir Daja.
Goals: 51' Enis Gavazaj 0-1, 55' Guillaume Hoarau 1-1, 90+5' Roger Assalé 2-1.
Referee: Simon Evans (WAL)   Attendance: 8,029

07.12.17   NSK Olimpiyskyi, Kiev: Dinamo Kiev – Partizan 4-1 (3-1)
Dinamo Kiev: Georgiy Bushchan, Josip Pivaric, Evgen Khacheridi, Tamás Kádár, Tomasz
Kedziora, Mikola Morozyuk, Vitaliy Buyalskiy (66' Denys Garmash), Viktor Tsygankov (83'
Derlis González), Volodymyr Shepeliev, Júnior Moraes, Mykola Shaparenko (77' Artem
Besedin). Coach: Aleksandr Khatskevich.
Partizan: Vladimir Stojkovic, Miroslav Vulicevic, Milan Mitrovic, Nemanja Miletic (I),
Everton Luiz (77' Petar Djurickovic), Marko Jevtovic, Seydouba Soumah, Danilo Pantic,
Nemanja G.Miletic (II), Léandro Tawamba Kana, Theophilus Solomon (66' Ognjen
Ozegovic). Coach: Miroslav Djukic.
Goals: 6' Mikola Morozyuk 1-0, 28', 31' Júnior Moraes 2-0, 3-0, 45+4' M. Jevtovic 3-1 (p),
77' Júnior Moraes 4-1 (p).
Referee: Pawel Gil (POL)   Attendance: 14,678.

323

GROUP C

14.09.17 WIRSOL Rhein-Neckar-Arena, Sinsheim:
1899 Hoffenheim – Sporting Braga 1-2 (1-1)
1899 Hoffenheim: Oliver Baumann, Ermin Bicakcic (46' Benjamin Hübner), Pavel Kaderábek, Håvard Nordtveit (69' Philipp Ochs), Kevin Vogt, Lukas Rupp, Nico Schulz, Florian Grillitsch (56' Eugen Polanski), Kerem Demirbay, Sandro Wagner, Andrej Kramaric.
Coach: Julian Nagelsmann.
Sporting Braga: Matheus Magalhães, Raúl Silva, Ricardo Esgaio, Marcelo Goiano, Nuno Sequeira, Lazar Rosic, Nikola Vukcevic, João Carlos (78' André Horta), Danilo Barbosa, Dyego Sousa (61' Fransérgio), Paulinho (83' Ahmed Hassan 'Koka'). Coach: Abel Ferreira.
Goals: 24' Sandro Wagner 1-0, 45+1' João Carlos 1-1, 50' Dyego Sousa 1-2.
Referee: Bobby Madden (SCO)   Attendance: 15,714.

14.09.17 Basaksehir Fatih Terim Stadyumu, Istanbul:
Istanbul Basaksehir F.K. – PFC Ludogorets Razgrad 0-0
Istanbul Basaksehir F.K.: Volkan Babacan, Gaël Clichy, Alexandru Epureanu, Júnior Caiçara, Joseph Attamah, Emre Belözoglu, Márcio Mossoró (80' Stefano Napoleoni), Gökhan Inler, Edin Visca, Emmanuel Adebayor (65' Mevlüt Erdinç), Eljero Elia (73' Kerim Frei).
Coach: Abdullah Avci.
PFC Ludogorets Razgrad: Jorge Broun, Cosmin Moti, Cicinho, Igor Plastun, Svetoslav Dyakov, Anicet Andrianantenaina, Wanderson, Natanael Pimienta, Jacek Góralski (77' Lucas Sasha), João Paulo (59' Claudiu Keserü), Jody Lukoki (86' Gustavo Campanharo).
Coach: Dimitar Dimitrov.
Referee: Stefan Johannesson (SWE)   Attendance: 6,804.

28.09.17 Ludogorets Arena, Razgrad: PFC Ludogorets Razgrad – 1899 Hoffenheim 2-1 (0-1)
PFC Ludogorets Razgrad: Jorge Broun, Cosmin Moti, Cicinho, Igor Plastun, Svetoslav Dyakov, Gustavo Campanharo (80' Jacek Góralski), Anicet Andrianantenaina, Wanderson (87' Claudiu Keserü), Natanael Pimienta, Marcelinho (90+1' Lucas Sasha), Jody Lukoki.
Coach: Dimitar Dimitrov.
1899 Hoffenheim: Oliver Baumann, Pavel Kaderábek (56' Philipp Ochs), Stefan Posch, Eugen Polanski, Håvard Nordtveit, Steven Zuber (56' Dennis Geiger), Kevin Vogt, Lukas Rupp, Nico Schulz, Andrej Kramaric, Mark Uth (74' Felix Passlack). Coach: Julian Nagelsmann.
Goals: 2' Pavel Kaderábek 0-1, 46' Svetoslav Dyakov 1-1, 72' Jody Lukoki 2-1.
Referee: Pawel Raczkowski (POL)   Attendance: 6,155.

28.09.17 Estádio Municipal de Braga, Braga:
Sporting Braga – Istanbul Basaksehir F.K. 2-1 (1-1)
Sporting Braga: Matheus Magalhães, Raúl Silva, Ricardo Ferreira, Ricardo Esgaio, Marcelo Goiano, Nuno Sequeira (20' Bruno Xadas), Nikola Vukcevic, João Carlos (79' Ricardo Horta), Danilo Barbosa, Paulinho, Ahmed Hassan 'Koka'. Coach: Abel Ferreira.
Istanbul Basaksehir F.K.: Volkan Babacan, Manuel Da Costa (46' Joseph Attamah), Gaël Clichy, Alexandru Epureanu, Júnior Caiçara, Emre Belözoglu, Márcio Mossoró (81' Mahmut Tekdemir), Gökhan Inler, Edin Visca, Eljero Elia, Mevlüt Erdinç (74' Mehmet Batdal).
Coach: Abdullah Avci.
Goals: 26' Ahmed Hassan 'Koka' 1-0, 28' Emre Belözoglu 1-1, 89' Fransérgio 2-1.
Referee: Matej Jug (SVN)   Attendance: 10,376.

19.10.17   WIRSOL Rhein-Neckar-Arena, Sinsheim:
1899 Hoffenheim – Istanbul Basaksehir F.K. 3-1 (0-0)
1899 Hoffenheim: Oliver Baumann, Benjamin Hübner, Pavel Kaderábek, Stefan Posch (69'
Steven Zuber), Kevin Vogt, Nico Schulz, Kerem Demirbay (63' Philipp Ochs), Nadiem Amiri,
Dennis Geiger (72' Eugen Polanski), Sandro Wagner, Mark Uth. Coach: Julian Nagelsmann.
Istanbul Basaksehir F.K.: Mert Günok, Gaël Clichy (81' Alparslan Erdem), Alexandru
Epureanu, Júnior Caiçara, Joseph Attamah, Gökhan Inler, Tunay Torun, Kerim Frei, Irfan
Kahveci (63' Mahmut Tekdemir), Mevlüt Erdinç (63' Stefano Napoleoni), Mehmet Batdal.
Coach: Abdullah Avci.
Goals: 52' Benjamin Hübner 1-0, 59' Nadiem Amiri 2-0, 75' Nico Schulz 3-0,
90+3' Stefano Napoleoni 3-1.
Referee: Aleksey Eskov (RUS)   Attendance: 21,167.

19.10.17   Estádio Municipal de Braga, Braga:
Sporting Braga – PFC Ludogorets Razgrad 0-2 (0-1)
Sporting Braga: Matheus Magalhães, Jefferson, Raúl Silva, Ricardo Ferreira, Ricardo Esgaio,
Marcelo Goiano (59' Bruno Xadas), Fransérgio (73' André Horta), Nikola Vukcevic, João
Carlos (58' Fábio Martins), Paulinho, Ahmed Hassan 'Koka'. Coach: Abel Ferreira.
PFC Ludogorets Razgrad: Renan, Cosmin Moti, Cicinho, Igor Plastun, Rafael Forster, Anicet
Andrianantenaina, Wanderson, Natanael Pimienta (85' Lucas Sasha), Jacek Góralski,
Marcelinho (74' Svetoslav Dyakov), Jody Lukoki (83' Claudiu Kererü).
Coach: Dimitar Dimitrov.
Goals: 25' Cosmin Moti 0-1, 56' Raul Silva 0-2 (og).
Referee: Davide Massa (ITA)   Attendance: 8,623.

02.11.17   Basaksehir Fatih Terim Stadyumu, Istanbul:
Istanbul Basaksehir F.K. – 1899 Hoffenheim 1-1 (0-0)
Istanbul Basaksehir F.K.: Mert Günok, Gaël Clichy, Alexandru Epureanu, Alparslan Erdem,
Júnior Caiçara, Gökhan Inler, Tunay Torun (62' Edin Visca), Kerim Frei, Irfan Kahveci (81'
Márcio Mossoró), Stefano Napoleoni (81' Eljeo Elia), Mevlüt Erdinç. Coach: Abdullah Avci.
1899 Hoffenheim: Oliver Baumann, Justin Hoogma, Håvard Nordtveit, Steven Zuber, Kevin
Vogt (23' Stefan Posch), Nico Schulz, Florian Grillitsch, Kerem Demirbay (74' Dennis
Geiger), Nadiem Amiri (58' Philipp Ochs), Sandro Wagner, Andrej Kramaric.
Coach: Julian Nagelsmann.
Goals: 47' Florian Grillitsch 0-1, 90+3' Edin Visca 1-1.
Referee: Harald Lechner (AUT)   Attendance: 5,214.

02.11.17   Ludogorets Arena, Razgrad: PFC Ludogorets Razgrad – Sporting Braga 1-1 (0-0)
PFC Ludogorets Razgrad: Jorge Broun, Cosmin Moti, Cicinho, Igor Plastun, Anicet
Andrianantenaina, Wanderson (85' Georgi Terziev), Natanael Pimienta, Jacek Góralski,
Marcelinho (73' Svetoslav Dyakov), Jody Lukoki, Virgil Misidjan (89' Gustavo Campanharo).
Coach: Dimitar Dimitrov.
Sporting Braga: Matheus Magalhães, Jefferson, Raúl Silva, Ricardo Ferreira, Ricardo Esgaio,
Marcelo Goiano, Nikola Vukcevic, Danilo Barbosa (78' Ahmed Hassan 'Koka'), Bruno Xadas
(58' Ricardo Horta), Dyego Sousa (65' Fransérgio), Paulinho. Coach: Abel Ferreira.
Goals: 68' Marcelinho 1-0, 83' Fransérgio 1-1.
Referee: Vladislav Bezborodov (RUS)   Attendance: 7,544.

23.11.17 Estádio Municipal de Braga, Braga: Sporting Braga – 1899 Hoffenheim 3-1 (1-0)
Sporting Braga: Matheus Magalhães, Jefferson, Raúl Silva, Ricardo Ferreira, Ricardo Esgaio,
Marcelo Goiano, Fransérgio, Nikola Vukcevic, João Carlos (77' Fábio Martins), Danilo
Barbosa, Paulinho (71' Dyego Sousa). Coach: Abel Ferreira.
1899 Hoffenheim: Oliver Baumann, Stefan Posch, Håvard Nordtveit (46' Serge Gnabry),
Steven Zuber (66' Ádám Szalai), Kevin Vogt, Nico Schulz, Florian Grillitsch, Kerem
Demirbay, Nadiem Amiri, Dennis Geiger (52' Mark Uth), Andrej Kramaric.
Coach: Julian Nagelsmann.
Goals: 1' Marcelo Goiano 1-0, 74' Mark Uth 1-1, 81', 90+3' Fransérgio 2-1, 3-1.
Referee: Andre Marriner (ENG)   Attendance: 10,054.
Sent off: 90+7' Ádám Szalai.

23.11.17 Ludogorets Arena, Razgrad:
          PFC Ludogorets Razgrad – Istanbul Basaksehir F.K. 1-2 (0-2)
PFC Ludogorets Razgrad: Renan, Cosmin Moti, Cicinho, Igor Plastun, Anicet
Andrianantenaina, Wanderson, Natanael Pimienta, Jacek Góralski (82' Gustavo Campanharo),
Marcelinho, Jody Lukoki (46' Claudiu Keserü), Virgil Misidjan. Coach: Dimitar Dimitrov.
Istanbul Basaksehir F.K.: Mert Günok, Alexandru Epureanu, Alparslan Erdem, Júnior Caiçara,
Joseph Attamah, Gökhan Inler, Edin Visca (90+3' Manuel Da Costa), Kerim Frei, Irfan
Kahveci, Stefano Napoleoni (67' Márcio Mossoró), Mevlüt Erdinç (87' Eljeo Elia).
Coach: Abdullah Avci.
Goals: 20' Edin Visca 0-1, 27' Kerim Frei 0-2, 65' Marcelinho 1-2.
Referee: Miroslav Zelinka (CZE)   Attendance: 7,520.

07.12.17   WIRSOL Rhein-Neckar-Arena, Sinsheim:
           1899 Hoffenheim – PFC Ludogorets Razgrad 1-1 (1-0)
1899 Hoffenheim: Gregor Kobel, Ermin Bicakcic, Alexander Rossipal, Simon Lorenz, Justin
Hoogma, Eugen Polanski, Håvard Nordtveit, Robert Zulj (69' Johannes Bühler), Philipp Ochs
(56' Meris Skenderovic), Felix Passlack, Robin Hack (76' David Otto).
Coach: Julian Nagelsmann.
PFC Ludogorets Razgrad: Renan, Cosmin Moti, Cicinho, Igor Plastun, Svetoslav Dyakov,
Anicet Andrianantenaina, Wanderson (87' Georgi Terziev), Natanael Pimienta, Jacek Góralski
(46' Claudiu Keserü), Marcelinho (88' Lucas Sasha), Virgil Misidjan.
Coach: Dimitar Dimitrov.
Goals: 25' Philipp Ochs 1-0, 62' Wanderson 1-1.
Referee: Orel Grinfeld (ISR)   Attendance: 7,814.
Sent off: 83' Claudiu Keserü.

07.12.17   Basaksehir Fatih Terim Stadyumu, Istanbul:
           Istanbul Basaksehir F.K. – Sporting Braga 2-1 (1-0)
Istanbul Basaksehir F.K.: Mert Günok, Gaël Clichy, Alexandru Epureanu, Júnior Caiçara,
Joseph Attamah, Márcio Mossoró, Gökhan Inler, Edin Visca (85' Stefano Napoleoni), Kerim
Frei, Irfan Kahveci (60' Emre Belözoglu), Mevlüt Erdinç (60' Mehmet Batdal).
Coach: Abdullah Avci.
Sporting Braga: Matheus Magalhães, Jefferson, Raúl Silva, Ricardo Esgaio, Bruno Viana,
Nikola Vukcevic, Danilo Barbosa, André Horta (72' João Carlos), Bruno Xadas (85' Ahmed
Hassan 'Koka'), Dyego Sousa, Fábio Martins (72' Ricardo Horta). Coach: Abel Ferreira.
Goals: 10' Edin Visca 1-0, 55' Raul Silva 1-1, 77' Emre Belözoglu 2-1 (p).
Referee: John Beaton (SCO)   Attendance: 5,241.

326

GROUP D

14.09.17 Ernst-Happel-Stadion, Wien: Austria Wien – AC Milan 1-5 (0-3)
Austria Wien: Osman Hadzikic, Heiko Westermann (42' Alexandar Borkovic, 86' Petar
Gluhakovic), Florian Klein, Christoph Martschinko, Abdul Kadiri Mohammed, Raphael
Holzhauser, Tarkan Serbest, Dominik Prokop, Jin-Hyun Lee (74' David De Paula), Felipe
Pires, Christoph Monschein. Coach: Thorsten Fink.
AC Milan: Gianluigi Donnarumma, Leonardo Bonucci, Cristián Zapata, Ignazio Abate, Luca
Antonelli, Alessio Romagnoli (74' Mateo Musacchio), Lucas Biglia, Hakan Çalhanoglu,
Franck Kessié (62' Giacomo Bonaventura), Nikola Kalinic (62' Suso), André Silva.
Coach: Vincenzo Montella.
Goals: 7' Hakan Çalhanoglu 0-1, 10', 20' André Silva 0-2, 0-3, 47' Alexandar Borkovic 1-3,
56' André Silva 1-4, 63' Suso 1-5.
Referee: Serdar Gözübüyük (HOL)   Attendance: 31,409.

14.09.17 Stadion HNK Rijeka, Rijeka: HNK Rijeka – AEK Athen 1-2 (1-1)
HNK Rijeka: Andrej Prskalo, Marko Vesovic, Dario Zuparic, Josip Elez, Leonard Zhuta,
Zoran Kvrzic (73' Boadu Maxwell Acosty), Josip Misic (81' Florentin Matei), Filip Bradaric,
Alexander Gorgon, Mario Gavranovic (59' Mate Males), Héber. Coach: Matjaz Kek.
AEK Athen: Giannis Anestis, Ognjen Vranjes, Uros Cosic, Hélder Lopes, Jakob Johansson,
Lazaros Christodoulopoulos (78' Astrit Ajdarevic), Petros Mantalos, Michalis Bakakis, André
Simões, Marko Livaja (86' Sergio Araújo), Viktor Klonaridis (60' Anastasios Bakasetas).
Coach: Manolo Jiménez.
Goals: 16' Petros Mantalos 0-1, 29' Josip Elez 1-1, 62' Lazaros Christodoulopoulos 1-2.
Referee: John Beaton (SCO)   Attendance: 5,932.

28.09.17 Stadio Giuseppe Meazza, Milano: AC Milan – HNK Rijeka 3-2 (1-0)
AC Milan: Gianluigi Donnarumma, Leonardo Bonucci, Mateo Musacchio, Ignazio Abate,
Alessio Romagnoli, Hakan Çalhanoglu (46' Giacomo Bonaventura), Franck Kessié (71' José
Mauri), Manuel Locatelli, Fabio Borini, André Silva (82' Suso), Patrick Cutrone.
Coach: Vincenzo Montella.
HNK Rijeka: Sumon Sluga, Marko Vesovic, Dario Zuparic, Josip Elez, Leonard Zhuta, Zoran
Kvrzic (58' Boadu Maxwell Acosty), Domagoj Pavicic (71' Mate Males), Josip Misic, Filip
Bradaric, Héber, Jakov Puljic (80' Matic Crnic). Coach: Matjaz Kek.
Goals: 14' André Silva 1-0, 53' Mateo Musacchio 2-0, 84' Boadu Maxwell Acosty 2-1,
90' Josip Elez 2-2 (p), 90+4' Patrick Cutrone 3-2.
Referee: Orel Grinfeld (ISR)   Attendance: 23,917.

28.09.17 Olympiako Stadio Spyros Louis, Athen: AEK Athen – Austria Wien 2-2 (1-1)
AEK Athen: Giannis Anestis, Rodrigo Galo, Ognjen Vranjes, Uros Cosic (23' Adam
Tzanetopoulos, 80' Anastasios Bakasetas), Jakob Johansson, Lazaros Christodoulopoulos,
Astrit Ajdarevic (53' Konstantinos Galanopoulos), Petros Mantalos, Michalis Bakakis, Sergio
Araújo, Marko Livaja. Coach: Manolo Jiménez.
Austria Wien: Patrick Pentz, Florian Klein, Christoph Martschinko, Abdul Kadiri Mohammed,
David De Paula (90+1' Jin-Hyun Lee), Raphael Holzhauser, Tarkan Serbest, Ismael Tajouri
Shradi, Felipe Pires, Christoph Monschein (70' Kevin Friesenbichler), Ibrahim Alhassan
Abdullahi (59' Dominik Prokop). Coach: Thorsten Fink.
Goals: 28' Marko Livaja 1-0, 43' Christoph Monschein 1-1, 49' Ismael Tajouri Shradi 1-2,
90' Marko Livaja 2-2.
Referee: Pael Gil (POL)   Attendance: 16,954.

327

19.10.17 Stadio Giuseppe Meazza, Milano: AC Milan – AEK Athen 0-0
AC Milan: Gianluigi Donnarumma, Leonardo Bonucci, Mateo Musacchio, Ricardo Rodríguez,
Davide Calabria, Giacomo Bonaventura (73' Franck Kessié), Hakan Çalhanoglu, Manuel
Locatelli, André Silva (62' Nikola Kalinic), Suso (83' Fabio Borini), Patrick Cutrone.
Coach: Vincenzo Montella.
AEK Athen: Giannis Anestis, Rodrigo Galo, Ognjen Vranjes, Hélder Lopes, Adam
Tzanetopoulos, Jakob Johansson, Lazaros Christodoulopoulos (64' Sergio Araújo), Petros
Mantalos (90+3' Konstantinos Galanopoulos), Michalis Bakakis, André Simões, Marko Livaja
(76' Anastasios Bakasetas). Coach: Manolo Jiménez.
Referee: Andreas Ekberg (SWE)   Attendance: 20,812.

19.10.17 Ernst-Happel-Stadion, Wien: Austria Wien – HNK Rijeka 1-3 (0-2)
Austria Wien: Patrick Pentz, Heiko Westermann, Florian Klein, Abdul Kadiri Mohammed,
David De Paula (59' Ismael Tajouri Shradi), Thomas Salamon, Raphael Holzhauser, Tarkan
Serbest (77' Dominik Prokop), Kevin Friesenbichler, Felipe Pires, Christoph Monschein.
Coach: Thorsten Fink.
HNK Rijeka: Sumon Sluga, Marko Vesovic, Dario Zuparic, Josip Elez (70' Roberto Puncec),
Leonard Zhuta, Mate Males, Josip Misic (77' Domagoj Pavicic), Filip Bradaric, Alexander
Gorgon, Mario Gavranovic, Boadu Maxwell Acosty (79' Zoran Kvrzic). Coach: Matjaz Kek.
Goals: 21', 31' Mario Gavranovic 0-1, 0-2, 90' Kevin Friesenbichler 1-2,
90+2' Zoran Kvrzic 1-3.
Referee: Sandro Schärer (SUI)   Attendance: 20,690.

02.11.17 Olympiako Stadio Spyros Louis, Athen: AEK Athen – AC Milan 0-0
AEK Athen: Giannis Anestis, Rodrigo Galo, Ognjen Vranjes, Uros Cosic, Hélder Lopes, Jakob
Johansson, Lazaros Christodoulopoulos (60' Marko Livaja), Michalis Bakakis, André Simões,
Sergio Araújo (79' Georgios Giakoumakis), Anastasios Bakasetas (66' Konstantinos
Galanopoulos). Coach: Manolo Jiménez.
AC Milan: Gianluigi Donnarumma, Leonardo Bonucci, Mateo Musacchio, Ricardo Rodríguez,
Alessio Romagnoli, Riccardo Montolivo, Hakan Çalhanoglu, Manuel Locatelli (67' Franck
Kessié), Fabio Borini, André Silva (81' Nikola Kalinic), Patrick Cutrone (46' Suso).
Coach: Vincenzo Montella.
Referee: Jorge Sousa (POR)   Attendance: 40,538.

02.11.17 Stadion HNK Rijeka, Rijeka: HNK Rijeka – Austria Wien 1-4 (0-1)
HNK Rijeka: Andrej Prskalo, Marko Vesovic, Roberto Puncec, Dario Zuparic, Leonard Zhuta,
Domagoj Pavicic, Josip Misic, Filip Bradaric, Alexander Gorgon (84' Jakov Puljic), Héber
(53' Florentin Matei), Boadu Maxwell Acosty (55' Zoran Kvrzic). Coach: Matjaz Kek.
Austria Wien: Patrick Pentz, Heiko Westermann, Petar Gluhakovic, Abdul Kadiri Mohammed,
Thomas Salamon, Raphael Holzhauser, Tarkan Serbest, Ismael Tajouri Shradi (86' Manprit
Sarkaria), Dominik Prokop (90' Ibrahim Alhassan Abdullahi), Kevin Friesenbichler (70'
Christoph Monschein), Felipe Pires. Coach: Thorsten Fink.
Goals: 41' Dominik Prokop 0-1, 61' Domagoj Pavicic 1-1, 62' Dominik Prokop 1-2,
73' Tarkan Serbert 1-3, 83' Christoph Monschein 1-4.
Referee: Jakob Kehlet (DEN)   Attendance: 7,912.
Sent off: 72' Josip Misic.

23.11.17 Stadio Giuseppe Meazza, Milano: AC Milan – Austria Wien 5-1 (3-1)
AC Milan: Gianluigi Donnarumma, Leonardo Bonucci (80' Gustavo Gómez), Cristián Zapata,
Mateo Musacchio, Ricardo Rodríguez (64' Luca Antonelli), Lucas Biglia, Hakan Çalhanoglu,
Franck Kessié, Fabio Borini (74' Manuel Locatelli), André Silva, Patrick Cutrone.
Coach: Vincenzo Montella.
Austria Wien: Patrick Pentz, Alexandar Borkovic, Abdul Kadiri Mohammed, David De Paula,
Thomas Salamon (69' Petar Gluhakovic), Raphael Holzhauser (86' Jin-Hyun Lee), Tarkan
Serbest, Dominik Prokop, Felipe Pires (78' Ismael Tajouri Shradi), Christoph Monschein,
Ibrahim Alhassan Abdullahi. Coach: Thorsten Fink.
Goals: 21' Christoph Monschein 0-1, 27' Ricardo Rodríguez 1-1, 36' André Silva 2-1,
42' Patrick Cutrone (42'), 70' André Silva 4-1, 90+3' Patrick Cutrone 5-1.
Referee: Andris Treimanis (LAT)   Attendance: 17,932.

23.11.17 Olympiako Stadio Spyros Louis, Athen: AEK Athen – HNK Rijeka 2-2 (1-2)
AEK Athen: Giannis Anestis, Dmitro Chigrinskiy, Rodrigo Galo (30' Marko Livaja), Ognjen
Vranjes, Hélder Lopes, Lazaros Christodoulopoulos (85' Patricio Rodriguez), Michalis
Bakakis, André Simões, Konstantinos Galanopoulos (68' Panagiotis Kone), Sergio Araújo,
Anastasios Bakasetas. Coach: Manolo Jiménez.
HNK Rijeka: Andrej Prskalo, Marko Vesovic, Dario Zuparic, Josip Elez, Leonard Zhuta, Mate
Males, Domagoj Pavicic (90+2' Matic Crnic), Filip Bradaric, Alexander Gorgon, Mario
Gavranovic (81' Jakov Puljic), Boadu Maxwell Acosty (70' Zoran Kvrzic).
Coach: Matjaz Kek.
Goals: 8', 26' Alexander Gorgon 0-1, 0-2, 45+2' Sergio Araújo 1-2,
55' Lazaros Christodoulopoulos 2-2.
Referee: Mattias Gestranius (FIN)   Attendance: 17,100.

07.12.17 Stadion HNK Rijeka, Rijeka: HNK Rijeka – AC Milan 2-0 (1-0)
HNK Rijeka: Simon Sluga, Marko Vesovic, Dario Zuparic, Josip Elez, Leonard Zhuta, Mate
Males, Zoran Kvrzic (86' Charis Mavrias), Domagoj Pavicic, Mario Gavranovic (81' Matic
Crnic), Jakov Puljic, Boadu Maxwell Acosty (76' Roberto Puncec). Coach: Matjaz Kek.
AC Milan: Marco Storari, Gabriel Paletta, Cristián Zapata, Luca Antonelli (80' Riccardo
Forte), Alessio Romagnoli, Davide Calabria, Lucas Biglia, Manuel Locatelli, Niccolò
Zanellato (74' Ignazio Abate), André Silva, Patrick Cutrone. Coach: Gennaro Gattuso.
Goals: 7' Jakov Puljic 1-0, 47' Mario Gavranovic 2-0.
Referee: István Vad (HUN)   Attendance: 8,021.

07.12.17 Ernst-Happel-Stadion, Wien: Austria Wien – AEK Athen 0-0
Austria Wien: Patrick Pentz, Michael Blauensteiner, Abdul Kadiri Mohammed, Thomas
Salamon (88' Manprit Sarkaria), Raphael Holzhauser, Tarkan Serbest, Ismael Tajouri Shradi
(72' Lucas Venuto), Dominik Prokop, Kevin Friesenbichler (77' Christoph Monschein), Felipe
Pires, Ibrahim Alhassan Abdullahi. Coach: Thorsten Fink.
AEK Athen: Panagiotis Tsintotas, Dmitro Chigrinskiy, Rodrigo Galo, Ognjen Vranjes, Hélder
Lopes, Lazaros Christodoulopoulos (64' Anastasios Bakasetas), Michalis Bakakis, André
Simões, Konstantinos Galanopoulos, Sergio Araújo (74' Viktor Klonaridis), Marko Livaja (90'
Panagiotis Kone). Coach: Manolo Jiménez.
Referee: Craig Pawson (ENG)   Attendance: 23,133.

GROUP E

14.09.17 Neo GSP Stadium, Nicosia: Apollon Limassol – Olympique Lyon 1-1 (0-0)
Apollon Limassol: Bruno Vale, Valentin Roberge, Jander, Alex da Silva (77' Nicolás
Martínez), André Schembri (85' Emilio Zelaya), Héctor Yuste, Antonio Jakolis (54' Adrián
Sardinero), Esteban Sachetti, Alef, João Pedro, Anton Maglica. Coach: Sofronis Avgousti.
Olympique Lyon: Anthony Lopes, Jérémy Morel, Marcelo, Rafael, Fernando Marçal, Jordan
Ferri (78' Tanguy NDombèlé), Lucas Tousart, Memphis Depay, Mariano Díaz (78' Bertrand
Traoré), Nabil Fekir, Maxwell Cornet. Coach: Bruno Génésio.
Goals: 53' Memphis Depay 0-1 (p), 90+3' Adrián Sardinero 1-1.
Referee: Miroslav Zelinka (CZE)   Attendance: 5,134.

14.09.17 MAPEI Stadium, Reggio nell'Emilia: Atalanta – Everton FC 3-0 (3-0)
Atalanta: Etrit Berisha, Andrea Masiello (77' Mattia Caldara), Rafael Tolói, José Palomino,
Timothy Castagne, Hans Hateboer, Alejandro Darío Gómez, Marten de Roon, Remo Freuler,
Bryan Cristante (82' Jasmin Kurtic), Andrea Petagna (79' Andreas Cornelius).
Coach: Gian Piero Gasperini.
Everton FC: Maarten Stekelenburg, Phil Jagielka, Leighton Baines, Michael Keane, Mason
Holgate, Morgan Schneiderlin (66' Sandro Ramírez), Gylfi Sigurdsson, Muhamed Besic,
Nikola Vlasic, Wayne Rooney (66' Davy Klaassen), Dominic Calvert-Lewin (76' Kevin
Mirallas). Coach: Ronald Koeman.
Goals: 27' Andrea Masiello 1-0, 41' Alejandro Darío Gómez 2-0, 44' Bryan Cristante 3-0.
Referee: Vladislav Bezborodov (RUS)   Attendance: 14,890.

28.09.17 Goodison Park, Liverpool: Everton FC – Apollon Limassol 2-2 (1-1)
Everton FC: Jordan Pickford, Leighton Baines, Ashley Williams, Jonjoe Kenny, Mason
Holgate, Morgan Schneiderlin, Gylfi Sigurdsson, Idrissa Gueye (46' Nikola Vlasic), Tom
Davies (67' Davy Klaassen), Wayne Rooney, Sandro Ramírez (67' Dominic Calvert-Lewin).
Coach: Ronald Koeman.
Apollon Limassol: Bruno Vale, Valentin Roberge, Héctor Yuste, Giorgos Vasiliou (83' Emilio
Zelaya), Antonio Jakolis (61' André Schembri), Esteban Sachetti (77' Jander), Alef, Allan,
João Pedro, Anton Maglica, Adrián Sardinero. Coach: Sofronis Avgousti.
Goals: 12' Adrián Sardinero 0-1, 21' Wayne Rooney 1-1, 66' Nikola Vlasic 2-1,
88' Héctor Yuste 2-2.
Referee: Tamás Bognar (HUN)   Attendance: 27,034.
Sent off: 86' Valentin Roberge.

28.09.17 Groupama Stadium, Décines-Charpieu: Olympique Lyon – Atalanta 1-1 (1-0)
Olympique Lyon: Anthony Lopes, Jérémy Morel, Marcelo, Kenny Tete, Ferland Mendy,
Tanguy NDombèlé, Lucas Tousart, Houssem Aouar (70' Memphis Depay), Bertrand Traoré
(85' Maxwell Cornet), Mariano Díaz (70' Myziane Maolida), Nabil Fekir.
Coach: Bruno Génésio.
Atalanta: Etrit Berisha, Andrea Masiello, José Palomino, Leonardo Spinazzola, Hans Hateboer,
Mattia Caldara, Alejandro Darío Gómez, Marten de Roon, Remo Freuler, Bryan Cristante (46'
Timothy Castagne), Andrea Petagna (61' Josip Ilicic). Coach: Gian Piero Gasperini.
Goals: 45' Bertrand Traoré 1-0, 57' Alejandro Darío Gómez 1-1.
Referee: Daniel Siebert (GER)   Attendance: 27,715.

19.10.17 MAPEI Stadium, Reggio nell'Emilia: Atalanta – Apollon Limassol 3-1 (1-0)
Atalanta: Etrit Berisha, Andrea Masiello, José Palomino, Leonardo Spinazzola, Hans Hateboer,
Mattia Caldara, Alejandro Darío Gómez (80' Jasmin Kurtic), Josip Ilicic (86' Andreas
Cornelius), Remo Freuler, Bryan Cristante (70' Marten de Roon), Andrea Petagna.
Coach: Gian Piero Gasperini.
Apollon Limassol: Bruno Vale, Jander, André Schembri (81' Adrián Sardinero), Héctor Yuste,
Antonio Jakolis, Esteban Sachetti, Alef, Andrei Pitian, Allan (57' Alex da Silva), João Pedro,
Anton Maglica (56' Emilio Zelaya). Coach: Sofronis Avgousti.
Goals: 12' Josip Ilicic 1-0, 59' André Schembri 1-1, 64' Andrea Petagna 2-1,
66' Remo Freuler 3-1.
Referee: Georgi Kabakov (BUL)   Attendance: 13,803.

19.10.17 Goodison Park, Liverpool: Everton FC – Olympique Lyon 1-2 (0-1)
Everton FC: Jordan Pickford, Ashley Williams, Cuco Martina, Michael Keane, Mason
Holgate, Morgan Schneiderlin (57' Gylfi Sigurdsson), Davy Klaassen (46' Ademola
Lookman), Nikola Vlasic, Tom Davies, Kevin Mirallas (68' Sandro Ramírez), Dominic
Calvert-Lewin. Coach: Ronald Koeman.
Olympique Lyon: Anthony Lopes, Marcelo, Fernando Marçal, Kenny Tete, Mouctar Diakhaby,
Lucas Tousart, Houssem Aouar, Bertrand Traoré, Memphis Depay (89' Tanguy NDombèlé),
Nabil Fekir (61' Jordan Ferri), Myziane Maolida (70' Maxwell Cornet).
Coach: Bruno Génésio.
Goals: 6' Nabil Fekir 0-1 (p), 69' Ashley Williams 1-1, 75' Bertrand Traoré 1-2.
Referee: Bas Nijhuis (HOL)   Attendance: 27,159.

02.11.17 Neo GSP Stadium, Nicosia: Apollon Limassol – Atalanta 1-1 (0-1)
Apollon Limassol: Bruno Vale, Alex da Silva (76' Anton Maglica), Héctor Yuste, Giorgos
Vasiliou, Esteban Sachetti, Alef, Allan, Emilio Zelaya, João Pedro, Fotis Papoulis (58'
Antonio Jakolis), Adrián Sardinero (64' André Schembri). Coach: Sofronis Avgousti.
Atalanta: Etrit Berisha, Andrea Masiello, José Palomino, Leonardo Spinazzola, Hans Hateboer,
Mattia Caldara, Josip Ilicic (54' Riccardo Orsolini), Remo Freuler, Jasmin Kurtic (69' Robin
Gosens), Bryan Cristante (81' Marten de Roon), Andrea Petagna. Coach: Gian Piero Gasperini.
Goals: 35' Josip Ilicic 0-1 (p), 90+4' Emilio Zelaya 1-1.
Referee: Andris Treimanis (LAT)   Attendance: 5,658.

02.11.17 Groupama Stadium, Décines-Charpieu: Olympique Lyon – Everton FC 3-0 (0-0)
Olympique Lyon: Anthony Lopes, Marcelo, Rafael, Ferland Mendy, Mouctar Diakhaby,
Tanguy NDombèlé (77' Jordan Ferri), Lucas Tousart, Bertrand Traoré (70' Mariano Díaz),
Memphis Depay, Nabil Fekir (62' Houssem Aouar), Maxwell Cornet. Coach: Bruno Génésio.
Everton FC: Jordan Pickford, Ashley Williams, Cuco Martina (43' Muhamed Besic), Jonjoe
Kenny, Mason Holgate, Aaron Lennon (71' Nikola Vlasic), Morgan Schneiderlin, Gylfi
Sigurdsson, Idrissa Gueye (61' Dominic Calvert-Lewin), Beni Baningime, Ademola Lookman.
Coach: David Unsworth.
Goals: 68' Bertrand Traoré 1-0, 76' Houssem Aouar 2-0, 88' Memphis Depay 3-0.
Referee: Orel Grinfeld (ISR)   Attendance: 48,103.
Sent off: 80' Morgan Schneiderlin.

23.11.17   Groupama Stadium, Décines-Charpieu:
Olympique Lyon – Apollon Limassol 4-0 (2-0)
Olympique Lyon: Anthony Lopes, Jérémy Morel (46' Lucas Tousart), Marcelo, Rafael,
Fernando Marçal, Mouctar Diakhaby, Tanguy NDombèlé, Bertrand Traoré (16' Houssem
Aouar), Memphis Depay (74' Myziane Maolida), Mariano Díaz, Nabil Fekir.
Coach: Bruno Génésio.
Apollon Limassol: Bruno Vale, Valentin Roberge, Jander, André Schembri (72' Nicolás
Martínez), Héctor Yuste, Antonio Jakolis, Esteban Sachetti, Alef, João Pedro, Anton Maglica
(17' Emilio Zelaya), Adrián Sardinero (72' Alex da Silva). Coach: Sofronis Avgousti.
Goals: 29' Mouctar Diakhaby 1-0, 32' Nabil Fekir 2-0, 67' Mariano Díaz 3-0,
90' Myziane Maolida 4-0.
Referee: Pawel Raczkowski (POL)   Attendance: 26,972.

23.11.17   Goodison Park, Liverpool: Everton FC – Atalanta 1-5 (0-1)
Everton FC: Joel Robles, Ashley Williams, Cuco Martina, Michael Keane, Jonjoe Kenny (69'
Morgan Feeney), Davy Klaassen (62' Nikola Vlasic), Tom Davies, Beni Baningime, Wayne
Rooney, Kevin Mirallas (79' Dominic Calvert-Lewin), Sandro Ramírez.
Coach: David Unsworth.
Atalanta: Etrit Berisha, Andrea Masiello (61' Mattia Caldara), Rafael Tolói, José Palomino,
Timothy Castagne, Hans Hateboer (70' Robin Gosens), Alejandro Darío Gómez, Marten de
Roon, Remo Freuler, Bryan Cristante (82' Andreas Cornelius), Andrea Petagna.
Coach: Gian Piero Gasperini.
Goals: 12', 64' Bryan Cristante 0-1, 0-2, 71' Sandro Ramírez 1-2, 86' Robin Gosens 1-3,
88', 90+4' Andreas Cornelius 1-4, 1-5.
Referee: Jakob Kehlet (DEN)   Attendance: 17,431.

Alejandro Darío Gómez missed a penalty kick (48')

07.12.17   Neo GSP Stadium, Nicosia: Apollon Limassol – Everton FC 0-3 (0-2)
Apollon Limassol: Tasos Kissas, Valentin Roberge, Jander, André Schembri (60' Emilio
Zelaya), Esteban Sachetti, Andrei Pitian, Allan, João Pedro, Fotis Papoulis, Adrián Sardinero
(60' Antonio Jakolis), Nicolás Martínez (75' Ioannis Pittas). Coach: Sofronis Avgousti.
Everton FC: Joel Robles, Morgan Feeney, Morgan Schneiderlin, Muhamed Besic, Davy
Klaassen, Harry Charsley (90+1' Alex Denny), Nikola Vlasic, Fraser Hornby (82' Nathan
Broadhead), Beni Baningime, Kevin Mirallas (88' Anthony Gordon), Ademola Lookman.
Coach: Sam Allardyce.
Goals: 21' 28' Ademola Lookman 0-1, 0-2, 87' Nikola Vlasic 0-3.
Referee: Sébastien Delferière (BEL)   Attendance: 4,237.

07.12.17   MAPEI Stadium, Reggio nell'Emilia: Atalanta – Olympique Lyon 1-0 (1-0)
Atalanta: Etrit Berisha, Andrea Masiello, Rafael Tolói, Leonardo Spinazzola, Hans Hateboer,
Mattia Caldara, Alejandro Darío Gómez, Josip Ilicic (83' José Palomino), Remo Freuler, Bryan
Cristante (87' Marten de Roon), Andrea Petagna (75' Jasmin Kurtic).
Coach: Gian Piero Gasperini.
Olympique Lyon: Anthony Lopes, Marcelo, Rafael, Ferland Mendy, Mouctar Diakhaby,
Jordam Ferri, Tanguy NDombèlé, Memphis Depay (68' Houssem Aouar), Mariano Díaz (75'
Amine Gouiri), Nabil Fekir, Maxwel Cornet (45+1' Willem Geubbels). Coach: Bruno Génésio.
Goal: 10' Andrea Petagna 1-0.
Referee: Aleksey Eskov (RUS)   Attendance: 13,925.

GROUP F

14.09.17 Andruv stadion, Olomouc: FC FASTAV Zlín – FC Sheriff 0-0
FC FASTAV Zlín: Stanislav Dostál, Zoran Gajic, Ondrej Baco, Petr Jirácek, Robert Matejov,
Vukadin Vukadinovic, Daniel Holzer, Mirzad Mehanovic (83' Adnan Dzafic), Ibrahim Traoré,
Ubong Moses Ekpai (68' Lukás Bartosák), Lukás Zelezník (62' Dame Diop).
Coach: Bohumil Páník.
FC Sheriff: Zvonimir Mikulic, Petru Racu, Ante Kulusic, Mateo Susic, Veaceslav Posmac,
Cristiano, Josip Brezovec (73' Yuri Kendysh), Jeremy de Nooijer, Gheorghe Anton, Stefan
Mugosa (81' Vitalie Damascan), Jairo (87' Zlatko Tripic). Coach: Roberto Bordin.
Referee: Andrew Dallas (SCO)   Attendance: 4,499.

14.09.17 Telia Parken, København: FC København – Lokomotiv Moskva 0-0
FC København: Robin Olsen, Peter Ankersen, Nicolai Boilesen, Michael Lüftner, Denis
Vavro, Ján Gregus, Kasper Kusk (62' Rasmus Falk), Zeca (86' William Kvist), Benjamin
Verbic, Pieros Sotiriou, Andrija Pavlovic (81' Martin Pusic). Coach: Ståle Solbakken.
Lokomotiv Moskva: Guilherme Marinato, Taras Mykhalyk, Maciej Rybus, Nemanja
Pejcinovic, Solomon Kverkvelia, Manuel Fernandes, Dmitriy Tarasov, Igor Denisov, Vladislav
Ignatyev, Aleksey Miranchuk (82' Anton Miranchuk), Jefferson Farfán (71' Éder).
Coach: Yuriy Semin.
Referee: Hüseyin Göcek (TUR)   Attendance: 17,285.

28.09.17 RZD Arena, Moskva: Lokomotiv Moskva – FC FASTAV Zlín 3-0 (3-0)
Lokomotiv Moskva: Guilherme Marinato, Nemanja Pejcinovic, Solomon Kverkvelia, Manuel
Fernandes, Dmitriy Tarasov, Igor Denisov, Vladislav Ignatyev (88' Boris Rotenberg), Aleksey
Miranchuk (78' Aleksandr Kolomeytsev), Jefferson Farfán (46' Anton Miranchuk), Éder,
Mikhail Lysov. Coach: Yuriy Semin.
FC FASTAV Zlín: Stanislav Dostál, Zoran Gajic, Ondrej Baco, Petr Jirácek, Robert Matejov
(65' Milos Kopecny), Vukadin Vukadinovic, Daniel Holzer, Ibrahim Traoré, Ubong Moses
Ekpai, Lukás Zelezník (46' Mirzad Mehanovic), Dame Diop (79' Jean-David Beauguel).
Coach: Bohumil Páník.
Goals: 2', 6, 17' Manuel Fernandes 1-0 (p), 2-0, 3-0.
Referee: Simon Lee Evans (WAL)   Attendance: 10,065.

28.09.17 Bolshaya Sportivnaya Arena, Tiraspol: FC Sheriff – FC København 0-0
FC Sheriff: Zvonimir Mikulic, Petru Racu, Ante Kulusic, Mateo Susic, Veaceslav Posmac,
Cristiano, Josip Brezovec (81' Ziguy Badibanga), Yuri Kendysh, Gheorghe Anton (63' Jeremy
de Nooijer), Stefan Mugosa (70' Vitalie Damascan), Jairo. Coach: Roberto Bordin.
FC København: Robin Olsen, Pierre Bengtsson, Peter Ankersen, Michael Lüftner, Denis
Vavro, William Kvist, Kasper Kusk (69' Nicolai Boilesen), Zeca, Benjamin Verbic (82' Uros
Matic), Martin Pusic (45' Rasmus Falk), Pieros Sotiriou. Coach: Ståle Solbakken.
Referee: Clayton Pisani (MLT)   Attendance: 5,070.

333

19.10.17 Andruv stadion, Olomouc: FC FASTAV Zlín – FC København 1-1 (1-1)
FC FASTAV Zlín: Zdenek Zlámal, Tomás Janícek, Zoran Gajic, Ondrej Baco, Petr Jirácek, Daniel Holzer, Milos Kopecny, Mirzad Mehanovic (77' Adnan Dzafic), Ibrahim Traoré (86' Lukás Zelezník), Ubong Moses Ekpai, Dame Diop (67' Vukadin Vukadinovic).
Coach: Bohumil Páník.
FC København: Stephan Andersen, Pierre Bengtsson, Peter Ankersen, Michael Lüftner, Denis Vavro, William Kvist, Ján Gregus, Uros Matic (83' Danny Amankwaa), Youssef Toutouh, Andrija Pavlovic (67' Pieros Sotiriou), Carlo Holse (67' Rasmus Falk).
Coach: Ståle Solbakken.
Goals: 11' Dame Diop 1-0, 19' Peter Ankersen 1-1.
Referee: Oliver Drachta (AUT)   Attendance: 6,245.

19.10.17 Bolshaya Sportivnaya Arena, Tiraspol: FC Sheriff – Lokomotiv Moskva 1-1 (1-1)
FC Sheriff: Zvonimir Mikulic, Ante Kulusic, Mateo Susic, Veaceslav Posmac, Cristiano, Josip Brezovec (69' Wilfried Balima), Yuri Kendysh, Gheorghe Anton, Stefan Mugosa (87' Vitalie Damascan), Jairo (81' Petru Racu), Ziguy Badibanga. Coach: Roberto Bordin.
Lokomotiv Moskva: Guilherme Marinato, Maciej Rybus, Nemanja Pejcinovic, Solomon Kverkvelia, Manuel Fernandes, Dmitriy Tarasov, Igor Denisov, Vladislav Ignatyev, Anton Miranchuk, Jefferson Farfán, Éder (61' Aleksandr Kolomeytsev). Coach: Yuriy Semin.
Goals: 17' Anton Miranchuk 0-1, 31' Ziguy Badibanga 1-1.
Referee: István Vad (HUN)   Attendance: 10,500.

02.11.17 Telia Parken, København: FC København – FC FASTAV Zlín 3-0 (1-0)
FC København: Robin Olsen, Pierre Bengtsson, Peter Ankersen, Michael Lüftner, Denis Vavro, Uros Matic, Kasper Kusk (64' Rasmus Falk), Zeca, Youssef Toutouh (72' Danny Amankwaa), Benjamin Verbic, Pieros Sotiriou (64' Andrija Pavlovic).
Coach: Ståle Solbakken.
FC FASTAV Zlín: Stanislav Dostál, Tomás Janícek (54' Josef Hnanícek), Zoran Gajic, Ondrej Baco, Petr Jirácek, Vukadin Vukadinovic, Daniel Holzer, Milos Kopecny, Ibrahim Traoré, Ubong Moses Ekpai (75' Lukás Zelezník), Dame Diop (64' Mirzad Mehanovic).
Coach: Bohumil Páník.
Goals: 40' Michael Lüfter 1-0, 49', 90+2' Benjamin Verbic 2-0, 3-0.
Referee: Nikola Dabanovic (MNE)   Attendance: 16,189.

02.11.17 RZD Arena, Moskva: Lokomotiv Moskva – FC Sheriff 1-2 (1-1)
Lokomotiv Moskva: Guilherme Marinato (33' Nikita Medvedev), Nemanja Pejcinovic, Solomon Kverkvelia, Manuel Fernandes, Dmitriy Tarasov (55' Dmitriy Barinov), Igor Denisov, Vladislav Ignatyev, Aleksey Miranchuk, Anton Miranchuk (73' Éder), Jefferson Farfán, Mikhail Lysov. Coach: Yuriy Semin.
FC Sheriff: Zvonimir Mikulic, Petru Racu, Ante Kulusic, Mateo Susic, Veaceslav Posmac, Cristiano (87' Victor), Josip Brezovec (66' Wilfried Balima), Yuri Kendysh, Gheorghe Anton, Jairo (78' Jeremy de Nooijer), Ziguy Badibanga. Coach: Roberto Bordin.
Goals: 26' Jefferson Farfán 1-0, 41' Ziguy Badibanga 1-1, 58' Josip Brezovec 1-2.
Referee: Sebastien Delferière (BEL)   Attendance: 10,118.

23.11.17   RZD Arena, Moskva: Lokomotiv Moskva – FC København 2-1 (1-1)
Lokomotiv Moskva: Anton Kochenkov, Vitaliy Denisov, Taras Mykhalyk (80' Nemanja
Pejcinovic), Solomon Kverkvelia, Manuel Fernandes, Igor Denisov, Vladislav Ignatyev,
Aleksandr Kolomeytsev, Aleksey Miranchuk (90+2' Dmitriy Barinov), Anton Miranchuk (74'
Dmitriy Tarasov), Jefferson Farfán. Coach: Yuriy Semin.
FC København: Robin Olsen, Peter Ankersen, Nicolai Boilesen, Michael Lüftner, Denis
Vavro, William Kvist, Uros Matic (78' Kasper Kusk), Zeca, Benjamin Verbic, Pieros Sotiriou,
Carlo Holse (70' Martin Pusic). Coach: Ståle Solbakken.
Goals: 17' Jefferson Farfán 1-0, 31' Benjamin Verbic 1-1, 51' Jefferson Farfán 2-1.
Referee: Javier Estrada Fernández (ESP)   Attendance: 10,696.

23.11.17   Bolshaya Sportivnaya Arena, Tiraspol: FC Sheriff – FC FASTAV Zlín 1-0 (1-0)
FC Sheriff: Zvonimir Mikulic, Petru Racu, Ante Kulusic, Mateo Susic, Veaceslav Posmac,
Cristiano, Josip Brezovec (70' Jeremy de Nooijer), Yuri Kendysh, Gheorghe Anton, Jairo (84'
Wilfried Balima), Ziguy Badibanga (90+2 Vitalie Damascan). Coach: Roberto Bordin.
FC FASTAV Zlín: Zdenek Zlámal, Zoran Gajic, Lukás Bartosák (80' Robert Bartolomeu),
Josef Hnanícek (85' Ibrahim Traoré), Ondrej Baco, Petr Jirácek, Robert Matejov, Adnan
Dzafic, Mirzad Mehanovic, Ubong Moses Ekpai (53' Daniel Holzer), Lukás Zelezník.
Coach: Bohumil Páník.
Goal: 11' Jairo 1-0.
Referee: Ola Nilsen (NOR)   Attendance: 5,485.

07.12.17   Andruv stadion, Olomouc: FC FASTAV Zlín – Lokomotiv Moskva 0-2 (0-0)
FC FASTAV Zlín: Zdenek Zlámal, Zoran Gajic, Josef Hnanícek, Petr Jirácek, Robert Matejov
(79' Adnan Dzafic), Vukadin Vukadinovic, Daniel Holzer, Milos Kopecny, Petr Hronek (65'
Tomás Janícek), Ibrahim Traoré, Dame Diop (72' Ubong Moses Ekpai).
Coach: Bohumil Páník.
Lokomotiv Moskva: Anton Kochenkov, Nemanja Pejcinovic, Solomon Kverkvelia, Manuel
Fernandes, Igor Denisov, Vladislav Ignatyev, Aleksandr Kolomeytsev (45+1' Dmitriy
Tarasov), Aleksey Miranchuk, Anton Miranchuk (59' Éder), Jefferson Farfán (81' Boris
Rotenberg), Mikhail Lysov. Coach: Yuriy Semin.
Goals: 70' Aleksey Miranchuk 0-1, 75' Jefferson Farfán 0-2.
Referee: Mete Kalkavan (TUR)   Attendance: 4,682.
Sent off: 57' Zoran Gajic.

07.12.17   Telia Parken, København: FC København – FC Sheriff 2-0 (0-0)
FC København: Robin Olsen, Peter Ankersen, Nicolai Boilesen, Michael Lüftner, Denis
Vavro, William Kvist, Rasmus Falk (81' Nicolaj Thomsen), Zeca, Benjamin Verbic (89' Uros
Matic), Federico Santander (82' Andrija Pavlovic), Pieros Sotiriou. Coach: Ståle Solbakken.
FC Sheriff: Zvonimir Mikulic, Petru Racu (62' Vitalie Damascan), Ante Kulusic, Mateo Susic,
Veaceslav Posmac, Cristiano, Josip Brezovec (55' Jeremy de Nooijer), Yuri Kendysh,
Gheorghe Anton (86' Stefan Mugosa), Jairo, Ziguy Badibanga. Coach: Roberto Bordin.
Goals: 56' Pieros Sotiriou 1-0, 59' Michael Lüftner 2-0.
Referee: Serdar Gözübüyük (HOL)   Attendance: 14,246.
Sent off: 69' Jairo.

Ziguy Badibanga missed a penalty kick (78').

335

GROUP G

14.09.17 Yaakov Turner Toto Stadium, Beer Sheva:
Hapoel Be'er Sheva – FC Lugano 2-1 (1-0)
Hapoel Be'er Sheva: Guy Haimov, Mihály Korhut, Loai Taha, Shir Tzedek, Dor Elo (70'
Hatem Abd Elhamed), John Ogu, Maharan Radi, Maor Melikson, Daniel Einbinder (85'
Vladimir Broun), Tomás Pekhart (66' Niv Zrihan), Anthony Nwakaeme. Coach: Barak Bakhar.
FC Lugano: David Da Costa, Fulvio Sulmoni, Vladimir Golemic, Steve Rouiller (46' Eloge
Yao), Dragan Mihajlovic, Jonathan Sabbatini, Davide Mariani (71' Radomir Milosavljevic),
Mario Piccinocchi, Domen Crnigoj (46' Mattia Bottani), Alexander Gerndt, Younés Bnou
Marzouk. Coach: Pierluigi Tami.
Goals: 2' Daniel Einbinder 1-0, 60', 67' Shir Tzedek 2-0 (p), 2-1 (og).
Referee: Tony Chapron (FRA)   Attendance: 14,752.

Tomás Pekhart missed a penalty kick (12')

14.09.17 Arena Nationala, Bucuresti: Steaua Bucuresti – Viktoria Plzen 3-0 (2-0)
Steaua Bucuresti: Florin Nita, Junior Maranhão, Romario Benzar, Bogdan Planic, Mihai
Balasa, Mihai Pintilii, Constantin Budescu (83' Dennis Man), Dragos Nedelcu, Denis Alibec
(74' Harlem Gnohéré), Catalin Golofca, Florinel Coman (57' Ovidiu Popescu).
Coach: Nicolae Dica.
Viktoria Plzen: Ales Hruska, Radim Rezník, Tomás Hajek, David Limbersky, Lukás Hejda,
Milan Petrzela (80' Martin Zeman), Daniel Kolár, Jan Kopic, Diego Zivulic (61' Tomás
Horava), Patrik Hrosovsky, Jakub Reznícek (61' Marek Bakos). Coach: Pavel Vrba.
Goals: 21', 44' Constantin Budescu 1-0 (p), 2-0, 73' Denis Alibec 3-0.
Referee: Andris Treimanis (LAT)   Attendance: 20,714.

28.09.17 swissporarena, Luzern: FC Lugano – Steaua Bururesti 1-2 (1-0)
FC Lugano: David Da Costa, Fabio Daprelà, Fulvio Sulmoni, Vladimir Golemic, Cristian
Ledesma, Dragan Mihajlovic, Mattia Bottani (71' Radomir Milosavljevic), Jonathan Sabbatini,
Davide Mariani (75' Antonini Culina), Domen Crnigoj (75' Younés Bnou Marzouk),
Alexander Gerndt. Coach: Pierluigi Tami.
Steaua Bucuresti: Florin Nita, Junior Maranhão, Romario Benzar, Bogdan Planic, Mihai
Balasa, Filipe Teixeira, Mihai Pintilii, Constantin Budescu (81' Lucian Filip), Florin Tanase,
Ovidiu Popescu (46' Dennis Man), Harlem Gnohéré (66' Florinel Coman).
Coach: Nicolae Dica.
Goals: 14' Mattia Bottani 1-0, 58' Constantin Budescu 1-1, 64' Junior Maranhão 1-2.
Referee: Sergey Boyko (UKR)   Attendance: 2,680.

28.09.17 Doosan Aréna, Plzen: Viktoria Plzen – Hapoel Be'er Sheva 3-1 (1-0)
Viktoria Plzen: Ales Hruska, Radim Rezník, Tomás Hajek, Lukás Hejda, Milan Havel, Milan
Petrzela (62' Martin Zeman), Daniel Kolár (74' Andreas Ivanschitz), Tomás Horava, Jan
Kopic, Patrik Hrosovsky, Michal Krmencík (85' Marek Bakos). Coach: Pavel Vrba.
Hapoel Be'er Sheva: David Goresh, Mihály Korhut, Hatem Abd Elhamed, Loai Taha, Dor Elo,
John Ogu, Maharan Radi, Maor Melikson (80' Isaac Cuenca), Vladimir Broun (80' Michael
Ohana), Tomás Pekhart, Ben Sahar (62' Anthony Nwakaeme). Coach: Barak Bakhar.
Goals: 29' Milan Petrzela 1-0, 69' Anthony Nwakaeme 1-1, 76' Jan Kopic 2-1,
89' Marek Bakos 3-1.
Referee: István Vad (HUN)   Attendance: 10,314.

19.10.17 swissporarena, Luzern: FC Lugano – Viktoria Plzen 3-2 (0-0)
FC Lugano: David Da Costa, Fabio Daprelà, Vladimir Golemic, Steve Rouiller, Cristian
Ledesma, Dragan Mihajlovic, Mattia Bottani (71' Alexander Gerndt), Davide Mariani, Mario
Piccinocchi, Domen Crnigoj (85' Marco Padalino), Carlinhos (73' Jonathan Sabbatini).
Coach: Pierluigi Tami.
Viktoria Plzen: Ales Hruska, Roman Hubník, Radim Rezník, Tomás Hajek, Milan Havel,
Milan Petrzela (56' Jan Kopic), Daniel Kolár (56' Michal Krmencík), Václav Pilar (70' Martin
Zeman), Ales Cermák, Patrik Hrosovsky, Marek Bakos. Coach: Pavel Vrba.
Goals: 63' Mattia Bottani 1-0, 69' Carlinhso 2-0, 76' Michal Krmencik 2-1,
88' Alexander Gerndt 3-1, 90' Marek Bakos 3-2.
Referee: Srdan Jovanovic (SER)   Attendance: 2,535.

19.10.17 Yaakov Turner Toto Stadium, Beer Sheva:
Hapoel Be'er Sheva – Steaua Bucuresti 1-2 (0-0)
Hapoel Be'er Sheva: David Goresh, Mihály Korhut, Ben Bitton (74' Isaac Cuenca), Hatem
Abd Elhamed, Loai Taha, John Ogu (30' Maharan Radi), Maor Melikson, Daniel Einbinder,
Vladimir Broun, Ben Sahar (68' Tomás Pekhart), Anthony Nwakaeme. Coach: Barak Bakhar.
Steaua Bucuresti: Florin Nita, Marko Momcilovic, Bogdan Planic, Mihai Balasa, Dragos
Nedelcu, Filipe Teixeira, Constantin Budescu, Romario Benzar (25' Gabriel Enache), Florin
Tanase (69' Harlem Gnohéré), Ovidiu Popescu, Dennis Man (58' Florinel Coman).
Coach: Nicolae Dica.
Goals: 70', 75' Harlem Gnohéré 0-1, 0-2, 87' Isaac Cuenca 1-2.
Referee: Kevin Blom (HOL)   Attendance: 15,117.

02.11.17 Doosan Aréna, Plzen: Viktoria Plzen – FC Lugano 4-1 (3-1)
Viktoria Plzen: Ales Hruska, Radim Rezník, Tomás Hajek, David Limbersky, Lukás Hejda,
Milan Petrzela, Tomás Horava (86' Diego Zivulic), Jan Kopic (74' Václav Pilar), Ales
Cermák, Patrik Hrosovsky, Michal Krmencík (65' Jakub Reznícek). Coach: Pavel Vrba.
FC Lugano: David Da Costa, Fabio Daprelà, Fulvio Sulmoni, Vladimir Golemic, Cristian
Ledesma (83' Radomir Milosavljevic), Dragan Mihajlovic, Mattia Bottani, Jonathan Sabbatini,
Davide Mariani, Alexander Gerndt (76' Younés Bnou Marzouk), Carlinhos (62' Bálint
Vécsei). Coach: Pierluigi Tami.
Goals: 4' Michal Krmencík 1-0, 15' Davide Mariani 1-1, 19' Michal Krmencík 2-1,
45' Tomás Horava 3-1, 56' Ales Cermák 4-1.
Referee: Jonathan Lardor (BEL)   Attendance: 9,483.

02.11.17 Arena Nationala, Bucuresti: Steaua Bucuresti – Hapoel Be'er Sheva 1-1 (1-1)
Steaua Bucuresti: Florin Nita, Ionut Larie, Junior Maranhão, Lucian Filip, Mihai Balasa, Mihai
Pintilii, Gabriel Enache, Constantin Budescu, Denis Alibec (70' Harlem Gnohéré), Florinel
Coman (65' Florin Tanase), Dennis Man (46' Filipe Teixeira). Coach: Nicolae Dica.
Hapoel Be'er Sheva: David Goresh, Miguel Vítor (70' Michael Ohana), Mihály Korhut, Hatem
Abd Elhamed, Loai Taha, Dor Elo, Maharan Radi, Daniel Einbinder, Isaac Cuenca (76' Maor
Melikson), Ben Sahar (82' Elyaniv Barda), Anthony Nwakaeme. Coach: Barak Bakhar.
Goals: 31' Florinel Coman 1-0, 37' Ben Sahar 1-1.
Referee: Halis Özkahya (TUR)   Attendance: 27,134.

23.11.17 swissporarena, Luzern: FC Lugano – Hapoel Be'er Sheva 1-0 (0-0)
FC Lugano: Joël Kiassumbua, Fulvio Sulmoni, Vladimir Golemic, Steve Rouiller, Dragan
Mihajlovic, Mattia Bottani (76' Cristian Ledesma), Jonathan Sabbatini, Bálint Vécsei, Davide
Mariani, Mario Piccinocchi (90+2' Antonini Culina), Carlinhos (54' Alexander Gerndt).
Coach: Pierluigi Tami.
Hapoel Be'er Sheva: David Goresh, Miguel Vítor, Mihály Korhut, Ben Bitton, Hatem Abd
Elhamed, John Ogu (46' Tomás Pekhart), Maharan Radi, Daniel Einbinder (57' Michael
Ohana), Isaac Cuenca (73' Maor Melikson), Ben Sahar, Anthony Nwakaeme.
Coach: Barak Bakhar.
Goal: 50' Carlinhos 1-0.
Referee: Harald Lechner (AUT)   Attendance: 3,011.

23.11.17 Doosan Aréna, Plzen: Viktoria Plzen – Steaua Bucuresti 2-0 (0-0)
Viktoria Plzen: Ales Hruska, Roman Hubník, Radim Rezník, David Limbersky, Lukás Hejda,
Milan Petrzela (88' Diego Zivulic), Daniel Kolár (83' Ales Cermák), Tomás Horava, Jan
Kopic, Patrik Hrosovsky, Jakub Reznícek (66' Marek Bakos). Coach: Pavel Vrba.
Steaua Bucuresti: Andrei Vlad, Junior Maranhão, Lucian Filip (46' Florin Tanase), Bogdan
Planic, Mihai Balasa, Gabriel Enache, Ovidiu Popescu, Dennis Man, Denis Alibec, Catalin
Golofca (46' Dragos Nedelcu), Florinel Coman (64' Constantin Budescu).
Coach: Nicolae Dica.
Goals: 49' Milan Petrzela 1-0, 76' Jan Kopic 2-0.
Referee: Ivan Bebek (CRO)   Attendance: 10,197.

07.12.17 Arena Nationala, Bucuresti: Steaua Bucuresti – FC Lugano 1-2 (0-2)
Steaua Bucuresti: Andrei Vlad, Ionut Larie, Junior Maranhão, Mihai Balasa, Dragos Nedelcu,
Gabriel Enache, William Amorim (41' Harlem Gnohéré), Florin Tanase (61' Marko
Momcilovic), Ovidiu Popescu, Catalin Golofca (46' Dennis Man), Florinel Coman.
Coach: Nicolae Dica.
FC Lugano: David Da Costa, Fabio Daprelà, Vladimir Golemic, Dominik Kovacic, Eloge Yao
(87' Younés Bnou Marzouk), Mattia Bottani, Bálint Vécsei, Davide Mariani, Mario
Piccinocchi (41' Jonathan Sabbatini), Antonini Culina (74' Dragan Mihajlovic), Radomir
Milosavljevic. Coach: Pierluigi Tami.
Goals: 3' Fabio Daprelá 0-1, 32' Bálint Vécsei 0-2, 60' Harlem Gnohéré 1-2.
Referee: Nikola Dabanovic (MNE)   Attendance: 13,231.

07.12.17 Yaakov Turner Toto Stadium, Beer Sheva:
          Hapoel Be'er Sheva – Viktoria Plzen 0-2 (0-1)
Hapoel Be'er Sheva: Guy Haimov, Mihály Korhut, Hatem Abd Elhamed, Loai Taha, Dor Elo,
Maharan Radi, Daniel Einbinder (59' Maor Melikson), Vladimir Broun, Isaac Cuenca (67' Niv
Zrihan), Tomás Pekhart, Michael Ohana. Coach: Barak Bakhar.
Viktoria Plzen: Ales Hruska, Roman Hubník, Radim Rezník, David Limbersky, Lukás Hejda,
Milan Petrzela (58' Václav Pilar), Daniel Kolár (77' Ales Cermák), Tomás Horava, Jan Kopic,
Patrik Hrosovsky, Michal Krmencík (89' Marek Bakos). Coach: Pavel Vrba.
Goals: 29' Lukás Hejda 0-1, 83' Tomás Horava 0-2.
Referee: Aleksandar Stavrev (MKD)   Attendance: 10,542.

338

GROUP H

14.09.17   Stadion Rajko Mitic, Beograd: Crvena Zvezda – BATE Borisov 1-1 (0-0)
Crvena Zvezda: Milan Borjan, Vujadin Savic, Milan Rodic, Filip Stojkovic, Mitchell Donald,
Nenad Krsticic (89' Nenad Milijas), Damien Le Tallec, Slavoljub Srnic (77' Aleksandar
Pesic), Guélor Kanga, Richmond Boakye, Nemanja Radonjic (72' Ricardinho).
Coach: Vladan Milojevic.
BATE Borisov: Denis Scherbitski, Denis Polyakov, Nemanja Milunovic, Vitaly Gayduchik,
Aleksey Rios, Igor Stasevich (83' Maksim Volodko), Stanislav Dragun, Aleksandr Volodko
(61' Nikolay Signevich), Mirko Ivanic, Vitaliy Rodionov (74' Dmitriy Baga), Mikhail
Gordeychuk. Coach: Aleksandr Yermakovich.
Goals: 54' Nemanja Radonjic 1-0, 72' Nikolay Signevich 1-1.
Referee: Evgen Aranovskiy (UKR)   Attendance: 40,284.

14.09.17   Emirates Stadium, London: Arsenal FC – 1. FC Köln 3-1 (0-1)
Arsenal FC: David Ospina, Per Mertesacker, Nacho Monreal, Héctor Bellerín, Rob Holding
(46' Sead Kolasinac), Mohamed Elneny, Alex Iwobi (68' Jack Wilshere), Ainsley Maitland-
Niles, Theo Walcott (83' Reiss Nelson), Alexis Sánchez, Olivier Giroud.
Coach: Arsène Wenger.
1. FC Köln: Timo Horn, Konstantin Rausch, Jonas Hector (35' Milos Jojic), Dominique
Heintz, Lukas Klünter (76' Yuya Osako), Jorge Meré, Matthias Lehmann, Marco Höger,
Leonardo Bittencourt, Simon Zoller (65' Marcel Risse), Jhon Córdoba. Coach: Peter Stöger.
Goals: 9' Jhon Córdoba 0-1, 49' Sead Kolasinac 1-1, 67' Alexis Sánchez 2-1,
82' Héctor Bellerín 3-1.
Referee: Javier Estrada Fernández (ESP)   Attendance: 59,359.

28.09.17   RheinEnergieStadion, Köln: 1. FC Köln – Crvena Zvezda 0-1 (0-1)
1. FC Köln: Timo Horn, Konstantin Rausch, Pawel Olkowski (76' Christian Clemens),
Frederik Sørensen, Dominique Heintz, Jorge Meré (46' Leonardo Bittencourt), Matthias
Lehmann, Milos Jojic, Salih Özcan, Jhon Córdoba, Sehrou Guirassy (46' Yuya Osako).
Coach: Peter Stöger.
Crvena Zvezda: Milan Borjan, Filip Stojkovic, Srdan Babic, Mitchell Donald, Nenad Krsticic
(78' Uros Racic), Damien Le Tallec, Slavoljub Srnic, Marko Gobeljic, Guélor Kanga,
Richmond Boakye (63' Aleksandar Pesic), Nemanja Radonjic (73' Nemanja Milic).
Coach: Vladan Milojevic.
Goal: 30' Richmond Boakye 0-1.
Referee: Bas Nijhuis (HOL)   Attendance: 46,195.

28.09.17   Borisov Arena, Borisov: BATE Borisov – Arsenal FC 2-4 (1-3)
BATE Borisov: Denis Scherbitski, Denis Polyakov (24' Maksim Volodko), Nemanja
Milunovic, Vitaly Gayduchik, Aleksey Rios, Igor Stasevich, Stanislav Dragun, Aleksandr
Volodko (85' Dmitriy Baga), Mirko Ivanic, Vitaliy Rodionov (55' Nikolay Signevich),
Mikhail Gordeychuk. Coach: Aleksandr Yermakovich.
Arsenal FC: David Ospina, Per Mertesacker, Shkodran Mustafi, Rob Holding, Jack Wilshere,
Mohamed Elneny, Ainsley Maitland-Niles, Joseph Willock (89' Edward Nketiah), Theo
Walcott, Olivier Giroud, Reiss Nelson (79' Marcus McGuane). Coach: Arsène Wenger.
Goals: 9', 22' Theo Walcott 0-1, 0-2, 25' Rob Holding 0-3, 28' Mirko Ivanic 1-3,
49' Olivier Giroud 1-4 (p), 67' Mikhail Gordeychuk 2-4.
Referee: Daniel Stefanski (POL)   Attendance: 13,100.

19.10.17   Borisov Arena, Borisov: BATE Borisov – 1. FC Köln 1-0 (0-0)
BATE Borisov: Denis Scherbitski, Denis Polyakov, Nemanja Milunovic, Vitaly Gayduchik,
Maksim Volodko, Aleksey Rios, Igor Stasevich, Stanislav Dragun, Aleksandr Volodko (74'
Dmitriy Baga), Mirko Ivanic (68' Mikhail Gordeychuk), Nikolay Signevich (85' Vitaliy
Rodionov). Coach: Aleksandr Yermakovich.
1. FC Köln: Timo Horn, Konstantin Rausch, Dominic Maroh, Pawel Olkowski, Dominique
Heintz, Christian Clemens (61' Sehrou Guirassy), Marco Höger, Milos Jojic (70' Leonardo
Bittencourt), Salih Özcan, Simon Zoller, Yuya Osako. Coach: Peter Stöger.
Goal: 55' Aleksey Rios 1-0.
Referee: Hüseyin Göçek (TUR)   Attendance: 11,783.

19.10.17   Stadion Rajko Mitic, Beograd: Crvena Zvezda – Arsenal FC 0-1 (0-0)
Crvena Zvezda: Milan Borjan, Vujadin Savic (66' Srdan Babic), Milan Rodic, Filip Stojkovic,
Mitchell Donald, Nenad Krsticic, Damien Le Tallec, Slavoljub Srnic (83' Marko Gobeljic),
Guélor Kanga, Richmond Boakye (80' Aleksandar Pesic), Nemanja Radonjic.
Coach: Vladan Milojevic.
Arsenal FC: Petr Cech, Mathieu Debuchy, Rob Holding, Jack Wilshere, Francis Coquelin (90'
Ben Sheaf), Mohamed Elneny, Ainsley Maitland-Niles, Joseph Willock (89' Marcus
McGuane), Theo Walcott, Olivier Giroud, Reiss Nelson. Coach: Arsène Wenger.
Goal: 85' Olivier Giroud 0-1.
Referee: Benoît Bastien (FRA)   Attendance: 50,327.
Sent off: 80' Milan Rodic.

02.11.17   RheinEnergieStadion, Köln: 1. FC Köln – BATE Borisov 5-2 (1-2)
1. FC Köln: Timo Horn, Konstantin Rausch, Dominic Maroh, Frederik Sørensen, Dominique
Heintz, Matthias Lehmann, Christian Clemens (46' Yuya Osako), Leonardo Bittencourt, Salih
Özcan, Simon Zoller (83' Pawel Olkowski), Sehrou Guirassy (69' Milos Jojic).
Coach: Peter Stöger.
BATE Borisov: Denis Scherbitski, Denis Polyakov, Nemanja Milunovic, Vitaly Gayduchik
(82' Jasse Tuominen), Aleksey Rios, Igor Stasevich, Stanislav Dragun, Aleksandr Volodko
(70' Vitaliy Rodionov), Mirko Ivanic, Mikhail Gordeychuk (60' Maksim Volodko), Nikolay
Signevich. Coach: Aleksandr Yermakovich.
Goals: 16' Simon Zoller 1-0, 31' Nemanja Milunovic 1-1, 33' Nikolay Signevich 1-2,
54' Yuya Osako 2-2, 63' Sehrou Guirassy 3-2, 82' Yuya Osako 4-2, 90' Milos Jojic 5-2.
Referee: Aleksandar Stavrev (MKD)   Attendance: 45,200.

02.11.17   Emirates Stadium, London: Arsenal FC – Crvena Zvezda 0-0
Arsenal FC: Matt Macey, Mathieu Debuchy, Rob Holding, Jack Wilshere, Francis Coquelin,
Mohamed Elneny, Ainsley Maitland-Niles, Joseph Willock (68' Edward Nketiah), Theo
Walcott, Olivier Giroud, Reiss Nelson. Coach: Arsène Wenger.
Crvena Zvezda: Milan Borjan, Vujadin Savic, Filip Stojkovic, Mitchell Donald, Nenad
Krsticic, Damien Le Tallec, Slavoljub Srnic (86' Uros Racic), Marko Gobeljic, Guélor Kanga
(70' Nemanja Milic), Richmond Boakye, Nemanja Radonjic (89' Aleksandar Pesic).
Coach: Vladan Milojevic.
Referee: Luca Banti (ITA)   Attendance: 58,285.

23.11.17   RheinEnergieStadion, Köln: 1. FC Köln – Arsenal FC 1-0 (0-0)
1. FC Köln: Timo Horn, Dominic Maroh (38' Konstantin Rausch), Frederik Sørensen, Lukas Klünter, Jorge Meré, Jannes Horn, Milos Jojic, Salih Özcan, Yuya Osako (73' Matthias Lehmann), Jhon Córdoba (56' Pawel Olkowski), Sehrou Guirassy. Coach: Peter Stöger.
Arsenal FC: David Ospina, Per Mertesacker, Mathieu Debuchy (84' Edward Nketiah), Calum Chambers (67' Reiss Nelson), Rob Holding, Jack Wilshere, Francis Coquelin, Mohamed Elneny, Ainsley Maitland-Niles, Danny Welbeck (46' Alex Iwobi), Olivier Giroud.
Coach: Arsène Wenger.
Goal: 62' Sehrou Guirassy 1-0 (p).
Referee: Vladislav Bezborodov (RUS)   Attendance: 45,300.

23.11.17   Borisov Arena, Borisov: BATE Borisov – Crvena Zvezda 0-0
BATE Borisov: Denis Scherbitski, Denis Polyakov, Jurica Buljat, Nemanja Milunovic, Aleksey Rios, Igor Stasevich, Stanislav Dragun, Aleksandr Volodko (56' Dmitriy Baga), Mirko Ivanic, Vitaliy Rodionov (62' Nikolay Signevich), Mikhail Gordeychuk (79' Maksim Volodko). Coach: Aleksandr Yermakovich.
Crvena Zvezda: Milan Borjan, Vujadin Savic, Milan Rodic, Filip Stojkovic, Mitchell Donald, Nenad Krsticic, Damien Le Tallec, Slavoljub Srnic (89' Uros Racic), Guélor Kanga, Nemanja Milic (65' Aleksandar Pesic), Richmond Boakye (90+3' Marko Gobeljic).
Coach: Vladan Milojevic.
Referee: Svein Moen (NOR)   Attendance: 12,000.

07.12.17   Stadion Rajko Mitic, Beograd: Crvena Zvezda – 1. FC Köln 1-0 (1-0)
Crvena Zvezda: Milan Borjan, Vujadin Savic, Milan Rodic, Filip Stojkovic, Mitchell Donald, Nenad Krsticic, Damien Le Tallec, Slavoljub Srnic (81' Marko Gobeljic), Branko Jovicic (64' Aleksandar Pesic), Guélor Kanga (89' Uros Racic), Richmond Boakye.
Coach: Vladan Milojevic.
1. FC Köln: Timo Horn, Konstantin Rausch, Pawel Olkowski (65' Lukas Klünter), Frederik Sørensen, Jannes Horn, Matthias Lehmann, Christian Clemens (71' Anas Ouahim), Milos Jojic, Salih Özcan, Yuya Osako, Sehrou Guirassy. Coach: Stefan Ruthenbeck.
Goal: 22' Slavoljub Srnic 1-0.
Referee: Bobby Madden (SCO)   Attendance: 51,364.

07.12.17   Emirates Stadium, London: Arsenal FC – BATE Borisov 6-0 (3-0)
Arsenal FC: David Ospina, Mathieu Debuchy, Calum Chambers, Rob Holding, Jack Wilshere, Francis Coquelin, Mohamed Elneny (76' Joseph Willock), Ainsley Maitland-Niles, Theo Walcott (71' Reiss Nelson), Danny Welbeck (77' Edward Nketiah), Olivier Giroud.
Coach: Arsène Wenger.
BATE Borisov: Denis Scherbitski, Denis Polyakov, Nemanja Milunovic, Maksim Volodko, Aleksey Rios, Igor Stasevich (69' Jasse Tuominen), Stanislav Dragun, Mirko Ivanic (76' Evgeni Yablonski), Evgeniy Berezkin, Vitaliy Rodionov (56' Nikolay Signevich), Mikhail Gordeychuk. Coach: Aleksandr Yermakovich.
Goals: 11' Mathieu Debuchy 1-0, 37' Theo Walcott 2-0, 43' Jack Wilshere 3-0, 51' Denis Polyakov 4-0 (og), 64' Olivier Giroud 5-0 (p), 74' Mohamed Elneny 6-0.
Referee: Robert Schörgenhofer (AUT)   Attendance: 25,909.

341

GROUP I

14.09.17 Stade Vélodrome, Marseille: Olympique Marseille – Atiker Konyaspor 1-0 (0-0)
Olympique Marseille: Yohann Pelé, Adil Rami, Rolando, Hiroki Sakai, Jordan Amavi,
Boubacar Kamara, Dimitri Payet (89' André Zambo Anguissa), Luiz Gustavo, Florian Thauvin
(75' Lucas Ocampos), Morgan Sanson, Valère Germain (81' Bouna Sarr). Coach: Rudi García.
Atiker Konyaspor: Serkan Kirintili, Ali Turan, Ferhat Öztorun, Nejc Skubic, Volkan Findikli
(61' Jens Jønsson), Mehdi Bourabia, Wilfred Moke Abro, Musa Araz (46' Deni Milosevic),
Ömer Sahiner (72' Imoh Ezekiel), Moryké Fofana, Malick Evouna. Coach: Mustafa Akçay.
Goal: 48' Adil Rami 1-0.
Referee: Gediminas Mazeika (LTU)   Attendance: 8,549.

14.09.17 Estádio Dom Afonso Henriques, Guimarães:
Vitória Guimarães – Red Bull Salzburg 1-1 (1-1)
Vitória Guimarães: Douglas Jesus, Victor García, Pedrão, Jubal, Ghislain Konan, Paolo
Hurtado (57' Kiko), Alhassan Wakaso (79' Rafael Miranda), Guillermo Celis, David Teixeira,
Sebastián Rincón (67' Héldon), Raphinha. Coach: Pedro Martins.
Red Bull Salzburg: Alexander Walke, Andreas Ulmer, Paulo Miranda, Stefan Lainer, Duje
Caleta-Car, Valon Berisha, Diadie Samassekou, Hannes Wolf (84' Christoph Leitgeb),
Amadou Haïdara (86' Xaver Schlager), Fredrik Gulbrandsen (65' Patson Daka), Munas
Dabbur. Coach: Marco Rose.
Goals: 25' Pedrão 1-0, 45' Valon Berisha 1-1.
Referee: Äliyar Agayev (AZE)   Attendance: 13,972.

28.09.17 Konya Büyüksehir Belediye Stadyumu, Konya:
Atiker Konyaspor – Vitória Guimarães 2-1 (1-0)
Atiker Konyaspor: Serkan Kirintili, Ali Turan, Nejc Skubic, Petar Filipovic, Mehdi Bourabia,
Musa Araz (76' Vedat Bora), Jens Jønsson, Deni Milosevic (90+1' Volkan Findikli), Ömer
Sahiner, Moryké Fofana, Patrick Eze (80' Malick Evouna). Coach: Mustafa Akçay.
Vitória Guimarães: João Miguel, João Aurélio, Pedrão (46' Moreno), Jubal, Ghislain Konan,
Paolo Hurtado, Alhassan Wakaso (46' Francisco Ramos), Guillermo Celis, Oscar Estupiñán
(71' Hélder Ferreira), Héldon, Raphinha. Coach: Pedro Martins.
Goals: 24' Musa Araz 1-0, 48' Deni Milosevic 2-0, 74' Paolo Hurtado 2-1.
Referee: Aleksandar Stavrev (MKD)   Attendance: 21,116.

28.09.17 Red Bull Arena, Wals-Siezenheim:
Red Bull Salzburg – Olympique Marseille 1-0 (0-0)
Red Bull Salzburg: Alexander Walke, Andreas Ulmer, Paulo Miranda, Stefan Lainer, Duje
Caleta-Car, Valon Berisha, Xaver Schlager (59' David Atanga), Diadie Samassekou, Hannes
Wolf, Amadou Haïdara, Munas Dabbur. Coach: Marco Rose.
Olympique Marseille: Yohann Pelé, Patrice Evra, Adil Rami, Rolando, Boubacar Kamara, Luiz
Gustavo (77' André Zambo Anguissa), Florian Thauvin (74' Clinton N'Jie), Morgan Sanson,
Maxime Lopez (79' Kostas Mitroglou), Valère Germain, Bouna Sarr. Coach: Rudi García.
Goal: 73' Munas Dabbur 1-0.
Referee: Ivan Bebek (CRO)   Attendance: 11,832.

19.10.17   Konya Büyüksehir Belediye Stadyumu, Konya:
Atiker Konyaspor – Red Bull Salzburg 0-2 (0-1)
Atiker Konyaspor: Serkan Kirintili, Ali Turan, Ferhat Öztorun, Nejc Skubic, Petar Filipovic,
Mehdi Bourabia, Jens Jønsson (71' Ali Çamdali), Deni Milosevic, Ömer Sahiner, Moryké
Fofana (76' Imoh Ezekiel), Patrick Eze (62' Musa Araz). Coach: Mustafa Akçay.
Red Bull Salzburg: Alexander Walke, Andreas Ulmer, Paulo Miranda, Stefan Lainer, Duje
Caleta-Car, Valon Berisha, Diadie Samassekou, Hannes Wolf (71' Xaver Schlager), Amadou
Haïdara (78' Takumi Minamino), Fredrik Gulbrandsen (88' Marc Rzatkowski), Munas
Dabbur. Coach: Marco Rose.
Goals: 5' Fredrik Gulbrandsen 0-1, 80' Munas Dabbur 0-2.
Referee: Craig Pawson (ENG)   Attendance: 23,354.

19.10.17   Stade Vélodrome, Marseille: Olympique Marseille – Vitória Guimarães 2-1 (1-1)
Olympique Marseille: Steve Mandanda, Patrice Evra (58' Jordan Amavi), Adil Rami, Aymen
Abdennour, Boubacar Kamara, Luiz Gustavo, Lucas Ocampos, Morgan Sanson (82' André
Zambo Anguissa), Maxime Lopez, Valère Germain (88' Clinton N'Jie), Bouna Sarr.
Coach: Rudi García.
Vitória Guimarães: João Miguel, João Aurélio, Jubal, Marcos Valente, Ghislain Konan, Rafael
Miranda (79' Guillermo Celis), Alhassan Wakaso, Francisco Ramos (63' Hélder Ferreira),
Rafael Martins (72' David Texeira), Héldon, Raphinha. Coach: Pedro Martins.
Goals: 17' Rafael Martins 0-1, 28' Lucas Ocampos 1-1, 76' Maxime Lopez 2-1.
Referee: Stefan Johannesson (SWE)   Attendance: 13,359.

02.11.17   Red Bull Arena, Wals-Siezenheim: Red Bull Salzburg – Atiker Konyaspor 0-0
Red Bull Salzburg: Cican Stankovic, Andreas Ulmer, Paulo Miranda, Stefan Lainer, Duje
Caleta-Car, Valon Berisha, Diadie Samassekou, Hannes Wolf (69' Takumi Minamino),
Amadou Haïdara (74' Reinhold Yabo), Fredrik Gulbrandsen (87' Xaver Schlager), Munas
Dabbur. Coach: Marco Rose.
Atiker Konyaspor: Serkan Kirintili, Ferhat Öztorun, Nejc Skubic, Selim Ay, Mehdi Bourabia,
Wilfred Moke Abro, Musa Araz (62' Moryké Fofana), Jens Jønsson (46' Ali Çamdali), Deni
Milosevic (89' Volkan Findikli), Ömer Sahiner, Malick Evouna. Coach: Mehmet Özdilek.
Referee: Paolo Mazzoleni (ITA)   Attendance: 8,773.

02.11.17   Estádio Dom Afonso Henriques, Guimarães:
Vitória Guimarães – Olympique Marseille 1-0 (0-0)
Vitória Guimarães: João Miguel, João Aurélio (83' Victor García), Jubal, Marcos Valente,
Ghislain Konan, Paolo Hurtado (89' Moreno), Alhassan Wakaso, Francisco Ramos, Rafael
Martins, Héldon, Raphinha (71' Hélder Ferreira). Coach: Pedro Martins.
Olympique Marseille: Steve Mandanda, Adil Rami, Aymen Abdennour, Jordan Amavi,
Boubacar Kamara, Luiz Gustavo (83' Kostas Mitroglou), Morgan Sanson, Maxime Lopez (76'
Hiroki Sakai), Valère Germain, Bouna Sarr, Clinton N'Jie (67' Florian Thauvin).
Coach: Rudi García.
Goal: 80' Paolo Hurtado 1-0.
Referee: Tamás Bognar (HUN)   Attendance: 14,181.
Sent off: 0' Patrice Evra (before the start of the match), 87' Boubacar Kamara.

343

23.11.17   Konya Büyüksehir Belediye Stadyumu, Konya:
Atiker Konyaspor – Olympique Marseille 1-1 (0-0)
Atiker Konyaspor: Serkan Kirintili, Ferhat Öztorun, Nejc Skubic, Petar Filipovic, Volkan
Findikli (59' Ali Çamdali), Mehdi Bourabia, Wilfred Moke Abro, Musa Araz, Deni Milosevic,
Moryké Fofana (80' Imoh Ezekiel), Malick Evouna (69' Ömer Sahiner).
Coach: Mehmet Özdilek.
Olympique Marseille: Steve Mandanda, Adil Rami, Rolando, Hiroki Sakai, Jordan Amavi,
Luiz Gustavo, Florian Thauvin (69' Clinton N'Jie), Lucas Ocampos (65' Dimitri Payet),
Morgan Sanson, André Zambo Anguissa (84' Bouna Sarr), Valère Germain.
Coach: Rudi García.
Goals: 82' Nejc Skubic 1-0 (p), 90+3' Wilfred Moke Abro 1-1 (og).
Referee: Sergey Karasev (RUS)   Attendance: 18,000.
Sent off: 80' Jordan Amavi.

23.11.17   Red Bull Arena, Wals-Siezenheim: Red Bull Salzburg – Vitória Guimarães 3-0 (2-0)
Red Bull Salzburg: Alexander Walke, Andreas Ulmer, Stefan Lainer, Duje Caleta-Car, Marin
Pongracic, Valon Berisha, Xaver Schlager, Amadou Haïdara, Fredrik Gulbrandsen (61' Hwang
Hee-Chan), Munas Dabbur (86' Samuel Tetteh), Takumi Minamino (71' Marc Rzatkowski).
Coach: Marco Rose.
Vitória Guimarães: Douglas Jesus, Victor García, Pedrão (60' Héldon), Ghislain Konan, Paolo
Hurtado (60' Jubal), Alhassan Wakaso, Guillermo Celis, Francisco Ramos, Rafael Martins,
Fábio Sturgeon, Raphinha (72' Hélder Ferreira). Coach: Pedro Martins.
Goals: 26' Munas Dabbur 1-0, 45+1' Andreas Ulmer 2-0, 67' Hwang Hee-Chan 3-0.
Referee: Andrew Dallas (SCO)   Attendance: 6,474.

07.12.17   Estádio Dom Afonso Henriques, Guimarães:
Vitória Guimarães – Atiker Konyaspor 1-1 (0-1)
Vitória Guimarães: Douglas Jesus, Victor García, Pedrão, Jubal, João Vigário (46' João
Aurélio), Paolo Hurtado, Guillermo Celis, Francisco Ramos (76' Hélder Ferreira), Rafael
Martins (74' Oscar Estupiñán), Héldon, Raphinha. Coach: Pedro Martins.
Atiker Konyaspor: Serkan Kirintili, Ali Turan, Ferhat Öztorun (46' Nejc Skubic), Selim Ay,
Ali Çamdali (63' Moryké Fofana), Mehdi Bourabia, Wilfred Moke Abro, Vedat Bora (81'
Deni Milosevic), Musa Araz, Ömer Sahiner, Malick Evouna. Coach: Mehmet Özdilek.
Goals: 15' Mehdi Nourabia 0-1, 77' Ali Turan 1-1 (og).
Referee: Daniel Siebert (GER)   Attendance: 9,040.

07.12.17   Stade Vélodrome, Marseille: Olympique Marseille – Red Bull Salzburg 0-0
Olympique Marseille: Steve Mandanda, Adil Rami, Rolando, Hiroki Sakai, Luiz Gustavo,
Lucas Ocampos, Morgan Sanson (68' Dimitri Payet), Maxime Lopez, André Zambo Anguissa,
Bouna Sarr, Clinton N'Jie (76' Valère Germain). Coach: Rudi García.
Red Bull Salzburg: Alexander Walke, Andreas Ulmer, Paulo Miranda, Stefan Lainer, Duje
Caleta-Car, Valon Berisha, Xaver Schlager, Diadie Samassekou (61' Reinhold Yabo), Amadou
Haïdara (77' Christoph Leitgeb), Fredrik Gulbrandsen (59' Hwang Hee-Chan), Munas Dabbur.
Coach: Marco Rose.
Referee: Aleksey Kulbakov (BLS)   Attendance: 23,865.

GROUP J

14.09.17 Olympiastadion Berlin, Berlin: Hertha BSC – Athletic Bilbao 0-0
Hertha BSC: Thomas Kraft, Sebastian Langkamp, Peter Pekarík, Marvin Plattenhardt, Karim Rekik, Salomon Kalou (85' Genki Haraguchi), Fabian Lustenberger, Vladimír Darida, Mitchell Weiser, Ondrej Duda, Vedad Ibisevic (76' Mathew Leckie). Coach: Pál Dárdai.
Athletic Bilbao: Iago Herrerín, Balenziaga, Etxeita, Aymeric Laporte, Lekue, San José, Mikel Vesga, Iñigo Córdoba (71' Raúl García), Aduriz, Muniain (90' Ager Aketxe), Iñaki Williams (85' Susaeta). Coach: José Ángel Ziganda.
Referee: Ivan Kruzliak (SVK)   Attendance: 28,832.

14.09.17 Arena L'viv, L'viv: Zorya Lugansk – Östersunds FK 0-2 (0-0)
Zorya Luhansk: Andriy Lunin, Vyacheslav Checher, Artem Sukhotsky, Artem Gordienko, Oleksandr Svatok, Artem Gromov, Dmytro Grechyshkin (53' Igor Kharatin), Oleksandr Andrievsky (73' Zeljko Ljubenovic), Oleksandr Karavayev, Iury, Maksym Lunyov (84' Vladyslav Kabayev). Coach: Yuriy Vernydub.
Östersunds FK: Aly Keita, Tom Pettersson, Sotirios Papagiannopoulos, Ronald Mukiibi (67' Gabriel Somi), Brwa Nouri (80' Alhaji Gero), Fouad Bachirou, Jamie Hopcutt (57' Samuel Laryeal Mensah), Hosam Aiesh, Ken Sema, Curtis Edwards, Saman Ghoddos.
Coach: Graham Potter.
Goals: 50' Saman Ghoddos 0-1, 90+4' Alhaji Gero 0-2.
Referee: Stephan Klossner (SUI)   Attendance: 5,097.

28.09.17 San Mamés Barria, Bilbao: Athletic Bilbao – Zorya Lugansk 0-1 (0-1)
Athletic Bilbao: Iago Herrerín, Eneko Bóveda, Etxeita (56' Iturraspe), Saborit (65' Iñigo Córdoba), Aymeric Laporte, Raúl García, San José, Beñat (78' Ager Aketxe), Aduriz, Muniain, Iñaki Williams. Coach: José Ángel Ziganda.
Zorya Luhansk: Andriy Lunin, Evgeniy Opanasenko, Artem Sukhotsky, Oleksandr Svatok, Artem Gromov (64' Vladyslav Kochergin), Dmytro Grechyshkin, Oleksandr Andrievsky, Igor Kharatin, Oleksandr Karavayev, Silas (53' Artem Gordienko), Maksym Lunyov (83' Vyacheslav Checher). Coach: Yuriy Vernydub.
Goal: 26' Igor Kharatin 0-1.
Referee: Halis Özkahya (TUR)   Attendance: 32,462.

28.09.17 Jämtkraft Arena, Östersund: Östersunds FK – Hertha BSC 1-0 (1-0)
Östersunds FK: Aly Keita, Tom Pettersson, Sotirios Papagiannopoulos, Ronald Mukiibi (76' Samuel Laryeal Mensah), Gabriel Somi (56' Dennis Widgren), Brwa Nouri (88' Ludvig Fritzson), Fouad Bachirou, Ken Sema, Curtis Edwards, Saman Ghoddos, Alhaji Gero.
Coach: Graham Potter.
Hertha BSC: Thomas Kraft, Sebastian Langkamp (62' Vladimír Darida), Peter Pekarík, Niklas Stark, Jordan Torunarigha, Per Skjelbred, Fabian Lustenberger, Alexander Esswein (65' Ondrej Duda), Mitchell Weiser, Valentino Lazaro (78' Valentin Stocker), Vedad Ibisevic. Coach: Pál Dárdai.
Goal: 22' Brwa Nouri 1-0 (p).
Referee: Luca Banti (ITA)   Attendance: 8,009.

19.10.17 Jämtkraft Arena, Östersund: Östersunds FK – Athletic Bilbao 2-2 (0-1)
Östersunds FK: Aly Keita, Tom Pettersson, Sotirios Papagiannopoulos, Ronald Mukiibi, Dennis Widgren, Brwa Nouri (89' Samuel Laryeal Mensah), Fouad Bachirou, Ken Sema, Curtis Edwards, Saman Ghoddos, Alhaji Gero. Coach: Graham Potter.
Athletic Bilbao: Iago Herrerín, Balenziaga (46' Eneko Bóveda), Etxeita, Aymeric Laporte, Lekue, Raúl García, Susaeta, Iturraspe, Mikel Vesga (77' Beñat), Iñigo Córdoba (66' Iñaki Williams), Aduriz. Coach: José Ángel Ziganda.
Goals: 14' Aduriz 0-1, 52' Alhaji Gero 1-1, 64' Curtis Edwards 2-1, 89' Iñaki Williams 2-2.
Referee: István Kovács (ROM)   Attendance: 7,870.

19.10.17 Arena L'viv, L'viv: Zorya Lugansk – Hertha BSC 2-1 (1-0)
Zorya Luhansk: Andriy Lunin, Evgeniy Opanasenko, Artem Sukhotsky, Vasiliy Pryyma (22' Oleksandr Svatok), Artem Gordienko, Dmytro Grechyshkin, Igor Kharatin (63' Oleksandr Andrievsky), Oleksandr Karavayev, Silas, Iury, Maksym Lunyov (81' Artem Gromov). Coach: Yuriy Vernydub.
Hertha BSC: Rune Jarstein, Peter Pekarík, Marvin Plattenhardt, Karim Rekik, Niklas Stark, Fabian Lustenberger, Alexander Esswein (58' Salomon Kalou), Mitchell Weiser, Valentino Lazaro, Arne Maier, Davie Selke (58' Vedad Ibisevic). Coach: Pál Dárdai.
Goals: 42' Silas 1-0, 56' Davie Selke 1-1, 79' Oleksandr Svatok 2-1.
Referee: Liran Liany (ISR)   Attendance: 9,521.

02.11.17 San Mamés Barria, Bilbao: Athletic Bilbao – Östersunds FK 1-0 (0-0)
Athletic Bilbao: Iago Herrerín, Balenziaga, Aymeric Laporte, Lekue, Unai Núñez, Raúl García (88' Ager Aketxe), San José (62' Susaeta), Iturraspe, Iñigo Córdoba, Aduriz, Iñaki Williams (73' Mikel Rico). Coach: José Ángel Ziganda.
Östersunds FK: Aly Keita, Tom Pettersson, Sotirios Papagiannopoulos, Ronald Mukiibi, Dennis Widgren (79' Gabriel Somi), Brwa Nouri (79' Hosam Aiesh), Fouad Bachirou, Ken Sema, Curtis Edwards, Saman Ghoddos, Alhaji Gero (74' Jamie Hopcutt).
Coach: Graham Potter.
Goal: 70' Aduriz 1-0.
Referee: Pawel Gil (POL)   Attendance: 32,354.
Sent off: 89' Unai Núñez.

02.11.17 Olympiastadion Berlin, Berlin: Hertha BSC – Zorya Lugansk 2-0 (1-0)
Hertha BSC: Thomas Kraft, Peter Pekarík, Niklas Stark, Jordan Torunarigha, Maximilian Mittelstädt, Salomon Kalou (59' Genki Haraguchi), Valentin Stocker, Alexander Esswein (79' Palko Dárdai), Ondrej Duda (74' Per Skjelbred), Arne Maier, Davie Selke. Coach: Pál Dárdai.
Zorya Luhansk: Andriy Lunin, Evgeniy Opanasenko, Artem Sukhotsky, Oleksandr Svatok, Dmytro Grechyshkin, Oleksandr Andrievsky, Igor Kharatin, Oleksandr Karavayev (74' Leonidas), Silas (56' Artem Gordienko), Iury, Maksym Lunyov (60' Artem Gromov). Coach: Yuriy Vernydub.
Goals: 16', 73' Davie Selke 1-0, 2-0.
Referee: John Beaton (SCO)   Attendance: 20,358.

23.11.17 San Mamés Barria, Bilbao: Athletic Bilbao – Hertha BSC 3-2 (1-2)
Athletic Bilbao: Iago Herrerín, Balenziaga, Etxeita, Aymeric Laporte, Lekue, San José (46'
Iturraspe), Mikel Rico, Ager Aketxe (46' Susaeta), Iñigo Córdoba (80' Raúl García), Aduriz,
Iñaki Williams. Coach: José Ángel Ziganda.
Hertha BSC: Thomas Kraft, Sebastian Langkamp, Marvin Plattenhardt, Karim Rekik,
Maximilian Mittelstädt, Fabian Lustenberger, Mathew Leckie (72' Alexander Esswein),
Mitchell Weiser, Valentino Lazaro (80' Vedad Ibisevic), Arne Maier, Davie Selke.
Coach: Pál Dárdai.
Goals: 26' Mathew Leckie 0-1, 35' Aduriz 1-1 (p), 36' Davie Selke 1-2, 66' Aduriz 2-2 (p),
82' Iñaki Williams 3-2.
Referee: Paolo Tagliavento (ITA)   Attendance: 38,928.

23.11.17 Jämtkraft Arena, Östersund: Östersunds FK – Zorya Lugansk 2-0 (1-0)
Östersunds FK: Aly Keita, Tom Pettersson, Sotirios Papagiannopoulos, Ronald Mukiibi,
Gabriel Somi (90+2' Dennis Widgren), Brwa Nouri, Fouad Bachirou, Ken Sema, Curtis
Edwards, Saman Ghoddos, Alhaji Gero (85' Samuel Laryeal Mensah). Coach: Graham Potter.
Zorya Luhansk: Andriy Lunin, Evgeniy Opanasenko, Artem Sukhotsky, Artem Gordienko,
Oleksandr Svatok, Artem Gromov (46' Maksym Lunyov), Dmytro Grechyshkin, Oleksandr
Andrievsky (61' Ruslan Babenko), Igor Kharatin, Oleksandr Karavayev, Iury (72' Silas).
Coach: Yuriy Vernydub.
Goals: 40' Dmytro Grechyshkin 1-0 (og), 78' Saman Ghoddos 2-0.
Referee: Kevin Blom (HOL)   Attendance: 7,754.

07.12.17 Arena L'viv, L'viv: Zorya Lugansk – Athletic Bilbao 0-2 (0-0)
Zorya Luhansk: Andriy Lunin, Artem Sukhotsky, Artem Gordienko, Oleksandr Svatok, Artem
Gromov, Ruslan Babenko (75' Vladyslav Kochergin), Oleksandr Andrievsky, Igor Kharatin,
Oleksandr Karavayev, Iury (62' Silas), Maksym Lunyov (46' Vladyslav Kabayev).
Coach: Yuriy Vernydub.
Athletic Bilbao: Iago Herrerín, Balenziaga, Aymeric Laporte, Lekue, Unai Núñez, Raúl García
(90+3' Ager Aketxe), Susaeta, San José, Mikel Rico, Aduriz (89' Sabin Merino), Iñaki
Williams (79' Iñigo Córdoba). Coach: José Ángel Ziganda.
Goals: 70' Aduriz 0-1, 86' Raúl García 0-2.
Referee: Ruddy Buquet (FRA)   Attendance: 8,428.

07.12.17 Olympiastadion Berlin, Berlin: Hertha BSC – Östersunds FK 1-1 (0-0)
Hertha BSC: Jonathan Klinsmann, Peter Pekarík, Niklas Stark (64' Per Skjelbred), Jordan
Torunarigha, Maximilian Mittelstädt, Fabian Lustenberger, Alexander Esswein, Genki
Haraguchi (80' Mitchell Weiser), Valentino Lazaro, Ondrej Duda, Palko Dárdai (77' Justin
Kade). Coach: Pál Dárdai.
Östersunds FK: Aly Keita, Tom Pettersson, Sotirios Papagiannopoulos, Ronald Mukiibi (90'
Frank Arhin), Gabriel Somi (78' Jamie Hopcutt), Brwa Nouri, Fouad Bachirou, Ken Sema,
Curtis Edwards, Saman Ghoddos, Alhaji Gero (46' Dennis Widgren). Coach: Graham Potter.
Goals: 58' Sotirios Papagiannopoulos 0-1, 61' Peter Pekarík 1-1.
Referee: Tiago Martins (POR)   Attendance: 15,686.

Brwa Nouri missed a penalty kick (87')

347

GROUP K

14.09.17 <u>Gelredome, Arnhem:</u> Vitesse – Lazio Roma 2-3 (1-0)
<u>Vitesse:</u> Remko Pasveer, Alexander Büttner, Guram Kashia, Maikel van der Werff, Fankaty
Dabo (83' Charlie Colkett), Matt Miazga, Navarone Foor, Thomas Bruns (88' Mason Mount),
Tim Matavz (79' Luc Castaignos), Bryan Linssen, Milot Rashica. Coach: Henk Fraser.
<u>Lazio Roma:</u> Thomas Strakosha, Stefan de Vrij, Jordan Lukaku (65' Senad Lulic), Bastos,
Adam Marusic, Davide Di Gennaro (62' Sergej Milinkovic-Savic), Marco Parolo, Luis
Alberto, Alessandro Murgia, Luiz Felipe (46' Ciro Immobile), Felipe Caicedo.
Coach: Simone Inzaghi.
<u>Goals:</u> 33' Tim Matavz 1-0, 51' Marco Parolo 1-1, 57' Bryan Linssen 2-1,
67' Ciro Immobile 2-2, 75' Alessandro Murgia 2-3.
<u>Referee:</u> Liran Liany (ISR)   Attendance: 19,867.

14.09.17 <u>Regenboogstadion, Waregem:</u> SV Zulte Waregem – OGC Nice 1-5 (0-3)
<u>SV Zulte Waregem:</u> Nicolas Leali, Timothy Derijck, Davy De fauw, Brian Hamalainen,
Michaël Heylen, Onur Kaya (75' Sander Coopman), Nill De Pauw (74' Grigoris Kastanos),
Julien De Sart, Idrissa Doumbia, Peter Olayinka, Aaron Leya Iseka (84' Ivan Saponjic).
Coach: Francky Dury.
<u>OGC Nice:</u> Yoan Cardinale, Christophe Jallet, Dante, Maxime Le Marchand, Arnaud Souquet,
Nampalys Mendy (84' Bassem Srarfi), Jean Michaël Seri (77' Adrien Tameze), Alain Saint-
Maximin, Pierre Lees-Melou, Mario Balotelli, Alassane Pléa (77' Ignatius Ganago).
Coach: Lucien Favre.
<u>Goals:</u> 16', 20' Alassane Pléa 0-1, 0-2, 28' Dante 0-3, 46' Aaron Leya Iseka 1-3,
69' Allan Saint-Maximin 1-4, 74' Mario Balotelli 1-5.
<u>Referee:</u> Ali Palabiyik (TUR)   Attendance: 9,072.

28.09.17 <u>Stadio Olimpico, Roma:</u> Lazio Roma – SV Zulte Waregem 2-0 (1-0)
<u>Lazio Roma:</u> Thomas Strakosha, Stefan Radu, Jordan Lukaku (79' Senad Lulic), Patric, Adam
Marusic, Davide Di Gennaro (54' Ciro Immobile), Marco Parolo, Luis Alberto (54' Sergej
Milinkovic-Savic), Alessandro Murgia, Luiz Felipe, Felipe Caicedo. Coach: Simone Inzaghi.
<u>SV Zulte Waregem:</u> Nicolas Leali, Timothy Derijck, Davy De fauw, Brian Hamalainen,
Marvin Baudry (84' Ivan Saponjic), Michaël Heylen, Nill De Pauw (46' Peter Olayinka),
Sander Coopman, Grigoris Kastanos (46' Onur Kaya), Idrissa Doumbia, Aaron Leya Iseka.
Coach: Francky Dury.
<u>Goals:</u> 18' Felipe Caicedo 1-0, 90' Ciro Immobile 2-0.
<u>Referee:</u> Harald Lechner (AUT)

Match was played behind closed doors.

28.09.17 <u>Allianz Riviera, Nice:</u> OGC Nice – Vitesse 3-0 (2-0)
<u>OGC Nice:</u> Yoan Cardinale, Christophe Jallet, Dante, Maxime Le Marchand, Arnaud Souquet,
Jean Michaël Seri (73' Adrien Tameze), Alain Saint-Maximin (79' Bassem Srarfi), Pierre
Lees-Melou, Vincent Koziello, Mario Balotelli (73' Ignatius Ganago), Alassane Pléa.
Coach: Lucien Favre.
<u>Vitesse:</u> Remko Pasveer, Alexander Büttner (46' Lassana Faye), Guram Kashia, Fankaty Dabo,
Matt Miazga, Thulani Serero (78' Mukhtar Ali), Navarone Foor, Thomas Bruns, Tim Matavz,
Bryan Linssen (86' Mason Mount), Milot Rashica. Coach: Henk Fraser.
<u>Goals:</u> 16' Alassane Pléa 1-0, 45' Allan Saint-Maximin 2-0, 82' Alassane Pléa 3-0.
<u>Referee:</u> Aleksey Eskov (RUS)   Attendance: 15,006.

19.10.17 Allianz Riveira, Nice: OGC Nice – Lazio Roma 1-3 (1-1)
OGC Nice: Yoan Cardinale, Christophe Jallet (88' Bassem Srarfi), Dante, Maxime Le Marchand, Marlon, Patrick Burner, Wesley Sneijder, Nampalys Mendy, Rémi Walter, Pierre Lees-Melou (71' Alassane Pléa), Mario Balotelli. Coach: Lucien Favre.
Lazio Roma: Thomas Strakosha, Stefan Radu, Patric, Bastos, Nani (60' Ciro Immobile), Davide Di Gennaro (60' Luis Alberto), Senad Lulic, Sergej Milinkovic-Savic, Alessandro Murgia, Luiz Felipe, Felipe Caicedo (75' Lucas Leiva). Coach: Simone Inzaghi.
Goals: 4' Mario Balotelli 1-0, 5' Felipe Caicedo 1-1, 65', 89' Sergej Milinkovic-Savic 1-2, 1-3.
Referee: Craig Thomson (SCO)   Attendance: 21,386.

19.10.17 Regenboogstadion, Waregem: SV Zulte Waregem – Vitesse 1-1 (1-1)
SV Zulte Waregem: Louis Bostyn, Timothy Derijck, Brian Hamalainen, Sandy Walsh (70' Davy De fauw), Michaël Heylen, Onur Kaya (89' Ivan Saponjic), Gertjan De Mets, Julien De Sart, Sander Coopman, Peter Olayinka, Aaron Leya Iseka (55' Nill De Pauw).
Coach: Francky Dury.
Vitesse: Remko Pasveer, Alexander Büttner (83' Lassana Faye), Guram Kashia, Fankaty Dabo, Matt Miazga, Thulani Serero, Thomas Bruns (77' Charlie Colkett), Mason Mount, Bryan Linssen, Luc Castaignos, Milot Rashica. Coach: Henk Fraser.
Goals: 23' Guram Kashia 1-0 (og), 27' Thomas Bruns 1-1.
Referee: Ivan Bebek (CRO)   Attendance: 9,488.

02.11.17 Stadio Olimpico, Roma: Lazio Roma – OGC Nice 1-0 (0-0)
Lazio Roma: Thomas Strakosha, Stefan de Vrij, Jordan Lukaku (74' Marco Parolo), Patric, Adam Marusic, Nani (59' Sergej Milinkovic-Savic), Lucas Leiva, Luis Alberto, Alessandro Murgia (59' Senad Lulic), Luiz Felipe, Felipe Caicedo. Coach: Simone Inzaghi.
OGC Nice: Walter Benítez, Christophe Jallet, Dante, Maxime Le Marchand, Arnaud Souquet, Wesley Sneijder (66' Arnaud Lusamba), Nampalys Mendy, Rémi Walter, Pierre Lees-Melou (80' Mario Balotelli), Vincent Koziello (86' Adrien Tameze), Alassane Pléa.
Coach: Lucien Favre.
Goal: 90+2' Maxime Le Marchand 1-0 (og).
Referee: Luca Banti (ITA)   Attendance: 21,327.

02.11.17 GelreDome, Arnhem: Vitesse – SV Zulte Waregem 0-2 (0-1)
Vitesse: Remko Pasveer, Alexander Büttner, Guram Kashia (67' Navarone Foor), Fankaty Dabo, Matt Miazga, Thulani Serero (58' Lassana Faye), Thomas Bruns, Mason Mount, Bryan Linssen, Luc Castaignos (35' Tim Matavz), Milot Rashica. Coach: Henk Fraser.
SV Zulte Waregem: Louis Bostyn, Davy De fauw (87' Michaël Heylen), Sandy Walsh, Marvin Baudry, Kingsley Madu, Onur Kaya (77' Idrissa Doumbia), Gertjan De Mets, Nill De Pauw (27' Brian Hamalainen), Julien De Sart, Sander Coopman, Peter Olayinka.
Coach: Francky Dury.
Goals: 3' Marvin Baudry 0-1, 70' Onur Kaya 0-2.
Referee: Evgen Aranovskiy (UKR)   Attendance: 17,906.
Sent off: 22' Kingsley Madu, 52' Alexander Büttner.

23.11.17   Stadio Olimpico, Roma: Lazio Roma – Vitesse 1-1 (1-1)
Lazio Roma: Ivan Vargic, Dusan Basta (86' Alessio Miceli), Jordan Lukaku, Patric, Bastos,
Nani (54' Senad Lulic), Luis Alberto (68' Adam Marusic), Luca Crecco, Alessandro Murgia,
Luiz Felipe, Simone Palombi. Coach: Simone Inzaghi.
Vitesse: Remko Pasveer, Guram Kashia, Matt Miazga, Julian Lelieveld (81' Fankaty Dabo),
Lassana Faye, Thulani Serero, Navarone Foor, Mason Mount, Tim Matavz (62' Luc
Castaignos), Bryan Linssen, Milot Rashica (69' Mitchell van Bergen). Coach: Henk Fraser.
Goals: 13' Bryan Linssen 0-1, 42' Luis Alberto 1-1.
Referee: Ali Palabiyik (TUR)   Attendance: 8,226.

23.11.17   Allianz Riveira, Nice: OGC Nice – SV Zulte Waregem 3-1 (2-0)
OGC Nice: Walter Benítez, Christophe Jallet, Dante, Maxime Le Marchand, Arnaud Souquet,
Patrick Burner (78' Arnaud Lusamba), Jean Michaël Seri (74' Adrien Tameze), Pierre Lees-
Melou, Vincent Koziello, Mario Balotelli (85' Marlon), Alassane Pléa. Coach: Lucien Favre.
SV Zulte Waregem: Louis Bostyn, Davy De fauw, Brian Hamalainen, Sandy Walsh, Marvin
Baudry, Michaël Heylen, Nill De Pauw (78' Alessandro Cordaro), Sander Coopman, Grigoris
Kastanos (46' Julien De Sart), Idrissa Doumbia (79' Ivan Saponjic), Aaron Leya Iseka.
Coach: Francky Dury.
Goals: 5', 31' Mario Balotelli 1-0 (p), 2-0, 81' Brian Hamalainen 2-1, 86' Adrien Tameze 3-1.
Referee: Luca Banti (ITA)   Attendance: 20,274.

07.12.17   Regenboogstadion, Waregem: SV Zulte Waregem – Lazio Roma 3-2 (1-0)
SV Zulte Waregem: Louis Bostyn, Davy De fauw, Sandy Walsh (87' Ivan Saponjic), Marvin
Baudry, Michaël Heylen, Kingsley Madu (46' Brian Hamalainen), Onur Kaya, Nill De Pauw,
Sander Coopman, Idrissa Doumbia (46' Julien De Sart), Aaron Leya Iseka.
Coach: Francky Dury.
Lazio Roma: Ivan Vargic, Dusan Basta, Jordan Lukaku, Patric, Bastos, Luca Crecco (55'
Felipe Anderson), Alessandro Murgia, Luiz Felipe (65' Wallace), Alessio Miceli (55' Lucas
Leiva), Felipe Caicedo, Simone Palombi. Coach: Simone Inzaghi.
Goals: 6' Nill De Pauw 1-0, 60' Michaël Heylen 2-0, 67' Felipe Caicedo 2-1,
76' Lucas Leiva 2-2, 83' Aaron Leya Iseka 3-2.
Referee: Charalambos Kalogeropoulos (GRE)   Attendance: 8,845.

07.12.17   GelreDome, Arnhem: Vitesse – OGC Nice 1-0 (0-0)
Vitesse: Remko Pasveer, Guram Kashia, Matt Miazga, Julian Lelieveld, Lassana Faye, Thomas
Oude Kotte, Thomas Bruns, Charlie Colkett (46' Navarone Foor), Mason Mount, Tim Matavz
(68' Milot Rashica), Luc Castaignos. Coach: Henk Fraser.
OGC Nice: Yoan Cardinale, Dante, Racine Coly, Patrick Burner, Malang Sarr, Wylan Cyprien,
Vincent Koziello, Arnaud Lusamba (88' Romain Perraud), Jean-Victor Makengo, Bassem
Srarfi (79' Rémi Walter), Alassane Pléa (66' Mohamed Diaby). Coach: Lucien Favre.
Goal: 84' Luc Castaignos 1-0.
Referee: Sandro Schärer (SUI)   Attendance: 17,564.

350

GROUP L

14.09.17 <u>Estadio Municipal de Anoeta, San Sebastián:</u>
Real Sociedad – Rosenborg BK 4-0 (3-0)
<u>Real Sociedad:</u> Gerónimo Rulli, De la Bella, Diego Llorente, Álvaro Odriozola, Aritz
Elustondo, Xabi Prieto (58' Juanmi), Canales, Illarramendi, Zurutuza (77' Igor Zubeldía),
Carlos Vela, Willian José (68' Jon Bautista). Coach: Eusebio Sacristán.
<u>Rosenborg BK:</u> André Hansen, Tore Reginiussen, Jørgen Skjelvik, Vegar Hedenstad, Birger
Meling, Mike Jensen, Anders Konradsen (62' Marius Lundemo), Anders Trondsen, Nicklas
Bendtner, Yann-Erik De Lanlay (74' Pål Helland), Samuel Adegbenro (82' Milan Jevtovic).
Coach: Kåre Ingebrigtsen.
<u>Goals:</u> 9' Diego Llorente 1-0, 10' Zurutuza 2-0, 41' Jørgen Skjelvik 3-0 (og),
77' Diego Llorente 4-0.
<u>Referee:</u> Paolo Mazzoleni (ITA)   Attendance: 21,479.

14.09.17 <u>Telekom Arena, Skopje:</u> Vardar Skopje – Zenit St.Petersburg 0-5 (0-3)
<u>Vardar Skopje:</u> Filip Gacevski, Boban Grncarov, Vladica Brdarovski (44' Darko Glisic),
Hovhannes Hambardzumyan, Tigran Barseghyan, Nikola Gligorov (64' Visar Musliu), Jambul
Jigauri, Darko Velkoski, Dejan Blazevski (70' Ytalo), Juan Felipe Alves, Boban Nikolov.
Coach: Cedomir Janevski.
<u>Zenit St.Petersburg:</u> Andrei Lunev, Branislav Ivanovic (78' Denis Terentyev), Domenico
Criscito, Miha Mevlja (82' Yuriy Zhirkov), Emanuel Mammana, Christian Noboa, Matías
Kranevitter, Daler Kuzyaev, Aleksandr Kokorin (64' Emiliano Rigoni), Artem Dzyuba,
Dmitriy Poloz. Coach: Roberto Mancini.
<u>Goals:</u> 6', 21' Aleksandr Kokorin 0-1, 0-2, 39' Artem Dzyuba 0-3,
66' Branislava Ivanovic 0-4, 89' Emiliano Rigoni 0-5.
<u>Referee:</u> Jakob Kehlet (DEN)   Attendance: 11,118.

28.09.17 <u>Stadion Krestovskyi, St.Petersburg:</u> Zenit St.Petersburg – Real Sociedad 3-1 (2-1)
<u>Zenit St.Petersburg:</u> Andrei Lunev, Branislav Ivanovic, Domenico Criscito, Miha Mevlja,
Emanuel Mammana, Leandro Paredes (88' Artem Dzyuba), Matías Kranevitter, Daler
Kuzyaev, Emiliano Rigoni (73' Aleksandr Erokhin), Aleksandr Kokorin, Sebastián Driussi
(80' Dmitriy Poloz). Coach: Roberto Mancini.
<u>Real Sociedad:</u> Gerónimo Rulli, De la Bella, Diego Llorente, Álvaro Odriozola, Aritz
Elustondo, Xabi Prieto (65' Juanmi), Canales, Zurutuza, Rubén Pardo (74' Illarramendi),
Adnan Januzaj, Jon Bautista (61' Willian José). Coach: Eusebio Sacristán.
<u>Goals:</u> 5' Emiliano Rigoni 1-0, 24' Aleksandr Kokorin 2-0, 41' Diego Llorente 2-1,
60' Aleksandr Kokorin 3-1.
<u>Referee:</u> Andre Marriner (ENG)   Attendance: 50,487.

28.09.17 Lerkendal Stadion, Trondheim: Rosenborg BK – Vardar Skopje 3-1 (1-0)
Rosenborg BK: André Hansen, Tore Reginiussen, Jørgen Skjelvik, Vegar Hedenstad, Birger
Meling, Mike Jensen, Anders Konradsen (78' Anders Trondsen), Marius Lundemo (86' Jacob
Rasmussen), Nicklas Bendtner, Yann-Erik De Lanlay (78' Milan Jevtovic), Samuel
Adegbenro. Coach: Kåre Ingebrigtsen.
Vardar Skopje: Filip Gacevski, Boban Grncarov, Hovhannes Hambardzumyan (85' Vanja
Markovic), Tigran Barseghyan (76' Filip Stojchevski), Visar Musliu, Nikola Gligorov, Jambul
Jigauri, Besir Demiri, Dejan Blazevski, Juan Felipe Alves, Boban Nikolov (76' Besar Iseni).
Coach: Cedomir Janevski.
Goals: 25' Nicklas Bendtner 1-0 (p), 56' Anders Konradsen 2-0, 68' Vegar Hedenstad 3-0,
90+1' Juan Felipe Alves 3-1.
Referee: Georgi Kabakov (BUL)   Attendance: 16,038.

19.10.17 Telekom Arena, Skopje: Vardar Skopje – Real Sociedad 0-6 (0-3)
Vardar Skopje: Filip Gacevski, Boban Grncarov, Evgen Novak, Hovhannes Hambardzumyan,
Darko Glisic (73' Besir Demiri), Tigran Barseghyan, Nikola Gligorov, Jambul Jigauri, Ytalo
(64' Vanja Markovic), Juan Felipe Alves, Boban Nikolov (46' Dejan Blazevski).
Coach: Cedomir Janevski.
Real Sociedad: Gerónimo Rulli, De la Bella, Diego Llorente, Aritz Elustondo, Andoni
Gorosabel, Xabi Prieto, Canales, Illarramendi (64' Rubén Pardo), Igor Zubaldía, Willian José
(60' Jon Bautista), Mikel Oyarzabal (57' Adnan Januzaj). Coach: Eusebio Sacristán.
Goals: 12' Mikel Oyarzabal 0-1, 34', 42', 55', 59' Willian José 0-2, 0-3, 0-4, 0-5,
90' De la Bella 0-6.
Referee: Äliyar Agayev (AZE)   Attendance: 20,368.

19.10.17 Stadion Krestovskyi, St.Petersburg: Zenit St.Petersburg – Rosenborg BK 3-1 (1-0)
Zenit St.Petersburg: Andrei Lunev, Branislav Ivanovic, Domenico Criscito, Miha Mevlja,
Emanuel Mammana, Leandro Paredes (83' Christian Noboa), Matías Kranevitter, Daler
Kuzyaev, Emiliano Rigoni, Aleksandr Kokorin (86' Dmitriy Poloz), Sebastián Driussi (62'
Aleksandr Erokhin). Coach: Roberto Mancini.
Rosenborg BK: André Hansen, Tore Reginiussen, Johan Bjørdal, Vegar Hedenstad (82' Alex
Gersbach), Jacob Rasmussen, Birger Meling, Mike Jensen, Anders Konradsen, Anders
Trondsen (80' Pål Helland), Nicklas Bendtner, Samuel Adegbenro (80' Marius Lundemo).
Coach: Kåre Ingebrigtsen.
Goals: 1', 68', 75' Emiliano Rigoni 1-0, 2-0, 3-0, 88' Pål Helland 3-1.
Referee: Tobias Stieler (GER)   Attendance: 46,211.

02.11.17 Estadio Municipal de Anoeta, San Sebastián:
        Real Sociedad – Vardar Skopje 3-0 (1-0)
Real Sociedad: Gerónimo Rulli, De la Bella, Raúl Navas, Iñigo Martínez, Andoni Gorosabel,
Canales, Zurutuza (46' Illarramendi), Igor Zubaldía, Willian José (62' Jon Bautista), Juanmi,
Mikel Oyarzabal (70' Adnan Januzaj). Coach: Eusebio Sacristán.
Vardar Skopje: Filip Gacevski, Boban Grncarov, Evgen Novak, Hovhannes Hambardzumyan,
Darko Glisic (64' Darko Velkoski), Tigran Barseghyan (75' Dejan Blazevski), Jambul Jigauri,
Vanja Markovic (64' Visar Musliu), Ytalo, Juan Felipe Alves, Boban Nikolov.
Coach: Cedomir Janevski.
Goals: 31' Juanmi 1-0, 69' De la Bella 2-0, 81' Jon Bautista 3-0.
Referee: Robert Schörgenhofer (AUT)   Attendance: 17,242.

02.11.17   Lerkendal Stadion, Trondheim: Rosenborg BK – Zenit St.Petersburg 1-1 (0-0)
Rosenborg BK: André Hansen, Tore Reginiussen, Jørgen Skjelvik, Jacob Rasmussen, Birger
Meling, Mike Jensen, Anders Trondsen, Morten Konradsen (86' Alex Gersbach), Nicklas
Bendtner, Pål Helland (71' Milan Jevtovic), Samuel Adegbenro (88' Johan Bjørdal).
Coach: Kåre Ingebrigtsen.
Zenit St.Petersburg: Andrei Lunev, Domenico Criscito, Igor Smolnikov, Miha Mevlja,
Emanuel Mammana, Christian Noboa (87' Artem Dzyuba), Oleg Shatov (75' Sebastián
Driussi), Aleksandr Erokhin (82' Matías Kranevitter), Leandro Paredes, Emiliano Rigoni,
Aleksandr Kokorin. Coach: Roberto Mancini.
Goals: 55' Nicklas Bendtner 1-0 (p), 90+3' Aleksandr Kokorin 1-1.
Referee: Serdar Gözübüyük (HOL)   Attendance: 18,597.

23.11.17   Lerkendal Stadion, Trondheim: Rosenborg BK – Real Sociedad 0-1 (0-0)
Rosenborg BK: André Hansen, Tore Reginiussen, Johan Bjørdal (87' Alex Gersbach), Vegar
Hedenstad, Jacob Rasmussen (78' Jørgen Skjelvik), Birger Meling, Mike Jensen, Anders
Trondsen, Nicklas Bendtner, Samuel Adegbenro, Jonathan Levi (64' Milan Jevtovic).
Coach: Kåre Ingebrigtsen.
Real Sociedad: Gerónimo Rulli, De la Bella, Raúl Navas, Iñigo Martínez, Álvaro Odriozola,
Xabi Prieto, Canales (85' Igor Zubaldía), Illarramendi, Willian José (75' Jon Bautista), Juanmi
(62' Carlos Vela), Mikel Oyarzabal. Coach: Eusebio Sacristán.
Goal: 90' Mikel Oyarzabal 0-1.
Referee: Daniel Stefanski (POL)   Attendance: 18,307.

23.11.17   Stadion Krestovskyi, St.Petersburg: Zenit St.Petersburg – Vardar Skopje 2-1 (2-0)
Zenit St.Petersburg: Yuriy Lodygin, Miha Mevlja, Denis Terentyev, Emanuel Mammana (87'
Maksim Karpov), Yuriy Zhirkov, Christian Noboa, Oleg Shatov (46' Sebastián Driussi),
Aleksandr Erokhin, Emiliano Rigoni, Artem Dzyuba (73' Matías Kranevitter), Dmitriy Poloz.
Coach: Roberto Mancini.
Vardar Skopje: Filip Gacevski, Boban Grncarov, Evgen Novak, Hovhannes Hambardzumyan,
Tigran Barseghyan (85' Filip Stojchevski), Jambul Jigauri (90+2' Petar Petkovski), Vanja
Markovic, Besir Demiri, Ytalo (79' Dejan Blazevski), Juan Felipe Alves, Boban Nikolov.
Coach: Cedomir Janevski.
Goals: 16' Dmitriy Poloz 1-0, 43' Emiliano Rigoni 2-0, 90+3' Dejan Blazevski 2-1.
Referee: Bart Vertenten (BEL)   Attendance: 38,196.

Artem Dzyuba missed a penalty kick (27')

07.12.17   Estadio Municipal de Anoeta, San Sebastián:
           Real Sociedad – Zenit St.Petersburg 1-3 (0-1)
Real Sociedad: Gerónimo Rulli, Iñigo Martínez, Kévin Rodrigues (61' De la Bella), Diego
Llorente, Álvaro Odriozola, Xabi Prieto, Illarramendi, Zurutuza (68' Canales), Adnan Januzaj,
Willian José, Mikel Oyarzabal (58' Juanmi). Coach: Eusebio Sacristán.
Zenit St.Petersburg: Yuriy Lodygin, Branislav Ivanovic, Domenico Criscito, Igor Smolnikov
(62' Yuriy Zhirkov), Miha Mevlja, Christian Noboa (62' Daler Kuzyaev), Aleksandr Erokhin,
Matías Kranevitter, Emiliano Rigoni, Aleksandr Kokorin, Dmitriy Poloz (76' Leandro
Paredes). Coach: Roberto Mancini.
Goals: 35' Aleksandr Erokhin 0-1, 58' Willian José 1-1, 64' Branislav Ivanovic 1-2,
85' Leandro Paredes 1-3.
Referee: Liran Liany (ISR)   Attendance: 20,609.

07.12.17 Telekom Arena, Skopje: Vardar Skopje – Rosenborg BK 1-1 (1-1)
Vardar Skopje: Filip Gacevski, Boban Grncarov, Evgen Novak, Tigran Barseghyan, Visar
Musliu, Nikola Gligorov, Besir Demiri, Dejan Blazevski (84' Jambul Jigauri), Ytalo, Juan
Felipe Alves, Boban Nikolov (80' Vanja Markovic). Coach: Cedomir Janevski.
Rosenborg BK: André Hansen, Tore Reginiussen, Jørgen Skjelvik, Vegar Hedenstad, Jacob
Rasmussen, Birger Meling, Alex Gersbach (90+2' Jonathan Levi), Anders Trondsen, Morten
Konradsen (71' Yann-Erik De Lanlay), Nicklas Bendtner, Samuel Adegbenro (90+2' Erik
Botheim). Coach: Kåre Ingebrigtsen.
Goals: 9' Ytalo 1-0, 45+2' Nicklas Bendtner 1-1 (p).
Referee: Sergey Boyko (UKR)   Attendance: 7,839.

ROUND OF 32

*CSKA Moskva, Atlético Madrid, Red Bull Leipzig, Sporting CP, SSC Napoli, Spartak Moskva,
Celtic FC, Borussia Dortmund entered the UEFA Europa League after finishing in third-place
in their respective UEFA Champions League groups.*

13.02.18 Stadion Rajko Mitic, Beograd: Crvena Zvezda – CSKA Moskva 0-0
Crvena Zvezda: Milan Borjan, Vujadin Savic, Milan Rodic, Filip Stojkovic, Mitchell Donald,
Nenad Krsticic, Damien Le Tallec, Branko Jovicic, Aleksandar Pesic (85' Uros Racic),
Mohamed Ben Nahouhane, Nemanja Radonjic (78' Slavoljub Srnic). Coach: Vladan Milojevic.
CSKA Moskva: Igor Akinfeev, Vasiliy Berezutksi, Viktor Vasin, Mário Fernandes, Pontus
Wernbloom, Bibras Natcho, Alan Dzagoev, Aleksandr Golovin, Konstantin Kuchaev, Ahmed
Musa, Vitinho (85' Fedor Chalov). Coach: Viktor Goncharenko.
Referee: Pawel Raczkowski (POL)   Attendance: 35,642.

15.02.18 Astana Arena, Astana: FK Astana – Sporting CP 1-3 (1-0)
FK Astana: Nenad Eric, Yuriy Logvinenko, Marin Anicic, Igor Shitov, Dmitriy Shomko,
Abzal Beysebekov, Marin Tomasov (86' Roman Murtazaev), Ivan Maevski, László
Kleinheisler (56' Marko Stanojevic), Djordje Despotovic (64' Sergiy Maliy), Patrick Twumasi.
Coach: Stanimir Stoilov.
Sporting CP: Rui Patrício, Fábio Coentrão (58' Rodrigo Battaglia), André Pinto, Sebastián
Coates, Cristiano Piccini, William Carvalho, Bruno Fernandes, Seydou Doumbia (61' Fredy
Montero), Bryan Ruiz, Marcos Acuña, Gelson Martins (85' Rúben Ribeiro).
Coach: Jorge Jesus.
Goals: 7' Marin Tomasov 1-0, 48' Bruno Fernandes 1-1 (p), 50' Gelson Martins 1-2,
56' Seydou Doumbia 1-3.
Referee: Ruddy Buquet (FRA)   Attendance: 29,737.
Sent off: 62' Yuriy Logvinenko.

15.02.18 Signal-Iduna-Park, Dortmund: Borussia Dortmund – Atalanta Bergamo 3-2 (1-0)
Borussia Dortmund: Roman Bürki, Lukasz Piszczek, Sokratis Papastathopoulos, Ömer Toprak, Jeremy Toljan, Gonzalo Castro, André Schürrle, Julian Weigl (81' Mahmoud Dahoud), Christian Pulisic (85' Alexander Isak), Marco Reus (62' Mario Götze), Michy Batshuaya. Coach: Peter Stöger.
Atalanta Bergamo: Etrit Berisha, Andrea Masiello, Rafael Tolói, Leonardo Spinazzola, Hans Hateboer, Mattia Caldara (85' José Palomino), Papu Gómez (76' Robin Gosens), Josip Ilicic (89' Andrea Petagna), Marten de Roon, Remo Freuler, Bryan Cristante. Coach: Gian Piero Gasperini.
Goals: 30' André Schürrle 1-0, 51', 56' Josip Ilicic 1-1, 1-2, 65', 90+1' M. Batshuayi 2-2, 3-2.
Referee: Daniel Stefanski (POL)   Attendance: 62,500.

15.02.18 Allianz Riviera, Nice: OGC Nice – Lokomotiv Moskva 2-3 (2-1)
OGC Nice: Walter Benítez, Dante, Marlon (46' Patrick Burner), Racine Coly, Malang Sarr, Jean Michaël Seri, Wylan Cyprien (82' Nampalys Mendy), Allan Saint-Maximin, Pierre Lees-Melou, Mario Balotelli, Alassane Pléa (70' Adrien Tameze). Coach: Lucien Favre.
Lokomotiv Moskva: Guilherme Marinato, Vitaliy Denisov (46' Maciej Rybus), Nemanja Pejcinovic, Solomon Kverkvelia, Manuel Fernandes, Igor Denisov, Vladislav Ignatyev, Aleksandr Kolomeytsev (46' Jefferson Farfán), Aleksey Miranchuk, Anton Miranchuk, Ari (71' Éder). Coach: Yuriy Semin.
Goals: 4', 28' Mario Balotelli 1-0, 2-0 (p), 45', 69', 77' Manuel Fernandes 2-1 (p), 2-2, 2-3.
Referee: István Kovács (ROM)   Attendance: 16,918.
Sent off: 66' Racine Coly.

15.02.18 Otkrytiye Arena, Moskva: Spartak Moskva – Athletic Bilbao 1-3 (0-3)
Spartak Moskva: Artem Rebrov, Serdar Taşçi, Andrey Eshchenko, Ilya Kutepov, Dmitriy Kombarov, Denis Glushakov (75' Sofiane Hanni), Lorenzo Melgarejo (58' Zé Luís), Fernando, Roman Zobnin, Quincy Promes, Luiz Adriano. Coach: Massimo Carrera.
Athletic Bilbao: Iago Herrerín, Etxeita, De Marcos, Yeray Álvarez, Lekue, Raúl García, Susaeta (68' San José), Iturraspe, Mikel Rico, Aduriz, Iñaki Williams (83' Sabin Merino). Coach: José Ángel Ziganda.
Goals: 22', 39' Aduriz 0-1, 0-2, 45+1' Ilya Kutepov 0-3 (og), 1-3 Luiz Adriano (60').
Referee: Benoît Bastien (FRA)   Attendance: 43,145.

15.02.18 Estadio Municipal de Anoeta, San Sebastián:
          Real Sociedad – Red Bull Salzburg 2-2 (0-1)
Real Sociedad: Gerónimo Rulli, Héctor Moreno (76' Aritz Elustondo), Kévin Rodrigues, Diego Llorente, Álvaro Odriozola, Xabi Prieto, Illarramendi, Igor Zubeldía, Juanmi (46' Adnan Januzaj), Jon Bautista (68' Agirretxe), Mikel Oyarzabal. Coach: Eusebio Sacristán.
Red Bull Salzburg: Alexander Walke, Andreas Ulmer, Stefan Lainer, André Ramalho (71' Marin Pongracic), Duje Caleta-Car, Reinhold Yabo (76' Takumi Minamino), Xaver Schlager, Diadie Samassekou, Amadou Haïdara, Munas Dabbur, Hwang Hee-Chan (46' Fredrik Gulbrandsen). Coach: Marco Rose.
Goals: 27' Mikel Oyarzabal 0-1 (og), 57' Álvaro Odriozola 1-1, 80' Adnan Januzaj 2-1, 90+4' Takumi Minamino 2-2.
Referee: Bobby Madden (SCO)   Attendance: 19,790.

355

15.02.18 Ludogorets Arena, Razgrad: PFC Ludogorets Razgrad – AC Milan 0-3 (0-1)
PFC Ludogorets Razgrad: Renan, Cosmin Moti, Cicinho, Igor Plastun, Svetoslav Dyakov,
Lucas Sasha, Anicet Andrianantenaina, Marcelinho (78' Gustavo Campanharo), Jody Lukoki
(81' Svetoslav Kovachev), Virgil Misidjan, Jakub Swierczok (46' Wanderson).
Coach: Dimitar Dimitrov.
AC Milan: Gianluigi Donnarumma, Leonardo Bonucci, Ignazio Abate (60' Ricardo
Rodríguez), Alessio Romagnoli, Davide Calabria, Lucas Biglia, Giacomo Bonaventura, Hakan
Çalhanoglu (75' Fabio Borini), Franck Kessié, Suso, Patrick Cutrone (65' André Silva).
Coach: Gennaro Gattuso.
Goals: 45' Patrick Cutrone 0-1, 64' Ricardo Rodríguez 0-2 (p), 90+2' Fabio Borini 0-3.
Referee: Milorad Mazic (SER)   Attendance: 7,887.

15.02.18 Jämtkraft Arena, Östersund: Östersunds FK – Arsenal FC 0-3 (0-2)
Östersunds FK: Aly Keita, Tom Pettersson, Sotirios Papagiannopoulos, Ronald Mukiibi,
Dennis Widgren (73' Doug Bergqvist), Samuel Laryeal Mensah, Brwa Nouri (46' Tesfaldet
Tekie), Ken Sema, Curtis Edwards, Saman Ghoddos, Alhaji Gero (46' Jamie Hopcutt).
Coach: Graham Potter.
Arsenal FC: David Ospina, Nacho Monreal (73' Sead Kolasinac), Shkodran Mustafi, Calum
Chambers, Héctor Bellerín, Mesut Özil, Henrikh Mkhitaryan (84' Reiss Nelson), Mohamed
Elneny, Alex Iwobi, Ainsley Maitland-Niles, Danny Welbeck (83' Edward Nketiah).
Coach: Arsène Wenger.
Goals: 13' Nacho Monreal 0-1, 24' Sotirios Papagiannopoulos 0-2 (og), 58' Mesut Özil 0-3.
Referee: David Fernández Borbalán (ESP)   Attendance: 7,665.

Tom Pettersson missed a penalty kick (90+1')

15.02.18 Stade Vélodrome, Marseille: Olympique Marseille – Sporting Braga 3-0 (1-0)
Olympique Marseille: Yohann Pelé, Adil Rami, Rolando, Jordan Amavi (59' Hiroki Sakai),
Dimitri Payet (78' André Zambo Anguissa), Luiz Gustavo, Bouna Sarr, Lucas Ocampos,
Maxime Lopez, Valère Germain (70' Florian Thauvin), Clinton N'Jie. Coach: Rudi García.
Sporting Braga: Matheus Magalhães, Ricardo Esgaio, Diogo Figueiras, Nuno Sequeira, Lazar
Rosic, Bruno Viana, Nikola Vukcevic, João Carlos Teixeira (72' André Horta), Danilo
Barbosa, Dyego Sousa (75' Ahmed Hassan 'Koka'), Paulinho (61' Wilson Eduardo).
Coach: Abel Ferreira.
Goals: 4', 69' Valère Germain 1-0, 2-0, 74' Florian Thauvin 3-0.
Referee: Serdar Gözübüyük (HOL)   Attendance: 21,731.

15.02.18 Telia Parken Stadium, København: FC København – Atlético Madrid 1-4 (1-2)
FC København: Robin Olsen, Peter Ankersen, Nicolai Boilesen, Michael Lüftner, Denis
Vavro, William Kvist, Ján Gregus, Rasmus Falk (62' Federico Santander), Viktor Fischer (72'
Andrija Pavlovic), Robert Skov (73' Pierre Bengtsson), Pieros Sotiriou.
Coach: Ståle Solbakken.
Atlético Madrid: Moyà, Juanfran, Diego Godín, José Giménez, Lucas Hernández, Saúl, Koke
(78' Gabi), Thomas Partey, Kevin Gameiro (70' Vitolo), Antoine Griezmann, Ángel Correa
(59' Yannick Ferreira-Carrasco). Coach: Diego Simeone.
Goals: 15' Viktor Fischer 1-0, 21' Saúl 1-1, 37' Kevin Gameiro 1-2,
71' Antoine Griezmann 1-3, 77' Vitolo 1-4.
Referee: Aleksei Kulbakov (BLS)   Attendance: 34,912.

15.02.18   Olympiako Stadio Spyros Louis, Athens: AEK Athen – Dinamo Kiev 1-1 (0-1)
AEK Athen: Vassilis Barkas, Rodrigo Galo, Vassilios Lambropoulos, Ognjen Vranjes,
Michalis Bakakis, André Simões, Konstantinos Galanopoulos (79' Astrit Ajdarevic), Marko
Livaja, Anastasios Bakasetas, Viktor Klonaridis (52' Lazaros Christodoulopoulos), Georgios
Giakoumakis (58' Sergio Araújo). Coach: Manolo Jiménez.
Dinamo Kiev: Denis Boyko, Mikola Morozyuk, Evgen Khacheridi, Tamás Kádár, Tomasz
Kedziora, Denys Garmash (78' Artem Besedin), Derlis González, Vitaliy Buyalskiy, Viktor
Tsygankov, Volodymyr Shepeliev, Júnior Moraes (90+1' Mykola Shaparenko).
Coach: Aleksandr Khatskevich.
Goals: 19' Viktor Tsygankov 0-1, 80' Astrit Ajdarevic 1-1.
Referee: Carlos del Cerro Grande (ESP)   Attendance: 30,518.

15.02.18   Celtic Park, Glasgow: Celtic FC – Zenit St.Petersburg 1-0 (0-0)
Celtic FC: Dorus de Vries, Mikael Lustig, Jozo Simunovic, Kieran Tierney, Kristoffer Ajer,
Scott Brown, James Forrest, Callum McGregor, Olivier Ntcham, Kouassi Eboue (73' Charly
Musonda), Moussa Dembélé (84' Odsonne Édouard). Coach: Brendan Rodgers.
Zenit St.Petersburg: Andrei Lunev, Domenico Criscito, Igor Smolnikov, Miha Mevlja,
Emanuel Mammana, Aleksandr Erokhin, Leandro Paredes, Daler Kuzyaev (62' Matías
Kranevitter), Emiliano Rigoni (62' Sebastián Driussi), Aleksandr Kokorin, Anton Zabolotnyi.
Coach: Roberto Mancini.
Goal: 78' Callum McGregor 1-0.
Referee: Damir Skomina (SVN)   Attendance: 56,743

15.02.18   Stadio San Paolo, Napoli: SSC Napoli – Red Bull Leipzig 1-3 (0-0)
SSC Napoli: Pepe Reina, Christian Maggio, Kalidou Koulibaly, Lorenzo Tonelli, Elseid Hysaj
(54' Mário Rui), Marek Hamsik (54' Lorenzo Insigne), Piotr Zielinski, Marko Rog, Adam
Ounas (61' Allan), Amadou Diawara, José Callejón. Coach: Maurizio Sarri.
Red Bull Leipzig: Péter Gulácsi, Willi Orban, Lukas Klostermann, Dayot Upamecano, Kevin
Kampl, Marcel Sabitzer, Bruma (79' Emil Forsberg), Konrad Laimer, Naby Keïta (86' Diego
Demme), Yussuf Poulsen (82' Jean-Kévin Augustin), Timo Werner. Coach: Ralph Hasenhüttl.
Goals: 52' Adam Ounas 1-0, 61' Timo Werner 1-1, 74' Bruma 1-2, 90+3' Timo Werner 1-3.
Referee: Artur Soares Dias (POR)   Attendance: 14,554.

15.02.18   Groupama Stadium, Décines-Charpieu:
           Olympique Lyon – Villarreal CF 3-1 (0-0)
Olympique Lyon: Anthony Lopes, Jérémy Morel, Marcelo, Rafael (85' Ferland Mendy),
Fernando Marçal, Tanguy NDombèlé, Lucas Tousart, Houssem Aouar (73' Memphis Depay),
Bertrand Traoré (77' Maxwel Cornet), Mariano Díaz, Nabil Fekir. Coach: Bruno Génésio.
Villarreal CF: Sergio Asenjo, Mario Gaspar, Jaume Costa, Víctor Ruíz, Álvaro González,
Denis Cheryshev (74' Roberto Soriano), Trigueros, Samu Castillejo (54' Enes Ünal), Rodri
Hernández, Pablo Fornals (88' Dani Raba), Carlos Bacca. Coach: Javi Calleja.
Goals: 46' Tanguy NDombèlé 1-0, 49' Nabil Fekir 2-0, 63' Pablo Fornals 2-1,
82' Memphis Depay 3-1.
Referee: Viktor Kassai (HUN)   Attendance: 46,846.

357

15.02.18 Stadion Partizana, Beograd: Partizan – Viktoria Plzen 1-1 (0-0)
Partizan: Vladimir Stojkovic, Miroslav Vulicevic, Milan Mitrovic, Nemanja Miletic (I),
Slobodan Urosevic, Zoran Tosic, Marko Jevtovic, Seydouba Soumah (71' Djordje Ivanovic),
Marko Jankovic, Danilo Pantic, Léandro Tawamba Kana (90' Svetozar Markovic).
Coach: Miroslav Djukic.
Viktoria Plzen: Ales Hruska, Roman Hubník, Radim Rezník, David Limbersky, Lukás Hejda,
Milan Petrzela (61' Martin Zeman), Daniel Kolár (78' Ales Cermák), Tomás Horava, Jan
Kopic, Patrik Hrosovsky, Michal Krmencík (90+1' Tomás Chory). Coach: Pavel Vrba.
Goals: 58' Léandro Tawamba Kana 1-0, 81' Radim Rezník 1-1.
Referee: Anastasios Sidiropoulos (GRE)   Attendance: 17,165.
Sent off: 85' Milan Mitrovic.

15.02.18 Arena Nationala, Bucuresti: FC Steaua Bucuresti – Lazio Roma 1-0 (1-0)
Steaua Bucuresti: Andrei Vlad, Junior Maranhão, Valerica Gaman, Romario Benzar, Bogdan
Planic, Mihai Pintilii (46' Filipe Teixeira), Constantin Budescu, Florin Tanase (58' Florinel
Coman), Dragos Nedelcu, Harlem Gnohéré (81' Cristian Tanase), Dennis Man.
Coach: Nicolae Dica.
Lazio Roma: Thomas Strakosha, Dusan Basta, Martín Cáceres, Jordan Lukaku (75' Senad
Lulic), Bastos, Luiz Felipe, Lucas Leiva, Sergej Milinkovic-Savic, Alessandro Murgia, Nani
(56' Felipe Anderson), Felipe Caicedo (56' Ciro Immobile). Coach: Simone Inzaghi.
Goal: 29' Harlem Gnohéré 1-0.
Referee: Deniz Aytekin (GER)   Attendance: 33,455.

21.02.18 VEB Arena, Moskva: CSKA Moskva – Crvena Zvezda 1-0 (1-0)
CSKA Moskva: Igor Akinfeev, Vasiliy Berezutksi, Sergey Ignashevich, Viktor Vasin (26'
Kirill Nababkin), Mário Fernandes, Pontus Wernbloom, Bibras Natcho, Alan Dzagoev,
Konstantin Kuchaev, Ahmed Musa, Vitinho (77' Georgi Milanov).
Coach: Viktor Goncharenko.
Crvena Zvezda: Milan Borjan, Vujadin Savic, Milan Rodic, Filip Stojkovic, Mitchell Donald
(78' Slavoljub Srnic), Nenad Krsticic, Damien Le Tallec, Branko Jovicic (88' Uros Racic),
Aleksandar Pesic, Mohamed Ben Nahouhane, Nemanja Radonjic (88' Luka Adzic).
Coach: Vladan Milojevic.
Goal: 45+1' Alan Dzagoev 1-0.
Referee: Jorge de Sousa (POR)   Attendance: 18,753.

22.02.18 RZD Arena, Moskva: Lokomotiv Moskva – OGC Nice 1-0 (1-0)
Lokomotiv Moskva: Guilherme Marinato, Nemanja Pejcinovic, Solomon Kverkvelia, Jefferson
Farfán (24' Aleksandr Kolomeytsev), Manuel Fernandes, Igor Denisov, Maciej Rybus,
Vladislav Ignatyev, Aleksey Miranchuk (84' Dmitriy Tarasov), Anton Miranchuk, Ari (64'
Éder). Coach: Yuriy Semin.
OGC Nice: Walter Benítez, Dante, Romain Perraud, Patrick Burner, Malang Sarr, Jean
Michaël Seri (84' Ihsan Sacko), Wylan Cyprien, Allan Saint-Maximin (78' Adrien Tameze),
Pierre Lees-Melou, Mario Balotelli, Alassane Pléa (79' Jean-Victor Makengo).
Coach: Lucien Favre.
Goal: 30' Igor Denisov 1-0.
Referee: Pavel Krákovec (CZE)   Attendance: 18,104.

22.02.18 Estadio Wanda Metropolitano, Madrid: Atlético Madrid – FC København 1-0 (1-0)
Atlético Madrid: Jan Oblak, Juanfran, Diego Godín, José Giménez, Sergi González, Gabi,
Vitolo, Koke (46' Saúl), Fernando Torres, Kevin Gameiro (68' Thomas Partey), Ángel Correa
(60' Nicolás Gaitán). Coach: Diego Simeone.
FC København: Stephan Andersen, Pierre Bengtsson, Peter Ankersen, Michael Lüftner, Denis
Vavro, William Kvist (46' Robert Skov), Ján Gregus, Viktor Fischer (46' Rasmus Falk),
Nicolaj Thomsen, Pieros Sotiriou (80' Jonas Wind), Andrija Pavlovic. Coach: Ståle Solbakken.
Goal: 7' Kevin Gameiro 1-0.
Referee: Gediminas Mazeika (LTU)   Attendance: 44,035.

22.02.18 NSK Olimpiyskyi, Kiev: Dinamo Kiev – AEK Athen 0-0
Dinamo Kiev: Denis Boyko, Mikola Morozyuk, Evgen Khacheridi, Tamás Kádár, Tomasz
Kedziora, Denys Garmash, Derlis González, Vitaliy Buyalskiy, Viktor Tsygankov, Volodymyr
Shepeliev (76' Artem Besedin), Júnior Moraes (90+3' Mykola Shaparenko).
Coach: Aleksandr Khatskevich.
AEK Athen: Vassilis Barkas, Dmitro Chigrinskiy, Rodrigo Galo, Vassilios Lambropoulos,
Masoud Shojaei, Lazaros Christodoulopoulos (74' Georgios Giakoumakis), Michalis Bakakis,
André Simões, Konstantinos Galanopoulos (80' Astrit Ajdarevic), Sergio Araújo, Anastasios
Bakasetas (70' Viktor Klonaridis). Coach: Manolo Jiménez.
Referee: Matej Jug (SVN)   Attendance: 27,024.

22.02.18 Stadion Krestovskyi, Saint Petersburg: Zenit St.Petersburg – Celtic FC 3-0 (2-0)
Zenit St.Petersburg: Andrei Lunev, Branislav Ivanovic (87' Igor Smolnikov), Domenico
Criscito, Miha Mevlja, Emanuel Mammana, Leandro Paredes, Matías Kranevitter, Daler
Kuzyaev, Emiliano Rigoni (84' Sebastián Driussi), Aleksandr Kokorin, Anton Zabolotnyi (76'
Aleksandr Erokhin). Coach: Roberto Mancini.
Celtic FC: Dorus de Vries, Mikael Lustig, Jozo Simunovic, Kieran Tierney, Kristoffer Ajer,
Scott Brown, James Forrest (71' Charly Musonda), Callum McGregor (62' Scott Sinclair),
Olivier Ntcham, Kouassi Eboue (46' Tom Rogic), Moussa Dembélé. Coach: Brendan Rodgers.
Goals: 8' Branislav Ivanovic 1-0, 27' Daler Kuzyaev 2-0, 61' Aleksandr Kokorin 3-0.
Referee: Antonio Mateu Lahoz (ESP)   Attendance: 50,492

22.02.18 Red Bull Arena, Leipzig: Red Bull Leipzig – SSC Napoli 0-2 (0-1)
Red Bull Leipzig: Péter Gulácsi, Bernardo, Dayot Upamecano, Ibrahima Konaté, Kevin
Kampl, Diego Demme, Marcel Sabitzer, Bruma (74' Emil Forsberg), Konrad Laimer, Yussuf
Poulsen (90+1' Stefan Ilsanker), Timo Werner (85' Jean-Kévin Augustin).
Coach: Ralph Hasenhüttl.
SSC Napoli: Pepe Reina, Raúl Albiol, Christian Maggio, Mário Rui (68' Elseid Hysaj),
Lorenzo Tonelli, Marek Hamsik (65' José Callejón), Allan, Piotr Zielinski, Amadou Diawara
(82' Jorginho), Dries Mertens, Lorenzo Insigne. Coach: Maurizio Sarri.
Goals: 33' Piotr Zielinksi 0-1, 86' Lorenzo Insigne 0-2.
Referee: Anthony Taylor (ENG)   Attendance: 36,163.

22.02.18 Estadio de la Cerámica, Villarreal: Villarreal CF – Olympique Lyon 0-1 (0-0)
Villarreal CF: Sergio Asenjo, Daniele Bonera, Mario Gaspar, Jaume Costa, Álvaro González,
Javi Fuego (74' Dani Raba), Trigueros (56' Denis Cheryshev), Rodri Hernández, Pablo Fornals
(46' Samu Castillejo), Carlos Bacca, Enes Ünal. Coach: Javi Calleja.
Olympique Lyon: Anthony Lopes, Jérémy Morel, Marcelo, Rafael, Ferland Mendy, Tanguy
NDombèlé (77' Houssem Aouar), Lucas Tousart, Bertrand Traoré, Memphis Depay, Mariano
Díaz (82' Jordan Ferri), Nabil Fekir (87' Myziane Maolida). Coach: Bruno Génésio.
Goal: 85' Bertrand Traoré 0-1.
Referee: Luca Banti (ITA)   Attendance: 17,028.
Sent off: 78' Jaume Costa.

22.02.18 Doosan Aréna, Plzen: Viktoria Plzen – Partizan 2-0 (0-0)
Viktoria Plzen: Ales Hruska, Roman Hubník, Radim Rezník, David Limbersky, Lukás Hejda,
Daniel Kolár (87' Ales Cermák), Martin Zeman (72' Milan Petrzela), Tomás Horava, Jan
Kopic, Patrik Hrosovsky, Michal Krmencík (84' Tomás Chory). Coach: Pavel Vrba.
Partizan: Vladimir Stojkovic, Miroslav Vulicevic, Bojan Ostojic, Nemanja Miletic (I), Sasa
Zdjelar, Slobodan Urosevic, Zoran Tosic, Marko Jevtovic (65' Ognjen Ozegovic), Marko
Jankovic (78' Seydouba Soumah), Danilo Pantic, Léandro Tawamba Kana.
Coach: Miroslav Djukic.
Goals: 67' Michal Krmencík 1-0, 90+4' Ales Cermák 2-0.
Referee: Jakob Kehlet (DEN)   Attendance: 10,185.

22.02.18 Stadio Olimpico, Roma: Lazio Roma – FC Steaua Bucuresti 5-1 (3-0)
Lazio Roma: Thomas Strakosha, Dusan Basta, Martín Cáceres (26' Bastos), Stefan de Vrij,
Patric, Lucas Leiva, Senad Lulic, Marco Parolo, Luis Alberto (67' Alessandro Murgia), Felipe
Anderson (74' Felipe Caicedo), Ciro Immobile. Coach: Simone Inzaghi.
Steaua Bucuresti: Andrei Vlad, Junior Maranhão, Valerica Gaman (61' Mihai Balasa),
Romario Benzar, Bogdan Planic, Filipe Teixeira, Dragos Nedelcu (46' Lucian Filip),
Constantin Budescu, Harlem Gnohéré, Florin Tanase (46' Florinel Coman), Dennis Man.
Coach: Nicolae Dica.
Goals: 7' Ciro Immobile 1-0, 35' Bastos 2-0, 42' Ciro Immobile 3-0, 51' Felipe Anderson 4-0,
71' Ciro Immobile 5-0, 82' Harlem Gnohéré 5-1.
Referee: Slavko Vincic (SVN)   Attendance: 27,597.

22.02.18 Estádio José Alvalade, Lisboa: Sporting CP – FK Astana 3-3 (1-1)
Sporting CP: Rui Patrício, Jérémy Mathieu, Fábio Coentrão, André Pinto, Stefan Ristovski,
Rúben Ribeiro (46' Marcos Acuña), Rodrigo Battaglia, Bruno Fernandes, João Palhinha (74'
Rafael Leão), Bryan Ruiz (60' William Carvalho), Bas Dost. Coach: Jorge Jesus.
FK Astana: Nenad Eric, Marin Anicic, Igor Shitov, Dmitriy Shomko, Abzal Beysebekov,
Evgeni Postnikov, Marin Tomasov, Ivan Maevski, László Kleinheisler (60' Marko Stanojevic),
Djordje Despotovic (66' Aleksey Shchetkin), Patrick Twumasi (87' Roman Murtazaev).
Coach: Stanimir Stoilov.
Goals: 3' Bas Dost 1-0, 37' Marin Tomasov 1-1, 53', 63' Bruno Fernandes 2-1, 3-1,
80' Patrick Twumasi 3-2, 90+4' Dmitriy Shomko 3-3.
Referee: Tamás Bognár (HUN)   Attendance: 30,456.

22.02.18 MAPEI Stadium – Città del Tricolore, Reggio nell'Emilia:
Atalanta Bergamo – Borussia Dortmund 1-1 (1-0)
Atalanta Bergamo: Etrit Berisha, Andrea Masiello, Rafael Tolói (88' Andreas Cornelius),
Leonardo Spinazzola, Hans Hateboer, Mattia Caldara, Papu Gómez, Josip Ilicic, Marten de
Roon (87' Andrea Petagna), Remo Freuler, Bryan Cristante. Coach: Gian Piero Gasperini.
Borussia Dortmund: Roman Bürki, Lukasz Piszczek, Sokratis Papastathopoulos, Ömer Toprak,
Jeremy Toljan (46' Marcel Schmelzer), Nuri Sahin, Mario Götze, André Schürrle, Mahmoud
Dahoud (82' Alexander Isak), Christian Pulisic (59' Marco Reus), Michy Batshuaya.
Coach: Peter Stöger.
Goals: 11' Rafael Tolói 1-0, 83' Marcel Schmelzer 1-1.
Referee: Jesús Gil Manzano (ESP)   Attendance: 17,492.

22.02.18 San Mamés Barria, Bilbao: Athletic Bilbao – Spartak Moskva 1-2 (0-1)
Athletic Bilbao: Iago Herrerín, Etxeita, De Marcos, Saborit, Yeray Álvarez, Lekue, Raúl
García (84' Aduriz), Susaeta, Iturraspe, Mikel Rico (53' San José), Iñaki Williams (90+2'
Iñigo Córdoba). Coach: José Ángel Ziganda.
Spartak Moskva: Aleksandr Selikhov, Serdar Tasçi (10' Ilya Kutepov), Salvatore Bocchetti,
Andrey Eshchenko, Dmitriy Kombarov, Denis Glushakov, Sofiane Hanni (59' Zé Luís),
Roman Zobnin, Quincy Promes, Mario Pasalic (74' Lorenzo Melgarejo), Luiz Adriano.
Coach: Massimo Carrera.
Goals: 44' Luiz Adriano 0-1, 57' Etxeita 1-1, 85' Lorenzo Melgarejo 1-2.
Referee: Tobias Stieler (GER)   Attendance: 36,873.

22.02.18 Red Bull Arena, Wals-Siezenheim: Red Bull Salzburg – Real Sociedad 2-1 (1-1)
Red Bull Salzburg: Alexander Walke, Andreas Ulmer, Stefan Lainer, André Ramalho, Jérôme
Onguéné, Reinhold Yabo (62' Valon Berisha), Xaver Schlager, Diadie Samassekou, Amadou
Haïdara, Munas Dabbur, Hwang Hee-Chan (90' Fredrik Gulbrandsen). Coach: Marco Rose.
Real Sociedad: Gerónimo Rulli (77' Toño), De La Bella (46' Diego Llorente), Raúl Navas,
Álvaro Odriozola, Aritz Elustondo, Canales, Illarramendi, Zurutuza, Adnan Januzaj, Agirretxe
(71' Jon Bautista), Mikel Oyarzabal. Coach: Eusebio Sacristán.
Goals: 10' Munas Dabbur 1-0, 28' Raúl Navas 1-1, 74' Valon Berisha 2-1 (p).
Referee: Sergei Karasev (RUS)   Attendance: 13,912.
Sent off: 71' Raúl Navas.

22.02.18 Stadio Giuseppe Meazza, Milano: AC Milan – PFC Ludogorets Razgrad 1-0 (1-0)
AC Milan: Antonio Donnarumma, Cristián Zapata, Ignazio Abate, Ricardo Rodríguez, Alessio
Romagnoli (74' Leonardo Bonucci), Riccardo Montolivo, Franck Kessié (56' José Mauri),
Manuel Locatelli, Fabio Borini, André Silva, Patrick Cutrone (56' Nikola Kalinic).
Coach: Gennaro Gattuso.
PFC Ludogorets Razgrad: Jorge Broun, Cosmin Moti, Cicinho, Georgi Terziev, Anicet
Andrianantenaina (82' Svetoslav Dyakov), Wanderson, Natanael Pimienta, Jacek Góralski,
Marcelinho (63' Gustavo Campanharo), Virgil Misidjan (71' Jody Lukoki), Jakub Swierczok.
Coach: Dimitar Dimitrov.
Goal: 21' Fabio Borini 1-0.
Referee: Alberto Undiano Mallenco (ESP)   Attendance: 17,453.

22.02.18 Emirates Stadium, London: Arsenal FC – Österlunds FK 1-2 (0-2)
Arsenal FC: David Ospina, Sead Kolasinac, Calum Chambers, Héctor Bellerín, Rob Holding,
Henrikh Mkhitaryan, Jack Wilshere (76' Joseph Willock), Mohamed Elneny, Alex Iwobi
(90+2' Reiss Nelson), Ainsley Maitland-Niles (46' Granit Xhaka), Danny Welbeck.
Coach: Arsène Wenger.
Östersunds FK: Aly Keita, Tom Pettersson, Sotirios Papagiannopoulos, Ronald Mukiibi (73'
Dino Islamovic), Dennis Widgren, Brwa Nouri, Jamie Hopcutt (81' Frank Arhin), Hosam
Aiesh (52' Tesfaldet Tekie), Ken Sema, Curtis Edwards, Saman Ghoddos.
Coach: Graham Potter.
Goals: 22' Hosam Aiesh 0-1, 23' Ken Sema 0-2, 47' Sead Kolasinac 1-2.
Referee: Ivan Kruzliak (SVK)   Attendance: 58,405.

22.02.18 Estádio Municipal de Braga, Braga:
        Sporting Braga – Olympique Marseille 1-0 (1-0)
Sporting Braga: Matheus Magalhães, Jefferson, Raúl Silva, Ricardo Esgaio, Marcelo Goiano
(73' Fábio Martins), Bruno Viana, Nikola Vukcevic, Ricardo Horta (73' Bruno Xadas), André
Horta, Wilson Eduardo, Ahmed Hassan 'Koka' (54' Paulinho). Coach: Abel Ferreira.
Olympique Marseille: Yohann Pelé, Adil Rami, Rolando, Hiroki Sakai, Luiz Gustavo, Bouna
Sarr, Lucas Ocampos, Morgan Sanson (84' Dimitri Payet), Maxime Lopez, Valère Germain
(73' Florian Thauvin), Clinton N'Jie (46' André Zambo Anguissa). Coach: Rudi García.
Goal: 31' Ricardo Horta 1-0.
Referee: Svein Oddvar Moen (NOR)   Attendance: 9,016.

ROUND OF 16

08.03.18 Estadio Wanda Metropolitano, Madrid:
        Atlético Madrid – Lokomotiv Moskva 3-0 (1-0)
Atlético Madrid: Axel Werner, Juanfran, Filipe Luís, José Giménez, Lucas Hernández, Saúl,
Koke, Thomas Partey, Diego Costa (75' Kevin Gameiro), Antoine Griezmann (67' Vitolo),
Ángel Correa (75' Fernando Torres). Coach: Diego Simeone.
Lokomotiv Moskva: Guilherme Marinato, Verdan Corluka, Nemanja Pejcinovic, Solomon
Kverkvelia, Manuel Fernandes, Igor Denisov, Maciej Rybus, Vladislav Ignatyev (53' Mikhail
Lysov), Aleksey Miranchuk, Anton Miranchuk (71' Aleksandr Kolomeytsev), Éder.
Coach: Yuriy Semin.
Goals: 22' Saúl 1-0, 47' Diego Costa 2-0, 90' Koke 3-0).
Referee: Jakob Kehlet (DEN)   Attendance: 40,767.

08.03.18 VEB Arena, Moskva: CSKA Moskva – Olympique Lyon 0-1 (0-0)
CSKA Moskva: Igor Akinfeev, Sergey Ignashevich, Aleksey Berezutski, Kirill Nababkin,
Pontus Wernbloom, Bibras Natcho, Alan Dzagoev (82' Kristijan Bistrovic), Georgi Milanov
(73' Vitinho), Aleksandr Golovin, Konstantin Kuchaev, Ahmed Musa (87' Fedor Chalov).
Coach: Viktor Goncharenko.
Olympique Lyon: Anthony Lopes, Jérémy Morel, Marcelo, Fernando Marçal, Kenny Tete,
Tanguy NDombèlé, Lucas Tousart, Houssem Aouar, Bertrand Traoré (76' Maxwell Cornet),
Memphis Depay (85' Myziane Maolida), Mariano Díaz (89' Ferland Mendy).
Coach: Bruno Génésio.
Goal: 68' Marcelo 0-1.
Referee: Antonio Mateu Lahoz (ESP)   Attendance: 13,990

08.03.18 Signal-Iduna-Park, Dortmund: Borussia Dortmund – Red Bull Salzburg 1-2 (0-0)
Borussia Dortmund: Roman Bürki, Sokratis Papastathopoulos, Marcel Schmelzer, Ömer
Toprak, Gonzalo Castro, Mario Götze (61' Christian Pulisic), André Schürrle, Julian Weigl,
Mahmoud Dahoud, Marco Reus, Michy Batshuaya (61' Maximilian Philipp).
Coach: Peter Stöger.
Red Bull Salzburg: Alexander Walke, Andreas Ulmer, Stefan Lainer, André Ramalho, Duje
Caleta-Car, Valon Berisha, Xaver Schlager (73' Takumi Minamino), Diadie Samassekou,
Amadou Haïdara (90+1' Reinhold Yabo), Munas Dabbur, Hwang Hee-Chan (69' Fredrik
Gulbrandsen). Coach: Marco Rose.
Goals: 49', 56' Valon Berisha 0-1 (p), 0-2, 62' André Schürrle 1-2.
Referee: Slavko Vincic (SVN)   Attendance: 53,700.

08.03.18 Stadio Giuseppe Meazza, Milano: AC Milan – Arsenal FC 0-2 (0-2)
AC Milan: Gianluigi Donnarumma, Leonardo Bonucci, Ricardo Rodríguez, Alessio
Romagnoli, Davide Calabria (79' Fabio Borini), Lucas Biglia, Giacomo Bonaventura, Hakan
Çalhanoglu (62' Nikola Kalinic), Franck Kessié, Suso, Patrick Cutrone (69' André Silva).
Coach: Gennaro Gattuso.
Arsenal FC: David Ospina, Laurent Koscielny, Shkodran Mustafi, Sead Kolasinac (62' Ainsley
Maitland-Niles), Calum Chambers (85' Mohamed Elneny), Mesut Özil (80' Rob Holding),
Henrikh Mkhitaryan, Jack Wilshere, Aaron Ramsey, Granit Xhaka, Danny Welbeck.
Coach: Arsène Wenger.
Goals: 15' Henrikh Mkhitaryan 0-1, 45+4' Aaron Ramsey 0-2.
Referee: Clément Turpin (FRA)   Attendance: 72.821.

08.03.18 Stadio Olimpico, Roma: Lazio Roma – Dinamo Kiev 2-2 (0-0)
Lazio Roma: Thomas Strakosha, Dusan Basta (74' Patric), Stefan Radu, Stefan de Vrij, Jordan
Lukaku, Wallace (85' Nani), Lucas Leiva, Felipe Anderson, Sergej Milinkovic-Savic,
Alessandro Murgia (74' Marco Parolo), Ciro Immobile. Coach: Simone Inzaghi.
Dinamo Kiev: Denis Boyko, Mikola Morozyuk, Josip Pivaric, Tamás Kádár, Tomasz
Kedziora, Mykyta Burda, Denys Garmash, Vitaliy Buyalskiy, Viktor Tsygankov, Mykola
Shaparenko (67' Júnior Moraes), Artem Besedin. Coach: Aleksandr Khatskevich.
Goals: 52' Viktor Tsygankov 0-1, 54' Ciro Immobile 1-1, 62' Felipe Anderson 2-1,
79' Júnior Moraes 2-2.
Referee: Ivan Kruzliak (SVK)   Attendance: 21,562.
Sent off: 90+6' Denys Garmash.

08.03.18 Red Bull Arena, Leipzig: Red Bull Leipzig – Zenit St.Petersburg 2-1 (0-0)
Red Bull Leipzig: Péter Gulácsi, Willi Orban, Lukas Klostermann, Dayot Upamecano, Emil
Forsberg, Diego Demme, Bruma (75' Marcel Sabitzer), Konrad Laimer (46' Bernardo), Naby
Keïta, Timo Werner, Jean-Kévin Augustin (79' Yussuf Poulsen). Coach: Ralph Hasenhüttl.
Zenit St.Petersburg: Andrei Lunev, Branislav Ivanovic, Domenico Criscito, Miha Mevlja,
Emanuel Mammana, Aleksandr Erokhin, Matías Kranevitter, Daler Kuzyaev, Emiliano Rigoni
(80' Dmitriy Poloz), Aleksandr Kokorin, Anton Zabolotnyi (57' Sebastián Driussi).
Coach: Roberto Mancini.
Goals: 56' Bruma 1-0, 77' Timo Werner 2-0, 86' Domenico Criscito 2-1.
Referee: Ovidiu Hategan (ROM)   Attendance: 19,877.

08.03.18 Stade Vélodrome, Marseille: Olympique Marseille – Athletic Bilbao 3-1 (2-1)
Olympique Marseille: Steve Mandanda, Adil Rami, Rolando, Hiroki Sakai, Jordan Amavi,
Dimitri Payet, Luiz Gustavo, Lucas Ocampos, Maxime Lopez (86' Bouna Sarr), Valère
Germain (71' André Zambo Anguissa), Florian Thauvin (62' Clinton N'Jie).
Coach: Rudi García.
Athletic Bilbao: Iago Herrerín, Balenziaga (69' Lekue), Etxeita, De Marcos, Yeray Álvarez,
Raúl García (78' Mikel Vesga), Susaeta (62' Iñigo Córdoba), San José, Beñat, Aduriz, Iñaki
Williams. Coach: José Ángel Ziganda.
Goals: 1' Lucas Ocampos 1-0, 13' Dimitri Payet 2-0, 45+3' Aduriz 2-1 (p),
57' Lucas Ocampos 3-1.
Referee: Jorge de Sousa (POR)   Attendance: 37,657.

08.03.18 Estádio José Alvalade, Lisboa: Sporting CP – Viktoria Plzen 2-0 (1-0)
Sporting CP: Rui Patrício, Jérémy Mathieu, Fábio Coentrão (86' Rúben Ribeiro), Sebastián
Coates, Stefan Ristovski, William Carvalho, Bruno Fernandes, Bryan Ruiz (79' Bruno César),
Fredy Montero, Marcos Acuña (57' Rodrigo Battaglia), Gelson Martins. Coach: Jorge Jesus.
Viktoria Plzen: Ales Hruska, Roman Hubník, Radim Rezník, David Limbersky, Lukás Hejda,
Milan Petrzela (62' Tomás Chory), Daniel Kolár (75' Jan Kovarík), Martin Zeman (82' Ales
Cermák), Tomás Horava, Patrik Hrosovsky, Michal Krmencík. Coach: Pavel Vrba.
Goals: 45+1', 49' Fredy Montero 1-0, 2-0.
Referee: Aleksei Kulbakov (BLS)   Attendance: 26,090.

15.03.18 RZD Arena, Moskva: Lokomotiv Moskva – Atlético Madrid 1-5 (1-1)
Lokomotiv Moskva: Anton Kochenkov, Verdan Corluka (75' Nemanja Pejcinovic), Solomon
Kverkvelia, Jefferson Farfán (46' Éder), Manuel Fernandes, Igor Denisov, Maciej Rybus,
Aleksandr Kolomeytsev (63' Dmitriy Tarasov), Aleksey Miranchuk, Anton Miranchuk,
Mikhail Lysov. Coach: Yuriy Semin.
Atlético Madrid: Axel Werner, Juanfran (46' Sime Vrsaljko), Filipe Luís (62' Lucas
Hernández), Diego Godín, José Giménez, Gabi, Saúl (61' Antoine Griezmann), Koke, Thomas
Partey, Fernando Torres, Ángel Correa. Coach: Diego Simeone.
Goals: 16' Ángel Correa 0-1, 20' Maciej Rybus 1-1, 47' Saúl 1-2,
65', 70' Fernando Torres 1-3 (p), 1-4, 85' Antoine Griezmann 1-5.
Referee: Artur Soares Dias (POR)   Attendance: 22,041.

15.03.18 NSC Olimpiyskiy Stadium, Kiev: Dinamo Kiev – Lazio Roma 0-2 (0-1)
Dinamo Kiev: Denis Boyko, Mikola Morozyuk (57' Derlis González), Josip Pivaric, Tamás
Kádár (45' Artem Shabanov), Tomasz Kedziora, Mykyta Burda, Vitaliy Buyalskiy, Viktor
Tsygankov, Volodymyr Shepeliev, Júnior Moraes, Artem Besedin (70' Dieumerci Mbokani).
Coach: Aleksandr Khatskevich.
Lazio Roma: Thomas Strakosha, Stefan Radu, Stefan de Vrij, Patric (72' Adam Marusic), Luiz
Felipe, Lucas Leiva, Senad Lulic (69' Jordan Lukaku), Marco Parolo, Luis Alberto, Felipe
Anderson, Ciro Immobile (82' Felipe Caicedo). Coach: Simone Inzaghi.
Goals: 23' Lucas Leiva 0-1, 83' Stefan de Vrij 0-2.
Referee: Jesús Gil Manzano (ESP)   Attendance: 52,639.

15.03.18   Krestovsky Stadium, St.Petersburg: Zenit St.Petersburg – Red Bull Leipzig 1-1 (1-1)
Zenit St.Petersburg: Andrei Lunev, Branislav Ivanovic, Domenico Criscito, Igor Smolnikov
(85' Dmitriy Poloz), Miha Mevlja, Yuriy Zhirkov, Leandro Paredes, Matías Kranevitter,
Emiliano Rigoni (90' Aleksandr Erokhin), Aleksandr Kokorin (8' Anton Zabolotnyi),
Sebastián Driussi. Coach: Roberto Mancini.
Red Bull Leipzig: Péter Gulácsi, Willi Orban (46' Ibrahima Konaté), Lukas Klostermann,
Bernardo, Dayot Upamecano, Emil Forsberg, Diego Demme (71' Stefan Ilsanker), Bruma,
Naby Keïta, Timo Werner, Jean-Kévin Augustin (90+1' Yussuf Poulsen).
Coach: Ralph Hasenhüttl.
Goals: 22' Jean-Kévin Augustin 0-1, 45+1' Sebastián Driussi 1-1.
Referee: Daniele Orsato (ITA)   Attendance: 44,092.

Timo Werner missed a penalty kick (82').

15.03.18   San Mamés Barria, Bilbao: Athletic Bilbao – Olympique Marseille 1-2 (0-1)
Athletic Bilbao: Iago Herrerín, Etxeita, De Marcos, Yeray Álvarez (44' Unai Núñez), Lekue,
Beñat (79' Mikel Vesga), Iturraspe, Mikel Rico (23' Susaeta), Iñigo Córdoba, Aduriz, Iñaki
Williams. Coach: José Ángel Ziganda.
Olympique Marseille: Steve Mandanda, Adil Rami, Rolando, Hiroki Sakai, Jordan Amavi,
Dimitri Payet, Luiz Gustavo (56' André Zambo Anguissa), Lucas Ocampos, Maxime Lopez
(78' Morgan Sanson), Kostas Mitroglou, Florian Thauvin (67' Bouna Sarr).
Coach: Rudi García.
Goals: 38' Dimitri Payet 0-1 (p), 52' Lucas Ocampos 0-2, 74' Iñaki Williams 1-2.
Referee: Anthony Taylor (ENG)   Attendance: 40,580.
Sent off: 76' Aduriz.

15.03.18   Doosan Aréna, Plzen: Viktoria Plzen – Sporting CP 2-1 (1-0, 2-0)
Viktoria Plzen: Ales Hruska, Radim Rezník (105' Lukás Hejda), Tomás Hajek, Milan Havel,
Daniel Kolár, Martin Zeman (100' Milan Petrzela), Tomás Horava, Jan Kovarík, Jan Kopic,
Patrik Hrosovsky, Marek Bakos (83' Michal Krmencík). Coach: Pavel Vrba.
Sporting CP: Rui Patrício, Jérémy Mathieu, Fábio Coentrão, André Pinto, Radoslav Petrovic
(67' Cristiano Piccini), Rodrigo Battaglia, Bruno Fernandes, Bryan Ruiz (99' Rúben Ribeiro),
Bas Dost, Marcos Acuña (76' Fredy Montero), Gelson Martins. Coach: Jorge Jesus.
Goals: 6', 65' Marek Bakos 1-0, 2-0, 105+2' Rodrigo Battaglia 2-1.
Referee: Tobias Stieler (GER)   Attendance: 9,370.

Bas Dost missed a penalty kick (90+2').

Sporting CP won after extra time.

15.03.18 Groupama Stadium, Décines-Charpieu: Olympique Lyon – CSKA Moskva 2-3 (0-1)
Olympique Lyon: Anthony Lopes, Marcelo, Fernando Marçal (70' Ferland Mendy), Kenny
Tete, Mouctar Diakhaby, Jordan Ferri (68' Myziane Maolida), Tanguy NDombèlé, Lucas
Tousart, Memphis Depay (65' Bertrand Traoré), Mariano Díaz, Maxwell Cornet.
Coach: Bruno Génésio.
CSKA Moskva: Igor Akinfeev, Vasiliy Berezutksi (46' Georgiy Shchennikov), Sergey
Ignashevich, Aleksey Berezutski, Kirill Nababkin, Pontus Wernbloom, Bibras Natcho, Alan
Dzagoev (90+4' Astemir Gordyushenko), Aleksandr Golovin, Konstantin Kuchaev, Ahmed
Musa (73' Vitinho). Coach: Viktor Goncharenko.
Goals: 39' Aleksandr Golovin 0-1, 58' Maxwell Cornet 1-1, 60' Ahmed Musa 1-2,
65' Pontus Wernbloom 1-3, 71' Mariano Díaz 2-3
Referee: Bobby Madden (SCO)   Attendance: 38,622.

CSKA Moskva won on away goals.

15.03.18 Red Bull Arena, Wals-Siezenheim: Red Bul Salzburg – Borussia Dortmund 0-0
Red Bull Salzburg: Alexander Walke, Andreas Ulmer, Stefan Lainer, André Ramalho, Duje
Caleta-Car, Valon Berisha, Xaver Schlager (79' Hannes Wolf), Diadie Samassekou, Amadou
Haïdara (82' Reinhold Yabo), Munas Dabbur, Hwang Hee-Chan (66' Fredrik Gulbrandsen).
Coach: Marco Rose.
Borussia Dortmund: Roman Bürki, Lukasz Piszczek, Sokratis Papastathopoulos, Marcel
Schmelzer, Dan-Axel Zagadou, Gonzalo Castro (62' Raphaël Guerreiro), Mario Götze (46'
Maximilian Philipp), André Schürrle, Mahmoud Dahoud, Marco Reus (46' Alexander Isak),
Michy Batshuaya. Coach: Peter Stöger.
Referee: Benoît Bastien (FRA)   Attendance: 29,520.

15.03.18 Emirates Stadium, London: Arsenal FC – AC Milan 3-1 (1-1)
Arsenal FC: David Ospina, Nacho Monreal, Laurent Koscielny (11' Calum Chambers),
Shkodran Mustafi, Héctor Bellerín, Mesut Özil (79' Sead Kolasinac), Henrikh Mkhitaryan (69'
Mohamed Elneny), Jack Wilshere, Aaron Ramsey, Granit Xhaka, Danny Welbeck.
Coach: Arsène Wenger.
AC Milan: Gianluigi Donnarumma, Leonardo Bonucci, Ricardo Rodríguez, Alessio
Romagnoli, Riccardo Montolivo, Hakan Çalhanoglu (70' Giacomo Bonaventura), Franck
Kessié (79' Manuel Locatelli), Fabio Borini, André Silva, Suso, Patrick Cutrone (67' Nikola
Kalinic). Coach: Gennaro Gattuso.
Goals: 35' Hakan Çalhanoglu 0-1, 39' Danny Welbeck 1-1 (p), 71' Granit Xhaka 2-1,
86' Danny Welbeck 3-1.
Referee: Jonas Eriksson (SWE)   Attendance: 58,973.

QUARTER-FINALS

05.04.18 Red Bull Arena, Leipzig: Red Bull Leipzig – Olympique Marseille 1-0 (1-0)
Red Bull Leipzig: Péter Gulácsi, Dayot Upamecano, Ibrahima Konaté, Lukas Klostermann,
Naby Keïta, Emil Forsberg (83' Marcel Sabitzer), Bruma, Konrad Laimer (74' Bernardo),
Diego Demme, Timo Werner, Jean-Kévin Augustin (70' Kevin Kampl).
Coach: Ralph Hasenhüttl.
Olympique Marseille: Yohann Pelé, Hiroki Sakai, Boubacar Kamara, Jordan Amavi, Lucas
Ocampos, Morgan Sanson, Dimitri Payet (86' Maxime Lopez), Luiz Gustavo, André Zambo
Anguissa, Kostas Mitroglou (80' Valère Germain), Bouna Sarr. Coach: Rudi García.
Goal: 45+1' Timo Werner 1-0.
Referee: Alberto Undiano Mallenco (ESP)   Attendance: 34,043.

05.04.18 Emirates Stadium, London: Arsenal FC – CSKA Moskva 4-1 (4-1)
Arsenal FC: Petr Cech, Laurent Koscielny, Nacho Monreal, Shkodran Mustafi, Héctor
Bellerín, Henrikh Mkhitaryan (61' Alex Iwobi), Aaron Ramsey, Jack Wilshere (74' Mohamed
Elneny), Mesut Özil, Granit Xhaka, Alexandre Lacazette (74' Danny Welbeck).
Coach: Arsène Wenger.
CSKA Moskva: Igor Akinfeev, Sergey Ignashevich, Aleksey Berezutski, Vasiliy Berezutksi,
Georgiy Shchennikov, Pontus Wernbloom, Alan Dzagoev (65' Vitinho), Aleksandr Golovin,
Bibras Natcho (74' Georgi Milanov), Konstantin Kuchaev, Ahmed Musa (83' Khetag
Khosonov). Coach: Viktor Goncharenko.
Goals: 9' Aaron Ramsey 1-0, 15' Aleksandr Golovin 1-1, 23' Alexandre Lacazette 2-1 (p),
28' Aaron Ramsey 3-1, 35' Alexandre Lacazette 4-1.
Referee: Pavel Královec (CZE)   Attendance: 58,285.

05.04.18 Estadio Wanda Metropolitano, Madrid: Atlético Madrid – Sporting CP 2-0 (2-0)
Atlético Madrid: Jan Oblak, Diego Godín, Stefan Savic, Lucas Hernández, Juanfran, Koke,
Saúl, Gabi, Antoine Griezmann (90' Vitolo), Ángel Correa (53' Kevin Gameiro), Diego Costa
(87' Thomas Partey). Coach: Diego Simeone.
Sporting CP: Rui Patrício, Sebastián Coates, Fábio Coentrão (80' Rúben Ribeiro), Jérémy
Mathieu, Cristiano Piccini, Bruno Fernandes (87' Fredy Montero), William Carvalho (45'
Marcos Acuña), Rodrigo Battaglia, Bryan Ruiz, Gelson Martins, Bas Dost. Coach: Jorge Jesus.
Goals: 1' Koke 1-0, 40' Antoine Griezmann 2-0.
Referee: Sergei Karasev (RUS)   Attendance: 53,301.

05.04.18 Stadio Olimpico, Roma: Lazio Roma – Red Bull Salzburg 4-2 (1-1)
Lazio Roma: Thomas Strakosha, Stefan de Vrij, Dusan Basta (65' Patric), Stefan Radu, Luiz
Felipe, Lucas Leiva, Marco Parolo, Senad Lulic, Sergej Milinkovic-Savic, Ciro Immobile (85'
Felipe Caicedo), Luis Alberto (65' Felipe Anderson). Coach: Simone Inzaghi.
Red Bull Salzburg: Alexander Walke, Duje Caleta-Car, André Ramalho, Andreas Ulmer,
Stefan Lainer, Amadou Haïdara (82' Hannes Wolf), Diadie Samassekou, Valon Berisha, Xaver
Schlager, Munas Dabbur, Fredrik Gulbrandsen (70' Takumi Minamino). Coach: Marco Rose.
Goals: 8' Senad Lulic 1-0, 30' Valon Berisha 1-1 (p), 49' Marco Parolo 2-1,
71' Takumi Minamino 2-2, 74' Felipe Anderson 3-2, 76' Ciro Immobile 4-2.
Referee: Ovidiu Hategan (ROM)   Attendance: 42,538.

12.04.18 Stade Vélodrome, Marseille: Olympique Marseille – Red Bull Leipzig 5-2 (3-1)
Olympique Marseille: Yohann Pelé, Hiroki Sakai, Boubacar Kamara, Jordan Amavi, Morgan
Sanson, Dimitri Payet (83' André Zambo Anguissa), Luiz Gustavo, Florian Thauvin (63'
Lucas Ocampos), Maxime Lopez, Kostas Mitroglou, Bouna Sarr (28' Adil Rami).
Coach: Rudi García.
Red Bull Leipzig: Péter Gulácsi, Dayot Upamecano (66' Bernardo), Ibrahima Konaté, Lukas
Klostermann, Marcel Sabitzer (59' Yussuf Poulsen), Naby Keïta, Stefan Ilsanker, Bruma,
Diego Demme (54' Emil Forsberg), Kevin Kampl, Jean-Kévin Augustin.
Coach: Ralph Hasenhüttl.
Goals: 2' Bruma 0-1, 6' Stefan Ilsanker 1-1 (og), 9' Bouna Sarr 2-1, 38' Florian Thauvin 3-1,
55' Jean-Kévin Augustin 3-2, 60' Dimitri Payet 4-2, 90+4' Hiroki Sakai 5-2.
Referee: Björn Kuipers (HOL)   Attendance: 61,882.

12.04.18 VEB Arena, Moskva: CSKA Moskva – Arsenal FC 2-2 (1-0)
CSKA Moskva: Igor Akinfeev, Sergey Ignashevich, Aleksey Berezutski, Kirill Nababkin,
Vasiliy Berezutksi, Alan Dzagoev (38' Vitinho), Aleksandr Golovin, Kristijan Bistrovic (72'
Bibras Natcho), Konstantin Kuchaev, Ahmed Musa, Fedor Chalov (79' Georgi Milanov).
Coach: Viktor Goncharenko.
Arsenal FC: Petr Cech, Laurent Koscielny, Nacho Monreal, Shkodran Mustafi, Héctor
Bellerín, Aaron Ramsey, Jack Wilshere (69' Calum Chambers), Mesut Özil, Mohamed Elneny,
Alexandre Lacazette (77' Alex Iwobi), Danny Welbeck. Coach: Arsène Wenger.
Goals: 39' Fedor Chalov 1-0, 2-0 Kirill Nababkin 2-0, 75' Danny Welbeck 2-1,
90+2' Aaron Ramsey 2-2.
Referee: Felix Zwayer (GER)   Attendance: 29,284.

12.04.18 Estádio José Alvalade, Lisboa: Sporting CP – Atlético Madrid 1-0 (1-0)
Sporting CP: Rui Patrício, Sebastián Coates, André Pinto, Stefan Ristovski (79' Seydou
Doumbia), Jérémy Mathieu (26' Radoslav Petrovic), Bruno Fernandes, Marcos Acuña,
Rodrigo Battaglia, Bryan Ruiz (70' Rúben Ribeiro), Gelson Martins, Fredy Montero.
Coach: Jorge Jesus.
Atlético Madrid: Jan Oblak, Diego Godín, Stefan Savic, Lucas Hernández (46' Sime Vrsaljko),
Juanfran, Koke, Saúl, Gabi, Antoine Griezmann, Diego Costa (52' Fernando Torres), Vitolo
(60' Ángel Correa). Coach: Diego Simeone.
Goal: 28' Fredy Montero 1-0.
Referee: Milorad Mazic (SER)   Attendance: 28,437.

12.04.18 Red Bull Arena, Wals-Siezenheim: Red Bul Salzburg – Lazio Roma 4-1 (0-0)
Red Bull Salzburg: Alexander Walke, Duje Caleta-Car, André Ramalho, Andreas Ulmer,
Stefan Lainer, Amadou Haïdara, Reinhold Yabo (84' Takumi Minamino), Valon Berisha,
Xaver Schlager, Munas Dabbur, Hwang Hee-Chan (79' Fredrik Gulbrandsen).
Coach: Marco Rose.
Lazio Roma: Thomas Strakosha, Stefan de Vrij, Dusan Basta (60' Jordan Lukaku), Stefan
Radu, Luiz Felipe, Lucas Leiva (78' Nani), Marco Parolo, Senad Lulic, Sergej Milinkovic-
Savic (69' Felipe Anderson), Ciro Immobile, Luis Alberto. Coach: Simone Inzaghi.
Goals: 55' Ciro Immobile 0-1, 56' Munas Dabbur 1-1, 72' Amadou Haïdara 2-1,
74' Hwang Hee-Chan 3-1, 76' Stefan Lainer 4-1.
Referee: Damir Skomina (SVN)   Attendance: 29,520.

SEMI-FINALS

26.04.18   Stade Vélodrome, Marseille: Olympique Marseille – Red Bull Salzburg 2-0 (1-0)
Olympique Marseille: Yohann Pelé, Jordan Amavi, Adil Rami, Lucas Ocampos (52' André
Zambo Anguissa), Morgan Sanson, Dimitri Payet, Luiz Gustavo, Florian Thauvin (81' Valère
Germain), Maxime Lopez (60' Clinton N'Jie), Kostas Mitroglou, Bouna Sarr.
Coach: Rudi García.
Red Bull Salzburg: Alexander Walke, Duje Caleta-Car, André Ramalho, Andreas Ulmer,
Stefan Lainer, Amadou Haïdara (81' Reinhold Yabo), Diadie Samassekou, Valon Berisha,
Munas Dabbur, Hannes Wolf (68' Xaver Schlager), Hwang Hee-Chan (60' Fredrik
Gulbrandsen). Coach: Marco Rose.
Goals: 15' Florian Thauvin 1-0, 63' Clinton N'Jie 2-0.
Referee: William Collum (SCO)   Attendance: 62,312.

26.04.18   Emirates Stadium, London: Arsenal FC – Atlético Madrid 1-1 (0-0)
Arsenal FC: David Ospina, Laurent Koscielny, Nacho Monreal, Shkodran Mustafi, Héctor
Bellerín, Aaron Ramsey, Jack Wilshere, Mesut Özil, Granit Xhaka, Alexandre Lacazette,
Danny Welbeck. Coach: Arsène Wenger.
Atlético Madrid: Jan Oblak, Diego Godín, Sime Vrsaljko, Lucas Hernández, José Giménez,
Thomas Partey, Koke, Saúl, Antoine Griezmann (85' Fernando Torres), Ángel Correa (75'
Stefan Savic), Kevin Gameiro (65' Gabi). Coach: Diego Simeone.
Goals: 61' Alexandre Lacazette 1-0, 82' Antoine Griezmann 1-1.
Referee: Clément Turpin (FRA)   Attendance: 59,066.
Sent off: 10' Sime Vrsaljko.

Diego Simeone was sent to the stands (13').

03.05.18   Red Bull Arena, Wals-Siezenheim:
           Red Bul Salzburg – Olympique Marseille 2-1 (0-0,2-0)
Red Bull Salzburg: Alexander Walke, Duje Caleta-Car, André Ramalho, Andreas Ulmer (96'
Marin Pongracic), Stefan Lainer, Amadou Haïdara, Diadie Samassekou, Valon Berisha, Xaver
Schlager (84' Takumi Minamino), Munas Dabbur, Fredrik Gulbrandsen (69' Hwang Hee-
Chan). Coach: Marco Rose.
Olympique Marseille: Yohann Pelé, Jordan Amavi, Adil Rami, Lucas Ocampos, Morgan
Sanson (102' Rolando), Dimitri Payet, Luiz Gustavo, Florian Thauvin, Maxime Lopez (67'
André Zambo Anguissa), Bouna Sarr, Valère Germain (84' Clinton N'Jie). Coach: Rudi García
Goals: 53' Amadou Haïdara 1-0, 65' Bouna Sarr 2-0 (og), 116' Rolando 2-1.
Referee: Sergei Karasev (RUS)   Attendance: 29,520.
Sent off: 119' Amadou Haïdara.

Olympique Marseille qualified through extra time.

03.05.18 Estadio Wanda Metropolitano, Madrid: Atlético Madrid – Arsenal FC 1-0 (1-0)
Atlético Madrid: Jan Oblak, Diego Godín, Lucas Hernández, José Giménez, Thomas Partey
(90+3' Stefan Savic), Koke, Saúl, Gabi, Antoine Griezmann, Diego Costa (83' Fernando
Torres), Vitolo (74' Ángel Correa). Coach: Diego Simeone.
Arsenal FC: David Ospina, Laurent Koscielny (12' Calum Chambers), Nacho Monreal,
Shkodran Mustafi, Héctor Bellerín, Aaron Ramsey, Jack Wilshere (68' Henrikh Mkhitaryan),
Mesut Özil, Granit Xhaka, Alexandre Lacazette, Danny Welbeck. Coach: Arsène Wenger.
Goal: 45+2' Diego Costa 1-0.
Referee: Gianluca Rocchi (ITA)   Attendance: 64,196.

FINAL

16.05.18 Parc Olympique Lyonnais, Décines-Charpieu:
         Olympique Marseille – Atlético Madrid 0-3 (0-1)
Olympique Marseille: Steve Mandanda, Adil Rami, Jordan Amavi, Dimitri Payet (32' Maxime
Lopez), Luiz Gustavo, Bouna Sarr, Lucas Ocampos (55' Clinton N'Jie), Morgan Sanson,
André Zambo Anguissa, Valère Germain (74' Kostas Mitroglou), Florian Thauvin.
Coach: Rudi García.
Atlético Madrid: Jan Oblak, Diego Godín, Sime Vrsaljko (46' Juanfran), José Giménez, Lucas
Hernández, Gabi, Saúl, Koke, Diego Costa, Antoine Griezmann (90' Fernando Torres), Ángel
Correa (88' Thomas Partey). Assistant Coach: Germán Burgos.
Goals: 21', 49' Antoine Griezmann 0-1, 0-2, 89' Gabi 0-3.
Referee: Björn Kuipers (HOL)   Attendance: 55,768

FAIRS CUP / UEFA CUP / EUROPA LEAGUE WINNERS

Fairs Cup (1958-1971), UEFA-Cup (1972-2009), Europa League (2010-2018).

1958	FC Barcelona	Spain
1960	FC Barcelona	Spain
1961	AS Roma	Italy
1962	Valencia CF	Spain
1963	Valencia CF	Spain
1964	Real Zaragoza	Spain
1965	Ferencvárosi TC	Hungary
1966	FC Barcelona	Spain
1967	Dinamo Zagreb	Croatia
1968	Leeds United	England
1969	Newcastle United	England
1970	Arsenal FC	England
1971	Leeds United	England
1972	Tottenham Hotspur	England
1973	Liverpool FC	England

1974	Feyenoord	Netherlands
1975	Borussia Mönchengladbach	Germany
1976	Liverpool FC	England
1977	Juventus	Italy
1978	PSV	Netherlands
1979	Borussia Mönchengladbach	Germany
1980	Eintracht Frankfurt	Germany
1981	Ipswich Town	England
1982	IFK Göteborg	Sweden
1983	RSC Anderlecht	Belgium
1984	Tottenham Hotspur	England
1985	Real Madrid	Spain
1986	Real Madrid	Spain
1987	IFK Göteborg	Sweden
1988	Bayer Leverkusen	Germany
1989	SSC Napoli	Italy
1990	Juventus	Italy
1991	Internazionale	Italy
1992	AFC Ajax	Netherlands
1993	Juventus	Italy
1994	Internazionale	Italy
1995	Parma AC	Italy
1996	Bayern München	Germany
1997	FC Schalke 04	Germany
1998	Internazionale	Italy
1999	Parma AC	Italy
2000	Galatasaray	Turkey
2001	Liverpool FC	England
2002	Feyenoord	Netherlands
2003	FC Porto	Portugal
2004	Valencia CF	Spain
2005	CSKA Moskva	Russia
2006	Sevilla FC	Spain
2007	Sevilla FC	Spain
2008	Zenith St. Petersburg	Russia
2009	Shakhtar Donetsk	Ukraine
2010	Atlético Madrid	Spain
2011	FC Porto	Portugal
2012	Atlético Madrid	Spain
2013	Chelsea FC	England
2014	Sevilla FC	Spain
2015	Sevilla FC	Spain
2016	Sevilla FC	Spain
2017	Manchester United	England
2018	Atlético Madrid	Spain

ALL-TIME WINNERS – COUNTRY

Spain	16
England	12
Italy	10
Germany	6
Netherlands	4
Sweden	2
Portugal	2
Russia	2
Hungary	1
Croatia	1
Belgium	1
Turkey	1
Ukraine	1

ALL-TIME WINNERS – CLUB

Sevilla FC	5
Atlético Madrid	3
FC Barcelona	3
Juventus	3
Internazionale	3
Liverpool FC	3
Valencia CF	3
Leeds United	2
Borussia Mönchengladbach	2
IFK Göteborg	2
Tottenham Hotspur	2
Real Madrid	2
Parma AC	2
Feyenoord	2
FC Porto	2
AS Roma	1
Real Zaragoza	1
Ferencvárosi TC	1
Dinamo Zagreb	1
Newcastle United	1
Arsenal FC	1
PSV	1
Eintracht Frankfurt	1
Ipswich Town	1
RSC Anderlecht	1
Bayer Leverkusen	1
SSC Napoli	1
AFC Ajax	1
Bayern München	1
FC Schalke 04	1
Galatasaray	1
CSKA Moskva	1
Zenith St. Petersburg	1
Shakhtar Donetsk	1
Chelsea FC	1
Manchester United	1